Strong Interest Inventory
Applications and Technical Guide

STRONG INTEREST INVENTORY™

Applications and Technical Guide

Form T317 of the *Strong Vocational Interest Blanks*®

Lenore W. Harmon
Jo-Ida C. Hansen
Fred H. Borgen
Allen L. Hammer

Contributing Authors
Diane W. DeWitt
Nadya A. Fouad
Robbie M. Kaplan

Consulting Psychologists Press, Inc.

Published by Stanford University Press
Stanford, California 94305

Distributed by Consulting Psychologists Press, Inc.
3803 E. Bayshore Road
Palo Alto, California 94303

Strong Interest Inventory of the *Strong Vocational Interest Blanks®*, Form T317. Copyright © 1933, 1938, 1945, 1946, 1966, 1968, 1974, 1981, 1985, 1994 by the Board of Trustees of the Leland Stanford Junior University. All rights reserved. Printed under license from Stanford University Press, Stanford, California 94305.

No part of this publication may be reproduced in any form or manner without prior written permission from Consulting Psychologists Press, Inc.

ISBN 0-89106-070-7

Printed in the United States of America.
00 99 98 97 96   14 13 12 11 10 9 8 7 6 5 4 3 2

Strong Interest Inventory is a trademark and *Strong Vocational Interest Blanks* is a registered trademark of Stanford University Press.

 is a trademark of Consulting Psychologists Press, Inc.

Myers-Briggs Type Indicator and MBTI are registered trademarks of Consulting Psychologists Press, Inc.

California Psychological Inventory is a trademark of Consulting Psychologists Press, Inc.

Microsoft and Windows are registered trademarks of Microsoft Corporation.

Monopoly is a registered trademark of Parker Borthers.

Text from Jo-Ida C. Hansen's and David P. Campbell's *Manual for the Strong Interest Inventory*, 4th edition (1985) and Jo-Ida C. Hansen's *User's Guide for the Strong Interest Inventory*, revised edition (1992) has been incorporated into this work.

Portions of John Holland's copyrighted publications, including *Making Vocational Choices: The Theory of Careers* (1973) and *The Self-Directed Search* (1970), have been adapted and incorporated into this work by special permission of the author.

Director of Test Publishing: T. R. Prehn
Strong Project Director: Diane G. Silver
Editors: Jude Berman, Janelle Rohr
Copyeditor: Beverly Zegarski
Proofreaders: Mary Gendron, Elizabeth Judd
Director of Research: Joseph Zelan
Data Collection Staff: Lynn Lawrence, Judy Manton, Yvonne daSilva
Data Management and Analysis: Mary C. Usher
Data Analysts: Mark S. Majors, Ashar Mitchell, T. V. Ramesh
Design: Mark Ong, Side by Side Studios
Print Production Director: Laura Ackerman-Shaw
Production: Elysia Cooke
Manufacturing: Gloria Forbes, Leslie Dozier-Jackson, Sylvia Rodriguez

Contents

List of Figures and Tables viii
Preface xiii
Acknowledgments xv

Chapter 1
Interest Measurement and the *Strong Interest Inventory* 1

E. K. Strong, Jr., and the *SVIB* 1
What Does the *Strong* Do? 2
Why Use Assessment Instruments in Career Counseling? 3
Why Use Interest Inventories? 3
How Psychological Research Has Made Use of the *Strong* 5
Possibilities for Use of the *Strong* in Research 7
References 8

Chapter 2
What's New in 1994 9

Overview of Data Collection 9
Items 10
General Reference Samples (GRSs) 11
General Occupational Themes (GOTs) 11
Basic Interest Scales (BISs) 12
Occupational Scales (OSs) 13
Personal Style Scales 18
Administrative Indexes 20
Profile 21
Conclusion 22
References 22

Chapter 3
Overview of the *Strong* Materials 23

Guidelines for Using the *Strong* 23
Limits on Using the *Strong* 24
Strong Materials 24
Translations 30
References 31

Chapter 4
Items: The Foundation of the Inventory 33

Item Format 33
Selecting Items for the 1994 *Strong* 33
How Items Are Used in the Inventory 35
Conclusion 42
Reference 42

Chapter 5
The General Occupational Themes 43

Theory, Content, and Interpretation of the General Occupational Themes 43
History of the General Occupational Themes 51
References 68

Chapter 6
The Basic Interest Scales 69

Content and Interpretation of the Basic Interest Scales 69
Revisions of the Basic Interest Scales for the 1994 *Strong* 70

Definitions of the Basic Interest Scales 70
Using the Basic Interest Scales
  in Counseling 78
Using the Basic Interest Scales in Assessing
  Leisure Interests 80
Research to Revise and Evaluate the Basic
  Interest Scales 80
Relationships of the Basic Interest Scales to the
  General Occupational Themes 83
Reliability 83
Validity 85
References 104

Chapter 7
The Occupational Scales 105

Using the Occupational Scales 105
The Development of the Occupational
  Scales 107
Characteristics of the Final Scales 120
Reliability 130
Concurrent Validity 130
Predictive Validity 150
Unpredictable Scales 153
The Future of the Occupational Scales 154
References 154

Chapter 8
The Personal Style Scales 155

Content and Interpretation of the Personal Style
  Scales 155
Research on the Personal Style Scales 161
References 173

Chapter 9
The Administrative Indexes 175

The Total Responses Index 175
The "Like," "Indifferent," and "Dislike" Percent
  Indexes 175
The Infrequent Responses Index 179

Chapter 10
General Strategies for Interpreting
the *Strong* 181

Effect of Interpreting the *Strong* 181
A Career-Counseling Sequence 182
Orienting the Client to Administration of the
  Strong 184
Preparing for Interpretation of the Profile:
  A Checklist 185

Interpreting the *Strong* Profile 187
Using the Theme Codes to Generalize to Other
  Occupations 192
Using the Personal Style Scales 193
Using the *Strong* to Explore Developmental
  Issues 195
Conclusion 195
References 195

Chapter 11
Challenges in Interpreting the *Strong* 197

Flat Profiles 197
Elevated Profiles 203
Diametrically Opposed Interests 207
Inconsistencies Among the Types of *Strong*
  Scales 208
Challenges Involving the Personal Style
  Scales 211
References 213

Chapter 12
Using the *Strong* with Adults 215

Vocational/Technical Career Exploration 215
Career Development in Organizations 216
Career Change 221
Outplacement 224
Training and Education 225
Retirement 227
Conclusion 227
References 228

Chapter 13
Using the *Strong* with College Students 231

Why Students Take the *Strong* 231
When Students Should Take the *Strong* 232
Using the *Strong* to Choose a Major 232
Using the *Strong* to Choose a Career 237
Using the *Strong* to Change a Major 240
Using the *Strong* to Counsel Graduate
  Students 240
Using the *Strong* to Identify Extracurricular
  Activities 242
Conclusion 242
References 242

Chapter 14
Using the *Strong* with High School Students 245

Age and Reading Level 246
Administration and Interpretation 246

When to Use the *Strong* with High School
  Students   247
Conclusion   253
References   253

Chapter 15
Cross-Cultural Use of the *Strong*   255

Cross-Cultural Counseling Use of
  the *Strong*   255
Review of Research on Cross-Cultural
  Interests   258
Data Collected in 1992–1993 for Racial and
  Ethnic Minority Groups   261
Conclusions and Future Needs   275
References   276

Chapter 16
Using the *Strong* with People Who Have Disabilities   281

Administration   282
Interpretation   283
Situations in Which the *Strong* Is Useful with
  Workers Who Have Disabilities   283
Research on the Vocational Interests of People
  Who Have Disabilities   288
Conclusion   289
References   289

Chapter 17
The Importance of Gender in Interpreting the *Strong*   291

Historical Perspective   291
Types of Gender Differences   292
Representing Gender Differences on
  the *Strong*   292
Using Gender Differences in Interpretation   293
The Nature of the Differences Between
  Women's and Men's Interests   297
Conclusion   306
References   307

Appendix A
Occupational Scales Samples, DOT Codes, and Related Job Titles   309

Appendix B
Occupations and Their Theme Codes   377

Index   385

Item Booklet/Answer Sheet

Profile for Robin Byrd

Figures and Tables

Figures

4.1 Percentage of "Like" Responses to the Item "Artist"   37
4.2 Percentage of "Like" Responses to the Item "Farmer"   38
4.3 Percentage of "Like" Responses to the Item "Public Speaking"   39
5.1 Correlations Between the General Occupational Themes, Arranged in Hexagonal Order   51
5.2 Alpha Reliabilities for Original and Revised General Occupational Themes   54
5.3 Test-Retest Reliabilities of Original and Revised General Occupational Themes   55
5.4 Rank-Ordered Occupations on the Realistic GOT   60
5.5 Rank-Ordered Occupations on the Investigative GOT   60
5.6 Rank-Ordered Occupations on the Artistic GOT   61
5.7 Rank-Ordered Occupations on the Social GOT   61
5.8 Rank-Ordered Occupations on the Enterprising GOT   62
5.9 Rank-Ordered Occupations on the Conventional GOT   62
5.10 Profiles of GOT Mean Scores for Six Academic Majors   64
5.11 Rank-Ordered Means of 24 Majors on the Realistic GOT   65
5.12 Rank-Ordered Means of 24 Majors on the Investigative GOT   65
5.13 Rank-Ordered Means of 24 Majors on the Artistic GOT   66
5.14 Rank-Ordered Means of 24 Majors on the Social GOT   66
5.15 Rank-Ordered Means of 24 Majors on the Enterprising GOT   67
5.16 Rank-Ordered Means of 24 Majors on the Conventional GOT   67
6.1 Rank-Ordered Occupations on the Agriculture BIS   92
6.2 Rank-Ordered Occupations on the Nature BIS   92
6.3 Rank-Ordered Occupations on the Military Activities BIS   93
6.4 Rank-Ordered Occupations on the Athletics BIS   93
6.5 Rank-Ordered Occupations on the Mechanical Activities BIS   94
6.6 Rank-Ordered Occupations on the Science BIS   94
6.7 Rank-Ordered Occupations on the Mathematics BIS   95
6.8 Rank-Ordered Occupations on the Medical Science BIS   95
6.9 Rank-Ordered Occupations on the Music/Dramatics BIS   96
6.10 Rank-Ordered Occupations on the Art BIS   96
6.11 Rank-Ordered Occupations on the Applied Arts BIS   97
6.12 Rank-Ordered Occupations on the Writing BIS   97
6.13 Rank-Ordered Occupations on the Culinary Arts BIS   98
6.14 Rank-Ordered Occupations on the Teaching BIS   98

6.15 Rank-Ordered Occupations on the Social Service BIS 99
6.16 Rank-Ordered Occupations on the Medical Service BIS 99
6.17 Rank-Ordered Occupations on the Religious Activities BIS 100
6.18 Rank-Ordered Occupations on the Public Speaking BIS 100
6.19 Rank-Ordered Occupations on the Law/Politics BIS 101
6.20 Rank-Ordered Occupations on the Merchandising BIS 101
6.21 Rank-Ordered Occupations on the Sales BIS 102
6.22 Rank-Ordered Occupations on the Organizational Management BIS 102
6.23 Rank-Ordered Occupations on the Data Management BIS 103
6.24 Rank-Ordered Occupations on the Computer Activities BIS 103
6.25 Rank-Ordered Occupations on the Office Services BIS 104
7.1 Distribution and Overlap of Scores for Females in the GRS and Female Physicists Scored on the Female Physicist Scale 147
8.1 Relationship of Work Style to the Themes on the Hexagon 157
8.2 Rank-Ordered Occupations on the Work Style Scale 168
8.3 Rank-Ordered Occupations on the Learning Environment Scale 168
8.4 Rank-Ordered Occupations on the Leadership Style Scale 169
8.5 Rank-Ordered Occupations on the Risk Taking/Adventure Scale 169
8.6 Four Occupations Illustrating Diverse Patterns of Personal Style Scales 170
8.7 Rank-Ordered Means of 24 Majors on the Work Style Scale 171
8.8 Rank-Ordered Means of 24 Majors on the Learning Environment Scale 171
8.9 Rank-Ordered Means of 24 Majors on the Leadership Style Scale 172
8.10 Rank-Ordered Means of 24 Majors on the Risk Taking/Adventure Scale 172
10.1 A Career-Counseling Sequence 184
10.2 Preinterpretation Checklist 186
10.3 Steps in Interpreting the *Strong* 187
11.1 Snapshot for Client 1, Showing a Flat Profile 200

11.2 Realistic, Investigative, Artistic, and Social Occupational Scales for Client 2, Showing an Elevated Profile 205
12.1 Snapshot and Personal Style Scales for Client 1, a Small Business Owner 220
12.2 Snapshot for Client 2, a Retired Architect 228
13.1 Snapshot for Client 1, a College Student Choosing a Major 236
13.2 Snapshot for Client 2, a College Student Choosing a Career 239
14.1 Snapshot and Administrative Indexes for Client 1, Confirming a High School Student's Choice of College Major 248
14.2 Snapshot for Client 2, a High School Student Reconsidering Her Choice of College Major 249
14.3 Snapshot for Client 3, a High School Student Entering the Workforce 251
15.1 Snapshot for Client 1, an Asian-American Female 259
15.2 Scores on the GOTs and BISs of Latino/Hispanic Male Police Officers and Other Male Police Officers in the Occupational Sample 272
15.3 Scores on the GOTs and BISs of Asian Female Dentists and Other Female Dentists in the Occupational Sample 273
15.4 Scores on the GOTs and BISs of African-American Female Librarians and Other Female Librarians in the Occupational Sample 274
15.5 Profile Scores of African-American Female School Administrators and Other Female School Administrators in the Occupational Sample 277
16.1 Investigative Occupational Scales and Personal Style Scales for Client 1, a Scientist Reassessing His Work Duties 284
16.2 Realistic and Investigative Occupational Scales for Client 2, an Accountant Seeking a Career Change 286
16.3 Enterprising Occupational Scales for Client 3, a Flight Attendant Changing Careers Due to Disability 287
17.1 Snapshot for Client 1, a Woman Reentering the Workforce 297
17.2 Percentage of "Like" Responses to the Item "Operating Machinery" 299

Tables

Note: All scores contained in tables are expressed as standard scores. Their derivation is explained in Chapters 5, 6, and 7.

2.1 New Items on Form T317 ($N = 35$)   10
2.2 Changes in the Basic Interest Scales   12
2.3 New Occupations ($N = 14$ Occupations, $N = 26$ Scales)   13
2.4 Occupational Groups Resampled for the 1994 *Strong* ($N = 36$)   14
2.5 Changes in the Occupational Scales   15
2.6 Occupational Scales with Correlations < .70 and Percentage of Items for Each Scale for Which a "Dislike" Response Is Scored Positively   17
2.7 Occupational Scales with Group Mean Differences > 7 Points   18
2.8 Mean Differences Between 1985 and 1994 Occupational Scales   19
3.1 Narrative Reports and Support Material for the 1994 *Strong*   31
4.1 Original Items and Their Potential Replacements Appearing on the Research Version   34
4.2 Percentage of "Like" Responses to the Items "Farmer" and "Artist" for the 1930s–1940s, 1960s, 1970s–1980s, and 1990s for 20 Occupational Samples   41
5.1 Intercorrelations Between the General Occupational Themes   52
5.2 Comparisons of 1985 and 1994 General Occupational Themes: Correlations, Internal Consistency Reliabilities, and Test-Retest Reliabilities   53
5.3 Means, Standard Deviations, and Interpretive Boundaries for the General Occupational Themes for the General Reference Samples   56
5.4 Test-Retest Reliability Statistics in Four Samples for the General Occupational Themes   57
5.5 Three-Year Test-Retest Reliability Statistics for the General Occupational Themes (Original Version)   58
5.6 Correlations Between the General Occupational Themes and *Vocational Preference Inventory* Scales   59
6.1 Comparisons of 1985 and 1994 Basic Interest Scales: Correlations and Internal Consistency Reliabilities   82
6.2 Means, Standard Deviations, and Interpretive Boundaries for the Basic Interest Scales for the General Reference Sample   84
6.3 Intercorrelations Between the Basic Interest Scales for Women and Men   86
6.4 Correlations Between the General Occupational Themes and the Basic Interest Scales for Women and Men   87
6.5 Test-Retest Reliability Statistics in Four Samples for the Basic Interest Scales   88
7.1 Demographic Characteristics of the General Reference Samples   110
7.2 Scale Characteristics, Three- to Six-Month Reliability Coefficients, Concurrent Validities (Percent Overlap), and Minimum and Maximum Possible Scores for the 1994 Occupational Scales   114
7.3 Data Used to Classify Occupational Scales: General Occupational Theme Scale Means and Percent Highest Score on GOT Scales   122
7.4 Test-Retest Reliability Statistics in Four Samples for the 211 Occupational Scales   131
7.5 Tilton Percent Overlap   148
7.6 Percentages of 132 Overlaps (Q) Among Selected Occupational Scales Falling into Various Intervals for Females and Males   149
7.7 Summary of *SVIB* and *SVIB-SCII* Predictive Validity Studies   152
8.1 Brief Definitions of Poles for the Personal Style Scales   156
8.2 Means, Standard Deviations, and Score Boundaries for the Personal Style Scales for the General Reference Sample   162
8.3 Intercorrelations of the Personal Style Scales for the General Reference Sample   163
8.4 Correlations Between the Personal Style Scales and the General Occupational Themes for Women and Men   164
8.5 Correlations Between the Personal Style Scales and the Basic Interest Scales for Women and Men   165
8.6 Internal Consistency Reliabilities for the Personal Style Scales   166
8.7 Test-Retest Reliability Statistics in Four Samples for the Personal Style Scales   167
8.8 Learning Environment Scores by Educational Level and Gender   167
9.1 Means and Standard Deviations of the "Like," "Indifferent," and "Dislike" Percent Indexes   176

9.2 Intercorrelations of the "Like" Percent Indexes for the Eight Booklet Parts and Subtotal   178

9.3 Score Distributions on the Infrequent Responses Indexes   180

10.1 Selected Items from the Mathematician Scales Illustrating How a Theme Code Suggests Day-to-Day Likes and Dislikes   191

11.1 Possible Reasons for Flat Profiles   199

11.2 Possible Reasons for Elevated Profiles   204

11.3 A Sample of Items Weighted Positively and Negatively on the Male Mathematician Scale   210

12.1 Occupations on the *Strong* Not Requiring a Four-Year College Degree for Entry   216

12.2 Example of Using Appendix A to Identify Additional Vocational Occupations   217

12.3 Reasons for Making a Career Change   222

12.4 Obstacles to a Career Change   223

13.1 Examples of Direct and Indirect Links Between *Strong* Occupational Scales and College Majors   234

15.1 Sample Sizes and Demographic Data for the Four Largest Racial and Ethnic Groups in the *Strong* Sample   263

15.2 Occupational Samples with > 10% Combined Ethnic Membership and Specific Ethnic Groups That Compose ≥ 5% of an Occupational Sample   264

15.3 Response Differences Between Ethnic Sample and General Reference Sample   265

15.4 Means and Standard Deviations on General Occupational Themes, Basic Interest Scales, and Personal Style Scales for the GRS, Whites, and Specific Ethnic Groups   267

15.5 Overlap in Items Differentiating Occupational Groups—Specific Ethnic Group Members and All Other Members of the Occupation—from the GRS   270

15.6 Top Ten Items Differentiating Occupational Groups—Specific Ethnic Group Members and All Other Members of the Occupation—from the GRS   271

17.1 Response Comparisons to the Item "Operating Machinery" for Five Pairs of Female and Male Samples   298

17.2 Items Showing Large Difference Between Women and Men in the Same Occupations   301

17.3 Mean Scores on and Correlations Between the 102 Pairs of Women's and Men's Occupational Scales   302

17.4 Summary of Correlations Between Scores on Female and Male Scales for the Female and Male GRSs (1994) and Women-in-General and Men-in-General (1985)   305

17.5 Overlapping Items in Most and Least Highly Correlated Female and Male Occupational Scales   306

17.6 Occupational Scales with Score Differences ≥ 10 Between Females and Males in the GRSs   307

Preface

The 1994 revision of the *Strong Interest Inventory* is the latest in the ongoing revision of the most widely used interest inventory in the history of career measurement. One of the hallmarks of the *Strong* is the commitment on the part of the developers and the publisher to continual improvement, refinement, and updating of the inventory.

This revision has spanned over five years of concentrated effort and has involved literally hundreds of professionals and practitioners. The 1994 *Strong*, the result of all this effort, contains new Basic Interest Scales, more Occupational Scales, and a new set of scales called the Personal Style Scales. Also, this version of the inventory was constructed using larger samples than were previously used; it has greater reliability, has fewer items, and offers an easier to use, more attractive Profile than earlier editions of the *Strong*.

The process used to develop the 1994 *Strong* was, however, different in many ways from the method used for previous revisions. Two closely interwoven themes provided the motivating force behind many of our efforts and decisions along the way. The first of these themes was inclusion—inclusion of more and different kinds of people in the research and development phases as well as inclusion of data and interpretive information about how the *Strong* can be used with specific populations in published material. The second theme was balance—balance between innovation and tradition and between science and practice. A brief description of how these two themes influenced the development of the 1994 *Strong* will give the reader a flavor of the long, complex, but eminently challenging revision process.

Many individuals contributed to the *Strong* revision. More researchers and scholars were involved than ever before. A team approach to development was adopted from the beginning. We found it productive to combine the skills, knowledge, and talents of people from all over the country and to discuss the issues that arose in a collegial forum. Some team members were delighted to spend hours discussing the technical aspects of interest measurement. Fortunately, other team members reined in some of our more esoteric discussions and pointed us in the direction of practical and timely solutions to problems. These researchers and scholars created and tested items, developed scales, and analyzed data from over 67,000 people.

Another important group were a board of prestigious researchers and practitioners who served on the *Strong* Research Advisory Board. The members of this board, who are among the most prolific and well-respected researchers in career theory and measurement, advised the revision team at every step along the way. They grappled with difficult measurement issues, always struggling to balance innovation with tradition.

Still another group that must be mentioned are the publishing professionals at Consulting Psychologists Press, Inc., and Stanford University Press who organized and managed the revision process. This team prepared, mailed, and processed thousands of copies of the research form used to collect data from the occupational samples. This group also coordinated the revision, designed the new *Strong* Profile, and developed other reports and materials to support the revised inventory.

Finally, but perhaps most important, were the hundreds of career professionals, practicing in a wide variety of settings and with a diversity of clients, who freely gave of their time to help shape the next generation of one of their primary career counseling tools. This group included professionals from high schools, community colleges, universities, outplacement firms, private practice, government agencies, and human resources departments in businesses and nonprofit organizations. They provided information on what they wanted to change as well as what they wanted to keep, on how they and their clients use information on a Profile, and on what new scales they wanted as well as what old scales they did not want. With every problem that faced the revision team, this question was always asked: How will this help the users of the *Strong* to better serve their clients?

This guide itself is another representation of the attempt to include and balance both research and practice. The general plan of the guide is to introduce the various elements of the inventory and then to feature them in a detailed discussion of counseling applications for which the *Strong* is used. There is much technical material here—new research and new data. Nonetheless, we have tried to keep the counselor's perspective foremost in mind, even within the more technical chapters.

Although previous publications of the *Strong* manuals and user's guides included some discussion of the use of the *Strong* with different populations, this guide includes, for the first time, in-depth presentations of how the inventory can be used with specific populations, including diverse cultural groups, adults, college students, high school students, people with disabilities, and women. These chapters represent much of the latest information on career practice and research with these groups of people.

It is up to the users of the *Strong*, both current and future, to decide whether we have achieved our goal of creating a revised *Strong Interest Inventory* that represents the best of science and practice and a useful balance of innovation and tradition.

Finally, we dedicate our efforts to the memory of E. K. Strong and to those who kept the tradition alive with the previous revisions of the inventory. Strong was clearly fascinated, as we are, by the interests of people in various occupations and by the many challenges inherent in determining those interests. Although the time and effort devoted to this revision by the team were enormous, we only have to step back to realize that our labor seems minuscule compared to that of E. K. Strong. Data that we have been able to compute in hours (and transmit across the country in minutes) took Strong weeks or months to calculate. That our methods are very different from those of Strong does not keep us from wishing that he could have joined us at the numerous meetings held over the course of the revision.

We are honored to have been given the opportunity to continue in E. K. Strong's tradition—one that continually reflects change in both the science of interest measurement and the world of work.

—**Lenore W. Harmon, Fred H. Borgen, & Allen L. Hammer**
August 1994

Acknowledgments

Lenore W. Harmon would like to thank David Coon and Amanda Kim for their superior research assistance. She would also like to acknowledge Robert Most, whose willingness to share his extensive knowledge of the *Strong* and its history provided insights and perceptions that facilitated the development of this revision.

Fred H. Borgen would like to thank the following individuals who provided invaluable research assistance: David A. C. Donnay, Jeff Hinds, Kristin A. Long, Lori P. Montross, and Lon Olsen.

The authors and contributing writers as well as the *Strong* team members at Consulting Psychologists Press, Inc., would like to give particular thanks to the counselors who helped gather appropriate case studies for the *Applications and Technical Guide* and to the clients themselves who were willing to take the *Strong* and share their results with us. Their participation is greatly appreciated.

The authors would especially like to acknowledge the important contributions Jo-Ida Hansen has made to the *Strong* over the years. She was the principal investigator of the 1981 and 1985 revisions of the inventory. Dr. Hansen, like the other researchers on the *Strong Interest Inventory* who preceded her, built on the solid foundation of the instrument. It was with the 1985 revision that more nonprofessional and vocational/technical Occupational Scales were added and new reference samples were developed. Although Dr. Hansen was not directly involved in this revision, her ideas as well as her prose are evident in it.

CHAPTER 1

Interest Measurement and the Strong Interest Inventory

The idea of measuring people's interests has been around since World War I, when military psychologists wrestled with the problem of how to determine which recruits should be cooks and which should be members of the cavalry. Most of us recognize that the type of man who likes the job of cooking (there were no women in the armed services in WWI) is different from the type of man who likes the job of riding and tending horses, and the idea of classifying people by their interests has some intuitive appeal. After WWI, it became clear to some of those same psychologists that the idea had important implications for civilians as well. If it were possible to measure people's vocational interests and to use those data along with information about abilities and values, it might be possible to perform two important, interrelated services. First, individuals could be helped in making educational and career plans. Second, the common interests of people working in various occupations could be described. These ideas led to the development of the *Strong*. What follows here will discuss, in general, what the *Strong Vocational Interest Blanks® (SVIB)*—which in its current version is known as the *Strong Interest Inventory*—is and how it can be used. ◆

E. K. Strong, Jr., and the SVIB

The *SVIB*, one of the first interest inventories to be developed, was introduced in 1927 by E. K. Strong, Jr., who had been one of those military psychologists (Most, 1993). E. K. Strong was an academic and a researcher who spent most of his career at Stanford University. He believed in grounding his work firmly in empirical research and in updating his materials and scoring procedures periodically. His approach to the care and maintenance of the interest inventory he developed is captured in a story told by one of his daughters. During the Great Depression of the 1930s, the faculty at Stanford were forced to take rather substantial salary reductions to avoid layoffs. Professor Strong had a family to support, but he also had an interest inventory to nurture. People who wanted to take the relatively new *SVIB* sent their responses, along with a dollar to pay for the service and postage, to Professor Strong's home. When he came home for lunch each day, he would open the mail and carefully stack up the incoming dollars to be devoted to the further development of the inventory. He never diverted any of those dollars to allay the problems of maintaining his family on a substantially reduced income. This story shows very clearly the importance he attached to nurturing the *Strong* with further research. In fact, Strong brought out the first revision of his inventory in 1938, during those Depression years.

A further testimony to Strong's commitment to his interest inventory is contained in a letter found in archives at Stanford University Press. Lewis Terman, writing to Donald Super about his review of Strong's book, *Vocational Interests of Men and Women* (Strong, 1943), said:

> *I have been in close touch with Strong's work on interests since he began it and on the golf course have discussed many aspects of the matter with him. From this close-quarter observation I have been throughout tremendously impressed by Strong's determination to stick to the job until he had it carried as far as possible. Never has he considered his own financial interests in the matter, for he has put back into the research all his profits on the Hollerith scoring of the tests for other people. The total of this runs to at least $50,000 and perhaps $75,000. My impression is that he has even spent a good part of his small royalties on the test blanks in the same way. (Lewis Terman, correspondence to Donald Super, June 15, 1945)*

What Does the Strong Do?

Although, in purpose and design, the current version of the *Strong* is remarkably similar to the one introduced over 50 years ago, over the years it has taken on elements that relate it to recent theoretical developments. Because the instrument is constantly updated, the scores received by an individual today compare that person's interests with those of people who have responded to the inventory recently and who may be in occupations that did not exist in Dr. Strong's day. Thus, in no way is the *Strong* limited by its evolutionary antiquity; it remains today the most scientifically sound, thoroughly researched, and widely used interest inventory.

The *Strong Interest Inventory* (Form T317) is a carefully constructed questionnaire that inquires about a respondent's level of interest in a wide range of familiar *items* (i.e., words or short phrases describing occupations, occupational activities, hobbies, leisure activities, school subjects, and types of people). For each of the 317 items, the respondent is asked to indicate his or her preferences from among three response categories on an *answer sheet*. The answers are then analyzed by computer (the *Strong* cannot be scored by hand) to derive scores on measures of interest type, called *scales*. The results are printed on a report called a *Profile*, which presents the scale scores in an organized format and offers interpretive information. Although the Profile is largely self-explanatory, it is helpful to have a counselor guide the respondent to an understanding of the scales and an interpretation of the scores. This *Applications and Technical Guide* provides counselors and research psychologists with practical information about using the *Strong* drawn from clinical knowledge, case studies, and occupational information; in addition, it presents technical information about the development and validation of the scales necessary for a thorough understanding and evaluation of the inventory.

The *Strong* uses a person's responses to the items to compare her or his pattern of responses to the patterns of responses of people of different types and in different occupations. This combination of information from the individual compared with information about other people allows us to make assumptions about whether that individual is likely to find satisfaction in the work typically done in a given occupation. Although most people can answer quite easily the *Strong's* questions about what specific things they like and dislike, few understand how their individual patterns of likes and dislikes are related to the patterns of people working in various occupations. Neither do they understand specific occupations well enough to know how their likes and dislikes are related to the activities pursued in those occupations. The power of the *Strong* thus rests on two assumptions: (1) that the day-to-day activities typical of a specific occupation are reflected in the interests of the people who are employed in it and (2) that those who have a similar pattern of interests will be satisfied in that occupation if they have compatible values and the necessary knowledge and abilities.

The *Strong* gives the respondent five main types of information: first, scores on six General Occupational Themes, which reflect the respondent's overall *orientation* to work; second, scores on 25 Basic Interest Scales, which report consistency of interests or aversions in 25 specific *areas*, such as art, science, and public speaking; third, scores on 211 Occupational Scales representing 109 different occupations, which indicate degree of similarity between the respondent's interests and the characteristic interests of women and men working in those *occupations*; fourth, scores on four Personal Style Scales, which measure aspects of the *style* with which an individual likes to learn, work, assume leadership, and take risks; and fifth, three types of Administrative Indexes, which help to identify *invalid* or unusual Profiles for special attention. Scores are arranged on the Profile in a format that encourages the respondent to note overall trends, to see how these trends are related to the world of work, and to employ these findings in a program of career exploration. The emphasis is on organizing the information in a way that best helps the respondent develop a general strategy toward approaching educational and career decisions.

Why Use Assessment Instruments in Career Counseling?

At the most general level, career counseling involves learning about oneself and the world of work. Typically, learning about oneself in this context means obtaining information about one's interests, needs, and abilities. Psychological testing is one technique used to obtain such information; other techniques include biographical interviews, recollection of previous experiences, exploring occupational-information resources, direct observation of others in the workplace, discussing work environments with people in a variety of occupations, and fantasizing about an ideal job. Because psychological testing offers several substantial advantages over other methods of data gathering, it is incorporated into all major approaches to career counseling as an integral component of the client's self-exploration (Crites, 1974). Among these advantages are the following:

1. Counselors can be taught to use tests more easily than they can be trained to use other methods of observation, such as rating scales or structured interviews.
2. Tests are more objective than are other methods of observation; this is not to say that tests cannot be influenced by the prejudices or beliefs of the test constructors, but biases of that sort can be controlled to a greater extent and are open to continued investigation by the psychological profession.
3. Tests afford the counselor both structure and focus in conducting the interview; they facilitate the interchange of information.
4. Observations made through tests are more easily communicated than observations made through other means.
5. Tests reduce the time needed for the gathering of information necessary for effective counseling; in other words, they provide a welcome shortcut to that information.
6. Because tests provide norms, they provide a standard of comparison for the individual in self-evaluation.
7. Tests can sometimes uncover predispositions that might not surface in interviews and might not otherwise be recognized by the respondents themselves prior to testing.

Thus, interest inventories, as a major class of tests, can be used effectively for a variety of purposes. What follows is a review of several of the more common applications.

Why Use Interest Inventories?

Interest inventories should perform one or both of two principal functions in career counseling. First, they should provide people with information about themselves and their relationship to the working world, information that will lead them to greater self-understanding and to better decisions about the course of their lives. Second, interest inventories should provide people who must make decisions about others (e.g., counselors, teachers, administrators, human resources managers, supervisors) with comparable information as well as strategies for interpreting it, so that the decisions these people make are ones that consider the unique qualities of each individual.

Interest inventories, in particular the *Strong*, can be used in many ways to serve these functions. Although the following discussion does not exhaust the possibilities, it lists those applications that have been found to be most effective.

An Aid in Making Educational and Occupational Choices

By far the most common use of the *Strong* is to help people make educational and occupational choices. People must make decisions about the course of their lives. Because choices about educational major and eventual occupation may have more impact on people's lives than any other decisions they make, these choices should be well informed.

When people make these decisions, they should have access to good occupational information, professional advice, and the best possible data about themselves. The *Strong* has been designed specifically for these situations, and the information it provides about a person's pattern of interests is directly applicable to making educational and occupational choices. Of course, other information, such as experiences and abilities, also should be considered in making these choices; the Profile offers a measure of *interests*, not abilities.

While some counselors use interest inventories only with people who are uncertain about what they want to do, many other clients who have already made firm decisions can be reassured by seeing their choices confirmed. One common reaction to the Profile is, "Yes, my scores look reasonable; that's about what I figured. This information is reassuring."

The *Strong* can be used with a variety of age groups—including high school students, college students, and adults—and with people from all walks of life. It is used by a variety of institutions to assess interests: high schools, colleges and universities, social service agencies, community organizations, corporations, consulting firms, employment agencies, and the military services. It can be used in career counseling that leads to decisions such as selecting a major or training program, choosing an occupation, making a mid-career change, or preparing for retirement (Hansen, 1984).

A Vehicle for Discussion

Many people seeking vocational guidance feel more comfortable in counseling sessions if the initial discussion is structured, and they are grateful for an organized assessment of their interest patterns. Inventory scores provide a focus that moves conversation quickly to areas that concern the client. Many counselors, especially inexperienced ones, also appreciate the focusing qualities of the *Strong* Profile scores. Of course, inventories should not be used as a crutch, but that is seldom a problem once the counselor has gained some experience.

Although experienced teachers and counselors can guide discussions with students quite adroitly even without the aid of inventories, many parents do not have the same facility. Interest inventory scores can present the parent with specific information about the student's interests—information that may not have surfaced in earlier discussions—and the Profile offers the student an opportunity to explain personal feelings in ways not usually possible. For example, several years ago, one university student reported with considerable relief that his *Strong* results had helped him convince his parents that he had good reason for not wanting to go to medical school. He was from a family with a long history of physicians—a parent, two siblings, a grandparent, and two other relatives had all gone to medical school—but he had never wanted to be a doctor. Whenever he said this to his family, they always responded, "Sure, we all felt that way when we were your age. After you get into it, you'll like it." Although years of protest had not availed, the evidence provided by his Profile—that his interests were quite different from those of physicians—convinced his family members that he was not destined to follow in the family tradition. With no further protest on their part, he took his degree in architecture and today is contentedly designing schools and industrial facilities.

In a similar situation, a student whose parents were advising her to enter nursing training had set her sights higher—she wanted to go to medical school. She used her *Strong* scores (and tests of ability) to demonstrate to them that her interests (and aptitudes) were similar to those of physicians and other biological scientists. Shown this evidence, the parents agreed to support her plans.

A Stimulus for Self-Exploration and the Exploration of Related Life Issues

Scores on the *Strong* may also be used to identify preferences for nonwork activities and situations, such as interests in vocational or recreational activities, interests in living or work environments, or interests that reflect preferences for types of people. Using the *Strong* to organize interests in all areas of life helps a person learn to integrate various life roles and to maximally satisfy his or her interests.

A Selection Device for Those Who Must Make Decisions About Others

Within the educational system, students are most often assigned to programs on the basis of their intellectual abilities. Looking at a student's interests, however, reveals another type of information about whether a specific program is appropriate for that student. For instance, suppose a female student wants to enter the automotive repair curriculum in her high school, but her counselor has encouraged her to take secretarial studies or a college preparatory course instead. If she is academically eligible for the automotive repair curriculum and her *Strong* scores show that her interests are compatible with those of workers in such an occupation, her counselor may be more willing to authorize the student's transfer into the program.

Within the world of work, people are most often hired for their ability to do the tasks associated with a particular job. The use of information demonstrating which applicants have interests most like those of others in similar positions may help to select employees like those who are known to be satisfied and have some tenure in similar positions.

Precisely how test scores should be used in educational and employee selection varies according to the situation and the training and experience of the person who is making the decision. Such decisions are important for all concerned and should be made by people with professional training. Using the inventory simply as a "go/no go" selection device, and making each decision on the basis of a fixed cutoff score, is not recommended.

For selection purposes, the inventory should be used as only part of a general screening process developed by someone with professional training. Similarly, using an inventory to make placement decisions about people already in an educational or employment setting is handled best by a trained personnel worker who studies the respondent's scores, then discusses them with him or her along with other considerations dictated by the practical setting.

A Tool to Help People Understand Their Job Dissatisfaction

Some people are dissatisfied with their jobs because they are in positions that fail to allow them outlets for their dominant interests or because they feel they have little in common with their colleagues. Many times a Profile can identify the problem by showing the individual how she or he is different. For example, when an accountant is shown that her interests lean more toward the artistic than those of most executives, she has information that can help her contend with the routine of her job. Even if she feels she cannot change careers, she can take steps to improve her situation, perhaps by becoming active in the local art institute during her off hours or by seeking employment as an accountant in an art-related firm, such as an advertising agency. What plan she develops depends on her imagination and energy, but the Profile scores can provide her with a direction.

How Psychological Research Has Made Use of the Strong

The *Strong* has been part of hundreds of research studies over more than half a century. Research has focused on individual, occupational, group, institutional, cultural, and societal trends and changes.

Studying Change Within an Individual

Interest inventories can be used in case studies of change (or lack of change) over time, where a single person is seen as representing a generalized phenomenon with significance in the counseling setting. For instance, an individual whose scores showed a change from Investigative to Social interests over the course of ten years had, in the interim, engaged in a new style of collective decision making within his engineering research group and had attended a number of training sessions to help him function more effectively in that format. That interests can change in response to organizational socialization is worth underscoring with case study evidence.

Studying Characteristic Interests of People in Particular Occupations

Detailed information about an occupation is useful for many purposes, such as helping people decide if they would like employment in that occupation, planning recruiting efforts to attract to the occupation those people who would be most likely to remain, or identifying people already in the occupation who might be more happily and more effectively assigned elsewhere.

Data on a new Occupational Scale, such as its item response percentages, scale means, and intercorrelations with existing scales, provide information about the dominant interests of people in that occupation. For example, interest inventory data from a sample of women geologists showed that their likes were concentrated in academic areas such as science and mathematics as well as in nature, outdoor, and mechanical activities. Their aversions focused on social service and religious activities and on traditional home and family activities. They also showed an aversion to Enterprising endeavors, such as merchandising and sales.

Studying Change in Groups

Interest inventories have been used to test groups at one point in time and then to retest them at a later time to see how they have changed. In a study by the American Association of Medical Colleges, 2,800 medical school students were tested upon entering and retested four years later, upon graduation (Hutchins, 1964). The result, discussed in more detail in Campbell (1971), indicated that these students showed a decline in both scientific and social service interests (areas in which they had scored very high initially), and a mild increase in adventuresome interests. These findings run counter to expectations and afford an interesting basis for further research into issues of professional socialization and the validity of scores obtained when the respondent is an applicant for a position for which the selection is highly competitive—both topics that can be studied by looking at differences in groups over time.

Interest inventories are not precise enough, however, to detect small, subtle, short-term changes in groups. Because the items for the inventory are selected for long-term stability and validity, small day-to-day shifts are not reflected in the scores. For example, teachers who test students before and after a specific course to determine the impact of the course usually will find that *Strong* scores show little, if any, change. Most people's interests, as measured by the *Strong*, are quite stable over the short term. Over a longer period, such as two or three years, changes may occur in some people—especially young people—and inventory scores generally reflect those changes.

Studying Change in Institutions

Interest inventories can be used to compare different high school or college classes, pools of applicants, or volunteer groups at various times. For example, a study that examined the characteristics of freshman classes at Dartmouth College over a 20-year period (Campbell, 1969) showed that the more recent classes were much more academically oriented—with stronger interests in science and the arts—than were their predecessors, who were more attracted to business endeavors.

Studying General Societal Trends

When samples tested in the 1930s and 1940s are compared with analogous samples tested in the 1960s, 1970s, and 1980s, estimates of general change within society can be drawn. The results of such studies (Campbell, 1966; Hansen, 1981, 1982) show that vocational interest patterns are much more stable over long time spans than the average person (or psychologist, for that matter) might think.

Studying Cross-Cultural Influences

Various studies have used the *Strong* to compare occupations in other countries. For some of these, the inventory has been translated into another language; for others—studies in Ireland and Pakistan, for example—the English-language version was used. Examples include Lonner's work with German-speaking psychologists and accountants (Lonner, 1968, 1969), Shah's work with Pakistani physicians and engineers (Shah, 1971), Hanlon's study of Irish students (Hanlon, 1971), Stauffer's work with the German and French translations of the *Strong* (Stauffer, 1973), and Fouad's work with the Spanish translation (Fouad, 1984; Fouad, Cudeck, & Hansen, 1984). The results of these studies show considerable similarity of interests across several countries among people in the same occupation. In general, these findings indicate that American norms are usable in other countries as representations of the interests of specific occupations there.

One problem in using earlier editions of the *Strong* cross-culturally was that a few items (e.g., "Be a cheerleader" or "Work with Democrats") were peculiarly American and bemused or irritated foreign respondents. Although the number of such items was too small to have an appreciable effect on scoring, the loss of goodwill was substantial. This problem was addressed in the development of the 1974 edition of the *Strong*, and many troublesome items were eliminated. Consequently, problems have been minimal with recent translations into other languages (Hansen & Fouad, 1984); most items (e.g., "Operating machinery," "Writing reports," and "Watching an open-heart operation") translate easily into other languages and elicit the same responses as they do in English. Chapter 15 discusses in more detail the translation and validation of the *Strong* into other languages.

Possibilities for Use of the Strong in Research

The items on the *Strong* provide a rich source of information for future study about the cognitive processes of individuals, the match between interest patterns and counseling interventions, the impact of interests on interpersonal relationships and group behavior, and the design of work environments and leisure activities around interests.

Studying Cognitive Processes Related to Interests

Item-level data from the *Strong* can be used to study:

1. *Cognitive structures regarding the world of work and how these structures change over time.* For example, does an occupation or occupational task, represented by an interest inventory item, drop out of a cluster of items with which it has previously been associated if technological change renders the item obsolete? Or does it remain a part of the cluster as long as respondents can remember what the item means?
2. *The development of different cognitive schema for evaluating interest inventory items.* What is common to the development of individuals who all view a set of items the same way, and what differentiates them from individuals who all view that set of items in the opposite way? For instance, what is common in the background of individuals who score very high on one of the General Occupational Themes scales, and what differentiates them from those who score very low?
3. *Emerging similarities and differences in cognitive schemas among groups of people.* For instance, are the interests of men and women in the same occupation converging or diverging?

Selecting Counseling Interventions

The *Strong* scales also provide a rich source of information that can be used to guide counseling interventions. Research in matching people with different types of interests with different types of counseling intervention indicate that such matches improve counseling outcomes (Kivlighan et al., 1981). The General Occupational Themes scales can be used to identify an individual's global interests and to select counseling techniques that will improve the counseling process for that individual, whether in a one-to-one or group session.

Studying Interpersonal Relationships

Marriages between people with similar interests might be more successful than marriages between people with dissimilar interests. Parents and children with different patterns of interest might need more help in communicating with each other than do those with similar interests. Research possibilities in such areas are almost endless.

Studying the Behavior Type Composition of Groups

Groups exhibiting heterogeneous interest patterns may be more or less efficient than are groups with homogeneous patterns. The characteristics of the individuals within any group have an impact on overall group behavior, and interest inventories can help in studying such issues.

Designing Jobs Around the Interests of People

Interest inventories are a systematic means of asking people what they like and dislike. Such information should be useful—indeed, crucial—in designing tasks and work environments that people find appealing. Given our current level of knowledge, this may at the moment be a grandiose goal. Still, if we know, for example, that psychologists have strong artistic interests, departments of psychology and psychological clinics might do well to allocate some portion of their supply budgets to making their environments more aesthetically exciting. Similarly, if we know that people in sales have high levels of adventuresome interests, designing sales incentives that capitalize on that knowledge could increase productivity.

Similar but more subtle modifications of working environments have been made by workers themselves, often through decades of gradual change. By learning to shape environments more systematically, we could have a greater impact sooner and create a greater diversity in work environments. In the absence of forces to the contrary, it is conformity, not diversity, that is the rule in most contemporary work settings. The better we can document that different people, or different subgroups of people, like different things, the more successfully we can adapt their work environments.

Designing Leisure Activities Around Interests

Leisure activities provide people with opportunities to use the same interests they use in the world of work or to use interests that are not utilized in their workplaces. Research on the relationship of interests to leisure activities can help determine which activities are used to satisfy work-related versus nonwork-related interests. This in turn may lead to an understanding of how the kind of leisure activities that individuals use is related to their satisfaction with work.

References

Campbell, D. P. (1966). The stability of vocational interests within occupations over long time spans. *Personnel and Guidance Journal, 44,* 1012–1019.

Campbell, D. P. (1969). The vocational interests of Dartmouth College freshmen: 1947–67. *Personnel and Guidance Journal, 47,* 527–530.

Campbell, D. P. (1971). *Handbook for the Strong Vocational Interest Blank.* Stanford, CA: Stanford University Press.

Crites, J. O. (1974). Career counseling: A review of major approaches. *The Counseling Psychologist, 4,* 3–23.

Fouad, N. A. (1984). Comparison of interests across cultures. *Dissertation Abstracts International,* 4503A (84–13), 777.

Fouad, N. A., Cudeck, R., & Hansen, J. C. (1984). Convergent validity of the Spanish and English forms of the SCII for bilingual Hispanic high school students. *Journal of Counseling Psychology, 31,* 339–348.

Hanlon, R. J. (1971). *Validation of the Strong Vocational Interest Blank for use in the Irish Republic.* Unpublished doctoral dissertation, Social Science Research Centre, University College, Galway, Ireland.

Hansen, J. C. (1981, August). *Changing interests: Myth or reality?* Paper presented at meetings of the American Psychological Association, Los Angeles.

Hansen, J. C. (1982, July). *The effect of history on the vocational interests of women.* Paper presented at meetings of the International Congress of Applied Psychology, Edinburgh, Scotland.

Hansen, J. C. (1984). *User's guide for the SVIB-SCII.* Stanford, CA: Stanford University Press.

Hansen, J. C., & Fouad, N. A. (1984). Translation and validation of the Spanish form of the Strong-Campbell Interest Inventory. *Measurement and Evaluation in Guidance, 16,* 192–197.

Hutchins, E. B. (1964). The AAMC longitudinal study: Implications for medical education. *Journal of Medical Education, 39,* 265–277.

Kivlighan, D. M., Jr., Hageseth, J. A., Tipton, R. M., & McGovern, T. V. (1981). Effects of matching treatment approaches and personality types in group vocational counseling. *Journal of Counseling Psychology, 28,* 315–320.

Lonner, W. J. (1968). The SVIB visits German, Austrian, and Swiss psychologists. *American Psychologist, 23,* 164–179.

Lonner, W. J. (1969). Bericht über Untersuchungen mit der deutschen Fassung des Strong Vocational Interest Blank for Men (SVIB). *Psychologische Rundschau, 20,* 151–156.

Most, R. (1993). Edward K. Strong: A thoroughly applied psychologist. *The Industrial Organizational Psychologist, 30,* 37–40.

Shah, I. (1971). A cross-cultural comparative study of vocational interests. *Dissertation Abstracts International, 31* (8-B), 5049.

Stauffer, E., (Trans. and Ed.) (1973). [E. K. Strong, Jr., and D. P. Campbell.] *Questionnaire d'intérets vocationnels: Manuel d'instructions.* Issy-les-Moulineaux, France.

Strong, E. K. (1943). *Vocational Interests of Men and Women.* Stanford, CA: Stanford University Press.

CHAPTER 2

What's New in 1994

The *Strong* has developed a loyal following of users over the years, probably due, at least in part, to a commitment to updating and improving the inventory on the part of everyone associated with it since its introduction, beginning with E. K. Strong. In addition, the various revisions of the *Strong* have been heavily researched, both by its developers and by other scholars. This chapter is written for those loyal users and researchers who are familiar with the 1985 *Strong* and Form T325. New users will not need to read this chapter to use the 1994 revision, although they may find it of interest. Since this chapter assumes a level of knowledge about the *Strong* that is typical of past users (thus avoiding the need to explain concepts introduced in subsequent chapters), a first-time user may find it necessary to read or refer to other chapters in order to understand the material presented here.

It is important to note that this guide replaces both the manual (Hansen & Campbell, 1985) and user's guide (Hansen, 1992) associated with the 1985 *Strong*. This change is intended to convince the reader that the practical applications and technical foundation of the *Strong* go hand in hand, since the belief is that the most skilled users of the *Strong*, whether for practice or research, are those who are best informed about its technical and psychometric bases.

This chapter gives a brief overview of data collection for the 1994 *Strong*. The chapter then introduces changes that have been made to the inventory at several levels: the items, the General Reference Samples (GRSs), the General Occupational Themes (GOTs), the Basic Interest Scales (BISs), the Occupational Scales (OSs), the new Personal Style Scales, the Administrative Indexes, and the Profile. ◆

Overview of Data Collection

During 1992 and 1993, over 55,000 people in 50 occupations completed a research version of the *Strong*. In part, the purpose of the revision was to update items on the Item Booklet/Answer Sheet, increase the *Strong*'s coverage by developing new Occupational Scales (OSs) representing emerging and growth occupations, and collect data from contemporary occupational groups for existing OSs that were based on old criterion groups. This data collection effort is the basis for many of the changes reported in this chapter as well as for the work reported in subsequent chapters. The extent of the effort and expense involved in revising the *Strong* is evidence of the commitment on the part of the publishers to keep the inventory up-to-date and innovative, qualities that have characterized the *Strong* since its inception.

Items

The research form of the *Strong* used for data collection in 1992 and 1993 contained all the 325 items from Form T325. A few of these items were altered slightly for purposes of improving language usage (e.g., "Dancing teacher" was changed to "Dance teacher"). An additional 54 items were included for two purposes: first, to provide more contemporary items that would tap the same content areas as previous items (e.g., "Typist" was replaced by "Word processor") and, second, to cover new content areas that might contribute to the various scales (e.g., the new item "Bilingual teacher"). Among these 54 items were a set that reflected work dimensions. These dimensions can be measured by asking individuals to indicate their preferences for one of each pair that can be formed from working with people, ideas, data, or things.

After considerable analysis to determine the best items, 317 were selected for the 1994 *Strong*. Of these 317, 282 are the same or very slightly modified items from the 1985 *Strong* and 35 are new items. Six of these new items—those that measure work dimensions—became a new part on the Item Booklet/Answer Sheet. Forty-three items have been deleted from the previous version; a few of these were replaced by similar new items, and the rest were deleted because they did not work as well as the items that were retained. The new items are listed in Table 2.1.

The item pool for the 1994 *Strong* appears more contemporary than its predecessor. Some items that appeared on the 1985 *Strong* (e.g., "Pursuing bandits in a sheriff's posse") were deleted because they were out of date. Some of the items included on the research form (e.g., "Spending time with family") were not used in the final Item Booklet/Answer Sheet

Table 2.1 New Items on Form T317 (*N* = 35)

Part I. Occupations
Accountant
Bilingual teacher
Civil service employee (replaces City or state employee)
Clothes designer (replaces Children's clothes designer and Costume designer)
Computer programmer
Customer service representative
Day care worker
Financial analyst
Forest ranger (replaces the activity Being a forest ranger)
Paralegal
Paramedic
Security guard
Special education teacher
Word processor (replaces Typist)

Part II. School Subjects
Business
Computer science
Health education

Part III. Activities
Learning more about the foods I eat
Repairing electronics equipment
Taking care of children
Competitive sports

Part IV. Leisure Activities
Shopping for the latest fashions
Playing team sports with friends

Part V. Types of People
Physically disabled people

Part VI. Preference Between Two Activities
Working full time vs. Working part time
Being friends with a research scientist vs. Being friends with a sales executive (replaces Being married to a research scientist vs. Being married to a sales executive)
Being responsible for earning money to support the family vs. Being responsible for caring for children
Working for nonprofit organizations vs. Working for profit-oriented organizations

Part VII. Your Characteristics
Can communicate easily with people of different cultures

Part VIII. Preference in the World of Work

Ideas vs. Data	Things vs. People
Data vs. People	Ideas vs. Things
People vs. Ideas	Things vs. Data

because nearly everyone endorsed them. Others (e.g., "Foreigners") were deleted to avoid giving offense. Most of the deleted items and some new items that were tried out but not included in the final revision were simply not as effective as those that were retained. (See Chapter 4 for a more detailed discussion of item selection.)

General Reference Samples (GRSs)

Whenever the *Strong* is revised, an important consideration is how to form the comparison group that will be used to develop new OSs and to norm the GOTs, BISs, and OSs. For the 1985 *Strong*, the male and female comparison groups were called the Men-in-General and Women-in-General groups. Each was composed of 300 members, selected to equally represent members of professional and nonprofessional occupational groups. In addition, the Men-in-General and Women-in-General groups were matched on occupational title. The item responses of these comparison groups were used in the selection of items for the 1985 OSs.

For the 1994 *Strong*, the male and female General Reference Samples (GRSs)—so named to differentiate them from the 1985 Men-in-General and Women-in-General groups—were based on the people who had been inventoried for the current revision. Whereas previous comparison groups used people inventoried in earlier years, the 1994 GRSs were made up completely of respondents from the 1990s. The major differences between the GRSs and the previous Women-in-General and Men-in-General groups stem from this fact.

After selecting representatives of each occupational criterion group that met the selection criteria detailed in Chapter 7, approximately 40,000 occupational group members were available. These groups were not equally represented, however; some had over 1,000 members and others less than 100 (see Appendix A for a description of each occupational group), but the median sample size for the entire set of criterion samples was 250. Had all the available respondents been used in the GRSs, the occupational groups would have been unequally weighted, so 200 members of each occupational criterion group were selected randomly to be included in the gender-appropriate GRS. In a few occupational criterion groups, fewer than 200 respondents were available, and in those cases, all the members of the group were used. The result was two GRSs composed of 9,467 women and 9,484 men.

In general, the rationale behind the development of the 1994 GRSs differed in two important ways from the rationale used for previous samples. First, since large-capacity computers could handle many cases at once, very large GRSs were developed, rather than the relatively small groups of 300 used previously. In this way, the influence of any one respondent was minimized. Second, since the comparison groups should represent contemporary interests, no attempt was made to approximate earlier comparison groups.

In a comparison of the response percentages between the 1985 Men-in-General and Women-in-General groups and the 1994 GRSs on the 325 items to which they all responded, 14 items differentiated the two groups of females and 19 items differentiated the two groups of males at 15 percent or greater. However, the average difference was about 3 to 5 percent over the 325 items. It is important to note that the respondents in the 1994 GRS responded "Dislike" to a larger percentage of items and "Like" to a smaller percentage than did those respondents in the 1985 Women-in-General and Men-in-General groups. This fact has some implications for the OSs that are discussed later in this chapter.

General Occupational Themes (GOTs)

The GOTs retain the same names and relationship to Holland's theoretical structure as the previous scales. The actual items have been changed somewhat to enhance reliability, and in some cases the scales are longer. However, their item content matches that of the previous scales in order to maintain content and construct validity. As a result, the scales can be interpreted just as were the scales on the 1985 *Strong*.

The new GOT scales were constructed by deleting items that were weakly correlated with the existing scales and adding items that were more highly correlated (see Chapter 5). On the new GOTs, Cronbach's alpha (a measure of homogeneity) has been increased to .90 or more for all six scales, a level previously reached by only two scales.

Table 2.2 Changes in the Basic Interest Scales

Scale by GOT	New Scale	Dropped Scale	Item Changes	Theme Change	Name Change
Realistic					
Adventure[a]		√	√		
Athletics			√	Formerly S	
Mechanical Activities			√		
Nature			√		
Investigative					
Mathematics			√		
Science			√		
Artistic					
Applied Arts	√				
Art			√		
Culinary Arts	√				
Music/Dramatics			√		
Writing			√		
Social					
Domestic Arts		√			
Medical Service			√	Formerly I	
Religious Activities			√		
Social Service			√		
Teaching			√		
Enterprising					
Law/Politics			√		
Organizational Management			√		Formerly Business Management
Sales			√		
Conventional					
Computer Activities	√				
Data Management	√				
Office Services			√		Formerly Office Practices

Note: No changes were made to the Agriculture, Military Activities, Medical Science, Merchandising, and Public Speaking scales.
[a] Moved to Personal Style Scales and renamed Risk Taking/Adventure.

Test-retest reliabilities have also been improved by these changes. When all the individuals in the 1994 GRSs are scored on the 1985 and 1994 GOT scales, the median correlations for parallel scales are .95 for females and .96 for males.

Basic Interest Scales (BISs)

The BISs on the 1994 revision are quite similar to those on the 1985 *Strong*. The BIS revisions were guided by factor analyses of the items using very large samples. In general, the scales were treated to the same type of analyses as the GOTs to increase length and enhance reliability (see Chapter 6). As a result, a few of the items in some scales were changed, with weaker items deleted and new items added. In addition, some new scales were added and one was deleted.

The number of BISs increased from 23 to 25. As shown in Table 2.2, four new scales were created: Applied Arts (Artistic Theme), Culinary Arts (Artistic Theme), Computer Activities (Conventional Theme), and Data Management (Conventional Theme). (Basic Interest Scales in Table 2.2 are listed in alphabetical order under the appropriate Theme.) Note that the two new scales associated with the Conventional Theme increased the number of BISs associated with the Conventional Theme from one to three. Two of the BISs that were retained were renamed to better represent the content of the scales: Business Management became Organizational Management and Office Practices became Office Services.

The Medical Service scale was moved from the Investigative to the Social Theme, and the Athletics scale was moved from the Social to the Realistic Theme. In 1985 the correlations were actually higher between Medical Service and the Social Theme than between Medical Service and the Investigative Theme, although the difference was not great. Because the correlations continued to be higher, a decision was made to place the Medical Service scale under the Social Theme. The Adventure scale from the 1985 *Strong* was also moved to a new group of Personal Style Scales and renamed Risk Taking/Adventure (described later in this chapter). Another scale, Domestic Arts, was dropped.

Of the 21 BISs retained in the 1994 *Strong*, five do not have any new items. For the remaining 16 scales, correlations between scores on the 1985 scales and 1994 scales computed for the combined GRSs are all above .95. The median correlation between the 21 old and new scales is .987.

Occupational Scales (OSs)

New data were collected from 50 occupations for the 1994 *Strong*, which has 211 OSs, compared with 207 for the 1985 *Strong*. Fourteen occupations are represented on the 1994 *Strong* that were not included in the earlier version (see Table 2.3). These occupations were added to represent contemporary occupations

Table 2.3 New Occupations
(N = 14 Occupations, N = 26 Scales)

Actuary
Audiologist
Auto Mechanic
Bookkeeper
Child Care Provider
Community Service Organization Director
Corporate Trainer
Gardener/Groundskeeper
Medical Records Technician
Paralegal
Plumber
Small Business Owner
Technical Writer
Translator

Note: There are male and female scales for each occupation except for Child Care Provider (female only) and Plumber (male only).

(e.g., Corporate Trainer and Technical Writer) and occupations in which considerable growth is expected in the future (e.g., Paralegal and Medical Records Technician). Although the goal was to collect data from both males and females in each of the targeted occupational groups, that was not achieved in every case because it was sometimes difficult to reach the minority gender in particular occupations. Two of the 14 new occupations (Child Care Provider and Plumber) are represented by members of one gender only, thus bringing the total of new scales based on new data to 26.

Four other new scales were developed based on data previously collected from eight groups of military enlistees in specific branches of the military and six groups of military officers in specific branches of the military. These are Military Enlisted Personnel (male and female) and Military Officer (male and female). Combining the data eliminated the considerable amount of overlap that existed among the military scales on the 1985 *Strong*.

Thirty-six of the newly sampled occupational groups represent occupations for which scales appeared on the 1985 *Strong*. Many of the oldest occupational groups were resampled, as were some

Table 2.4 Occupational Groups Resampled for the 1994 Strong (N = 36)

Accountant	Librarian
Advertising Executive	Life Insurance Agent
Architect	Marketing Executive
Banker	Nurse, RN
Biologist	Nursing Home Administrator
Business Education Teacher	Occupational Therapist
Chemist	Parks and Recreation Coordinator[a]
Computer Programmer/Systems Analyst	Pharmacist
Credit Manager	Physical Therapist
Dentist	Physicist
Elementary School Teacher[a]	Police Officer
Engineer	Public Relations Director
Farmer	Radiologic Technologist
Flight Attendant	School Administrator
Forester	Social Worker
Housekeeping & Maintenance Supervisor[a]	Special Education Teacher
Human Resources Director[a]	Speech Pathologist
Lawyer	Veterinarian

Note: The names of the occupational groups as they appear on the 1994 Profile are used here.
[a] See Table 2.5 for previous name of this scale.

more recent ones. Some occupational groups (e.g., Banker, Architect, and Librarian) were resampled because they had undergone considerable change over a relatively short time (see Table 2.4). Computer Programmer and Systems Analyst were combined because their activities and functions overlap and the distinction between these two designations is often not made in the field. Since over 46 percent of the scales are based on newly collected data, almost half the *Strong* scales now use the latest, most up-to-date information. Those for which no new data were collected had more recent samples and represent jobs that have not changed significantly since their criterion samples were collected.

Six pairs of the OSs were renamed, as shown in Table 2.5. Some changes, such as Executive Housekeeper becoming Housekeeping & Maintenance Supervisor, were made to give a clearer sense of the nature of the occupation. Other changes, such as Beautician becoming Hair Stylist, were made to provide the contemporary name.

As Table 2.5 shows, seven pairs of military scales were combined to make the two pairs of scales described earlier. In a few cases, an OS was deleted in favor of a more broadly based occupational group (e.g., YWCA/YMCA Director was replaced by Community Service Organization Director). Four other occupations that were on the 1985 Profile (i.e., Bus Driver, Chamber of Commerce Executive, Funeral Director, and IRS Agent) were also dropped. A total of 24 scales representing 12 occupations were deleted.

In all, 109 occupational groups were retained from the 1985 *Strong*, representing 57 occupations. Fifty-two groups consisted of both male and female samples; five groups consisted of samples representing one gender only. Since every OS was revised by comparing the occupational group members' responses to the 1985 *Strong* items with those of the new GRSs, different scales resulted even though they were based on data from occupational groups that had been retained.

Table 2.5 Changes in the Occupational Scales

Old Name	New Name
Dropped Occupations	
Bus Driver	*(Not applicable)*
Chamber of Commerce Executive	
Funeral Director	
IRS Agent	
Combined Occupations	
Air Force Enlisted Personnel	Military Enlisted Personnel
Army Enlisted Personnel	
Marine Corps Enlisted Personnel	
Navy Enlisted Personnel	
Air Force Officer	Military Officer
Army Officer	
Navy Officer	
Subsumed Under Broader Category	
YWCA/YMCA Director	Community Service Organization Director
Renamed Occupations	
Executive Housekeeper	Housekeeping & Maintenance Supervisor
Personnel Director	Human Resources Director
Beautician	Hair Stylist
Guidance Counselor	High School Counselor
Elementary Teacher	Elementary School Teacher
Recreation Leader	Parks and Recreation Coordinator

As described in Chapter 7, some changes were made in the strategy for selecting items based on preliminary analyses conducted before the scales were built. The new OSs were constructed to be shorter than the previous scales in order to shorten the inventory and decrease overlap among scales without sacrificing reliability or concurrent validity, as traditionally measured by Tilton's overlap. Since the scales are shorter, it was possible that they might result in a greater overlap in scores among the OSs, even though they separate the occupational groups adequately from the GRSs, a result exactly opposite of the one intended. For example, in the case of psychologists and sociologists, who may have many similar interests, longer scales—with more items—might help to differentiate them, whereas shorter scales could result in clients getting quite similar scores on both scales.

To assess the possibility that greater overlap might result from scales with fewer items, 12 1994 OSs for each gender were selected to represent the six Holland types. Then males in the 12 occupations were scored on all 12 scales, and overlaps between scores were computed. The median difference between men in the 12 occupations scored on the 12 scales was over 2 standard deviations. The differences ranged from less than half a standard deviation between OSs representing adjacent Holland Themes, as one would predict from Holland's theory, to over 4 standard deviations. (See Chapter 5 for a description of Holland's theory as it applies to the *Strong*.)

The latter difference characterized how male Fine Artists scored on the Athletic Trainer scale for males, for example.

A comparable analysis was completed for the females in the 12 occupations, and the findings were similar to those of the men. On the basis of this study, a tentative conclusion is that the shorter scales did not result in greater overlap between OS scores but rather had the intended effect of producing good separation between OSs. Additional research is needed to confirm these findings.

Because the OSs were developed to decrease overlap among them, users may notice that individuals who take the 1994 *Strong* get fewer high scores on the OSs than they might have on the 1985 *Strong*. Individuals who obtain few high scores on the OSs should be encouraged to generalize from their GOT and BIS scores to occupations that do not appear on the Profile.

Counselors experienced in using the 1985 *Strong* should be aware that some of the 1994 OSs may operate somewhat differently from their earlier counterparts, despite the fact that they have acceptable reliability and concurrent validity (see Chapter 7, Table 7.2). The 1994 male and female GRSs were scored on all of the OSs that appear on both the 1985 and the 1994 *Strong*, and their scores on matching scales were correlated. The mean correlation for the female GRS was .83; for the male GRS it was .82. Scales with correlations lower than .70 are listed in Table 2.6. For females, the Musician and Florist scales had the lowest correlations; for males, Musician and Marketing Executive had the lowest.

One potential reason for the modest correlations reported in Table 2.6 is the tendency for the GRS to respond with fewer "Like" and more "Dislike" responses than the previous comparison groups. Fewer "Dislike" items appear on the OSs because they are constructed by using only those items that differentiate the occupational group from the GRS. So, if the GRS has more "Dislike" responses, then the OSs will have more "Like" responses. It is interesting to note that 18 out of the 22 scales listed in Table 2.6 were based on data collected from occupational groups before 1985. Having fewer "Dislike" items on OSs will have the greatest effect on those individuals with a high "Dislike" response percentage. When taking the 1994 *Strong*, these people will generally receive lower scores than they would have received on the same scales that appeared on the 1985 inventory. On the 1985 version, those people with high "Dislike" response rates tended to get high scores on scales that had a high proportion of items scored in the "Dislike" direction.

Scales that are more balanced in their proportion of "Like" and "Dislike" responses are probably preferable to those with extreme proportions of "Like" or "Dislike" responses because they are less vulnerable to response sets. It is worth noting that similar phenomena were noted after the 1985 revision (Creaser & Jacobs, 1987) and indeed after the first revision subsequent to the death of E. K. Strong (Williams, Kirk, & Frank, 1968).

Another way to look at the differences between the 1985 and 1994 OSs is to compare standard scores on the 1985 and 1994 scales for the same group of people. Table 2.7 presents a summary of the scales with the greatest difference between mean scores on male and female scales for the appropriate GRS. Differences greater than 7 points appear in the table. The three occupations for which scales for both genders had relatively high differences were Fine Artist, Florist, and Horticultural Worker. In most of the comparisons, the earlier scale had the higher score, as indicated by positive differences. It is also important to note that the average scores for members of the GRSs on these scales were relatively low. For the female scales, none of the 1994 mean scores reached the mid-range of 30 to 40 (which would be interpreted as having some interest in the occupation). For the male scales, two 1994 mean scores reached the mid-range: Business Education Teacher and Credit Manager, for both of which the 1994 means were higher than the 1985 means.

Although there are differences in mean scores on certain scales, these differences may not be important because for the typical person as represented by the GRSs, scores will fall into the mid-range or dissimilar range. Those who have interests similar to people in the occupations will score higher and their scores will represent their similarity to members of the occupational groups.

As shown in Tables 2.6 and 2.7, most of the scales for which there were differences between 1985 and 1994 scales were those for which new occupational samples were *not* collected for the 1994 revision. However, each of the six RIASEC Themes had a different mix or proportion of the two kinds of retained scales (i.e., those that were resampled and those that

Table 2.6 Occupational Scales with Correlations < .70 (1985 vs. 1994 Scales) and Percentage of Items for Each Scale for Which a "Dislike" Response Is Scored Positively

Scale Name	Correlation[a]	Percentage of "Dislike" Items	
		1985	1994
Female Scales			
Florist	.55	68.4	35.0
Musician	.63	54.7	23.5
Sociologist	.64	46.8	14.8
Beautician/Hair Stylist	.65	70.9	37.2
Geographer	.68	52.7	14.0
College Professor	.68	61.4	27.0
Horticultural Worker	.69	50.9	22.2
Physical Therapist[b]	.69	42.1	27.0
Lawyer[b]	.69	56.7	17.1
Male Scales			
Musician	.48	58.8	33.9
Marketing Executive[b]	.54	67.3	39.3
Florist	.58	66.7	34.1
Geographer	.60	61.3	28.9
Chiropractor	.61	41.4	14.9
Psychologist	.61	61.3	25.0
Banker[b]	.64	45.8	48.9
College Professor	.66	53.7	17.9
Restaurant Manager	.67	58.5	23.8
Travel Agent	.67	63.6	33.3
Broadcaster	.68	63.8	27.1
Photographer	.69	55.2	30.6
Investments Manager	.69	62.7	42.2

[a] Correlations for female scales are based on the scores of the female General Reference Sample ($N = 9,467$); correlations for male scales, on the scores of the male General Reference Sample ($N = 9,484$).
[b] New occupational sample in 1994.

were not). To test whether this different mix of scales might have an overall effect on the OSs within any given Theme, the differences between 1985 and 1994 OS scores were examined for each Theme. Table 2.8 shows the results.

On the average, scores on OSs in the Investigative and Artistic Themes were slightly lower in 1994 than in 1985. Scores on OSs in the Realistic and Enterprising Themes were also lower in 1994 than in 1985, although to a lesser degree. Scores on OSs in the Social and Conventional Themes were slightly higher.

While Tables 2.6, 2.7, and 2.8 indicate that some scales on the 1994 Profile will behave differently from their 1985 counterparts, it is important to note that of 181 comparisons, only 20 appear in Table 2.7, which used a cutoff of 7 standard score points for inclusion. Sixteen that had low correlations in Table 2.6 do not even appear in Table 2.7. Table 2.8 shows that the modest differences averaged over

Table 2.7 Occupational Scales with Group Mean Differences > 7 Points (1985 vs. 1994 Scales)

Scale Name	1985 Mean Scores	1994 Mean Scores	Difference Between Mean Scores
Female Scales			
Florist	35	21	14
Artist, Fine	28	17	11
Horticultural Worker	35	24	11
Beautician/Hair Stylist	34	25	9
Musician	34	25	9
Medical Illustrator	21	13	8
Medical Technician	32	24	8
Vocational Agriculture Teacher	30	23	7
Male Scales			
Artist, Commercial	28	16	12
Life Insurance Agent	17	28	−11
Mathematician	26	15	11
Geologist	33	23	10
Horticultural Worker	32	22	10
Geographer	33	24	9
Business Education Teacher	23	31	−8
Credit Manager	29	37	−8
Artist, Fine	25	18	7
Florist	30	23	7
Mathematics Teacher	30	23	7
Physician	31	24	7

Note: Means of female scales are based on the standard scores of the female General Reference Sample (*N* = 9,467); means of male scales, on the standard scores of the male General Reference Sample (*N* = 9,484).

Holland Themes ranged from −2.7 to 3.24 standard score points. (All scores in tables in this guide are standard scores, unless otherwise noted.)

Personal Style Scales

The Personal Style Scales are a new category of scales on the 1994 *Strong* that were designed to suggest particular environments in which individuals like to learn and to work and types of activities people find satisfying. This category replaces the Special Scales on the 1985 *Strong*. The two Special Scales, Introversion-Extroversion and Academic Comfort, have been deleted. Two of the new scales, Work Style and Learning Environment, bear some relationship to the earlier scales, but are not strictly speaking replacements for those scales. Counselors who have become expert in the use of the two deleted scales need to understand the differences clearly. In addition, the Leadership Style scale is entirely new, and the Risk Taking/Adventure scale has been moved from the BISs, where it was called Adventure. Like the BISs, all the new scales are presented with box-and-whisker graphs; however, descriptions of each end of the scales are also provided, thus creating bipolar scales. (See Chapter 8 for descriptions of these scales as well as information about their development and relationship to the GOTs and BISs.)

Table 2.8 Mean Differences Between 1985 and 1994 Occupational Scales by Theme and Gender

		Occupational Sample Data Collected for					
		1985		1994		Total	
Theme Code	Gender	N of Scales	Mean Score Difference	N of Scales	Mean Score Difference	N of Scales	Mean Score Difference
R	Female	6	3.50	4	−3.00	10	0.90
	Male	5	3.20	5	−1.20	10	1.00
	Combined	11	3.36	9	−2.00	20	0.95
I	Female	15	3.00	7	−0.14	22	2.00
	Male	13	4.31	7	0.00	20	2.80
	Combined	28	3.61	14	−0.70	42	2.38
A	Female	10	3.80	5	0.40	15	2.67
	Male	12	4.42	5	0.40	17	3.24
	Combined	22	4.14	10	0.40	32	2.97
S	Female	7	1.14	9	−1.33	16	−0.25
	Male	8	1.13	9	−3.33	17	−1.24
	Combined	15	1.13	18	−2.33	33	−0.76
E	Female	14	3.14	5	−2.80	19	1.58
	Male	13	1.77	5	−3.40	18	0.33
	Combined	27	2.48	10	−3.10	37	0.97
C	Female	4	4.00	6	−2.50	10	0.10
	Male	2	3.00	5	−5.00	7	−2.70
	Combined	6	3.67	11	−3.64	17	−1.06
	Total N of Scales	109		72		181	

Note: Positive mean differences indicate higher scores on the 1985 scales, while negative differences indicate higher scores on the 1994 scales. Scores for male scales are based on the male General Reference Sample; scores for the female scales, on the female General Reference Sample.

Work Style Scale

This scale was developed to differentiate those who like to work with people from those who prefer to work with ideas, data, or things. The scale is somewhat similar to the Introversion-Extroversion scale from the 1985 *Strong*, although the correlations between the two scales are only −.58 for women and −.66 for men in the GRS. Note that these correlations are negative because the Work Style scale is scored so that higher scores characterize those who like to work with people, whereas the Introversion-Extroversion scale was scored so that people who prefer more solitary work environments scored high. Actually, the Work Style scale is related nearly as highly to the Leadership Style scale as to the Introversion-Extroversion scale. For women and men the correlations between Work Style and Leadership Style are .52 and .61, respectively.

Although it was normed on the combined GRS, the Work Style scale has rather large gender differences. On average, women score toward the works with people pole more often than do men. College students also tend to score more toward the works with people pole than do employed adults. Counselors need to keep these differences in mind when interpreting the results of the Work Style scale. In particular, they need to be aware that the same score carries different meanings for men and for women as well as for college students and adults.

Learning Environment Scale

The Learning Environment scale was developed to distinguish between people with high levels of formal academic education and those with practical training and minimal formal education. Members of the GRS with different levels of education have appropriately different mean scores on this scale (see Chapter 8, Table 8.8). The scale is similar to but not exactly like the Academic Comfort scale; for members of the GRS, the correlation between the two scales is .64 for women and .69 for men. The new scale has fewer items that have to do with liking scientific occupations and school subjects than did the Academic Comfort scale.

In a small informal study by A. L. Hammer (1994) of 44 adults scored on both the Academic Comfort scale and the Learning Environment scale ($r = .74$), those who scored close to either end of the scale on Academic Comfort maintained similar scores on the Learning Environment scale. However, those who scored approximately 40 to 50 on the Academic Comfort scale (the low to moderate range) tend to score more toward the academic pole of the Learning Environment scale. Those previously in the low to moderate range who changed the most seemed to be well educated and verbal people who enjoy books, reading, and learning in general.

Interpretation of the Learning Environment scale may differ somewhat from interpretation of the Academic Comfort scale since the scores characteristic of various levels of education appear to be somewhat lower on the former scale than on the latter. On the Learning Environment scale, scores of about 50 characterize employed adults with bachelor's and master's degrees, while people with high school or technical training usually score below 40. Those with Ph.D. degrees score about 56 on the average, while college undergraduates have average scores under 50.

Leadership Style Scale

The Leadership Style scale, which emerged from the factor analysis of the items on the *Strong*, reflects an individual's preferred leadership role. Individuals scoring toward the directs others (right) pole are comfortable taking charge and enjoy motivating others. People who score toward the leads by example (left) pole prefer to lead by example and would rather complete tasks themselves than assign them to others. Because this scale is new, more data are needed reflecting the variety of leadership styles represented by the left pole.

Risk Taking/Adventure Scale

The Risk Taking/Adventure scale, which had been the Adventure Basic Interest Scale on the 1985 *Strong*, was placed among the Personal Style Scales because it seemed to express a style of working rather than an interest in a certain type of work. The scale is similar to that which previously appeared among the BISs.

Administrative Indexes

Some changes have been made in the Administrative Indexes that the experienced user should note. These changes are described briefly here. However, the indexes are described in detail in Chapter 9.

Total Responses

The number of total responses needed for a confident interpretation of the Profile is now 300, as the number of items on the inventory has decreased from 325 to 317. On the 1985 *Strong*, the cutoff was 305.

Infrequent Responses Scale

New infrequency scales have been developed for both women and men. As in the past, the counselor should explore any score that is a negative number for inappropriate response sets or attitudes on the part of the respondent. It is important to note that the 1994 *Strong* will show a few more negative scores than did the 1985 version because the point at which the index becomes negative has been set so that up to 1 percent of each of the GRSs will obtain a negative score. For the 1985 *Strong* the percentage receiving negative scores was set closer to 0. A study by Miller and Foxworth (1992) found that, among a small group of college women, instructions to respond randomly did not result in any negative scores on the 1985 Infrequent Responses scale. The new Infrequent Responses scale may modestly increase the number of Profiles targeted for further exploration due to unusual response styles.

Like/Indifferent/Dislike (LID) Percentages

As in the 1985 *Strong*, the LID response percentages to sections of the Item Booklet/Answer Sheet are provided on the Profile. The major change in the response percentage indexes involves the calculation for the total of these percentages. As discussed in the "Items" section of this chapter, the Preference in the World of Work section was added to the Item Booklet/Answer Sheet. Thus there are now eight parts instead of seven on the inventory and consequently eight parts in the Administrative Indexes. Part VI (Preference Between Two Activities) and the new Part VIII are not scored in the same format as the others; both extremes of items in these two parts represent an endorsement of something, while right-hand extreme answers (either a "Dislike" or "No" response) for all the other parts represent a lack of endorsement. Based on evidence from correlations among the LID percentages for the parts, the "total" now contains only the sum of Parts I through V and VII rather than the sum of all parts of the inventory, and this is called the Subtotal. The percentages for Parts VI and VIII are included in the Administrative Indexes—each part listed separately—but are less meaningful in interpreting the respondent's overall endorsement rates. However, response percentages for Parts I through V, VII, and the Subtotal should be interpreted as they were previously (see Chapter 9).

Profile

The *Strong* Profile was redesigned to make it easier for counselors to use and for clients to understand by improving the presentation of the information. These changes resulted from feedback gathered from counselors who used the *Strong* as well as from those who were unfamiliar with the inventory. Prototypes were prepared of alternative ways of presenting information, and these were shown to groups of career counselors from various settings (e.g., high schools, community colleges, universities, government agencies, businesses, and outplacement firms) throughout the United States before design and format changes were finalized.

The Profile now begins with a page called the Snapshot. The Snapshot provides a graphic summary of the client's results on the GOTs, BISs, and OSs. A reference to the Personal Style Scales also appears on the page.

The General Occupational Themes and the Basic Interest Scales, which formerly appeared on two pages, are now all printed on one page. As in the 1985 version of the *Strong*, the BISs are categorized by Theme. Such an organization provides counselors with the option of focusing the clients solely on the GOTs and BISs; clients are not distracted by their results on the Occupational Scales. To give clients the flavor of each Theme, a brief definition of each is now printed after the name of the Theme.

Another change in the GOTs and BISs on the 1994 Profile is that the number of interpretive comment categories has been reduced from seven to five, as is apparent on the Snapshot, the first page of the Profile. The comments have been rephrased to present a lack of interest in an area in a less negative light and to emphasize that the *Strong* is not a test of ability but rather an inventory of interests. This goal was accomplished by changing "low" to "little" and by adding the word *interest* to each comment. The elimination of two categories—"Moderately High" and "Moderately Low"—also makes the interpretation more direct and avoids making perhaps unnecessarily fine distinctions for the client.

Another change for the GOTs and BISs is that the boundaries used to determine which interpretive comment is printed now match the graphical presentation of the box-and-whisker graphs for each gender. For example, a comment of "Average Interest" corresponds to a score plotted in the box that defines the middle 50 percent of the scores, and a comment of "High Interest" corresponds to a score plotted on the thin line or "whisker" that identifies scores from the 50th to the 75th percentiles. (See Chapters 5 and 6 for a detailed description.) Also, to increase the clients' understanding of the scores, the phrases "Less Interest" and "More Interest" have been added above each numeric scale, with arrows indicating a continuum of interest. Again, such labeling reinforces for clients that the *Strong* is an instrument measuring their interest.

In the Occupational Scales section of the Profile, the scales are still grouped under the appropriate Themes, but within each Theme the occupations are listed alphabetically for ease in locating specific scales. The majority (166) of the Occupational Scales appear under the same Theme as they did on the 1985 Profile. Only 17 are now listed under a different Theme. (Note that 26 OSs are new to the *Strong*.) For most of these 17 OSs, the first and second letters of their Theme codes appear in reverse order compared to the sequence of letters in the codes on the 1985 *Strong*. For example, the male Veterinarian scale had been coded RI and is now coded IR. The scale whose code is most different from the earlier code is female Dental Hygienist. On the 1985 Profile the code was SCI, but it is now EIS. Such changes occurred because the codes themselves reflect the makeup of the members of the occupational group as well as the procedure used to assign the codes. See Chapter 7 for a discussion of how Theme codes are assigned to Occupational Scales and their usefulness in the counseling process.

As with the GOTs and BISs, the interpretive comment categories in the OS section have been reduced from seven to five, with the elimination of the "Moderately Similar" and "Moderately Dissimilar" categories. In this case, above the numeric scale, the phrases "Dissimilar Interests" and "Similar Interests" with arrows showing the continuum of interests replace the specific interpretive comments. The ranges shown have also been adjusted. Whereas the category boundaries used on the 1985 Profile read 15, 25, 30, 40, 45, 55, they now read 15, 20, 30, 40, 50, 55. This change was made so that 50, which represents the mean score of those in an occupational group on their own Occupational Scale, would appear as one of boundaries (e.g., female commercial artists score 50 on average on the female Commercial Artist Occupational Scale). Counselors can now point to this boundary and emphasize that any of the client's scores that fall at or above this point are at or above the mean for the occupational criterion group.

Another revision in the presentation of the Occupational Scales is that the heading "Your Scores" replaces "Standard Scores" above the client's numeric scores, thus replacing a technical label with one more readily understandable by clients. Likewise, the label "Theme Codes" now appears above the column of codes.

Another change in the *Strong* is the placement of validity indexes—the Infrequent Responses and the Total Responses. Because these indexes are primarily for use by the counselor and are generally of little interest to the client, they were moved from the top of the first page of the 1985 Profile to the bottom of the last page of the current Profile. Similarly, the Administrative Indexes were moved to this last page and now appear under the heading "Summary of Item Responses." (For a detailed description of each page of the Profile, see Chapter 3.)

Conclusion

The 1994 revision of the *Strong* continues in the tradition of all the earlier revisions. Changes were made for two primary reasons: (1) to maintain the contemporary focus of the *Strong*, complete with the latest information from some of the fastest growing and evolving occupations; and (2) to enhance use of the information by making the presentation more accessible. The hope is that users will find that the changes enhance their use of the *Strong* and the usefulness of the inventory for their clients.

References

Creaser, J. W., & Jacobs, M. (1987). Score discrepancies between the 1981 and 1985 editions of the Strong-Campbell Interest Inventory. *Journal of Counseling Psychology, 34*, 288–292.

Hammer, A. L. (1994). [A comparison of scores on the Learning Environment scale and the Academic Comfort scale]. Unpublished raw data.

Hansen, J. C. (1992). *User's guide for the Strong Interest Inventory* (rev. ed.). Stanford, CA: Stanford University Press.

Hansen, J. C., & Campbell, D. P. (1985). *Manual for the Strong Interest Inventory* (4th ed.). Stanford, CA: Stanford University Press.

Miller, M. J., & Foxworth, C. L. (1992). Effects of response set on the Infrequent Response Index of the Strong Interest Inventory. *Journal of Employment Counseling, 29*, 162–165.

Williams, P. A, Kirk, B. A., & Frank, A. C. (1968). New men's SVIB: A comparison with the old. *Journal of Counseling Psychology, 15*, 287–294.

CHAPTER 3

Overview of the Strong Materials

This chapter provides a detailed description of the materials that have been developed for the 1994 version of the *Strong* at the time of publication of the revision. Preceding that description are suggested guidelines for using the *Strong* and a discussion of the limits of the inventory. ◆

Guidelines for Using the Strong

In general, the *Strong* is easy to administer and can be used with a wide range of age groups and diverse populations. Taking an average of only 35 to 40 minutes to complete, it can be given individually or in groups.

Appropriate Age for Testing

The *Strong* can be used with high school students, college students, and adults; thus, the appropriate age for using the instrument spans 50 years or more. The inventory usually is not administered to students who have not yet entered the eighth grade (ages 13 to 14), since most people's interest patterns have not developed enough to be identified before that age. Stability of interests increases with age; however, even in the eighth grade there is considerable stability in the configuration of an individual's Profile (Hansen & Stocco, 1980).

Counselors who wish to stimulate eighth-, ninth-, or tenth-graders to think about career planning can use the *Strong* as an introduction to the world of work and the process of career choice. The *Strong*'s General Occupational Themes (GOTs) and Basic Interest Scales (BISs) will indicate the emerging interests of 13-, 14-, and 15-year-olds even if their interests have not developed sufficiently to yield many high scores on the Occupational Scales (OSs).

Most high school counselors administer the *Strong* to eleventh- or twelfth-graders (16-, 17-, and 18-year-olds) to help them make decisions about postsecondary training, education, or employment. At these ages, most students' interests are beginning to solidify, and the Profile results are useful for long-range educational and career-planning purposes. In fact, remarkable levels of interest stability have been found for people tested over a 12-year interval—first as college freshmen and then later as working adults (Swanson & Hansen, 1988).

Reading Level

A readability analysis was conducted on the *Strong* Item Booklet/Answer Sheet. The overall reading level was found to fall between the eighth- and ninth-grade levels. Of course, some people who read at this level may not have an attention span sufficiently long to complete the inventory in one sitting, but the validity of the *Strong* will not be compromised by allowing them to complete the inventory in two or more shorter sessions.

Although the readability level of the instructions in the Item Booklet/Answer Sheet fell below the eighth-grade level, the overall level was somewhat higher because of the vocabulary found in the item sections of the inventory. Not all the vocabulary used in the inventory is familiar to everyone, especially students in the lower grades or people who are not proficient in English. If a client is unfamiliar with a few items (e.g., occupations in Part I, such as "City planner," "Civil engineer," or "Labor arbitrator," or school subjects in Part II, such as "Calculus" or "Physiology"), it is permissible to offer definitions or explanations for those items. The client will then be better able to estimate accurately her or his preference or aversion to the items, and the Profile scores will be more meaningful than if the client just guessed the meaning of those items.

Appropriate Time for Readministering the Strong

Although for most people interests are stable even as early as the eighth or ninth grade, it is not always easy to distinguish people whose interests are stable from those whose interests are unstable. Therefore, periodic reevaluation of interests is warranted. Reconfirmation of known interests is as useful in the career-counseling process as is the discovery of new interests, and many clients find a comparison of several *Strong* inventories taken within a year or two of one another to be interesting and illuminating.

Limits on Using the Strong

Professionals using the *Strong* need to be as aware of the limits of the inventory as they are of the many benefits that recommend its use. Keeping these limitations in mind can help the counselor avoid inappropriate uses of the inventory.

The *Strong* is a measure of interests, not abilities. While the professional counselor probably views this fact as a defining, rather than limiting, feature of the *Strong*, it may be a source of frustration for some clients. These clients, who may be less vocationally mature than others, may expect the career counselor to administer an instrument that can tell them what they are "good at" and therefore what they "should" do.

Since the *Strong* is a measure of interests, it is limited by the stability or development of the underlying interests in the populations among which it is used. This fact should be kept in mind when using the *Strong* with young students who may not have yet developed stable occupational interests. With such groups, the GOTs and the BISs will probably provide the best point of departure for a discussion of interests. (See Chapter 14 on using the *Strong* with high school students.)

The effectiveness of the *Strong* is also limited by the extent to which respondents do not understand the items. Thus, it is of limited usefulness among populations whose native language is not English and among those who have inadequate knowledge of the occupations found on the *Strong*.

The *Strong*, like other interest inventories, is further limited by the sampling procedures used to collect responses from occupational members. Ideally, it would be desirable to identify the entire population of a given occupation and then sample randomly from this base. Although this process was not possible, efforts were made in norming the *Strong* to identify large samples of members of the target occupations and then to use multiple wave sampling to ensure the greatest possible response.

Finally, the *Strong* is limited in the number of occupations for which it provides comparisons. Obviously, no inventory could possibly include all of the occupations (more than 12,000) found in the *Dictionary of Occupational Titles*. An inventory should, however, provide a means for results to be generalized to many other occupations, and the *Strong* fulfills this function. Every effort has also been made to ensure that all occupational types are adequately represented: although Realistic occupations predominate in the world of work, the number of occupations within each of the six major Theme codes of the *Strong* is roughly equal. Inclusion of occupations on the *Strong* was guided by the need to represent vocational/technical as well as professional occupations.

Strong Materials

At the time of publication, the 1994 edition of the *Strong* includes the following materials:

▲ a combined Item Booklet/Answer Sheet (Form T317);
▲ the *Strong* Profile, for reporting all the person's scores on the *Strong*;
▲ two narrative reports that provide more focused and individualized interpretations of the person's results;

- other support materials to facilitate the client's understanding of his or her results and to aid the counselor in interpretation;
- *Strong* scoring and reporting software to enable users to administer, score, and provide results on-site.

Item Booklet/Answer Sheet

Use of the 1994 *Strong* begins with a respondent completing Form T317 of the Item Booklet/Answer Sheet. This booklet contains both the items and places for the client's response and is computer scannable, thus eliminating the need for a separate booklet and answer sheet. Each computer-generated report has its own Item Booklet/Answer Sheet. The report to be generated from a particular Item Booklet is always listed on the front cover of the booklet. Having a separate booklet for each report simply ensures that the correct report is generated when the answers are scanned. When completed, the booklet is mailed to one of the publisher's scoring centers for computer scoring. There is also a separate booklet for use with the on-site scoring software (described later) when paper-and-pencil administration is desired. Since each booklet uses Form T317, all the items and instructions are identical, and the following description applies to all of them. The Item Booklet/Answer Sheet is shown at the back of this guide.

Instructions

The general goal of the instructions is to direct respondents to consider only their interests when answering the items. They are reminded that the *Strong* is not a test of abilities. Some minor changes in language, grammar, and punctuation have been made in the instructions for the 1994 version of the Item Booklet/Answer Sheet. In the introductory set of instructions, for example, the phrase "your scores" was changed to "your results" in an attempt to remove the association with tests.

Demographics

The first page of the 1985 *Strong* Item Booklet/Answer Sheet asked only for the client's name, gender (required for scoring), age, date of inventory administration, and an identification number (optional). These questions are retained on the current answer sheet, along with additional demographic questions, including an optional question asking the client to identify his or her ethnicity and one asking for the highest level of education completed. Four questions were also added to identify the work or employment status of the respondent, including work role, hours per week in paid employment, satisfaction with employment, and number of years employed in that line of work. The respondent is asked for his or her zip code as well.

These additional demographic questions were designed to aid in the collection of normative information as well as to facilitate research on use of the *Strong* with different populations. The intended use of the new demographic items is explained on the answer sheet. In addition, responses to these items are considered optional; clients who do not feel comfortable answering them are not required to do so.

Item Sections

The *Strong* items are grouped in eight parts, each comprising a different kind of item. The response format for most of the items consists of "Like," "Indifferent," and "Dislike" (exceptions are noted in the following discussion of Parts I to VIII). Chapter 9 and the application chapters (10 to 17) in this guide discuss how the client's response rate to each of these sets of items can be used in counseling. (For a description of how items were selected for the *Strong,* see Chapter 4.)

Part I. Occupations (135 items). All the items in this part are names of occupations. This set of items exhibits the greatest measurement power; that is, these items elicit more variability in response from one occupation to the next than do any other set of items. The responses of people to these occupational names signal their own particular occupational orientation.

Part II. School Subjects (39 items). The school subjects cover a wide range of educational situations, including academic and other areas. Most people, even students as young as 13 or 14, have little trouble deciding how they feel about a given subject, even though they may never have studied it.

Part III. Activities (46 items). This part contains a diverse collection of activities, such as "Doing research work," "Interviewing job applicants," and "Repairing electronics equipment." This is another powerful section; people from different occupations have widely varying response percentages to these items.

Part IV. Leisure Activities (29 items). These items cover leisure activities, hobbies, games, sports, physical activities, and a variety of entertainments. Some examples are "Symphony concerts," "Camping," and "Playing team sports with friends." Many of the items in this section provoke striking differences in the characteristic responses of people from different occupations.

Part V. Types of People (20 items). This part asks whether the respondent would enjoy day-to-day contact with various types of people such as "Highway construction workers," "High school students," and "Artistic people." One of the components of interest in an occupation is the characteristics of the people in that occupation.

Part VI. Preference Between Two Activities (30 items). The items in this section ask the respondent to contrast two activities or circumstances, such as "Taking a chance" versus "Playing it safe," and "Outside work" versus "Inside work." The two choices are printed opposite one another, and respondents are asked to choose the one that they like better, or to mark "=" if they like or dislike both the same or can't decide. When a respondent is asked to choose between two activities, she or he is forced to decide which activity is preferred even though the respondent may like both of them.

Part VII. Your Characteristics (12 items). The respondent is asked to read a statement such as "Usually start activities of my group," and to respond either "Yes," "?," or "No" to indicate if the statement is an apt self-description. Respondents are instructed to use the question mark "?" when they cannot decide whether the statement describes them. Interviews with people who have taken the *Strong* indicate that almost everyone seems to answer this section honestly.

Part VIII. Preference in the World of Work (6 items). This section of items is new to the *Strong*. The items comprise six pairs of work dimensions, representing all possible pairings of ideas, data, people, and things. Respondents are asked to choose which they prefer, or to mark "=" if they like or dislike both the same or can't decide. These items were added to explore two theoretical interest dimensions suggested by Prediger (1982). He reviewed the literature and suggested that two dimensions anchored by data versus ideas and people versus things provide an explanation for the relationship between the interests and occupations of individuals. The new items were ultimately used to form the groups compared to construct the new Work Style scale of the *Strong* (see Chapter 8). They have also proved useful in differentiating occupational groups—as expected from Prediger's data.

The Strong Profile

The *Strong* Profile has been extensively redesigned. The changes were the result of discussions with literally hundreds of *Strong* users from high schools, vocational schools, colleges, government agencies, and businesses across the country. For no previous version of the *Strong* were users so extensively consulted. The process included conducting individual and group interviews with users as well as nonusers to determine what they and their clients wanted on a Profile, reviewing prototypes of various designs, and eliciting reactions and recommendations for change.

The goals of redesigning the *Strong* Profile were to:

- ▲ explain results in plain language, while remaining true to the underlying measurement principles;
- ▲ improve the overall visual appeal so that clients would not be overwhelmed by numerical data;
- ▲ organize information to allow for maximum flexibility in conducting individual and group interpretations;
- ▲ help users interpret the Profile by adding such elements as definitions and keys;
- ▲ identify relationships among the *Strong* scales through visual cues such as color coding;
- ▲ effectively present the new Personal Style Scales;
- ▲ provide a more useful overview of the meaning of *Strong* results on the back of the Profile, including suggestions on how to undertake career exploration.

A sample Profile that contains a client's scores is shown at the end of this guide.

Strong Snapshot

The *Strong* Snapshot, the first page of the Profile, serves as a summary of the client's highest scores on the three major sets of *Strong* scales: the General Occupational Themes, the Basic Interest Scales, and the Occupational Scales. Both clients and counselors can see, almost at a glance, an overview of the client's *Strong* results. (See Chapter 10 and the application chapters that follow for suggestions on how to interpret the Snapshot.)

Demographics. In the top right corner of the Snapshot is demographic information taken from the client's answer sheet: name, identification number (if filled in on the answer sheet), age, gender, date tested, and date scored. The remaining pages of the Profile contain only the client's name and, if available, the identification number.

General Occupational Themes (GOTs). The six GOTs are presented from highest to lowest, ranked by interpretive comment ("Very High Interest" to "Very Little Interest"). Within the interpretive comment category, the GOTs are ranked by score. The client's interpretive comment is indicated on the Snapshot by a checkmark (✓) placed in the appropriate box. To the right of the boxes are brief definitions of each GOT, which help the client understand and remember how to distinguish between the Themes. Although these definitions are based on the item content of the scale, they do not capture the full richness of the Theme (see Chapter 5 for detailed descriptions of the Themes). Nonetheless, they do explain simply to clients the Holland type terminology. To the left of the name of the GOT is the first letter of that Theme, cueing clients to the coding system.

Below the results of the GOTs is the Theme code, consisting of one to three letters that represent the individual's highest GOTs. This code is derived by listing the first letter of each GOT on which the client scored "Average Interest" or above, ranked by interpretive comment. If two or more Themes have the same interpretive comment (e.g., "High Interest"), then the ranking relies on the standard scores. If more than three GOTs fit the criteria just described, only the top three are used to compute the code. A code is not computed if the client has no GOT scores of "Average Interest" or above. Text explaining the purpose of the Theme codes appears instead.

To the left of the list of GOTs is text that varies depending on the individual's results. Two versions of text can be printed. One version prints if the client has any GOTs with scores in the "Average Interest" category or above. This text explains what the GOTs measure and provides some suggestions for how to use the Theme code. The other version prints for those persons who have *no* GOTs in the "Average Interest" or above category. The texts of these paragraphs suggest some reasons for the pattern of scores.

Basic Interest Scales (BISs). The BIS section of the Snapshot provides a list of the individual's five highest BISs, rank ordered from highest to lowest, by interpretive comment ("Very High Interest" to "Very Little Interest"). Within interpretive comment category, the BISs are ranked by score. The client's interpretive comment is indicated on the Snapshot by a checkmark (✓) placed in the appropriate box. To the right of the boxes are brief definitions of each scale that can help the client immediately understand the differences among these scales. Although these definitions are based on the item content of the scales, again they do not capture the richness of the BISs. However, the definitions serve an important purpose, as they give clients common descriptions for what may be unfamiliar BIS names. (See Chapter 6 for detailed descriptions of these scales.) To the left of the name of each BIS in this list is the first letter of the Theme with which that scale is most closely associated. These codes can help the client and counselor identify overall patterns in the client's results.

To the left of the results is printed text that varies depending on the individual's results. Two versions of text can be printed. One version prints if an individual has any BISs with scores in the "Average Interest" category or above. This text explains what the BISs measure. The other version prints for those persons who have *no* BISs in the "Average Interest" or above category. The texts of these paragraphs suggest some reasons for the pattern of scores.

Occupational Scales (OSs). The OS section of the Snapshot provides a list of the client's ten highest OSs, ranked from highest to lowest by interpretive comment category ("Very Similar" to "Very Dissimilar"). Within an interpretive comment category, the OSs are ranked by score. The client's result on each scale is indicated on the Snapshot by a checkmark (✓) placed in the appropriate box.

To the left of the name of each scale is the Theme code, consisting of one to three letters, indicating the Theme(s) characteristic of those employed in that occupation. (See Chapter 7 for an explanation of how these codes were derived.)

To the left of the OSs is printed text that varies depending on the individual's results. As for the GOTs and BISs, two versions of text can be printed. One version prints if there are any OSs in the "Mid-range," "Similar," or "Very Similar" categories (a score of 30 or above). This text explains what the OSs measure and provides some suggestions about how to use the Theme codes. The other version prints for those persons who have *no* OSs in the "Mid-range" or similar categories. The texts of these paragraphs suggest some reasons for the pattern of scores. The texts also discuss how clients might use the Occupational Scales information as they consider career choices.

Personal Style Scales. To the right of the OSs section on the Snapshot, a paragraph is printed informing clients that the *Strong* includes another set of scales, the Personal Style Scales, the results of which may help them in career exploration. Clients are instructed to turn to the last page of the Profile, page 6, to see their results on these scales.

Validity Check. In addition to the sets of scales just described, the *Strong* also includes a number of scales that can help the counselor assess the validity of an individual's Profile. The results of these scales are printed on page 6 of the Profile and are described later in this chapter. However, note that if any of these scales indicates a potential problem with the validity of the Profile, an alert is printed in the bottom right corner of the Snapshot directing the counselor to review the Summary of Item Responses on page 6.

General Occupational Themes/ Basic Interest Scales

Page 2 of the *Strong* Profile contains the client's results on the 6 General Occupational Themes and all 25 of the Basic Interest Scales. On this page, the Basic Interest Scales are grouped under the Theme to which they are most closely related.

Key. Appearing in the upper right corner of page 2, just below the demographic information, is a legend. This legend, labeled "KEY (Sample Scores)," is designed to make the Profile more understandable to the client, especially if she or he is reviewing results after a counseling session. As the title implies, this key shows clients how to read the information provided for each scale—the meaning of the numbers and symbols appearing on this page.

GOT and BIS Results. Printed next to the name of each GOT is a brief description of that Theme for ease in understanding the terminology. Printed below each GOT and BIS name is one of five interpretive comments that range from "Very High Interest" to "Very Little Interest." These interpretive comments are based on the distributions of the appropriate-gender General Reference Samples (GRS). The comment printed on the *Strong* Profile corresponds to the particular percentile band in the appropriate GRS in which the client's score falls. The percentiles in the GRS for each interpretive comment are as follows:

Very High Interest	91st and above
High Interest	76th to 90th
Average Interest	26th to 75th
Little Interest	11th to 25th
Very Little Interest	10th and below

For each GOT and BIS, two box-and-whisker graphs are presented. The upper box shows the results for the female GRS; the lower box, the results for the male GRS. Each graph contains three pieces of information: the mean of the sample, indicated by the vertical space near the middle of the thick rectangle; the middle 50 percent of the scores for that gender, represented by the thick box itself; and the middle 80 percent of scores for that gender, represented by the thinner lines (or "whiskers") that extend in both directions from the ends of the box. It should be noted that the boundaries that were used to construct the box-and-whisker graphs correspond to the percentile boundaries that define the interpretive comments.

The client's numerical score on the scale, which compares him or her to the combined male/female GRS, is printed to the right of the box-and-whisker graphs. The dot representing the client's score is plotted on the appropriate graph based on the client's gender.

Occupational Scales

Pages 3, 4, and 5 contain the client's results for the 211 OSs on the *Strong*.

Key. Appearing in the upper right corner of page 3, just below the demographic information, is the key. As with the key on page 2 of the Profile, this key shows clients how to read the information provided on this page—the meaning of the numbers and symbols. For each of the three pages of OS results, the key uses an example from one of the scales on that page to explain the Theme codes associated with each of the OSs. These keys also illustrate that some of the scales have different codes for males and females and that some are single-gender scales.

Occupational Scale Results. Presentation of the OSs is organized by Theme, with two Themes per page. The OSs are listed in alphabetical order within each Theme to enable users to locate scales quickly. To the left of each scale name in the "Theme Codes" column are the Theme codes for females (first column) and males (second column). The client's scores on both the female and male scales are printed in the "Your Scores" column to the right of the scale names. Labeling these columns "Theme Codes" and "Your Scores," respectively, should help reduce the number of questions to the counselor about the information presented in these columns. For scales that have a different Theme code for each gender, the Theme code for the other gender is printed in parentheses in the "Your Scores" column. For a few occupations it was not possible to find satisfactory occupational samples for both genders; these are noted by an asterisk in this column.

The client's score on the same-gender OS is plotted with a dot in one of the seven columns to the right of the "Your Scores" column. At the top of these columns are the following numbers, from left to right: 15, 20, 30, 40, 50, and 55. The width of the columns is designed to visually approximate a normal distribution of scores, with the mid-range column in the middle the widest and the two end columns, representing the tails of the distribution, the narrowest. One of the vertical lines in the rightmost columns is placed at 50, which is the mean of the occupational sample on that OS. For example, the mean for the sample of female carpenters is 50 on the female Carpenter OS. A score from 40 to 49, inclusive, is "Similar," while a score of 50 and above is "Very Similar." A score of 30 to 39 is mid-range. Likewise, a score of 20 to 29, inclusive, is "Dissimilar," while a score below 20 is "Very Dissimilar."

On each of the three pages on which the OSs are presented, the right column has been designed so that the client and counselor can record notes as they proceed through the interpretation.

Personal Style Scales

Page 6 of the Profile contains the client's results on the four Personal Style Scales: Work Style, Learning Environment, Leadership Style, and Risk Taking/Adventure. Presentation of the client's results on these four scales employs the same box-and-whisker graphs as used for the GOTs and BISs on page 2 of the Profile. The upper and lower graphs represent the distribution of female and male scores, respectively. In addition, to facilitate interpretation of these scales, anchors have been created that indicate the meaning of scores toward each pole of the scale. Unlike the GOTs and BISs, interpretive comments are not provided with these scales, since the meaning of the scores is indicated by the placement of the dot and by the scale anchors.

Summary of Item Responses

This section of the Profile is primarily intended for use by the counselor. On the left are the Administrative Indexes. These are the response percentages for each of the three response options for each of the eight parts of the *Strong* Item Booklet/Answer Sheet. The first five parts (i.e., Occupations, School Subjects, Activities, Leisure Activities, Types of People), along with Part VII (Your Characteristics), are averaged and reported on a "subtotal" line. The first five parts use the "Like," "Indifferent," and "Dislike" response format, while the Your Characteristics section uses the "Yes," "?," "No" format, which is similar to the Like/Indifferent/Dislike format. The response percentages for Part VI (Preference Between Two Activities) and Part VIII (Preference in the World of Work) are reported separately and not included in the total, since a response format that asks clients to choose between two preferences has a different meaning than do the other formats.

To the right of the response percentage indexes is a count of the Total Responses out of 317 that the client marked on his or her answer sheet. The client's score on the Infrequent Responses index is also provided. (See Chapter 9 for an explanation of these indexes.)

Understanding Your Results on the Strong

The back of each page of the Profile contains an overview and preliminary interpretation of the results. The text on the back of each page is intended to help the client understand the results on the front of that page. Several tables and charts are included to make the material more visually appealing and to further facilitate the client's understanding of the meaning of his or her results. A short exercise is also provided that can help the client integrate the information on the Profile and use the results to begin his or her career exploration.

Narrative Reports

Computer-generated narrative reports are available through the publisher's mail-in scoring service, as well as through the software system described in the next section. When ordered through the mail-in service, the *Strong* Profile is returned to the client along with any narrative report. The narrative reports serve to further individualize reporting of the client's results. They can help the client focus on the overall pattern of his or her *Strong* results, while also highlighting particular patterns and providing a more in-depth explanation of the most salient information. The reports include additional information, such as related occupations and suggestions for further career exploration. In addition, they provide a printed interpretation that the client can take away from the counseling session and refer to later. Specific reports and additional support materials are described in Table 3.1.

Support Materials

As for previous versions of the *Strong*, additional support materials are available to help clients and counselors better understand the meaning and implications of the results (see Table 3.1). Additional materials will also be developed to help users in different settings interpret and extend the results. These will include resource binders and applications guides for professionals from specific settings (e.g., colleges, organizations), introductory booklets for the client, and videotapes.

In the past, support materials have been based on extensive field experience and in many cases were suggested by users themselves. For example, *Using the Strong in Organizations* (Hirsh, 1986) was created to meet the needs of professionals conducting group interpretations of the *Strong*. The script for workshop leaders, as well as every group exercise, was extensively tested in real workshops in a variety of settings and then altered based on feedback from participants. This tradition of field testing materials with practitioners will continue with the 1994 *Strong*. Additional support materials will be developed after practitioners have had sufficient time to use the new *Strong*, and it has been determined what types of products would be most helpful. Contact the publisher for information about the most recent materials.

Software

A software system using a Microsoft® Windows® environment is available under a license from the publisher for total on-site management of the *Strong*. This system provides three options for administration of the *Strong:* on-line administration, with the items being presented to the client on the computer screen; use of a printed Item Booklet/Answer Sheet followed by key-in of the client's responses; use of an Item Booklet/Answer Sheet that can be scanned into the computer on-site.

Once the client's responses have been entered into the computer using one of these three methods, the professional can select the reports desired for immediate printing, for example the *Strong* Profile and individualized narrative reports (e.g., the Interpretive Report and the Professional Report). The Profile can also be printed on four-color preprinted forms purchased from the publisher that are identical to the Profile available with mail-in scoring. The software provides local customization options for printing.

To facilitate not only the selection and preparation of the appropriate reports but also the management of client information, client information and item responses are collected into a database. In addition, the database will help the professional track the administrations of the *Strong* and other assessment tools that are available through the system, for example, the *Myers-Briggs Type Indicator*® and the *California Psychological Inventory*™.

The client software module (the part of the software system used by the client when taking the items on-line) can be networked or installed from a floppy disk for administration of the *Strong* at multiple computers. These results can then be transferred to a computer containing the licensed software to produce the appropriate reports and to be included in the database.

Overall, use of the software system provides a fast, accurate, and efficient means of administering and scoring the *Strong* and of producing high-quality individualized reports for clients.

Translations

The 1985 *Strong* was translated into a number of different languages for both commercial and research

Table 3.1 Narrative Reports and Support Material for the 1994 *Strong*

Title	Description
Interpretive Report	Reports client's scores on the *Strong* scales and provides individualized interpretation of those scores; lists related occupations with DOT codes for those occupations on which the client scored highest; suggests a series of individualized "Next Steps" for client's career exploration.
Professional Report	Designed for clients who desire to pursue an occupation or career that typically requires at least a four-year college degree for entry; reports the client's scores on the professional occupations on the *Strong*; computes an Occupational Scales code based on the client's high scores on those occupations and then uses the code to suggest similar occupations for further exploration; describes how individuals with a similar code might function in an organization; incorporates the results of the four Personal Style Scales.
Profile	Basic report of client's results on the inventory that contains all scales and indexes. Back of each page offers interpretive information for client.
Profile, Skills Confidence Edition	Regular *Strong* Profile plus a page of *Skills Confidence Inventory* results. *Skills Confidence Inventory* reports client's confidence in performing tasks associated with six Holland Themes. Also compares confidence in skills on a particular Theme to interest in the Theme.
Strong and MBTI Career Report	Integrates client's highest *Strong* Theme and Personal Style Scales results with four-letter personality type from *Myers-Briggs Type Indicator* results. Lists occupations suggested by the two instruments and offers personalized strategies for career exploration, based on *Strong* and MBTI results.
Career Exploration: A Journey of Discovery	One-page, two-sided worksheet, designed to help the client get involved in the interpretive process; outlines a career exploration process to help the client integrate information from the *Strong* Profile with other information such as values, skills, and family issues; uses the metaphor of a journey to encourage the client to explore many sources of information and to convey the idea that career exploration is a process, not a one-time event
Exploring Career Options with the *Strong Interest Inventory* (rev. ed.)	Videotape that explains each of the types of scales on the *Strong*. Also answers questions clients frequently ask, such as the meaning of scores indicating little interest and how to make use of results for career planning.
Skills Confidence Inventory Manual	Explains research done to construct and validate the *Skills Confidence Inventory*. Also offers suggestions for administering and interpreting the *Skills Confidence Inventory* together with the *Strong*.
Strong Interest Inventory Resource: Strategies for Group and Individual Interpretations in Business and Organizational Settings	Binder that contains complete workshop script and individual interpretation tips customized for making *Strong* presentations to business audiences. Includes exercises and reproducible masters for overheads and handouts. Offers tips on focusing interpretation toward such workplace issues as downsizing, self-employment, gender and family issues, and retirement planning.
Strong Interest Inventory Resource: Strategies for Group and Individual Interpretations in College Settings	Binder with complete workshop scripts and individual interpretation suggestions customized for using the *Strong* with college students. Contains exercises and reproducible masters for overheads and handouts. Suggests how to adapt interpretations to address concerns of adult and reentry students, students with disabilities, racial and ethnic minority students, and other college populations.
Strong and MBTI Career Development Guide (rev. ed.)	Updated guide for counselors that reports on research done on using the MBTI and the 1994 edition of the *Strong* together in career counseling.

Table 3.1 Narrative Reports and Support Material for the 1994 *Strong* (continued)	
Title	**Description**
Strong and MBTI Career Development Workbook (rev. ed.)	Client workbook that contains worksheets to help individuals use results from both instruments to assess themselves, evaluate work tasks and environments, identify occupations to explore, and stay motivated while in the process of career development
Where Do I Go Next? Using Your *Strong* Results to Manage Your Career	Client booklet that explains the General Occupational Themes and Basic Interest Scales, offers advice on using the Personal Style Scales to find satisfying work environments, and lists additional occupations—organized by Holland Theme—for exploration. Next Steps section helps client use *Strong* results to explore career options.

purposes. Translations of the 1994 *Strong* will follow. Permission to translate any part of the *Strong* for any reason must be requested in writing from the publisher. (For more information on translations of the *Strong*, see Chapter 15.)

References

Hansen, J. C., & Stocco, J. L. (1980). Stability of vocational interests of adolescents and young adults. *Measurement and Evaluation in Guidance, 13,* 173–178.

Hirsh, S. K. (1986). *Using the Strong in organizations.* Palo Alto, CA: Consulting Psychologists Press.

Prediger, D. J. (1982). Dimensions underlying Holland's hexagon: Missing link between interests and occupations? *Journal of Vocational Behavior, 21,* 259–287.

Swanson, J. L., & Hansen, J. C. (1988). Stability of vocational interests over 4-year, 8-year, and 12-year intervals. *Journal of Vocational Behavior, 33,* 185–202.

CHAPTER 4

Items: The Foundation of the Inventory

Vocational interest inventories are effective because different people respond differently to the various inventory items, and people who have found satisfying work in an occupation tend to respond to items in a way that is characteristic of others in their occupation. These basic premises, illustrated and documented in the following pages, are the foundation for the entire enterprise of interest measurement. For the user, a knowledge of how items contribute to the scales can be an invaluable aid to understanding and interpreting the inventory. ◆

Item Format

The items on the *Strong* Item Booklet/Answer Sheet, which fall into eight parts, have three different response formats. Most parts (e.g., Occupations, School Subjects, Activities, Leisure Activities, and Types of People) utilize a Like/Indifferent/Dislike response format. Two parts, Preference Between Two Activities and Preference in the World of Work, require the respondent to choose between two alternatives, and the part Your Characteristics uses a Yes/?/No response format. For each item, the proportion of a group of individuals giving each response is an important piece of information about that item as well as about that group of people.

Selecting Items for the 1994 Strong

For the 1994 revision of the *Strong*, a research version of the *Strong* containing all 325 items from the 1985 inventory as well as an additional 54 items was given to over 55,000 people. This sampling resulted in a final selection of 317 of the 379 items that appeared on the research version. (See Chapter 2 for a list of all the new items added to the 1994 inventory as well as those deleted from the 1985 inventory.)

For a number of reasons, it was necessary to modify some old items and add some new items. New items were written to broaden the coverage of the item content of the *Strong*. For example, the research version of the *Strong* included items (e.g., "Paralegal" and "Security guard") that extended the number of occupations requiring less than four years of college, items (e.g., "Day care worker" and "Bilingual teacher") that reflected occupations of growing importance in our society, and leisure activities (e.g., "Biking" and "Walking") that reflected contemporary fitness trends.

Some of the new items were written to replace original items that worked well but seemed outdated. Examples from the 1985 *Strong* include "Repairing a clock," an item that is outdated since most clocks are now electronic and are often thrown away rather than repaired; "Foreigners," an item that sounds somewhat pejorative; and "Being married to a research scientist vs. Being married to a sales executive," an item that could be viewed as sexist. Reworded items are listed in Table 4.1. When replacement items were

Table 4.1 Original Items and Their Potential Replacements Appearing on the Research Version

Original Item/ New Item	Retained on Form T317	Response Percentages of Females (N = 7,500 approx.)			Response Percentages of Males (N = 7,500 approx.)		
		Like	Indifferent	Dislike	Like	Indifferent	Dislike
Repairing a clock	√	24	31	45	35	32	33
Repairing electronics equipment	√	14	26	60	30	34	36
Foreigners		44	43	13	39	46	15
People from a different culture		62	34	4	56	39	5
Being married to a research scientist vs. Being married to a sales executive		49	27	24	47	31	22
Being friends with a research scientist vs. Being friends with a sales executive	√	55	22	23	56	22	22
Income tax accountant	√	14	21	65	14	27	59
Accountant	√	30	20	50	26	25	49
Opera singer	√	21	21	58	16	19	65
Musical performer		49	25	26	45	25	30

written, both the original and the replacement were included on the research version so that responses to each could be compared.

The research version was much longer than desirable for an interest inventory because of the presence of both new and replacement items. Since previous experience had shown that the length of a scale is less important than the quality of its items (Hansen & Campbell, 1985), it was necessary to identify the best items to include without adding to the overall length of the inventory. Therefore, all 379 items were analyzed in four ways to select the best items for final inclusion in the *Strong*. These analyses are described here.

1. To eliminate items that did not work well, the response percentages of a large heterogeneous group of respondents to each item were considered. Any item that was extremely popular or extremely unpopular would not work well because it would not differentiate between occupational groups. All the items that appeared on the 1985 *Strong* had previously survived a similar analysis, but some of the new items written for the research version (e.g., "Spending time with family," to which nearly everyone responded "Like") were abandoned because everyone answered them the same way. However, a few such items were retained so that a scale of infrequently used items could be developed. (See Chapter 9 for a discussion of this scale.)

2. A second analysis examined people's responses to the original and reworded items on the research version. Since it was not possible to assume that responses would be the same for similar items, each change had to be checked and verified. This verification process was accomplished by including the new items along with their potential replacements to determine if people would respond with the same percentage of "Like" endorsements to the reworded items. The response percentages for the pairs of original and replacement items are given in Table 4.1.

This analysis of response percentages was used as the basis for deciding which version of the items to include or whether both should appear on the revised version of the inventory. For instance, while the percentage of men responding "Like" to "Repairing electronic equipment" was similar to that for "Repairing a clock," women responded "Like" less frequently to the new item. Both of these items were retained based on other criteria. While men *and* women responded "Like" more frequently to "People from a different culture" than to "Foreigners," both of these items were deleted because, although the former was intended as a replacement for the latter, it did not appear on many scales (see the analysis described next). Both males and females responded similarly to the items using "being married to" and "being friends with" in the stem; the newer item was chosen to make the *Strong* appear to be more up-to-date.

The analysis of potential replacement items also made it possible to determine whether specific and general occupational titles elicited different patterns of "Like," "Indifferent," and "Dislike" responses. For example, the original items "Income tax accountant" and "Opera singer" were liked less by both men and women than the newer, more general items "Accountant" and "Musical performer," apparently because their greater specificity appealed to fewer people. The pairs of items (i.e., "Income tax accountant" and "Accountant") did not act as synonyms, as had been expected. The items "Accountant," "Income tax accountant," and "Opera singer" were retained in the 1994 *Strong* because they had acceptable response distributions and were useful in constructing the Occupational Scales (OSs). "Musical performer" was dropped because it was used in very few scales. (The analysis reported next discusses how often items appear on scales.)

3. Because of the efficiency of modern computers, it was possible to construct tentative scales using all the items on the research form to determine how many OSs would include each item. A few items that were not eliminated in the first analysis did not appear on many of these tentative scales. Such items were considered candidates for deletion if they appeared to contribute to less than five scales. The magnitude of the differentiation was considered as well; an item that contributed to only two scales might be retained if it was one of the most differentiating items for those scales, whereas an item that contributed to four scales with a weaker differentiating power might be deleted.

4. Once an item was suggested for deletion, it was checked against the preliminary General Occupational Theme scales (GOTs) and Basic Interest Scales (BISs) to make sure that none of the scales would be reduced in reliability or validity if the item were deleted. Since the GOTs and BISs are shorter than the OSs, an item that was integral to one or more of these scales was usually retained.

As a result of these analyses, some items that would have been acceptable except for the availability of better items were not selected; others were deleted even though they had performed well in earlier versions of the inventory.

How Items Are Used in the Inventory

In exploring item functioning, it is important to remember that items are used in two ways in the inventory. First, using statistical procedures (e.g., factor analysis), they can be clustered so that those items to which people respond similarly are placed together on a scale. Such procedures were used to develop the GOTs (see Chapter 5) and the BISs (see Chapter 6).

Second, using empirical procedures, items that differentiate members of a particular occupational group from workers at large can be identified and grouped together on scales. Such procedures form the basis of the OSs (see Chapter 7). Both "Like" and "Dislike" responses can appear on OSs, and responses can be weighted both positively and negatively. The result is that the content of the OSs is much more diverse than that of the other types of scales.

To understand how the items perform in the OSs, it is useful to know how they (1) characterize occupational groups, (2) characterize a large heterogeneous sample of employed adults called the General Reference Sample (GRS), and (3) differentiate between specific occupational groups and the GRS.

Establishing Characteristic Item Responses for Occupational Groups

Each *Strong* scale is represented by a group of people who are at least 25 years old, have at least three years of experience in the occupation, perform activities that typify the occupation, and describe themselves as satisfied with the occupation. Except for occupations in which one gender group is highly underrepresented, the *Strong* scales for each occupation contain separate scales for men and women. Although men and women in the same occupation respond similarly to some items, they respond differently to others, thus creating a need for the construction of separate scales.

People in different occupations are characterized by different average responses to each item. Average item response percentages for a number of occupational samples are plotted in Figures 4.1 through 4.3 for a "Like" response to three items: "Artist," "Farmer," and "Public speaking." Note that the vertical axes of the three figures differ due to the shapes of the distributions and the numbers of occupational samples presented. As a result, the reader should consult the figures to learn the overall shapes of the three distributions, but should not make comparisons among them based on the height of the distributions. The intervals on the horizontal axis represent the percentage of "Like" responses to the item in question. For example, with regard to the item "Artist," Figure 4.1 shows that 80 of the female occupational samples had a "Like" response percentage falling between 41 and 50. The five highest and five lowest ranking samples for each gender are identified for each item, illustrating the occupational differences in responses to these items. (The six lowest response percentages for females are given in Figure 4.2 because the fourth, fifth, and sixth lowest "Like" response percentages are tied at 19 percent.)

For the items "Artist" and "Farmer," the graphs include 620 and 622 samples, respectively, collected over the history of the *Strong*. In both graphs, about 41 percent of the samples are female and about 59 percent are male. Most of the samples included are the adult occupational groups that took research versions of the *Strong* from 1927 to 1993 to develop the OSs; the others are miscellaneous samples that were collected for various research projects. Collectively, these samples represent a diverse array of employed female and male adults. Except for unusual groups, such as astronauts and famous football coaches, the samples contain more than 75 people, and in many cases more than 1,000.

Since data have been collected for more men's occupational groups than women's over the years, it is not appropriate to make a direct comparison of the height of the bars for male and female groups within Figures 4.1 and 4.2. It is more appropriate to look at the shape of the distribution for each gender separately. In Figure 4.3, only the 211 occupational samples used to develop scales for the 1994 *Strong* are included. Since the number of male and female occupational groups represented in this figure is nearly equal, it is appropriate to make a direct comparison of the bars representing the male and female occupational groups.

Figure 4.1 shows item response percentages for the "Artist" item. Psychometrically, this item is an excellent one because it produces a broad distribution of responses: in some occupations, almost everyone responded "Like" to this item; in others, almost no one did. In contrast are those items to which nearly everyone responded in the same manner; such items, which elicit minimal discrimination among people or among groups and therefore do not contribute to the purpose of the inventory, have been dropped. Most items produce roughly the same spread as does the "Artist" item, over 90 percentage points from the lowest to the highest response sample. However, the shapes of the distributions vary, as a comparison of Figures 4.1 through 4.3 indicates. (Another item distribution is given in Figure 17.2.)

The "Farmer" item (see Figure 4.2 on page 38) is an example of an item with a different pattern of mean responses for the groups represented. While the range of responses is broad, the mean response rates of most of the groups fall between 11 and 50 percent. This item is useful chiefly because it separates agricultural from other occupations. Unlike the "Artist" item, it does not differentiate well among the other occupations across a broad response range.

Figure 4.3 (on page 39) shows that items representing school subjects differentiate among occupational groups in a manner similar to the items shown in Figures 4.1 and 4.2. The item "Public speaking" distributes 211 occupational groups over 80 percentage points. These 211 samples are the same ones used in developing the current occupational samples. While male and female occupational samples are distributed over most of the range, the distribution is flatter for males than for females.

The data on average item response percentages for all items found on the *Strong* illustrate several important points:

1. *The popularity of the individual item responses varies greatly from occupation to occupation.*
   The distributions in Figures 4.1 through 4.3

Items: The Foundation of the Inventory **37**

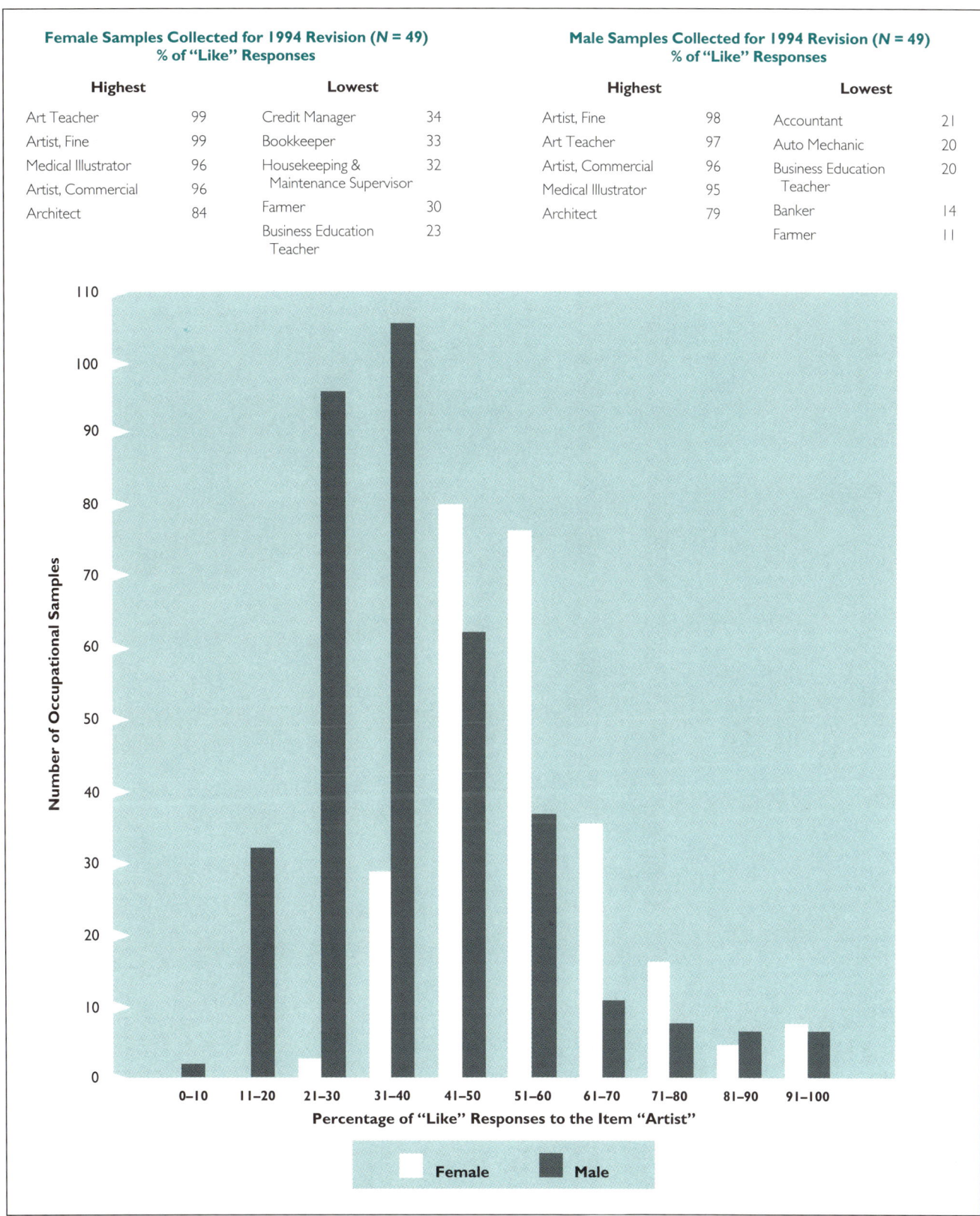

Figure 4.1 Percentage of "Like" Responses to the Item "Artist" for 620 Occupational Samples Collected over the History of the *Strong*

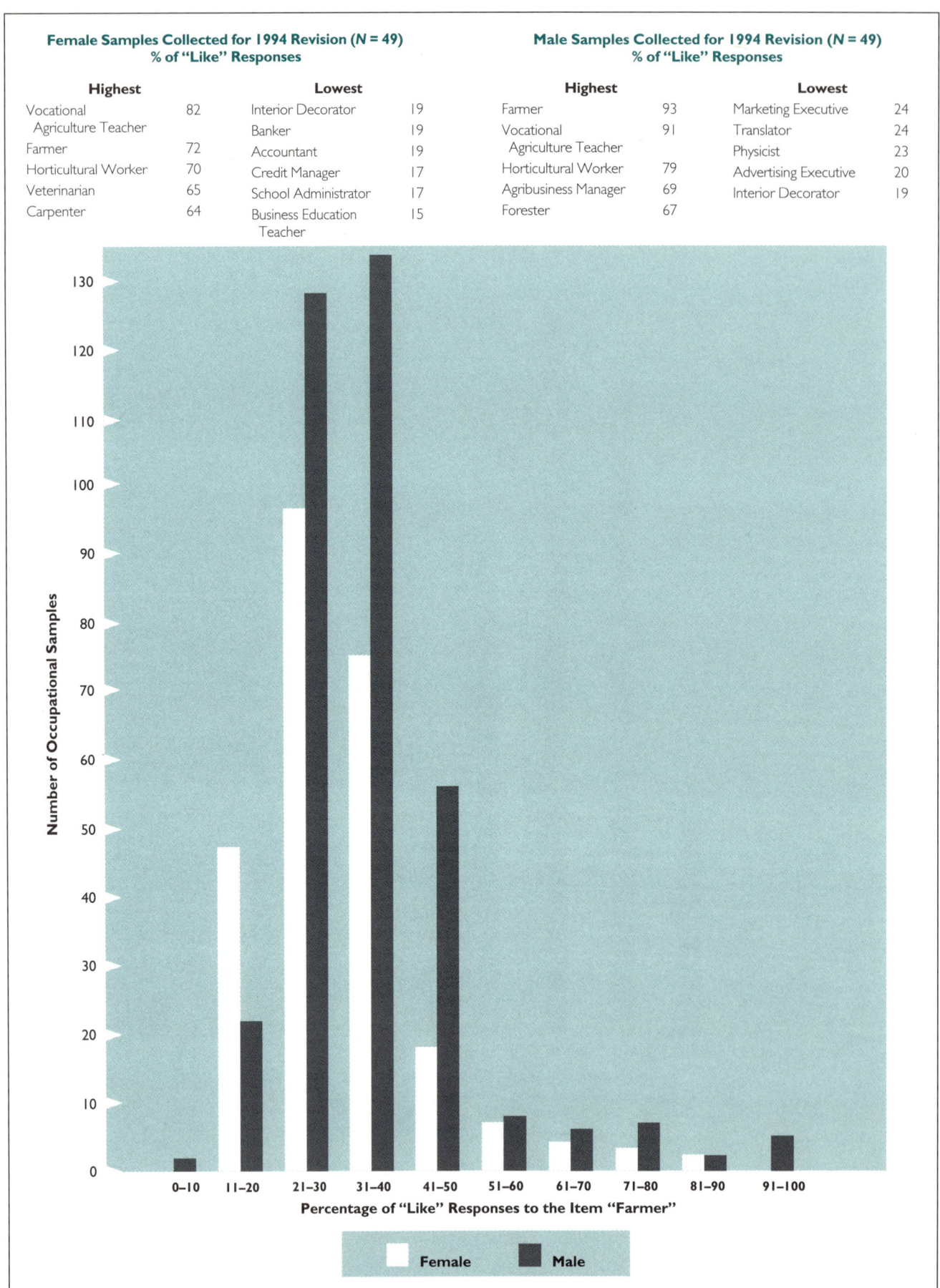

Figure 4.2 Percentage of "Like" Responses to the Item "Farmer" for 622 Occupational Samples Collected over the History of the *Strong*

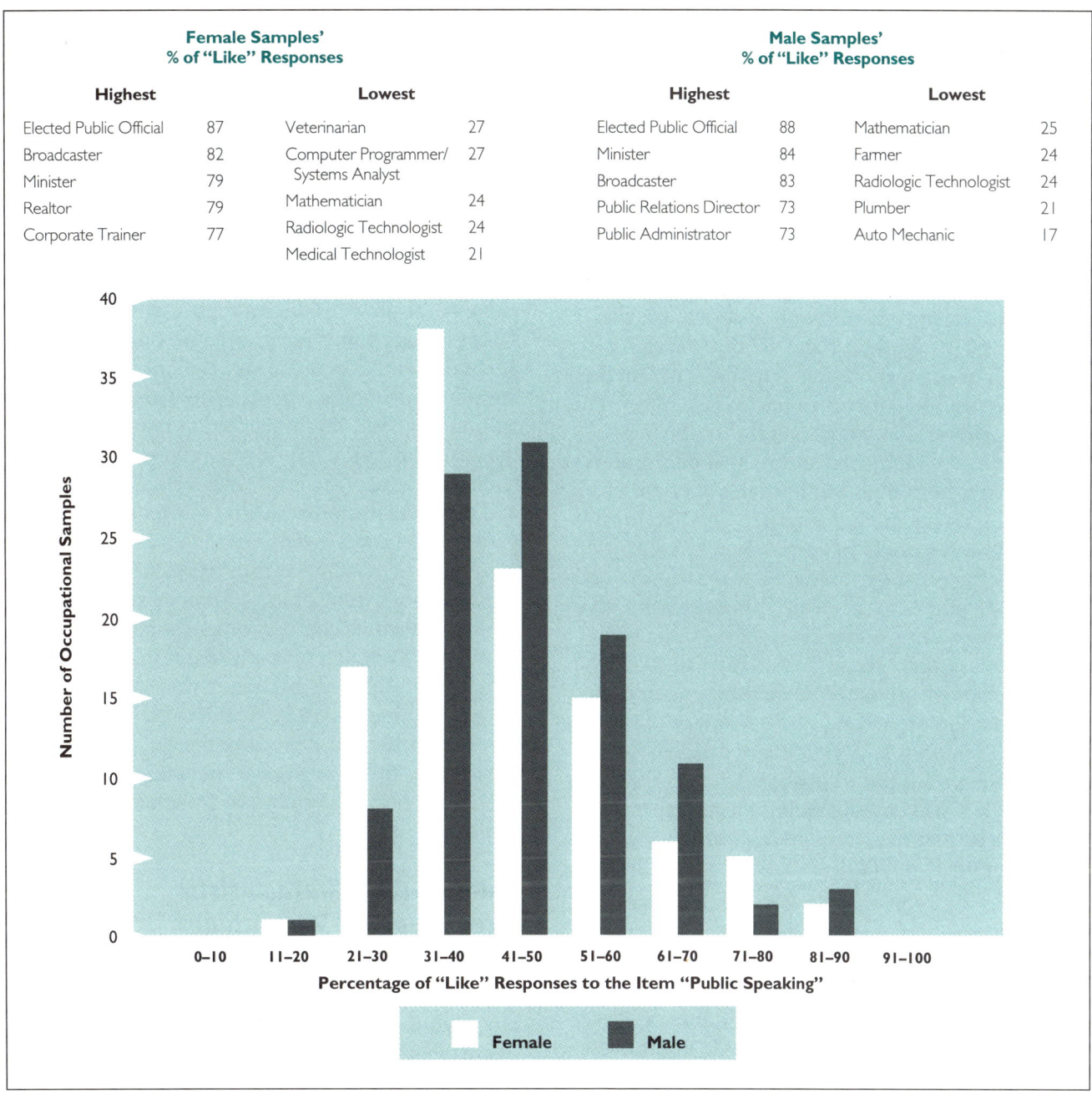

Figure 4.3 Percentage of "Like" Responses to the Item "Public Speaking" for 211 Occupational Samples

are typical, showing a wide range of "Like" responses extending from lows of 4 to 5 percent to highs of over 95 percent. Most of the *Strong* items show similar ranges. The power of the individual items to discriminate between occupations directly establishes the usefulness of the inventory. Valid scales can be constructed only from individually effective items.

2. *The content of each item response is appropriate for the occupations highly endorsing or rejecting it.* Occupational samples respond to the *Strong* items as one would expect: artists endorse artistic items; scientists, scientific items; and mechanics, mechanical items. The rank ordering of the five highest scoring and five lowest scoring male and female occupational samples from the 1994 *Strong* (see Figures 4.1 through 4.3) emphasizes the general reasonableness of their item endorsements.

Because this information is so reasonable, it is sometimes seen as trivial. People often ask, "Why did you go to all that trouble to prove the obvious? Don't you already know that farmers will say they like to be farmers, and artists that they like to be artists?" However, much of what seems obvious becomes apparent only *after* the data have been organized. The chief benefit of the systematic, empirical approach is that concepts can be quantified, then compared quantitatively and qualitatively.

3. *The responses to each item vary in their characteristics, especially in average popularity and in the range of spread they create among the occupational samples.* It is clear from comparing the shapes of the distributions in Figures 4.1 and 4.2 that the average number of occupations that respond "Like" to the item "Artist" is higher than the average number of occupations that respond "Like" to the item "Farmer," even though some occupational groups respond at both high and low rates of endorsement for each item. In contrast, no occupational groups represented in Figure 4.3 are characterized by the very high and very low percentages of "Like" responses to the item "Public speaking" that characterize some occupations for the other two items. Since these characteristics vary considerably and independently across the inventory items, the construction of the OSs took advantage of these item differences. As long as the individual item response spreads the occupational groups across a relatively broad range of endorsement percentages, there is no ideal item response pattern for the occupational samples.

4. *For the most part, responses to the items are stable over time.* An occupational sample tested in one decade gives about the same responses as does another sample from the same occupation tested three to four decades later. Table 4.2 presents data on the stability of the "Like" response to the items "Artist" and "Farmer" over time. Four different samples of the same gender in the same 20 occupational groups were tested, each in different decades: one in the 1930s or 1940s, generally by Strong; a second in the 1960s, by Campbell; a third in the 1970s or 1980s, by Hansen; and finally one in the 1990s for the current revision. More male than female occupational groups are represented, largely because the coverage of women's occupations in the early *Strong* was limited.

Table 4.2 shows the range, in percentage points, covered by the first three samples and then assesses whether the response percentage of the current occupational group falls outside that range and, if so, by how much. For the item "Farmer," four of the response percentages for the new occupational samples fall outside the range of the previous three samples, although none by more than 3 points. It is worth noting that three of the four differences are in the negative direction, which means that the response percentage of the current group extended the range of the previous three occupations at the lower end. For the item "Artist," five of the response percentages for the new occupational samples fall outside the range of the previous three samples, two of them by 12 percentage points in the negative direction. Some of the differences over time are undoubtedly due to sampling differences, not occupational shifts. The samples were not always selected or tested in exactly the same way in the four investigations. Still, the differences over time are impressively small.

These data demonstrate that the item response percentages from a given occupational sample can be used safely over many years to represent that occupation. Although none of the current occupational samples for which comparisons are available shifted substantially enough to imply that it would make a difference in OS construction, several of the groups ranged over more than 20 points in their response percentages to these items over the years. This finding suggests that occupational item response rates should be checked periodically using new occupational samples.

Establishing Characteristic Item Response Percentages for the General Reference Sample

To select items for the OSs, the responses of a heterogeneous group of workers are needed as basis of comparison with more homogeneous groups of workers in specific occupations. For this revision of the *Strong*, that heterogeneous group was called the General Reference Sample (GRS), and it represented relatively equally all the 98 occupational samples collected for the revision. (The GRS is discussed in detail in Chapter 7.) In addition, how the item responses of the GRS cluster together is the basic data used in constructing the GOTs and BISs (see Chapters 5 and 6).

The response patterns of the GRS are helpful in describing this relatively heterogeneous group. The most popular item on the *Strong*, "Can write a concise, well-organized report" (in Part VII, Your Characteristics), was endorsed by 80 percent of the men

Table 4.2 Percent "Like" Responses to the Items "Farmer" and "Artist" for the 1930s–1940s, 1960s, 1970s–1980s, and 1990s for 20 Occupational Samples

Sample	Gender	"Farmer" Item						"Artist" Item					
		30s–40s	60s	70s–80s	90s	Range[a]	Change[b]	30s–40s	60s	70s–80s	90s	Range	Change
Accountant	M	25	25	39	35	14	—[c]	20	26	32	21	12	—
Advertising Executive	M	25	22	29	20	7	–2	56	68	70	67	14	—
Architect	M	27	28	42	28	15	—	87	88	82	79	6	–3
Banker	M	41	30	41	39	11	—	13	26	34	14	21	—
Business Education Teacher	F	22	17	26	15	9	–2	36	39	35	23	4	–12
Chemist	M	36	27	37	33	10	—	25	46	39	29	21	—
Dentist	M	32	37	49	40	17	—	41	55	48	44	14	—
Engineer	M	26	30	51	39	25	—	28	42	35	33	14	—
Farmer	M	88	97	100	93	12	—	11	13	18	11	7	—
Forester	M	47	64	73	67	26	—	21	37	34	27	16	—
Lawyer	F	31	22	32	23	10	1	47	50	52	54	5	2
Lawyer	M	26	35	45	33	19	–3	19	37	44	39	25	—
Librarian	F	31	26	35	27	9	—	57	64	60	51	7	–6
Life Insurance Agent	F	21	19	28	25	9	—	32	53	57	39	25	—
Life Insurance Agent	M	29	28	38	34	10	—	21	22	28	23	7	1
Nurses, RN	F	33	29	41	34	12	—	53	54	55	41	2	–12
Personnel Director	M	27	32	36	30	9	—	32	40	33	33	8	—
Physicist	M	25	23	47	23	24	—	37	53	43	43	16	—
Police Officer	M	27	32	44	38	17	—	16	30	29	22	14	—
School Administrator	M	37	39	46	39	9	—	16	26	30	26	14	—
Mean		32.8	33.1	44.0	35.8	13.7		33.4	43.5	42.9	36.0	12.6	

[a] Range is calculated from 1930s–1940s to 1970s–1980s.
[b] Change indicates the amount of deviation between the 1990s percent "Like" response and the range from previous years.
[c] "—" indicates that the 1990s percent "Like" response falls within the range.

and women in the GRS. For the next most popular item, "Drawing a definite salary vs. Receiving a commission on what is done" (in Part VI, Preference Between Two Activities), a definite salary was endorsed by 76 percent of the GRS. The least popular items for this group were "Security guard," "Nurse's aide/Orderly," and "Dental assistant" (all in Part I, Occupations), each of which was endorsed by only 4 percent of the GRS. These few examples suggest that members of the GRS saw themselves as relatively verbally skilled, were security conscious in today's economic conditions, and disliked occupations that do not require extensive schooling. These responses are not necessarily typical of employed workers in general but are typical of the relatively highly educated members of the GRS.

Building Occupational Scales

One of the ways that interest inventory data are most frequently used is in the comparison of item response percentages between two or more samples. Each of the OSs is a collection of items that have shown large differences in response percentage between a sample of people in that occupation and a reference sample. But to identify items that are suitable for that OS, there must be a basis for establishing what is meant by "large differences."

Item percentage differences are calculated by systematically comparing the "Like" and "Dislike" response percentages of the two samples (the occupational sample and GRS), one item at a time. The difference on the "Indifferent" response, which is rarely if ever the largest difference of the three responses, is ignored at this step. As discussed in Chapter 7, it is sometimes used, if large enough, to refine the item weights. The comparison of "Like" and "Dislike" responses yields, for each item, two percentage differences: one between the two "Like" percentages, one between the two "Dislike" percentages. The larger of the two differences becomes the ranking of that item with respect to other items and toward its possible selection for an OS based on the responses of the occupational sample. An item is called a "12 percent item," a "30 percent item," and so on, reflecting the size of the larger difference.

Substantial experience has shown that differences of 10 percent or less can usually be ignored. Samples tested and retested over short periods typically yield about a dozen item response differences of 10 percent or larger between test and retest. Consequently, ignoring differences of this size (or less) eliminates the risk of selecting items that reflect only the normal fluctuations within a sample. In general, 12 percent items are barely important (about four items will differ between test and retest at this level), and 16 percent items are important (usually no items will differ on short test and retest intervals at this level). Every extra point above this percentage becomes more important; 20 percent items, for example, are extremely important.

For constructing Occupational Scales, "important" means that the item responses reflect a real difference between the samples, one that will be replicated on repeated sampling and will manifest itself in behaviors that differentiate between the individuals making up the two samples (i.e., they will choose different activities, not only on paper but also in their actual behavior). These guidelines for the use of item response differences are based on the assumption that both samples contain at least 200 people. If the samples are smaller, the item percentage differences should be increased, ideally to at least 18 to 20 percent for samples as small as 50.

Also important in the construction of an OS is the number of items across the full range of the inventory that exhibit these response differences. The number should be sufficient to provide a reliable scale but not so great as to promote unnecessary overlap among the scales. For the 1994 *Strong*, an average scale length of 45 items was found to be sufficient (see Chapter 7, Table 7.2).

Conclusion

The item responses of any group of respondents provide a window through which the most prevalent likes and dislikes of people in a group can be seen. Item responses are also the foundation upon which the structure of interest measurement rests. The more users understand what the items say about occupational groups and how they were used in constructing scales, the more proficient those users will be in using the *Strong*.

Reference

Hansen, J. C., & Campbell, D. P. (1985). *Manual for the Strong Interest Inventory* (4th ed.). Stanford, CA: Stanford University Press.

CHAPTER 5

The General Occupational Themes

The first part of this chapter is designed to help the reader understand the content and implications of the General Occupational Themes (GOTs). It briefly describes the origins of the Themes in John L. Holland's (1973, 1985a) theory of vocational choice and their addition to the 1974 *Strong* (Campbell & Holland, 1972; Hansen & Johansson, 1972). Next, the six GOT scales are described, including the variety of behaviors and preferences associated with each. Various interpretive strategies using the Themes are discussed.

The second half of the chapter addresses how the GOTs were created and presents research evidence for their reliability, validity, and interpretation. In the 1994 *Strong*, special attention was given to increasing the reliability of the GOTs. Cronbach alpha reliabilities for all the Themes have been increased to .90 or higher, and test-retest reliabilities have been increased. At the same time, efforts have been made to maintain the construct validity of the scales so that their meaning remains constant for counseling use and for theory and research. ◆

Theory, Content, and Interpretation of the General Occupational Themes

The homogeneous scales of the *Strong*—the GOTs and Basic Interest Scales (BISs)—were developed to provide a parsimonious organization for the *Strong* Profile and to offer additional means of explaining high and low scores on the Occupational Scales (OSs). The Theme scales were developed by first examining definitions of each Theme type and then selecting from the *Strong* item pool those items that best reflected that definition. The creation of the GOTs merged Strong's empiricism and Holland's theory and represented an important milestone in interest measurement (Borgen, 1991).

Holland's Theory

Holland's theory—presented in *Making Vocational Choices: A Theory of Careers* (1973)—is based on four main assumptions:

1. In our culture, most people can be categorized into six types—Realistic, Investigative, Artistic, Social, Enterprising, and Conventional—and each person may be characterized by one type or some combination of these types.

2. Occupational environments can be divided into the same six types, and each environment is dominated by a particular type of person. Thus, the peronality types of co-workers, as much as job requirements, establish the working tenor of a given occupation.

3. People search for environments that let them exercise their skills and abilities, express their attitudes and values, take on problems and roles they find stimulating and satisfying, and avoid chores or responsibilities they find distasteful or formidable.
4. Behavior is determined by an interaction between a person's personality and the characteristics of his or her working environment. Factors such as job performance, satisfaction, and stability are influenced by this interaction.

Since a classification system of only six types is insufficient to fully represent the diversity of human personalities and working environments, Holland expanded his classification to incorporate combinations of the six types, such as Realistic-Investigative, Artistic-Social, and Enterprising-Social-Conventional. In theory, using all possible combinations of the six types, 720 classifications can be established. In practice, the use of the most strongly manifested one, two, or three types seems sufficient for most purposes.

Holland's theory organizes the six types by placing them at the six points of a hexagon (see Figure 5.1 on page 51), with those presumed to be most closely related located adjacent to each other, and those most dissimilar located across the hexagon from each other. The order in which they fall around the hexagon is frequently called the R-I-A-S-E-C order, each letter being the first letter of the type name. The corresponding GOTs use the same names: for example, Realistic Theme, or simply R Theme.

Relationships between the types, or between the GOTs representing the types, can be described according to the spatial distance separating them. Thus, types adjacent to one another on the hexagon (e.g., Realistic and Investigative) have more in common with one another than do types opposite each other (e.g., Realistic and Social). However, even types adjacent to one another occasionally have some descriptors that are in opposition. The most notable examples are the Artistic and Social types: the former like to work alone and independently, while the latter like to work with people and be the center of attention.

Matching Interest Types with Job Types

Occupations or jobs can also be categorized in terms of the six types. The requirements of each job establish what its type will be. For example, testing large samples of engineers with the *Strong* results in coding them Realistic-Investigative (RI), indicating that the occupation combines Realistic interests in mechanical activities, machinery, and concrete problems with Investigative interests in math, science, and abstract problems.

The process of self-exploration and world-of-work examination in career counseling involves matching a client's Holland type with that person's job type. However, Holland's model of career exploration goes beyond simply matching people and jobs. His theory also suggests matching an individual's interests with that person's preferred learning environments, family environments, leisure activities, and living environments. Discrepancies between the person's interests (as summarized by the GOTs) and his or her environment (whether work, leisure, or living environment) may lead to dissatisfaction. For example, an Enterprising-Realistic type who satisfies her Enterprising interests as a Life Insurance Agent may spend her leisure time in Realistic activities that require mechanical skills and ingenuity to produce tangible products. If for some reason she is expected to attend theater performances and art showings, she may find herself bored and feel obligated rather than entertained.

Definitions of the Themes

Generally, people are not pure types. In fact, *most people have interests that are a combination of two or more Themes.* Consequently, people with combinations of interests may find that only some of the descriptors for the Themes (described later in this chapter) on which they scored high on the *Strong* fit what they know about themselves. One way to help people identify the combination of descriptors that best fits them is to use the interpretive information for each type that appears on the back of page 2 of the Profile; ask the person to underline each descriptor that seems to fit and cross out those that do not.

The definitions and examples presented here were derived in part from the work of several authors, most notably Holland (1973), Hansen and Campbell (1985), Gottfredson and Holland (1989), and Hansen (1992). These materials were also enhanced using analyses of the 1994 *Strong* data, including the tables and figures in the latter half of this chapter. The new Personal Style Scales (see Chapter 8) permitted analyses that were particularly informative for understanding and describing the GOTs. These descriptions are best viewed as prototypes capturing general constructs and expectations, with room for variability in individual cases.

Realistic (R Theme): *building, repairing, working outdoors*

Realistic people like activities, jobs, and co-workers who represent such interest areas as mechanical, construction, and repair activities; nature and the outdoors; and adventurous, physical activities. They enjoy working with tools, machines, and equipment. They are interested in action rather than thought and prefer concrete problems to ambiguous, abstract problems. They tend to score toward the takes chances pole of the Risk Taking/Adventure scale and to score toward the works with ideas/data/things pole of the Work Style scale (see Chapter 8 for a discussion of these and two other Personal Style Scales).

Typical work activities
- Doing jobs that produce tangible results
- Operating or designing heavy equipment or huge machines
- Using tools that require fine motor coordination and manual dexterity (e.g., dentist's drill, surgeon's scalpel, jeweler's tweezers)
- Operating precision machinery (e.g., drill press, x-ray machine)
- Fixing, building, and repairing

Potential competencies
- Mechanical abilities and ingenuity
- Problem solving with tools and machines
- Psychomotor skills
- Poise with outdoor and adventurous activities
- Physical strength

Self-concept and values
- Emotionally stable and reliable
- Practical, thrifty, and persistent
- Shy, modest
- Likely to avoid being the center of attention
- Uncomfortable talking about themselves
- Inclined to take physical risks
- Likely to maintain traditional values
- Slow to accept radical new ideas

Environments
- Manufacturing or industrial firms with tangible products
- Construction industry
- Mining and energy industries
- Transportation fields (e.g., air, trucking, local transit)
- Engineering and technical firms
- The outdoors; small, rural communities
- Situations calling for minimal interaction with others
- Situations permitting casual dress
- Organizations structured with clearly drawn lines of authority (e.g., armed forces, enforcement agencies, protection occupations)

Typical hobbies
- Repairing old things (e.g., cars, machines, appliances)
- Building and rebuilding
- Reading magazines and books about outdoor sports, cars, airplanes, boats
- Hunting, fishing, camping, rock climbing
- Operating powerful recreational vehicles (e.g., speedboats, motorcycles, snowmobiles)
- Physically dangerous activities (e.g., skydiving, mountain climbing, auto racing)

Sample Realistic occupations

R	Auto Mechanic
R	Gardener/Groundskeeper
R	Plumber
R	Police Officer
R	Rancher
RI	Electrician
RI	Engineer
RI	Forester
RI	Machinist
RI	Radiologic Technologist
RS	Vocational Agriculture Teacher
RS	Industrial Arts Teacher
RE	Building Contractor
RE	Horticultural Worker
RE	Military Officer
RSI	Cabinetmaker

Typical R-Theme items
- "Auto mechanic"
- "Electronics technician"
- "Agriculture"

- "Repairing a clock"
- "Popular mechanics magazines"

Investigative (I Theme): researching, analyzing, inquiring

Investigative people have a strong scientific, inquiring orientation. They enjoy gathering information, uncovering new facts or theories, and analyzing and interpreting data. They are most comfortable in academic or research environments and enjoy pursuing advanced degrees. They prefer to rely on themselves in their work rather than on others in a group project. They dislike selling and repetitive activities. They tend to score toward the works with ideas/data/things pole of the Work Style scale and toward the academic pole of the Learning Environment scale. Since the I Theme is not correlated with leadership style, that scale can add important new information about preferred work roles.

Typical work activities
- Performing ambiguous or abstract tasks
- Solving problems through thinking
- Working independently
- Doing scientific or laboratory work
- Conducting research and analyses
- Collecting and organizing data

Potential competencies
- Scientific ability
- Analytical skills
- Mathematical skills
- Writing skills
- Perseverance in solving difficult, abstract problems

Self-concept and values
- Independent, self-motivated
- Reserved, introspective
- Analytical, curious
- Task oriented (becoming absorbed in the job)
- Confident of scholarly and intellectual abilities
- Original, creative
- Nonconformist values and attitudes

Environments
- Unstructured organizations that allow freedom in work styles
- Research and design laboratories and firms
- Universities and colleges
- Medical facilities
- Computer-related industries
- Scientific foundations and think tanks

Typical hobbies
- Work (may be consumed by a job, working 12- to 14-hour days as well as weekends, with little time for leisure, family, or social activities)
- Complex activities that require learning many facts, details, and principles (e.g., skiing, sailing, scuba diving)
- Computers (evaluating, programming, discussing)
- Reading
- Astronomy
- Chess
- Bird watching

Sample Investigative occupations
IA	College Professor
IA	Physician
IA	Psychologist
IC	Pharmacist
IR	Chemist
IC	Chiropractor
IR	Dentist
IR	Medical Technician
IR	Optometrist
IR	Research & Development Manager
IR	Respiratory Therapist
IR	Veterinarian
IRA	Geologist
IRA	Physicist
IRS	Science Teacher
IRC	Medical Technologist

Typical I-Theme items
- "Author of technical books"
- "Chemistry"
- "Mathematics"
- "Zoology"
- "Doing research work"

Artistic (A Theme): *creating or enjoying art, drama, music, writing*

Artistic people value aesthetic qualities and have a great need for self-expression. This type, more than any other, includes people who enjoy being spectators or observers (in this case, of the arts) rather than participants. Artistic types frequently express their artistic interests in leisure or recreational activities as well as in vocational activities or environments. With their typical verbal-linguistic bent, they are quite comfortable in academic or intellectual environments, as reflected in their Learning Environment scores. It is important to recognize that the spectrum of the A Theme has a threefold content: visual arts, music/dramatics, and writing.

Typical work activities
- Composing, writing
- Creating artwork (e.g., painting, sculpting, photography)
- Working independently
- Acting, performing
- Playing musical instruments, decorating, designing

Potential competencies
- Creativity, imagination
- Verbal-linguistic skills
- Musical ability
- Artistic ability
- Dramatics

Self-concept and values
- Independent, nonconforming
- Impulsive, expressive
- Romantic, free-spirited
- Intuitive, complicated
- Sensitive, emotional
- Drawn to beauty and aesthetic qualities

Environments
- Unstructured, flexible organizations that allow self-expression
- Artistic studios (preferably their own)
- Theaters and concert halls
- Institutions that teach artistic skills (e.g., universities, music and dance schools, art institutes)
- Museums, libraries, and galleries
- Advertising, public relations, and interior-decorating firms

Typical hobbies
- Drawing, sketching, painting
- Photography
- Attending dance and musical concerts
- Going to theaters, museums, and galleries
- Reading
- Writing poetry or stories
- Collecting artwork
- Playing a musical instrument
- Dancing

Sample Artistic occupations
A	Artist, Commercial
A	Artist, Fine
A	Lawyer
A	Librarian
A	Musician
A	Reporter
AS	Art Teacher
AE	Advertising Executive
AE	Broadcaster
AE	Technical Writer
ASE	English Teacher
ARI	Architect
ARE	Photographer
AIR	Medical Illustrator
AES	Corporate Trainer

Typical A-Theme items
- "Author of novels"
- "Interior decorator"
- "Literature"
- "Symphony concerts"
- "Magazines about art or music"

Social (S Theme): *helping, instructing, caregiving*

Social people, unlike the first three types in the RIASEC hexagon, like to work with people; they enjoy working in groups, sharing responsibilities, and being the center of attention. Central characteristics are helping, nurturing, and caring for others, and teaching and instructing, especially of young people. Social types like to solve problems through discussions of feelings and interactions with others. They may also enjoy working with people through leading, directing, and persuading. Thus, a person with a high S Theme is likely also to score toward the works with people pole of the Work Style scale and to score toward the directs others pole of the Leadership Style scale.

Typical work activities
- Teaching, explaining
- Enlightening, guiding
- Helping, facilitating
- Selecting and training
- Informing, organizing
- Solving problems, leading discussions

Potential competencies
- Social and interpersonal skills
- Verbal ability
- Teaching skills
- Listening skills
- Ability to empathize with and understand others

Self-concept and values
- Humanistic, idealistic
- Ethical, responsible
- Tactful, cooperative
- Kind, generous
- Understanding, insightful
- Friendly, cheerful
- Concerned for the welfare of others

Environments
- Social service agencies
- Schools
- Religious organizations
- Human resources departments
- Medical service and health care facilities
- Mental health clinics

Typical hobbies
- Entertaining others
- Attending conventions
- Doing volunteer and community service work
- Organizing social events (e.g., picnics, excursions, neighborhood parties)
- Artistic and Realistic activities (Research has shown that employees who work in social services have a propensity toward burnout [Matthews, 1990]; often they feel a need for the solitude of R-Theme and A-Theme activities as avocational pursuits.)

Sample Social occupations

S	Child Care Provider
S	Elementary School Teacher
S	Public Health Nurse
SE	Community Service Organization Director
SE	High School Counselor
SE	Home Economics Teacher
SE	Parks and Recreation Coordinator
SR	Physical Education Teacher
SI	Student Personnel Worker
SA	Occupational Therapist
SA	Social Worker
SA	Speech Pathologist
SEA	Social Science Teacher
SCA	Nurse, LPN
SRE	Agricultural Extension Agent
SIR	Physical Therapist

Typical S-Theme items
- "High school teacher"
- "Social worker"
- "Special education teacher"
- "Helping others overcome their difficulties"
- "Taking care of children"

Enterprising (E Theme): selling, managing, persuading

Enterprising people are verbally facile in selling and leading. They seek positions of leadership, power, and status. They enjoy working with other people and leading them toward organizational goals and economic success. The E Theme is clearly linked with a Work Style of working with people and a Leadership Style of directing others. Enterprising people may like to take financial and interpersonal risks and to participate in competitive activities.

They are quite different from I types (opposite on the hexagon) and dislike scientific activities and long periods of intellectual effort. Scientists (e.g., physicists, biologists, mathematicians, geologists, and chemists) score low on the E Theme, reflecting that they have little interest in selling, leading, and working with people.

Typical work activities
- Selling, purchasing
- Political maneuvering
- Entertaining clients
- Leading committees, groups, organizations, companies
- Giving speeches, talks, presentations
- Managing people and projects

Potential competencies
- Verbal skills suited to public speaking, persuading, and selling
- Social and interpersonal skills
- Leadership skills
- Personal resiliency, high energy, optimism
- Ability to focus on organizational goals, including profit

Self-concept and values
- Status conscious
- Ambitious, competitive
- Sociable, talkative
- Witty, argumentative
- Aggressive
- Adventuresome, risk taking
- Optimistic, energetic, popular
- Attracted to money, power, and material possessions

Environments
- Industrial and manufacturing firms
- Government and political organizations
- Seats of power and finance (e.g., large corporations, executive offices, brokerage firms)
- Retail and wholesale firms (e.g., auto dealerships, department stores, real estate firms)
- Fund-raising organizations
- Independently owned businesses

Typical hobbies
- Belonging to clubs and organizations
- Sporting events, as participant or spectator
- Entertaining and socializing
- Political activities
- Attending conventions

Sample Enterprising occupations
E	Life Insurance Agent
E	Realtor
E	Traveling Salesperson
EC	Buyer
EC	Store Manager
ER	Auctioneer
EA	Marketing Executive
ES	Sales Manager
ECR	Agribusiness Manager
ECR	Purchasing Agent
ECR	Restaurant Manager
ECA	Travel Agent
ECS	Housekeeping & Maintenance Supervisor
EIS	Dental Hygienist
EAS	Flight Attendant
EAC	Florist

Typical E-Theme items
- "Auto salesperson"
- "Sales manager"
- "Stockbroker"
- "Customer service representative"
- "People who have made fortunes in business"

Conventional (C Theme): accounting, organizing, processing data

Conventional people especially like activities that require attention to organization, data systems, detail, and accuracy. They often enjoy mathematics and data management activities such as accounting and investment management. Like Enterprising people, they work well in large organizations, but unlike Enterprising people, they do not show a distinct preference for or against leadership positions. Interest in leadership is quite variable among those high on the C Theme, making the Leadership Style scale valuable in assessing potential work roles.

The C Theme contrasts with the A Theme opposite it on the hexagon: the C Theme reflects a preference for organization, while the A Theme involves preferences for unstructured, creative tasks. Thus, many people with strong Artistic interests have low scores on the C Theme; these include commercial and fine artists, medical illustrators, advertising executives, public relations directors, and art teachers.

Typical work activities
- Conducting a financial analysis
- Operating office machines
- Organizing office procedures
- Keeping records and financial books
- Writing business reports
- Making charts and graphs

Potential competencies
- Efficiency, organization
- Management of systems and data
- Mathematical skills
- Persistence and patience with detailed paperwork
- Operation of office machines
- Perfectionism

Self-concept and values
- Conscientious, persevering
- Practical
- Self-contained, conservative
- Orderly, systematic
- Precise, accurate
- Careful, controlled
- Careful about money and material possessions

Environments
- Large corporations
- Business offices
- Financial institutions (e.g., banks, credit companies)
- Accounting firms
- Quality control and inspection departments
- Structured organizations with well-ordered chains of command

Typical hobbies
- Collecting (e.g., stamps, coins)
- Home-improvement projects
- Building models (e.g., airplanes, doll houses, electric trains)
- Civic and fraternal organizations
- Games (e.g., Monopoly®) with clear-cut rules

Sample Conventional occupations

C	Bookkeeper
C	Medical Records Technician
C	Clerical Worker
C	Proofreader
CE	Accountant
CE	Administrative Assistant
CE	Banker
CE	Certified Public Accountant
CE	Credit Manager
CE	Store Salesperson
CI	Actuary
CSE	Dental Assistant
CES	Business Education Teacher
CES	Food Service Manager
CES	Nursing Home Administrator
CES	Secretary

Typical C-Theme items
- "Cashier in bank"
- "Private secretary"
- "Statistician"
- "Financial analyst"
- "Developing business systems"

Weighting of the Theme Items

Each GOT is composed of 20 or more items. A "Like" response to one of the items constituting a Theme *raises* a person's score (weight = +1), a "Dislike" response *lowers* the score (weight = –1), and an "Indifferent" response *has no effect* on the score (weight = 0). In other words, if a person says "Like" to the item "Auto mechanic," which is weighted on the R Theme, this person's score on the R Theme increases; a "Dislike" response to the same item results in a decrease in the R-Theme score. (A thorough description of the scale construction method for the GOTs and reliability and validity data are reported in a later section of this chapter.)

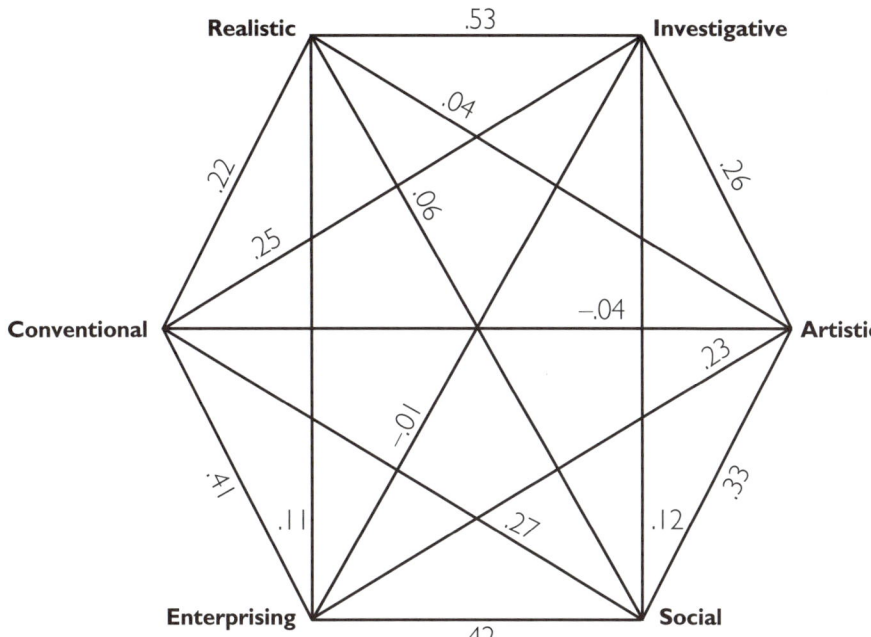

Figure 5.1 Correlations Between the General Occupational Themes, Arranged in Hexagonal Order

Note: Correlations Based on General Reference Sample of 9,467 Women and 9,484 Men.

Interpreting GOT Scores

Of the various types of scales on the *Strong*, the GOTs are the most general, covering six broad dimensions. Thus, the six GOT scores provide a global view of the client's interests and occupational orientation. High scores suggest the general range of activities the person will enjoy, the type of occupational environment she or he will find most comfortable, the problems she or he will be most willing to tackle, and the kinds of people who will be most appealing as co-workers.

Counselors can use the GOT scores to help clients understand what activities are valued by people of a particular type, what kinds of jobs or occupations fit them, what environments (whether work, play, or living environments) are comfortable for them, and what kinds of co-workers would appeal to them. Counselors may find the GOTs particularly useful for young people and for those who are unclear about their general vocational direction. Clients can use the GOT scores to consider how their vocational interests fit with their life-style. Some people find that their work and leisure activities, living and play environments, and the types of people they enjoy are all compatible. Others have more diverse interests; these people need to determine how that diversity can find expression in their lives. As respondents integrate their interest scores with what they already know about themselves (e.g., past activities, jobs, accomplishments, and general life histories), unique patterns of interest should begin to emerge.

To understand each GOT type or combination of types better, the counselor should study the descriptions presented in this chapter and the occupations and academic major fields scoring high and low on each scale (see Figures 5.4 through 5.9, 5.11 through 5.16, and Appendix B). Remember, most people do not score high on just one Theme: many have two or three high scores—usually on adjacent Themes—some people have few high scores, and some have none. (Refer to Chapters 10 and 11 for general strategies to use in interpreting the *Strong* as well as specific suggestions for handling challenging situations.)

History of the General Occupational Themes

At its inception in 1927, the *Strong Vocational Interest Blank* was an empirical, atheoretical instrument. Although E. K. Strong, Jr., developed scales that had impressive validity and reliability statistics and great

Table 5.1 Intercorrelations Between the General Occupational Themes

Scale	Realistic	Investigative	Artistic	Social	Enterprising	Conventional
Realistic	—	.57	.23	.08	.08	.23
Investigative	.51	—	.30	.09	–.05	.20
Artistic	.06	.30	—	.26	.25	–.14
Social	.13	.19	.36	—	.40	.22
Enterprising	.19	.04	.21	.43	—	.36
Conventional	.27	.32	.02	.31	.47	—

Note: Correlations above the diagonal are based on 9,467 women; those below the diagonal are based on 9,484 men.

utility, his Profile presented a person's scores with only the laconic statement that "this score represents the degree of similarity between your interests and [those of] workers in this occupation." The person was left to decide, with the aid of a counselor, what those interests were for each occupation. Nevertheless, the empirical success of the early *Strong* inventory obscured the lack of an organizing theory.

The Strong and Occupational Theory

Strong realized in the late 1930s that systematic clustering of the scales was necessary. He was gathering data on more and more occupations, and he wanted to arrange their scales in groupings that would make interpretations more fruitful. His first tentative step toward a theory was to gather the scales into groups on the Profile. Guided to some extent by factor analyses carried out by L. L. Thurstone, he formed the groups by using scale intercorrelations. Despite wide use, these groupings lacked a theoretical structure and left out some occupations that defied grouping. What was needed was an organizing structure that would be at once global and parsimonious, one that would embrace all existing *Strong* scales as well as any that would be developed in the future. Strong attempted this in a different manner with his Group Scales but later dropped them when he found their psychometric qualities disappointing.

In an attempt to develop an occupational classification system closely tied to psychometric research, Holland (1959) proposed six basic categories of occupational interests, categories closely resembling the dimensions usually seen in research on vocational interests with the *Strong Blank*. Over the years, he refined and expanded his classifications in a theory encompassing the broad area of educational and vocational behavior, retaining as its foundation the original six categories (Holland, 1965, 1973). He has described its genesis:

The formulation for the types grew out of my experience as a vocational counselor and a clinician, and out of my construction of a personality inventory from interest material. After reviewing the vocational literature—especially factor-analytic studies of personality and vocational interests—I concluded that it might be useful to categorize people into six types.

The present types are analogous in some ways to those proposed earlier by Adler, Fromm, Jung, Sheldon, and others. They differ from these earlier typologies in their origin—which is largely our vocational literature—and in their definitions. The six major factors identified in Guilford's comprehensive factor analysis of human interest—mechanical, scientific, social welfare, clerical, business, and aesthetic—approximate the present types. To the best of my knowledge, Guilford's factor analysis is the most explicit forerunner of the present typology (Holland, 1966, pp. 15, 10).

Holland's classification system was an extension of the trait and factor theory that dominated occupational theory from the 1920s to the 1950s. That approach, at its worst and simplest, implied that the main goal of vocational counseling is to match people and jobs—in other words, to see that round pegs find their way into round holes. Holland's theory, which considers the individual's total life-style and the global occupational environment, offered a more sophisticated approach. Although the concept of matching the individual to a setting was still salient, Holland addressed other concerns, especially developmental issues. He described the effects of different environments on various types: for example, he pointed out that Investigative types usually do well in school because they have attitudes and values compatible with those of their teachers and thus find the atmosphere supportive; in contrast, Realistic types

Table 5.2 Comparisons of 1985 and 1994 General Occupational Themes: Correlations for Parallel Scales, Internal Consistency Reliabilities, and 3–6 Month Test-Retest Reliabilities

		1985 Scale			1994 Scale		
Scale	Correlation	Number of Items	Cronbach Alpha	Test-Retest	Number of Items	Cronbach Alpha	Test-Retest
Realistic	.972	20	.903	.904	23	.929	.919
Investigative	.946	20	.857	.891	20	.908	.907
Artistic	.976	20	.912	.917	33	.938	.907
Social	.944	20	.850	.850	23	.900	.854
Enterprising	.957	20	.867	.837	22	.902	.841
Conventional	.932	20	.827	.853	21	.902	.868

Note: Scale correlations and Cronbach alphas are based on the General Reference Sample of 18,951 women and men. Test-retest reliabilities are based on a sample of 191 employed women and men.

tend to do poorly because the match between their dominant characteristics and the dominant characteristics of academic environments is poor. (See also several recent writers, such as Chartrand [1991], Rounds and Tracey [1990], Spokane [1987], and Walsh and Holland [1992], for related modern perspectives on the trait and factor paradigm.)

Construction of the Original GOT Scales

The GOTs were first introduced into the *Strong* in 1974. A detailed account of the initial construction of the 1974 GOT scales for men is given in Campbell and Holland (1972); a similar project for women is reported by Hansen and Johansson (1972). Essentially, what was done in both projects was to select 20 items to represent each type on the basis of the descriptions given by Holland (1966). A variety of statistical evidence was used in the selection of specific items: item intercorrelations, popularity of the items among occupations of designated Holland types, and item-scale correlations.

Scale intercorrelations for the 1994 GOTs are presented in Table 5.1. On the strength of similar correlation results, Holland and his colleagues (Cole, Whitney, & Holland, 1971) suggested that his types be arranged in a hexagon, as shown in Figure 5.1 on page 51. Although the sides of the hexagon may not be as regular as Holland's theory suggests, the patterns of intercorrelations support the overall structure; the strongest correlations usually occur between adjacent scales, the weakest usually between scales directly opposite each other.

The introduction of the GOTs to the *Strong* provided a structure that was helpful in understanding both the BISs and the OSs and that could be used to organize the Profile scores, since each of the BISs and OSs was assigned a code type based on the six Themes. (Using data from Table 7.3, Chapter 7 explains how this was done.) Essentially, each OS was assigned to a code type corresponding to the highest Theme scores of the people in that occupation. Arranging the scales on the Profile in the RIASEC order further facilitated the interpretation of the scores and patterns of scores.

Revision of the GOTs

Until the 1994 revision of the *Strong*, only minor changes had been made to the GOTs (see Hansen & Campbell, 1985). For this revision, several analyses were conducted to evaluate the items in the existing GOTs to determine whether the reliabilities of the scales could be enhanced. An analysis was made to determine how well each of the 20 items in each scale was working, and additional items to enhance each scale were sought. To increase scale homogeneity, as measured by Cronbach alpha, item-scale correlations were examined. As a result, a number of weakly correlated items were deleted and a number of new, stronger items were added to each scale. An attempt was also made to minimize correlations among adjacent scales on the hexagon to maintain the spatial meaning of scale relationships within the hexagon. Finally, an effort was made to retain the traditional content of the scales. Thus, for

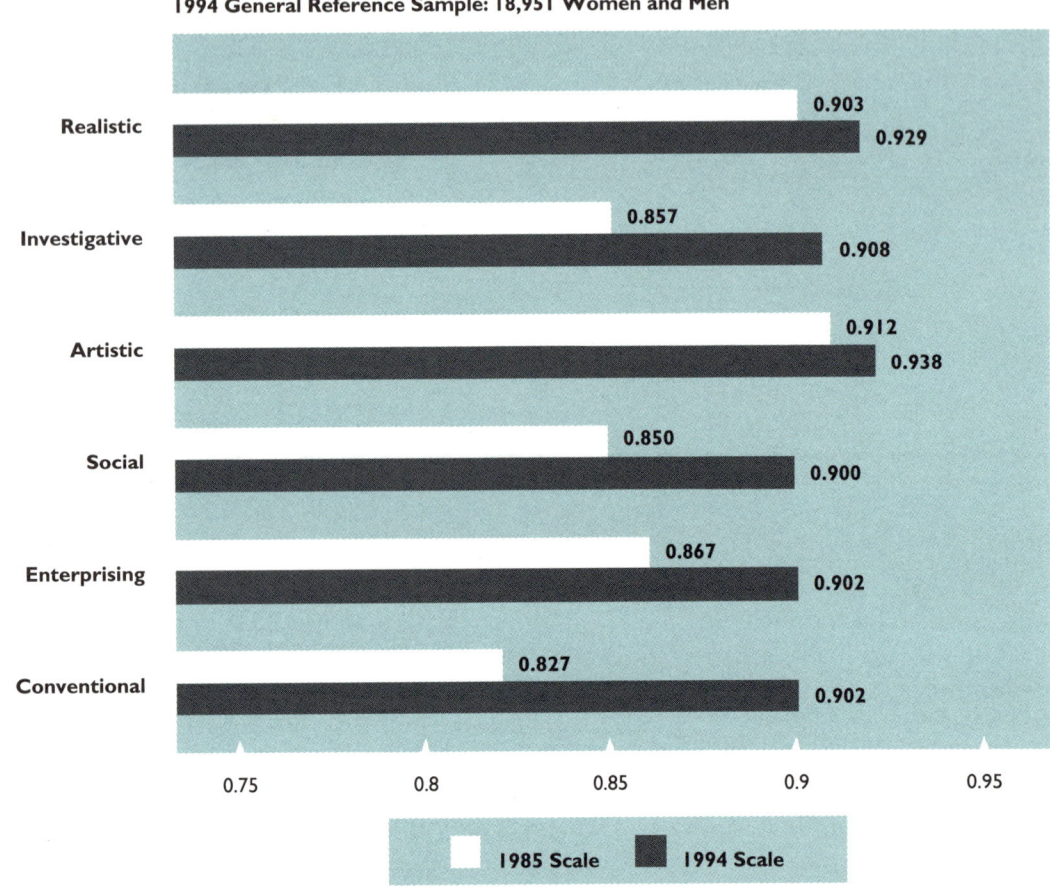

Figure 5.2 Alpha Reliabilities of Original and Revised General Occupational Themes

example, the threefold content in the Artistic scale (i.e., art, music/dramatics, and writing) was maintained. Further, the item content in Holland's (1985b) *Vocational Preference Inventory (VPI)* was examined to ensure some consistency with the basic content Holland uses to operationalize his theory.

Current evidence suggests the psychometric characteristics of the GOTs have been improved, while the traditional construct meaning of these scales has been maintained. Table 5.2 shows the correlations between the original (1985) and revised (1994) GOTs. It is evident that despite the fine-tuning of the scales, the correlations between parallel scales remain high, ranging from .932 for Conventional to .976 for Artistic.

The increases in Cronbach alpha reliability achieved for the 1994 revised GOT scales are displayed in Table 5.2 and Figure 5.2. Notably, alphas for all scales are now .90 or better; two of the original scales, Realistic and Artistic, were already at that level. But for the remaining GOTs, especially Social and Conventional, the major improvement in the internal consistencies is expected to improve their utility for counseling and research.

Improving the internal consistency reliabilities of the new GOTs also appears to have had a slight positive effect on the test-retest reliabilities of the scales. Table 5.2 and Figure 5.3 show the increases in the test-retest reliabilities for a national sample of 191 working adults over a 3- to 6-month interval (this sample is described in detail later in the chapter). The stability of all the scales is high, and especially high (above .90) for the Realistic, Investigative, and Artistic scales. The implication for counseling use is that these are potent dimensions of individual differences, likely to be quite stable over some time, especially for working adults. Furthermore, these dimensions are now measured with improved reliability in the 1994 *Strong*.

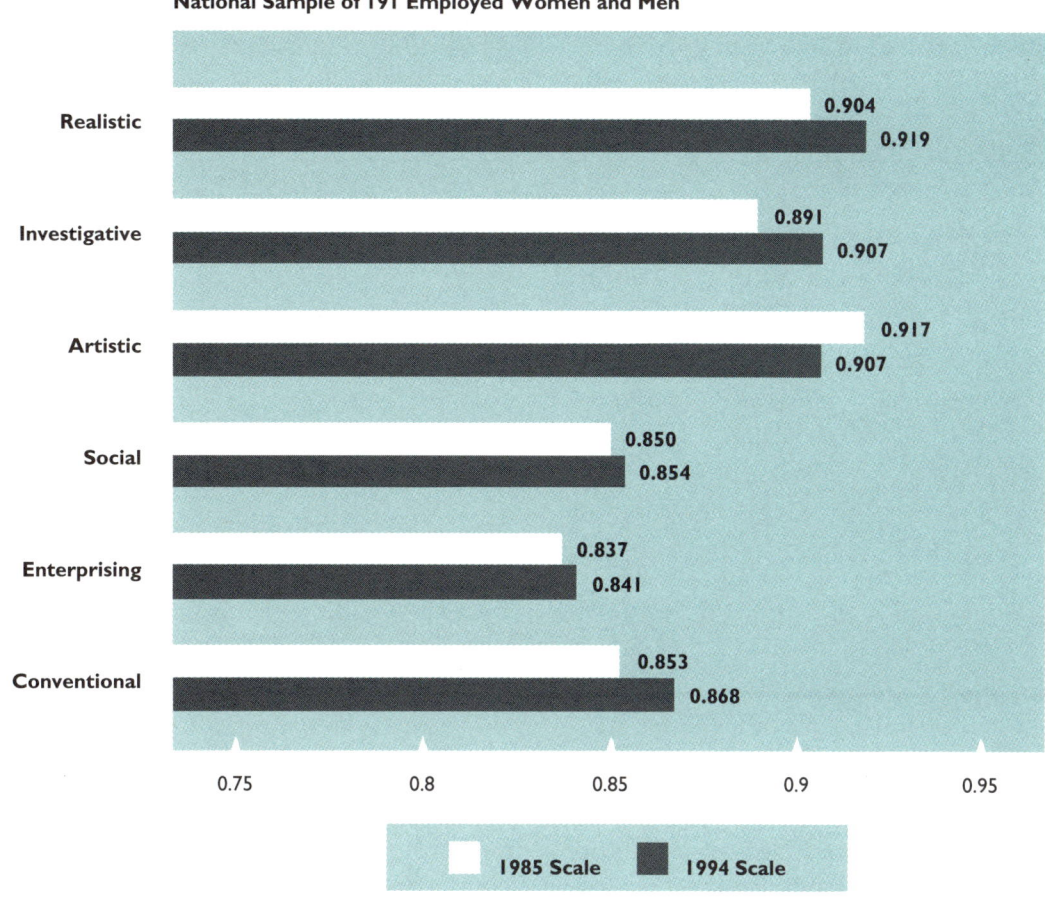

Figure 5.3 Test-Retest Reliabilities (3–6 month) of Original and Revised General Occupational Themes

Norming the Scales

The combined General Reference Sample (GRS) of 18,951 people (9,467 women and 9,484 men) was used to create standard scores on the GOTs (see Chapter 7 for a discussion of formation of the GRS). For this group of people, raw score means and standard deviations on the six scales were used in a standardization formula that converts all scores into distributions with standard score means of 50 and standard deviations of 10. By this formula

$$\text{standard score} = \left(\frac{X - Mc}{SDc}\right)10 + 50$$

where X is an individual's raw score, and Mc and SDc are the combined GRS raw score mean and raw score standard deviation. Thus, a respondent's scores on the GOTs can be compared quickly on common numerical measures; a standard score of 60, for example, falls one standard deviation (50 plus 10) above the combined mean, no matter which of the Themes is being scored.

Table 5.3 on page 56 lists the means and standard deviations of the Women's and Men's GRSs and the ranges used to define each interpretive category. (All scores in tables in this guide are standard scores, unless otherwise noted.)

Test-Retest Reliability

The test-retest reliability of the 1994 *Strong* scales was evaluated using four different samples that varied in several ways, including age, employment status, length of the test-retest interval, and whether or not a career intervention occurred during the retest interval.

Test-Retest Reliability Samples

Samples A and B had no specific career development experiences during the retest interval, but the samples differed in age, work status, and test-retest interval. Samples C and D differed from the others in that

Table 5.3 Means, Standard Deviations, and Interpretive Boundaries for the General Occupational Themes for the General Reference Samples by Gender

Scale	Gender	Mean	S.D.	Very Little Interest (0–10)	Little Interest (11–25)	Average Interest (26–75)	High Interest (76–90)	Very High Interest (91–100)
Realistic	Female	46.7	9.1	33–35	36–39	40–53	54–59	60–73
	Male	53.3	9.8	33–39	40–45	46–60	61–66	67–73
Investigative	Female	49.0	10.3	28–35	36–40	41–57	58–62	63–69
	Male	51.0	10.0	28–36	37–43	44–59	60–64	65–69
Artistic	Female	52.6	9.4	27–39	40–45	46–60	61–64	65–70
	Male	47.4	10.0	27–33	34–39	40–54	55–60	61–70
Social	Female	51.3	10.1	28–38	39–43	44–59	60–65	66–75
	Male	48.7	9.7	28–36	37–41	42–55	56–62	63–75
Enterprising	Female	50.4	9.8	33–37	38–42	43–57	58–64	65–80
	Male	49.6	10.1	33–36	37–41	42–56	57–64	65–80
Conventional	Female	50.6	10.5	34–37	38–42	43–57	58–66	67–80
	Male	49.4	9.5	34–37	38–42	43–55	56–63	64–80

Note: Ns = 9,467 women, 9,484 men; numbers in parentheses are percentiles.

each involved a college career development class and were similar to each other in that they included college students with a career development experience, retested after three months.

The sample differences can be expected to have some effects on the retest reliabilities, and particularly on the level of means for specific *Strong* scales. Scale means for Sample A can be expected to be close to the standard score means of 50 established for the GRS. Such a close pattern should not be expected for all scales for the three college samples because of their younger age, predominantly female gender composition, stage of career development, and preponderance of majors in specific fields, such as psychology.

The diversity of these samples expands the generalizability of the scales and increases the robustness of their reliability. The samples are described here and are referred to in subsequent chapters where reliability results are presented for specific types of scales.

Sample A. This sample was a national sample of 191 employed adults (110 women, 81 men) in 15 diverse occupations who were retested after an interval of three to six months. They were respondents in the 1994 *Strong* renorming who indicated an interest in participating in additional research. Fifteen occupations were selected to represent diversity across the interest domain and also educational level. These occupations were Auto Mechanic, Advertising Executive, Chemist, Child Care Provider, Farmer, Flight Attendant, Human Resources Director, Life Insurance Agent, Medical Records Technician, Registered Nurse, Paralegal, Physical Therapist, Small Business Owner, Technical Writer, and Translator. From these occupations, 231 people were selected and sent a retest *Strong;* 191 responded, for a response rate of 83 percent. This sample can be considered a representative subset of the GRS of 18,951.

Sample B. This sample included 84 college students (54 women, 30 men) in a psychological measurement course who retook the *Strong* after a one-month interval. They were students at Iowa State University enrolled in four sections of an upper-level undergraduate course, consisting primarily of junior and senior psychology majors.

Sample C. This sample consisted of 79 college students (56 women, 23 men) in a career development course at the University of North Carolina at Greensboro, who were retested after a three-month interval. They ranged in age from 18 to 25, with one 30-year-old, and were sophomores, juniors, or seniors. They were students in a career development class and had intervening experiences typical of such classes.

Table 5.4 Test-Retest Reliability Statistics in Four Samples for the General Occupational Themes

Theme	Test-Retest Correlation	Test		Retest	
		Mean	S.D.	Mean	S.D.
Sample A: Employed Adults, 3–6 months (N = 110 women, 81 men)					
Realistic	.92	49.8	10.9	50.7	11.0
Investigative	.91	50.3	10.6	51.6	10.4
Artistic	.91	50.4	10.6	51.2	10.6
Social	.85	50.1	9.8	50.3	10.0
Enterprising	.84	50.7	9.8	51.0	9.6
Conventional	.87	50.5	9.8	51.5	10.2
Sample B: College Students, 1 month (N = 54 women, 30 men)					
Realistic	.88	44.1	9.0	44.8	9.3
Investigative	.84	47.6	9.2	48.0	9.9
Artistic	.86	51.8	9.7	51.9	10.2
Social	.84	54.9	10.1	55.1	10.2
Enterprising	.86	52.6	11.3	52.9	11.6
Conventional	.86	48.4	10.2	48.7	10.1
Sample C: College Students, 3 months (N = 56 women, 23 men)					
Realistic	.78	40.9	7.8	43.7	8.7
Investigative	.85	40.6	9.1	41.7	9.7
Artistic	.91	44.1	9.0	46.0	10.3
Social	.89	54.3	12.1	53.0	12.5
Enterprising	.77	53.0	10.2	56.2	10.1
Conventional	.78	49.2	9.9	51.5	11.1
Sample D: College Students, 3 months (N = 61 women, 26 men)					
Realistic	.84	42.8	9.1	43.0	9.2
Investigative	.86	42.1	10.0	42.3	10.2
Artistic	.86	50.0	10.5	50.8	10.5
Social	.82	52.4	9.9	53.9	11.0
Enterprising	.74	54.6	9.8	55.4	11.0
Conventional	.82	50.4	10.1	50.8	11.0

Sample D. This group of 87 college students (61 women, 26 men) in a career development course at the University of Illinois were retested after a three-month interval. They were in the freshman through senior years. This sample was similar to Sample C from Greensboro, with a similar retest interval following a typical career development course.

Test-Retest Reliability Results

Table 5.4 shows results for the GOTs for the four test-retest reliability samples. These results show a high level of stability of scores, sufficient to support the use of the GOTs in counseling and career planning with individuals. The highest level of test-retest stability occurred for the sample of employed adults (Sample A), even though many respondents in this

Table 5.5 Three-Year Test-Retest Reliability Statistics for the General Occupational Themes (Original Version)

Theme	Test-Retest Correlation	Test		Retest	
		Mean	S.D.	Mean	S.D.
Employed, Adult Sample (*N* = 65 women, 75 men)					
Realistic	.82	51	10.9	51	11.0
Investigative	.78	52	8.9	52	9.6
Artistic	.87	51	10.4	51	10.9
Social	.82	48	10.7	47	10.2
Enterprising	.80	50	9.1	50	9.3
Conventional	.79	49	9.8	49	10.7

Source: Hansen & Campbell, 1985, p. 30.

sample had the longest retest intervals. This result is not surprising since Sample A was the most diverse, covering a range of occupations, with means of approximately 50, like the GRS. Moreover, these were employed adults, settled in work roles, and less likely to be undergoing the typical career changes of college students.

None of the college samples had the level of interest diversity that would maximize test-retest correlations. Each of these samples was drawn from a specific course, leading to some distinctiveness about the pattern of mean GOTs. To the extent the sample means for a General Occupational Theme deviated from 50, there was some restrictiveness of range in the scores, thus lowering the level of test-retest correlation. Table 5.4 shows lower mean scores for the college samples on the Realistic and Investigative scales, especially for the samples from career development classes (Samples C and D). In contrast, the college samples had means above 50 on the Social and Enterprising scales.

Despite the special limitations of the college samples for showing maximum test-retest reliability, the results generally demonstrate the stability of the GOTs. Sample B probably gives the most meaningful results for the college samples because the mean scores are closer to 50 and the sample did not involve a career intervention, as occurred for Samples C and D. For Sample B, the one-month test-retest reliabilities of the GOTs ranged from .84 to .88, a level that supports the use of the scales in individual career planning.

Since the revised General Occupational Themes have only recently been developed, data on them are not available for test-retest reliabilities over a number of years. However, because the revised GOTs were designed to be very similar to the original GOTs and because the correlations between the parallel original and revised GOTs are very high (see Table 5.2), it is informative to examine longer-term test-retest reliabilities for the original General Occupational Themes. Table 5.5 shows three-year test-retest reliabilities for a diverse sample of employed adults collected by the Center for Interest Measurement Research at the University of Minnesota and published in the 1985 *Strong* manual (Hansen & Campbell, 1985). These results show that the typical test-retest reliability was about .81, a figure high enough to indicate that the Theme scores are generally stable over three years but low enough to indicate that some shifting did occur.

Validity

An extensive number of studies over the past two decades speak directly or indirectly to the validity of the GOTs. Many studies used the GOT measures of the six Holland RIASEC dimensions; the most extensive and rigorous of these analyses suggested that the GOTs provide the best published inventory measures of the RIASEC hexagon (Tracey & Rounds, 1993). Other researchers, especially Holland and associates, used other inventories (e.g., Holland's *VPI*) to measure the RIASEC dimensions.

Table 5.6 Correlations Between the General Occupational Themes (Original Version) and *Vocational Preference Inventory* Scales (Based on 97 People)

VPI Scales	*Strong* General Occupational Themes					
	Realistic	Investigative	Artistic	Social	Enterprising	Conventional
Realistic	.73	.40	−.05	.20	.39	.44
Investigative	.38	.77	.09	.02	.06	.27
Artistic	−.13	.09	.78	.15	−.08	−.20
Social	.15	.03	.09	.72	.20	.21
Enterprising	.38	.14	−.15	.28	.79	.63
Conventional	.32	.20	−.37	.16	.41	.76

Source: Hansen & Campbell, 1985, p. 31.

Table 5.6 reports data collected at the University of Minnesota's Center for Interest Measurement Research, where 97 respondents completed both the *Vocational Preference Inventory* and the *Strong* (an earlier version with the original GOTs). Correlations between the same-named GOTs and *VPI* scales were high (median = .765), indicating that the two inventories measure similar interest dimensions (Hansen & Campbell, 1985). These results illustrate the large overlap between various inventories measuring the RIASEC dimensions.

One early study used the *Edwards Personal Preference Schedule (EPPS)*, an instrument based on Murray's need theory, to identify personality characteristics associated with the GOTs (Utz & Korben, 1976). Although few of the product-moment correlation coefficients between the *EPPS* and *Strong* scales were even moderately high (only 3 out of 182 were over .30), several were significant in the expected direction on the basis of definitions of the GOTs. For example, the R Theme correlated negatively with Affiliation; the I Theme correlated positively with Achievement; the A Theme correlated negatively with Order and positively with Change; the S Theme negatively with Autonomy and positively with Nurturance and Dominance; the E Theme positively with Dominance; and the C Theme negatively with Autonomy and positively with Endurance.

Another study (Varca & Shaffer, 1982) used adolescent and adult participants to show that the GOTs are useful for identifying avocational activities in which an individual will participate. These researchers found that people picked avocational and leisure activities that were congruent with their GOT types and that, like vocational interests, avocational interests were stable over time.

Occupational Differences on GOTs

Because the revised GOTs for 1994 have improved reliability, it is reasonable to expect that they would also show modestly improved validity. Although future studies are necessary to confirm this expectation, both the concurrent and construct validity of the 1994 GOTs can be directly evaluated by examining the rankings of mean occupational groups on the 1994 *Strong*. Figures 5.4 through 5.9 (shown on pages 60–62) display for each GOT the 15 highest-ranking and 15 lowest-ranking occupations of the 109 occupations on the 1994 *Strong*. Seven of these occupations are represented by a single gender and are displayed as single-gender occupations. For the remaining 102 occupations, a combined mean has been calculated by equally weighting the female and male means on each GOT (these gender-based means are shown in Table 7.3). For all instances in Figures 5.4 through 5.9, standardized scores were derived from the combined GRS of women and men.

Combining occupational means by gender provides for a succinct and readily interpretable display and facilitates making general inferences about the GOTs without focusing on gender differences. While gender differences on the GOTs are present in diverse general samples, within a single occupation the peak scores are often similar for women and men. This pattern is generally the case for the occupations ranking in the highest 15 GOTs, as shown in Figures 5.4 through 5.9.

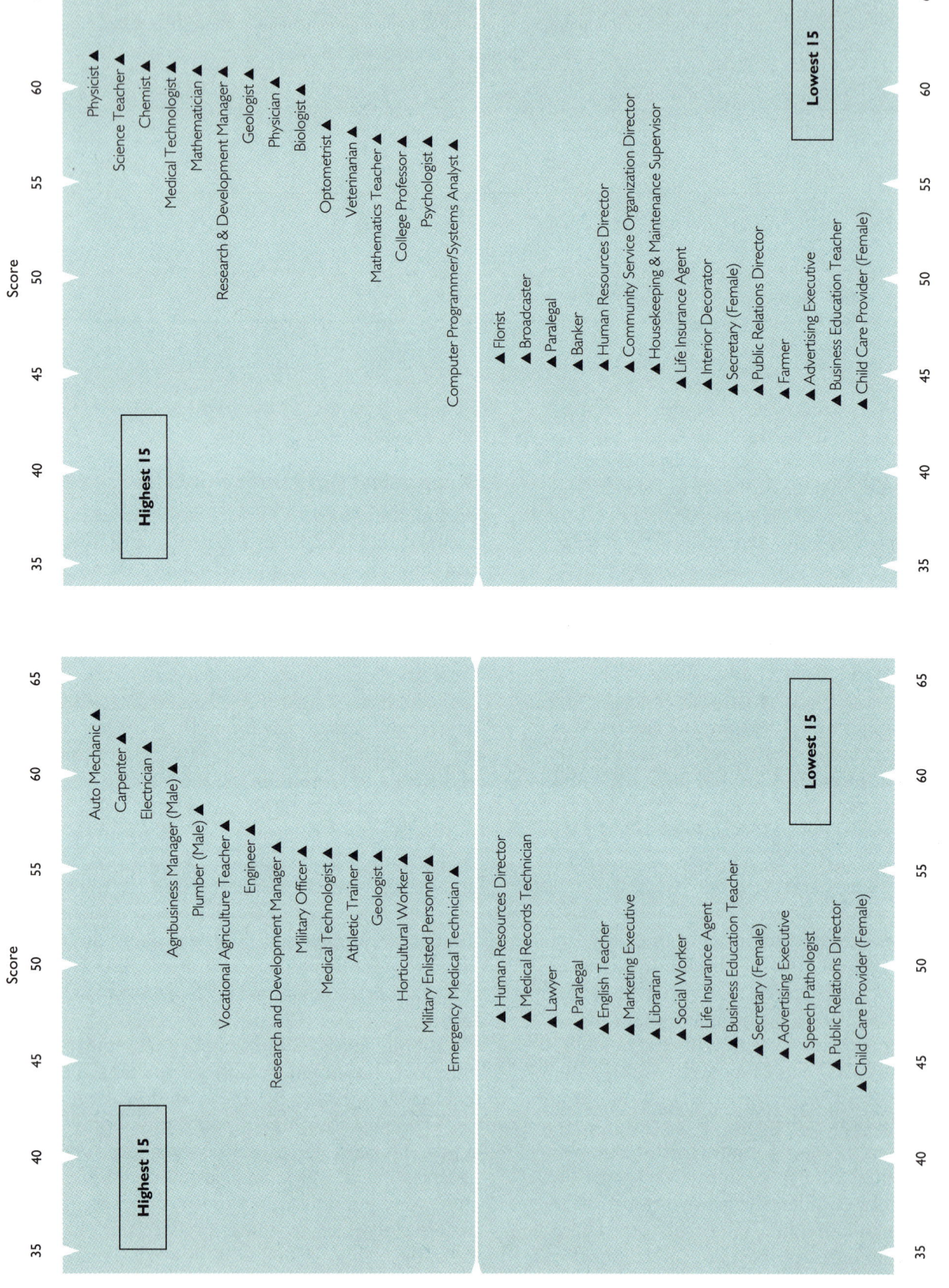

Figure 5.4 Rank-Ordered Occupations on the Realistic GOT:
The 15 Highest and 15 Lowest Occupational Means of 109 Occupations

Figure 5.5 Rank-Ordered Occupations on the Investigative GOT:
The 15 Highest and 15 Lowest Occupational Means of 109 Occupations

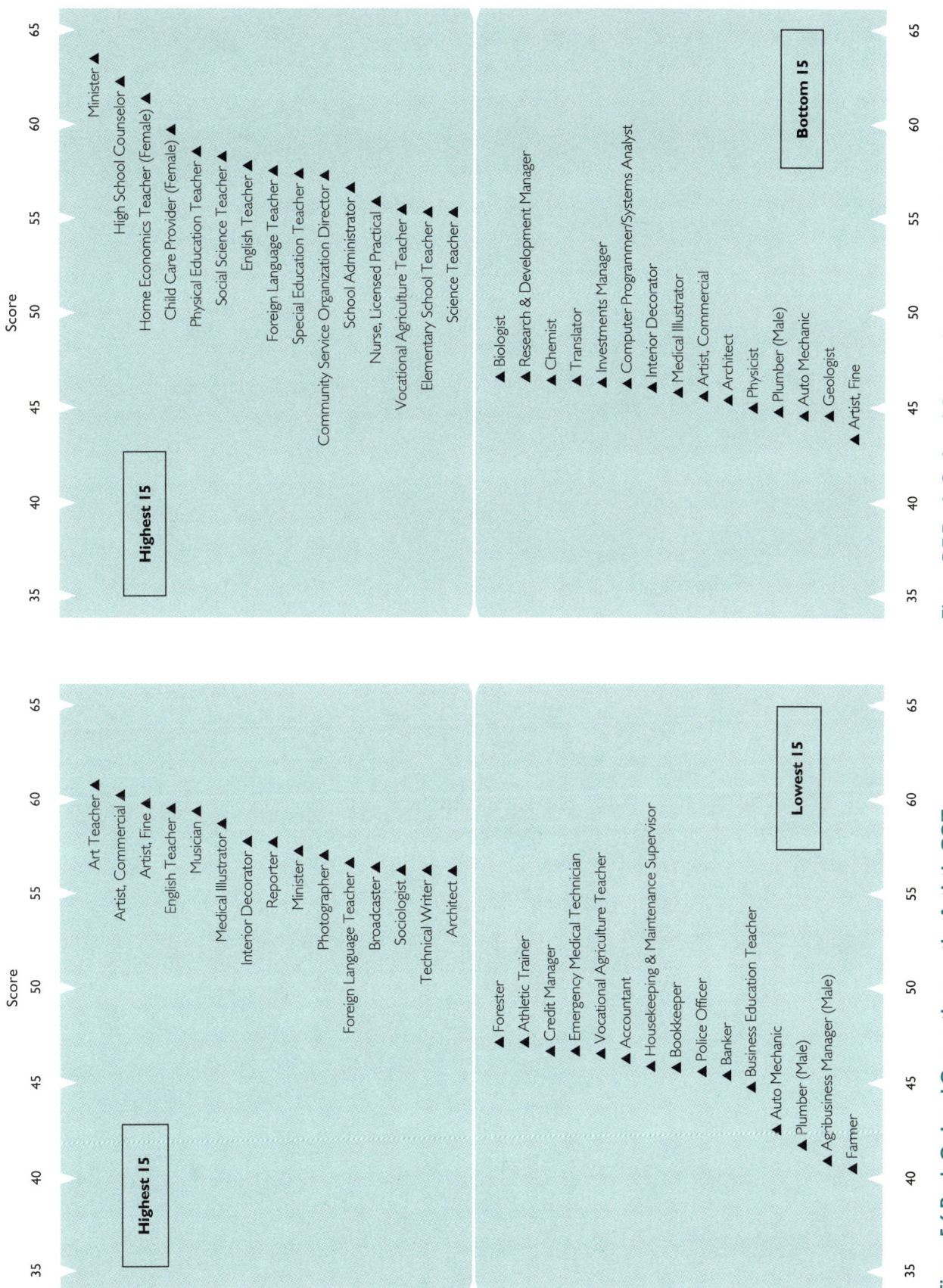

Figure 5.6 Rank-Ordered Occupations on the Artistic GOT:
The 15 Highest and 15 Lowest Occupational Means of 109 Occupations

Figure 5.7 Rank-Ordered Occupations on the Social GOT:
The 15 Highest and 15 Lowest Occupational Means of 109 Occupations

61

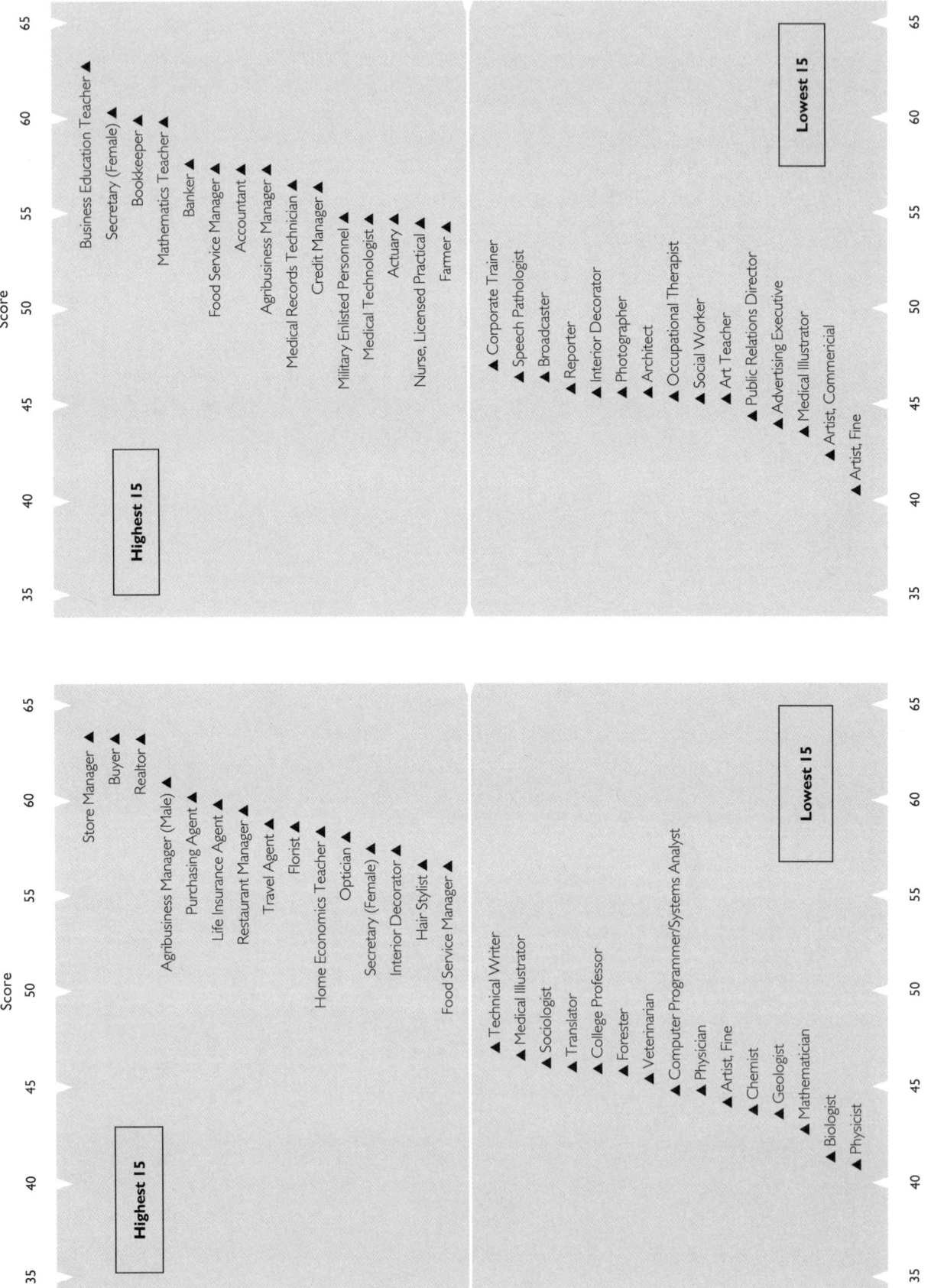

Figure 5.8 Rank-Ordered Occupations on the Enterprising GOT:
The 15 Highest and 15 Lowest Occupational Means of 109 Occupations

Figure 5.9 Rank-Ordered Occupations on the Conventional GOT:
The 15 Highest and 15 Lowest Occupational Means of 109 Occupations

Differences on GOTs for Academic Majors

The concurrent and construct validity of the GOTs can also be addressed by examining the mean GOT differences for people in different major concentrations of study. Respondents to the 1994 renorming of the *Strong* provided information about their major field of education and training. They coded their majors by choosing from a list of 27 possibilities. Two of these choices (Structural Work/Construction and Transportation) were dropped from the analysis because of low sample sizes; the category of "Other" was also dropped. Thus, it was possible to calculate mean GOTs for 24 educational majors for 16,994 of the 18,951 people in the GRS. Figure 5.10 on page 64 shows the GOT Profiles for six academic majors, each one with a peak score on a different GOT scale.

Some comments about the strengths and limits of these data are appropriate. A major strength of the data is its derivation from a large national sample using the revised *Strong* with employed adults in diverse fields. A potential limitation is that some of the major choices available on the coding sheet (e.g., Business, Medicine/Health Services) were quite general and thus failed to capture the interest differences within the general field. A second potential limitation is that since these respondents spanned the full age range of working adults, the educational experience of some occurred many years earlier. Nevertheless, because of their scope and uniqueness, these are valuable data for showing the validity and counseling uses of the GOTs for educational planning. They show for most major fields substantial differences in GOT patterns that conform to theoretical expectations and provide another line of evidence for the validity of the GOTs.

While Figure 5.10 shows the GOT mean Profile for each of six selected educational majors, it is informative to display the same mean data quite differently by ranking the majors on each GOT. This is done in Figures 5.11 through 5.16 on pages 65–67. Again, these figures support the validity and utility of the GOTs, with quite substantial differences across major fields, ranked in theoretically and intuitively meaningful ways.

64 Chapter 5

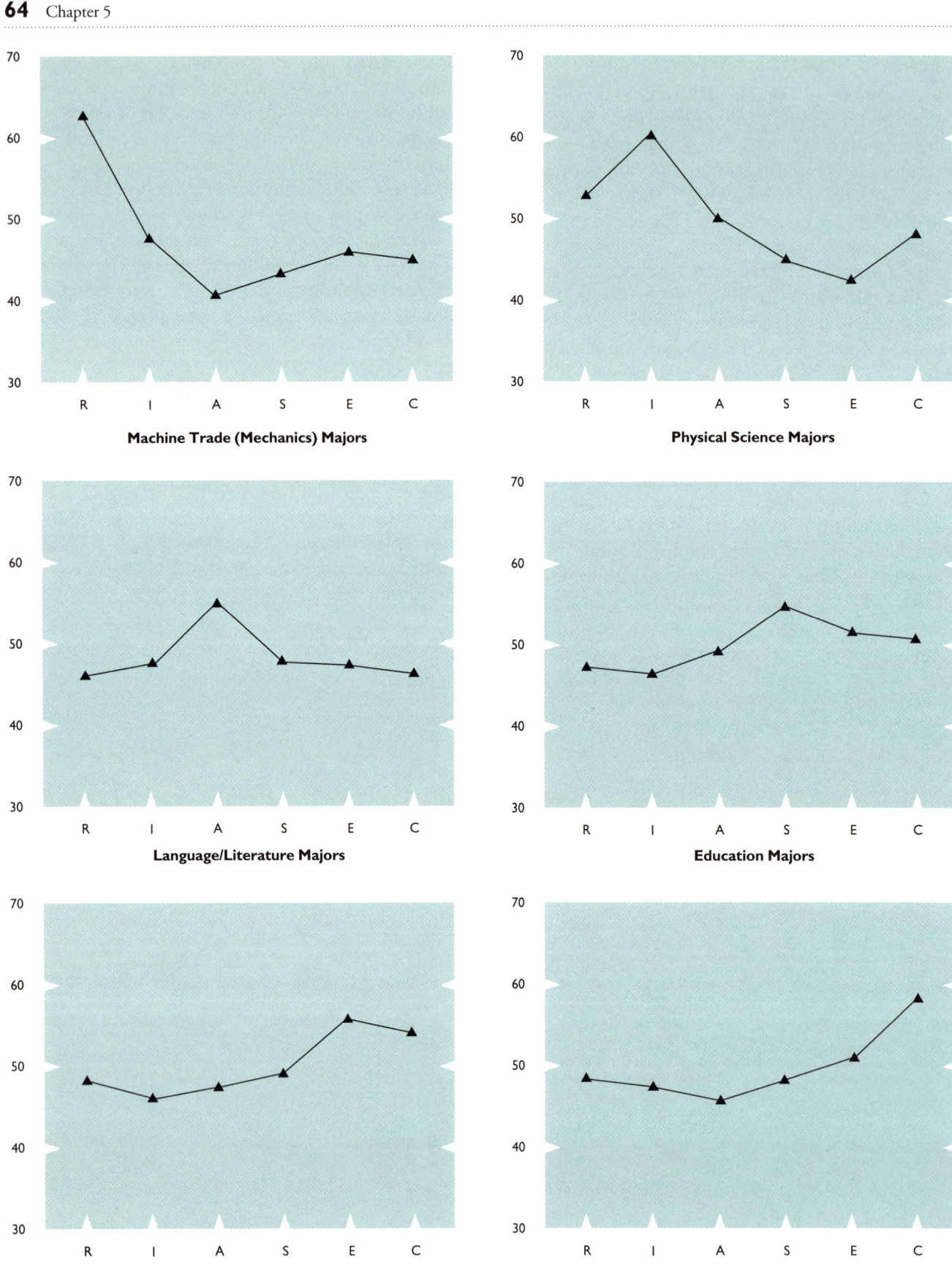

Figure 5.10 Profiles of GOT Mean Scores for Six Selected Academic Majors, Illustrating Peak Scores on Each of the Six GOT Scales

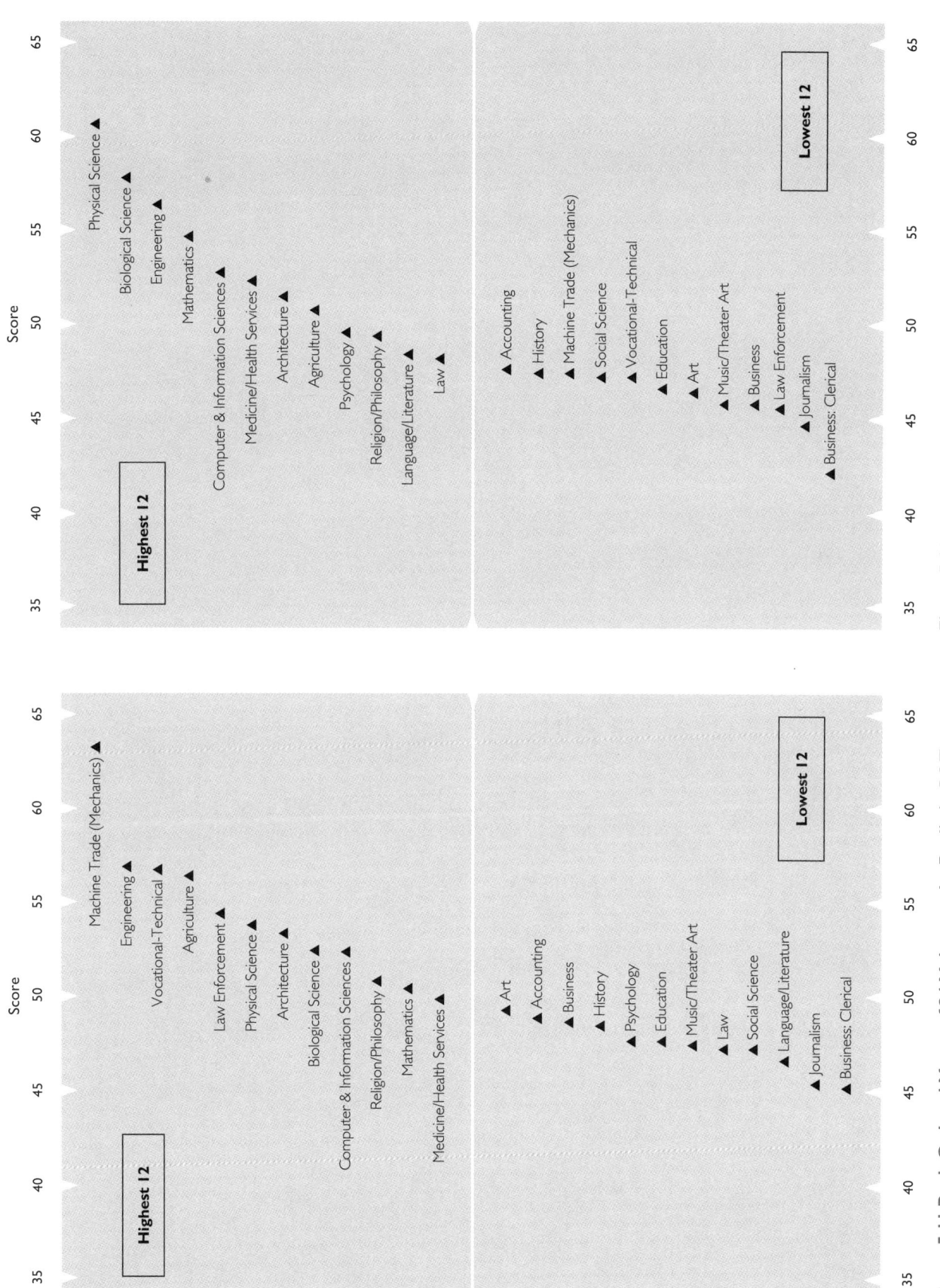

Figure 5.11 Rank-Ordered Means of 24 Majors on the Realistic GOT

Figure 5.12 Rank-Ordered Means of 24 Majors on the Investigative GOT

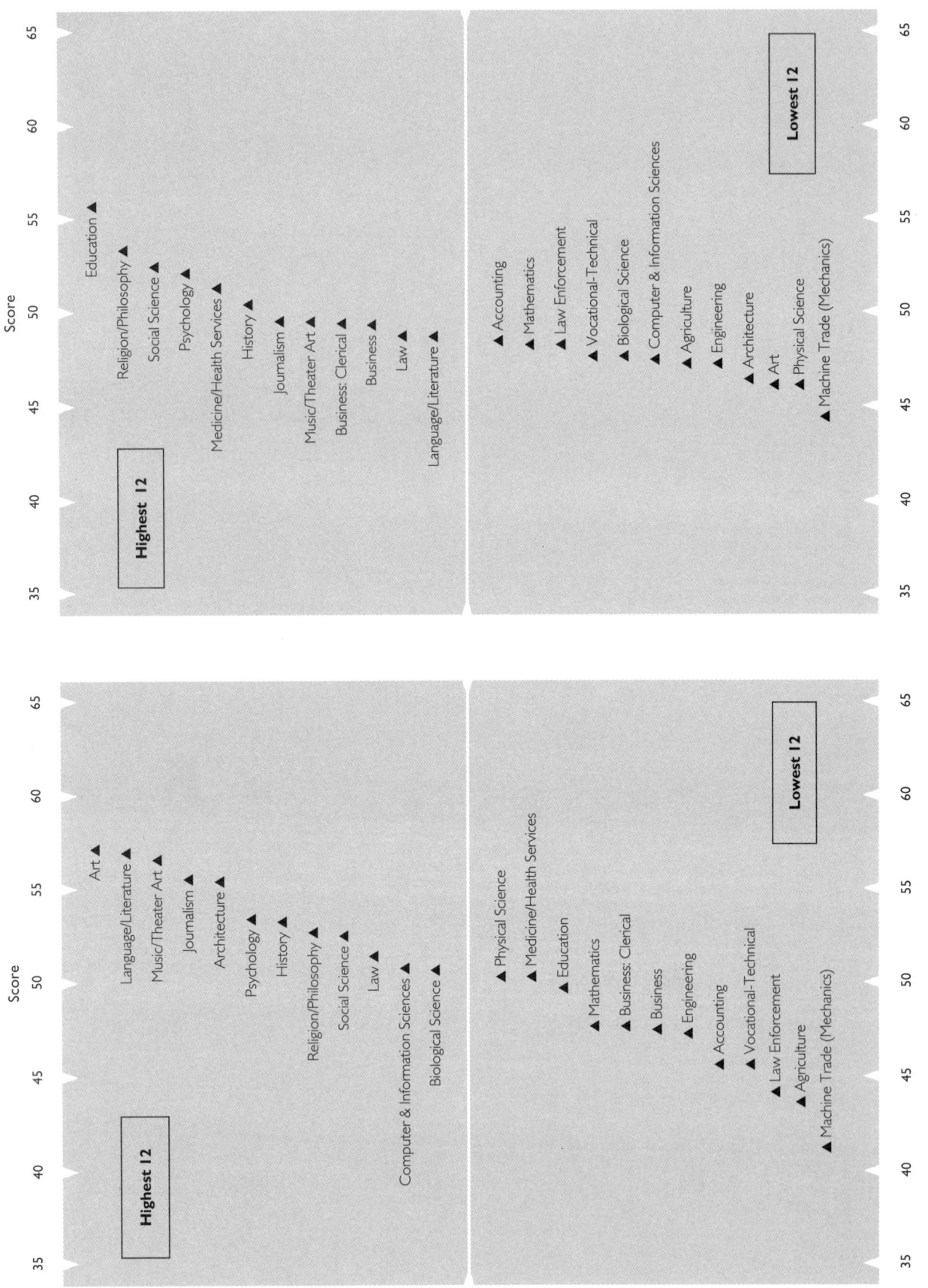

Figure 5.13 Rank-Ordered Means of 24 Majors on the Artistic GOT

Figure 5.14 Rank-Ordered Means of 24 Majors on the Social GOT

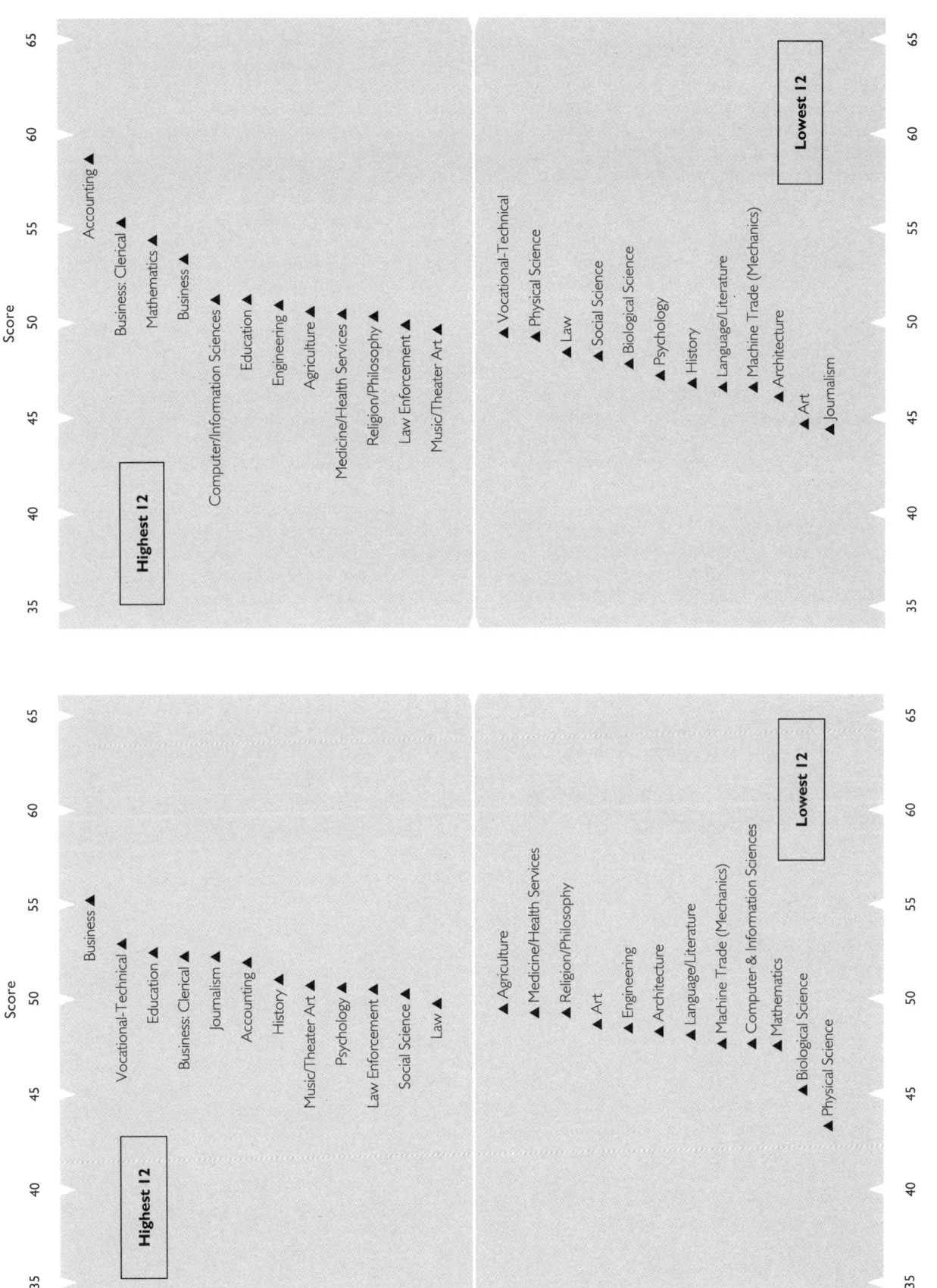

Figure 5.15 Rank-Ordered Means of 24 Majors on the Enterprising GOT

Figure 5.16 Rank-Ordered Means of 24 Majors on the Conventional GOT

References

Borgen, F. H. (1991). Megatrends and milestones in vocational behavior: A 20-year counseling psychology retrospective. *Journal of Vocational Behavior, 39,* 263–290.

Campbell, D. P., & Holland, J. L. (1972). A merger in vocational interest research: Applying Holland's theory to Strong's data. *Journal of Vocational Behavior, 2,* 353–376.

Chartrand, J. M. (1991). The evolution of trait-and-factor career counseling: A person x environment fit approach. *Journal of Counseling and Development, 69,* 518–524.

Cole, N. S., Whitney, D. R., & Holland, J. L. (1971). A spatial configuration of occupations. *Journal of Vocational Behavior, 1,* 1–9.

Gottfredson, G. D., & Holland, J. L. (1989). *Dictionary of Holland occupational codes* (2nd ed.). Odessa, FL: Psychological Assessment Resources.

Hansen, J. C. (1992). *User's guide for the Strong Interest Inventory* (rev. ed.). Stanford, CA: Stanford University Press.

Hansen, J. C., & Campbell, D. P. (1985). *Manual for the Strong Interest Inventory* (4th ed.). Stanford, CA: Stanford University Press.

Hansen, J. C., & Johansson, C. B. (1972). The application of Holland's vocational model to the Strong Vocational Interest Blank for Women. *Journal of Vocational Behavior, 2,* 479–493.

Holland, J. L. (1959). A theory of vocational choice. *Journal of Counseling Psychology, 6,* 35–45.

Holland, J. L. (1965). *Manual for the Vocational Preference Inventory.* Palo Alto, CA: Consulting Psychologists Press.

Holland, J. L. (1966). *The psychology of vocational choice.* Waltham, MA: Blaisdell.

Holland, J. L. (1973). *Making vocational choices: A theory of careers.* Englewood Cliffs, NJ: Prentice-Hall.

Holland, J. L. (1985a). *Making vocational choices* (2nd ed.). Englewood Cliffs, NJ: Prentice-Hall.

Holland, J. L. (1985b). *Manual for the Vocational Preference Inventory.* Odessa, FL: Psychological Assessment Resources.

Matthews, D. B. (1990). A comparison of burnout in selected occupational fields. *The Career Development Quarterly, 38,* 230–239.

Rounds, J. B., & Tracey, T. J. (1990). From trait-and-factor to person-environment fit counseling: Theory and process. In W. B. Walsh & S. H. Osipow (Eds.), *Career counseling: Contemporary topics in vocational counseling* (pp. 1–44). Hillsdale, NJ: Erlbaum.

Spokane, A. R. (Ed.). (1987). Conceptual and methodological issues in person-environment fit research [Special issue]. *Journal of Vocational Behavior, 31,* 217–221.

Tracey, T. J., & Rounds, J. B. (1993). Evaluating Holland's and Gati's vocational-interest models: A structural meta-analysis. *Psychological Bulletin, 113,* 229–246.

Utz, P., & Korben, D. (1976). The construct validity of the Occupational Themes on the Strong-Campbell Interest Inventory. *Journal of Vocational Behavior, 9,* 31–42.

Varca, P. E., & Shaffer, G. S. (1982). Holland's theory: Stability of avocational interests. *Journal of Vocational Behavior, 21,* 288–298.

Walsh, W. B., & Holland, J. L. (1992). A theory of personality and work environments. In W. B. Walsh, K. H. Craik, & R. H. Price (Eds.), *Person-environment psychology: Models and perspectives* (pp. 35–69). Hillsdale, NJ: Erlbaum.

CHAPTER 6

The Basic Interest Scales

This chapter begins with a practical emphasis on describing the content and interpretation of the 25 Basic Interest Scales (BISs) in the 1994 *Strong Interest Inventory*. The revisions made for the 1994 *Strong* are also discussed. For the first time since their introduction in the 1960s, the BISs have been substantially analyzed and updated. However, long-time users of the inventory can rest assured that interpretations of the scales can be made much as before. The latter half of the chapter focuses on the research conducted to create the BISs and to evaluate the reliability and validity of the scales. ◆

Content and Interpretation of the Basic Interest Scales

The Basic Interest Scales can be looked upon as subdivisions of the General Occupational Themes (GOTs). For example, the Agriculture, Nature, Athletics, Military Activities, and Mechanical Activities scales are all coded Realistic because each is closely related statistically to the R Theme. Similarly, all of the Basic Interest Scales are arranged on the Profile in groups under the General Occupational Theme to which they are related (see page 2 of the *Strong* Profile at the back of this guide).

Each of the BISs covers a specific area of content and, like the GOTs, is composed of homogeneous (i.e., statistically correlated) items. However, the GOTs are generally broader and more diverse in content span, while the BISs are more focused on a specific interest domain. This difference is well illustrated in the Artistic GOT, which contains items measuring art, music/dramatics, and writing, whereas the BISs separately measure each of these domains in three specific scales.

Each Basic Interest Scale's name provides a good clue to the item content of that scale. For example, the Mechanical Activities scale includes the following items:

▲ "Auto mechanic"
▲ "Mechanical engineer"
▲ "Operating machinery"
▲ "Solving mechanical puzzles"
▲ "Have mechanical ingenuity (inventiveness)"

The consistency of item content within a scale can be illustrated by the Office Services scale also, which includes items such as:

▲ "Bank teller"
▲ "Hospital records clerk"
▲ "Typewriting/Word processing"
▲ "Operating office machines"
▲ "Checking printed material for errors"

Revisions of the Basic Interest Scales for the 1994 Strong

For the current revision, considerable efforts were made to evaluate whether the BISs could be enhanced. At the same time, so that users already familiar with the *Strong* could readily adapt to any changes, continuity with the previous BISs was maintained. As a result, the prior scales were retained whenever possible; one scale was deleted completely, and four new scales were added. In some instances, scales were rearranged on the Profile. In other instances, the name of the scale was changed (see Chapter 2, Table 2.2 for a listing of all changes to the BISs).

Prior users of the BISs might ask:

▲ Do the 1994 scales have the same meaning as the prior versions?

▲ Can one continue to interpret the scales in the ways that prior literature and experience have supported for earlier versions of the scales?

The answer to these questions is yes, based on the high correlations between the 1985 and 1994 scales. These correlations are discussed later in the chapter.

Definitions of the Basic Interest Scales

The title of a BIS gives a fair sense of the meaning for that scale, but knowledge of the scale's item content and of the kinds of people who score high on that scale provides a more thorough understanding of the interest factor measured. (In referring to occupational means, scores of 58 or higher are typically used to designate a "high" score. These references are to the mean occupational scores, as shown in Figures 6.1 through 6.25, at the end of this chapter.) Understanding of a scale is also enhanced by examining its correlations with other BISs and with the GOTs and Personal Style Scales. The following discussion presents each of the 25 BISs—including the 4 new ones—in the order that they appear on the Profile.

Realistic BISs

Agriculture

The core content of the Agriculture scale is typified by its name: working in farming or ranching settings. The scale also has a subtheme of enjoying physically active work in outdoor settings. The Agriculture and Nature BISs correlate moderately highly, with both sharing the outdoor content of the R Theme. However, the scales do tap somewhat different content, which is well reflected in their names. The Agriculture scale emphasizes farming and ranching, while the Nature scale has the flavor of enjoying the beauty of nature, love of the outdoors, and biology.

People with scores of "High Interest" or "Very High Interest" on the Agriculture scale include vocational agriculture teachers, horticultural workers, farmers, agribusiness managers, foresters, gardeners/groundskeepers, and veterinarians. Although farmers score very high on Agriculture, they have only average scores on Nature. High scores for Agriculture are also obtained by physical education teachers and athletic trainers, reflecting the outdoor and physical activity flavor of the scale.

Items on the Agriculture scale reflect active physical labor in an outdoor environment. Such items include:

▲ "Farmer"
▲ "Rancher"
▲ "Agriculture"
▲ "Outside work"
▲ "Physical activity"

People who score high on the Agriculture scale frequently prefer to live in a rural rather than a metropolitan area. If they are city dwellers, they typically have a favorite spot somewhere away from the city to which they retreat during leisure time.

Nature

The items on the Nature scale reflect appreciation for the beauty of nature and an interest in outdoor recreational activities rather than in active outdoor farming work as in the Agriculture scale. The scale's content reflects an interest in plants, wildlife, and biology. Scores of "High Interest" and "Very High Interest" on the Nature scale might be seen in people who also have an interest in science, especially its biological aspects. The scale often has important implications for how (and where) people like to spend their leisure time.

People scoring high on the Nature scale include some in the same occupations scoring high on the Agriculture scale: vocational agriculture teachers, horticultural workers, foresters, and gardeners/groundskeepers. Also scoring high on the Nature scale are biologists, science teachers, and medical illustrators. Notably absent from the highest scorers on the Nature scale, in contrast to the Agriculture scale, are farmers, physical education teachers, and athletic trainers. Someone with a high score on the Nature scale combined with a lower score on the Agriculture scale may enjoy the outdoors as a more recreational participant rather than as a physically vigorous worker. More vigorous and dangerous activity might be expected as scores on the Athletics BIS move higher and scores on the Risk Taking/Adventure scale (one of the Personal Style Scales) move toward the takes chances pole. (See Chapter 8 for a discussion of the Personal Style Scales.)

Some Nature scale items include:

- ▲ "Landscape gardener"
- ▲ "Nature study"
- ▲ "Raising flowers and vegetables"
- ▲ "Forest ranger"
- ▲ "Camping"

People with scores of "High Interest" or "Very High Interest" on the Nature scale are interested in recreational activities such as rock climbing, camping, canoeing, hunting, and fishing. Like people who score high on the Agriculture scale, they often prefer to live in rural areas or small communities; they may choose weekend retreats beside a lake, in the mountains, or on a river.

Occasionally Nature interests are expressed in conjunction with an interest in art. For the artistically skilled, nature may serve as a source of inspiration or as a subject matter for their sketches, paintings, or poems. Others with an aesthetic appreciation or eye for nature may choose photography as a mechanism for capturing the beauty of nature. A good example is the occupational group of medical illustrators, who score high on the Nature scale but only average on the Agriculture BIS.

Military Activities

Interest in a structured environment that has a well-ordered, clearly defined chain of command is characteristic of people with high scores on the Military Activities scale. Such people also like to be in a position of authority, with power or control over others.

A high score on the Military Activities scale does not guarantee that a person also will score high on the Military Officer or Military Enlisted Personnel Occupational Scales (OSs). These two military scales are each composed of over 35 items; of these, only 5 are items representing military activities (e.g., "Drilling soldiers"). Even responding "Like" to all 5 of these items would not be sufficient to score high without other interests similar to those of military officers or military enlisted personnel. What this says is that there is much to a military occupation that is not military.

People with scores of "High Interest" or "Very High Interest" on the Military Activities scale include military officers, military enlisted personnel, airline pilots, highway patrol officers, police officers, and others in law enforcement and protection occupations.

Items on the Military Activities scale include:

- ▲ "Military officer"
- ▲ "Military drill"
- ▲ "Drilling soldiers"
- ▲ "Drilling in a military company"

The Military Activities scale is one BIS with a high minimum score; the lowest score possible on the scale is 42. This score compares with possible minimum scores on other scales ranging from 24 to 38. Consequently, it is important to alert clients with scores of 42 on the Military Activities scale that they have scored as low as possible. High scores are relatively rare for women in the general population. It is only in military, law enforcement, and related occupations that both women and men show high average scores.

Athletics

This scale represents an all-consuming interest in sports. People who score high on the Athletics scale are avid fans who may not even participate in sports, although they probably have some past athletic experience, especially in team sports. They tend to enjoy being spectators at a variety of sporting events ranging from boxing matches, football games, golf tournaments, and ski races to gymnastics meets, swimming meets, weight-lifting competitions, and wrestling tournaments. People who participate only in solitary sports such as running or who are interested in only one sport to the exclusion of all others probably will not score high on this scale.

People who score high on Athletics respond "Like" to a range of sports-related items such as:

- ▲ "Athletic director"
- ▲ "Professional athlete"
- ▲ "Golf"

- "Playing team sports with friends"
- "Sports pages in the newspaper"

People with scores of "High Interest" or "Very High Interest" on the scale include coaches, physical education teachers, athletic trainers, recreation leaders, and community service organization directors. Many people in Enterprising occupations also score above average on the Athletics scale. They may use their interest in athletics as a common denominator when socializing with business clients, either discussing their favorite college or professional teams or relating their own memories as a player. This characteristic has been especially true for men; some women who have entered high levels of business have also chosen to involve themselves in this aspect of the business world.

Mechanical Activities

The Mechanical Activities scale is one of the easiest to interpret; it measures interest in activities that require working not only with large equipment and machinery but also with small precision instruments such as those used by a surgeon or dentist. The Mechanical Activities scale is nearly synonymous with the Realistic GOT. High scorers like building, repairing, tinkering, and generally using a wide range of tools and materials. The scale represents a preference for working with things rather than people and thus is associated with scores toward the works with ideas/data/things pole of the Work Style scale.

Occupations in which both women and men receive scores of "High Interest" or "Very High Interest" on the Mechanical Activities scale include auto mechanics, carpenters, electricians, engineers, geologists, physicists, research and development managers, medical technologists, mathematics teachers, and military officers.

Items on the Mechanical Activities scale include:

- "Auto mechanic"
- "Mechanical engineer"
- "Operating machinery"
- "Solving mechanical puzzles"
- "Have mechanical ingenuity (inventiveness)"

Investigative BISs

Science

The Science scale is a measure of interest in the natural sciences, especially the physical sciences, and in scientific research. The scale is highly correlated with the Investigative GOT and thus shares many of its descriptors. The Science scale is negatively correlated with the Work Style scale; high scorers on Science often prefer working alone and with scientific material rather than with people directly.

Occupations with scores of "High Interest" or "Very High Interest" on this scale, such as biologists, chemists, geologists, and physicists, emphasize scientific theory, the search for basic truths, and an experimental approach to solving problems and understanding the universe. Other groups that may not be seen as traditional, prototypic natural scientists also score high on the Science scale and often have science integral to their work: medical technologists, science teachers, mathematicians, research and development managers, physicians, computer programmers/systems analysts, and medical technicians.

Items on the Science scale include:

- "Astronomer"
- "Laboratory technician"
- "Chemistry"
- "Physics"
- "Performing scientific experiments"

Mathematics

One scale that is very specifically described by its name is the Mathematics scale; it measures an interest in working with numbers and performing statistical analyses. Although most of the occupations that score high on the Mathematics scale are of the Investigative type, such as chemists, mathematicians, actuaries, geologists, and physicists, occupations with other primary Holland codes also have an interest in mathematics as one of their clusters of interests. For example, engineers, coded as Realistic-Investigative (RI), score high on the Mathematics scale, as do accountants, coded Conventional-Enterprising (CE). The majority of people with high Mathematics scores tend to score toward the works with ideas/data/things pole of the Work Style scale. Profiles that differ from this pattern invite a thoughtful discussion of the implications.

Items on the Mathematics scale relate in an obvious manner to the scale name, for example:

- "Statistician"
- "Algebra"
- "Arithmetic"

- ▲ "Calculus"
- ▲ "Geometry"

Medical Science

While the Science scale measures interest primarily in the physical sciences, the Medical Science scale measures an interest in the biological sciences and medical fields.

Items on the Medical Science scale include:

- ▲ "Biologist"
- ▲ "Physician"
- ▲ "Physiology"
- ▲ "Zoology"
- ▲ "Watching an open-heart operation"

Occupations that have scores of 58 or higher on the Medical Science scale typically require a strong educational background in the biological as well as physical sciences. The list of such medical specialties is quite extensive and includes dentists, dental hygienists, athletic trainers, medical technologists, physicians, pharmacists, optometrists, physical therapists, respiratory therapists, chiropractors, emergency medical technicians, and veterinarians. Also scoring high are science teachers and medical illustrators.

Artistic BISs

Music/Dramatics

People who score high on the Music/Dramatics scale enjoy participating in a wide range of performance activities or being part of the audience who enjoys watching others perform. Music/Dramatics is a central feature of the A Theme, along with the expected content of Art as well as that of Writing. Although the verbal-linguistic content of the Writing scale might not be expected within the Artistic Theme, in fact, all these areas are correlated. Thus, it is not unusual to have either all high or all low scores across all of these areas.

Items on the Music/Dramatics scale include:

- ▲ "Actor/Actress"
- ▲ "Opera singer"
- ▲ "Jazz or rock concerts"
- ▲ "Magazines about art or music"
- ▲ "Ballet dancers"

As the items indicate, the Music/Dramatics scale incorporates a wide range of musical and theatrical interests. A person committed to only one type of theater (e.g., musicals), one type of dance (e.g., modern), or one type of music (e.g., classical) probably would not score high on this scale. People with scores of "High Interest" or "Very High Interest" include fine artists, commercial artists, art teachers, and musicians.

Art

This scale measures an appreciation for art; like the Music/Dramatics scale, an interest in art may be expressed through creating an artwork or through enjoying and collecting art. The Art scale is the BIS most closely allied with the Artistic GOT. People with scores of "High Interest" or "Very High Interest" on the Art scale include architects, commercial artists, fine artists, art teachers, interior decorators, medical illustrators, and photographers.

Items on the Art scale include:

- ▲ "Art museum director"
- ▲ "Art teacher"
- ▲ "Cartoonist"
- ▲ "Interior decorator"
- ▲ "Sculptor"

Applied Arts

The Applied Arts scale, new to the *Strong* in 1994, is very similar to the Art BIS. These are the two most similar BISs, both in terms of correlation and item overlap. The subtle difference in the Applied Arts scale comes from its broad emphasis on visual creativity and spatial visualization. Thus, the Applied Arts scale is somewhat less tied to the A Theme and more related to the R Theme and the I Theme than is the Art scale. Although there will rarely be a difference of more than 8 points between a client's scores on the Applied Arts and Art scales, such a difference deserves special attention. A score on the Applied Arts scale that is higher than one on the Art scale invites consideration of occupational activities under the R Theme and the I Theme that involve spatial visualization.

Items on the Applied Arts scale include:

- ▲ "Architect"
- ▲ "Cartoonist"
- ▲ "Illustrator"
- ▲ "Photographer"
- ▲ "Mechanical drawing"

People with scores of "High Interest" or "Very High Interest" on the Applied Arts scale are medical illustrators, architects, photographers, art teachers, commercial artists, fine artists, technical writers, and interior decorators.

Writing

The Writing scale represents an interest in literature, reading, and language from the perspectives of appreciation and creation. High scorers often are comfortable in academic learning environments. People with scores of "High Interest" or "Very High Interest" on the scale are in occupations with a verbal-linguistic orientation: English teachers, reporters, public relations directors, technical writers, sociologists, ministers, translators, and librarians.

An interest (or disinterest) in writing and language can be important in the way people work and communicate in a whole range of occupational roles; therefore, the Writing scale can have major import for many career choices. Thus, for example, an engineer who enjoys writing will have a different menu of satisfying occupational roles than one who does not.

While the Writing scale covers communication by written word, the Public Speaking scale addresses oral communication preferences. Together the Writing and Public Speaking scales can stimulate thought about how one would prefer to express oneself at work or even in leisure activities. Adding information from such Personal Style Scales as the Work Style scale and Leadership Style scale gives an even more complete picture.

Items on the Writing scale include:

- ▲ "Author of children's books"
- ▲ "Editor"
- ▲ "Poet"
- ▲ "English composition/Writing"
- ▲ "Writing a one-act play"

Culinary Arts

The Culinary Arts scale directly measures interests in cooking and entertaining. It has been added as a new BIS, grouped in the Artistic area, although it is also correlated with the Social and Enterprising GOTs. This scale partially replaces the old Domestic Arts scale, which had a heterogeneous content, including cooking and entertaining. The hosting/entertaining component of the Culinary Arts scale is linked to the Work Style and Leadership Style scales. Thus, those scoring high on Culinary Arts may tend to score toward the works with people pole of the Work Style scale and toward the directs others pole of the Leadership Style scale.

People with scores of "High Interest" or "Very High Interest" on the Culinary Arts scale include home economics teachers, chefs, dietitians, food service managers, and restaurant managers.

Items on the Culinary Arts scale include:

- ▲ "Preparing dinner for guests"
- ▲ "Cooking"
- ▲ "Trying new cooking recipes"
- ▲ "Entertaining others"
- ▲ "Learning more about the foods I eat"

Social BISs

Teaching

Educators representing a wide range of disciplines score high on the Teaching scale: for example, foreign language teachers, high school counselors, home economics teachers, mathematics teachers, art teachers, music teachers, school administrators, and special education teachers. Note that college professors are not included in this list of high-scoring occupations; their average score on the scale is lower—just 53. This pattern makes sense when one understands that high scores on the Teaching scale signal an interest not just in "teaching" but more specifically in "teaching young people" in smaller classrooms with considerable student-teacher interaction. Thus, the Teaching scale is distinctly an S-Theme scale, while college professors typically fit in the I Theme.

Items on the Teaching scale include:

- ▲ "Elementary school teacher"
- ▲ "High school teacher"
- ▲ "School principal"
- ▲ "Teaching children"
- ▲ "Have patience when teaching others"

Social Service

The Social Service scale is closely related to the Social GOT; the two use many of the same descriptors. A high score on the Social Service scale indicates a humanistic, altruistic interest in working with and helping people. High scorers are likely to score toward the works with people pole of the Work Style scale and toward the directs others pole of the Leadership Style scale.

Items on the Social Service scale include:

- ▲ "Social worker"
- ▲ "Youth organization staff member (e.g., YMCA, YWCA, YMHA, YWHA)"
- ▲ "Sociology"
- ▲ "Helping others overcome their difficulties"
- ▲ "Contributing to charities"

People with scores of "High Interest" or "Very High Interest" on this scale are high school counselors, ministers, social workers, special education teachers, child care providers, community service organization directors, social science teachers, and licensed practical nurses.

Medical Service

The Medical Service scale was previously categorized as an I-Theme scale, but on the 1994 Profile it has been moved to the S-Theme cluster to reflect its strong social and service flavor. Unlike the Medical Science scale, the Medical Service scale does not measure liking of high-level medical and biological science courses but rather focuses on direct service to sick people in medical settings. Usually respondents who scored high on the I Theme will not score high on Medical Service if they also score low on the S Theme.

Items on the Medical Service scale include:

- ▲ "Dental assistant"
- ▲ "Nurse's aide/Orderly"
- ▲ "Taping a sprained ankle"
- ▲ "Giving first aid assistance"
- ▲ "Physically sick people"

People with mean scores of 58 or more on this scale include licensed practical nurses, emergency medical technicians, dental assistants, athletic trainers, registered nurses, respiratory therapists, medical technicians, physical therapists, radiologic technologists, medical technologists, dental hygienists, and chiropractors. While people who score high on the Medical Service scale generally want to have close contact with patients, those who score high only on the Science and Medical Science scales typically are more research and laboratory oriented and have minimal personal interest in the patient.

Religious Activities

The Religious Activities scale reflects an interest in spiritual or religious concerns, especially through organized activities. Items include, for example:

- ▲ "Religious leader (e.g., minister, priest, rabbi)"
- ▲ "Worker in religious vocation"
- ▲ "Religious studies"
- ▲ "Young people's religious group"
- ▲ "Religious people"

The items on the Religious Activities scale were revised in 1985. The original wording of the items used primarily Judeo-Christian terms; the wording of the items on the 1994 Item Booklet/Answer Sheet is more generic and is intended to elicit more reliable answers from respondents.

People with scores of "High Interest" or "Very High Interest" on the Religious Activities scale in past samples have been directly involved with the clergy: directors of religious education, ministers, nuns, and priests. The 1994 *Strong* includes one such occupation: ministers, who score distinctly high, with a mean score of 67 ("Very High Interest"). Interestingly, licensed practical nurses and high school counselors also have mean scores of 58 or more ("High Interest"). Moreover, a number of teachers also have mean scores of 56 or 57 on the Religious Activities scale; these include English teachers, foreign language teachers, and social science teachers.

Enterprising BISs

Public Speaking

The Public Speaking scale measures an interest in persuading others through verbal activities, a willingness to be in the limelight, and a desire to influence people's thoughts and viewpoints. The scale has a distinctly E-Theme flavor. The scale is correlated with several of the Personal Style Scales: a preference toward the works with people pole of the Work Style scale, toward the academic pole of the Learning Environment scale, and especially toward the directs others pole of the Leadership Style scale.

People who score highest on the scale are those who frequently make public presentations to others:

broadcasters, elected public officials, public administrators, ministers, and public relations directors. Also scoring quite high (55–57) are realtors; lawyers; corporate trainers; school administrators; and people in many high school occupations such as high school counselors, social science teachers, and English teachers.

However, there are some interesting exceptions among the teaching occupations: college professors average considerably lower (women = 49, men = 53), as do elementary school teachers, special education teachers, and business education teachers. The E-Theme flavor of this scale explains such scoring patterns since other Themes predominate for the latter four occupations. College professors are the Investigative type, elementary and special education teachers are the Social type, and business education teachers are the Conventional type. Thus, not all people who spend a large portion of their working day speaking in front of others should be expected to have high scores on the Public Speaking scale, especially those for whom other Themes predominate.

One's inclination toward public speaking can have a major impact within a particular career choice. For example, professors who score very high on the scale might work very differently from professors with low scores. The Public Speaking and Writing scales can be used together to clarify preferences for oral and written means of communication. Adding scores on the Personal Style Scales, especially Work Style and Leadership Style, expands the interpretive possibilities.

Items on the Public Speaking scale include:

▲ "Public relations director"
▲ "TV announcer"
▲ "Public speaking"
▲ "Making a speech"
▲ "Expressing judgments publicly, regardless of what others say"

Law/Politics

High scores on the Public Speaking scale are frequently matched by high scores on the Law/Politics scale; both reflect an interest in debates and arguments designed to sell concepts (as opposed to selling tangible products). High scorers are likely to score toward the directs others pole on the Leadership Style scale and to score toward the academic pole of the Learning Environment scale. The Personal Style Scales of Work Style and Risk Taking/Adventure provide important additional information about how an interest in law/politics might be expressed. People who score low on this BIS usually avoid conflicts and confrontations.

Items on the Law/Politics scale include:

▲ "Criminal lawyer"
▲ "Governor of a state"
▲ "Political science"
▲ "Discussing politics"
▲ "Heading a civic improvement program"

People with scores of "High Interest" or "Very High Interest" on the Law/Politics scale include elected public officials, lawyers, public administrators, school administrators, sociologists, and social science teachers.

Merchandising

This scale measures an interest in wholesale and retail activities, selling tangible products rather than services or concepts. This BIS most typifies the E Theme, and descriptors of the E Theme can also be applied here. High scorers tend to score toward the works with people pole of the Work Style scale and toward the directs others pole of the Leadership Style scale. The Merchandising and Sales scales both entail selling, but in somewhat different settings. Those people who score high on the Merchandising scale like selling in structured, store-like settings and are not likely to enjoy being required to make unsolicited sales contacts unless they also have high scores on the Sales scale.

People who score highest on the Merchandising scale include buyers, store managers, purchasing agents, florists, travel agents, restaurant managers, interior decorators, and opticians. Realtors also score high on the Merchandising scale (women = 62, men = 59), but score even a full standard deviation higher on the Sales scale (women = 72, men = 70), reflecting their very rare level of comfort with making sales contacts.

Items include:

▲ "Advertising executive"
▲ "Retailer"
▲ "Travel agency manager"
▲ "Wholesaler"
▲ "Buying merchandise for a store"

Sales

The major difference between the Sales and Merchandising scales is that people who score high on the Sales scale like to take their product to others without prior invitation. They can handle the rejection that often occurs in these situations and will keep calling on new customers until they make a sale. Those who score high on the Sales scale and also score high on the Social Service or Religious Activities scales typically cannot sell simply for the sake of selling; rather, they have high ideals and need to believe that the product they are selling will benefit the buyer.

People with scores of "High Interest" or "Very High Interest" on the Sales scale typically score toward the practical pole of the Learning Environment scale and prefer practical learning settings. All the Personal Style Scales provide helpful supplementary information about the way sales interest might be expressed. For example, many people with high scores on the Sales scale score toward the right pole (directs others) of the Leadership Style scale, but a substantial subset have Leadership Style scores that are in the middle of the scale or even toward the left pole (leads by example).

People with high scores on the Sales scale are led by the prototypic sales occupations of realtor and life insurance agent, each with very high average scores of around 70. Also with high scores (57–64) on the Sales scale are store managers, buyers, opticians, florists, restaurant managers, travel agents, hair stylists, purchasing agents, interior decorators, elected public officials, and small business owners.

Items on the Sales scale include:

▲ "Auto salesperson"
▲ "Sales manager"
▲ "Specialty salesperson"
▲ "Traveling salesperson"
▲ "Interviewing prospects in selling"

Organizational Management

The Organizational Management scale measures an interest in authority and power and in supervising, organizing, leading, or directing others. High scorers typically score toward the directs others pole of the Leadership Style scale and toward the works with people pole of the Work Style scale. Although these activities most frequently occur in traditional enterprising environments such as business, industrial, and manufacturing settings, managers with this style may also be found in schools, colleges, hospitals, social service agencies, government offices, and research laboratories. Scores on the other BISs, OSs, and Personal Style Scales provide information on the person's most appropriate management environment.

Items on the Organizational Management scale include:

▲ "Factory manager"
▲ "Office manager"
▲ "Interviewing job applicants"
▲ "Developing business systems"
▲ "Business magazines"

People with scores of "High Interest" or "Very High Interest" on this scale include business education teachers, executives, credit managers, store managers, human resources directors, public administrators, purchasing agents, restaurant managers, sales managers, realtors, and travel agents.

Conventional BISs

Data Management

This new Conventional scale measures processing and handling data and information, but with a larger component of management independence and decision making than the Office Services scale, previously the only Conventional scale. (Note that the 1985 BIS Office Practices was renamed Office Services in 1994.) The core content of the scale is managing financial, statistical, mathematical, or actuarial data to provide assessments or decisions. In contrast with the Office Services scale, those with high scores on the Data Management scale are more likely to score high on the Mathematics scale. Often the tasks require some advanced training such as accounting or mathematics.

The Data Management scale is not substantially correlated with any of the four Personal Style Scales. Thus, high scorers do not typically prefer to work with a particular personal style and are not likely to score toward either pole of the Work Style or Leadership Style scale. People who score high on the Data Management scale enjoy managing data, but they may or may not enjoy managing people. This pattern contrasts with the Organizational Management scale, on which high scores are typified by an orientation toward the E Theme, a tendency to score toward the works with people pole of the Work Style scale, and a tendency to score toward the directs others pole of the Leadership Style scale. Thus, the Data Management scale is best used in combination with the Personal Style Scales to determine the person's preferences for work style and leadership style.

People with scores of "High Interest" or "Very High Interest" on the Data Management scale include those involved with business accounting and data-intensive decision making (accountants, bookkeepers, business education teachers, investments managers, credit managers, and bankers) and those with a central mathematics component (actuaries and mathematics teachers).

Items on the Data Management scale include:

▲ "Accountant"
▲ "Business teacher"
▲ "Financial analyst"
▲ "Making statistical charts"
▲ "Things vs. Data"

Computer Activities

Computer Activities is a new Conventional scale that directly measures interests in working with computers. The content is quite specific and addresses the area of liking computers, computer science, and office machines. Given the rapid changes in computer technology, one might expect many people to be changing how they respond to such items. Generational differences may also be evident, with children and young people more exposed to computers, and therefore more comfortable with them, than older people might be. High scores are associated with the other Conventional domains of the Data Management and Office Services scales and also to some degree with the Mathematics, Science, and Mechanical Activities scales.

Those whose scores show "High Interest" or "Very High Interest" on the Computer Activities scale are a fairly diverse and relatively small group: secretaries, business education teachers, military enlisted personnel, and mathematics teachers. Commercial and fine artists, and others in the A Theme, are among those who show a distinct pattern of dislikes in this domain.

Items on the Computer Activities scale include:

"Computer operator"

"Computer programmer"

▲ "Word processor"
▲ "Computer science"
▲ "Operating office machines"

Office Services

The Office Services scale, formerly called Office Practices, is the BIS most closely related to the Conventional GOT. The scale measures an interest in clerical and office activities and includes items such as:

▲ "Bank teller"
▲ "Hospital records clerk"
▲ "Typewriting/Word processing"
▲ "Operating office machines"
▲ "Checking printed material for errors"

Occupational groups scoring high on the Office Services scale include business education teachers, secretaries, bookkeepers, dental assistants, food service managers, bankers, mathematics teachers, licensed practical nurses, and agribusiness managers. There are often substantial gender differences on this scale, even within the same occupational title. It appears that women and men may often have different roles (and/or preferences) in the office services area, even when holding the same occupational title. Thus, female bankers average 62.0 ("High Interest") on Office Services, while male bankers average only 52.9 ("Average Interest"). Another striking difference, likely reflecting quite traditional gender roles and preferences, is between female and male farmers; female farmers score 61.3 ("High Interest") and male farmers score 50.6 ("Average Interest"). See Chapter 17 for further discussion of gender issues regarding the *Strong* scales.

Using the Basic Interest Scales in Counseling

The BISs can be used to assist counselors and clients in understanding the underlying interests measured by the GOTs. The BISs can be used with clients in the same manner as the Themes—to identify activities, jobs, environments, and types of people that appeal to them. The BISs also can be very useful with the OSs, to interpret the content of the likes and dislikes that determine a client's results on the OSs.

The homogeneous item content of the BISs lends itself to straightforward interpretations about activities the client likes or dislikes: for example, items on the Art scale are concerned exclusively with artistic activities; items on the Mechanical Activities scale, with mechanical activities; and those on the Sales scale, with sales.

Since the BISs share the features of the GOTs, when a counselor understands the standard scores, norm groups, gender norming, and interpretive boundaries for one type of scale, that knowledge immediately applies to the other type of scale. The basic difference is that the six GOTs are broader in content, while the 25 BISs cover more specific content. The BISs cover more specific subthemes of the GOTs, with each GOT having three to five BISs grouped under it on the *Strong* Profile.

Implications of High Percentages of "Like" or "Dislike" Responses

High scores on the BISs are achieved primarily by answering "Like" to the items on a scale; low scores primarily by answering "Dislike." As with the GOTs, BIS items are weighted +1 for a "Like" response, –1 for a "Dislike" response, and 0 for an "Indifferent" response. The score on a scale increases if the respondent says "Like" and decreases if the respondent says "Dislike." An average score is obtained if the person responds "Like" to some items and "Dislike" to others; such a person probably has a tolerance, but not a great passion, for the activities represented by that scale.

Those clients who give an unusually high number of "Like" responses (i.e., 60 to 70 percent or higher), as indicated by the Administrative Indexes on page 6 of the Profile, will likely have scores in the "High Interest" or "Very High Interest" ranges on many GOTs and BISs. Although such scores indicate a positive response to a large number of activities in each area, they probably are not as clear an indicator of high interest as are scores in the same range that are the only high scores for the BIS. Allowances should be made in Profile interpretation when a person has responded with a high percentage of "Like" or "Dislike" responses. In such cases, the ranking of scores must be considered, as well as how high BIS scores are in general. The three or four highest—and lowest—scores are worth noting, no matter what, since these are the areas in which the individual has most consistently responded "Like" or "Dislike." For more information on the interpretation of elevated, flat, and depressed Profiles, refer to Chapter 11.

Plotting of Scores on the Profile

The method of plotting scores on page 2 of the Profile is designed to make the results easy to interpret, in a normative sense. Plotted scores in the extreme ranges indicate the most noteworthy BIS scores on each Profile. For each scale, the distributions of scores for the male and female General Reference Samples (GRSs) are indicated by the horizontal box-and-whisker graphs, as discussed in the later section "Norming the Scales." (Also see Chapter 3 for a detailed discussion of page 2 of the Profile.)

Identifying Underlying Themes

The BISs are particularly useful in providing a direct reflection of the salient content in a client's responses. These results provide a comprehensive and directly interpretable representation of the client's interests. The counselor might begin by examining the overall pattern of scores showing both high and little interest, paying attention to both the GOTs and BISs. Often clear patterns emerge; for example, the client may distinctly like many of the BIS subthemes within a GOT Theme, with many scores falling in the "High Interest" or "Very High Interest" range. Conversely, many people have a pattern of distinct dislikes, perhaps also patterned within a GOT Theme. Clear patterns of dislikes are as important as clear patterns of likes in interpreting a client's BIS results. When a pattern of BIS scores has been identified, counseling can focus on evaluating the accuracy of the pattern, exploring its meaning, and discerning implications for the client's vocational and life planning.

The process just described represents perhaps the most simple and obvious interpretive scenario for the BISs. Many other permutations and possibilities can develop out of the individual needs of clients and the versatility of counselors. For example, after looking at the broad pattern of likes and dislikes within a Theme, it may be valuable to consider the meaning of disparities within that Theme. Thus, a woman in premed may have scores of "High Interest" on the I Theme and the Science and Medical Science scales but only "Average Interest" in Mathematics. Counseling may focus on how she can best satisfy her interests within the medical field without emphasizing mathematical tasks.

At other times, the pattern of scores on the GOTs and BISs does not tell an unambiguous story. If the client is struggling with career identity and with achieving a fulfilling life-style, greater effort may be required to arrive at a satisfactory interpretation that is only dimly evident from the pattern of BIS scores. Another pattern that can present an interpretive challenge occurs when scores on only one or two BISs are above the "Average Interest" range. Depending on the client's circumstances, these elevated scores may or may not be helpful in confirming or creating career alternatives. An even more challenging, and often frustrating, pattern is the absence of any scores above "Average Interest." Perhaps more challenging yet are those Profiles on which all scores indicate "Little Interest" or "Very Little Interest." (See Chapter 11 for strategies to handle such challenges.)

After the client and counselor have discussed the results of the BISs, it is time to turn to the OSs to see which occupations have people with interests similar to the client's. Used in conjunction with the OSs, the BISs provide information about major themes in the individual's interests. (Chapter 10 offers interpretive strategies and methods for integrating the results of all the GOTs, BISs, and OSs.)

Using the Basic Interest Scales in Assessing Leisure Interests

The BISs may be used to help a client explore not only occupational interests but also avocational interests, and counselors should encourage their clients to consider both work and leisure interests as they examine their *Strong* results. Cairo (1979), in a study designed to determine the validity of the original BISs, found that the scales identify leisure interests as well as they identify occupational interests. Although the scales used to measure leisure activities were, in most cases, different from the scales used to measure occupations, 79 percent of the respondents had BIS scores that were congruent with occupational or avocational activities; and about half of the respondents who had congruent measured interests and occupations also had congruent measured interests and leisure activities. Cairo's findings suggest that the BISs may be used to explore the entire interest pattern of an individual rather than just occupational interests alone.

Research to Revise and Evaluate the Basic Interest Scales

The general research strategy used in developing the BISs involved grouping together items that correlated with each other and had similar content (Campbell, 1971; Campbell, Borgen, Eastes, Johansson, & Peterson, 1968). A scale formed by using clusters of statistically related items has three important characteristics: first, it represents, by virtue of its internal consistency, an important focus around which people can group their own interests; second, because the items are all drawn from one area, the content of the scale is easy to understand; and third, the concentration of related items in a single scale provides a more reliable measure than the same number of unrelated items would.

Thus, a key characteristic of the BISs is that they are homogeneous scales. For example, the Art scale includes, among others, the following items: "Artist," "Cartoonist," and "Interior decorator." These and other similar items were clustered together because most people tend to react to them either by responding "Like" to all (or nearly all) of them or "Indifferent" or "Dislike" to all (or nearly all) of them. The strength of this tendency to respond in a similar way to items can be measured by assigning weights of $+1$, 0, and -1, respectively, to the three possible responses for each item and then calculating the product-moment correlations between the items. Among 500 women in a general sample reported by Hansen and Campbell (1985), the correlation between "Artist" and "Cartoonist" was .47, between "Artist" and "Interior decorator" .52, and between "Cartoonist" and "Interior decorator" .27; the analogous figures among 500 men were .49, .45, and .37, respectively. Item intercorrelations of this size indicate a substantial relationship between the items.

Purpose and Origin of the Basic Interest Scales

One main purpose in developing the BISs was to improve the understanding of the OSs. The latter, which historically preceded the former, were constructed by gathering together into a scale all items that discriminate between an occupational sample and a GRS, no matter what the item content. The resulting scale, though powerful statistically, may be difficult to interpret because the items are quite varied. The Psychologist OS, for example, incorporates a wide range of items, including subgroups that reflect interests in science, social service, and the arts—all weighted positively—and other subgroups encompassing business and physical activities—all weighted negatively. A person can score high (or low) on this scale in countless ways, and only those counselors with extensive clinical experience can search out the factors underlying particular scores.

Kenneth Clark, in his work with the *Minnesota Vocational Interest Inventory* (Clark, 1961), proposed the use of two types of scales to overcome this problem: empirically developed, heterogeneous OSs, such as those that had always been part of the *Strong Vocational Interest Blanks (SVIB)*, and statistically developed homogeneous scales. Clark's rationale was that the combination of these two types of scales would provide more information than would either type used separately. For example, if a person scored high on an OS, such as the Psychologist scale, his or her scores on the homogeneous scales could be scanned to see precisely what combination of interests was present—science, social service, art, or whatever. The homogeneous scales could be used to describe the general patterns reflected in the scores of empirical scales. For this reason, the profile for the *Minnesota Vocational Interest Inventory* contained both types of scales; at the time it was published, it was the only inventory to do so (Clark & Campbell, 1965). Shortly thereafter, the *SVIB* Profile also was expanded to include both types of scales (Campbell, 1969).

The two types of scales serve different purposes, and to understand their complementary nature, one must understand the differences in their development and in their operating characteristics.

Constructing the 1968 Scales

To some extent, the BISs formed themselves; for the most part, the clusters of correlated items making up the scales fell out of the item-intercorrelation matrix. A few arbitrary decisions were made in borderline cases, especially in those instances where an item correlated highly with some items in a cluster but not with others. In a few instances an item was not used because it did not "feel" right for a given scale. For example, the item "Sculptor" correlated moderately with the Science items but was not added to that scale because it seemed out of place. Such decisions were rare; the bulk of the scale construction decisions were based on hard data.

The details of the construction of the BISs were first published in a 1968 monograph by Campbell, Borgen, Eastes, Johansson, and Peterson, and also given in Chapters 3 and 4 of the 1971 *Handbook for the Strong Vocational Interest Blank* (Campbell, 1971). Briefly, the procedure was as follows:

1. Item-intercorrelation matrices containing correlation coefficients between all possible pairs of items were generated for both female and male samples.

2. Frequency distributions of these correlations were made for each gender. The two distributions, presented in the handbook, were virtually identical, with means of about .03 and standard deviations of about .12. Because most of the correlations were less than .30, that figure was considered "high," and pairs of items with correlations of .30 or greater were considered closely related.

3. Scales were constructed by gathering together those items with intercorrelations of .30 or higher. In many cases, the selection criterion had to be dropped to .20, especially in those instances where, for example, item A correlated .30 with B and .30 with C, but B correlated only .20 with C.

The item-intercorrelation matrices for all of the original *SVIB* Basic Interest Scales are presented in the handbook; scanning them affords a good impression of the level of correlation one can expect when working with individual items.

Until Campbell's construction of a merged form of the *Strong* (Campbell, 1974), the instrument had separate booklets and scales for women and men. Thus, the 1968 BISs were constructed separately for the women's and men's booklets. In constructing the 1974 scales, the female and male *SVIB* scale sets were merged into a single set, usually by combining the parallel women's and men's scales. If a scale appeared on only one form of the *SVIB*, it was nonetheless retained in most cases (e.g., Domestic Arts appeared only on the women's form of the *SVIB*). Dropping or rewording of items in the booklet also led to minor changes in a few of the scales. (Scale-by-scale changes are given in the 1974 *Manual for the Strong-Campbell Interest Inventory*.)

This work resulted in the construction of 23 BISs ranging in length from 5 to 24 items, with a median length of 11 items. The BISs for the 1985 *Strong* had the same item content as the 1974 scales, but the 1985 scales were renormed on the 1985 GRS.

Table 6.1 Comparisons of 1985 and 1994 Basic Interest Scales: Correlations for Parallel Scales and Internal Consistency Reliabilities

Basic Interest Scale	Correlation	1985 Scale		1994 Scale	
		Number of Items	Cronbach Alpha	Number of Items	Cronbach Alpha
Agriculture	1.000[a]	6	.737	6	.737
Nature	.965	11	.795	8	.822
Military Activities	1.000[a]	5	.873	5	.873
Athletics	.963	12	.831	13	.893
Mechanical Activities	.989	24	.944	21	.938
Science	.995	17	.896	18	.904
Mathematics	.987	9	.892	11	.890
Medical Science	1.000[a]	8	.816	8	.816
Music/Dramatics	.992	13	.828	13	.841
Art	.993	14	.902	14	.897
Applied Arts	—[b]	—	—[b]	12	.867
Writing	.996	14	.903	15	.905
Culinary Arts	—[b]	—	—[b]	7	.799
Teaching	.969	9	.787	9	.814
Social Service	.955	11	.791	14	.851
Medical Service	.975	9	.793	12	.836
Religious Activities	.961	9	.907	7	.866
Public Speaking	1.000[a]	10	.817	10	.817
Law/Politics	.974	12	.859	14	.875
Merchandising	1.000[a]	13	.853	13	.853
Sales	.985	12	.809	11	.814
Organizational Management	.982	14	.846	17	.883
Data Management	—[b]	—	—[b]	17	.879
Computer Activities	—[b]	—	—[b]	5	.788
Office Services	.986	16	.866	19	.903

Note: Comparisons are based on General Reference Sample of 18,951 women and men.
[a] No change in item composition of the scale.
[b] Basic Interest Scale added to Profile in 1994.

Comparisons of the 1985 and 1994 Scales

The correlations between the 1985 and 1994 scales are shown in Table 6.1, for the 21 BISs retained from the 1985 Profile. Five of the 21 scales have no change in item content and thus are identical at the raw score level. Eight additional scales correlate .985 or higher with the 1985 scales. For the remaining 8 scales, the correlations range from .955 to .982. The median correlation for the 21 scales is .987. Thus, the 1994 revision of the BISs amounted to fine-tuning, without major change in the coverage of the scales.

This revision has somewhat improved the internal consistency reliabilities, or Cronbach alphas, for some of the scales. Table 6.1 shows alphas, as measures of internal consistency, for the 1985 and 1994 scales. These enhancements of alphas were achieved by dropping some items from the 1985 scales that were not highly correlated with the remaining items and/or adding new items that were highly correlated with the scale items and had similar content.

The polishing of the BISs for the 1994 revision followed the principles of the original construction of the scales (Campbell, Borgen, Eastes, Johansson, & Peterson, 1968), although the analysis was a less onerous task due to more modern computer technology. In addition, current technology enabled the use of much larger samples, presumably yielding greater stability and precision of results. Nevertheless, even after this more high-powered recent analysis, the original BISs, derived in more informal ways, were found to be quite robust, with the items and content remaining very similar over nearly three decades and across totally new samples.

Norming the Scales

The BISs have been renormed against the 1994 GRS, a sample of 9,467 women and 9,484 men (see Chapter 7 for a description of the GRS). For each scale, the mean and standard deviation of this combined-gender sample were set equal to 50 and 10, respectively, and all future scores are converted to this distribution for ready comparison.

As is the case with the GOTs, each BIS has an interpretive comment based on the level of interest the person shows. These comments are based on the distribution for the respondent's own gender, and the comments for the BISs correspond to the percentile bands used for the GOTs. Table 6.2 lists the standard score means and standard deviations of the GRSs for women and men and the ranges used to define each interpretive category. The extremes of the lower and upper bands for each scale are the minimum and maximum possible scores; these are the scores that will be earned by anyone answering all items "Dislike" or "Like," respectively—and thus on all scales they are the same for males and females.

The distributions of the GRSs for males and females are depicted on the Profile by two box-and-whisker graphs for each scale. The upper box represents the female distribution; the lower box, the male. For each distribution for each scale, the vertical space near the middle of the box indicates the mean; the thick portion of the box represents the middle 50 percent of the sample (from the 26th to the 75th percentiles); and the thin-line extensions (whiskers) represent the middle 80 percent (from the 11th to the 90th percentiles). With the use of standard scores, graphs, and interpretive comments, an individual's score may be compared with either the male or female distribution or the combined male and female distribution.

Relationships of the Basic Interest Scales to the General Occupational Themes

The BISs are grouped on the Profile into the six GOT categories, as indicated in the left column of Table 6.2 (pages 84–85). This grouping was based on the scale intercorrelations given in Tables 6.3 and 6.4 (pages 86–87). In most cases, the BISs in the same category correlate at least moderately with each other, and in some cases correlate so highly that the decision to create two scales instead of one was all but arbitrary. For example, the Merchandising and Sales scales, both of which fit easily into Holland's Enterprising category, might well have been combined; they were kept separate, even though their intercorrelation is high, because they have somewhat different item content and somewhat different meaning. Other pairs—Science and Medical Science, Art and Applied Arts, Teaching and Social Service—are similarly related. One can opt either for parsimony and a small number of scales or for purity of item content and a larger number. The two types of scales—the GOTs and BISs—provide the best of both approaches, and their high correlations suggest that the two types rest on the same underlying structure.

In Table 6.3 the intercorrelations between Basic Interest Scales grouped within the same GOT have been highlighted with a triangular color screen. These correlations are shown separately by gender, with those for women appearing in the upper triangles and those for men appearing in the lower triangles.

Reliability

The four samples used to evaluate test-retest reliability of the 1994 *Strong* included a three- to six-month retest on a national sample of working adults and three samples of college students at different universities, with retest intervals of one to three months. (See Chapter 5 for a detailed description of these samples.) The test-retest reliabilities for these samples for the BISs are shown in Table 6.5 (pages 88–90).

Table 6.2 Means, Standard Deviations, and Interpretive Boundaries for the Basic Interest Scales for the General Reference Sample

Theme	Basic Interest Scale	Gender	Mean	S.D.	Very Little Interest (0–10)	Little Interest (11–25)	Average Interest (26–75)	High Interest (76–90)	Very High Interest (91–100)
R	Agriculture	Female	48.3	10.0	31–33	34–39	40–54	55–62	63–68
		Male	51.8	9.9	31–37	38–44	45–59	60–64	65–68
R	Nature	Female	50.1	10.2	25–34	35–42	43–58	59–61	62–64
		Male	49.9	9.9	25–35	36–42	43–58	59–61	62–64
R	Military Activities	Female	47.4	7.7	None	42–43	44–49	50–56	57–78
		Male	52.9	11.0	None	42–43	44–60	61–67	68–78
R	Athletics	Female	47.2	9.1	31–34	35–39	40–54	55–60	61–68
		Male	52.8	10.0	31–37	38–44	45–61	62–64	65–68
R	Mechanical Activities	Female	46.8	8.9	35–36	37–39	40–52	53–59	60–73
		Male	53.2	10.0	35–39	40–45	46–60	61–67	68–73
I	Science	Female	48.8	9.9	30–35	36–40	41–56	57–62	63–71
		Male	51.2	10.0	30–37	38–43	44–59	60–64	65–71
I	Mathematics	Female	48.8	10.0	32–34	35–40	41–56	57–63	64–67
		Male	51.2	9.8	32–36	37–43	44–58	59–63	64–67
I	Medical Science	Female	49.7	10.0	32–35	36–41	42–57	58–63	64–69
		Male	50.6	9.9	32–36	37–42	43–58	59–63	64–69
A	Music/Dramatics	Female	52.4	9.6	29–39	40–45	46–60	61–64	65–70
		Male	47.6	9.9	29–34	35–39	40–54	55–61	62–70
A	Art	Female	52.8	9.3	29–39	40–45	46–60	61–64	65–67
		Male	47.2	9.9	29–33	34–39	40–55	56–60	61–67
A	Applied Arts	Female	50.9	10.1	28–35	36–43	44–58	59–63	64–67
		Male	49.1	9.9	28–35	36–41	42–57	58–62	63–67
A	Writing	Female	51.7	9.6	28–36	37–44	45–59	60–63	64–66
		Male	48.3	10.1	28–34	35–40	41–56	57–61	62–66
A	Culinary Arts	Female	53.4	8.9	25–40	41–46	47–58	59–62	63–65
		Male	46.5	9.7	25–33	34–39	40–54	55–58	59–65

The stability of scores over time is quite high, permitting these scales to be used for both research and counseling purposes.

Test-retest reliability of the earlier versions of the BISs has been thoroughly studied (Campbell, 1971; Hansen & Campbell, 1985). Because the 1994 BISs that have been retained are so highly correlated with the earlier versions, it can be expected that the results of studies of the earlier versions of the scales also generalize to the 1994 scales. The correlations range from the .50s, for 16-year-olds retested 36 years later, to the .90s, for samples tested and retested over a few weeks. The correlations vary mainly with the age of the person at the time of the first testing and the length of the retest interval, with the first factor being more important.

A study of the interests of high school and college students (Hansen & Stocco, 1980) demonstrated the effect of age on test-retest reliabilities. Although BIS median three-year test-retest correlations were lower for high school students ($r = .56$) and college students ($r = .68$) than for adults ($r = .82$), the

Table 6.2 Means, Standard Deviations, and Interpretive Boundaries for the Basic Interest Scales for the General Reference Sample (continued)

Theme	Basic Interest Scale	Gender	Mean	S.D.	Very Little Interest (0–10)	Little Interest (11–25)	Average Interest (26–75)	High Interest (76–90)	Very High Interest (91–100)
S	Teaching	Female	50.2	10.0	24–35	36–42	43–58	59–63	64–65
		Male	49.8	9.9	24–35	36–42	43–57	58–62	63–65
S	Social Service	Female	52.2	9.9	28–38	39–45	46–59	60–65	66–73
		Male	47.8	9.6	28–35	36–40	41–54	55–60	61–73
S	Medical Service	Female	50.6	10.5	32–37	38–42	43–57	58–64	65–80
		Male	48.9	9.7	32–36	37–41	42–55	56–62	63–80
S	Religious Activities	Female	50.1	9.9	36–37	38–41	42–57	58–65	66–70
		Male	49.8	10.2	36–36	37–41	42–57	58–65	66–70
E	Public Speaking	Female	48.7	9.8	32–36	37–41	42–55	56–62	63–73
		Male	51.2	10.0	32–37	38–43	44–58	59–65	66–73
E	Law/Politics	Female	48.3	9.8	31–35	36–40	41–55	56–62	63–72
		Male	51.7	9.8	31–38	39–43	44–59	60–65	66–72
E	Merchandising	Female	50.9	10.0	32–37	38–42	43–58	59–64	65–74
		Male	49.1	9.9	32–35	36–41	42–55	56–62	63–74
E	Sales	Female	49.2	9.4	38–38	39–42	43–54	55–63	64–87
		Male	50.8	10.5	38–38	39–42	43–57	58–65	66–87
E	Organizational Management	Female	49.4	9.9	28–36	37–42	43–57	58–62	63–73
		Male	50.6	10.1	28–36	37–42	43–58	59–64	65–73
C	Data Management	Female	49.2	10.1	32–36	37–40	41–56	57–63	64–75
		Male	50.8	9.9	32–37	38–42	43–58	59–64	65–75
C	Computer Activities	Female	49.9	10.4	34–35	36–40	41–56	57–63	64–71
		Male	50.1	9.7	34–35	36–41	42–56	57–64	65–71
C	Office Services	Female	51.8	10.8	36–39	40–43	44–58	59–67	68–82
		Male	48.2	8.8	36–38	39–41	42–53	54–61	62–82

Note: Sample consisted of 9,467 women and 9,484 men; numbers in parentheses are percentiles.

correlations were nonetheless sufficiently high to warrant the use of the BISs with young adults. However, with high school students especially, some score changes are likely over a three-year period.

Validity

There is no single index of validity for the BISs; instead, a variety of information has been drawn together to show that scores on these scales are reasonable and are related to the respondent's behavior.

Content Validity

The emphasis in constructing these scales was to pull together related items; hence, each scale is focused on one content area, and the items reflect this focus. For example, the Science scale contains items like "Astronomer," "Biologist," "Chemist," and "Working in a research laboratory." Obviously, these items have content validity; responses to them provide direct information about the person's feelings toward scientific activities. The same is true of the other scales.

Table 6.3 Intercorrelations Between the Basic Interest Scales for Women and Men (Decimal Points Omitted)

	AGR	NAT	MIL	ATH	MEC	SCI	MAT	MSC	MUS	ART	AAR	WRI	CUL	TEA	SSE	MSE	REL	PUB	LAW	MER	SAL	ORG	DAT	COM	OFF
Agriculture	—	67	18	31	38	27	06	27	03	10	22	01	08	04	08	27	05	−06	−06	−06	−01	−12	−06	05	−02
Nature	62	—	13	18	45	53	18	50	24	37	45	23	20	13	18	34	08	00	05	−03	−07	−10	−03	10	−04
Military Activities	19	12	—	27	30	16	12	20	03	−03	04	02	02	10	10	26	14	19	22	17	17	22	17	18	18
Athletics	29	11	24	—	21	06	10	22	05	−05	08	−07	15	19	21	28	05	21	21	25	22	25	14	09	09
Mechanical Activities	37	41	24	11	—	63	47	38	11	21	42	09	03	06	04	29	02	01	13	04	03	08	27	38	16
Science	13	45	12	00	61	—	61	63	20	26	44	25	01	13	02	34	04	00	14	−17	−20	−10	22	30	01
Mathematics	01	14	10	10	44	63	—	28	−03	−02	14	01	−02	06	−11	11	02	−02	13	−02	−03	11	64	47	28
Medical Science	21	50	19	21	36	60	29	—	23	22	32	17	15	20	23	68	08	12	20	03	−01	02	08	13	01
Music/Dramatics	−13	19	−01	−09	−01	19	−01	25	—	71	59	58	28	21	31	11	18	39	29	25	10	13	−11	−07	−15
Art	−05	32	−04	−16	11	26	−01	26	76	—	88	60	27	17	27	08	11	25	19	22	05	04	−14	−07	−17
Applied Arts	07	39	02	00	33	43	13	35	61	88	—	62	18	20	24	15	08	21	20	15	01	02	−05	05	−13
Writing	−14	18	01	−07	−03	25	06	22	65	65	66	—	16	28	34	02	19	46	42	20	05	18	−04	00	−08
Culinary Arts	06	30	07	09	09	11	02	26	40	39	32	28	—	23	34	22	16	23	16	35	23	27	06	03	10
Teaching	01	18	12	20	03	18	10	27	28	25	28	36	24	—	58	25	26	32	26	19	04	26	04	10	13
Social Service	06	25	14	22	04	09	−06	33	40	38	35	43	38	60	—	41	40	40	31	39	26	37	−01	07	18
Medical Service	24	41	25	22	35	40	16	70	23	21	27	14	34	33	50	—	21	25	05	11	10	09	05	24	26
Religious Activities	08	17	16	07	05	09	05	16	22	18	16	25	14	30	45	27	—	30	14	13	13	16	06	10	18
Public Speaking	−04	−05	25	26	−03	01	03	20	37	25	24	46	29	39	53	20	39	—	78	50	37	55	12	−03	00
Law/Politics	−03	06	27	29	08	12	15	26	26	17	20	41	22	32	43	17	21	79	—	43	30	54	29	05	04
Merchandising	04	07	24	28	11	−10	05	15	20	19	18	21	33	19	41	21	17	52	50	—	75	75	34	15	33
Sales	12	02	22	26	13	−16	02	25	03	00	01	02	19	01	26	14	13	38	35	78	—	63	27	12	31
Organizational Management	00	01	29	32	13	−04	16	14	11	05	07	17	26	26	41	18	18	58	61	81	66	—	55	27	45
Data Management	−03	00	18	22	23	23	62	15	−07	11	−02	03	07	09	07	12	04	22	37	45	34	60	—	53	64
Computer Activities	−01	14	16	04	43	45	53	25	07	08	17	09	13	15	13	31	13	09	14	21	12	27	50	—	69
Office Services	00	09	22	10	23	16	35	16	03	01	05	08	17	19	27	36	21	18	21	44	33	49	67	66	—

Note: Correlations above the diagonal are based on 9,467 women; those below are based on 9,484 men. The triangular color screens highlight correlations between BISs grouped within the same GOT. (Upper triangles show correlations for women; lower triangles, correlations for men.)

Table 6.4 Correlations Between the General Occupational Themes and the Basic Interest Scales for Women and Men (Decimal Points Omitted)

	General Occupational Theme and Gender											
	Realistic		Investigative		Artistic		Social		Enterprising		Conventional	
Basic Interest Scale	Female	Male	Female	Male	Female	Male	Female	Male	Female	Male	Female	Male
Agriculture	57	55	25	15	08	−09	10	13	−02	09	00	01
Nature	60	54	53	48	34	28	17	28	00	10	01	10
Military Activities	32	28	16	14	02	00	15	20	21	28	21	22
Athletics	26	17	12	07	02	−08	26	30	27	31	13	16
Mechanical Activities	95	96	58	54	18	05	06	10	08	16	29	32
Science	61	55	94	94	28	27	04	13	−12	−05	18	29
Mathematics	40	36	70	71	00	02	00	07	00	07	54	59
Medical Science	42	38	72	71	26	29	22	33	09	18	09	22
Music/Dramatics	15	−01	23	22	87	89	24	32	24	18	−13	01
Art	25	12	26	27	90	91	19	27	19	16	15	−01
Applied Arts	45	33	43	42	83	83	19	30	14	17	06	06
Writing	11	−03	25	27	80	84	25	34	20	18	−07	07
Culinary Arts	06	12	06	16	28	41	34	35	35	33	09	15
Teaching	06	03	16	22	25	33	78	78	22	21	12	19
Social Service	08	07	06	15	35	46	86	86	43	45	13	22
Medical Service	33	38	37	44	10	23	44	52	18	27	24	32
Religious Activities	03	07	05	12	18	24	56	61	16	19	15	19
Public Speaking	02	−01	07	10	42	41	38	52	52	54	04	21
Law/Politics	12	09	21	20	35	33	26	39	45	52	14	29
Merchandising	04	13	−09	00	27	24	35	38	95	95	33	44
Sales	03	16	−12	−07	09	03	25	25	84	86	29	34
Organizational Management	05	13	−03	05	14	13	38	42	79	82	50	55
Data Management	20	19	26	29	−11	−05	07	16	33	43	83	85
Computer Activities	32	36	27	41	−06	08	15	20	18	23	74	70
Office Services	12	20	00	17	−17	04	27	34	37	46	93	93

Note: Female correlations are based on 9,467 women; male correlations are based on 9,484 men.

Table 6.5 Test-Retest Reliability Statistics in Four Samples for the Basic Interest Scales

Basic Interest Scale	Test-Retest Correlation	Test Mean	Test S.D.	Retest Mean	Retest S.D.
Sample A: Employed Adults, 3–6 months (N = 110 women, 81 men)					
Agriculture	.82	49.7	9.9	49.7	9.8
Nature	.86	49.9	10.3	51.3	9.4
Military Activities	.87	50.1	10.4	50.7	10.8
Athletics	.94	48.8	10.4	49.3	10.3
Mechanical Activities	.92	49.5	10.7	50.7	11.0
Science	.92	50.5	10.4	51.5	10.5
Mathematics	.89	49.0	9.6	49.8	9.3
Medical Science	.84	50.8	10.0	52.3	9.9
Music/Dramatics	.87	50.7	10.7	51.2	10.7
Art	.91	49.9	10.1	50.9	10.0
Applied Arts	.86	49.5	10.3	50.5	10.4
Writing	.89	50.9	10.2	51.5	10.1
Culinary Arts	.80	50.8	9.3	51.2	9.1
Teaching	.80	49.3	10.1	48.9	10.3
Social Service	.84	51.2	9.9	51.2	9.8
Medical Service	.84	51.3	10.2	52.5	10.0
Religious Activities	.85	50.2	10.3	50.1	10.9
Public Speaking	.86	50.1	10.2	50.5	10.2
Law/Politics	.87	50.2	10.3	51.0	10.4
Merchandising	.84	50.4	9.7	50.5	9.8
Sales	.84	50.6	10.9	50.9	10.7
Organizational Management	.87	49.6	9.2	50.6	9.5
Data Management	.88	49.7	10.2	50.2	9.9
Computer Activities	.82	50.6	9.9	51.1	10.3
Office Services	.87	51.3	9.8	52.2	10.3
Sample B: College Students, 1 month (N = 54 women, 30 men)					
Agriculture	.81	45.8	9.0	45.5	9.1
Nature	.81	47.6	8.9	47.3	9.1
Military Activities	.89	48.4	10.0	48.0	9.4
Athletics	.93	52.5	9.9	52.6	9.7
Mechanical Activities	.88	44.0	9.2	44.9	9.9
Science	.88	47.8	9.3	48.3	9.8
Mathematics	.87	45.1	9.9	45.8	9.7
Medical Science	.85	52.1	10.3	52.3	10.7
Music/Dramatics	.86	52.2	9.8	52.8	10.0
Art	.86	52.1	10.1	52.2	10.3
Applied Arts	.85	49.8	10.5	50.0	10.8

Table 6.5 Test-Retest Reliability Statistics in Four Samples for the Basic Interest Scales (continued)

Basic Interest Scale	Test-Retest Correlation	Test		Retest	
		Mean	S.D.	Mean	S.D.

Sample B: College Students, 1 month (N = 54 women, 30 men) (continued)

Writing	.85	50.2	9.8	50.0	10.0
Culinary Arts	.83	53.4	9.3	53.1	9.4
Teaching	.83	54.0	9.5	53.4	10.1
Social Service	.86	59.1	9.2	58.9	9.6
Medical Service	.81	54.6	11.2	55.0	11.6
Religious Activities	.78	48.5	8.8	48.8	8.7
Public Speaking	.81	48.9	9.3	49.0	9.3
Law/Politics	.85	49.9	10.0	49.7	10.2
Merchandising	.86	51.7	9.8	52.1	10.5
Sales	.83	51.1	11.2	52.1	11.5
Organizational Management	.86	47.4	10.5	47.0	10.7
Data Management	.85	44.0	9.1	44.1	9.3
Computer Activities	.82	46.1	10.9	46.7	10.7
Office Services	.83	50.2	10.2	50.6	10.4

Sample C: College Students, 3 months (N = 56 women, 23 men)

Agriculture	.78	43.3	7.9	45.0	8.5
Nature	.81	40.1	10.0	42.4	11.4
Military Activities	.68	46.6	8.2	47.8	8.9
Athletics	.90	50.7	9.8	53.1	10.1
Mechanical Activities	.78	42.4	7.6	44.5	8.2
Science	.87	41.2	8.4	42.6	9.7
Mathematics	.78	43.4	7.9	43.6	8.8
Medical Science	.80	44.9	10.2	47.4	10.4
Music/Dramatics	.86	46.3	8.9	47.8	9.5
Art	.88	45.8	9.7	47.5	10.7
Applied Arts	.83	42.6	9.6	44.9	10.8
Writing	.87	42.7	9.6	43.5	9.6
Culinary Arts	.70	53.1	8.2	54.0	9.0
Teaching	.85	50.0	12.9	48.6	12.5
Social Service	.89	55.1	11.9	54.4	11.4
Medical Service	.79	49.2	10.2	50.4	11.5
Religious Activities	.91	50.4	10.1	49.7	10.9
Public Speaking	.86	46.7	9.3	49.6	9.8
Law/Politics	.89	46.5	10.4	48.9	11.1
Merchandising	.74	52.6	10.0	56.0	9.2
Sales	.79	54.1	10.7	57.0	11.2
Organizational Management	.79	49.0	10.3	51.4	10.0

Table 6.5 Test-Retest Reliability Statistics in Four Samples for the Basic Interest Scales (continued)

Basic Interest Scale	Test-Retest Correlation	Test		Retest	
		Mean	S.D.	Mean	S.D.
Sample C: College Students, 3 months (N = 56 women, 23 men) (continued)					
Data Management	.77	45.8	9.0	48.0	9.6
Computer Activities	.66	47.1	10.4	48.9	11.2
Office Services	.80	51.6	10.7	53.5	11.4
Sample D: College Students, 3 months (N = 61 women, 26 men)					
Agriculture	.77	42.8	7.8	43.0	8.4
Nature	.88	39.7	10.2	40.3	10.8
Military Activities	.73	47.5	8.1	47.7	8.2
Athletics	.90	54.0	10.3	54.4	9.6
Mechanical Activities	.82	44.2	8.9	43.9	8.8
Science	.85	41.8	9.7	41.7	10.1
Mathematics	.85	45.2	9.3	45.7	9.8
Medical Science	.85	45.6	11.6	45.6	11.6
Music/Dramatics	.88	51.6	10.1	52.1	10.0
Art	.85	49.2	10.5	50.2	10.2
Applied Arts	.79	47.6	10.8	48.5	10.7
Writing	.87	49.0	10.3	49.8	10.5
Culinary Arts	.79	52.7	9.5	52.3	9.2
Teaching	.86	50.9	11.7	51.4	12.3
Social Service	.76	53.7	10.2	55.9	10.5
Medical Service	.80	49.2	11.9	49.3	11.8
Religious Activities	.86	46.9	9.0	47.3	10.1
Public Speaking	.86	50.9	10.3	51.8	11.3
Law/Politics	.89	50.6	9.9	52.3	11.0
Merchandising	.75	54.6	9.8	55.3	10.0
Sales	.77	54.1	9.7	55.0	11.3
Organizational Management	.76	50.9	9.8	51.7	11.1
Data Management	.83	47.5	10.6	47.8	10.8
Computer Activities	.72	46.2	10.7	46.6	11.0
Office Services	.80	51.6	9.5	52.6	10.7

Concurrent Validity

Concurrent validity is the power of a psychological measure to discriminate between two groups whose behavior at the same point in time differs.

The concurrent validity of the BISs can be evaluated by comparing the scores of people who are currently in different occupations; if the scales are working as they should, such people should score high on scales relevant to their own occupations. Therefore, artists should score high on the Art scale; scientists, high on the Science scale; teachers, high on the Teaching scale. Further, people in unrelated occupations should score at only average levels or lower on scales not related to their occupations.

The validity of each BIS can be evaluated by ranking the means of the 109 occupational groups in the 1994 *Strong* on each scale. These results are shown in Figures 6.1 through 6.25 (pages 92–104). The figures show for each BIS the 15 highest-ranking and 15 lowest-ranking occupations for each scale. Seven of the 109 occupations have only a single gender, and for these occupations, the gender is identified on the figures. For the remaining occupations, a composite mean has been calculated by equally weighting the female and male means on each BIS. These are standardized scores from the combined General Reference Samples of women and men.

These figures give a succinct overview of the occupational differences on each BIS and speak to the concurrent and construct validity of each scale. The results suggest substantial validity for the BISs, with mean occupational scores often spread out over 2 to 2.5 standard deviations, or a range of 20 to 25 points. Counselors are encouraged to study these occupational rankings to expand their understanding of each BIS so they can better explain to clients the meaning of high and low scores.

Predictive Validity

Predictive validity can be viewed as the power of an inventory to discriminate statistically between two groups who will behave somewhat differently sometime in the future. The predictive validity of the Basic Interest Scales is not as good as their concurrent validity, since a long-range discrimination is harder to make than a concurrent one. Nevertheless, there is considerable agreement between the scores earned by people and their subsequent occupations. The domain measured by the scale is an arena where high scorers are likely to find satisfying employment. For example, young adults with high scores on the Science scale tend to end up in occupations of a generally scientific character. Similarly, those with high scores on the Sales scale are likely to end up in occupations with sales features. Studies documenting that conclusion are summarized in Campbell's *Handbook* (1971).

Most of the current *Strong* Basic Interest Scales are quite similar to the older *Strong* BISs; consequently, research findings based on earlier BISs can be generalized to the 1994 *Strong*. Hansen and Campbell (1985) and Campbell (1971) presented results that support the predictive validity of the Basic Interest Scales and their relative stability over changes in age. The four new Basic Interest Scales introduced in the 1994 *Strong*—Applied Arts, Culinary Arts, Data Management, and Computer Activities—are based on scale construction methods that are similar to those used with the original BISs and therefore also yield scales with high content validity and readily interpretable meaning. Thus, they can be expected to show useful predictive validity similar to the other Basic Interest Scales. High scorers on the Data Management scale, for example, can be expected to end up working in occupations with such activities. Future research will be conducted to confirm these kinds of expectations for the new BISs.

The more consistent the pattern of scores on different types of scales across the entire Profile, the more predictive the pattern is. Johnson and Johansson (1972) have shown that consistency between scores on the Basic Interest Scales and the Occupational Scales leads to greater predictive accuracy. A person with a high score on one of the Occupational Scales in the sales area—such as Realtor or Life Insurance Agent—and a score of "High Interest" or "Very High Interest" on the Sales Basic Interest Scale is more likely to enter sales work than is a person with an equally high score on these same Occupational Scales but a score of "Very Little Interest," "Little Interest," or "Average Interest" on the Sales Basic Interest Scale. Individuals with the latter pattern of scores are more likely to enter a people-oriented but nonsales occupation, such as public relations.

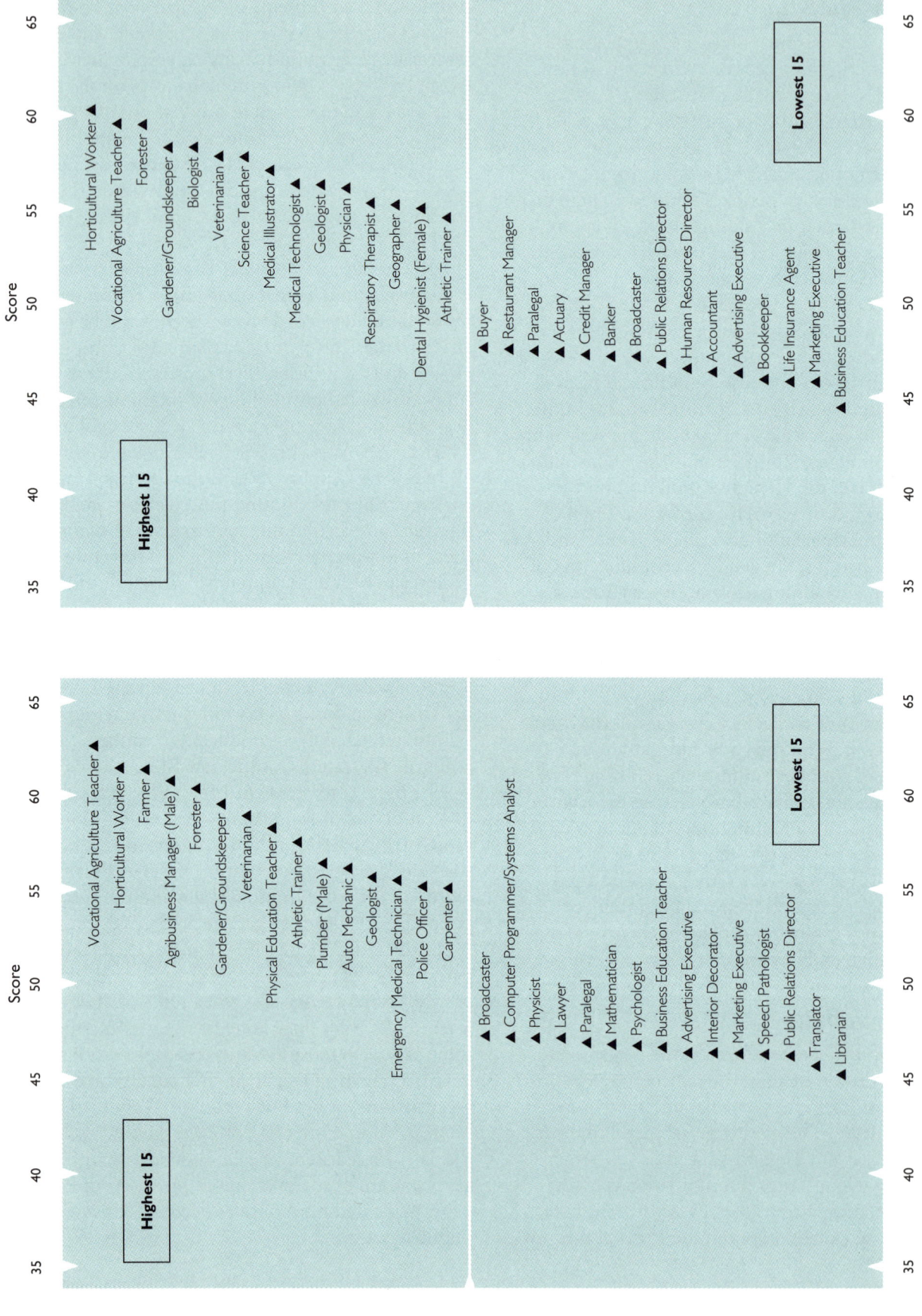

Figure 6.1 Rank-Ordered Occupations on the Agriculture BIS:
The 15 Highest and 15 Lowest Occupational Means of 109 Occupations

Figure 6.2 Rank-Ordered Occupations on the Nature BIS:
The 15 Highest and 15 Lowest Occupational Means of 109 Occupations

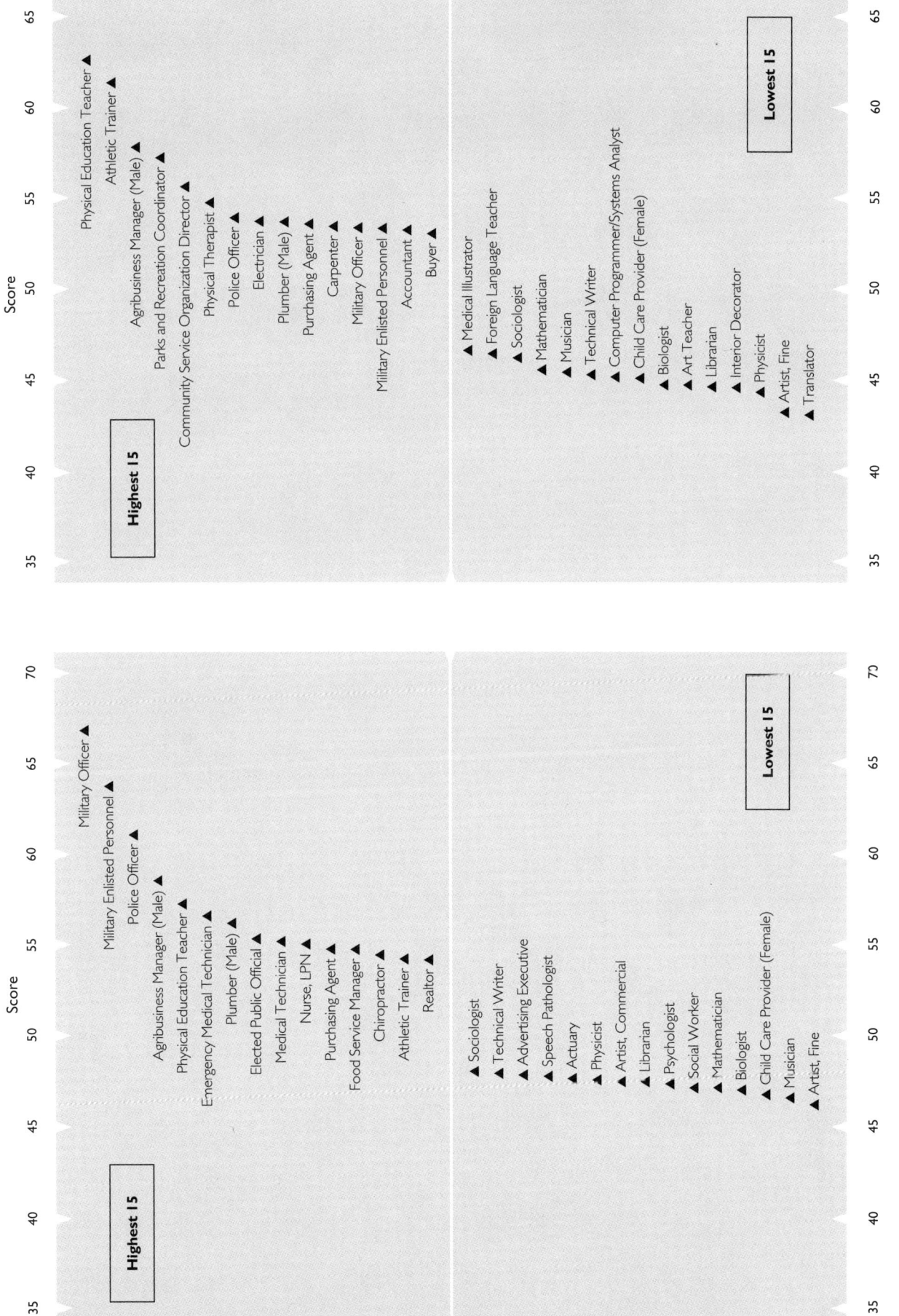

Figure 6.3 Rank-Ordered Occupations on the Military Activities BIS:
The 15 Highest and 15 Lowest Occupational Means of 109 Occupations

Figure 6.4 Rank-Ordered Occupations on the Athletics BIS:
The 15 Highest and 15 Lowest Occupational Means of 109 Occupations

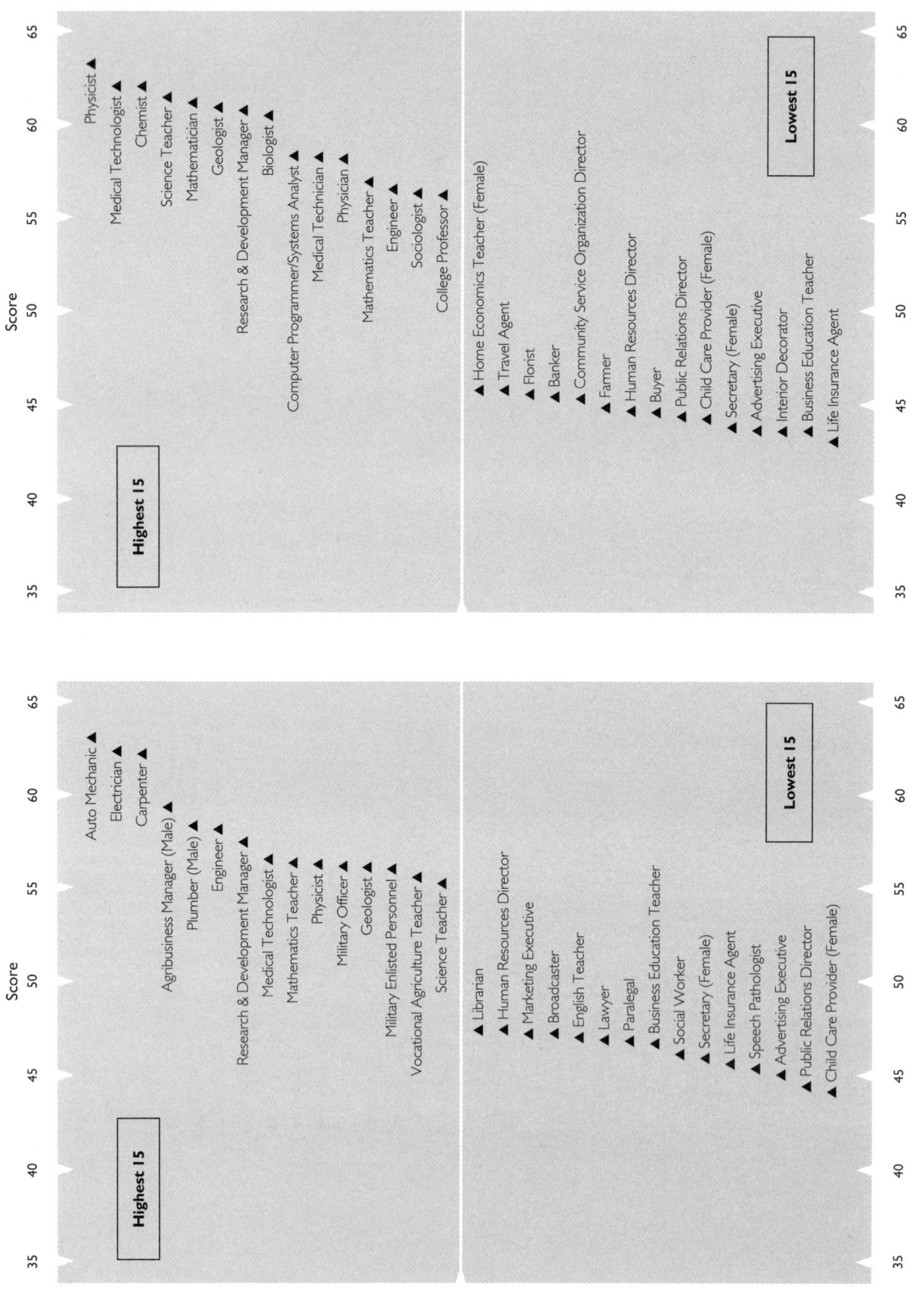

Figure 6.5 Rank-Ordered Occupations on the Mechanical Activities BIS: The 15 Highest and 15 Lowest Occupational Means of 109 Occupations

Figure 6.6 Rank-Ordered Occupations on the Science BIS: The 15 Highest and 15 Lowest Occupational Means of 109 Occupations

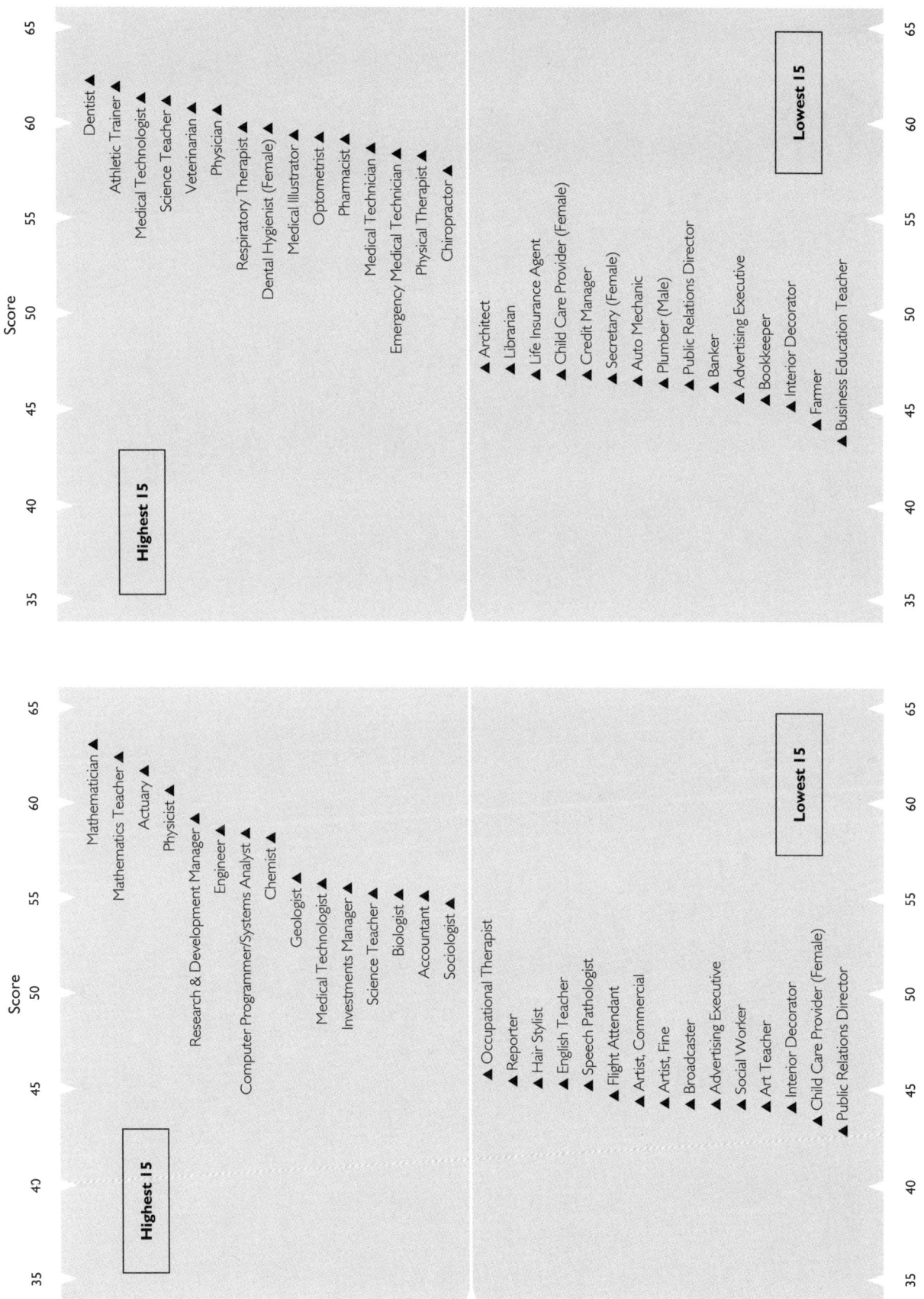

Figure 6.7 Rank-Ordered Occupations on the Mathematics BIS: The 15 Highest and 15 Lowest Occupational Means of 109 Occupations

Figure 6.8 Rank-Ordered Occupations on the Medical Science BIS: The 15 Highest and 15 Lowest Occupational Means of 109 Occupations

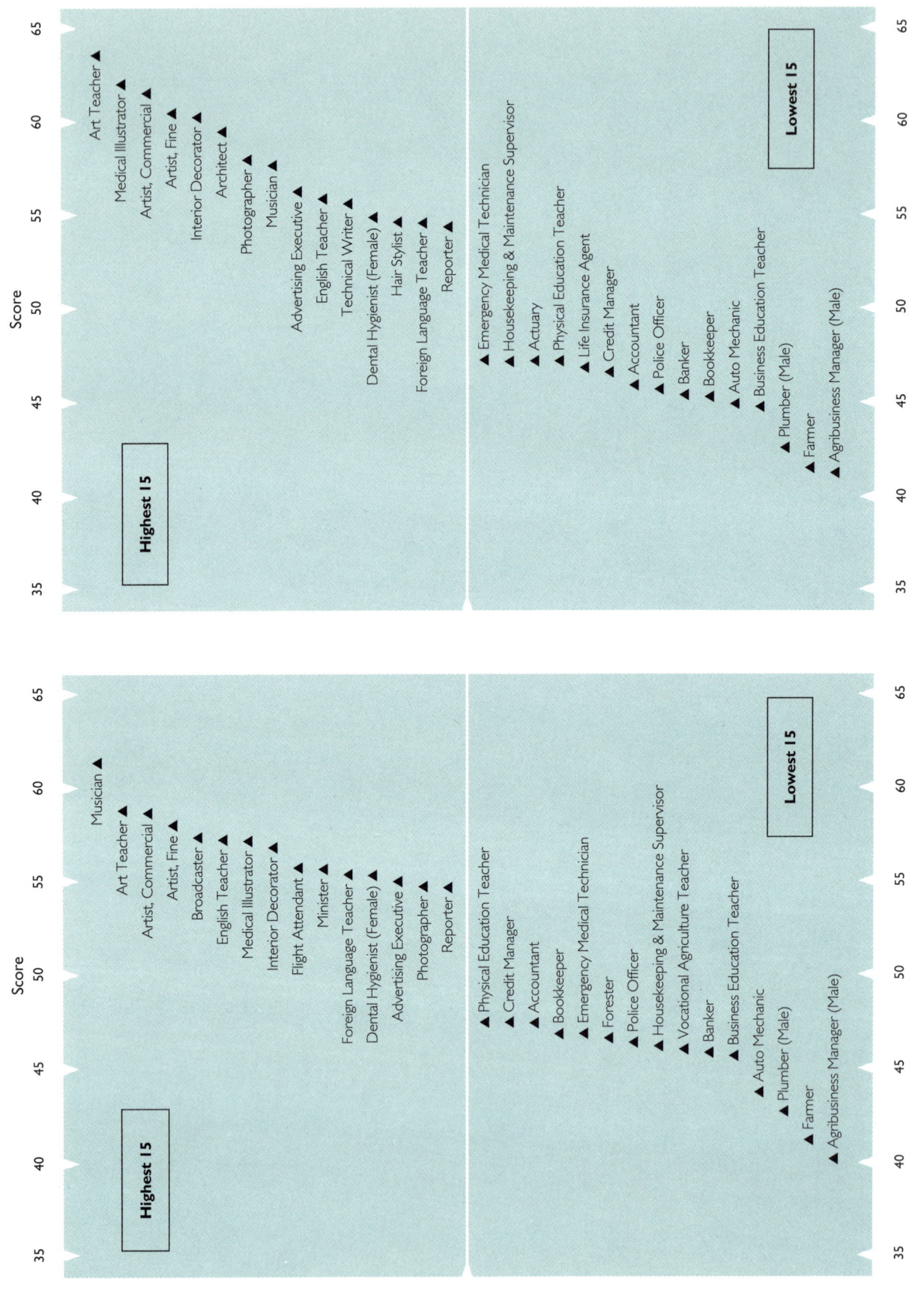

Figure 6.9 Rank-Ordered Occupations on the Music/Dramatics BIS: The 15 Highest and 15 Lowest Occupational Means of 109 Occupations

Figure 6.10 Rank-Ordered Occupations on the Art BIS: The 15 Highest and 15 Lowest Occupational Means of 109 Occupations

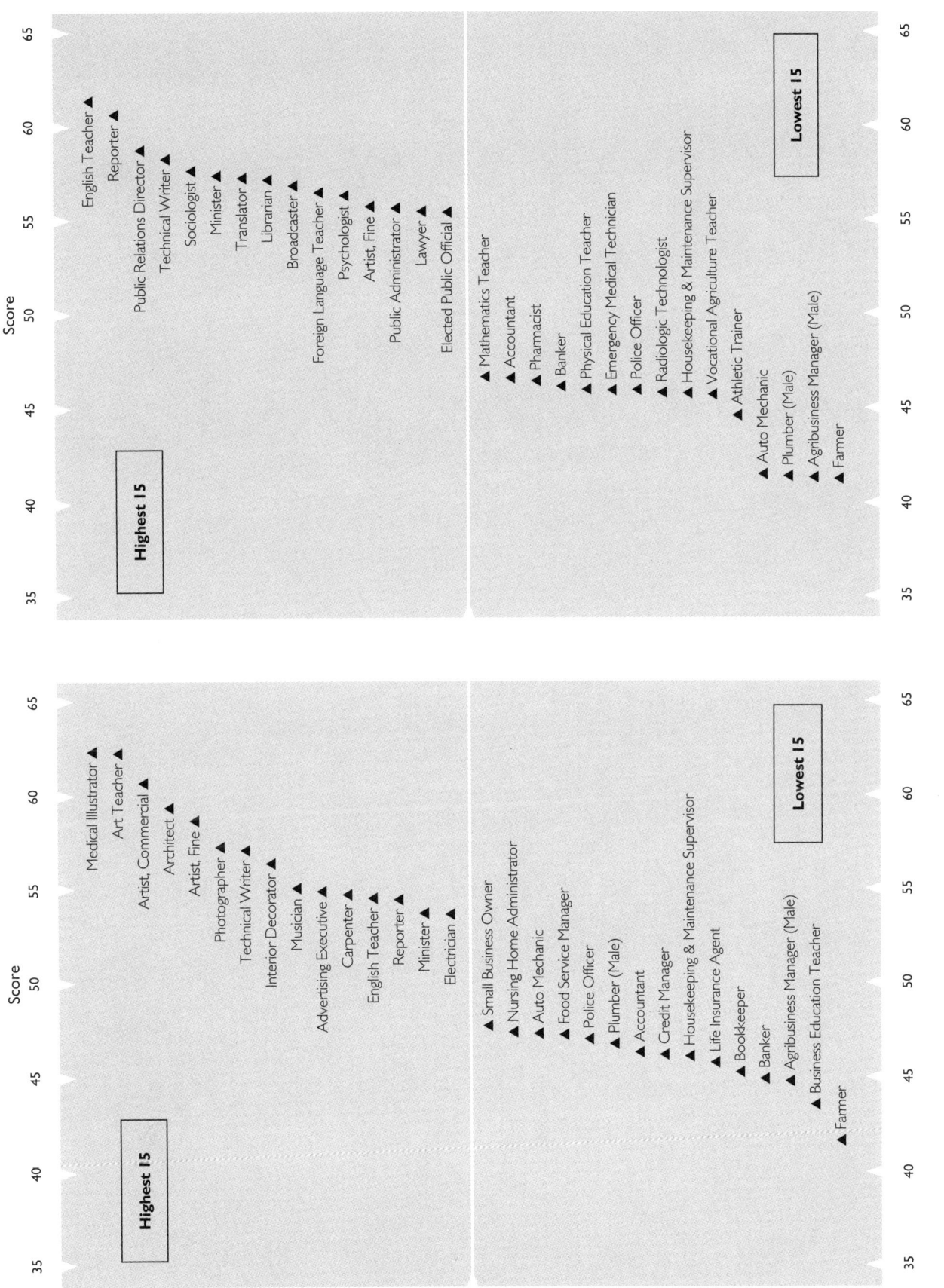

Figure 6.11 Rank-Ordered Occupations on the Applied Arts BIS:
The 15 Highest and 15 Lowest Occupational Means of 109 Occupations

Figure 6.12 Rank-Ordered Occupations on the Writing BIS:
The 15 Highest and 15 Lowest Occupational Means of 109 Occupations

97

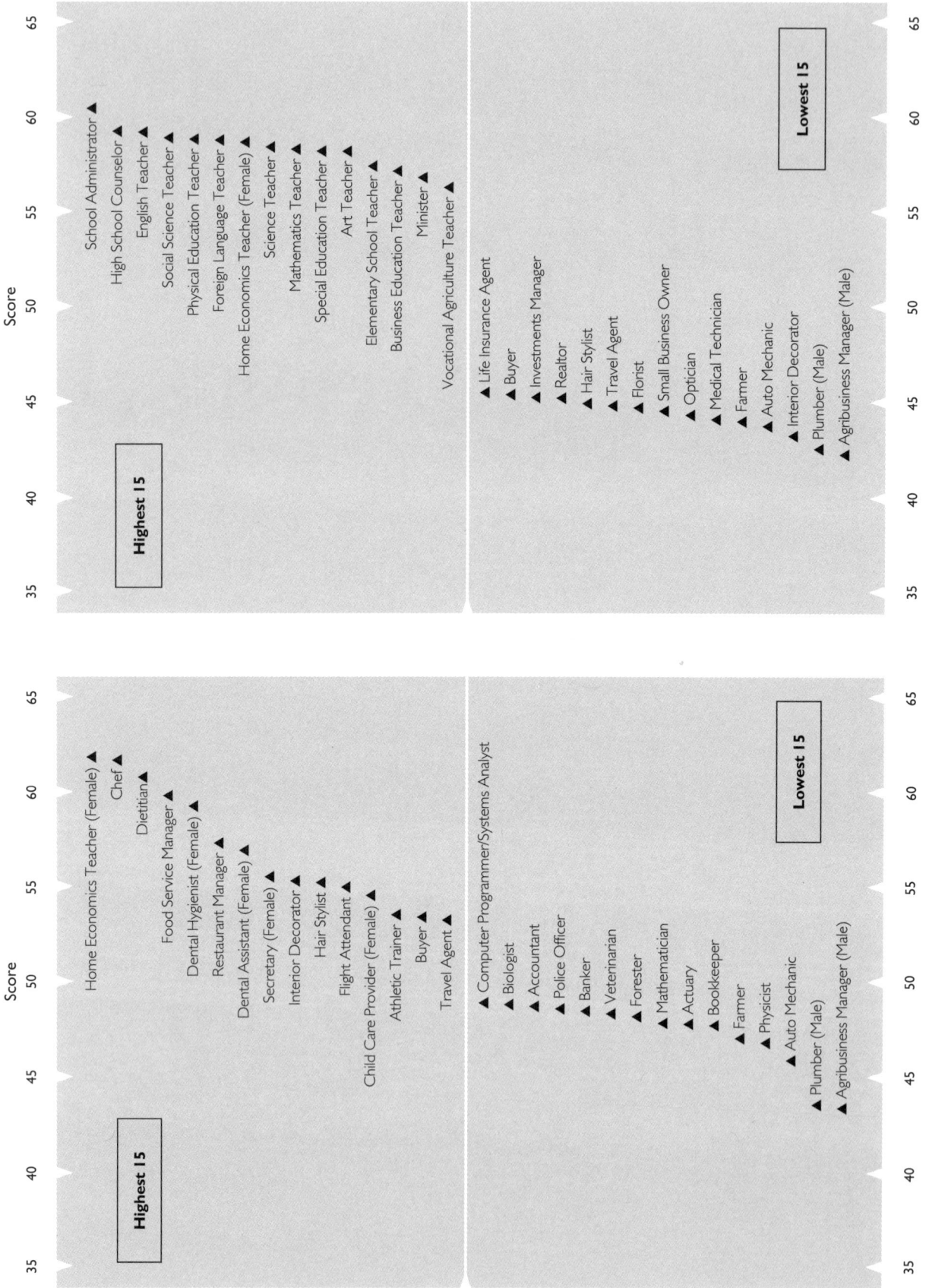

Figure 6.13 Rank-Ordered Occupations on the Culinary Arts BIS: The 15 Highest and 15 Lowest Occupational Means of 109 Occupations

Figure 6.14 Rank-Ordered Occupations on the Teaching BIS: The 15 Highest and 15 Lowest Occupational Means of 109 Occupations

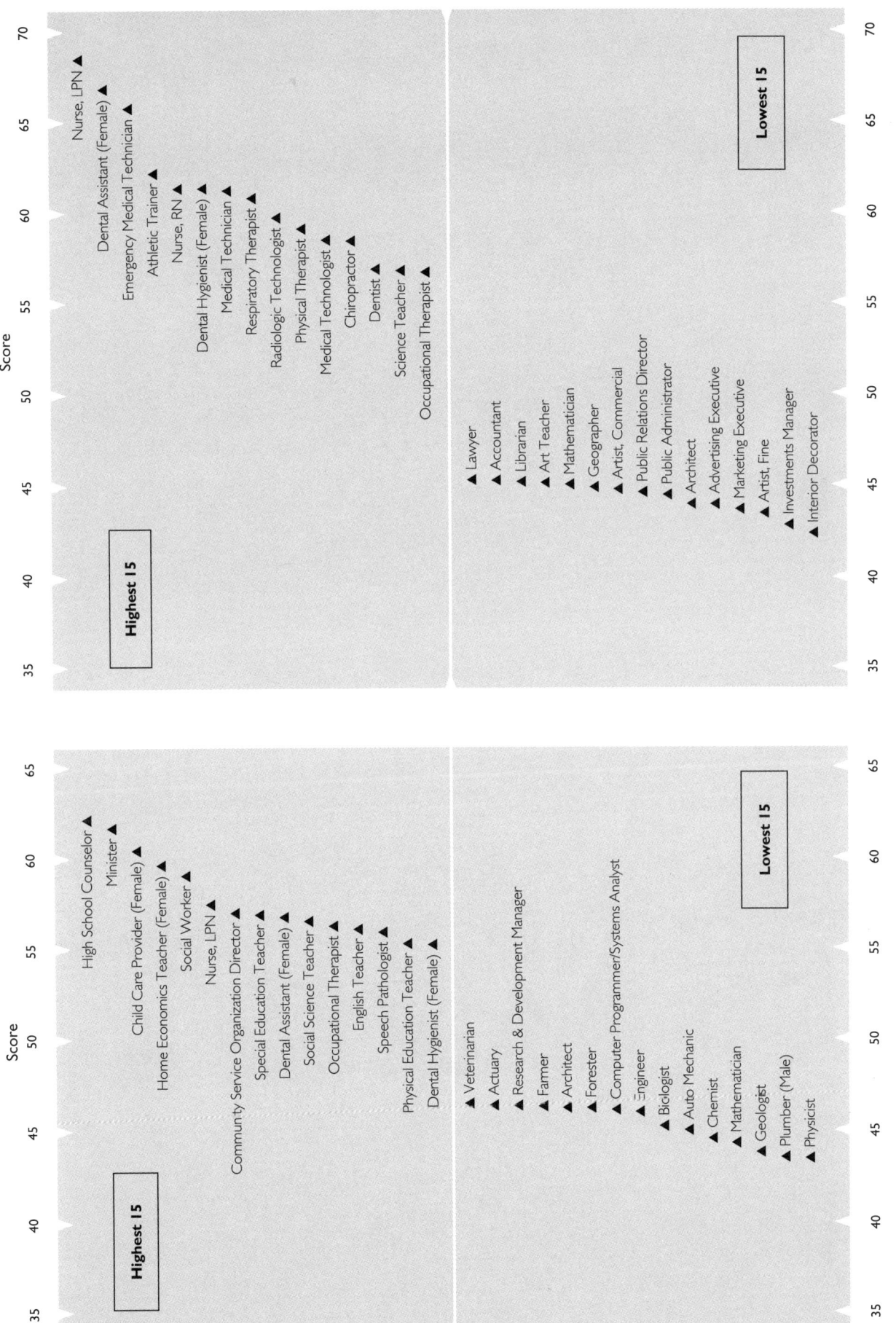

Figure 6.15 Rank-Ordered Occupations on the Social Service BIS: The 15 Highest and 15 Lowest Occupational Means of 109 Occupations

Figure 6.16 Rank-Ordered Occupations on the Medical Service BIS: The 15 Highest and 15 Lowest Occupational Means of 109 Occupations

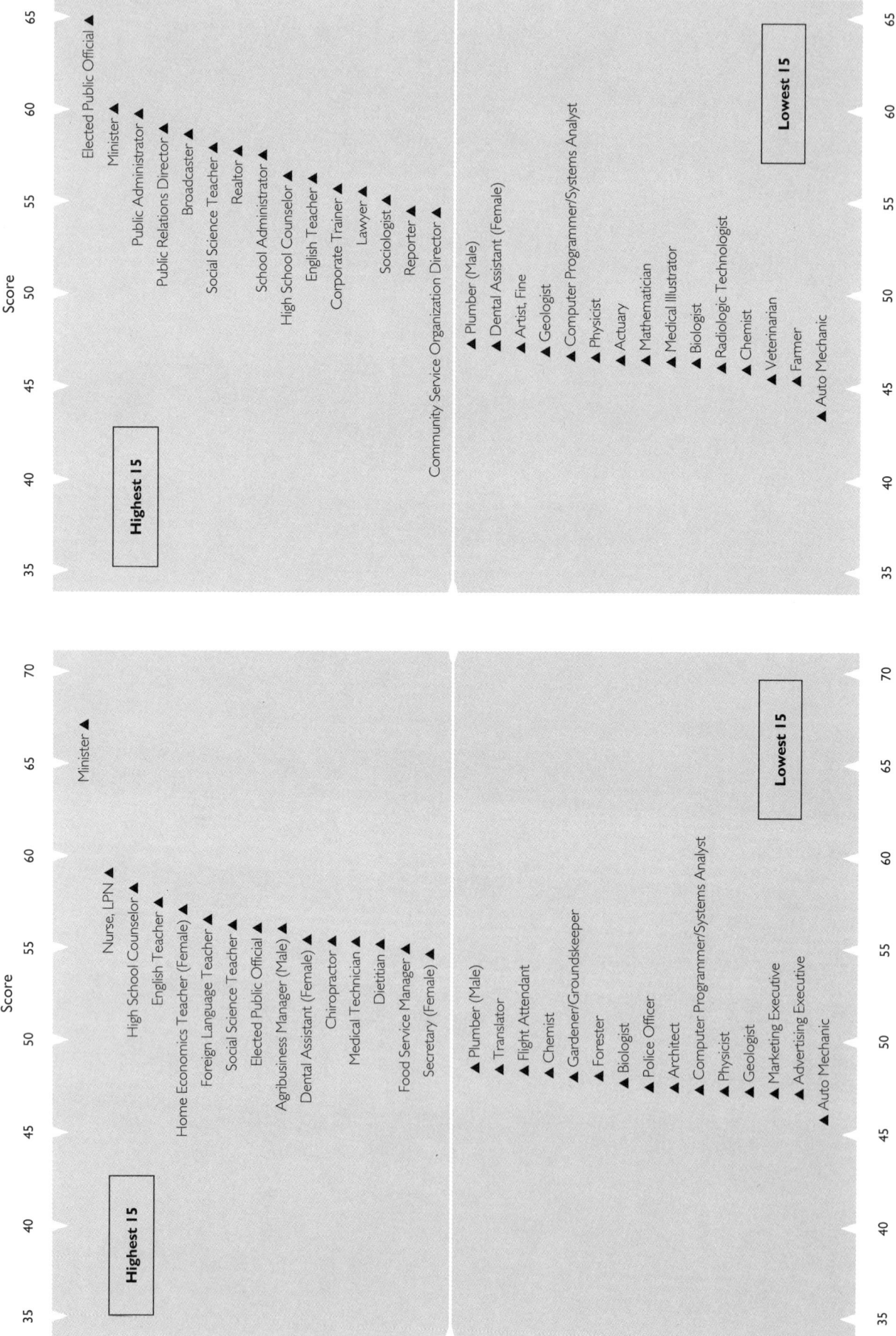

Figure 6.17 Rank-Ordered Occupations on the Religious Activities BIS:
The 15 Highest and 15 Lowest Occupational Means of 109 Occupations

Figure 6.18 Rank-Ordered Occupations on the Public Speaking BIS:
The 15 Highest and 15 Lowest Occupational Means of 109 Occupations

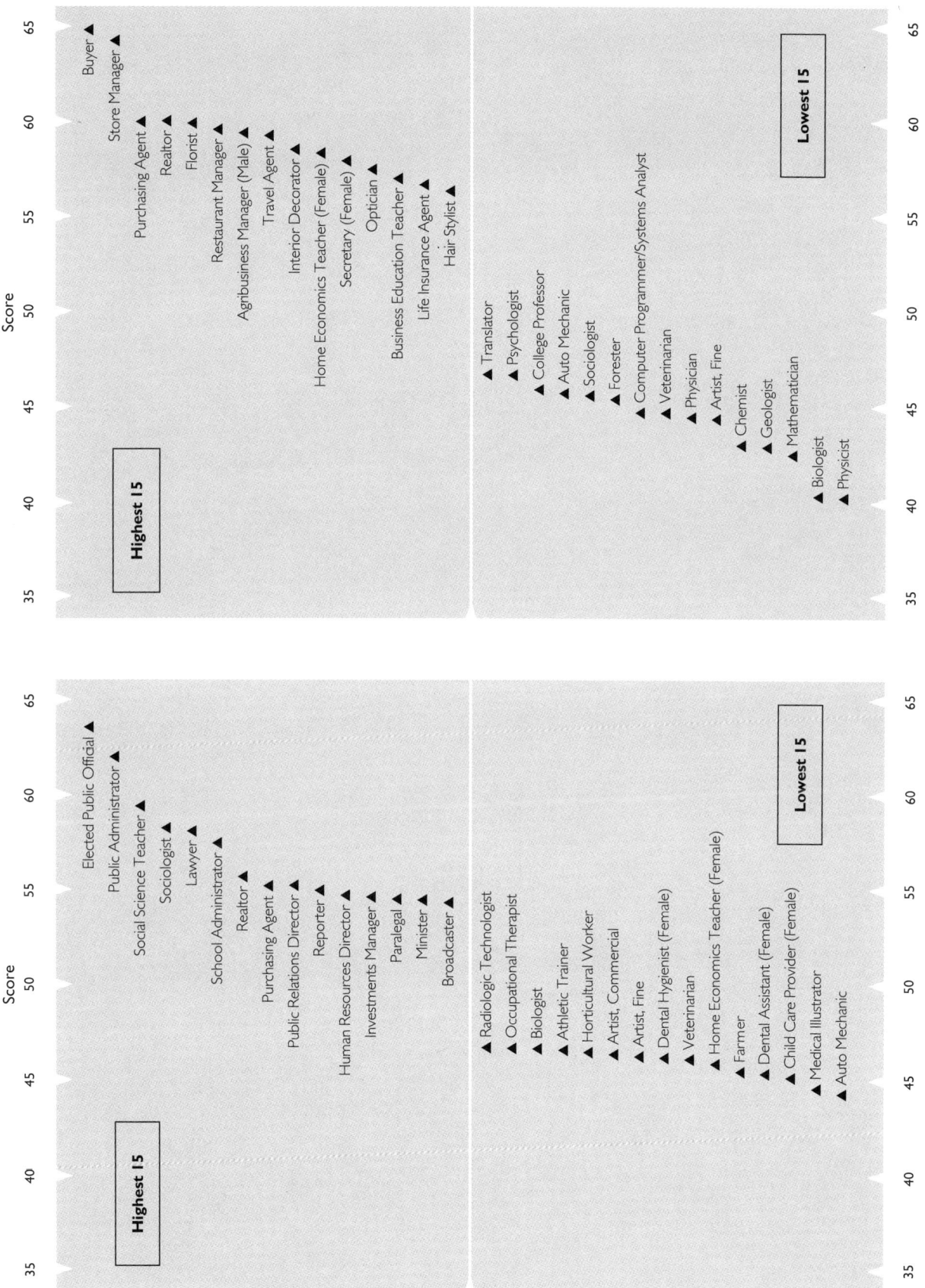

Figure 6.19 Rank-Ordered Occupations on the Law/Politics BIS: The 15 Highest and 15 Lowest Occupational Means of 109 Occupations

Figure 6.20 Rank-Ordered Occupations on the Merchandising BIS: The 15 Highest and 15 Lowest Occupational Means of 109 Occupations

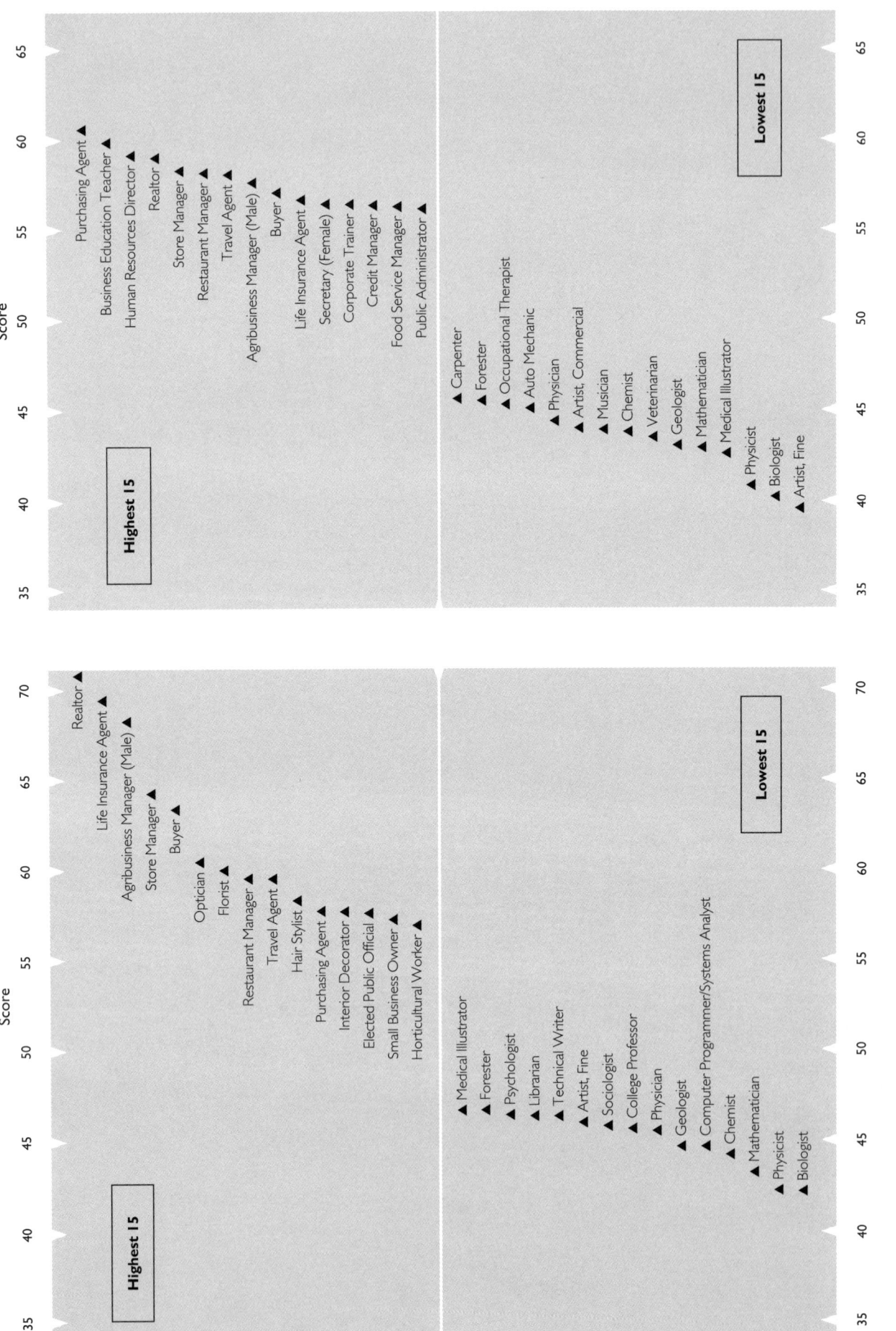

Figure 6.21 Rank-Ordered Occupations on the Sales BIS:
The 15 Highest and 15 Lowest Occupational Means of 109 Occupations

Figure 6.22 Rank-Ordered Occupations on the Organizational Management BIS: The 15 Highest and 15 Lowest Occupational Means of 109 Occupations

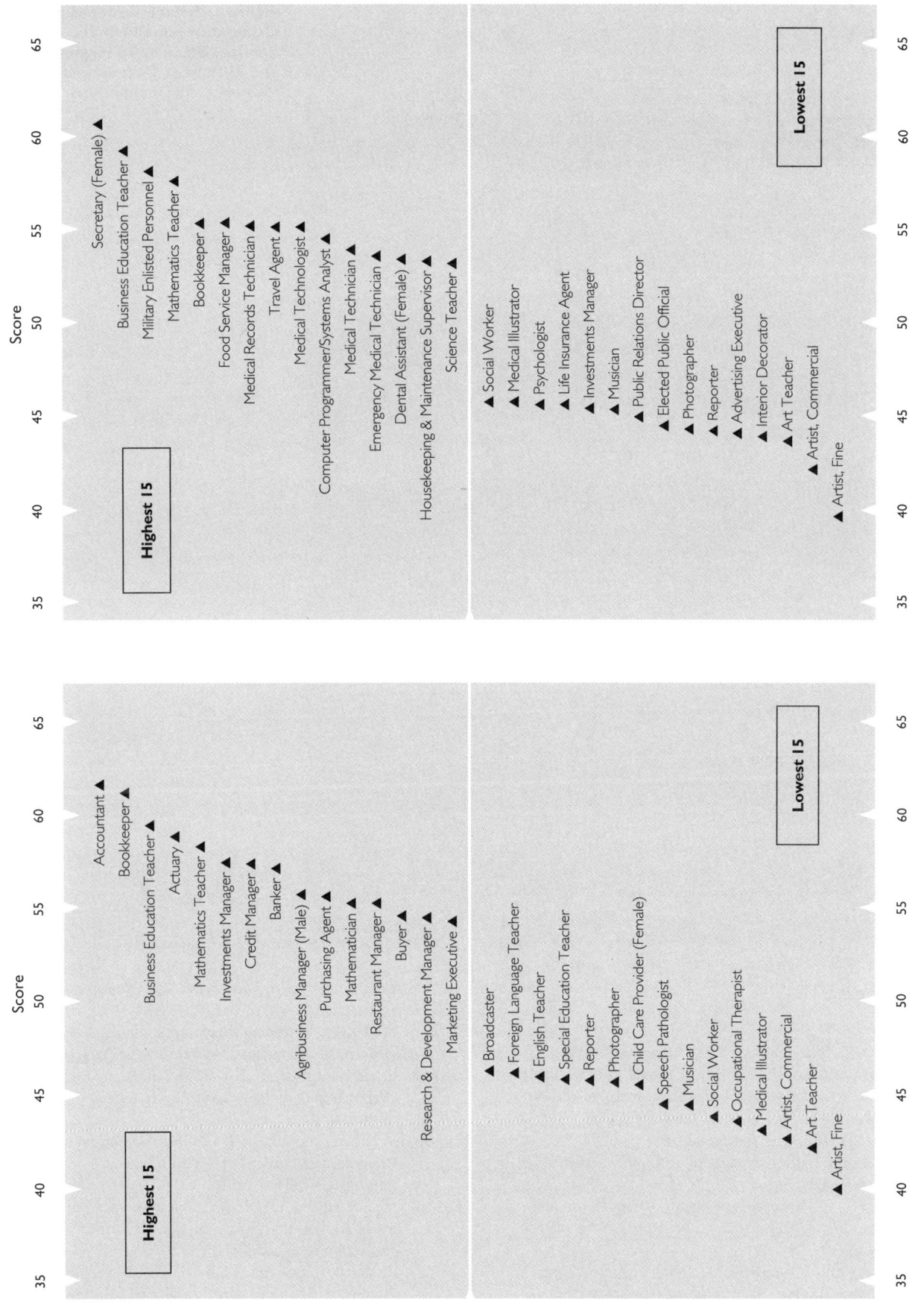

Figure 6.23 Rank-Ordered Occupations on the Data Management BIS: The 15 Highest and 15 Lowest Occupational Means of 109 Occupations

Figure 6.24 Rank-Ordered Occupations on the Computer Activities BIS: The 15 Highest and 15 Lowest Occupational Means of 109 Occupations

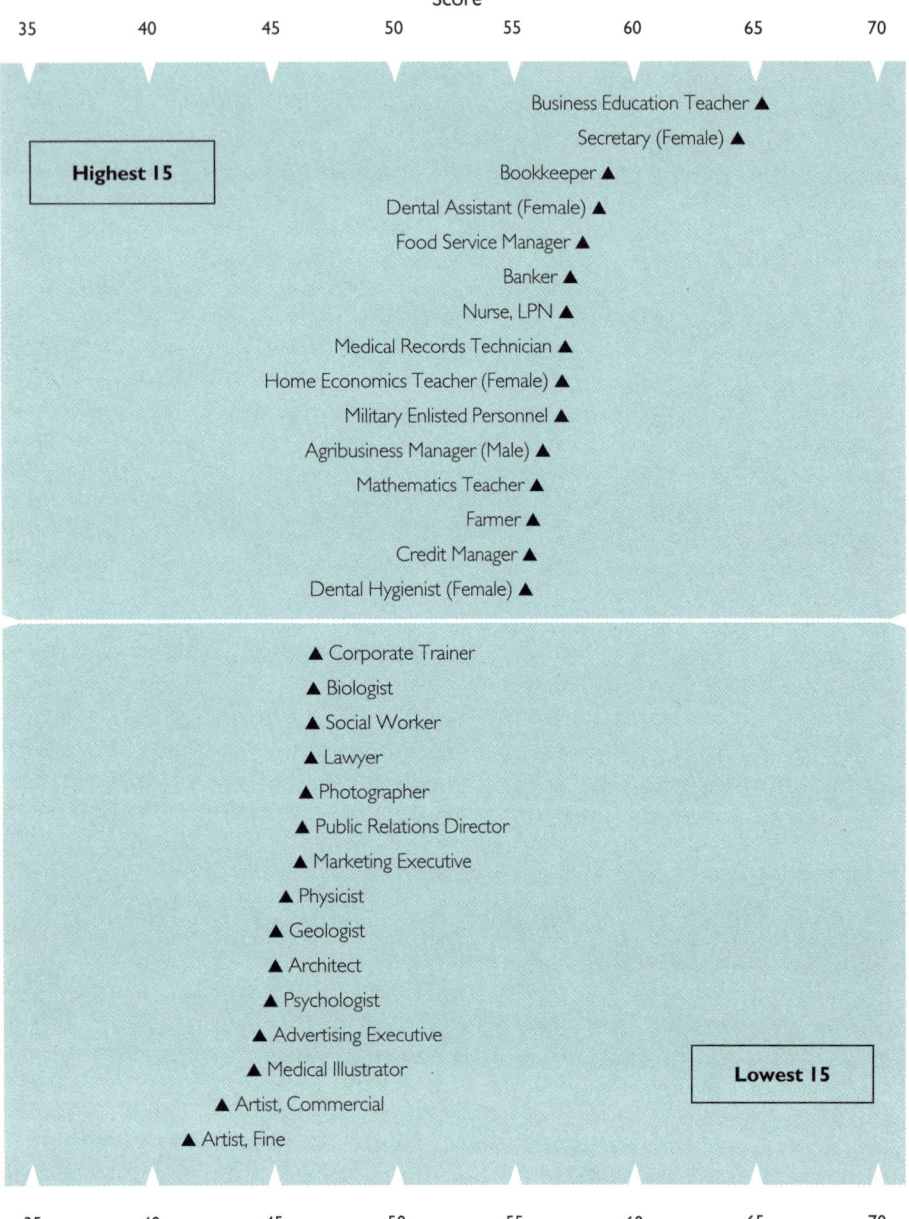

Figure 6.25 Rank-Ordered Occupations on the Office Services BIS: The 15 Highest and 15 Lowest Occupational Means of 109 Occupations

References

Cairo, P. C. (1979). The validity of the Holland and Basic Interest Scales of the Strong Vocational Interest Blank: Leisure activities versus occupational membership as criteria. *Journal of Vocational Behavior, 15,* 68–77.

Campbell, D. P. (1969). The vocational interests of Dartmouth College freshmen: 1947–67. *Personnel and Guidance Journal, 47,* 527–530.

Campbell, D. P. (1971). *Handbook for the Strong Vocational Interest Blank.* Stanford, CA: Stanford University Press.

Campbell, D. P. (1974). *Manual for the Strong-Campbell Interest Inventory.* Stanford, CA: Stanford University Press.

Campbell, D. P., Borgen, F. H., Eastes, S., Johansson, C. B., & Peterson, R. A. (1968). A set of Basic Interest Scales for the Strong Vocational Interest Blank for men. *Journal of Applied Psychology Monographs, 52* (6, Part 2).

Clark, K. E. (1961). *Vocational interests of nonprofessional men.* Minneapolis: University of Minnesota Press.

Clark, K. E., & Campbell, D. P. (1965). *Minnesota Vocational Interest Inventory.* New York: Psychological Corporation.

Hansen, J. C., & Campbell, D. P. (1985). *Manual for the Strong Interest Inventory* (4th ed.). Stanford, CA: Stanford University Press.

Hansen, J. C., & Stocco, J. (1980). Stability of vocational interests of adolescents and young adults. *Measurement and Evaluation in Guidance, 13,* 173–178.

Johnson, R. W., & Johansson, C. B. (1972). Moderating effect of basic interests on predictive validity of SVIB occupational scales. *Proceedings, 80th Annual Convention, American Psychological Association,* pp. 589–590.

CHAPTER 7

The Occupational Scales

The Occupational Scales (OSs) were the original scales developed by E. K. Strong. They have proven very effective over the years because they provide information about how an individual's responses compare with those of people actually employed in and satisfied with a particular occupation. For each revision of the *Strong Interest Inventory,* some OSs were dropped from the Profile, while others were added to it. The 1994 *Strong* contains 211 OSs—102 pairs with separate scales for men and women and 7 scales for occupations represented by only a single gender. This chapter begins with a description of how the scales are used; later sections explain how the scales for the 1994 *Strong* were developed. ◆

Using the Occupational Scales

The OSs are highly specific. The results of each of the 211 scales answer the basic question: "Does the respondent have likes and dislikes similar to men or women in this occupation?" Thus, the OSs enable a respondent to compare his or her interests with those of people from a diverse representation of occupations, including accountants, commercial artists, carpenters, engineers, psychologists, and small business owners, to name just a few. These scales generate a large amount of specific information about and for each respondent. To make the best use of these data, counselors need to know when it is appropriate to introduce information provided by the OSs and how to present that information so that it is most useful. To accomplish these tasks, the counselor must also be familiar with how these scales were developed.

The closer a client is to making a specific occupational choice, the more helpful the OSs will be. Even in these cases, it will still prove useful to discuss scores for the OSs in the context of the broader General Occupational Themes (GOTs) and Basic Interest Scales (BISs). For young people, or even some adults, who are involved in a general exploration of the world of work, it is usually most useful to turn first to the GOTs and the BISs before moving to an interpretation of the OSs. Scores on the GOTs and BISs provide a framework for the exploration of a wide range of occupations and for subsequently narrowing the focus of exploration and making specific decisions. This approach allows the client to leave open as many options as possible for as long as possible. Once the client is ready to take a more focused approach, information provided by the OSs can be introduced.

If the client is facing an imminent, occupationally relevant educational decision, an entry-level occupational choice, or a decision about career change or adjustment beyond the entry level, the OSs provide the most specific and detailed information. Decisions that represent a clear choice point between very different career paths should be examined especially carefully. For example, deciding to major in English may rule out, at least for the time being, a career as a chemist but will not rule out a career as an editor, author, journalist, or any number of occupations for which verbal or language skills are useful. Or, as another example, the decision to enroll in engineering may open up many opportunities in various engineering-related fields but will make a transition to occupations in the social sciences or the arts difficult. The client's pattern of results on the OSs will often be of great help in making such decisions because they provide the means of making specific comparisons between the client's interests and the interests of, for instance, English teachers and engineers.

Summary of Interpretation Procedures

A brief summary of the procedures for interpreting the OSs is presented here. A more detailed series of steps is found in Chapter 10 of this guide. Specific examples of how the OSs can be used with clients from specific populations are also found in the other applications chapters (12 through 17). The general method is to explore with the client each occupation for which a score of "Similar" interest (i.e., 40 or above) is obtained. One effective approach is to first look at those OSs that are related to the individual's highest GOT and BIS scores. This method is facilitated by the fact that the OSs are grouped together by Theme on the Profile so that their relationships to the GOTs are highlighted. Identifying high scores on a set of OSs that also correspond to a high score on the GOT to which those OSs are related provides a clear focus for the client's exploration. For example, if most of the occupations on which the client has scored "Similar" or above fall within the Investigative Theme or have *I* as part of their code, then both the client's general and specific interest patterns converge on this Theme. Additional scores of "High Interest" or "Very High Interest" on the BISs within the I Theme would provide additional confirmation of the importance of this Theme for the client.

Keep in mind, however, that a client's high scores on the OSs will not *necessarily* be related to the client's highest GOT scores. For example, a client's results on the OSs may indicate a similarity of interests to those of Accountant or Banker, both of which are coded as CE, reflecting Conventional and Enterprising interests. This same client, however, may demonstrate a high interest in the Artistic GOT and in some of the BISs within the Artistic Theme.

This apparent inconsistency is actually a valuable source of information. A number of reasons this pattern may occur and suggestions for interpreting it are found in Chapter 11. Nonetheless, two reasons are worth discussing here because they help elucidate the meanings of the OSs and the codes assigned to them. One reason is that for a few occupations, the Theme codes assigned to the OSs are somewhat arbitrary. Members of some occupational groups have one GOT on which they score much higher than the other scales, and most people in the occupation have that Theme as their highest GOT score. According to Holland, people for whom one Theme clearly predominates are said to have differentiated codes. For other occupational groups, however, the coding is less clear. For these occupational groups, their mean scores on two or three of the GOTs may be quite similar, and the frequencies of people in that occupation with different high-point codes will also be similar. (The Theme scores for occupational groups will be discussed in greater detail in this chapter in the section "Classifying Occupational Scales by GOT Code.") A client's high score on the female Emergency Medical Technician OS, coded RCI, may not necessarily be inconsistent with her "High Interest" in the Investigative GOT. Twenty-two percent of female Emergency Medical Technicians in the occupational criterion groups have Realistic as their highest GOT, but 21 percent have Investigative as their highest GOT.

A second reason that OS scores are sometimes unrelated to scores on the GOTs or BISs is the composition of the OSs. The OSs make greater use of "Dislike" responses than do the other kinds of scales. Also, since they were not developed to be conceptually consistent, the OSs have more heterogeneous item content than the other scales. Therefore, it may be productive to discuss each high OS score in terms of the client's perception of those aspects of the occupation that fit that individual's interests and those that do not.

For example, the female OS for Occupational Therapist (SAR) contains positively scored items that tap interests in social services and medical services (reflected by the S in the code), in artistic activities (A), and in working with one's hands (R). A respondent could score relatively high on the Occupational Therapist scale by answering "Like" to a few items in each of these areas while not liking enough of the items in any one area to obtain a high score on the Social, Artistic, or Realistic GOTs or BISs. The female Occupational Therapist scale also contains negatively scored items that indicate a dislike for business-related occupations and activities as well as activities involving the use of numbers. Thus, a client could also obtain a relatively high score on this scale by responding "Dislike" to these items, which would have very little effect on any high scores that might be obtained on the S, A, or R GOTs or BISs. When counseling a woman with a score of "Similar" interest on the Occupational Therapist scale, therefore, it might be helpful to explore her perceptions of the job, noting that employed occupational therapists have different types of likes and dislikes. This discussion could lead the client to a more differentiated view of the occupation as well as to a greater understanding of how her likes and dislikes are related to those of people in the occupation.

When interpreting the OSs, it is also important to remember that the same numerical scores have somewhat different meanings on the OSs than they do on the GOTs and BISs. For example, whereas 50 is the average standard score for the combined General Reference Samples (GRSs) for the GOTs and BISs, a score of 50 on the OSs is the average score for individuals employed in a given occupation. On the GOTs and BISs, a score of 50 is not remarkable; on the OSs, a score of 50 should command attention. As stated earlier, scores above 40 show that the client has some degree of similarity to people employed in the occupation and are thus worth noting. (A score of 40 would not indicate high interest on a GOT or BIS.)

Since the interests of males and females are somewhat different (see Chapter 17), separate OSs have been constructed for most occupations. Each individual is scored on both of the scales. and these scores are reported on the Profile. However, the scores plotted graphically will be those corresponding to the individual's gender, as it is these scores that are the most meaningful for interpretation. Nonetheless, a discussion of the differences between a client's scores on female and male scales may be instructive once the counselor understands the basis for those differences.

The Development of the Occupational Scales

The basic procedure used to develop an OS, devised by E. K. Strong, is to compare the responses of the members of an occupation to those of a general group of employed individuals to determine which items differentiate between the two groups. For example, most people in a particular occupational group may say "Like" to the item "Taking responsibility." If most employed people, however, also say "Like" to this item, then the results do not reveal much about what makes that occupation, and those employed in it, unique. (In fact, this item was deleted from the 1994 *Strong* because so many people endorsed it that it did not differentiate any occupation from the GRS.)

If, in contrast, most people in a particular occupation say "Like" to the item "Calculus," while most people in the general sample say "Dislike," then the results differentiate them from the larger group. (It should come as no surprise to learn that this item is on the Mathematician scale.) Thus, to develop an OS, three elements are necessary: a set of items to which individuals can respond to define their interests, item responses from a group of people employed in the occupation for which the scale is to be built, and item responses from a more diverse group of people employed in many occupations to be used as a comparison group.

Specifically, to develop or revise an OS for the *Strong*, eight steps were taken. Note that here these steps are presented sequentially for the purposes of exposition; however, there was more overlap among steps than this sequence implies. The steps are as follows:

1. Select the items for possible inclusion on the inventory.
2. Identify which occupational groups were targeted for possible inclusion on the *Strong*.
3. Administer the items to members of targeted occupational groups; some of these represent new occupations on the *Strong;* others represent a resampling and updating of occupations already appearing on the *Strong*.
4. Screen the occupational groups so that only those respondents who most typify the occupations are retained.
5. Form a more general group against which the specific occupational groups can be compared.
6. Compute the percentage of each occupational group giving each of the response options for each item as well as the response percentages for the general comparison group.
7. Determine a minimum percentage difference in item response between the occupational and

general comparison groups in order to select all items that produce the minimum—or greater—difference between the two groups, and assign scoring weights.

8. Score the occupational groups on the scale created by the differentiating items and then norm the scale by using the mean and standard deviation of each occupational group to establish standard scores for that OS.

The following sections present a detailed discussion about each of the steps just identified.

Step 1: Select Items

The first step in developing the OSs involved determining which items would be administered to the targeted occupational groups (both new and resampled). Since it was not possible to predict which items would differentiate any given occupation from the general group, knowledge of how past items performed with past occupational groups and general groups was used to guide item selection.

Thus, the initial item pool comprised the 325 items on the 1985 *Strong*. Added to this pool were a number of items that represented more contemporary occupations; others represented rewordings of items already in the pool. (See Chapter 2 for a more detailed description of item changes and Chapter 4 for a discussion of item technology.) In general, new items were added that appeared likely to differentiate the new occupations targeted for inclusion on the 1994 *Strong* or to improve the differentiation of occupations being resampled. For example, a number of new items that represented computer-related occupations and activities were added. Given the purposes and uses of the inventory, two important features of the item pool were that it continue to cover a broad range of occupations, school subjects, work activities, and leisure activities and that it elicit both "Like" and "Dislike" responses. The original and added items comprised the research version of the *Strong*.

Step 2: Target Specific Occupational Groups for Sampling

New occupations were targeted for possible inclusion on the 1994 *Strong*. Occupations were chosen primarily for two reasons: because the demand for more workers was predicted to be high in the near future, and to provide a broad range of occupational fields, both nonprofessional and professional. For example, one of the largest growing segments of the economy has been and continues to be the health care industry. Therefore, the occupations Medical Records Technician and Audiologist were added. Additional nonprofessional occupations, (e.g., Plumber and Child Care Provider) as well as professional occupations (e.g., Actuary, Paralegal, and Technical Writer) were also included in the sampling plans.

Ninety-three percent of the occupations represented by the OSs on the 1994 *Strong* can be found in *The Enhanced Guide for Occupational Exploration* (Maze & Mayall, 1991), which describes the 2,500 most important jobs in the United States. The few occupations represented by the OSs that are not listed in the guide or do not at least have similar titles to jobs that are listed have general names (e.g., Small Business Owner and Marketing Executive).

Seventy-two scales (counting both male and female scales for the same occupation) appearing on the 1985 *Strong* were also targeted for sampling. Generally, the older the sample for a given occupation, the more likely it was to be replaced by a new sample. Other, more recently sampled scales were also targeted for resampling because of the possibility that some of the basic tasks performed by those in the occupation had changed due to the advent of computers (e.g., Architect) or forces in the marketplace (e.g., Banker).

Note that simply targeting an occupation for sampling or resampling did not guarantee that an OS would actually be constructed. There are many circumstances that can result in a scale not being formed, such as lack of response from those surveyed or too few people meeting the screening criteria (Step 4 below). For example, the occupation Nurses' Aide was targeted but failed to yield enough answer sheets. (For a detailed description of changes in the occupations represented by the OSs, see Chapter 2. Also see Appendix A for a description of the composition of the final occupational groups.) Having an understanding of the makeup of the groups can enhance interpretation of the OS scores.

Step 3: Survey the Occupational Groups

Once it was determined that an occupation would be targeted for inclusion on the *Strong*, a source of names of people employed in that occupation was sought. The source varied with the occupation and included professional directories or mailing lists, lists of employees provided by large employers, lists of certified or registered members of an occupation, or lists of firms or agencies employing people in the occupation to be sampled.

After such a group had been identified, a sample was drawn. It was important to survey enough people so that, given the inevitable lack of response on the part of some, a large enough sample would remain to permit selection of typical members of an occupation.

A primary goal of this revision, as with other recent revisions of the *Strong*, was to collect enough data so that separate scales could be developed for men and women in the occupation. In rare cases it was possible to stratify the sampling by gender; however, most lists that can be used for sampling occupations do not identify individuals by gender. For those occupations in which there were known imbalances across gender, "oversampling" was necessary to ensure that adequate numbers were obtained from the gender that was underrepresented in that occupation. For the 1994 *Strong*, another primary goal was to include as many racial and ethnic group members as possible.

All members of the sample received a request to participate in the research, which was in some cases accompanied by a letter of endorsement by their organization, professional association, or employer; a copy of the research version of the *Strong* containing all items under consideration for the revision; and an envelope that allowed them to return the data directly to the scale developer. They were promised confidentiality, a copy of their Profile, and the chance to contribute to the development of the *Strong*. In some cases, additional mailings were necessary when the initial response was not sufficient.

Step 4: Screen the Occupational Samples

Once a sufficient number of people in an occupational group responded to the inventory, they were screened on a set of criteria that had proven useful in selecting occupational groups in the past: job satisfaction, experience, performing the job in a typical manner, and age. If respondents did not meet all the criteria, they were considered ineligible and were not included in the occupational sample.

Job Satisfaction

Because the *Strong* is used in career planning, the OSs should reflect the interests of satisfied workers if the scales are to be used as valid predictors. The most direct way to find out if workers are satisfied is to ask them. For the occupational samples for the 1994 *Strong*, the question was, "How do you feel about your work?" The response options were "I am very satisfied," "I am somewhat satisfied," "I am somewhat dissatisfied," and "I am very dissatisfied." For groups collected in earlier years, a slightly different form of this question was used. In both cases, any individual who indicated any degree of dissatisfaction was not included in the final occupational sample.

Experience

Almost all the occupational samples were restricted to workers who had at least three years of experience on the job. The assumption was that most individuals unsuited to a job would not stay that long, although this criterion meant that some well-suited employees with less than three years of experience were excluded.

Performing in a Typical Manner

The respondents were also screened to remove individuals who were not performing the duties typical of members of the occupation. Thus, the person trained as a lawyer who identified his primary occupation as writer of fiction or the nurse who was running a retail medical supply business was not included in the lawyer or nurse occupation, respectively. Although this circumstance usually affects less than 1 or 2 percent of the respondents in any occupational sample, it was considerably higher for a few occupations.

Age

In the past, the age criterion for inclusion in the sample was 25 to 60 years old for most occupational groups. In the data collection for the 1994 *Strong*, however, the upper age limit was relaxed to reflect the changing demographic trends of the 1990s. If they met the criteria of job satisfaction, experience, and typicality, workers over 60 were included in the sample. The lower age limit was usually ensured by the three-year experience criterion.

Response Rate

Occupational groups tend to have fairly different response rates. The proportion of workers who respond to a mailed request to complete an interest inventory is a function of a variety of factors. The response rate is lower when using older lists because of people having changed addresses and even occupations. Members of some occupations are more mobile than others, so even the most up-to-date list for some occupations is likely to contain inaccurate addresses. Members of particular occupational groups are simply more intrigued by the task than others; one man who sent a note with his completed inventory saying, "People like me don't like to do things like this," came from an occupational sample with one of the lower response rates.

Within occupational groups, factors that influence response rates probably work to improve the quality of occupational groups rather than decrease it. Individuals who have little attachment to their work, find little satisfaction in it, do not practice it in a typical way, or are planning to leave it often select themselves out of the sample by not responding. Random events (e.g., natural disasters, family emergencies, and health problems) probably affect members of all occupational groups in approximately the same proportions. While workers experiencing such problems might have made positive contributions, they probably do not differ in important ways from others in the same group not experiencing such problems.

Table 7.1 Demographic Characteristics of the General Reference Samples

Characteristics	Female (N = 9,467)		Male (N = 9,484)	
	Mean	S.D.	Mean	S.D.
Age	40.5	9.6	44.6	10.5
Age at which career decision was made	23.9	8.4	24.0	7.7
Years in occupation	13.8	8.4	18.2	10.3
Years in current position	8.2	7.5	11.2	9.6
	Percent		Percent	
Very satisfied with work	58.7		61.8	
Working 30+ hours per week	89.6		94.7	
Nonwhite	8.5		8.3	
With physical disability	2.9		5.0	
Less than a bachelor's degree	22.7		17.6	
Bachelor's degree	32.0		33.3	
Master's degree	28.9		28.0	
Professional or doctoral degree	16.4		21.1	

Step 5: Form the General Reference Samples

As stated earlier, OSs are formed by comparing the item responses of members of specific occupational groups with members of a more broadly based group of the same gender. For the 1994 *Strong*, these broader groups were the General Reference Samples (GRSs). The GRSs contained samples of approximately 200 members of each occupation for which new data were collected for this revision. The GRS of males numbered 9,484, and the GRS of females numbered 9,467. Demographic data for the two GRSs are noted in Table 7.1. Average ages were 40.5 and 44.6 years for females and males, respectively; they averaged 13.8 and 18.2 years in their occupations. About 60 percent of each group was very satisfied with their occupation, with the remainder being somewhat satisfied. The modal educational level for each group was the bachelor's degree. About 8 percent of each group was nonwhite. There were people with physical disabilities in each group.

For previous versions of the *Strong*, the comparison group for item selection and scale development consisted of a rather small number of carefully chosen individuals. Two strategies used in developing the new GRSs were to use much larger groups and to include only recent respondents in the GRSs.

Larger GRSs

The enormous increase in the capacity of computers in recent years has made it possible to use a much larger comparison group, thus protecting the GRSs from the limitations of small sample sizes. Since approximately 55,000 individuals in 98 occupations completed and returned answer sheets for this revision, their number formed the upper limit on the size of the combined GRS. However, the number of respondents in the respective occupational groups varied considerably due to the conditions under which the sample was selected. Since it was desirable that the occupational groups be equally represented in the GRS, 200 respondents from each group that contained more than 200 were randomly selected from the entire sample. For the eight occupations represented by fewer than 200 members (female auto mechanics, male bookkeepers, female and male farmers, female gardener/groundskeepers, male paralegals, male plumbers, and female police officers), the entire occupational sample was used in the GRS. Of these eight groups, five were represented by at least 100 members, and three by at least 90 members.

To assess the effect of this new method of constituting the GRSs, a study was conducted using data from the 1985 *Strong*. The purpose was to determine what effect this new method would have had if it had been used in 1985. Using the 1985 data, two GRSs (one for males and one for females) were composed by sampling approximately 200 members from each occupational group in the manner used in the 1994 revision. The response percentages of these two GRSs were computed and compared with the response percentages for the comparison groups actually used in developing the 1985 scales, that is, the Men-in-General and Women-in-General groups. (This process is explained later in this chapter in Step 7.)

Although the 1985 Men-in-General and Women-in-General groups were constructed very differently, the comparison between the 1985 and 1994 methods revealed that, for men, only one item had a response percentage difference greater than 10 percent; the average difference for "Like" and "Dislike" responses over all items was less than 1 percent. The same analysis for women indicated two items with a response percentage difference greater than 10 percent and an average difference for "Like" and "Dislike" responses over all items of less than 1 percent. This study demonstrated that the two methods produced extremely similar response percentages. The newer method, utilizing much larger comparison groups, was chosen for the 1994 *Strong* because it reduced the influence that any one individual or occupational group could have in the GRS.

Using Recent Respondents

Using only the most recently collected occupational groups in the GRSs is advantageous because the participants responded to all the items on revised Form T317 of the *Strong*. Items added for this revision can appear only on scales for which data were recently collected because occupational groups that were not resampled did not take the research version of the *Strong* and therefore did not respond to items that were added to the *Strong* as a result of analyzing responses to it. However, using only recently collected respondents in the GRSs restricted the GRSs to members of the 98 occupational groups for which data were recently collected. Thus, it was important to determine the extent to which occupational groups responded similarly over time.

Therefore, another study was conducted to examine response patterns over time. The responses of members of the 72 occupational samples that had been collected for this revision were compared with those of members of the samples from the same occupations previously represented on the *Strong* Profile. Occupations that appeared on both the 1985 and 1994 versions were called "matching" occupations. Combining all the matching occupations but keeping the genders separate showed that among the 325 items common to both instruments, 54 items differentiated between the two groups of females (i.e., those in the 1985 and 1994 occupational groups) and 61 items differentiated between the two groups of males. In general, the differences were most often in the direction of the 1994 group responding "Like" to fewer items or "Dislike" to more items.

In this analysis, the criterion used for determining a "difference" in response was 10 percent or more, although item response differences of 10 percent are not commonly used in scale construction; differences of 16 percent are more typical. However, since the purpose here was not to construct a scale but to explore differences, the criterion was relaxed so that more differences would have a chance to emerge. The differences that appeared point to either sampling differences or differences attributable to time. Since the occupations were the same over time, only glaring differences in the way the samples were collected could suggest differences in the samples themselves. Since an attempt was made to use sampling procedures similar to those used previously, the more likely explanation is that endorsements of some interest items have changed somewhat over time. For instance, "Aggressive people" was endorsed less by the 1994 respondents, while "Working regular hours" was endorsed more by this group. These results suggest that the responses of the general groups used as references samples do change somewhat over time and support the use of GRSs composed of recent respondents.

Step 6: Compute the Response Percentages

This step involved computing the response percentages for each item on the research version for each occupational group and for the male and female GRSs. Only those members of the occupational groups who satisfied the criteria in Step 4 were included in this computation. For example, for the item "Chemist" the percentage of people who responded "Like," "Indifferent," and "Dislike" in each occupational group and in the two GRSs was calculated.

Step 7: Determine Items and Assign Weights for the Occupational Scales

This step involved the actual construction of the OSs: that is, deciding exactly which items would be used to score the scales and whether each of the responses to those items would be weighted +1 or –1. First, however, it was necessary to identify the desirable scale characteristics. Empirical scale construction always involves a tradeoff between item validity and scale reliability. Emphasizing the former, which is directly related to scale validity, produces short scales; emphasizing the latter, which is based on test-retest correlations, produces long scales. The relative importance attached to the two factors has changed from time to time, depending on the inclinations and purposes of those conducting the revision. If scale validity is stressed, only those items showing large differences between the occupational group and the appropriate reference sample are weighted. If scale reliability is stressed, then as many items as possible are used, even those of moderate validity, because longer scales are more stable than shorter scales over time.

Because of the power and efficiency of modern computers, it was possible to explore these competing factors. The effect of scale length and cutoff point on the reliability and validity of the 1985 scales was examined using 1985 data (from Tables 6.1 and 6.3 of Hansen & Campbell, 1985). In these analyses, 30-day test-retest reliabilities were used as the reliability estimates. The degree of overlap in scores between the occupational groups and the appropriate In-General group was used as an index of concurrent validity, with less overlap indicating greater validity.

The results of this analysis (Harmon, Usher, & Borgen, 1994) suggested that only the length of the scale predicted reliability. The more items on the scale, the greater its test-retest reliability. Validity, in this case overlap, was predicted by both the number of items on the scale and the percentage cutoff point. The strongest predictor of overlap, however, was the cutoff point (i.e., the minimum percentage difference used to select items). This relationship between the cutoff point and overlap was negative. Thus, greater concurrent validity, as measured by degree of overlap, was associated with (1) a higher minimum percentage difference between an occupational group and a GRS and (2) a larger number of items. Setting a higher minimum percentage difference usually results in fewer items. However, because of the strong relationship between minimum percentage difference and overlap as an indicator of validity in this study, the best chance of minimizing item overlap among OSs was to use fewer items per scale.

With this research as background, the following procedures were used to construct the OSs.

Compare the Occupational Group with the GRS

The first step was to compare the sample's item responses with those of the appropriate-gender GRS. Using the response percentages for every item calculated in Step 6, the differences between the percentages of the two groups were calculated. For example, the result of comparing the occupational sample of female physicists to the GRS of females on the item "Computer science" was:

Sample	Item Response Percentage			
	Like	Indifferent	Dislike	Total
Female Physicist	72	25	3	100
Female GRS	44	35	21	100
Difference	**+28**	**–10**	**–18**	

Identify Items That Differentiate

The next step was to identify those items that differentiated the occupational sample and the GRSs at a significant level. This task raised the question of what would be a significant level and what would be the minimum cutoff percent difference. In previous revisions of the *Strong*, a 16 percent difference in the "Like" or "Dislike" response rate between the occupational group and reference sample was sufficient to produce scales of adequate length, usually 60 to 70 items. As a result, item responses that differentiated the two groups at 16 percent or greater were the starting point for constructing the 1994 scales.

Since the goal was to explore the possibility of using shorter scales of about 40 items, a range of percentage differences between the responses of the occupational group and GRS that would produce that many "Like" or "Dislike" responses was identified. With the use of computers, it was possible to examine a family of possible scales to select a final minimum percentage difference for each scale that would maximize reliability and validity while minimizing length. For each occupational group, four to six tentative scales containing 40 items were constructed, each scale using a slightly different minimum percent cutoff.

Each family of scales was examined to determine whether any potential scales were available that contained more than 40 to 50 items and that showed a 16 percent or greater difference between the two groups. If such a scale, or scales, existed, then the scales with the next highest minimum cutoff (17 percent) were examined to determine the number of items on each. Scales with successively higher minimum cutoffs were then examined (18 percent, 19 percent, and so on) until a scale was found for which the number of items had dropped to roughly 45. When there was no scale that contained more than 40 items and showed a 16 percent difference between groups, each family of scales was examined to determine whether or not a scale was available that contained fewer items and that showed a 16 percent difference or greater between the two groups. When no such scales were identified, those scales with a lower minimum cutoff were examined (e.g., starting with 15 percent and moving lower). Eventually, this procedure converged toward a minimum cutoff point at which about 40 to 50 items were available to form a scale. The final minimum cutoff ("Minimum % Difference") and number of items used for each scale are shown in Table 7.2.

Assign Scoring Weights

After the discriminating items were identified for each of the potential scales, the "Like" or "Dislike" response choice that showed the larger difference was weighted +1 or –1, depending on the direction of the difference. For example, the "Like" response to the item "Doing research work" received a +1 weight on the female Physicist scale. The opposite response choice (in this case, "Dislike") automatically was weighted in the opposite direction, even if the percent difference of that particular response was not above the minimum cutoff (that is, no matter how small the empirical difference). This technique, which assumes each item to be a miniature dimension, increases the reliability of the scale about .03 to .04 correlational points and does not affect validity (percent overlap) either way. Thus, for the item "Doing research work" on the female Physicist scale, the "Dislike" response was weighted –1.

Once the "Like" and "Dislike" choices for an item had been weighted, the "Indifferent" response choice was weighted, but only if the difference between the occupational group and the GRS for that response was sufficiently large. If the difference was positive, the "Indifferent" response was weighted +1; if negative, –1. Thus, the final weighting scheme for the item "Doing research work" on the female Physicist scale was:

Sample	Item Response Percentage		
	Like	Indifferent	Dislike
Female Physicist	94	5	1
Female GRS	32	26	42
Difference	**+62**	**–21**	**–41**
Item weights	+1	–1	–1

If a client answered "Like" to the item "Doing research work," she would be responding like female physicists, and her score on the female Physicist scale would increase (+1). Conversely, if she responded "Dislike" or "Indifferent," her score on this scale would decrease (–1). Of course, one of the interesting and useful features of the OSs is that they contain items that also identify things that members of the occupational samples *dislike*. For example, the item "Fashion model" is an aversion of female physicists; 75 percent respond "Dislike" to this item. Therefore, on the female Physicist scale the item was weighted as follows:

Sample	Item Response Percentage		
	Like	Indifferent	Dislike
Female Physicist	10	15	75
Female GRS	30	24	46
Difference	**–20**	**–9**	**+29**
Item weights	–1	0	+1

In this case, a client responding "Dislike" to the item "Fashion model" would be responding the same way that female physicists do, and the score on the female Physicist scale would increase (+1). Conversely, a "Like" response would result in the client receiving a score of –1 on the scale. For this item, the "Indifferent" response is weighted 0 because the item did not reach a satisfactory level of difference in response rate between the occupational sample and the GRS to be weighted.

Table 7.2 Scale Characteristics, Three- to Six-Month Reliability Coefficients, Concurrent Validities (Percent Overlap), and Minimum and Maximum Possible Scores for the 1994 Occupational Scales

Occupational Scale	Gender	Number of Items	Minimum % Difference	Three- to Six-Month Reliability[a]	Tilton % Overlap	Minimum Possible Score	Maximum Possible Score
Accountant	Female	44	16	.92	40	−5	79
Accountant	Male	41	16	.91	41	−10	76
Actuary	Female	40	16	.92	38	−5	80
Actuary	Male	40	16	.87	37	−12	79
Advertising Executive	Female	50	19	.92	39	−16	71
Advertising Executive	Male	63	19	.95	38	−12	75
Agribusiness Manager	Male	47	29	.85	18	−11	75
Architect	Female	44	19	.91	29	−32	79
Architect	Male	45	16	.92	29	−30	80
Artist, Commercial	Female	48	24	.93	25	−45	77
Artist, Commercial	Male	50	23	.92	19	−34	82
Artist, Fine	Female	52	25	.90	21	−39	74
Artist, Fine	Male	50	27	.90	19	−22	71
Art Teacher	Female	51	21	.86	18	−47	77
Art Teacher	Male	47	25	.90	21	−29	76
Athletic Trainer	Female	42	26	.87	17	−20	74
Athletic Trainer	Male	44	20	.88	20	−26	79
Audiologist	Female	40	10	.88	54	−21	90
Audiologist	Male	23	12	.82	60	−6	80
Auto Mechanic	Female	49	26	.95	19	−4	74
Auto Mechanic	Male	53	26	.93	27	−9	71
Banker	Female	46	17	.93	49	10	76
Banker	Male	45	16	.92	48	0	77
Biologist	Female	50	24	.93	28	−21	71
Biologist	Male	50	23	.91	28	−16	69
Bookkeeper	Female	33	17	.92	34	−4	78
Bookkeeper	Male	46	17	.92	35	−10	80
Broadcaster	Female	40	22	.91	41	1	71
Broadcaster	Male	59	17	.92	38	−16	78
Business Education Teacher	Female	56	22	.92	24	−5	70
Business Education Teacher	Male	61	20	.91	31	3	74
Buyer	Female	42	20	.91	23	−23	80
Buyer	Male	41	18	.88	29	−11	79
Carpenter	Female	42	25	.91	21	−13	74
Carpenter	Male	43	20	.89	27	−15	84

[a] Three- to six-month reliability data is based on Sample A of employed adults (N = 110 women, 81 men).

Table 7.2 Scale Characteristics, Three- to Six-Month Reliability Coefficients, Concurrent Validities (Percent Overlap), and Minimum and Maximum Possible Scores for the 1994 Occupational Scales (continued)

Occupational Scale	Gender	Number of Items	Minimum % Difference	Three- to Six-Month Reliability[a]	Tilton % Overlap	Minimum Possible Score	Maximum Possible Score
Chef	Female	42	18	.84	33	−30	86
Chef	Male	41	18	.81	28	−10	80
Chemist	Female	53	20	.95	34	−9	75
Chemist	Male	48	18	.94	35	−14	74
Child Care Provider	Female	35	16	.91	39	−16	78
Chiropractor	Female	45	19	.83	33	−3	78
Chiropractor	Male	47	16	.85	36	−12	79
College Professor	Female	63	17	.92	41	−14	79
College Professor	Male	39	16	.90	50	−10	74
Community Service Organization Director	Female	41	16	.92	51	−4	75
Community Service Organization Director	Male	45	18	.89	46	0	72
Computer Programmer/Systems Analyst	Female	48	18	.94	49	3	71
Computer Programmer/Systems Analyst	Male	50	20	.93	38	−9	70
Corporate Trainer	Female	49	17	.91	47	−14	71
Corporate Trainer	Male	32	15	.89	59	2	69
Credit Manager	Female	37	16	.92	49	3	82
Credit Manager	Male	42	16	.89	54	8	74
Dental Assistant	Female	46	20	.85	31	−3	78
Dental Hygienist	Female	67	16	.80	35	−16	84
Dentist	Female	38	16	.88	36	−16	75
Dentist	Male	48	16	.89	37	−14	79
Dietitian	Female	40	16	.81	37	−15	84
Dietitian	Male	46	20	.82	35	0	78
Elected Public Official	Female	44	23	.89	30	−6	70
Elected Public Official	Male	45	23	.88	31	−5	69
Electrician	Female	48	25	.92	27	−4	72
Electrician	Male	44	21	.92	31	−22	80
Elementary School Teacher	Female	24	16	.90	42	−15	78
Elementary School Teacher	Male	34	13	.88	43	−23	89
Emergency Medical Technician	Female	47	21	.88	27	−4	80
Emergency Medical Technician	Male	44	21	.91	35	−2	75

Table 7.2 Scale Characteristics, Three- to Six-Month Reliability Coefficients, Concurrent Validities (Percent Overlap), and Minimum and Maximum Possible Scores for the 1994 Occupational Scales (continued)

Occupational Scale	Gender	Number of Items	Minimum % Difference	Three- to Six-Month Reliability[a]	Tilton % Overlap	Minimum Possible Score	Maximum Possible Score
Engineer	Female	52	17	.94	45	8	73
Engineer	Male	40	15	.94	52	0	74
English Teacher	Female	60	20	.89	34	−24	72
English Teacher	Male	51	23	.90	32	−11	71
Farmer	Female	51	24	.93	31	2	76
Farmer	Male	45	31	.91	31	6	65
Flight Attendant	Female	42	18	.89	43	0	77
Flight Attendant	Male	60	18	.91	42	8	78
Florist	Female	40	17	.87	23	−27	87
Florist	Male	44	16	.86	20	−14	88
Food Service Manager	Female	43	21	.86	39	9	77
Food Service Manager	Male	37	22	.84	39	9	73
Foreign Language Teacher	Female	47	19	.84	30	−25	78
Foreign Language Teacher	Male	38	22	.85	31	−7	74
Forester	Female	42	19	.91	37	−12	77
Forester	Male	40	16	.91	42	−14	75
Gardener/Groundskeeper	Female	39	16	.90	47	1	79
Gardener/Groundskeeper	Male	38	16	.86	41	−7	85
Geographer	Female	50	17	.89	47	0	76
Geographer	Male	45	16	.86	30	−42	85
Geologist	Female	48	25	.94	31	−13	73
Geologist	Male	53	19	.94	30	−34	76
Hair Stylist	Female	43	20	.86	26	−12	89
Hair Stylist	Male	45	23	.89	26	−1	78
High School Counselor	Female	51	20	.87	41	−6	69
High School Counselor	Male	50	21	.86	35	−5	71
Home Economics Teacher	Female	46	22	.83	27	−12	73
Horticultural Worker	Female	36	20	.82	31	−21	80
Horticultural Worker	Male	53	16	.87	27	−32	89
Housekeeping & Maintenance Supervisor	Female	58	17	.91	42	−1	89
Housekeeping & Maintenance Supervisor	Male	40	15	.91	49	−1	88
Human Resources Director	Female	44	16	.92	49	−14	74
Human Resources Director	Male	42	17	.89	49	2	71

Table 7.2 Scale Characteristics, Three- to Six-Month Reliability Coefficients, Concurrent Validities (Percent Overlap), and Minimum and Maximum Possible Scores for the 1994 Occupational Scales (continued)

Occupational Scale	Gender	Number of Items	Minimum % Difference	Three- to Six-Month Reliability[a]	Tilton % Overlap	Minimum Possible Score	Maximum Possible Score
Interior Decorator	Female	59	19	.90	20	−38	82
Interior Decorator	Male	44	26	.94	20	−7	71
Investments Manager	Female	41	20	.90	30	−17	78
Investments Manager	Male	45	16	.85	36	−24	83
Lawyer	Female	41	17	.92	51	−9	71
Lawyer	Male	40	16	.92	51	−9	73
Librarian	Female	38	15	.92	52	−15	76
Librarian	Male	53	19	.94	42	−4	77
Life Insurance Agent	Female	43	19	.92	33	−6	75
Life Insurance Agent	Male	44	20	.91	32	−12	74
Marketing Executive	Female	50	16	.89	40	−21	81
Marketing Executive	Male	56	16	.91	42	−16	80
Mathematician	Female	52	23	.94	21	−30	75
Mathematician	Male	45	23	.92	20	−36	73
Mathematics Teacher	Female	48	20	.87	26	−11	75
Mathematics Teacher	Male	42	20	.87	27	−19	74
Medical Illustrator	Female	50	23	.89	18	−49	75
Medical Illustrator	Male	52	25	.86	15	−36	75
Medical Records Technician	Female	38	15	.87	51	10	83
Medical Records Technician	Male	38	14	.99	49	7	85
Medical Technician	Female	48	20	.87	24	−15	85
Medical Technician	Male	47	20	.89	33	−6	79
Medical Technologist	Female	39	23	.90	33	−7	73
Medical Technologist	Male	49	19	.90	40	1	69
Military Enlisted Personnel	Female	45	20	.86	37	12	82
Military Enlisted Personnel	Male	39	20	.87	39	2	80
Military Officer	Female	48	17	.88	39	7	78
Military Officer	Male	42	20	.90	43	−1	75
Minister	Female	45	25	.89	22	−19	68
Minister	Male	44	24	.87	34	−2	67
Musician	Female	51	17	.92	35	−30	80
Musician	Male	59	17	.92	36	−11	81
Nurse, LPN	Female	42	21	.87	22	−11	82
Nurse, LPN	Male	48	23	.82	25	7	76

Table 7.2 Scale Characteristics, Three- to Six-Month Reliability Coefficients, Concurrent Validities (Percent Overlap), and Minimum and Maximum Possible Scores for the 1994 Occupational Scales (continued)

Occupational Scale	Gender	Number of Items	Minimum % Difference	Three- to Six-Month Reliability[a]	Tilton % Overlap	Minimum Possible Score	Maximum Possible Score
Nurse, RN	Female	30	13	.88	43	–8	79
Nurse, RN	Male	33	16	.87	38	–6	77
Nursing Home Administrator	Female	40	16	.85	44	–4	78
Nursing Home Administrator	Male	31	15	.86	54	6	79
Occupational Therapist	Female	42	17	.89	42	–18	79
Occupational Therapist	Male	47	17	.89	41	–6	80
Optician	Female	46	17	.80	39	2	84
Optician	Male	58	16	.86	35	–8	85
Optometrist	Female	35	20	.90	47	3	74
Optometrist	Male	43	16	.88	37	–29	84
Paralegal	Female	41	13	.91	53	–5	81
Paralegal	Male	34	16	.83	44	–3	83
Parks and Recreation Coordinator	Female	38	16	.90	47	2	77
Parks and Recreation Coordinator	Male	38	15	.91	55	3	73
Pharmacist	Female	39	16	.90	43	–8	80
Pharmacist	Male	31	15	.85	49	0	78
Photographer	Female	45	18	.90	38	–16	80
Photographer	Male	49	17	.90	31	–22	85
Physical Education Teacher	Female	42	23	.89	16	–20	81
Physical Education Teacher	Male	39	21	.85	21	–23	77
Physical Therapist	Female	37	16	.90	37	–11	77
Physical Therapist	Male	31	16	.88	42	–4	69
Physician	Female	61	18	.93	31	–31	80
Physician	Male	44	19	.90	32	–22	78
Physicist	Female	56	27	.94	19	–26	74
Physicist	Male	53	24	.92	23	–26	70
Plumber	Male	51	20	.91	42	1	76
Police Officer	Female	45	18	.92	35	6	74
Police Officer	Male	48	17	.92	34	–12	85
Psychologist	Female	47	21	.89	35	–19	73
Psychologist	Male	52	19	.91	34	–18	75
Public Administrator	Female	54	19	.90	38	–11	74
Public Administrator	Male	48	20	.89	40	–4	70

Table 7.2 Scale Characteristics, Three- to Six-Month Reliability Coefficients, Concurrent Validities (Percent Overlap), and Minimum and Maximum Possible Scores for the 1994 Occupational Scales (continued)

Occupational Scale	Gender	Number of Items	Minimum % Difference	Three- to Six-Month Reliability[a]	Tilton % Overlap	Minimum Possible Score	Maximum Possible Score
Public Relations Director	Female	50	22	.94	31	−31	72
Public Relations Director	Male	50	21	.94	34	−16	72
Purchasing Agent	Female	43	20	.85	39	−1	77
Purchasing Agent	Male	42	21	.86	42	3	72
Radiologic Technologist	Female	39	16	.89	44	−2	86
Radiologic Technologist	Male	40	15	.92	47	3	81
Realtor	Female	41	27	.88	19	−12	73
Realtor	Male	43	21	.87	35	−1	71
Reporter	Female	52	19	.92	35	−23	76
Reporter	Male	42	19	.91	33	−15	75
Research & Development Manager	Female	44	22	.93	33	−11	75
Research & Development Manager	Male	62	17	.92	35	−17	76
Respiratory Therapist	Female	44	17	.86	39	−6	83
Respiratory Therapist	Male	49	17	.85	39	−13	80
Restaurant Manager	Female	46	20	.87	39	−4	80
Restaurant Manager	Male	42	21	.86	32	−7	78
School Administrator	Female	44	18	.89	46	−1	69
School Administrator	Male	63	17	.87	43	−7	74
Science Teacher	Female	49	20	.89	27	−17	73
Science Teacher	Male	47	20	.90	34	−7	72
Secretary	Female	50	18	.89	37	−4	79
Small Business Owner	Female	27	14	.87	61	16	84
Small Business Owner	Male	40	16	.88	48	0	84
Social Science Teacher	Female	50	19	.87	43	−1	69
Social Science Teacher	Male	56	17	.87	46	−4	73
Social Worker	Female	41	17	.89	44	−11	68
Social Worker	Male	44	18	.91	35	−13	76
Sociologist	Female	54	23	.90	29	−21	72
Sociologist	Male	59	20	.89	35	−18	76
Special Education Teacher	Female	33	15	.88	45	−18	79
Special Education Teacher	Male	35	16	.88	41	−9	77
Speech Pathologist	Female	40	15	.91	48	−18	73
Speech Pathologist	Male	43	18	.90	43	−14	78
Store Manager	Female	43	18	.88	39	2	75
Store Manager	Male	39	19	.89	33	2	74

Table 7.2 Scale Characteristics, Three- to Six-Month Reliability Coefficients, Concurrent Validities (Percent Overlap), and Minimum and Maximum Possible Scores for the 1994 Occupational Scales (continued)

Occupational Scale	Gender	Number of Items	Minimum % Difference	Three- to Six-Month Reliability[a]	Tilton % Overlap	Minimum Possible Score	Maximum Possible Score
Technical Writer	Female	40	16	.92	48	−13	70
Technical Writer	Male	70	16	.93	41	−14	83
Translator	Female	41	17	.92	40	−27	78
Translator	Male	54	18	.93	37	−6	78
Travel Agent	Female	60	16	.86	39	−10	80
Travel Agent	Male	51	16	.91	41	−5	82
Veterinarian	Female	59	17	.92	31	−27	79
Veterinarian	Male	39	16	.91	36	−18	78
Vocational Agriculture Teacher	Female	50	16	.86	27	−29	84
Vocational Agriculture Teacher	Male	59	21	.86	24	−17	77

These examples illustrate an important feature of the OSs: a high score on the OS is the result of a person's having both interests and aversions that match those of the occupational sample. Thus, a high score suggests that the respondent will have much in common with the members of that occupation.

Analyze Reliability and Validity of the Different Scales Within the Family and Choose the Final Scale

Once item weights had been assigned to each item in the potential scales, the reliabilities and validities for each of these scales were examined. From among these sets of scales for each occupational group, the scale that represented a moderate length and maximized reliability and validity was chosen.

One of the interesting findings that resulted from this procedure was that, in general, most occupational groups have a characteristic reliability and validity that do not change markedly even with rather large changes in the number of items. For example, for the female physicists, a 24 percent minimum cutoff resulted in a scale with 70 items, having a reliability of .945 and a 20 percent overlap with the female GRS. A scale using a minimum cutoff of 31 percent resulted in a scale with 35 items, a reliability of .938, and a 16 percent overlap with the female GRS. A scale using a minimum cutoff of 27 percent with 56 items, a reliability of .943, and a 19 percent overlap with the female GRS was the one that was ultimately selected, largely because it contained an intermediate number of items.

Step 8: Norm the Scales

Once the optimal scales were selected, they were normed by scoring the original occupational samples on the scales and using their raw score means and standard deviations in a standard score conversion formula that yielded a mean of 50 and a standard deviation of 10 for the occupational group. When an individual takes the *Strong*, his or her raw scores on each OS are converted to standard scores for easy comparison.

Characteristics of the Final Scales

The number of items, the minimum percentage difference between the occupational group and the GRS, the three- to six-month reliability, and the Tilton percent of overlap for all 211 OSs have been provided in Table 7.2. In addition, the minimum and maximum scores for each OS are presented there.

The median three- to six-month reliability coefficient for the 211 OSs is .90, with the middle 50 percent falling between .87 and .92, and 90 percent of the coefficients falling between .83 and .94. The median percentage of overlap on the 211 OSs is 36 percent, with the middle 50 percent falling between 30 and 42 percent overlap and 90 percent of the overlaps falling between 19 and 51 percent. Mean reliabilities and validities are quite similar for the OSs appearing on the 1985 *Strong* (see Hansen & Campbell, 1985, for those scales) and those appearing on the 1994, but it is worth noting that the 1985 scale reliabilities are for a 30-day test-retest period, whereas the 1994 scale reliabilities are for a three- to six-month period.

The largest difference between the 1985 and 1994 *Strong* is in the length of the scales, with the average being 55 items for the 1985 OSs and 46 for the 1994 OSs. It is noteworthy that an average decrease in scale length of nine items has not resulted in a decrease in average reliability or concurrent validity. As Table 7.2 shows, a few scales used relatively low cutoffs to make the best possible scales. The scales using the lowest percentage cutoffs were male and female Audiologist; female Elementary School Teacher; female Nurse, RN; and female Paralegal. Three of these scales have a Tilton overlap statistic of over 50 percent. These scales were maintained on the inventory because even the scale with the highest degree of overlap between the occupational sample and the GRS, 61 percent for the female Small Business Owner scale, results in a one standard deviation separation between the groups. (Later in this chapter, under the section "Concurrent Validity," the concept of overlap is discussed in greater detail.)

Classifying Occupational Scales by GOT Code

The Occupational Scales are ordered on the Profile in the six categories represented by the General Occupational Themes classification system (see Chapter 5). To the left of each Occupational Scale are two columns, labeled "Theme Codes," one for females and one for males. In these columns are one, two, or three letters that represent the General Occupational Themes most closely associated with that scale. Within each RIASEC category the Occupational Scales are listed alphabetically because it is easier to find an occupational scale by name than by code, especially if the user is not familiar with the codes of all of the OSs on the *Strong*.

In addition to providing a structure for organizing the OSs on the Profile, the codes also provide clients and counselors with a tool for helping clients better understand the world of work as well as expand their options by linking the occupations on the *Strong* to thousands of others. A discussion of how the codes can be used to understand the characteristics of occupations follows. (Note that Chapter 10 of this guide discusses in detail how the Theme codes can be used to help clients expand educational or career options.)

Assigning Codes

GOT codes were assigned to the OSs primarily on the basis of empirical data. Table 7.3 shows the data that were used in selecting the codes. For each occupational sample, the first set of six columns shows the mean scores on the GOTs based on the appropriate gender General Reference Sample; the second set of six columns presents the mean scores based on the combined GRSs (female and male); the last set of six columns shows the percent of people in each occupational sample with that GOT as their highest score. The mean scores of the occupational groups on each of the GOTs and the distribution of people in each of these groups according to their individual highest GOTs give somewhat different but complementary information. The former combines the scores of all of the individuals in each group for each GOT. The latter places each individual in only one of the six Themes depending on his or her highest score.

The preliminary guidelines for assigning codes to each occupational sample were based on the appropriate gender GOT means (from the first set of RIASEC scores in Table 7.3). These steps included identifying all GOTs for which the appropriate gender means were greater than 50, rank-ordering all of these GOTs, and assigning a code based on this ranking. This simple but precise method failed to resolve the problems of (1) two or more GOT means being essentially tied, (2) more than three letters being assigned to a code, and (3) differentiating between GOT means within a code.

Scales had different combinations of these three problems. For example, some scales had more than three letters in the code, with the last two or three ranked Themes essentially tied. (Scores were considered tied if they were within 1 point of each other, indicated by parentheses in Table 7.3.)

Table 7.3 Data Used to Classify Occupational Scales: General Occupational Theme Scale Means and Percent Highest Score on GOT Scales

Occupational Scale	Gender	Code[a]	Appropriate Gender-Normed GOT Mean						Combined Gender-Normed GOT Mean						Percent Highest Score					
			R	I	A	S	E	C	R	I	A	S	E	C	R	I	A	S	E	C
Accountant	Female	CE	49	49	46	48	51	57	46	48	49	49	51	58	11	8	9	10	17	45
Accountant	Male	CE	49	49	46	48	51	57	52	50	44	47	51	56	13	8	8	9	14	48
Actuary	Female	(CI)	50	55	47	49	48	55	47	54	50	50	48	56	12	29	10	10	9	30
Actuary	Male	(CI)	48	54	48	48	48	54	51	55	46	47	47	54	8	27	13	8	9	35
Advertising Executive	Female	AE	46	44	55	48	53	44	43	43	58	49	53	45	6	7	45	12	24	6
Advertising Executive	Male	AE	45	44	57	47	51	44	48	45	54	46	51	44	5	5	60	6	21	3
Agribusiness Manager	Male	E(CR)*	57	48	43	52	61	58	60	49	41	51	61	57	23	4	0	6	40	27
Architect	Female	(AR)I	55	53	56	45	47	46	51	52	58	46	48	46	28	17	40	5	5	5
Architect	Male	A(RI)	52	51	57	46	47	46	55	52	54	45	47	46	20	12	50	5	7	6
Artist, Commercial	Female	ARI	53	51	60	45	50	42	50	50	62	46	50	42	19	10	58	3	9	1
Artist, Commercial	Male	A	50	48	61	46	47	43	53	49	58	45	47	42	8	4	76	5	6	1
Artist, Fine	Female	AR*	52	51	59	43	45	40	48	50	61	44	45	41	19	15	60	2	3	1
Artist, Fine	Male	A	49	49	62	44	44	40	53	50	59	43	43	40	11	6	82	0	1	0
Art Teacher	Female	A(SE)*	54	49	60	55	54	46	50	48	62	56	54	46	17	3	47	15	13	5
Art Teacher	Male	AS	49	47	63	55	50	45	53	48	60	53	50	44	5	2	67	16	9	1
Athletic Trainer	Female	RIS*	60	57	47	54	49	51	55	56	50	55	49	51	45	20	6	15	7	7
Athletic Trainer	Male	S(IR)	53	53	46	55	49	50	56	54	44	54	49	49	19	20	3	33	12	13
Audiologist	Female	(IS)	49	52	50	52	49	48	45	51	53	54	49	48	11	22	19	26	11	11
Audiologist	Male	(IA)	50	52	51	50	50	49	53	53	48	49	50	48	16	24	19	15	16	10
Auto Mechanic	Female	R*	67	51	43	45	46	48	62	50	46	46	47	48	82	3	1	3	4	7
Auto Mechanic	Male	R	61	47	42	45	48	47	64	48	39	44	48	46	79	3	1	3	8	6
Banker	Female	CE	47	44	45	49	53	59	44	43	48	50	53	60	5	5	10	5	21	54
Banker	Male	CE	50	47	45	49	54	56	53	48	43	47	54	55	16	6	6	10	24	38
Biologist	Female	IRA	53	61	51	46	41	48	50	60	54	48	42	48	16	62	9	6	2	5
Biologist	Male	IA	49	59	52	47	41	48	53	60	49	46	41	47	8	63	16	6	2	5
Bookkeeper	Female	C	49	47	46	47	50	61	46	46	48	48	51	62	11	6	7	7	7	62
Bookkeeper	Male	C	47	47	46	46	50	59	51	48	43	45	50	58	9	6	4	5	14	62
Broadcaster	Female	AE	48	46	57	50	55	47	45	45	59	51	56	47	9	4	42	8	31	6
Broadcaster	Male	AE	47	46	56	49	52	46	50	47	54	48	52	46	7	5	45	10	26	7
Business Education Teacher	Female	CES	46	44	44	53	55	63	43	43	47	54	56	65	4	1	3	7	19	66
Business Education Teacher	Male	CES	45	43	46	54	57	62	49	44	43	52	57	61	4	2	5	10	21	58
Buyer	Female	EC	48	46	50	49	64	54	44	45	53	50	64	55	3	3	6	3	69	16
Buyer	Male	EC*	48	47	51	51	63	52	51	48	48	49	63	52	6	1	11	5	70	7
Carpenter	Female	R(IA)	66	55	54	49	46	47	61	54	56	51	46	48	82	3	6	4	3	2
Carpenter	Male	R(EA)*	59	50	52	51	52	50	62	51	49	49	52	49	53	5	10	9	15	8

[a] Parentheses indicate that mean scores are within 1 point of each other; asterisks indicate that the number of means > 50 exceeds the number of letters in the code.

**Table 7.3 Data Used to Classify Occupational Scales:
General Occupational Theme Scale Means and Percent Highest Score on GOT Scales** (continued)

Occupational Scale	Gender	Code[a]	Appropriate Gender-Normed GOT Mean						Combined Gender-Normed GOT Mean						Percent Highest Score					
			R	I	A	S	E	C	R	I	A	S	E	C	R	I	A	S	E	C
Chef	Female	(ERA)	54	49	54	49	54	49	51	48	56	51	54	49	27	3	26	15	17	12
Chef	Male	ER*	53	50	52	52	55	51	56	51	49	50	55	50	18	9	16	18	28	11
Chemist	Female	IR	55	63	49	46	43	49	51	62	52	47	44	49	20	66	4	3	3	4
Chemist	Male	IR	52	60	49	47	44	49	55	61	46	45	44	49	10	65	9	3	3	10
Child Care Provider	Female	S*	47	44	49	58	51	49	44	43	52	60	51	50	6	2	11	53	13	15
Chiropractor	Female	(IR)*	55	55	52	51	52	51	51	54	55	53	53	51	21	17	13	14	20	15
Chiropractor	Male	I(RA)**	53	55	53	52	52	49	56	56	50	50	51	48	19	21	23	17	13	7
College Professor	Female	I(AR)*	53	58	54	51	45	49	50	57	57	52	46	50	15	39	19	13	4	10
College Professor	Male	(IA)S	50	56	55	52	47	50	54	57	52	50	47	50	10	34	27	12	6	11
Community Service Organization Director	Female	SE	48	45	49	56	52	49	45	44	52	57	52	49	11	5	15	40	17	12
Community Service Organization Director	Male	SE	49	46	49	59	53	50	47	47	47	57	53	49	10	5	10	47	16	12
Computer Programmer/Systems Analyst	Female	IR	54	57	50	46	46	50	51	56	53	47	46	51	28	36	14	7	5	10
Computer Programmer/Systems Analyst	Male	I(AR)	52	57	53	46	44	50	56	58	50	45	44	49	18	39	24	4	3	12
Corporate Trainer	Female	(AE)S	47	47	55	52	54	46	44	46	57	53	54	47	9	8	33	17	26	7
Corporate Trainer	Male	(AES)	48	47	52	52	53	48	51	48	49	51	52	47	15	8	25	19	26	7
Credit Manager	Female	CE	48	45	47	50	54	57	45	44	49	51	54	58	8	3	9	13	23	44
Credit Manager	Male	(CE)	50	47	47	50	56	56	53	48	44	48	56	55	12	4	6	9	32	37
Dental Assistant	Female	(C(S)E)*	51	51	50	54	53	55	48	50	52	55	54	55	15	13	11	21	15	25
Dental Hygienist	Female	E(IS)*	51	53	52	53	55	52	48	52	54	54	55	53	18	14	11	16	26	15
Dentist	Female	I(RA)	53	57	53	49	49	48	50	56	55	51	49	48	21	36	20	9	8	6
Dentist	Male	IR	54	57	50	48	48	49	57	58	47	47	48	48	25	37	14	8	6	10
Dietitian	Female	I(ES)*	52	55	49	53	53	51	48	54	52	54	53	51	14	23	11	18	21	13
Dietitian	Male	(SEC)*	51	52	52	56	56	55	54	53	49	54	56	54	14	8	14	23	20	21
Elected Public Official	Female	E(AS)*	51	51	54	53	56	51	48	50	57	55	56	52	12	13	17	17	29	12
Elected Public Official	Male	(ES)A	49	48	52	55	56	49	52	49	49	54	56	49	10	5	19	21	36	9
Electrician	Female	RIA	65	56	54	48	47	48	61	55	57	49	48	48	69	14	11	2	2	2
Electrician	Male	RIC	59	53	47	50	50	51	62	54	45	48	50	50	58	9	4	8	11	10
Elementary School Teacher	Female	S	46	47	50	55	50	49	44	46	52	56	51	50	6	10	21	33	15	15
Elementary School Teacher	Male	S*	51	50	51	56	50	50	54	51	48	54	49	50	15	12	19	31	9	14
Emergency Medical Technician	Female	(RCI)*	55	54	47	53	50	54	51	53	50	54	50	55	22	21	8	18	8	23
Emergency Medical Technician	Male	RI*	56	53	46	52	50	52	59	54	43	50	50	51	34	16	5	15	12	18

Table 7.3 Data Used to Classify Occupational Scales: General Occupational Theme Scale Means and Percent Highest Score on GOT Scales (continued)

Occupational Scale	Gender	Code[a]	Appropriate Gender-Normed GOT Mean						Combined Gender-Normed GOT Mean						Percent Highest Score					
			R	I	A	S	E	C	R	I	A	S	E	C	R	I	A	S	E	C
Engineer	Female	RI*	60	58	49	48	49	51	55	57	51	49	49	51	42	29	7	6	6	10
Engineer	Male	(RI)	55	55	47	47	47	50	59	56	44	46	47	50	36	29	6	6	10	13
English Teacher	Female	(AS)E	47	47	58	57	54	50	44	46	61	59	55	50	4	6	35	26	20	9
English Teacher	Male	ASE	46	48	61	59	51	50	49	49	58	57	51	50	3	3	46	29	8	11
Farmer	Female	C(SE)	50	43	42	52	51	56	47	42	45	53	51	57	12	5	2	25	14	42
Farmer	Male	RC	57	45	39	45	50	52	60	46	36	44	49	51	56	2	1	6	13	22
Flight Attendant	Female	EAS	49	46	53	51	55	48	46	45	55	53	56	49	10	5	23	17	35	10
Flight Attendant	Male	(EA)S	48	46	56	51	56	49	52	47	53	50	55	48	12	4	36	10	30	8
Florist	Female	E(AC)	50	46	52	49	59	52	47	45	54	50	59	52	10	5	16	6	45	18
Florist	Male	E(AC)	49	46	52	50	59	52	53	47	49	49	58	51	13	4	19	6	43	15
Food Service Manager	Female	C(ES)*	52	48	47	55	55	57	48	47	49	56	55	58	15	6	4	18	21	36
Food Service Manager	Male	(CE)S*	52	50	49	53	58	57	56	51	47	52	58	56	14	6	9	13	27	31
Foreign Language Teacher	Female	(SA)E*	48	48	56	57	53	51	45	47	58	58	53	52	7	4	30	25	18	16
Foreign Language Teacher	Male	(SA)*	47	48	58	58	52	52	50	49	55	57	51	51	8	5	31	33	11	12
Forester	Female	(RI)	56	55	49	48	45	48	52	54	51	49	46	49	37	29	12	9	5	8
Forester	Male	(RI)	54	53	46	47	47	49	57	54	43	45	46	48	34	26	9	9	10	12
Gardener/Groundskeeper	Female	RC	56	50	49	46	50	51	52	49	52	48	51	52	33	10	17	4	11	25
Gardener/Groundskeeper	Male	RE	54	48	47	49	51	47	57	49	45	48	51	47	37	8	15	11	21	8
Geographer	Female	(IR)A	56	57	52	46	49	50	52	56	54	48	50	50	32	29	13	6	10	10
Geographer	Male	(IA)	49	54	53	48	48	50	52	55	50	47	47	50	10	30	24	12	8	16
Geologist	Female	IRA	59	62	52	44	44	47	54	61	54	44	44	48	33	51	6	4	3	3
Geologist	Male	IRA	54	60	52	45	43	47	57	61	49	44	43	47	23	57	13	2	2	3
Hair Stylist	Female	EC*	51	46	49	51	55	52	47	45	52	52	56	53	14	4	13	15	33	21
Hair Stylist	Male	(EA)*	48	47	57	50	58	51	51	48	55	49	58	50	9	3	36	10	30	12
High School Counselor	Female	SE*	49	50	52	61	55	52	46	49	55	62	56	53	8	6	9	41	23	13
High School Counselor	Male	SE*	49	49	53	63	54	53	52	50	50	62	54	52	8	4	10	54	12	12
Home Economics Teacher	Female	SE*	53	48	49	60	58	53	49	47	51	61	58	54	9	3	3	37	33	15
Horticultural Worker	Female	(RE)I*	56	53	51	50	55	51	52	52	54	52	55	52	24	16	10	10	24	16
Horticultural Worker	Male	(RE)I	56	53	50	50	55	50	59	54	47	49	55	50	29	10	12	11	27	11
Housekeeping & Maintenance Supervisor	Female	(EC)S	50	44	45	51	54	54	47	43	48	52	55	55	15	3	6	15	31	30
Housekeeping & Maintenance Supervisor	Male	(EC)S*	52	46	47	52	54	53	55	47	44	51	54	52	22	5	7	20	25	21

Table 7.3 Data Used to Classify Occupational Scales: General Occupational Theme Scale Means and Percent Highest Score on GOT Scales (continued)

Occupational Scale	Gender	Code[a]	Appropriate Gender-Normed GOT Mean						Combined Gender-Normed GOT Mean						Percent Highest Score					
			R	I	A	S	E	C	R	I	A	S	E	C	R	I	A	S	E	C
Human Resources Director	Female	E(AS)	46	45	51	51	54	49	43	44	54	52	54	50	7	8	22	18	31	14
Human Resources Director	Male	ES	48	46	49	52	55	49	52	47	46	51	54	49	15	6	14	20	31	14
Interior Decorator	Female	EA*	51	46	56	45	58	45	47	45	59	47	58	46	9	3	35	3	47	3
Interior Decorator	Male	AE	46	43	59	46	56	46	49	44	57	45	56	46	6	0	55	3	31	5
Investments Manager	Female	(EIR)*	53	54	52	44	53	49	49	53	54	46	54	50	25	24	15	2	26	8
Investments Manager	Male	(EC)I	48	51	50	48	52	53	52	52	48	47	52	52	13	15	17	13	20	22
Lawyer	Female	A	48	50	55	49	50	47	45	49	57	51	50	47	8	18	40	13	14	7
Lawyer	Male	A	46	50	54	49	49	48	50	51	51	48	49	47	7	18	36	13	15	11
Librarian	Female	A	49	50	54	48	49	49	46	49	56	49	49	50	13	13	35	12	13	14
Librarian	Male	A	44	48	57	48	47	49	48	49	54	47	47	49	5	11	50	9	9	16
Life Insurance Agent	Female	E	46	45	49	49	60	50	43	44	52	51	61	50	4	4	10	6	64	12
Life Insurance Agent	Male	E	46	45	46	50	59	49	50	46	43	48	59	49	7	6	6	10	58	13
Marketing Executive	Female	(EA)	47	50	53	47	54	49	44	49	55	48	54	49	8	18	25	7	31	11
Marketing Executive	Male	(EA)	46	49	53	48	54	49	49	50	50	47	53	49	8	13	27	10	34	8
Mathematician	Female	IRC*	55	62	51	48	43	53	51	61	53	50	44	54	15	60	7	4	2	12
Mathematician	Male	I(CA)*	51	60	52	48	43	53	54	61	50	46	42	52	11	50	14	7	1	17
Mathematics Teacher	Female	CIR*	56	58	48	55	52	61	52	57	51	56	52	63	16	21	3	8	8	44
Mathematics Teacher	Male	(CI)S*	54	57	48	55	50	58	58	58	45	54	50	57	15	20	8	13	8	36
Medical Illustrator	Female	(AI)R	54	57	56	43	46	43	50	56	59	45	47	43	19	41	32	3	5	0
Medical Illustrator	Male	AIR	53	56	61	48	47	44	56	57	59	47	46	44	12	18	62	4	2	2
Medical Records Technician	Female	C	47	48	46	49	50	57	44	47	49	51	51	57	9	8	10	14	16	43
Medical Records Technician	Male	C*	47	50	51	51	51	57	50	51	48	49	51	56	10	8	18	12	16	36
Medical Technician	Female	I(RC)	53	56	47	49	50	53	49	55	50	51	51	53	22	29	7	10	11	21
Medical Technician	Male	I(RE)*	55	58	48	51	53	52	58	59	46	50	53	52	23	30	4	11	18	14
Medical Technologist	Female	I(RC)	56	62	50	49	50	55	52	61	53	51	50	56	21	43	4	7	7	18
Medical Technologist	Male	IRC*	57	60	51	53	50	55	60	61	48	51	50	54	22	36	7	10	9	16
Military Enlisted Personnel	Female	C(RE)*	55	50	49	53	54	57	51	49	52	54	55	58	24	7	7	11	19	32
Military Enlisted Personnel	Male	RCE*	57	50	47	52	53	55	60	51	44	51	53	54	36	7	3	15	15	24
Military Officer	Female	R(EI)*	56	52	52	48	53	52	52	51	54	50	54	52	32	14	14	8	20	12
Military Officer	Male	R(EC)*	56	53	48	51	54	54	60	54	46	50	54	53	30	16	5	13	21	15
Minister	Female	SAR*	53	51	57	63	47	47	49	50	60	64	48	48	11	8	16	58	4	3
Minister	Male	SA*	51	50	57	64	53	53	54	51	55	63	52	52	6	3	18	54	7	12

Table 7.3 Data Used to Classify Occupational Scales: General Occupational Theme Scale Means and Percent Highest Score on GOT Scales (continued)

Occupational Scale	Gender	Code[a]	Appropriate Gender-Normed GOT Mean						Combined Gender-Normed GOT Mean						Percent Highest Score					
			R	I	A	S	E	C	R	I	A	S	E	C	R	I	A	S	E	C
Musician	Female	A*	50	51	59	50	48	48	47	50	61	51	49	49	9	10	51	10	9	11
Musician	Male	A	49	50	60	49	49	46	53	51	57	48	48	46	11	6	60	8	8	7
Nurse, LPN	Female	(SC)E	50	49	48	54	51	53	47	48	50	56	51	54	15	7	9	30	15	24
Nurse, LPN	Male	SCE*	49	52	52	58	53	56	52	53	49	56	53	55	12	12	13	32	7	24
Nurse, RN	Female	(SI)	49	52	50	52	48	49	46	51	52	54	48	50	13	21	18	26	10	12
Nurse, RN	Male	(SAI)	49	53	54	53	48	49	52	54	51	52	47	49	14	17	26	23	7	13
Nursing Home Administrator	Female	(C(E)S)	48	46	48	52	53	54	45	45	50	53	53	55	8	5	13	22	21	31
Nursing Home Administrator	Male	(CES)	50	48	48	53	53	54	54	49	46	51	53	53	16	7	10	20	19	28
Occupational Therapist	Female	S(AR)	51	50	52	55	47	46	48	49	54	56	48	46	16	10	19	36	11	8
Occupational Therapist	Male	SA*	51	51	53	55	48	46	54	52	51	53	47	45	17	10	25	33	9	6
Optician	Female	E(CR)	53	50	50	50	58	53	49	49	52	51	58	54	15	11	9	7	40	18
Optician	Male	ER*	55	52	49	50	58	52	59	53	47	49	58	51	26	13	9	6	37	9
Optometrist	Female	IR*	54	59	50	50	51	52	51	58	53	52	52	52	21	38	6	9	11	15
Optometrist	Male	IR*	53	57	50	51	52	51	56	58	48	50	51	50	20	32	7	12	14	15
Paralegal	Female	(CE)	47	45	50	50	51	51	44	44	53	51	52	52	8	5	26	17	20	24
Paralegal	Male	(CA)	47	47	52	49	50	53	51	48	49	48	50	52	13	5	24	16	14	28
Parks and Recreation Coordinator	Female	SE	50	46	49	55	52	48	47	45	51	56	52	48	17	6	12	37	18	10
Parks and Recreation Coordinator	Male	(SE)	50	47	49	53	52	49	53	48	46	52	52	48	17	7	14	31	20	11
Pharmacist	Female	I(CR)	51	57	48	49	49	51	47	56	51	50	49	52	13	43	9	11	10	14
Pharmacist	Male	I(CE)*	51	55	47	50	52	52	54	56	45	48	51	51	15	29	7	14	16	19
Photographer	Female	ARE	54	50	58	47	51	46	50	49	60	48	51	46	23	10	42	6	13	6
Photographer	Male	A(RE)	53	50	57	49	52	46	56	51	54	48	52	46	21	8	40	9	18	4
Physical Education Teacher	Female	(SR)C	58	53	47	57	51	54	53	52	50	59	51	55	33	10	2	26	9	20
Physical Education Teacher	Male	SR*	53	51	48	60	52	52	57	52	46	58	52	52	18	9	4	48	10	11
Physical Therapist	Female	(SI)R	51	54	50	53	47	47	47	53	53	55	47	47	17	24	17	28	7	7
Physical Therapist	Male	(SI)R*	52	54	51	54	48	48	56	55	48	52	48	48	21	21	17	25	6	10
Physician	Female	I(AR)	54	61	54	50	44	47	51	60	56	51	45	48	19	51	12	11	3	4
Physician	Male	IAR	52	60	55	50	45	49	55	61	52	48	45	48	13	49	21	7	3	7
Physicist	Female	IRA	56	63	51	45	40	48	52	62	53	46	41	48	22	67	6	1	1	3
Physicist	Male	I(RA)	52	61	52	45	41	48	55	62	49	44	41	48	11	67	13	2	1	6
Plumber	Male	R	55	47	44	46	50	48	58	48	42	45	49	47	52	10	5	13	13	7
Police Officer	Female	RE	53	47	46	49	51	48	49	46	49	50	52	49	34	4	9	17	24	12
Police Officer	Male	R	53	46	45	49	50	49	56	47	42	48	49	48	38	7	7	14	17	17

Table 7.3 Data Used to Classify Occupational Scales: General Occupational Theme Scale Means and Percent Highest Score on GOT Scales (continued)

Occupational Scale	Gender	Code[a]	Appropriate Gender-Normed GOT Mean						Combined Gender-Normed GOT Mean						Percent Highest Score					
			R	I	A	S	E	C	R	I	A	S	E	C	R	I	A	S	E	C
Psychologist	Female	IA*	51	58	56	51	47	48	47	57	58	53	48	48	12	41	24	13	6	4
Psychologist	Male	(IA)	49	56	56	50	47	48	52	57	54	49	47	48	11	30	32	13	7	7
Public Administrator	Female	A(ER)*	52	51	55	47	53	49	48	50	57	49	53	50	19	13	27	6	26	9
Public Administrator	Male	A(SE)*	50	51	56	54	53	52	53	52	53	53	53	51	10	12	25	22	18	13
Public Relations Director	Female	AE	45	44	57	49	54	43	42	43	59	51	54	44	5	3	48	13	29	2
Public Relations Director	Male	AE	44	44	56	50	52	46	48	45	53	48	52	45	5	4	47	14	23	7
Purchasing Agent	Female	E(CR)*	54	50	52	50	61	54	50	49	54	51	61	55	15	5	8	6	49	17
Purchasing Agent	Male	E(CR)*	54	50	49	52	59	54	57	51	47	51	59	53	16	6	8	12	41	17
Radiologic Technologist	Female	(RIS)	51	51	48	51	50	50	47	50	51	52	51	50	17	17	13	20	16	17
Radiologic Technologist	Male	(RI)	53	52	47	49	49	49	56	53	45	48	49	49	30	22	9	12	14	13
Realtor	Female	E*	49	46	52	51	64	52	45	45	54	53	64	53	3	2	4	5	76	10
Realtor	Male	E*	51	49	51	52	62	52	54	50	48	50	62	51	8	6	7	7	60	12
Reporter	Female	A	50	49	58	49	50	45	46	48	60	51	51	45	12	9	45	13	18	3
Reporter	Male	A	47	48	58	50	48	47	50	49	55	49	48	47	4	8	58	15	8	7
Research & Development Manager	Female	IR*	56	62	51	45	50	51	52	61	53	46	50	51	20	57	6	3	8	6
Research & Development Manager	Male	IRC	57	60	49	48	50	52	60	61	47	47	50	51	28	42	9	3	9	9
Respiratory Therapist	Female	(IR)A*	55	56	52	51	50	50	51	55	54	52	51	50	25	28	12	12	11	12
Respiratory Therapist	Male	I(RS)*	54	57	53	54	51	51	57	58	50	53	50	51	17	29	17	18	10	9
Restaurant Manager	Female	ECR*	52	48	51	51	60	55	48	47	54	52	60	56	14	5	8	9	39	25
Restaurant Manager	Male	ECR	51	46	48	50	59	53	54	47	46	49	59	52	14	6	8	7	53	12
School Administrator	Female	(SE)A	47	50	51	55	54	50	44	49	54	57	54	51	6	14	15	26	25	14
School Administrator	Male	S(EC)*	48	51	49	58	54	53	51	52	47	57	53	52	5	12	11	36	19	17
Science Teacher	Female	I(RS)*	55	63	50	55	50	53	51	62	53	57	50	53	13	52	5	15	6	9
Science Teacher	Male	I(RS)*	56	60	49	55	49	52	59	61	46	54	49	52	20	37	7	18	6	12
Secretary	Female	CES	49	45	50	52	57	59	46	44	53	53	57	60	8	3	9	8	31	41
Small Business Owner	Female	(CE)	50	47	49	48	54	53	47	46	52	49	54	54	12	9	17	6	24	32
Small Business Owner	Male	(RE)	54	48	45	47	54	50	57	49	43	45	53	50	35	6	8	6	30	15
Social Science Teacher	Female	S(EA)*	49	48	53	57	53	51	46	47	56	58	54	52	10	7	20	29	19	15
Social Science Teacher	Male	SEA*	49	47	52	59	54	51	52	48	50	58	53	50	10	3	17	38	20	12
Social Worker	Female	(SA)	47	46	54	54	48	45	44	45	56	55	48	45	8	7	31	32	14	8
Social Worker	Male	SA	46	46	55	57	48	46	50	47	52	55	48	45	7	6	33	39	10	5
Sociologist	Female	IAR	52	59	56	49	46	49	48	58	58	51	46	50	15	42	22	10	5	6
Sociologist	Male	AI*	48	55	57	52	47	52	52	56	54	51	46	51	4	23	35	19	6	13

Table 7.3 Data Used to Classify Occupational Scales: General Occupational Theme Scale Means and Percent Highest Score on GOT Scales (continued)

Occupational Scale	Gender	Code[a]	Appropriate Gender-Normed GOT Mean						Combined Gender-Normed GOT Mean						Percent Highest Score					
			R	I	A	S	E	C	R	I	A	S	E	C	R	I	A	S	E	C
Special Education Teacher	Female	SE	48	46	50	57	51	50	45	45	52	58	52	50	12	4	13	37	20	14
Special Education Teacher	Male	S(EA)	48	47	51	58	51	49	51	48	48	57	50	48	8	6	17	45	13	11
Speech Pathologist	Female	SA	45	48	51	55	49	47	42	47	54	56	49	47	4	11	23	43	10	9
Speech Pathologist	Male	(SA)	45	48	54	55	48	46	48	49	51	53	48	46	4	12	32	35	10	7
Store Manager	Female	E(CA)*	50	48	53	51	62	53	46	47	55	53	62	54	8	3	11	6	55	17
Store Manager	Male	ECS	50	47	50	51	64	54	53	48	47	50	64	53	7	4	5	7	63	14
Technical Writer	Female	AIR	51	53	56	47	47	48	48	52	58	49	48	48	17	22	36	8	8	9
Technical Writer	Male	AI	50	52	57	47	47	48	54	53	54	45	46	47	17	19	45	5	6	8
Translator	Female	A	49	50	55	46	46	47	46	49	58	48	47	48	13	17	47	7	8	8
Translator	Male	AI	47	52	55	46	46	50	50	53	53	45	46	50	8	22	40	7	6	17
Travel Agent	Female	E(CA)	49	47	53	48	60	53	45	46	55	50	60	54	9	5	15	6	48	17
Travel Agent	Male	ECA	48	46	51	49	58	54	51	47	49	48	57	53	9	4	18	7	38	24
Veterinarian	Female	IRA	55	59	51	46	44	47	52	58	53	47	45	48	29	43	13	5	2	8
Veterinarian	Male	IR	53	57	47	48	46	48	57	58	45	46	46	47	24	42	9	11	5	9
Vocational Agriculture Teacher	Female	R(SI)*	57	53	48	54	52	50	53	52	51	55	53	50	30	18	7	18	15	12
Vocational Agriculture Teacher	Male	RSE*	59	52	45	57	55	54	62	54	42	56	54	53	40	7	2	22	15	14

Differentiation between GOT means can cause coding problems in two circumstances. One is when one GOT is much higher than the rest, but all are above 50. For example, an occupational sample might have three scores greater than 50, but one of those scores is relatively higher than the other two. A code for this occupation could include all three Themes or only the highest Theme. The latter solution was chosen for the 1994 *Strong* based on the assumption that the differentiation of interests reflected by the relative levels of the GOTs is an important characteristic of the interests of the people in that occupation. A clear example is that of female auto mechanics. In this sample, two GOT scores exceeded 50: the mean for Realistic was 67, and the mean for Investigative was 51. So as not to diminish the importance of the significant difference between the two areas of interest, only a single code was chosen to represent the scale. Note that most distributions are not so peaked; the maximum score appearing in Table 7.3 is 67, and the minimum is 41.

The other circumstance causing a problem with differentiation is when the distribution of mean GOT scores is flat: in other words, when there is little differentiation. When GOT mean scores are closely clustered, code selection tends to be somewhat more arbitrary, and classification is probably less reliable. This problem is related to the issue of ties.

Because of such coding problems, the following additional guidelines were needed: (1) match the 1994 codes to those used on the 1985 Profile, (2) strive for consistency in the codes for men and women in the same occupation by assigning the same first letter code to each, and (3) use only the top three GOT means. These additional guidelines, along with the data in Table 7.3, were used to assign codes to those occupational samples for which the coding was problematic.

Traditionally, the number of letters appearing in a GOT code has been limited to three, which is reasonable given only six possibilities. When the number of GOT means greater than 50 exceeded three, only the top three were used. If the third and fourth GOT means were the same and at least 1 point lower than the second code, only the top two GOT means were coded. The female Home Economics Teacher scale typifies this case. The top four GOT means were S (60), E (58), R (53), and C (53). The code became SE, and in Table 7.3 an asterisk was placed beside the second letter code to indicate that more than two GOT means exceeded 50. Table 7.3 shows asterisks beside all codes for which the number of eligible mean scores exceeded the number of letters in the code.

Another case in which there were fewer letters in the code than eligible GOT means is illustrated by the female Interior Decorator scale. In this example, the E, A, and R Themes received scores of 58, 56, and 51, respectively. Arguments for including R as the third letter in the code could go either way. To resolve the issue, other sources of information were sought. The combined gender-normed GOT means and the distribution of highest scores in Table 7.3 corroborated the use of only two letters. The corresponding scale for males also only had two eligible scales—A (59) and E (56). The 1985 codes for female and male Interior Decorator were AE and A, respectively. To remain consistent with other sources of information, female Interior Decorator was coded with only two letters, EA.

When attempting to make the codes of both the male and female scale consistent when the scales have had rather flat GOT means, the question arose as to which Theme they would be placed in. For example, both the male and female Investments Manager scales had three GOT means that tied for first place. In this case, both were placed under the Enterprising Theme to remain consistent with the 1985 codes.

Another example of a pair of scales with flat GOT means is Nurse, RN. The two highest means for female Nurse, RN, were tied at 52 on the S and I scales, the same two Themes that composed the 1985 code for this scale. Male Nurse, RN, had three means that tied for highest score—A (54), I (53), and S (53). The 1985 code for male Nurse, RN, was ISR, which meant that on the 1985 Profile this scale was placed under a Theme different from female Nurse, RN. Due to the three-way tie in the mean scores for male Nurse, RN, it was possible to assign this scale a letter code that placed it in the same category as its opposite-gender counterpart. Whenever tied scores made it possible, male-female pairs of scales were placed under the same Theme on the Profile. However, a few occupations (e.g., Athletic Trainer, Dietitian, Farmer, Interior Decorator, Military Enlisted Personnel, Small Business Owner, and Sociologist) had significantly different top mean scores, which placed them in separate sections of the Profile.

The procedures just described provided a practical and user-friendly solution while honoring the complexity of interest patterns within an occupational sample. It should be emphasized, however, that no set of coding rules—including one that is empirical and verifiable—is perfect. Each rule solves some problems while at the same time creating others.

Differences in Theme Codes

Readers familiar with the GOT codes on the 1985 scales will note that the 1994 OSs are associated with longer codes. Because the codes are assigned based on empirical data, they do not match in all cases the codes previously used on the *Strong*. For the 211 occupational scales on the 1994 revision, 167 occupational scales have the same first letter code as they did in 1985, and 50 of these have exactly the same code for all letters. Eighteen scales have different first letters, although all but one of them have the old first letter in the new code. (Note that 26 on the 1994 *Strong* were not represented on the 1985 Profile.) These changes in coding may result from changes in the GOTs, the use of new occupational samples, different coding rules, or some combination of all of these factors.

The codes used on the 1994 *Strong* also may not match exactly codes derived from other sources. When comparing codes across sources, however, it is important to understand how the codes were assigned. Some published sources use expert judgments based on job descriptions instead of data from people actually working in those jobs.

Using Codes to Understand Occupations

Counselors are encouraged to examine the distributions of means and frequencies in Table 7.3. Flat distributions suggest that the occupation is more diverse in terms of the type of people who work in it. More peaked distributions suggest that the occupation attracts individuals with more focused interests. A counselor can tailor this information to a client's needs. For example, a client exhibiting a flat Profile might feel more comfortable in an occupation whose members exhibit a broad span of interests. In contrast, an individual with highly differentiated interests might decide, for whatever reason, to enter an occupation whose code is not congruent with his or her Theme code. This client might stand a better chance of finding a satisfying position in that occupation if it is one that contains people with diverse interests. Appendix B in the back of this guide also lists occupations by code. Counselors can refer to this list to identify additional occupations with particular codes.

Reliability

Reliability is an estimate of the stability of scores over time. Test-retest statistics were computed for each of the OSs and are reported in Table 7.2 (shown earlier) and Table 7.4. Table 7.2 contains only the test-retest correlations for a sample of 191 employed adults tested over a three- to six-month interval. On the average, three- to six-month reliabilities for the 1994 OSs were comparable to those reported over a 30-day interval for the 1985 OSs. Table 7.4 contains complete test-retest information, including means and standard deviations for each administration as well as test-retest correlations for four samples. Sample A was composed of the 191 employed adults just mentioned; Samples B, C, and D were college student samples tested over one- to three-month intervals. Samples C and D had intervening career development experiences. (See Chapter 5 for a detailed description of these samples.) Although the correlations for Samples B and D were somewhat lower than those for Sample A on the average, the high and low correlations for all the samples are for similar scales. The median correlations (not shown in Table 7.4) for Samples A through D were .90, .87, .85, and .84, respectively, and the ranges of correlations were .80 to .95, .70 to .93, .71 to .96, and .66 to .93, respectively. For all four samples the majority of the correlations suggested considerable stability over several months.

Swanson and Hansen (1988) completed an interesting study in which they established the test-retest reliability of individuals' scores on the 1985 *Strong* Profile by correlating scores from a current administration of the *Strong* with those resulting from an administration 12 years earlier. Such a study was possible because the items on the inventory had not changed over this time period.

These researchers found that for 242 females, the median correlation was .72 over all of the male and female OSs, ranging from –.04 to .96 for the individuals. For 167 males the median correlation was .73, ranging from .11 to .96. Overall, the OSs were remarkably reliable over the 12-year period, even though some individuals' Profiles did not show high reliability. Although these data are based on the 1985 *Strong*, there is little reason to believe that the 1994 OSs should behave differently. However, future studies should be done to confirm this prediction.

Concurrent Validity

Concurrent validity is the power of a scale to discriminate between people currently employed in different occupations. Two types of validity information are relevant: first, the contrast between the occupational samples and the GRSs; second, the mean scores of occupational samples on each other's scales.

Percent Overlap

The contrast between the occupational groups and GRSs usually is expressed in terms of *percent overlap*, a statistic suggested by Tilton (1937). This statistic, ranging from 0 to 100 percent, gives the percentage of scores in one distribution (occupational group) that are matched by scores in another distribution (GRS). If the scale discriminates perfectly between the two samples, so that their distributions are entirely separated, the overlap is 0 percent; if the scale does not discriminate at all and the two distributions are identical, the overlap is 100 percent.

Figure 7.1 (page 147) shows the overlap between the female GRS and the female physicist occupational group on the female Physicist scale. The overlap between these two groups, as reported in Table 7.2, is 19 percent. Note that because the GRS is so much larger than the occupational group, the figure shows the proportion of each group with each score rather than the actual number of people with each score. Although the two groups have scores that overlap in the interval of 16 to 65, the distributions are clearly different.

Table 7.4 Test-Retest Reliability Statistics in Four Samples for the 211 Occupational Scales

Occupational Scale	Gender	Test-Retest Correlation	Test Mean	Test S.D.	Retest Mean	Retest S.D.	Test-Retest Correlation	Test Mean	Test S.D.	Retest Mean	Retest S.D.
		Sample A: Employed Adults, 3–6 months (N = 110 women, 81 men)					Sample B: College Students, 1 month (N = 54 women, 30 men)				
Accountant	Female	.92	32.0	12.1	32.3	12.0	.91	26.7	12.5	27.6	12.1
Accountant	Male	.91	27.3	13.6	27.8	13.7	.90	21.5	14.0	21.9	13.9
Actuary	Female	.92	30.9	13.4	32.2	13.7	.90	24.1	13.2	24.8	12.5
Actuary	Male	.87	26.4	12.4	27.0	12.8	.87	21.2	12.5	22.0	12.0
Advertising Executive	Female	.92	28.4	13.0	27.4	13.5	.87	33.4	11.5	33.5	11.6
Advertising Executive	Male	.95	33.6	14.4	33.1	15.2	.93	38.5	12.9	37.8	13.4
Agribusiness Manager	Male	.85	18.5	12.0	19.1	11.6	.87	17.1	12.6	18.3	11.5
Architect	Female	.91	22.4	15.7	24.1	16.5	.87	18.9	13.3	20.0	13.3
Architect	Male	.92	25.7	14.8	27.2	15.0	.87	23.2	13.6	24.5	13.1
Artist, Commercial	Female	.93	14.5	19.4	15.3	20.4	.92	17.1	18.2	17.3	19.0
Artist, Commercial	Male	.92	20.4	17.7	20.7	18.9	.92	26.2	17.7	26.5	18.0
Artist, Fine	Female	.90	16.1	16.0	15.6	16.2	.88	15.9	16.8	15.8	16.4
Artist, Fine	Male	.90	21.4	14.7	20.5	14.9	.89	24.4	15.7	24.7	15.1
Art Teacher	Female	.86	8.9	18.6	9.8	18.9	.90	13.9	19.7	14.8	20.7
Art Teacher	Male	.90	22.7	19.0	23.8	19.7	.91	30.1	19.8	30.3	20.6
Athletic Trainer	Female	.87	18.7	16.7	20.8	17.0	.87	21.7	16.9	22.9	16.4
Athletic Trainer	Male	.88	15.9	15.3	17.2	15.5	.91	22.2	16.7	23.3	16.6
Audiologist	Female	.88	35.2	13.5	36.2	13.5	.85	40.7	13.2	40.8	12.9
Audiologist	Male	.82	40.1	12.7	41.6	11.9	.81	43.4	12.5	43.9	12.6
Auto Mechanic	Female	.95	28.2	14.2	29.1	15.2	.93	22.7	11.4	23.1	12.1
Auto Mechanic	Male	.93	21.1	14.1	21.3	14.4	.89	19.1	11.4	20.2	11.6
Banker	Female	.93	35.1	10.4	34.9	10.6	.91	34.3	9.4	34.9	9.8
Banker	Male	.92	32.4	12.2	32.6	12.3	.91	30.4	11.9	30.3	11.3
Biologist	Female	.93	24.8	16.0	24.8	16.5	.91	19.1	13.5	18.6	14.2
Biologist	Male	.91	25.3	13.9	25.0	13.8	.88	22.5	11.9	21.8	12.7
Bookkeeper	Female	.92	31.4	12.4	31.0	12.7	.87	23.4	10.9	24.1	10.9
Bookkeeper	Male	.92	28.1	13.2	28.0	13.1	.88	22.6	11.3	23.1	11.2
Broadcaster	Female	.91	31.6	13.9	32.0	14.1	.88	34.3	12.4	34.6	13.4
Broadcaster	Male	.92	32.9	14.9	32.9	15.3	.88	38.3	12.3	37.2	13.5

7.4 Test-Retest Reliability Statistics in Four Samples for the 211 Occupational Scales (continued)

Occupational Scale	Gender	Test-Retest Correlation	Test Mean	Test S.D.	Retest Mean	Retest S.D.	Test-Retest Correlation	Test Mean	Test S.D.	Retest Mean	Retest S.D.
		Sample A: Employed Adults, 3–6 months (N = 110 women, 81 men)					Sample B: College Students, 1 month (N = 54 women, 30 men)				
Business Education Teacher	Female	.92	24.7	10.2	24.8	10.8	.86	24.6	9.8	24.5	10.4
Business Education Teacher	Male	.91	33.0	9.8	32.7	10.3	.88	34.7	10.1	34.6	10.3
Buyer	Female	.91	17.0	15.4	17.7	16.0	.89	22.5	15.1	23.3	15.6
Buyer	Male	.88	25.0	15.2	25.9	15.3	.88	28.9	15.5	29.2	15.7
Carpenter	Female	.91	23.1	17.2	24.5	18.1	.86	18.1	13.2	19.2	13.6
Carpenter	Male	.89	20.0	14.1	21.6	14.5	.86	19.3	12.1	20.0	12.0
Chef	Female	.84	24.5	15.4	25.7	15.7	.85	27.2	14.4	27.7	14.8
Chef	Male	.81	30.3	12.6	30.8	13.1	.85	33.7	13.7	34.5	13.5
Chemist	Female	.95	30.7	15.6	31.1	16.1	.91	23.3	11.6	23.7	12.5
Chemist	Male	.94	25.7	15.7	26.2	16.1	.88	17.6	11.5	18.6	12.7
Child Care Provider	Female	.91	26.0	14.3	25.0	14.9	.89	36.8	13.8	36.5	14.3
Chiropractor	Female	.83	32.0	11.1	33.1	10.2	.76	28.8	11.6	29.4	11.8
Chiropractor	Male	.85	32.2	12.1	33.6	11.4	.81	35.1	11.7	35.6	11.9
College Professor	Female	.92	32.8	13.3	33.6	13.1	.86	28.5	11.0	28.5	11.4
College Professor	Male	.90	35.2	14.8	35.8	13.8	.80	32.0	11.0	31.7	11.3
Community Service Organization Director	Female	.92	34.6	11.6	33.9	11.8	.86	42.9	10.5	42.8	10.7
Community Service Organization Director	Male	.89	33.2	12.4	33.2	12.4	.89	41.0	12.7	40.9	12.4
Computer Programmer/ Systems Analyst	Female	.94	36.8	13.4	37.9	13.8	.92	30.1	11.3	30.7	11.8
Computer Programmer/ Systems Analyst	Male	.93	29.0	12.8	29.6	13.0	.89	21.8	10.7	22.7	11.3
Corporate Trainer	Female	.91	33.5	14.4	32.8	14.1	.87	36.3	11.3	35.4	11.9
Corporate Trainer	Male	.89	39.3	12.2	39.5	12.2	.87	41.4	10.8	40.5	11.7
Credit Manager	Female	.92	34.5	12.9	34.6	13.0	.90	31.8	11.5	32.2	11.6
Credit Manager	Male	.89	35.4	11.8	36.2	11.7	.88	33.8	11.9	33.3	11.8
Dental Assistant	Female	.85	26.5	11.1	27.9	11.2	.84	30.1	12.7	30.9	12.2
Dental Hygienist	Female	.80	26.4	12.3	28.3	11.8	.85	31.3	14.4	32.3	13.7

7.4 Test-Retest Reliability Statistics in Four Samples for the 211 Occupational Scales (continued)

Occupational Scale	Gender	Test-Retest Correlation	Test Mean	Test S.D.	Retest Mean	Retest S.D.	Test-Retest Correlation	Test Mean	Test S.D.	Retest Mean	Retest S.D.
		Sample A: Employed Adults, 3–6 months (N = 110 women, 81 men)					Sample B: College Students, 1 month (N = 54 women, 30 men)				
Dentist	Female	.88	29.8	14.0	31.2	14.0	.90	29.8	13.4	30.4	13.7
Dentist	Male	.89	28.2	13.3	30.2	13.3	.88	27.4	12.2	28.2	12.5
Dietitian	Female	.81	29.7	12.2	31.0	11.8	.87	30.7	14.5	31.1	14.8
Dietitian	Male	.82	34.6	11.4	35.6	11.4	.85	38.2	13.4	37.9	12.9
Elected Public Official	Female	.89	26.9	14.8	27.5	14.7	.84	27.2	13.9	26.5	14.0
Elected Public Official	Male	.88	25.7	12.7	26.3	13.0	.85	25.6	11.6	25.5	11.6
Electrician	Female	.92	29.3	15.2	30.9	15.9	.87	25.3	12.8	26.5	13.0
Electrician	Male	.92	16.4	17.6	17.0	17.8	.91	12.4	15.3	14.0	15.2
Elementary School Teacher	Female	.90	27.4	14.4	26.3	15.9	.90	37.9	14.6	37.0	15.7
Elementary School Teacher	Male	.88	33.3	14.7	33.0	15.6	.85	45.1	14.6	44.6	14.9
Emergency Medical Technician	Female	.88	28.6	12.8	29.9	12.6	.86	28.7	12.9	29.3	12.3
Emergency Medical Technician	Male	.91	27.9	12.4	28.9	12.7	.88	28.0	11.3	28.3	11.2
Engineer	Female	.94	36.4	14.7	38.0	14.9	.90	28.8	12.4	30.0	12.6
Engineer	Male	.94	29.7	15.0	30.9	15.5	.88	21.0	11.5	22.4	12.2
English Teacher	Female	.89	23.7	17.8	24.0	17.6	.84	26.9	15.7	26.9	16.7
English Teacher	Male	.90	29.4	16.8	29.6	17.0	.85	31.7	15.0	32.0	15.4
Farmer	Female	.93	29.7	10.2	29.6	10.2	.91	28.5	8.5	28.9	9.0
Farmer	Male	.91	26.6	11.3	26.4	11.2	.87	23.8	9.3	24.2	9.7
Flight Attendant	Female	.89	31.5	12.2	32.2	12.3	.86	37.7	11.3	37.3	11.8
Flight Attendant	Male	.91	40.4	11.1	41.0	11.7	.91	46.2	11.2	45.9	11.8
Florist	Female	.87	17.4	15.1	18.0	15.7	.87	20.3	14.7	21.2	14.9
Florist	Male	.86	27.0	12.8	27.9	13.3	.88	27.5	12.1	28.1	12.6
Food Service Manager	Female	.86	31.3	9.2	32.1	9.4	.84	31.7	10.7	33.0	10.8
Food Service Manager	Male	.84	34.4	9.9	35.3	10.0	.88	36.4	12.3	36.5	11.8
Foreign Language Teacher	Female	.84	22.3	14.4	21.9	15.6	.80	27.2	15.7	27.3	15.8
Foreign Language Teacher	Male	.85	31.8	12.3	31.9	13.0	.79	35.8	12.7	35.7	12.9
Forester	Female	.91	32.2	15.1	32.6	14.9	.90	25.3	12.7	25.7	12.6
Forester	Male	.91	27.1	14.2	27.5	13.8	.87	17.7	10.6	18.3	11.4

7.4 Test-Retest Reliability Statistics in Four Samples for the 211 Occupational Scales (continued)

Occupational Scale	Gender	Test-Retest Correlation	Test Mean	Test S.D.	Retest Mean	Retest S.D.	Test-Retest Correlation	Test Mean	Test S.D.	Retest Mean	Retest S.D.
		Sample A: Employed Adults, 3–6 months (N = 110 women, 81 men)					Sample B: College Students, 1 month (N = 54 women, 30 men)				
Gardener/Groundskeeper	Female	.90	37.6	12.7	38.9	12.6	.85	30.2	10.3	30.7	10.4
Gardener/Groundskeeper	Male	.86	30.7	11.9	31.5	11.5	.88	29.7	10.4	29.9	10.3
Geographer	Female	.89	36.6	13.3	38.4	13.1	.87	30.3	11.9	30.2	12.3
Geographer	Male	.86	24.0	16.4	25.3	15.0	.74	17.2	12.1	16.8	12.5
Geologist	Female	.94	28.0	16.8	29.6	17.4	.90	18.6	14.1	19.3	14.1
Geologist	Male	.94	20.2	16.5	21.2	17.0	.89	13.4	12.6	14.1	13.5
Hair Stylist	Female	.86	23.1	12.6	23.5	12.3	.86	27.7	13.2	28.4	12.6
Hair Stylist	Male	.89	31.6	12.7	32.5	13.4	.88	36.1	13.6	36.7	13.8
High School Counselor	Female	.87	29.4	13.9	29.6	14.3	.83	35.7	13.1	34.9	13.4
High School Counselor	Male	.86	31.0	13.5	30.9	14.0	.81	37.6	12.5	36.9	12.5
Home Economics Teacher	Female	.83	20.7	12.1	21.4	13.0	.86	26.5	15.6	27.2	14.8
Horticultural Worker	Female	.82	26.0	15.6	27.2	14.5	.83	19.0	15.4	21.0	14.4
Horticultural Worker	Male	.87	21.9	14.6	22.8	14.8	.84	17.7	13.5	19.2	12.8
Housekeeping & Maintenance Supervisor	Female	.91	32.9	11.0	32.9	10.9	.89	34.9	10.3	35.0	9.7
Housekeeping & Maintenance Supervisor	Male	.91	33.8	11.5	34.5	11.5	.89	36.5	11.5	36.1	10.4
Human Resources Director	Female	.92	32.7	14.5	32.4	14.9	.91	35.7	12.9	35.0	14.0
Human Resources Director	Male	.89	35.0	11.9	35.6	12.3	.87	37.3	10.9	36.4	11.7
Interior Decorator	Female	.90	14.7	15.6	15.8	16.1	.90	15.8	14.4	16.8	14.7
Interior Decorator	Male	.94	29.9	12.9	29.5	13.4	.93	34.7	12.1	34.8	12.3
Investments Manager	Female	.90	29.7	11.8	30.6	11.8	.86	24.8	10.0	24.4	10.4
Investments Manager	Male	.85	25.8	11.8	26.1	11.6	.80	18.9	11.0	18.9	9.8
Lawyer	Female	.92	35.0	15.4	35.7	15.6	.87	33.6	13.4	33.1	14.1
Lawyer	Male	.92	35.7	14.3	36.2	14.3	.88	35.9	12.6	34.7	12.9
Librarian	Female	.92	33.7	15.1	33.8	14.4	.90	27.0	13.3	26.9	13.1
Librarian	Male	.94	39.1	13.3	38.8	13.4	.90	38.3	12.1	38.0	12.4
Life Insurance Agent	Female	.92	29.8	13.0	29.6	13.5	.87	30.0	10.6	30.7	11.4
Life Insurance Agent	Male	.91	26.1	13.2	26.1	13.7	.89	28.4	10.9	28.9	11.5

7.4 Test-Retest Reliability Statistics in Four Samples for the 211 Occupational Scales (continued)

Occupational Scale	Gender	Test-Retest Correlation	Test Mean	Test S.D.	Retest Mean	Retest S.D.	Test-Retest Correlation	Test Mean	Test S.D.	Retest Mean	Retest S.D.
		Sample A: Employed Adults, 3–6 months (N = 110 women, 81 men)					Sample B: College Students, 1 month (N = 54 women, 30 men)				
Marketing Executive	Female	.89	31.7	12.6	31.0	12.6	.70	29.2	10.3	28.7	9.9
Marketing Executive	Male	.91	33.0	13.5	32.5	13.6	.83	31.6	10.4	31.0	11.6
Mathematician	Female	.94	19.9	17.7	20.4	18.1	.88	9.1	14.4	10.1	15.8
Mathematician	Male	.92	12.7	17.3	13.3	17.6	.84	6.4	12.8	7.0	13.7
Mathematics Teacher	Female	.87	24.6	13.2	25.6	12.9	.81	22.0	12.9	23.1	12.9
Mathematics Teacher	Male	.87	18.9	14.0	19.9	14.1	.79	16.8	13.0	17.8	13.2
Medical Illustrator	Female	.89	12.8	15.9	14.4	16.7	.90	9.5	16.8	9.4	16.9
Medical Illustrator	Male	.86	16.6	16.8	18.6	16.9	.86	17.9	18.1	19.2	17.8
Medical Records Technician	Female	.87	37.0	10.3	37.8	10.5	.87	35.8	9.6	36.8	9.8
Medical Records Technician	Male	.83	41.0	11.1	41.9	11.0	.81	41.0	11.1	40.8	11.6
Medical Technician	Female	.87	26.3	12.0	27.7	12.4	.82	22.5	12.5	23.8	12.9
Medical Technician	Male	.89	27.1	13.4	28.5	13.5	.88	23.4	13.7	24.6	13.7
Medical Technologist	Female	.90	28.4	15.5	30.5	15.8	.88	22.9	15.0	24.5	15.3
Medical Technologist	Male	.90	29.9	13.2	31.6	13.6	.87	26.9	12.6	27.7	12.4
Military Enlisted Personnel	Female	.86	34.7	10.5	36.2	10.4	.80	33.9	10.4	34.8	9.6
Military Enlisted Personnel	Male	.87	28.3	12.4	29.6	12.5	.83	26.3	11.3	27.2	11.0
Military Officer	Female	.88	35.7	12.7	37.3	12.6	.87	32.5	12.1	32.2	12.4
Military Officer	Male	.90	27.0	12.9	28.6	13.0	.87	23.2	13.0	23.9	13.0
Minister	Female	.89	19.2	16.4	19.5	16.7	.83	23.9	13.8	23.6	14.1
Minister	Male	.87	31.3	13.7	31.2	13.5	.84	34.8	11.2	34.9	11.5
Musician	Female	.92	23.0	18.2	23.3	18.1	.87	26.5	17.1	27.1	17.4
Musician	Male	.92	35.0	14.2	35.3	14.2	.89	40.0	13.6	40.0	13.4
Nurse, LPN	Female	.87	20.7	12.6	21.5	13.2	.81	24.0	14.1	24.7	13.9
Nurse, LPN	Male	.82	31.7	9.8	33.1	10.1	.80	35.5	11.3	36.4	10.7
Nurse, RN	Female	.88	32.3	13.7	32.5	14.0	.82	38.8	12.7	39.0	13.1
Nurse, RN	Male	.87	35.6	13.6	36.5	13.4	.78	41.5	13.3	41.4	12.9
Nursing Home Administrator	Female	.85	33.3	11.1	34.5	11.2	.80	34.8	11.8	35.5	12.0
Nursing Home Administrator	Male	.86	38.7	11.5	39.5	11.6	.76	39.4	10.6	39.4	10.8

7.4 Test-Retest Reliability Statistics in Four Samples for the 211 Occupational Scales (continued)

Occupational Scale	Gender	Test-Retest Correlation	Test Mean	Test S.D.	Retest Mean	Retest S.D.	Test-Retest Correlation	Test Mean	Test S.D.	Retest Mean	Retest S.D.
		Sample A: Employed Adults, 3–6 months (N = 110 women, 81 men)					Sample B: College Students, 1 month (N = 54 women, 30 men)				
Occupational Therapist	Female	.89	31.3	13.2	30.8	12.9	.87	37.9	13.7	37.6	12.8
Occupational Therapist	Male	.89	37.7	12.3	37.6	12.1	.89	46.4	13.0	46.3	12.3
Optician	Female	.80	32.5	11.4	34.1	11.2	.83	33.5	13.3	35.0	12.4
Optician	Male	.86	28.8	11.5	30.3	11.0	.84	27.7	12.1	28.9	11.4
Optometrist	Female	.90	36.5	13.1	38.3	13.3	.85	33.4	12.4	34.0	12.7
Optometrist	Male	.88	26.2	15.0	27.7	14.6	.86	24.3	14.7	25.5	15.1
Paralegal	Female	.91	35.5	13.1	35.2	13.1	.86	40.2	10.1	39.1	10.4
Paralegal	Male	.83	37.7	12.4	37.7	12.2	.81	37.9	11.0	36.5	11.2
Parks and Recreation Coordinator	Female	.90	36.0	11.6	36.1	11.5	.88	43.2	11.5	42.8	11.2
Parks and Recreation Coordinator	Male	.91	36.1	11.0	36.4	10.8	.89	41.7	10.3	41.5	10.6
Pharmacist	Female	.90	32.1	14.9	34.0	15.3	.82	32.2	13.5	33.7	13.4
Pharmacist	Male	.85	36.3	12.8	38.1	12.7	.82	38.0	13.3	39.0	13.4
Photographer	Female	.90	30.0	14.5	30.5	14.7	.85	28.8	13.3	29.4	13.5
Photographer	Male	.90	28.7	14.1	29.4	14.2	.87	29.8	13.2	30.8	13.9
Physical Education Teacher	Female	.89	21.7	16.6	22.2	16.4	.90	25.9	16.3	25.8	15.2
Physical Education Teacher	Male	.85	15.3	15.8	15.4	16.2	.88	24.3	17.1	24.2	16.3
Physical Therapist	Female	.90	30.0	13.6	30.6	13.4	.87	38.1	12.9	38.2	12.6
Physical Therapist	Male	.88	32.1	14.6	33.7	14.2	.87	37.9	13.8	38.3	13.6
Physician	Female	.93	25.8	15.7	26.7	15.9	.84	20.2	13.4	21.6	14.4
Physician	Male	.90	26.0	16.9	27.1	17.1	.81	21.6	14.7	23.5	15.2
Physicist	Female	.94	18.9	18.1	19.6	19.1	.92	10.6	14.1	11.1	15.4
Physicist	Male	.92	17.1	16.4	17.6	16.9	.87	9.7	12.2	10.3	13.2
Plumber	Male	.91	28.3	11.2	28.8	11.1	.87	25.9	9.1	26.6	9.8
Police Officer	Female	.92	35.8	11.0	36.0	11.3	.88	40.0	10.4	39.6	9.8
Police Officer	Male	.92	25.3	13.2	25.3	13.1	.85	28.4	11.6	27.5	10.9
Psychologist	Female	.89	28.7	14.7	29.9	13.9	.85	31.1	11.9	30.8	12.3
Psychologist	Male	.91	30.1	15.0	30.5	14.4	.88	32.0	12.2	31.0	12.4

7.4 Test-Retest Reliability Statistics in Four Samples for the 211 Occupational Scales (continued)

Occupational Scale	Gender	Test-Retest Correlation	Test		Retest		Test-Retest Correlation	Test		Retest	
			Mean	S.D.	Mean	S.D.		Mean	S.D.	Mean	S.D.
			Sample A: Employed Adults, 3–6 months (N = 110 women, 81 men)					Sample B: College Students, 1 month (N = 54 women, 30 men)			
Public Administrator	Female	.90	29.5	15.2	30.5	15.1	.86	28.2	13.7	27.7	14.0
Public Administrator	Male	.89	30.6	14.8	31.3	14.8	.84	31.6	13.2	31.1	14.2
Public Relations Director	Female	.94	22.6	18.4	22.1	18.7	.91	24.8	16.7	23.4	16.9
Public Relations Director	Male	.94	30.4	15.8	29.9	16.6	.91	33.4	13.8	32.6	15.0
Purchasing Agent	Female	.85	31.7	13.3	33.2	13.1	.87	31.4	14.9	31.7	14.7
Purchasing Agent	Male	.86	30.5	12.1	31.7	12.2	.85	31.1	12.8	30.4	12.9
Radiologic Technologist	Female	.89	33.1	11.7	34.3	12.0	.81	38.6	9.8	39.5	9.7
Radiologic Technologist	Male	.92	34.4	12.6	35.1	12.9	.90	36.7	10.3	37.7	10.7
Realtor	Female	.88	20.0	13.9	21.0	14.2	.85	19.8	15.1	20.6	15.0
Realtor	Male	.87	28.9	12.3	29.5	12.6	.88	30.6	12.3	30.8	13.0
Reporter	Female	.92	26.6	17.4	26.7	17.4	.88	28.3	15.5	28.6	16.1
Reporter	Male	.91	30.2	16.2	30.4	16.4	.85	32.1	15.4	31.9	15.6
Research & Development Manager	Female	.93	28.3	16.8	30.1	17.1	.88	22.0	15.2	23.2	15.7
Research & Development Manager	Male	.92	22.2	16.1	23.8	16.6	.89	15.6	14.2	16.8	14.9
Respiratory Therapist	Female	.86	33.0	14.5	35.1	14.4	.82	31.3	13.6	32.5	13.5
Respiratory Therapist	Male	.85	29.7	14.6	31.7	14.7	.79	30.8	14.5	31.4	14.5
Restaurant Manager	Female	.87	29.8	13.1	31.5	13.4	.87	29.8	14.1	30.6	13.9
Restaurant Manager	Male	.86	28.7	12.6	29.6	13.0	.90	31.2	13.8	31.5	13.5
School Administrator	Female	.89	34.3	12.8	34.4	12.9	.83	36.1	12.2	35.7	12.6
School Administrator	Male	.87	31.6	12.7	32.0	12.9	.84	33.0	12.8	32.2	12.9
Science Teacher	Female	.89	24.2	15.8	25.7	15.7	.83	22.3	14.5	22.6	15.1
Science Teacher	Male	.90	26.6	14.4	27.6	14.2	.87	25.5	13.0	26.0	13.2
Secretary	Female	.89	27.7	12.2	28.6	12.7	.87	28.7	13.8	30.0	14.1
Small Business Owner	Female	.87	40.2	10.7	41.1	11.1	.82	38.1	10.8	39.2	10.8
Small Business Owner	Male	.88	31.0	11.2	32.0	11.3	.86	28.8	9.5	30.3	9.5
Social Science Teacher	Female	.87	33.2	13.2	34.0	13.0	.80	35.1	11.9	34.3	12.3
Social Science Teacher	Male	.87	33.6	12.4	34.1	12.9	.83	38.5	11.3	37.7	11.3

7.4 Test-Retest Reliability Statistics in Four Samples for the 211 Occupational Scales (continued)

Occupational Scale	Gender	Test-Retest Correlation	Test Mean	Test S.D.	Retest Mean	Retest S.D.	Test-Retest Correlation	Test Mean	Test S.D.	Retest Mean	Retest S.D.
		Sample A: Employed Adults, 3–6 months (N = 110 women, 81 men)					Sample B: College Students, 1 month (N = 54 women, 30 men)				
Social Worker	Female	.89	31.7	12.7	30.2	13.3	.89	43.1	12.0	41.4	12.1
Social Worker	Male	.91	34.6	13.9	33.7	14.1	.91	45.8	13.0	44.6	12.9
Sociologist	Female	.90	25.1	16.0	26.0	15.4	.86	25.5	13.0	24.7	13.6
Sociologist	Male	.89	29.5	15.5	30.0	14.8	.85	30.1	13.0	29.6	13.4
Special Education Teacher	Female	.88	28.7	13.7	27.4	14.8	.87	42.1	14.3	41.6	14.3
Special Education Teacher	Male	.88	36.5	13.0	35.3	13.8	.87	48.8	13.6	48.1	13.7
Speech Pathologist	Female	.91	31.3	13.9	30.2	14.3	.91	42.6	13.2	41.3	13.2
Speech Pathologist	Male	.90	38.2	13.0	37.5	13.5	.89	48.6	12.1	46.9	12.1
Store Manager	Female	.88	29.5	12.2	30.6	12.5	.89	33.1	13.2	33.7	13.7
Store Manager	Male	.89	29.1	12.1	30.0	12.6	.88	30.5	13.6	30.9	14.3
Technical Writer	Female	.92	31.8	15.6	32.4	15.5	.89	29.9	14.1	30.2	14.2
Technical Writer	Male	.93	36.5	13.7	36.5	13.7	.90	34.6	12.6	34.7	12.3
Translator	Female	.92	29.1	15.7	29.2	16.1	.89	26.1	16.0	25.1	15.5
Translator	Male	.93	36.4	11.8	36.0	12.0	.91	32.1	11.7	31.9	11.4
Travel Agent	Female	.86	31.1	12.9	32.0	12.8	.86	32.3	13.4	32.5	13.6
Travel Agent	Male	.91	34.8	12.4	34.6	12.3	.86	36.6	12.3	36.1	12.6
Veterinarian	Female	.92	27.0	16.2	28.2	16.6	.90	22.6	14.1	23.5	14.6
Veterinarian	Male	.91	26.9	15.9	28.3	16.4	.86	23.7	14.0	24.1	14.6
Vocational Agriculture Teacher	Female	.86	23.5	15.3	24.4	14.5	.86	21.0	13.7	21.4	13.2
Vocational Agriculture Teacher	Male	.86	21.3	12.1	21.7	11.6	.81	17.7	10.6	18.2	10.1
		Sample C: College Students, 3 months (N = 56 women, 23 men)					Sample D: College Students, 3 months (N = 61 women, 26 men)				
Accountant	Female	.87	34.5	11.9	35.8	13.3	.88	35.9	13.3	35.9	13.5
Accountant	Male	.88	28.6	14.1	30.7	15.3	.87	30.8	14.1	31.5	14.4
Actuary	Female	.84	24.2	11.6	26.0	12.7	.83	26.0	11.4	26.2	13.1
Actuary	Male	.79	20.1	10.5	21.5	11.5	.78	23.2	11.2	23.5	12.2

7.4 Test-Retest Reliability Statistics in Four Samples for the 211 Occupational Scales (continued)

Occupational Scale	Gender	Test-Retest Correlation	Test		Retest		Test-Retest Correlation	Test		Retest	
			Mean	S.D.	Mean	S.D.		Mean	S.D.	Mean	S.D.
		Sample C: College Students, 3 months (N = 56 women, 23 men)					Sample D: College Students, 3 months (N = 61 women, 26 men)				
Advertising Executive	Female	.86	35.1	10.9	35.6	11.8	.76	38.3	10.1	38.6	11.8
Advertising Executive	Male	.90	34.7	11.1	35.7	11.9	.82	40.8	10.7	41.4	11.6
Agribusiness Manager	Male	.77	22.4	11.2	24.9	11.7	.76	18.9	10.9	19.0	10.8
Architect	Female	.82	10.4	12.7	12.3	13.7	.86	19.1	15.6	18.8	14.2
Architect	Male	.82	16.5	12.0	18.3	12.9	.88	21.4	15.0	21.2	14.7
Artist, Commercial	Female	.90	5.3	16.5	8.8	18.1	.85	14.8	18.1	15.0	18.7
Artist, Commercial	Male	.93	17.3	15.6	18.8	16.7	.83	24.2	14.9	25.1	16.0
Artist, Fine	Female	.85	8.1	14.6	8.1	14.6	.79	14.4	14.9	13.8	15.6
Artist, Fine	Male	.83	19.1	13.6	17.8	14.1	.80	21.3	12.9	21.7	14.3
Art Teacher	Female	.88	3.6	17.4	6.4	19.5	.85	9.4	21.1	11.1	20.0
Art Teacher	Male	.94	17.7	17.5	19.4	20.1	.87	25.6	19.1	26.7	19.3
Athletic Trainer	Female	.82	12.5	14.5	17.6	16.5	.83	17.2	18.8	17.5	18.2
Athletic Trainer	Male	.87	19.5	13.7	22.0	15.3	.85	18.5	15.9	18.6	15.8
Audiologist	Female	.86	37.0	14.3	36.1	14.1	.83	34.3	14.6	34.4	15.0
Audiologist	Male	.79	34.5	12.4	37.0	12.8	.78	35.9	15.2	36.1	15.4
Auto Mechanic	Female	.89	22.0	10.9	24.0	11.9	.86	21.8	11.3	21.6	11.1
Auto Mechanic	Male	.92	25.8	10.9	25.7	11.7	.91	20.5	10.8	20.1	11.7
Banker	Female	.85	43.4	9.3	43.7	9.9	.90	42.0	10.2	42.4	10.4
Banker	Male	.89	39.7	12.1	40.4	12.6	.87	38.1	12.9	38.1	12.9
Biologist	Female	.81	9.3	12.2	8.3	11.5	.88	8.4	12.9	8.5	13.9
Biologist	Male	.79	14.3	11.7	11.9	11.6	.87	12.7	12.0	12.7	12.9
Bookkeeper	Female	.85	31.3	11.8	32.5	12.5	.85	30.9	11.7	30.8	11.5
Bookkeeper	Male	.87	33.9	12.2	34.3	13.1	.87	32.8	13.2	32.5	13.2
Broadcaster	Female	.87	27.0	11.5	30.4	12.5	.88	35.9	12.9	37.1	13.0
Broadcaster	Male	.90	29.2	12.8	31.8	14.1	.88	38.1	12.8	38.8	13.0
Business Education Teacher	Female	.82	30.6	10.5	30.8	11.1	.89	29.3	10.5	30.8	11.2
Business Education Teacher	Male	.79	39.0	9.9	39.9	10.1	.85	39.0	10.0	40.0	10.6
Buyer	Female	.83	28.8	14.0	32.6	13.6	.81	30.0	13.6	30.7	14.6
Buyer	Male	.85	31.8	15.2	36.2	15.7	.79	35.4	13.8	36.0	15.3

139

7.4 Test-Retest Reliability Statistics in Four Samples for the 211 Occupational Scales (continued)

Occupational Scale	Gender	Test-Retest Correlation	Test Mean	Test S.D.	Retest Mean	Retest S.D.	Test-Retest Correlation	Test Mean	Test S.D.	Retest Mean	Retest S.D.
			Sample C: College Students, 3 months (N = 56 women, 23 men)					Sample D: College Students, 3 months (N = 61 women, 26 men)			
Carpenter	Female	.82	11.8	12.4	15.8	14.4	.83	16.2	15.1	15.9	14.3
Carpenter	Male	.81	19.1	10.5	21.9	11.8	.83	20.0	11.6	19.8	11.5
Chef	Female	.75	22.9	14.0	27.5	15.7	.73	24.8	15.1	25.0	14.2
Chef	Male	.77	33.2	11.7	36.0	13.0	.71	34.5	12.3	34.7	12.3
Chemist	Female	.83	18.0	10.2	17.8	10.4	.85	19.3	12.1	18.4	12.8
Chemist	Male	.80	12.9	9.9	12.0	10.1	.80	13.3	12.1	13.3	12.6
Child Care Provider	Female	.91	38.9	16.7	36.0	16.6	.85	34.4	12.8	35.2	14.9
Chiropractor	Female	.79	23.8	10.8	26.4	12.8	.84	24.1	12.7	25.0	13.1
Chiropractor	Male	.85	28.4	12.1	30.2	13.1	.82	30.3	12.9	30.7	13.5
College Professor	Female	.86	17.9	10.2	18.5	11.0	.84	21.1	13.2	22.2	13.2
College Professor	Male	.83	19.6	11.2	19.9	12.2	.88	24.4	14.0	25.3	14.1
Community Service Organization Director	Female	.81	45.2	9.4	45.0	9.0	.79	45.3	10.4	46.0	10.8
Community Service Organization Director	Male	.86	38.7	11.4	40.0	12.2	.81	41.0	11.7	42.1	11.6
Computer Programmer/ Systems Analyst	Female	.81	24.9	9.8	25.7	10.6	.85	26.8	11.3	26.4	11.7
Computer Programmer/ Systems Analyst	Male	.81	17.8	8.8	17.0	8.9	.87	17.9	11.1	17.5	11.3
Corporate Trainer	Female	.87	30.2	12.0	31.7	11.9	.86	35.7	12.0	37.3	13.4
Corporate Trainer	Male	.83	39.1	10.4	40.7	10.8	.84	41.5	11.5	42.8	12.3
Credit Manager	Female	.88	42.2	12.5	43.2	12.9	.87	41.1	13.0	41.7	13.5
Credit Manager	Male	.84	36.8	12.5	40.4	13.1	.81	39.1	11.9	40.2	12.9
Dental Assistant	Female	.81	33.1	11.7	34.6	11.6	.75	28.8	12.6	29.3	12.2
Dental Hygienist	Female	.82	29.2	13.2	32.1	13.5	.83	27.8	15.2	29.1	14.4
Dentist	Female	.87	20.6	13.7	23.3	14.4	.88	23.2	15.6	23.2	16.2
Dentist	Male	.85	20.2	12.9	22.3	13.3	.89	21.3	15.0	22.0	15.5
Dietitian	Female	.82	26.4	12.1	30.1	13.4	.85	25.3	13.7	25.8	14.1
Dietitian	Male	.80	37.9	12.2	40.3	13.3	.77	36.3	12.6	37.2	12.7

7.4 Test-Retest Reliability Statistics in Four Samples for the 211 Occupational Scales (continued)

Occupational Scale	Gender	Test-Retest Correlation	Test Mean	Test S.D.	Retest Mean	Retest S.D.	Test-Retest Correlation	Test Mean	Test S.D.	Retest Mean	Retest S.D.
		Sample C: College Students, 3 months (N = 56 women, 23 men)					Sample D: College Students, 3 months (N = 61 women, 26 men)				
Elected Public Official	Female	.86	21.3	12.1	24.2	13.9	.88	26.9	13.5	29.7	14.9
Elected Public Official	Male	.87	22.6	10.1	25.3	11.5	.87	28.1	11.0	30.1	12.4
Electrician	Female	.83	18.5	12.0	22.6	13.7	.84	23.4	13.8	23.2	12.8
Electrician	Male	.89	15.1	14.1	17.7	15.9	.82	14.7	13.9	13.3	12.4
Elementary School Teacher	Female	.90	37.9	17.5	35.0	17.9	.82	35.3	14.3	35.3	15.1
Elementary School Teacher	Male	.89	40.6	19.2	38.0	19.1	.80	38.2	15.5	38.7	16.9
Emergency Medical Technician	Female	.79	25.6	10.6	29.1	12.1	.78	25.3	13.1	25.0	13.2
Emergency Medical Technician	Male	.85	25.1	9.3	27.7	10.8	.83	24.7	11.4	24.2	11.3
Engineer	Female	.82	25.0	10.4	27.7	11.9	.84	27.6	12.9	27.4	12.7
Engineer	Male	.84	19.4	10.1	21.0	11.4	.82	20.5	12.1	20.3	12.5
English Teacher	Female	.89	15.8	15.7	17.7	16.7	.87	23.1	17.0	25.6	18.2
English Teacher	Male	.92	21.3	14.9	21.9	16.6	.89	28.7	16.2	30.2	17.0
Farmer	Female	.89	36.9	8.4	36.5	9.1	.84	30.6	8.7	29.8	8.4
Farmer	Male	.90	31.5	9.9	30.9	10.2	.86	25.7	10.2	24.9	10.1
Flight Attendant	Female	.79	38.0	10.5	41.6	9.3	.82	39.7	10.4	40.2	10.8
Flight Attendant	Male	.87	44.8	9.7	47.2	9.8	.84	46.9	9.2	47.1	10.0
Florist	Female	.80	23.3	13.8	27.3	12.9	.72	22.1	13.4	21.9	12.0
Florist	Male	.79	30.6	11.2	34.3	11.4	.77	29.0	10.9	29.2	10.9
Food Service Manager	Female	.81	35.2	10.0	36.8	10.6	.73	32.6	9.6	33.1	9.6
Food Service Manager	Male	.75	36.4	10.1	39.4	10.5	.74	38.0	9.9	38.4	10.5
Foreign Language Teacher	Female	.90	21.4	16.7	21.2	16.5	.85	23.5	15.5	25.9	16.3
Foreign Language Teacher	Male	.91	31.4	13.6	30.2	14.1	.87	32.2	12.4	34.1	13.6
Forester	Female	.85	18.4	11.4	19.2	12.7	.90	17.6	13.1	17.9	13.4
Forester	Male	.86	16.2	10.2	17.2	11.4	.84	12.4	10.8	12.2	10.9
Gardener/Groundskeeper	Female	.84	27.5	10.5	31.1	11.5	.84	27.8	10.3	27.3	10.4
Gardener/Groundskeeper	Male	.74	31.1	8.7	33.5	9.1	.80	27.9	9.8	27.6	9.7
Geographer	Female	.82	21.8	11.2	25.1	12.8	.78	25.4	12.2	26.0	12.3
Geographer	Male	.81	5.2	13.5	5.7	14.1	.86	7.7	14.0	9.9	14.4

7.4 Test-Retest Reliability Statistics in Four Samples for the 211 Occupational Scales (continued)

Occupational Scale	Gender	Test-Retest Correlation	Test Mean	Test S.D.	Retest Mean	Retest S.D.	Test-Retest Correlation	Test Mean	Test S.D.	Retest Mean	Retest S.D.
		Sample C: College Students, 3 months (N = 56 women, 23 men)					Sample D: College Students, 3 months (N = 61 women, 26 men)				
Geologist	Female	.84	11.6	12.2	14.2	13.6	.83	14.2	14.2	13.3	14.0
Geologist	Male	.81	6.2	12.2	5.4	12.1	.80	5.8	12.9	4.8	13.5
Hair Stylist	Female	.75	33.4	11.2	36.2	10.4	.79	29.9	11.0	30.0	10.5
Hair Stylist	Male	.85	35.7	11.8	38.7	11.5	.77	36.5	11.6	37.7	11.3
High School Counselor	Female	.88	29.6	14.1	30.4	13.3	.85	32.9	13.7	34.8	14.6
High School Counselor	Male	.89	31.7	14.3	31.1	13.9	.85	32.6	13.5	34.8	14.9
Home Economics Teacher	Female	.83	27.5	15.1	29.1	15.2	.82	25.2	15.1	26.6	14.8
Horticultural Worker	Female	.71	16.1	13.5	21.2	14.6	.79	14.7	14.3	14.3	14.2
Horticultural Worker	Male	.77	14.5	12.6	18.7	12.9	.82	13.2	13.2	12.3	12.6
Housekeeping & Maintenance Supervisor	Female	.85	43.4	9.5	44.0	9.3	.81	39.1	10.3	38.9	9.4
Housekeeping & Maintenance Supervisor	Male	.82	41.5	10.0	44.3	9.9	.74	38.3	9.9	37.9	10.5
Human Resources Director	Female	.87	35.9	12.7	37.9	12.1	.87	39.1	12.5	40.9	14.5
Human Resources Director	Male	.88	37.2	10.4	40.0	10.4	.88	39.7	11.1	41.6	12.2
Interior Decorator	Female	.88	13.4	14.4	18.2	14.7	.74	18.6	13.7	19.6	12.8
Interior Decorator	Male	.91	33.0	11.0	33.7	10.9	.84	34.9	10.9	35.6	10.6
Investments Manager	Female	.88	22.1	12.4	23.8	13.4	.81	27.4	11.3	27.7	11.1
Investments Manager	Male	.83	20.7	11.8	22.3	13.3	.82	23.9	12.8	24.8	12.8
Lawyer	Female	.89	26.0	13.8	28.7	14.2	.91	35.8	14.0	37.3	15.2
Lawyer	Male	.88	28.9	11.9	31.1	12.9	.90	38.1	13.1	39.7	14.1
Librarian	Female	.91	19.8	13.1	19.7	13.4	.91	24.4	15.1	25.9	15.1
Librarian	Male	.96	31.1	11.9	29.9	12.7	.93	34.1	12.4	35.3	12.2
Life Insurance Agent	Female	.88	35.4	11.7	38.0	12.6	.88	37.5	11.5	38.3	12.6
Life Insurance Agent	Male	.90	34.4	11.7	36.8	12.7	.88	36.5	12.1	37.1	12.8
Marketing Executive	Female	.90	29.0	12.8	30.9	13.1	.77	34.0	11.9	34.4	12.2
Marketing Executive	Male	.86	30.2	11.0	31.7	12.0	.83	34.8	13.0	36.6	13.3
Mathematician	Female	.82	2.1	11.9	1.7	12.2	.82	4.3	13.8	3.9	14.7
Mathematician	Male	.83	1.2	12.8	-1.7	11.7	.83	0.1	13.3	-0.2	13.5

7.4 Test-Retest Reliability Statistics in Four Samples for the 211 Occupational Scales (continued)

Occupational Scale	Gender	Test-Retest Correlation	Test Mean	Test S.D.	Retest Mean	Retest S.D.	Test-Retest Correlation	Test Mean	Test S.D.	Retest Mean	Retest S.D.
		Sample C: College Students, 3 months (N = 56 women, 23 men)					Sample D: College Students, 3 months (N = 61 women, 26 men)				
Mathematics Teacher	Female	.82	19.6	11.9	20.9	12.9	.81	20.2	12.8	20.2	13.0
Mathematics Teacher	Male	.80	14.0	11.5	14.6	13.0	.78	14.9	13.0	14.5	13.8
Medical Illustrator	Female	.81	-3.1	14.7	0.1	17.5	.88	1.4	17.9	1.3	17.9
Medical Illustrator	Male	.87	5.9	15.6	9.3	18.4	.87	11.5	19.0	12.2	18.8
Medical Records Technician	Female	.77	38.9	8.3	39.9	9.4	.82	36.7	9.1	36.9	10.0
Medical Records Technician	Male	.78	39.5	9.8	41.6	11.5	.73	39.4	10.0	40.3	10.7
Medical Technician	Female	.80	22.5	11.0	24.7	11.9	.78	18.6	12.2	17.4	12.4
Medical Technician	Male	.84	19.1	11.1	22.0	12.6	.83	17.4	13.3	17.4	13.4
Medical Technologist	Female	.86	16.5	12.9	19.1	14.3	.84	16.8	15.1	16.5	15.4
Medical Technologist	Male	.84	20.4	11.2	23.2	12.6	.84	20.8	13.3	20.6	13.5
Military Enlisted Personnel	Female	.71	33.6	9.0	36.5	11.0	.75	33.8	10.3	33.9	10.0
Military Enlisted Personnel	Male	.74	27.0	9.2	28.8	11.3	.73	24.9	10.4	24.5	9.6
Military Officer	Female	.79	27.2	10.6	31.0	12.4	.74	31.2	10.9	32.4	10.9
Military Officer	Male	.78	20.3	10.3	22.6	12.4	.75	22.8	10.8	23.5	11.1
Minister	Female	.89	13.1	15.1	13.8	15.7	.87	19.8	15.9	21.3	17.2
Minister	Male	.91	27.1	12.9	27.8	13.5	.87	31.6	12.7	33.1	14.0
Musician	Female	.90	13.7	15.5	14.7	17.0	.86	23.4	17.0	24.0	18.2
Musician	Male	.91	30.6	11.8	31.1	12.7	.90	35.7	13.2	36.4	13.9
Nurse, LPN	Female	.85	25.0	13.6	26.2	14.0	.75	21.5	12.8	21.8	13.3
Nurse, LPN	Male	.85	34.1	10.5	35.4	11.0	.78	32.5	11.0	33.5	11.2
Nurse, RN	Female	.88	30.5	13.0	30.1	14.0	.84	29.4	14.4	30.1	14.7
Nurse, RN	Male	.88	29.7	14.3	30.1	15.3	.86	29.6	15.2	30.8	16.1
Nursing Home Administrator	Female	.81	37.0	10.6	38.7	10.7	.66	35.2	10.4	36.1	11.2
Nursing Home Administrator	Male	.85	40.4	10.4	41.6	10.8	.71	39.8	9.6	40.6	11.0
Occupational Therapist	Female	.87	31.0	14.0	30.0	15.2	.83	28.8	15.1	30.2	15.8
Occupational Therapist	Male	.89	36.8	13.2	36.6	14.1	.85	36.6	13.9	37.2	14.9

7.4 Test-Retest Reliability Statistics in Four Samples for the 211 Occupational Scales (continued)

Occupational Scale	Gender	Test-Retest Correlation	Test		Retest		Test-Retest Correlation	Test		Retest	
			Mean	S.D.	Mean	S.D.		Mean	S.D.	Mean	S.D.
		Sample C: College Students, 3 months (N = 56 women, 23 men)					Sample D: College Students, 3 months (N = 61 women, 26 men)				
Optician	Female	.73	36.7	11.5	40.8	11.4	.69	35.2	11.5	35.6	11.0
Optician	Male	.75	29.7	10.2	32.9	10.5	.74	27.6	10.6	27.3	10.6
Optometrist	Female	.86	26.9	11.6	29.0	12.8	.83	28.2	13.0	27.9	12.8
Optometrist	Male	.84	17.7	14.0	20.2	14.5	.84	18.8	14.4	18.8	14.8
Paralegal	Female	.77	44.2	9.9	44.4	9.7	.86	44.2	11.8	45.1	11.6
Paralegal	Male	.79	36.9	10.4	37.8	11.3	.83	39.9	10.5	41.1	11.1
Parks and Recreation Coordinator	Female	.86	40.5	10.1	43.4	11.1	.82	43.0	11.1	43.8	11.1
Parks and Recreation Coordinator	Male	.83	41.0	9.4	43.5	9.8	.80	43.5	9.6	44.0	9.8
Pharmacist	Female	.84	27.8	13.5	28.8	13.5	.87	24.9	14.0	24.9	14.6
Pharmacist	Male	.83	32.4	12.5	34.8	13.6	.84	31.2	13.4	31.6	14.3
Photographer	Female	.88	18.1	12.4	20.6	13.1	.82	25.8	13.4	26.6	13.8
Photographer	Male	.86	21.5	12.3	24.8	13.5	.81	28.7	12.4	28.9	12.8
Physical Education Teacher	Female	.84	22.0	13.5	25.0	15.8	.84	24.1	16.7	24.4	16.1
Physical Education Teacher	Male	.87	19.6	14.6	21.3	16.3	.82	22.5	15.9	24.0	16.2
Physical Therapist	Female	.84	31.5	12.2	32.7	13.0	.84	32.5	14.7	32.8	14.2
Physical Therapist	Male	.85	29.1	13.2	32.2	14.2	.85	31.3	14.9	31.7	15.2
Physician	Female	.85	10.4	12.6	11.4	13.2	.90	12.5	15.2	12.2	16.2
Physician	Male	.85	8.6	14.5	11.1	15.7	.89	13.8	17.6	14.5	18.4
Physicist	Female	.82	2.8	11.9	2.6	12.3	.85	4.7	14.4	4.5	15.2
Physicist	Male	.75	3.0	11.3	1.4	10.5	.84	3.9	13.6	4.2	14.5
Plumber	Male	.93	32.7	10.1	33.0	10.9	.89	29.8	9.9	28.5	9.8
Police Officer	Female	.91	36.1	9.5	39.5	10.8	.89	39.3	10.2	39.8	10.5
Police Officer	Male	.90	31.4	10.6	33.4	11.2	.89	29.8	12.1	30.1	12.6
Psychologist	Female	.85	14.9	12.9	17.1	13.8	.85	21.4	14.0	23.1	13.8
Psychologist	Male	.87	15.7	12.6	17.1	13.8	.85	23.0	13.8	24.0	13.5
Public Administrator	Female	.90	20.1	12.7	23.9	14.2	.89	28.4	13.4	31.4	14.4
Public Administrator	Male	.87	22.6	12.5	25.8	13.7	.88	30.5	13.6	33.0	14.8

7.4 Test-Retest Reliability Statistics in Four Samples for the 211 Occupational Scales (continued)

Occupational Scale	Gender	Test-Retest Correlation	Test Mean	Test S.D.	Retest Mean	Retest S.D.	Test-Retest Correlation	Test Mean	Test S.D.	Retest Mean	Retest S.D.
		Sample C: College Students, 3 months (N = 56 women, 23 men)					Sample D: College Students, 3 months (N = 61 women, 26 men)				
Public Relations Director	Female	.90	18.7	15.9	21.6	16.0	.87	27.3	15.2	28.7	16.8
Public Relations Director	Male	.92	27.7	13.7	29.4	14.2	.87	35.0	13.5	36.6	14.8
Purchasing Agent	Female	.79	33.4	14.0	38.2	14.1	.75	36.0	13.1	36.8	14.1
Purchasing Agent	Male	.84	31.2	12.3	35.2	12.6	.81	34.8	11.8	36.0	12.9
Radiologic Technologist	Female	.82	39.7	10.5	38.8	10.1	.87	35.9	12.2	35.1	12.2
Radiologic Technologist	Male	.84	39.0	10.3	38.7	10.2	.87	33.7	12.0	32.5	12.0
Realtor	Female	.82	21.3	12.7	25.8	13.9	.81	24.5	13.6	26.0	15.0
Realtor	Male	.87	31.7	12.1	35.1	12.7	.82	35.3	11.5	36.3	12.6
Reporter	Female	.89	16.3	14.3	18.9	15.7	.88	26.2	14.9	28.4	15.4
Reporter	Male	.87	20.3	13.6	22.4	14.3	.87	29.4	15.0	32.0	15.1
Research & Development Manager	Female	.85	13.9	13.0	17.1	14.7	.84	16.3	14.3	16.9	14.8
Research & Development Manager	Male	.87	9.9	11.7	13.3	13.4	.82	12.8	13.6	13.1	13.4
Respiratory Therapist	Female	.84	25.2	12.9	28.3	14.6	.84	24.1	15.4	24.0	15.1
Respiratory Therapist	Male	.86	22.7	14.1	25.3	16.0	.82	22.4	16.4	23.1	16.0
Restaurant Manager	Female	.80	32.3	13.1	37.1	12.9	.77	34.5	12.9	35.4	13.9
Restaurant Manager	Male	.85	34.5	11.9	37.6	12.3	.78	36.7	11.2	37.2	12.4
School Administrator	Female	.89	32.9	11.6	34.9	12.4	.89	36.7	13.0	37.9	14.3
School Administrator	Male	.87	30.1	11.0	31.6	11.3	.87	32.7	12.7	34.3	13.7
Science Teacher	Female	.87	13.2	14.1	15.0	15.6	.86	13.1	15.9	13.6	16.2
Science Teacher	Male	.84	18.0	12.2	20.3	13.4	.86	18.5	14.2	18.3	14.2
Secretary	Female	.81	34.7	12.7	37.3	12.2	.80	34.0	11.6	34.8	12.3
Small Business Owner	Female	.80	42.0	11.3	45.4	11.4	.74	42.5	9.7	43.0	10.8
Small Business Owner	Male	.89	37.3	10.8	38.6	11.2	.81	34.9	9.7	33.9	9.5
Social Science Teacher	Female	.88	27.8	12.1	29.6	13.0	.89	32.6	13.0	34.6	14.1
Social Science Teacher	Male	.89	33.3	11.8	34.1	12.3	.86	36.7	11.6	38.5	13.1
Social Worker	Female	.83	37.3	12.3	35.1	12.9	.78	37.5	11.5	37.4	11.8
Social Worker	Male	.91	37.5	14.0	36.8	13.7	.85	38.5	12.4	39.3	12.9

7.4 Test-Retest Reliability Statistics in Four Samples for the 211 Occupational Scales (continued)

Occupational Scale	Gender	Test-Retest Correlation	Test Mean	Test S.D.	Retest Mean	Retest S.D.	Test-Retest Correlation	Test Mean	Test S.D.	Retest Mean	Retest S.D.
		Sample C: College Students, 3 months (N = 56 women, 23 men)					Sample D: College Students, 3 months (N = 61 women, 26 men)				
Sociologist	Female	.88	10.5	13.0	13.2	14.7	.88	18.2	14.9	20.3	15.2
Sociologist	Male	.89	15.4	14.0	16.8	14.9	.88	22.3	15.6	25.0	15.8
Special Education Teacher	Female	.92	40.2	17.8	36.8	18.0	.82	36.7	13.8	38.1	14.5
Special Education Teacher	Male	.92	44.6	17.1	41.8	16.4	.85	42.1	13.3	43.6	14.5
Speech Pathologist	Female	.90	39.7	15.6	36.0	15.8	.85	37.2	13.6	37.5	13.7
Speech Pathologist	Male	.91	43.1	13.7	41.7	14.3	.81	43.1	11.9	44.1	12.3
Store Manager	Female	.81	35.5	12.1	39.3	12.0	.79	37.6	11.8	38.4	13.0
Store Manager	Male	.84	32.6	12.8	36.4	13.4	.78	35.3	12.3	36.1	13.7
Technical Writer	Female	.89	17.0	13.2	18.2	14.6	.86	24.5	15.7	25.8	15.6
Technical Writer	Male	.89	23.8	12.0	23.8	13.1	.90	29.7	13.6	30.9	13.1
Translator	Female	.92	13.5	14.2	13.3	15.4	.86	19.8	15.7	21.7	15.9
Translator	Male	.92	26.8	10.6	25.1	11.7	.90	28.9	12.0	29.5	11.5
Travel Agent	Female	.80	33.4	12.3	37.4	12.8	.77	36.0	11.3	37.3	12.5
Travel Agent	Male	.83	39.3	10.5	41.9	11.1	.79	41.4	9.8	41.8	11.7
Veterinarian	Female	.87	11.6	13.9	12.9	14.6	.90	11.0	16.1	10.4	17.0
Veterinarian	Male	.86	14.5	14.3	16.2	15.2	.87	13.3	15.5	13.6	16.4
Vocational Agriculture Teacher	Female	.76	15.5	12.0	18.2	13.6	.84	12.9	15.1	13.4	14.9
Vocational Agriculture Teacher	Male	.76	17.8	9.3	19.2	9.8	.80	14.2	10.7	14.8	10.5

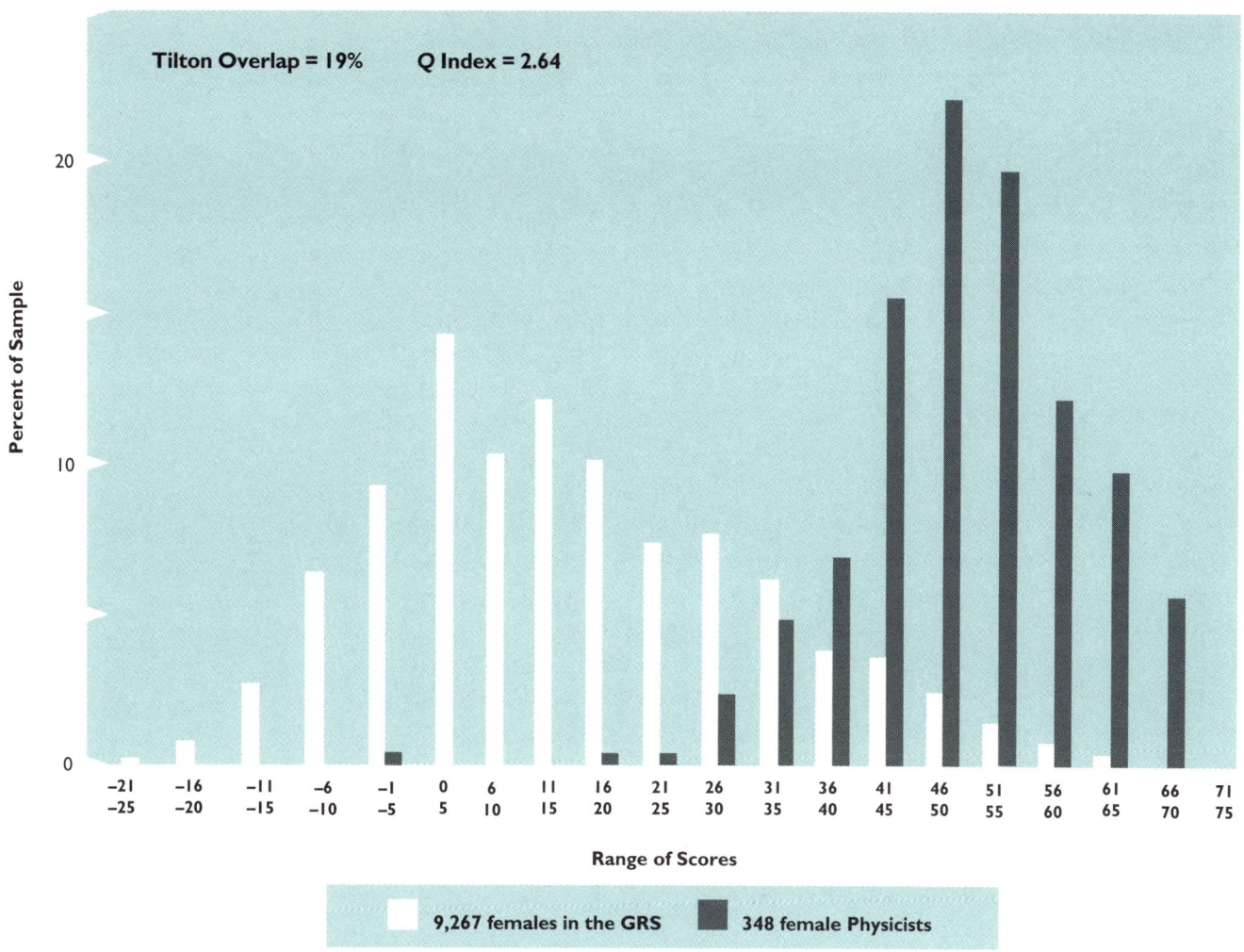

Figure 7.1 Distribution and Overlap of Scores for Females in the GRS (Excluding Female Physicists) and Female Physicists Scored on the Female Physicist Scale

Although the percent overlap can be calculated by actually counting the overlapping scores and converting the resulting figure to a percentage, Tilton provided a table that permits the calculation of this statistic using the means and standard deviations of the two samples in this formula:

$$Q = \frac{M_1 - M_2}{(SD_1 + SD_2)/2}$$

where M_1 and M_2 are the two mean scores, and SD_1 and SD_2 are the two standard deviations. The index Q is used to enter Tilton's overlap table to determine the percentage overlap of the two distributions. Use of this formula assumes that the two distributions are normally distributed, although experience suggests that the formula is quite robust even with skewed distributions. In fact, Elster and Dunnette (1971) showed that violations of two of the assumptions for Tilton's overlap (i.e., normality and equality of standard deviations) did not result in an underestimate of the overlap. Instead, the true and estimated overlaps tended to converge as mean differences increased. The other assumption of Tilton's overlap (i.e., equal Ns in the two distributions) was clearly violated when used to determine the concurrent validity of the *Strong* because the GRS is always much larger than the occupational group.

It is interesting to note that the Q statistic computed to find Tilton's overlap is analogous to Cohen's d statistic, a measure of effect size (Cohen, 1988). Cohen suggests that "the size of the groups is not a major issue as long as Ns are relatively large" (Cohen, 1988, p. 42). The Ns used in calculating overlaps for the OSs are very large.

Table 7.5 Tilton Percent Overlap

Q	%	Q	%	Q	%	Q	%
0.00	100	0.63	75	1.35	50	2.30	25
0.02	99	0.66	74	1.38	49	2.35	24
0.05	98	0.69	73	1.41	48	2.40	23
0.08	97	0.72	72	1.44	47	2.45	22
0.10	96	0.74	71	1.48	46	2.51	21
0.12	95	0.77	70	1.51	45	2.56	20
0.15	94	0.80	69	1.54	44	2.62	19
0.18	93	0.82	68	1.58	43	2.68	18
0.20	92	0.85	67	1.61	42	2.74	17
0.23	91	0.88	66	1.65	41	2.81	16
0.25	90	0.91	65	1.68	40	2.88	15
0.28	89	0.94	64	1.72	39	2.95	14
0.30	88	0.96	63	1.76	38	3.03	13
0.33	87	0.99	62	1.79	37	3.11	12
0.35	86	1.02	61	1.83	36	3.20	11
0.38	85	1.05	60	1.87	35	3.29	10
0.40	84	1.08	59	1.91	34	3.39	9
0.43	83	1.11	58	1.95	33	3.50	8
0.46	82	1.14	57	1.99	32	3.62	7
0.48	81	1.17	56	2.03	31	3.76	6
0.51	80	1.20	55	2.07	30	3.92	5
0.53	79	1.23	54	2.12	29	4.11	4
0.56	78	1.26	53	2.16	28	4.34	3
0.58	77	1.29	52	2.21	27	4.65	2
0.61	76	1.32	51	2.25	26	5.15	1

Note: See text for derivation of Q index.
Source: "The measurement of overlapping," by J. W. Tilton, 1937, *Journal of Educational Psychology, 28,* pp. 656–662.

Although Tilton's overlap has been used to describe the concurrent validity of the *Strong* OSs, recognizing that the Q statistic is an effect size raises questions about the appropriate variance estimate for the denominator of Q. Note that in their meta-analysis of treatment effects, Smith and Glass (1977) advocated the use of an effect size based on the standard deviation of the control group instead of an averaged standard deviation like the one used in Tilton's overlap statistic. The potential effect would be to increase the size of the denominator and decrease the effect size. Considering the GRSs as being analogous to the control group, since they have a larger standard deviation, the resulting statistic would show a smaller effect size. Although this would have been a reasonable way to estimate effect sizes, this method was not used since it would have made it difficult to compare overlaps with scales developed earlier.

In composing the GRSs, 200 people were randomly selected from each occupational group, or all the available group members were used if there were less than 200. Thus, the occupational groups that had *N*s near 200 overlapped almost completely with

Table 7.6 Percentages of 132 Overlaps (Q) Among Selected Occupational Scales Falling into Various Intervals for Females and Males

Q Interval	% of Female Scale Overlaps	% of Male Scale Overlaps
0–0.99	3	8
1.00–1.99	34	29
2.00–2.99	55	45
3.00–3.99	8	16
4.00–4.99	0	2

the GRS, even though the GRS would not necessarily overlap completely with the occupational group. To correct for this problem, members of each occupational group were systematically removed from the GRS when computing Tilton's overlap for their scale.

Table 7.5 shows the amount of separation, in terms of standard deviation units, associated with various levels of percent overlap. For example, a Q index of approximately 2.00, associated with a percent overlap of about 32, represents a separation of 2 standard deviations between the distributions, an enormous separation by usual standards of psychological research. (For purposes of comparison, 2 standard deviations correspond roughly to differences of 30 IQ points, or 6 inches in height, or 1.8 grade points on a 4-point scale, or the difference between the 16th and 86th percentiles.)

Table 7.2, shown earlier, provides the percent overlaps for the *Strong* OSs. The median overlap for both the female and the male scales was 36 percent. This degree of overlap is associated with a Q index of 1.83, which means that the scales separated the occupational samples from the GRSs by slightly less than 2 standard deviations, on the average. The best scale in this respect was the male Medical Illustrator scale, which had an overlap of only 15 percent (Q index = 2.88) between the occupational sample and the male GRS; the best female scale was Athletic Trainer, which had an overlap of only 17 percent (Q index = 2.74) between the occupational sample and the female GRS. Remember that the Q index is actually an effect size and that these numbers represent a separation of nearly 3 standard deviations between groups. The poorest scales in terms of concurrent validity were male Audiologist (Q = 1.05) and female Small Business Owner (Q = 1.02).

The wide range of percent overlaps shown in Table 7.2 indicates that the scales varied considerably in their concurrent validities. Scales with the highest validities (the lowest overlaps) tended to be those for occupations that were tightly defined and distinct from most other occupations (e.g., Medical Illustrator, Physicist, Fine Artist, and Interior Decorator). Scales with low validities (high overlaps) were those for occupations that were not as well defined (e.g., Small Business Owner).

Mean Scores of Occupations on Other Occupational Scales

Another important type of concurrent validity information is the mean scores of the occupational samples on each other's scales. This information is too voluminous to include in this guide, since scoring each of the 211 occupational samples on each of the 211 scales would produce 44,521 Q statistics. Instead, 12 male and female occupational samples representing all the GOT codes were each scored on the scales for the other 11 of the same gender, and Q statistics were computed. The analysis for each gender produced 132 Q statistics, which are summarized in Table 7.6.

For males the lowest Q or effect size was .21 for biologists and college professors scored on the College Professor scale; the highest was 4.19 for athletic trainers and fine artists scored on the Athletic Trainer scale. For females the lowest Q or effect size was .65 for chiropractors and licensed practical nurses scored on the Chiropractor scale; the highest was 3.45 for licensed practical nurses and technical writers scored on the Nurse, LPN, scale. Since low Q statistics denote greater overlap and high ones less overlap, these results seem reasonable and suggest that the scales separate occupational groups quite well, except when the groups might be expected to be somewhat similar.

Predictive Validity

The predictive validity of an OS is the scale's power to distinguish between people who will eventually enter different occupations—to distinguish, for example, between students who will become bankers and those who will become artists or farmers. This predictive power is an important attribute, because the inventory is generally used to help make long-term decisions; thus, it is important that there be data to support the long-range predictive power of these scales.

E. K. Strong's Studies of Validity

The *Strong* has a long history of research on predictive validity, beginning with E. K. Strong's attempts in the 1930s. He believed intensely in the value of empirical data and very early began collecting longitudinal data to use in studying the practical usefulness of his inventory. During the year following initial publication of the inventory (1927), Strong administered it to the senior class of Stanford University; five years later he asked these students which occupations they had entered to determine if the inventory had accurately predicted their career choices. The results were published in the *Journal of Educational Psychology* under the title "Predictive Value of the Vocational Interest Test" (Strong, 1935). In this report, Strong grappled (as every investigator has since) with the issue of what constitutes predictive validity. He said:

> Determination of the validity of a vocational test is fraught with many difficulties. What should be the criterion? At first thought "final vocational choice" appears to be the only ultimate criterion in guidance. But . . . one cannot assume that every man [or woman] eventually enters the occupation for which he [or she] is best fitted. If this were true there would be no great need for vocational tests. . . . Because final occupational choice cannot be accepted as a perfect criterion, it necessarily follows that a vocational test that correlates perfectly with final occupational choice is as faulty as the present system of finding one's livelihood (p. 332).

The fact that final occupational choice is not a perfect criterion is of crucial importance in understanding why the *Strong* (or any other interest inventory) cannot, by the nature of the problem, approach perfect predictive validity. Strong concluded, however, that a substantial relationship should exist between scores on his test and eventual occupational choice, and he argued that the following four propositions, if true, would constitute persuasive evidence of high validity:

1. People continuing in occupation X should obtain higher interest scores on the scale for X than they do on scales for any other occupations.
2. Interest scores on scale X should be higher for people continuing in occupation X than for people in occupation Y.
3. Interest scores on scale X should be higher for people continuing in occupation X than for people who change from occupation X to occupation Y.
4. People changing from occupation Y to occupation X should have scored higher on the X scale *prior to the change* than they scored on the Y scale.

Strong used the results of his five-year follow-up study of Stanford seniors to evaluate the inventory on these four propositions and concluded, as summarized in the 1938 manual for the *Strong*: "The first three propositions are true with respect to averages but, of course, there were some individual exceptions. . . . The fourth proposition is approximately true."

Several years later, Strong studied the predictive validity of the test for these students and several hundred of their peers (combined $N = 524$) over a longer time period and reported the results in his book *Vocational Interests 18 Years After College* (Strong, 1955). In general, his results supported the propositions he had advanced 20 years earlier.

Validity Studies Since E. K. Strong

Following Strong's lead, a number of other investigators have conducted studies of the validity of the inventory over long time periods. The usual paradigm is to test a group of students, put the data away, let several years pass, locate the students, ascertain their current occupations (and their perseverance, satisfaction, and success in those occupations), then study the degree of correspondence between their earlier scores and their current occupations. The basic finding of these studies has been that there is a substantial relationship between high scores on the OSs and the eventual occupation entered. Depending on how the hit rate is calculated, between one-half and two-thirds of all college students enter occupations that are predictable from their earlier scores on the *Strong*.

The level of accuracy is influenced, as might be expected, by various external factors. McArthur (1954), for example, showed that Harvard students from high socioeconomic backgrounds (those who attended private schools) were less predictable than other Harvard students (those from public schools). The former were more likely to enter occupations dictated by their family fortunes than they were to follow their own interests—sometimes, according to McArthur's observations, to the detriment of their occupational satisfaction. Campbell (1966) showed that predictability was higher for students who had well-defined interest patterns, an outcome that also appeared in Strong's 18-year follow-up of Stanford students.

Brandt and Hood (1968), using the files of the Counseling Service at the University of Iowa, demonstrated that students with severe emotional problems were less predictable than students who were not disturbed. Harmon (1969) provided evidence showing that, for women making a career commitment outside of the home, measured interests were as predictive of career choices as they were for men. Hansen and Swanson (1983) found that the predictive validity of the *Strong* for choosing a college major increased if the students were satisfied with their college experience and was greater for those students whose interests were most stable during the 3 1/2-year test-retest interval.

In general, these studies support Strong's original proposition that measured interests are predictive of occupational choice, and they extend his original work by documenting situations in which the predictive validity is higher or lower than average.

One of the last predictive validity studies on the *Strong Vocational Interest Blanks (SVIB)* (before its conversion to the merged-gender form) was conducted using subjects who had been students at the University of Missouri. Dolliver, Irvin, and Bigley (1972) searched the files of the Testing and Counseling Service for *SVIB*s completed at least nine years earlier and found 1,000 men who had been tested, on the average, 12 years earlier. The researchers managed to collect follow-up data from 130 of them who were in occupations for which the *SVIB* had a corresponding OS. (They actually received data from 220 men; 90 were in occupations with no *SVIB* scale.) Using classification methods developed by McArthur (1954), the researchers classified these men into three categories according to the predictive level of their earlier scores.

Their results are reported in Table 7.7, which also includes the results from several of the predictive validity studies just discussed. The data in the first row of Table 7.7 were taken from Strong's 18-year follow-up of Stanford students: "excellent" hits were those with standard scores of 45 or above on the scale for the occupation the individuals ultimately entered, "moderate" hits were standard scores of 40 to 44, and "poor" hits were scores of 39 or below. As mentioned earlier, McArthur (1954) split his sample of Harvard students into two groups: those who attended public high schools and those who attended private high schools. Brandt and Hood (1968) studied two groups: "normal" and "deviant" (so classified on the basis of their *Minnesota Multiphasic Personality Inventory [MMPI]* profiles).

Scanning the table gives a general picture of the level of predictive accuracy one can expect: the "excellent" and "moderate" hit rate centers around 65 percent, from McArthur's high of 61 percent for predicting job entry to Dolliver et al.'s low of 54 percent. The results, though ranging over 20 percentage points, are relatively consistent, especially given the variability in age of the subjects when tested, purpose of testing, particular techniques of investigators, percent of earlier sample reassessed, and variability of classification techniques. All things considered, the hit rate appears to be about 65 percent.

In an extension of this work, Dolliver and Kunce (1973) identified another source of error in validity studies that depend on following up individuals over time: that is, the characteristics of people who choose not to cooperate with the researcher. The researchers asked the question, "Who drops out of an *SVIB* follow-up study?", then answered it using data from the original testing of these dropouts. "We found [that] those in intellectual occupations and those with the most accurate *SVIB* results show greater likelihood of dropping out. . . . Those for whom the [earlier] *SVIB* was most accurate did not make themselves available for further study." Their data thus suggest that the level of predictive accuracy reported by follow-up studies is a conservative estimate of true validity.

Validity Studies Based on the SVIB-SCII

Most predictive validity studies for the *Strong* are based on initial and follow-up testing with the older forms of the *SVIB*. However, Spokane (1979)

Table 7.7 Summary of *SVIB* and *SVIB-SCII* Predictive Validity Studies: Percentages of Sample Falling in Three Hit Categories

Study[a]	Gender	N	Study Span (Years)	Excellent Hits (45+)	Moderate Hits (40–44)	Poor Hits (39–)
Strong (direct scale)	Male	524	18	48%	18%	34%
McArthur (total sample)	Male	60	14	45	20	35
McArthur (public school)	Male	31	14	61	13	26
Brandt & Hood (total)	Male	259	7	47	20	33
Brandt & Hood (normals)	Male	129	7	56	16	28
Dolliver et al. (total sample)	Male	130	12	42	12	46
Spokane (direct scale)	Female	120	3.5	42	17	41
Spokane (direct scale)	Male	236	3.5	59	12	29
Hansen & Swanson (total sample)	Female	245	3.5	44	14	42
Hansen & Swanson (total sample)	Male	183	3.5	38	26	36
Hansen & Swanson (satisfied)	Female, male	130	3.5	51	20	29
Hansen & Swanson (unsatisfied)	Female, male	298	3.5	38	15	47
Hansen & Swanson (stable profiles)	Female, male	95	3.5	59	7	34
Hansen & Swanson (unstable profiles)	Female, male	88	3.5	24	16	50
Hansen & Swanson (high AC scores)	Female, male	115	3.5	50	17	33
Hansen & Swanson (low AC scores)	Female, male	64	3.5	27	9	64

Source: Hansen & Campbell, 1985, p. 75.

[a] See text for an explanation of parenthetical qualifications.

examined the predictive validity of the 1974 *Strong-Campbell Interest Inventory (SCII)* for college women and men over a 3 1/2-year span. Excellent and moderate predictive validity was found for 59 percent of the females and 71 percent of the males. Spokane also found that students who stated interests consistent with their measured interests reported higher levels of job satisfaction.

Occupational entry or expressed occupational choice usually is identified as the criterion for prediction for the *Strong*. The usefulness of the 1981 *Strong* in exploring college majors was examined in a study that also considered concurrent validity, differential validity for females and males, and the moderating effect of interest stability (Hansen & Swanson, 1983). The validity hit rates were similar to those reported in previous studies, indicating that the *Strong* can be used with confidence for choosing a college major. Also, entry into both *direct* majors (those with a major clearly represented by an OS, e.g., psychology, geography, social work) and *indirect* majors (those not clearly represented, e.g., industrial relations, art history, music therapy) was predictive. This finding is especially important, since no interest inventory profile can provide a scale to measure interests in every occupation or major.

Thus, generalizing beyond the Profile with the related scales expands the usefulness of the instrument. The results, as summarized in Table 7.7, also show that the *Strong* is more predictive for students who are satisfied with their majors or who have stable interests during their college careers. Finally, the results suggest that as the number of OSs developed on female occupational samples has increased with each revision (57 scales in 1974, 76 in 1981, 105 in 1985), the predictive validity of the *Strong* for women has improved slightly. Thus, predictive validity hit rates for the merged-gender form of the *Strong* compare favorably with the older *SVIB* hit rates, which averaged around 65 percent.

Validity Studies Based on the Strong Interest Inventory

Since the publication of the *Strong* in 1985, a study of its concurrent validity for college major selection was reported by Hansen and Tan (1992). They essentially replicated the 1983 study by Hansen and Swanson mentioned earlier and found similar results supporting the earlier findings.

Recently, emphasis has been placed on exploration validity, the effect of an inventory in stimulating career exploration among its users. In a well-designed contrast group study by Randahl, Hansen, and Haverkamp (1993), students who were administered the *Strong* and received an interpretation of their results reported participating in more discussion and reading about careers that did the contrast group, which reported pursuing opportunities for vocational assessment over the ensuing year. From such findings, it appears that the use of the *Strong* may have encouraged students to engage in career exploration activities such as reading and discussion.

Predictive Validity and Scores on the Basic Interest Scales

Another study related to the predictive validity of the OSs was published by Johnson and Johansson (1972). They reanalyzed data from earlier studies of male students who had had high scores on either the Life Insurance Agent or Physicist scale. Ten years later, about 75 percent of these students were in occupations related to their scores on scales found on earlier Profiles. But what was more revealing was that whether a student with a high score on one OS went directly into that occupation or into a related occupation was influenced considerably by his or her score on the appropriate BIS. For example, a student with a high score on the Life Insurance Agent scale and a high score on the Sales BIS was likely to become a salesperson; another student with the same score on the Life Insurance Agent scale but a low score on the Sales scale (which meant that his or her common interests with salespeople were in areas other than sales) was more likely to enter a related occupation, such as advertising.

The principal result of Johnson and Johansson's study was to show that the more consistency there is between scores on the OSs and scores on the BISs, the more specific (and more confident) the counselor can be in predicting outcomes from the Profile.

Future Validity Studies

Studies similar to all of those discussed in this chapter can and should be undertaken with this revision of the *Strong*. In the meantime, it is worth noting that the *Strong* rests on a research base that seems to be cumulative. While previous studies have shown that revised Occupational Scales may behave somewhat differently than earlier ones (Creaser & Jacobs, 1987; Williams, Kirk, & Frank, 1968), no studies have shown that any revision of the *Strong* has decreased substantially the reliability or validity of the OSs.

Unpredictable Scales

One anomaly in working with empirical scales is that they do not always behave predictably. If several scales are constructed under precisely the same rules for item selection, weighting, and norming, then the scales should operate in similar fashion, yet sometimes they do not. Their validities, as measured by percent overlap between samples, may vary markedly; their reliabilities also vary, though these are usually more consistent than are the validities.

The most noticeable variation from one OS to another is in the population mean: that is, the average score earned on an OS by people not in that occupation. In every form of the inventory, there have been scales with high population means. On the 1938 men's form, for example, over 50 percent of high school senior boys scored at or above the mean on the Farmer scale.

On the 1946 women's form, high scores for young women were common on the Elementary Teacher and Secretary scales. On the 1966 men's form, the Physical Therapist and Computer Programmer scales showed many more high scores than the other scales, and on the 1969 women's form, the same was true for the Army Officer and Navy Officer scales. Much of what is known as "shrewd, clinical interpretive skill" comes from knowing about and having a reasonable explanation for these high population means. Such knowledge can be gained by a careful reading of this chapter, especially the data in Table 7.2.

Why scales with apparently similar items have different scale characteristics is something that remains unexplained. Although good counselors learn to overcome, and even profit from, these aberrations, it should not be forgotten that that is exactly what they are—aberrations. These scales are not intended to behave differently—they just do. Thus, counselors have to learn to deal with their idiosyncrasies. As counselors use the 1994 *Strong*, they will most surely identify unpredictable scales.

The Future of the Occupational Scales

An important goal for the future will be to refine further the techniques used to develop Occupational Scales so that the *Strong* Profile provides the best measurement of interests in a set of occupations. For this revision, technology has allowed those developing the OSs to examine and alter, when necessary, their methods of building scales—while still in the process of scale construction. It is hoped that these carefully examined methods have resulted in the best set of OSs yet developed for the *Strong*.

References

Brandt, J. E., & Hood, A. B. (1968). Effect of personality adjustment on the predictive validity of the Strong Vocational Interest Blank. *Journal of Counseling Psychology, 15,* 547–551.

Campbell, D. P. (1966). Occupations ten years later of high school seniors with high scores on the SVIB life insurance salesman scale. *Journal of Applied Psychology, 50,* 369–372.

Cohen, J. (1988). *Statistical power analysis for the behavioral sciences* (2nd ed.). Hillsdale, NJ: Erlbaum.

Creaser, J. W., & Jacobs, M. (1987). Score discrepancies between the 1981 and 1985 editions of the Strong-Campbell Interest Inventory. *Journal of Counseling Psychology, 34,* 288–292.

Dolliver, R. H., Irvin, J. A., & Bigley, S. E. (1972). Twelve-year follow-up of the Strong Vocational Interest Blank. *Journal of Counseling Psychology, 19,* 212–217.

Dolliver, R. H., & Kunce, J. E. (1973). Who drops out of an SVIB follow-up study? *Journal of Counseling Psychology, 20,* 188–189.

Elster, R. S., & Dunnette, M. D. (1971). The robustness of Tilton's measure of overlap. *Educational and Psychological Measurement, 31,* 685–697.

Hansen, J. C., & Campbell, D. P. (1985). *Manual for the Strong Interest Inventory* (4th ed.). Stanford, CA: Stanford University Press.

Hansen, J. C., & Swanson, J. L. (1983). Stability of interests and the predictive and concurrent validity of the 1981 Strong-Campbell Interest Inventory for college majors. *Journal of Counseling Psychology, 30,* 194–201.

Hansen, J. C., & Tan, R. N. (1992). Concurrent validity of the 1985 Strong Interest Inventory for college major selection. *Measurement and Evaluation in Counseling and Development, 25,* 53–57.

Harmon, L. W. (1969). The predictive power over 10 years of measured social service and scientific interests among college women. *Journal of Applied Psychology, 53,* 193–198.

Harmon, L. W., Usher, M. C., & Borgen, F. H. (1994). In search of the perfect occupational interest scale. Unpublished manuscript.

Johnson, R. W., & Johansson, C. B. (1972). Moderating effect of basic interests on predictive validity of SVIB occupational scales. *Proceedings, 80th Annual Convention, American Psychological Association,* pp. 589–590.

Maze, M., & Mayall, D. (compilers). (1991). *The enhanced guide for occupational exploration.* Indianapolis: JIST Works, Inc.

McArthur, C. (1954). Long term validity of the Strong Interest Test in two subcultures. *Journal of Applied Psychology, 38,* 346–354.

Randahl, G. J., Hansen, J. C., & Haverkamp, B. E. (1993). Instrumental behaviors following test administration and interpretation: Exploration validity of the Strong Interest Inventory. *Journal of Counseling and Development, 71,* 435–439.

Smith, M. L., & Glass, G. V. (1977). Meta-analysis of psychotherapy outcome studies. *American Psychologist, 32,* 752–760.

Spokane, A. R. (1979). Occupational preference and the validity of the Strong-Campbell Interest Inventory for college women and men. *Journal of Counseling Psychology, 26,* 312–318.

Strong, E. K., Jr. (1935). Predictive value of the Vocational Interest Test. *Journal of Educational Psychology, 26,* 332.

Strong, E. K., Jr. (1938). *Vocational Interest Blank for Men* (revised). Stanford, CA: Stanford University Press.

Strong, E. K., Jr. (1955). *Vocational interests 18 years after college.* Minneapolis: University of Minnesota Press.

Swanson, J. L., & Hansen, J. C. (1988). Stability of vocational interests over 4-year, 8-year, and 12-year intervals. *Journal of Vocational Behavior, 33,* 185–202.

Tilton, J. W. (1937). The measurement of overlapping. *Journal of Educational Psychology, 28,* 656–662.

Williams, P. A., Kirk, B. A., & Frank, A. C. (1968). New men's SVIB: A comparison with the old. *Journal of Counseling Psychology, 15,* 287–294.

CHAPTER 8

The Personal Style Scales

A distinctive innovation in the 1994 *Strong* is the introduction of the Personal Style Scales. Measuring preferences for and comfort with broad styles of living and working, these scales complement the traditional vocational interest scales that measure preferences for more specific aspects of the work itself. The four Personal Style Scales are Work Style, Learning Environment, Leadership Style, and Risk Taking/ Adventure.

The Personal Style Scales can help individuals explore how they go about learning, working, playing, or living in general. For some people, these scales may have less to do with specific educational or work settings than with how those people prefer to learn or work in general. In other cases, these scales can be helpful in showing people how their preferred styles differ from the mode of others within a work setting, especially if that setting is one in which most people show one distinctive style.

In the first part of this chapter, the content, interpretation, and implications of the Personal Style Scales are described. The second part focuses on how the scales were created and on the research evidence for their reliability, validity, and interpretation. ◆

Content and Interpretation of the Personal Style Scales

The four Personal Style Scales have many of the features of the General Occupational Themes (GOTs) and Basic Interest Scales (BISs). They have standard scores based on the General Reference Sample (GRS) of 18,951 women and men. On the *Strong* Profile, they also are reported using box-and-whisker graphs to show separate distributions for women and men; boxes show the middle 50 percent and whiskers show the middle 80 percent of scores for each gender. A distinguishing characteristic of the Personal Style Scales, however, is that they are construed as bipolar scales, with a distinctive style (or preference) associated with both the left and the right pole of each scale. The characteristics of the left and right poles for each scale are summarized in Table 8.1 on the following page.

Since the mean of these scales is 50 for general groups of people, scores that differ substantially from 50 (either above or below) typify one of the poles of that style. Thus, scores of 45 and below identify the left pole of the scales, and scores of 55 and above identify the right pole. More extreme scores (40 and below; 60 and above) even more clearly identify that particular style. Scores in the mid-range (46–54) occur for people with no predominant preference for

Table 8.1 Brief Definitions of Poles for the Personal Style Scales

Personal Style Scale	Left Pole	Right Pole
Work Style	Works with ideas/data/things	Works with people
Learning Environment	Practical	Academic
Leadership Style	Leads by example	Directs others
Risk Taking/Adventure	Plays it safe	Takes chances

one style or the other; they probably have a mix of preferences for that style or no strong preferences for a particular one.

The interpretive material in the following sections has been derived primarily from the tables and figures found in the second half of this chapter. Since the Risk Taking/Adventure scale has a history of over 25 years, most of its interpretive material was derived from previous sources (Douce & Hansen, 1988; Hansen, 1992; Hansen & Campbell, 1985). Since the other three Personal Style Scales were created for this revision of the *Strong*, amplification of their utility can be expected from future research and counseling use. Nonetheless, the database used here is extensive and rich and provides much information that clarifies the meaning and implications of these new scales.

Work Style Scale

The Work Style scale distinguishes individuals who prefer to work with people from those who prefer working with ideas, data, or things. Those who prefer to work with people endorse *Strong* items that represent people-oriented occupations and activities, including some items that refer to relating to others as helpers. The item "Can smooth out tangles and disagreements between people" clearly differentiates those who prefer to work with people from those who prefer to work alone. However, items that imply contact with others without directly involving a helping function (e.g., "Raising money for charity" and "Planning a large party") also identify the works with people pole of the scale. Those who prefer working alone (with ideas, data, or things), in contrast, endorse items in those particular domains. They like scientific and technical activities, see themselves as having mechanical ingenuity, and would prefer being a lighthouse keeper to being a headwaiter/hostess.

The Work Style scale is clearly and symmetrically joined to the RIASEC scales, falling as a bipolar axis across the hexagon (see Figure 8.1). The works with people pole links strongly to the E and S Themes. The works with ideas/data/things pole ties to the R and I Themes. Thus, the Work Style scale is an important, broad dimension bridging four of the RIASEC scales.

Students who score toward the works with people pole are often found in major fields such as education, journalism, business, and social sciences, although their mean scores are only moderately high (i.e., in the range of 53–56). Students who prefer to work with ideas, data, or things, in contrast, are often found in the physical sciences, machine trades, engineering, biological sciences, computer and information sciences, and mathematics. (See the last section of this chapter for a discussion of educational majors and their relationship to the Personal Style Scales.) These students' scores indicate a preference for working with ideas, data, or things (the left pole) and as such are distinctly different from the mean of 50 for all people in the norm group.

There are gender differences of more than one-half a standard deviation (6.2 standard score points) between females and males in the GRS, with females scoring more toward the works with people pole. As a result, it is especially important to note the gender-based box-and-whisker graphs on the Profile, showing the middle 50 percent and middle 80 percent of each sample. Interpretations of the Work Style scale need to attend to the appropriate band for each client.

Women who score 63 and above and men who score 59 and above on the Work Style scale are more than one standard deviation from the mean in terms of their preference for working with people. Women who score 43 and below and men who score 39 and below are more than one standard deviation from the mean in terms of their inclination to work with ideas, data, or things.

Scores can be used to help individuals determine whether they are more inclined to work with people or with ideas, data, or things. Interpretation of this

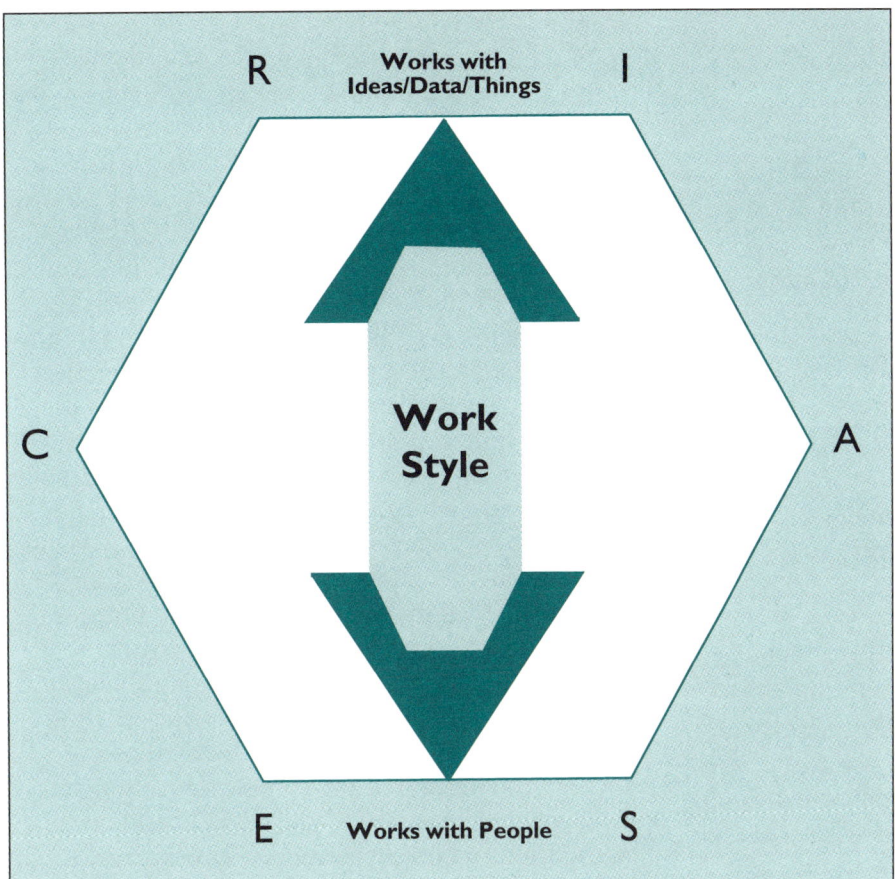

Figure 8.1 Relationship of Work Style to the Pattern of Themes on the Hexagon

scale can explain problems of adjustment when an individual is uncomfortable in a specific work setting. Although the standard deviation for occupational groups (ranging from 6.8 for male physicists to 9.3 for female engineers) is not as large as the standard deviation for the GRS, individuals in specific occupations score at various levels on the Work Style scale. The mean scores for college students can be nearly as much as one standard deviation above the mean for the group of working adults. This pattern probably reflects the special nature of the college samples, with a preponderance of women students in the social sciences.

It would be a mistake to assume that people should choose their occupations based on the Work Style scale. It may be just as productive to explore occupations of interest to the individual in relationship to the type of work settings offered within the occupation. Some social workers, for instance, may have research positions that put them in little contact with people. Likewise, some physicists may find themselves working with great numbers of people in educational or public information settings. Admittedly, such positions are rare, but they are worth discussing with clients whose Work Style scale scores do not seem to fit their vocational interests.

Sample Occupations Whose Members Prefer a Works with People Work Style

- Child Care Provider
- Community Service Organization Director
- Flight Attendant
- High School Counselor
- Human Resources Director
- Life Insurance Agent
- Social Worker

Sample Occupations Whose Members Prefer a Works with Ideas/Data/Things Work Style

- Biologist
- Chemist

- Computer Programmer/Systems Analyst
- Mathematician
- Physicist

Typical Work Style Items

- "Author of technical books" (works with ideas/data/things pole)
- "Customer service representative" (works with people pole)
- "Designer, electronic equipment" (works with ideas/data/things pole)
- "Doing research work" (works with ideas/data/things pole)
- "Flight attendant" (works with people pole)
- "Helping others overcome their difficulties" (works with people pole)

Learning Environment Scale

The Learning Environment scale differentiates people who prefer academic learning environments from those who prefer more practically oriented, hands-on learning situations. People who prefer to learn in academic settings express cultural, verbal, and research interests as well as an interest in teaching itself. People who prefer to learn in more practical settings express interests in clerical, technical, and physical activities. This scale reflects whether an individual is more comfortable in a practical or an academic learning setting. However, this scale is not an indicator of whether the person will be successful in one setting or the other.

The Learning Environment scale correlates to a certain extent with the deleted Academic Comfort scale from the 1985 *Strong*. The correlation between the two scales is .64 for women and .69 for men. One difference is that the Learning Environment scale has fewer items that have to do with liking scientific occupations and school subjects.

The Learning Environment scale correlates most strongly with the A Theme, reflecting the scale's central cultural and verbal content. Because of the Learning Environment scale's research content, it also correlates moderately with the I Theme.

There are large average differences in the Learning Environment scale across educational majors. Those scoring toward the academic pole include students with majors with a cultural/artistic, verbal, or research emphasis: language/literature, history, journalism, physical sciences, and social sciences. Those scoring toward the practical pole include students in such areas as the machine trades, vocational-technical majors, business (clerical), law enforcement, and agriculture.

The Learning Environment scale may be helpful to individuals who are exploring educational options. Scores of 55 and above typify individuals in occupations that require a great deal of academic preparation and individuals who have achieved the Ph.D. degree. Scores of 45 and below are common for individuals in many occupations that require practical training of limited duration (e.g., high school or technical training). Within occupations, the range of scores on this scale is fairly large, from about .66 to 1.2 standard deviations. Early evidence suggests that scores below 50 may occur often for college students. In three college samples used for reliability studies (see the last section of this chapter), means ranged from 40 to 47, all toward the practical pole.

An individual's score on the Learning Environment scale should not be used to restrict occupational choice. Rather, it is useful for a broadly focused exploration of preferences for learning environments. For instance, the medical field offers occupations requiring various types of training, from courses that last less than a year to advanced medical training requiring many years of academic work.

Sample Occupations Whose Members Prefer an Academic Learning Environment

- College Professor
- Geographer
- Lawyer
- Physicist
- Psychologist
- Public Administrator
- Sociologist

Sample Occupations Whose Members Prefer a Practical Learning Environment

- Agribusiness Manager
- Auto Mechanic
- Dental Assistant
- Farmer
- Hair Stylist
- Nurse, LPN
- Plumber

Typical Learning Environment Items
- "Algebra" (academic pole)
- "Art museum director" (academic pole)
- "Bank teller" (practical pole)
- "College professor" (academic pole)
- "Highway construction workers" (practical pole)
- "Operating machinery" (practical pole)

Leadership Style Scale

The Leadership Style scale is a new Personal Style Scale that, on one pole, reflects a preference for meeting, directing, persuading, and leading other people. People who score toward this directs others pole enjoy moving readily and gregariously into interpersonal settings and like to take initiative and take charge in an organizational setting. People who score toward the opposite pole—leads by example—are not comfortable taking charge of others. They prefer to do a task themselves rather than direct others to do it. They may lead by example rather than by giving directions.

The Leadership Style scale is quite highly correlated with the Introversion-Extroversion (IE) scale, which appeared in the 1985 *Strong* but has been removed from the 1994 version. People who score toward the directs others pole of the Leadership Style scale are likely to show preferences for the general E Theme, and specifically the Enterprising BISs of Public Speaking, Law/Politics, and Organizational Management. People who score toward the leads by example pole are disinterested in being persuasive or being in charge of others and tend to have little interest in these domains.

Students scoring toward the directs others pole of the Leadership Style scale are likely to major in areas such as journalism, social sciences, law, and history. Students scoring toward the leads by example pole are likely to major in fields such as machine trades, physical sciences, mathematics, biological sciences, and agriculture.

There are essentially no substantial gender differences on the Leadership Style scale. The means for females and males are virtually identical.

The Leadership Style scale can be particularly helpful in considering people's preferred leadership role within occupational settings, especially settings not typified by people scoring near either the left or right pole on this scale. These settings include those within the R, I, and C Themes that are not correlated with the Leadership Style scale. Thus, if someone with interests in one of these areas has a Leadership Style scale score above 55, that person might consider the special roles she or he could play within the occupation. For example, very few physicists have scores above 55 on the Leadership Style scale, but those who do are likely to play especially valuable roles within the profession. Likewise, since few physicists have a preference for working with people, a physicist with both a directive leadership style and a people-oriented work style would be quite rare and would be expected to show an interpersonal style atypical for physicists. This atypical physicist might play complementary roles that are helpful to colleagues and the physics profession itself.

Sample Occupations Whose Members Prefer a Directs Others Leadership Style
- Broadcaster
- Corporate Trainer
- Elected Public Official
- High School Counselor
- Minister
- Public Administrator
- Public Relations Director
- Realtor
- School Administrator

Sample Occupations Whose Members Prefer a Leads by Example Leadership Style
- Auto Mechanic
- Chemist
- Farmer
- Mathematician
- Physicist
- Plumber
- Radiological Technologist
- Veterinarian

Typical Leadership Style Items
- "Heading a civic improvement program" (directs others pole)
- "Making a speech" (directs others pole)
- "Meeting and directing people" (directs others pole)

- ▲ "People who assume leadership" (directs others pole)
- ▲ "Put drive into an organization" (directs others pole)

Risk Taking/Adventure Scale

The content of the Risk Taking/Adventure scale is a mix of physically risky activities, such as auto racing, and other more general items about risk taking and adventure. This scale was first developed by David Campbell et al. in 1968, so considerable experience and lore have developed about its implications and counseling use (Campbell, 1971; Douce & Hansen, 1988; Hansen, 1992; Hansen & Campbell, 1985). Until this revision, the scale was called Adventure and appeared with the Realistic BISs. It has now been renamed and moved to the Personal Style Scales section of the Profile.

There are substantial gender differences on this scale, with men averaging more than one-half standard deviation (6.2 standard score points) higher than women. Thus, it is important to attend to these gender differences on the Profile, evaluating that person's score relative to the box and whiskers for the person's gender.

Risk Taking/Adventure scores toward the takes chances pole tend to correlate significantly with other measures for which a high score indicates a willingness to (1) take risks, (2) act on the spur of the moment, (3) be spontaneous, and (4) sometimes act recklessly. People who score toward the takes chances pole also have a tendency to be independent, self-reliant, and rebellious when faced with restraints; to be outgoing; and to enjoy being the center of attention and doing things just for the fun of it. People who score near the plays it safe pole of the Risk Taking/Adventure scale generally avoid danger and risks and try to maximize their personal safety (Douce & Hansen, 1988).

With increasing subject age, Risk Taking/Adventure scores shift toward the plays it safe pole as people become more aware of the consequences of risk taking; thus, the scale is more predictive of current than of future behavior. Scores near the takes chances pole on Risk Taking/Adventure for people over the age of 30 indicate an enduring penchant for risks rather than merely youthful exuberance. For them, exploration should include gaining an understanding of ways to satisfy their need for risk taking.

Some people (e.g., skydivers) score toward the takes chances pole because they enjoy physical risk taking. Occupations in this category include police officers and astronauts. People who race cars, climb mountains (or jump off them, for example, by hang gliding), or go on dangerous treks (e.g., Will Steger, who has led dogsled expeditions to both the North and South Poles) are physical risk takers. Other people (e.g., salespeople and stockbrokers) who score in this range may also be financial risk takers. These people typically prefer to work for a commission, whereas a person scoring near the plays it safe pole on Risk Taking/Adventure would be reluctant to work for a commission and would choose a salaried position instead.

For some people, the Risk Taking/Adventure takes chances pole is expressed through a love for travel that may approach wanderlust (e.g., astronauts); for others, it is an indicator of willingness to take social risks or to try new activities without guarantees of success. For still others, such scores may reflect a need for autonomy and independence in their jobs as well as in their personal lives.

Scores toward the left pole of Risk Taking/Adventure (plays it safe) signal extreme discomfort in trying new activities without careful planning and without as many guarantees as possible. Part of the counseling process should include preparation and perhaps role playing to reduce these clients' fear of failing. A few successes generally lead to increased self-confidence and more willingness to try risky activities. This behavior is often the case, for example, with adults returning to school. At first, unsure how well they will compete with younger students, they choose a light course load or easy classes to test their skills. Then, with successful experience, their confidence often blossoms and they become strong students, willing to take more risks. In general, the best method for interpreting this scale is to offer clients several hypotheses explaining why people score toward one or the other pole and then ask them to identify the hypotheses that best fit what they know about themselves.

Sample Occupations Whose Members Prefer a Takes Chances Risk Taking/Adventure Style

- ▲ Athletic Trainer
- ▲ Auto Mechanic
- ▲ Carpenter
- ▲ Electrician

- Emergency Medical Technician
- Plumber
- Police Officer

Sample Occupations Whose Members Prefer a Plays It Safe Risk Taking/Adventure Style
- Dental Assistant
- Dental Hygienist
- Librarian
- Mathematician
- Nurse, LPN
- Speech Pathologist

Typical Risk Taking/Adventure Items
- "Auto racer" (takes chances pole)
- "Climbing along the edge of a steep cliff" (takes chances pole)
- "Jet pilot" (takes chances pole)
- "People who live dangerously" (takes chances pole)
- "Taking a chance" (takes chances pole)

Research on the Personal Style Scales

Research on the Personal Style Scales, discussed in the following sections, focuses on construction of the four scales, including norming, and presents correlations between the four scales and with the GOTs and BISs. Evidence of the scales' reliability and validity is also provided.

Constructing the Personal Style Scales

Although the four Personal Style Scales were designed to be used in similar ways, they were developed through two quite different psychometric strategies. The development of the first two scales, Work Style and Learning Environment, followed the prototypic empirical approach that dominated the early history of the *Strong*. Each was composed of items selected strictly according to a statistical criterion of group differences, just as the items in the Occupational Scales (OSs) were selected. The other two scales, Leadership Style and Risk Taking/Adventure, were developed in a different tradition. Like the BISs, they were built as homogeneous scales, bringing together correlated items with similar content.

Work Style Scale

The Work Style scale was constructed empirically using two contrasting groups of respondents to the *Strong*. Among the new items added to the Item Booklet/Answer Sheet for this revision were the six items in Part VIII, Preference in the World of Work, which ask the respondent to indicate preferences between all possible combinations of people, data, ideas, and things. From the responses of the 1994 GRS it was possible to identify individuals who consistently preferred one of the options over all the others. These individuals were collected into two groups, those who consistently preferred people ($N = 6,681$) and those who consistently preferred one of the other three options ($N = 5,574$). Item responses that differentiated between these two groups at the 16 percent level were identified. As a result, 51 items are scored on this scale.

Learning Environment Scale

Again using the empirical method of contrasted groups, the Learning Environment scale was developed to separate individuals in the 1994 GRS who had earned master's degrees and Ph.D. degrees ($N = 7,328$) from individuals whose highest degree was from a technical or trade school ($N = 422$). Forty-nine items that differentiated the two groups at 20 percent or greater response frequency differences were selected for the scale. Those scoring 55 and above on this scale tend to be more comfortable in formal, academic learning situations, while those scoring 45 and below tend to be more comfortable in less formal and more applied learning settings.

Leadership Style Scale

The possibility of building a Leadership Style scale was clearly evident from factor analyses of the *Strong* items. These factor analyses typically revealed a potent leadership dimension, appearing as one of the first eight factors and accounting for substantial individual differences. Using the guidance from the factor analyses, a 23-item homogeneous content scale was built by identifying items strongly correlated with the scale and with relatively consistent content but with construct breadth. The actual construction of the scale was done with random samples of about 2,000 from the full GRS of 18,951, with the evaluation of the scale later conducted with the full GRS.

Table 8.2 Means, Standard Deviations, and Score Boundaries for the Personal Style Scales for the General Reference Sample by Gender

Personal Style Scale	Gender	Mean	S.D.	Bottom 10% (0–10)	Next 15% (11–25)	Middle 50% (26–75)	Next 15% (76–90)	Top 10% (91–100)
Work Style	Female	53.1	9.6	20–39	40–46	47–60	61–65	66–78
	Male	46.9	9.4	20–34	35–40	41–53	54–59	60–78
Learning Environment	Female	50.0	10.4	1–35	36–42	43–57	58–62	63–78
	Male	50.0	9.5	1–36	37–43	44–56	57–62	63–78
Leadership Style	Female	50.1	10.0	18–36	37–43	44–58	59–62	63–72
	Male	50.0	10.0	18–36	37–43	44–57	58–62	63–72
Risk Taking/Adventure	Female	46.9	9.7	30–33	34–39	40–54	55–60	61–70
	Male	53.1	9.4	30–40	41–46	47–60	61–65	66–70

Note: General Reference Sample consisted of 9,467 women, 9,484 men; numbers in parentheses are percentiles.

Risk Taking/Adventure Scale

The Risk Taking/Adventure scale was first constructed in 1968 as one of the BISs (Campbell, Borgen, Eastes, Johansson, & Peterson, 1968; Campbell, 1971). Items for these homogeneous scales were selected by identifying items that correlated with each other and had similar content. The 1994 nine-item scale remains similar to the initial scale, although a number of its items have been reworded for modern usage. Campbell (1971, pp. 103–105) observed that the Adventure scale was the only scale with a clear personality flavor that could be successfully developed through this homogeneous strategy. Given this history, it is a natural evolution that the scale, now renamed Risk Taking/Adventure, should be moved into the new Personal Style Scales section of the Profile.

Norming the Personal Style Scales

Like the GOTs and BISs, the Personal Style Scales were normed on the GRS combined group containing both women and men ($N = 18,951$). Scores were converted to a mean of 50 and a standard deviation of 10. However, gender differences occurred on some of the scales; thus the Profile provides separate box-and-whisker graphs for women and men, just as it does for the GOTs and BISs. These graphs show, separately for women and men, the mean, middle 50 percent, and middle 80 percent of the distribution for each scale. Similarly, Table 8.2 shows, by gender, standard score means and standard deviations, as well as the standard score boundaries for the middle 50 percent and middle 80 percent shown on the Profile for each gender. There are essentially no gender differences for the Learning Environment and Leadership Style scales. As discussed earlier, substantial gender differences occur for the other two scales, however. Women tend to score toward the works with people pole of the Work Style scale, and men tend to score toward the takes chances pole of the Risk Taking/Adventure scale.

Correlations Between the Scales

Much can be learned about the meaning and interpretation of the new Personal Style Scales by examining their correlations with each other, and especially with other established scales on the *Strong*. These correlations show how the Personal Style Scales fit into the theoretical structure established for the six Holland types, as measured by the GOTs. They also show how the Personal Style Scales link to the more specific content of the BISs. These data speak to the concurrent and construct validity of the Personal Style Scales.

Relationship Between the Personal Style Scales

The intercorrelations of the four Personal Style Scales are shown, by gender, in Table 8.3. The table generally shows considerable independence between the scales. The highest correlation is between the Leadership Style and Work Style scales, with a higher correlation for men (.61) than for women (.52). Leadership Style also correlates moderately with Learning Environment, but interestingly, Work

Table 8.3 Intercorrelations of the Personal Style Scales for the General Reference Sample (Decimal Points Omitted)

Personal Style Scale	Work Style	Learning Environment	Leadership Style	Risk Taking/ Adventure
Work Style	—	−08	52	−05
Learning Environment	07	—	50	25
Leadership Style	61	49	—	32
Risk Taking/Adventure	03	12	31	—

Note: Correlations above the diagonal are based on 9,467 women; those below the diagonal are based on 9,484 men.

Style and Learning Environment are essentially uncorrelated. Risk Taking/Adventure is the least correlated of the Personal Style Scales, but it does correlate about .30 with Leadership Style for both women and men.

These modest scale intercorrelations suggest that for a group of individuals there will be considerable diversity in Profile patterns on the Personal Style Scales. That is, almost all combinations of patterns on each scale are possible. Some of the scales will also covary modestly. For example, a client's Profile might show scores on the Leadership Style and Work Style scales that either are both toward the left pole or both toward the right pole. Alternately, scores on the Leadership Style and Learning Environment scales could also show similar combinations. These various patterns provide rich hypotheses for counseling interpretation. For example, someone who scores toward the directs others pole of the Leadership Style scale and toward the takes chances pole of the Risk Taking/Adventure scale could be expected to lead with more flair and assertiveness than someone with a score toward the directs others pole of the Leadership Style scale and toward the plays it safe pole of the Risk Taking/Adventure scale. Subsequent research and experience will provide an expanded base for classifying and interpreting these various patterns.

Relationships to the General Occupational Themes

The relationships of the four Personal Style Scales to the six GOTs is shown, by gender, in Table 8.4 on page 164. Strong and fascinating relationships are evident across the two types of scales, which might be anticipated since Holland's theory of occupational types is also a personality theory (Holland, 1985). It is also important to note in Table 8.4 that the pattern of relationships is very similar for women and men. The relationships between the RIASEC scales and the Personal Style Scales can be summarized as follows:

High R-Theme interest	▲ Works with ideas/data/things Work Style
	▲ Takes chances Risk Taking/Adventure style
High I-Theme interest	▲ Works with ideas/data/things Work Style
	▲ Academic Learning Environment
High A-Theme interest	▲ Academic Learning Environment
	▲ Directs others Leadership Style
High S-Theme interest	▲ Works with people Work Style
	▲ Directs others Leadership Style
High E-Theme interest	▲ Works with people Work Style
	▲ Directs others Leadership Style
High C-Theme interest	▲ No clear relationship to Personal Style Scales

One of the most revealing patterns of relationships in Table 8.4 is for the Work Style scale. Not only are the linkages for women and men very similar, but two RIASEC scales are associated with the left pole of the Work Style scale, and two are associated with the right pole. R types and I types prefer working with ideas, data, or things; S types and E types prefer working with people.

Table 8.4 Correlations Between the Personal Style Scales and the General Occupational Themes for Women and Men (Decimal Points Omitted)

	Personal Style and Gender							
	Work Style		Learning Environment		Leadership Style		Risk Taking/ Adventure	
General Occupational Theme	Female	Male	Female	Male	Female	Male	Female	Male
Realistic	−39	−33	05	−11	−05	−07	44	41
Investigative	−46	−38	41	40	03	04	30	26
Artistic	11	21	65	70	35	33	30	15
Social	64	62	09	25	37	47	04	12
Enterprising	60	57	01	04	50	51	18	24
Conventional	07	10	−31	−07	−01	13	−09	02

Note: General Reference Sample consisted of 9,467 women and 9,484 men.

These linkages are shown schematically in Figure 8.1 (shown on page 157), in which the Work Style scale forms a superordinate axis that cuts across the RIASEC hexagon. This configuration will not come as a revelation to anyone familiar with Holland's theory (see Rounds & Tracey, 1993), but to have it emerge so clearly by serendipity is testament to the scientific robustness of these constructs and to the potential counseling utility of the Personal Style Scales. Enthusiasm, however, should be tempered with an important caution: a substantial item overlap exists between the Personal Style Scales and the GOTs and BISs. Thus, some of these correlations are likely inflated for theoretical purposes, although they do reflect the structure of the relationships among *Strong* scales and how they are likely to be related in counseling use.

Relationships to the Basic Interest Scales

Table 8.5 displays in a similar way the relationships between the Personal Style Scales and the 25 BISs. Recall that the BISs often measure specific content that is measured more generally in the GOTs; therefore, some parallels between Tables 8.4 and 8.5 are expected. Specifically, those BISs that are highly correlated (either negatively or positively) with a specific GOT should show a pattern of correlations with the Personal Style Scales that is similar to that which is evident for that GOT in Table 8.4. Thus, Mechanical Activities links with the Personal Style Scales, as the R Theme does. An interest in Merchandising is coupled with a works with people Work Style preference and an active Leadership Style, as is the E Theme.

In contrast, rich interpretive possibilities lie within the relationships shown in Table 8.5. Such possibilities speak to the discriminant validity of the many BISs that do not link to the Personal Style Scales in the way that other BISs within the same Theme do. Thus, Medical Science is only moderately correlated with the Personal Style Scales, a pattern that is quite different from the Science BIS. Similarly, Religious Activities is not highly correlated with any of the Personal Style Scales, unlike the Social Service BIS. These kinds of patterns are intuitively reasonable and contribute to the meaning and validity of both kinds of scales. Readers are encouraged to study Table 8.5 in some detail.

Reliability of the Personal Style Scales

Both internal consistency and test-retest reliability have been evaluated for the scales. Internal consistency reliabilities (Cronbach alphas) are shown in Table 8.6 (page 166) for the full GRS ($N = 18,951$). These alphas are high for the three long scales having 51, 49, and 23 items: Work Style, Learning Environment, and Leadership Style, respectively. The alpha (.78) is lower for the Risk Taking/Adventure scale, consisting of just nine items.

Test-retest reliabilities are shown in Table 8.7 (page 167) for four different test-retest samples, which are described in detail in Chapter 5. Sample A, the national sample of 191 employed adults, is similar to the GRS. College samples C and D had an intervening career development course during the retest interval. Mean scores for the employed adult sample are very close to 50, while the means for the college samples often diverge substantially

Table 8.5 Correlations Between the Personal Style Scales and the Basic Interest Scales for Women and Men (Decimal Points Omitted)

Basic Interest Scale Listed by Theme	Personal Style and Gender							
	Work Style		Learning Environment		Leadership Style		Risk Taking/ Adventure	
	Female	Male	Female	Male	Female	Male	Female	Male
Realistic								
Agriculture	−15	−06	−11	−27	−10	−08	29	30
Nature	−20	−06	17	09	−03	01	28	22
Military Activities	02	10	−05	−02	12	20	28	29
Athletics	21	29	−07	−08	23	25	46	47
Mechanical Activities	−42	−39	06	−07	−05	−08	33	31
Investigative								
Science	−56	−51	36	34	−06	−06	26	21
Mathematics	−39	−34	18	22	−04	00	10	10
Medical Science	−13	−02	19	22	07	14	33	33
Artistic								
Music/Dramatics	16	23	54	60	33	30	29	13
Art	06	14	51	55	22	21	21	09
Applied Arts	−10	01	48	50	16	17	29	22
Writing	09	18	69	75	37	34	19	09
Culinary Arts	39	37	10	21	27	32	06	12
Social								
Teaching	43	43	27	38	32	36	05	07
Social Service	63	64	16	31	42	50	09	14
Medical Service	16	20	−17	−01	04	16	18	24
Religious Activities	26	26	07	18	18	23	−06	−03
Enterprising								
Public Speaking	42	52	50	49	78	76	30	28
Law/Politics	24	36	52	49	63	63	34	33
Merchandising	59	57	04	07	48	48	15	21
Sales	48	45	−12	−12	37	39	12	20
Organizational Management	54	54	09	15	60	62	13	22
Conventional								
Data Management	−05	04	−07	03	10	18	00	07
Computer Activities	−10	−12	−19	02	−08	02	−03	06
Office Services	20	20	−44	−17	−06	08	−21	−08

Note: General Reference Sample consisted of 9,467 women and 9,484 men.

Table 8.6 Internal Consistency Reliabilities for the Personal Style Scales

Personal Style Scale	Number of Items	Cronbach Alpha
Work Style	51	.91
Learning Environment	49	.86
Leadership Style	23	.86
Risk Taking/Adventure	9	.78

Note: Figures are based on the combined General Reference Sample of 18,951 people.

from 50 for some of the scales. All the college samples, each drawn from a specific course in psychology or education, show a mean works with people Work Style scale preference and a practical Learning Environment scale preference. Despite the diversity across these retest samples, the stability of the Personal Style Scales is uniformly high and supports their use in individual counseling. It is noteworthy that the stability of the Risk Taking/Adventure scale is high despite its somewhat lower internal consistency reliability.

Validity of the Personal Style Scales

In this section, a specific focus is given to construct and concurrent validity by examining how known groups differ on the Personal Style Scales.

Educational Level Differences on the Learning Environment Scale

The Learning Environment scale was designed to differentiate people comfortable in formal academic settings from those who prefer learning in more practical or applied settings. Thus, one route to examining the validity of this Personal Style Scale is to look at differences on the scale for people with varying amounts of formal education. Table 8.8, using data from the General Reference Sample, shows a progression in scores from less to more education among both men and women on the Learning Environment scale. Because courses of study that have a more formal academic orientation tend to be longer, it can be inferred that the Learning Environment scale is differentiating among groups of more and less academically oriented individuals.

Occupational Differences on the Personal Style Scales

As for the General Occupational Themes (Chapter 5) and the Basic Interest Scales (Chapter 6), the validity of the Personal Style Scales was addressed by examining occupational and educational major field differences. Also, the 109 occupations on the *Strong* have been ranked on each scale, with the results shown in Figures 8.2 through 8.5 (pages 168–169). Also shown, in Figure 8.6 (page 170), are Personal Style Scales mean Profiles, by gender, for four occupations—auto mechanics, fine artists, elected public officials, and research & development managers. These results clearly support the validity of the Personal Style Scales.

Educational Major Differences on the Personal Style Scales

Figures 8.7 through 8.10 (pages 171–172) show the ranking of 24 educational majors on each of the Personal Style Scales. These are the 24 majors reported by 16,994 of the 18,951 people in the GRS (see Chapter 5 for a more complete description). For each scale, there are quite substantial differences across people majoring in the 24 areas of concentration. The most modest differences are for the Risk Taking/Adventure scale. The major differences in fields for the other three Personal Style Scales are large (more than one standard deviation); these differences strongly support the validity of the scales.

Table 8.7 Test-Retest Reliability Statistics in Four Samples for the Personal Style Scales

Personal Style Scale	Test-Retest Correlation	Test Mean	Test S.D.	Retest Mean	Retest S.D.
Sample A: Employed Adults, 3–6 months (N = 110 women, 81 men)					
Work Style	.92	50.5	9.7	50.1	10.1
Learning Environment	.91	50.0	10.5	49.9	9.8
Leadership Style	.88	50.0	10.3	50.3	10.0
Risk Taking/Adventure	.85	50.9	10.3	50.8	10.8
Sample B: College Students, 1 month (N = 54 women, 30 men)					
Work Style	.91	56.9	8.6	56.9	9.2
Learning Environment	.83	46.8	8.4	46.3	7.9
Leadership Style	.85	51.4	9.5	51.7	9.6
Risk Taking/Adventure	.87	53.5	10.2	53.8	10.5
Sample C: College Students, 3 months (N = 56 women, 23 men)					
Work Style	.86	59.1	8.2	58.9	8.0
Learning Environment	.87	39.9	8.3	40.2	8.0
Leadership Style	.86	48.5	9.3	51.1	10.3
Risk Taking/Adventure	.89	47.3	11.1	50.5	11.6
Sample D: College Students, 3 months (N = 61 women, 26 men)					
Work Style	.86	58.7	8.2	59.5	8.9
Learning Environment	.89	44.1	9.7	45.5	9.6
Leadership Style	.81	52.0	9.4	52.4	9.5
Risk Taking/Adventure	.88	52.6	12.1	52.4	11.4

Table 8.8 Learning Environment Scores by Educational Level and Gender

Educational Level	Women N	Women Mean	Women S.D.	Men N	Men Mean	Men S.D.	Total GRS N	Total GRS Mean	Total GRS S.D.
Less than high school	20	36.05	7.86	19	35.42	7.20	39	35.74	7.45
High school	338	36.17	9.93	252	37.04	8.62	590	36.55	9.40
Trade/technical training	241	38.60	9.58	181	39.26	8.65	422	38.89	9.19
Some college	869	44.51	9.76	666	44.40	8.95	1,535	44.46	9.42
Associate degree	545	43.68	9.83	442	44.26	8.62	987	43.94	9.31
Bachelor's degree	3,028	49.78	9.19	3,161	49.08	8.63	6,189	49.42	8.92
Master's degree	2,740	53.38	8.92	2,655	52.50	8.45	5,395	52.95	8.70
Professional degree (e.g., D.D.S., J.D., M.D., etc.)	777	52.77	9.31	853	51.58	8.86	1,630	52.15	9.09
Doctorate (e.g., Ph.D., Ed.D.)	781	57.76	7.20	1,152	56.01	7.50	1,933	56.72	7.43
Total	9,339	50.09	10.38	9,381	50.02	9.47	18,720	50.06	9.93

Note: Figures are based on General Reference Sample of 9,467 women and 9,484 men and exclude 128 women and 103 men for whom data on educational level was missing.

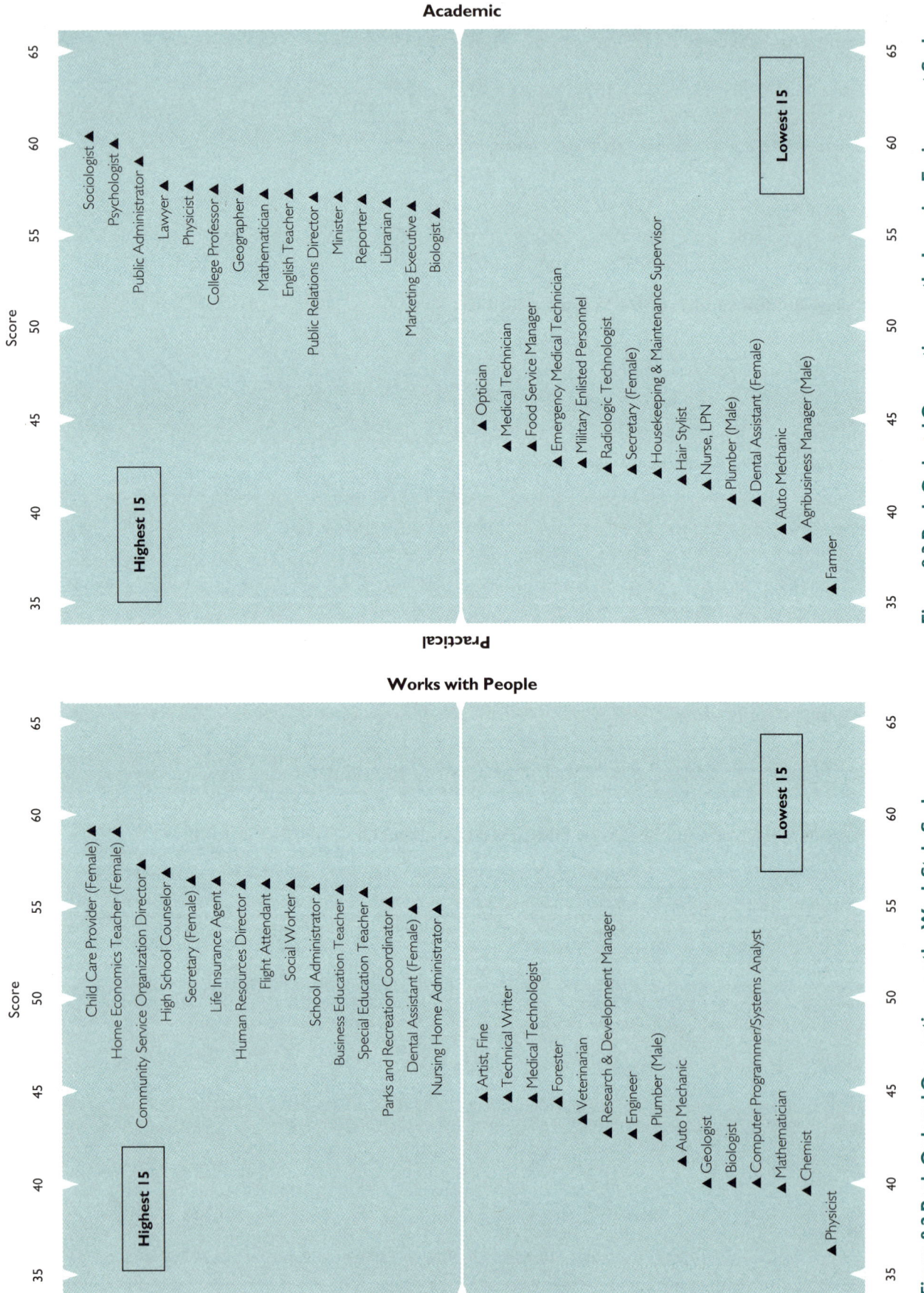

Figure 8.2 Rank-Ordered Occupations on the Work Style Scale: The 15 Highest and 15 Lowest Occupational Means of 109 Occupations

Figure 8.3 Rank-Ordered Occupations on the Learning Environment Scale: The 15 Highest and 15 Lowest Occupational Means of 109 Occupations

168

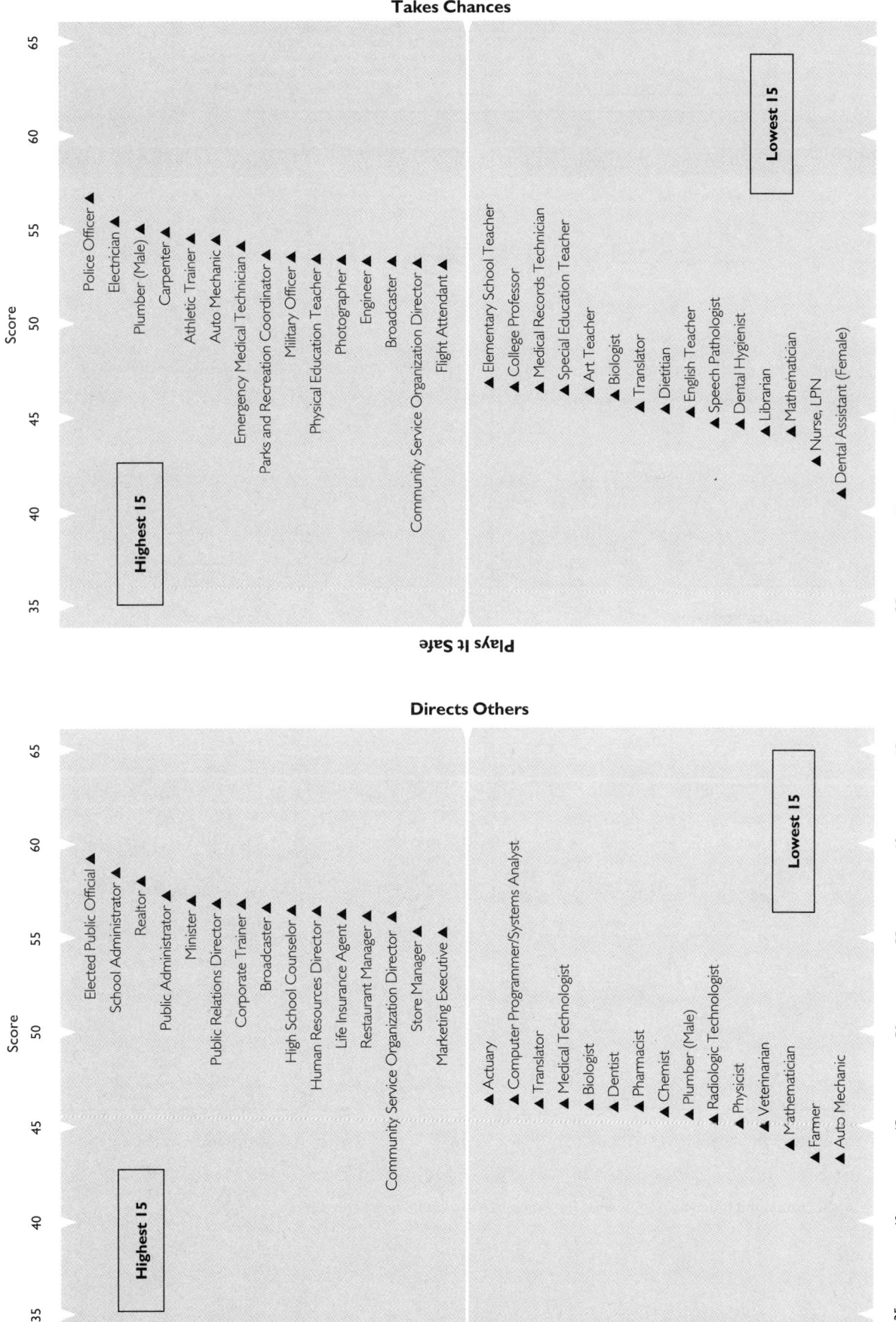

Figure 8.5 Rank-Ordered Occupations on the Risk Taking/Adventure Scale: The 15 Highest and 15 Lowest Occupational Means of 109 Occupations

Figure 8.4 Rank-Ordered Occupations on the Leadership Style Scale: The 15 Highest and 15 Lowest Occupational Means of 109 Occupations

169

170 Chapter 8

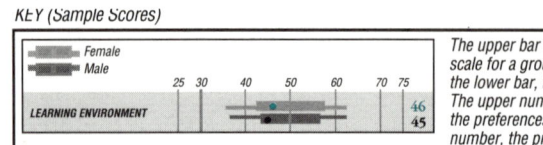

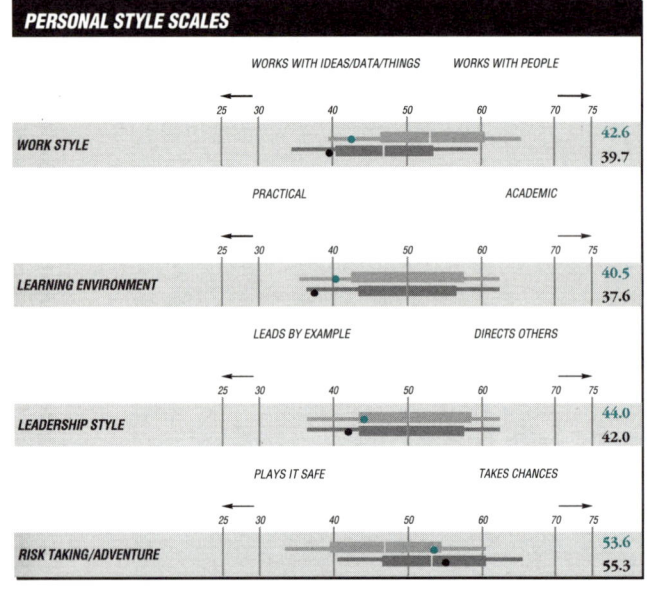

Auto Mechanic

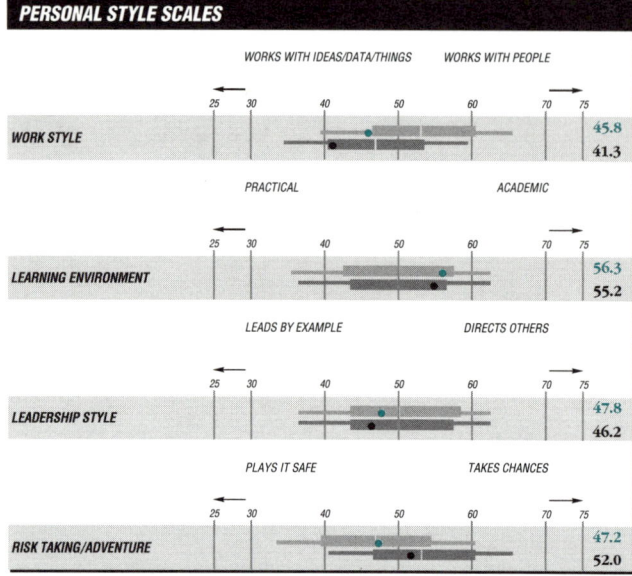

Fine Artist

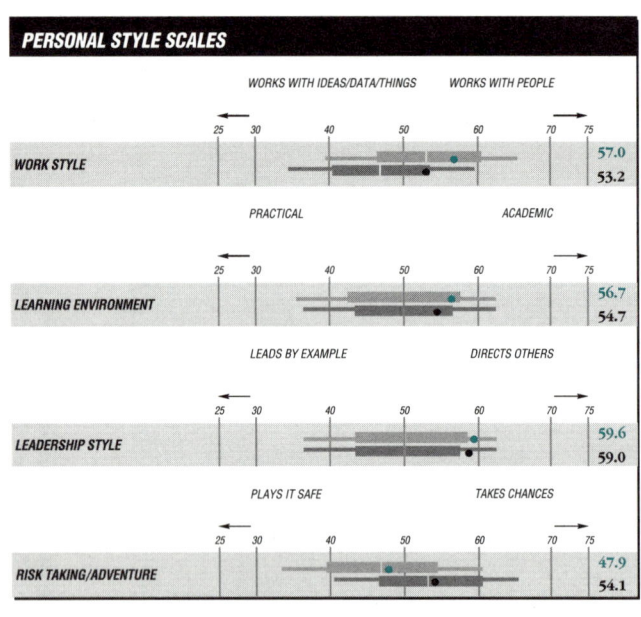

Elected Public Official

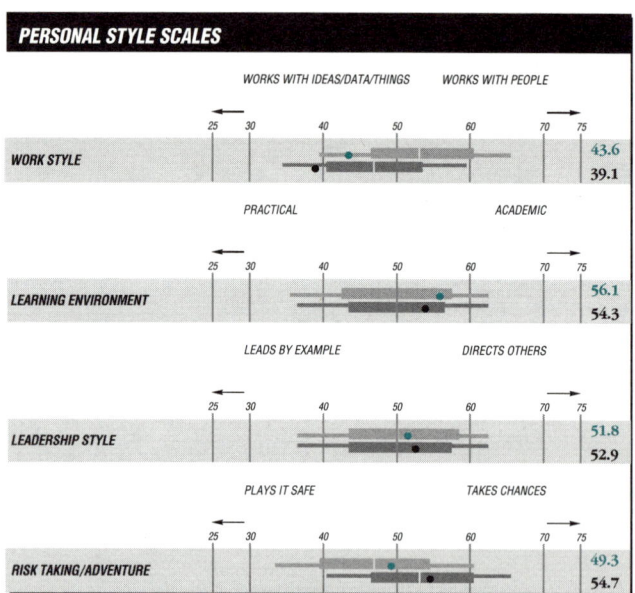

Research & Development Manager

Figure 8.6 Four Occupations Illustrating Diverse Patterns of Personal Style Scales

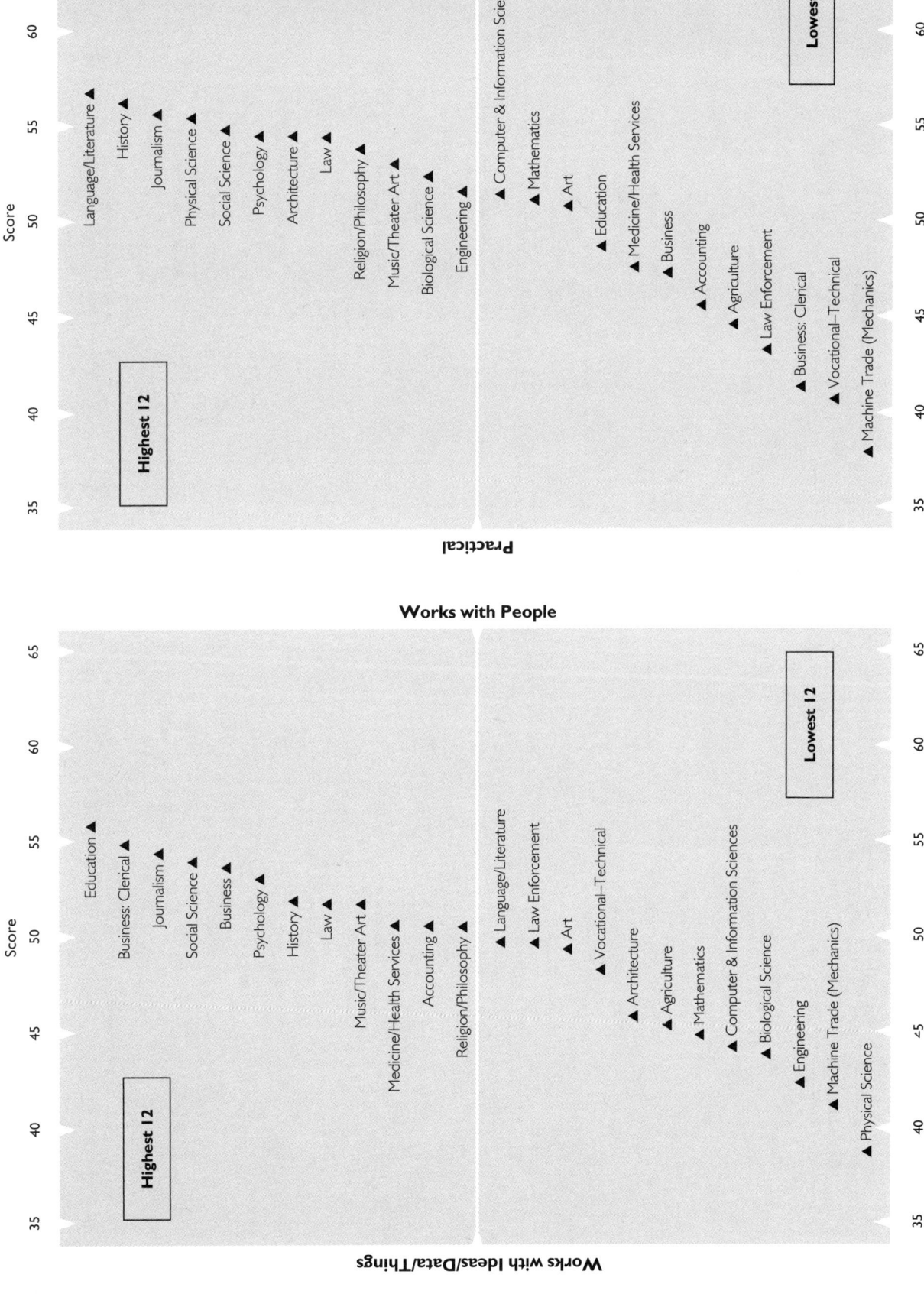

Figure 8.7 Rank-Ordered Means of 24 Majors on the Work Style Scale

Figure 8.8 Rank-Ordered Means of 24 Majors on the Learning Environment Scale

171

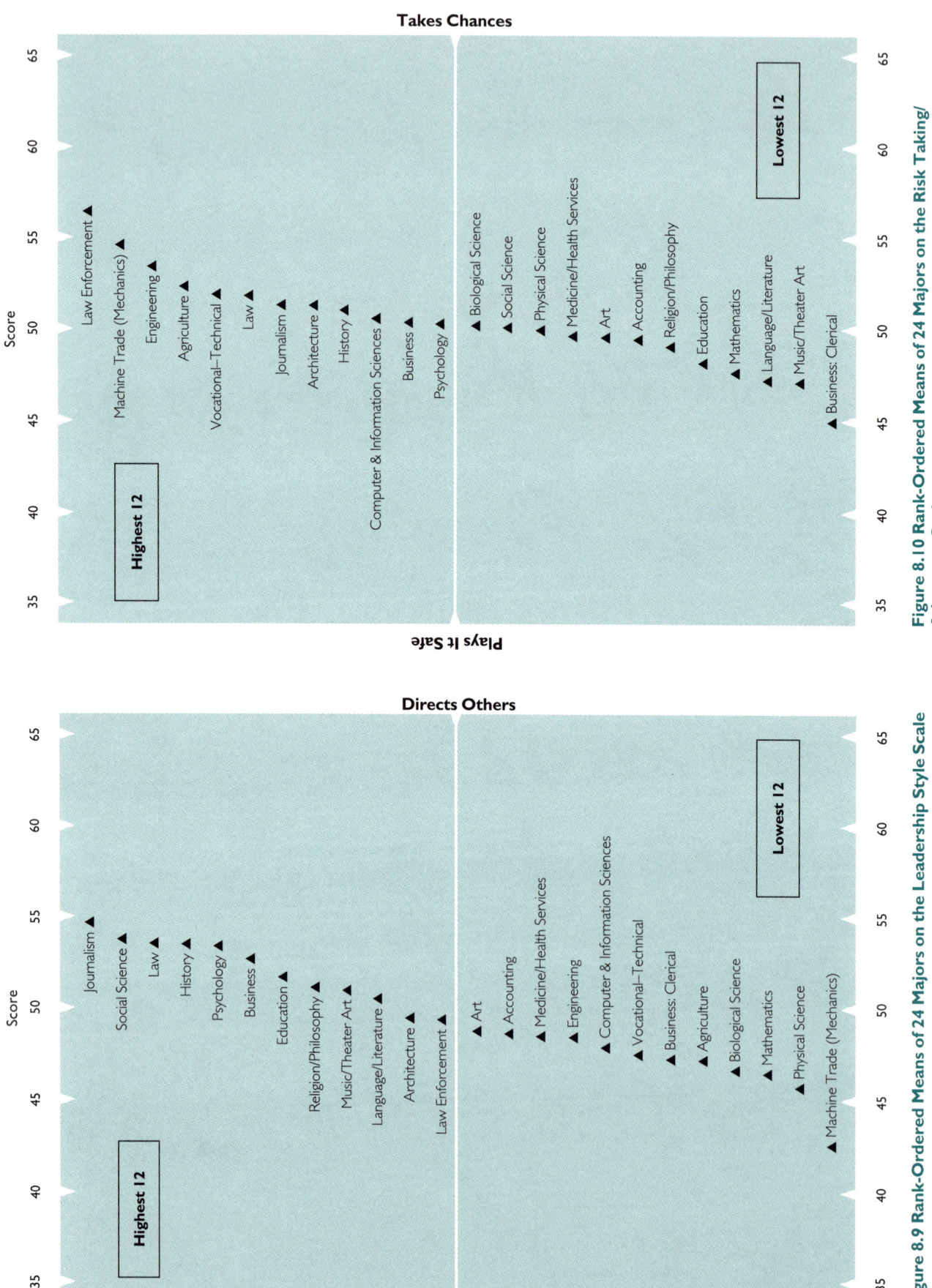

Figure 8.10 Rank-Ordered Means of 24 Majors on the Risk Taking/Adventure Scale

Figure 8.9 Rank-Ordered Means of 24 Majors on the Leadership Style Scale

References

Campbell, D. P. (1971). *Handbook for the Strong Vocational Interest Blank*. Stanford, CA: Stanford University Press.

Campbell, D. P., Borgen, F. H., Eastes, S., Johansson, C. B., & Peterson, R. A. (1968). A set of Basic Interest Scales for the Strong Vocational Interest Blank for men. *Journal of Applied Psychology Monographs, 52*(6), part 2.

Douce, L. A., & Hansen, J. C. (1988). Examination of the construct validity of the SVIB-SCII Adventure scale for college women. *Measurement and Evaluation in Counseling and Development, 20,* 171–174.

Hansen, J. C. (1992). *User's guide for the Strong Interest Inventory* (rev. ed.). Stanford, CA: Stanford University Press.

Hansen, J. C., & Campbell, D. P. (1985). *Manual for the Strong Interest Inventory* (4th ed.). Stanford, CA: Stanford University Press.

Holland, J. L. (1985). *Making vocational choices: A theory of vocational personalities and work environments.* Englewood Cliffs, NJ: Prentice-Hall.

Rounds, J., & Tracey, T. J. (1993). Prediger's dimensional representation of Holland's RIASEC circumplex. *Journal of Applied Psychology, 78,* 875–890.

CHAPTER 9

The Administrative Indexes

The *Strong* Administrative Indexes are routine checks performed by computer on each answer sheet to make certain that nothing has gone awry during the administration, completion, or processing of the Item Booklet/Answer Sheet. The indexes provide three statistics: total responses, the percentage of "Like," "Indifferent," and "Dislike" responses to each part of the inventory booklet, and infrequent responses. This information appears on page 6 of the Profile. How these three indexes are used in interpreting the Profile is discussed in the applications chapters of this guide. ◆

The Total Responses Index

The first of these indexes, Total Responses (TR), is the number of item responses on the answer sheet recognized by the computer. Since the *Strong* has 317 items, if every item were answered, the Total Responses number printed on the Profile would be 317. Occasionally, marks on the answer sheet are too light, and the computer will not recognize such responses. In some cases, the person taking the *Strong* may have overlooked a section of the Item Booklet/Answer Sheet or neglected to complete the inventory. A few answers may be omitted without appreciably affecting the scoring, but if the TR index drops below 300, the counselor should check the answer sheet to assess the problem. If there are fewer than 300 responses, an alert to the counselor is printed in the lower right corner of the Snapshot (page 1 of the Profile) and the notice "Insufficient Responses" is printed on page 6 of the Profile.

The "Like," "Indifferent," and "Dislike" Percent Indexes

The "Like," "Indifferent," and "Dislike" percent indexes show the percent of "Like," "Indifferent," and "Dislike" responses selected in each section of the inventory. These figures reflect the respondent's response style in filling in the inventory. Because the parts vary in response format, only Parts I through V and Part VII, which call for responses of "Like," "Dislike," or "Indifferent," or "Yes," "?," or "No," are included in the calculation of the Subtotal presented on the Profile. Since Parts VI and VIII involve a forced-choice response format, where response sets are less likely to operate, they are not included in the Subtotal. The discussion in the following sections applies mainly to the Subtotal and to those parts of the inventory that are not in a forced-choice response format.

Normal Response Ranges

Table 9.1 shows the means and standard deviations on the total "Like," "Indifferent," and "Dislike"

175

Table 9.1 Means and Standard Deviations on the "Like," "Indifferent," and "Dislike" Percent Indexes

Booklet Part	Gender	Response Percentage Index[a]					
		Like		Indifferent		Dislike	
		Mean	S.D.	Mean	S.D.	Mean	S.D.
I. Occupations	Female	26	12	26	14	48	18
	Male	24	13	30	16	46	20
	Combined	25	13	28	15	47	19
II. School Subjects	Female	41	17	29	15	30	18
	Male	38	18	34	16	28	19
	Combined	40	17	31	16	29	18
III. Activities	Female	38	15	31	14	31	14
	Male	34	15	36	15	30	16
	Combined	36	15	34	15	30	15
IV. Leisure Activities	Female	36	15	29	14	35	16
	Male	32	15	33	15	36	18
	Combined	34	15	31	15	35	17
V. Types of People	Female	38	19	41	19	21	15
	Male	34	19	43	20	23	16
	Combined	36	20	42	20	22	16
VII. Your Characteristics	Female	55	17	20	15	24	15
	Male	59	18	21	15	20	15
	Combined	57	18	21	15	22	15
Subtotal[b]	Female	33	12	29	12	38	14
	Male	31	12	32	13	37	16
	Combined	32	12	31	13	37	15
VI. Preference Between Two Activities	Female	41	12	24	17	35	11
	Male	43	12	23	17	34	10
	Combined	42	12	23	17	35	11
VIII. Preference in the World of Work	Female	43	18	14	22	43	17
	Male	45	19	16	24	39	17
	Combined	44	18	15	23	41	17

Note: Based on 9,467 women, 9,484 men, and combined group (9,467 women and 9,484 men).
[a] Parts VI through VIII of the Item Booklet/Answer Sheet have response formats different from the Like/Indifferent/Dislike format.
[b] The Subtotal response percentages are calculated on all items in Parts I through V and Part VII.

percent indexes for each part of the Item Booklet/Answer Sheet for the General Reference Samples (GRSs) of 9,467 women and 9,484 men. These figures suggest the normal ranges for each section. Although response percentages vary somewhat from part to part, the mean "Like" response rate to items in the Subtotal as shown in Table 9.1 and on the Profile (Parts I through V and Part VII use a Like/Indifferent/Dislike or Yes/?/No response format) is about 32 percent, and the standard deviation is about 12 percent.

Scores for most respondents will fall between the mean and plus or minus 1.5 standard deviations (that is, between approximately 14 and 50 percent). Consequently, a range of 14 to 50 percent for total "Like" responses is sufficient for most interpretive purposes.

The mean total "Dislike" responses average 37 percent, with a standard deviation of 15, so the range covered by 1.5 standard deviations is approximately 14 to 60. Indexes within these two ranges for "Like" and "Dislike" responses are normal; if response percentages fall outside these limits, the interpretation of portions of the Profile may have to be modified, as discussed later in this section. In both total "Like" and "Dislike" responses, the mean percentage for men is slightly lower than for women, while the men have slightly higher standard deviations of total "Dislike" responses than women.

High "Like" Percentages

A high percentage of "Like" responses for the entire inventory—for example, 65 percent or higher over several parts—will be reflected by a large number of high scores on the General Occupational Themes and the Basic Interest Scales. This pattern occurs because these scales assign positive weights only to the "Like" response, in contrast to the Occupational Scales, which also weight the "Dislike" response positively, depending on the direction of the difference between the occupational group and General Reference Samples. Although these scores do reflect what the respondent says she or he likes, the interpretation of the Profile may need to be modified. For example, if scores on 15 or 16 Basic Interest Scales are above 60, then the definition of a high score, usually regarded as any score above 58, needs to be altered for this individual. In such cases, only the three to five highest scores should be considered high. No single characteristic describes all persons with high "Like" percentages, but some combination of the adjectives "enthusiastic," "curious," "diverse," "unfocused," and "energetic" will fit many of them. Chapter 11 provides case studies and discussion relevant to elevated Profiles.

High "Dislike" Percentages

Conversely, if the "Dislike" response percentage is high over several parts, the General Occupational Themes and Basic Interest Scales scores will reflect "Little Interest" or "Very Little Interest." Persons with high "Dislike" percentages tend to fall into two categories: one includes those people with an intense occupational focus—they mark almost every item "Dislike" because they are interested in a single area, such as art, science, or mechanics; the other category includes those who have few likes in the world and who find virtually everything uninteresting or even repugnant. These two categories present two very different counseling challenges: the first category may describe a person who is already committed passionately to a fixed course, which could prove impractical if the chosen occupation is unavailable; the second category may also provide a formidable challenge because the person systematically rejects almost every choice offered. Chapter 11 presents more information on the interpretation of flat and depressed Profiles.

High "Indifferent" Percentages

Occasionally, a respondent will respond "Indifferent" to a large majority of items. These people usually report considerable vocational confusion or occasionally generalized apathy. The *Strong* is useful in identifying such problems, and the results can provide the counselor with the opportunity to explore why the client is indecisive or apathetic. Some counselors have found it helpful to have such a person retake the inventory, stressing that the "Indifferent" response should be avoided when possible. Although no empirical study has been made of the value of the results when clients are given these instructions, counselors who have adopted this approach have found that it helps to break the counseling impasse.

Extreme Cases

The "Like," "Indifferent," and "Dislike" percent indexes can provide other useful information, especially when percentages are either extremely high or extremely low. For example, occasionally a student answers "Dislike" to virtually every occupation in the first part of the inventory while at the same time choosing a more typical number of "Like," "Indifferent," and "Dislike" responses on the remaining parts of the inventory. Such an unusual response pattern should be noted by the counselor and explored with the student. In other cases, students may answer "Dislike" to most of the school subjects, suggesting another fruitful area of discussion for the counselor and client.

Differences Between Occupational Samples

The range of mean "Like," "Indifferent," and "Dislike" percentages among occupational samples is approximately equal to the standard deviation of the

Table 9.2 Intercorrelations of the "Like" Percent Indexes for the Eight Booklet Parts and Subtotal

Booklet Part	Booklet Part								
	I	II	III	IV	V	VII	Subtotal	VI	VIII
I. Occupations	—	.62	.67	.55	.49	.27	.92	.08	.01
II. School Subjects	.66	—	.59	.52	.43	.29	.77	.12	−.03
III. Activities	.69	.64	—	.67	.57	.41	.85	.09	.02
IV. Leisure Activities	.58	.56	.69	—	.57	.35	.74	.10	.05
V. Types of People	.52	.48	.61	.58	—	.33	.67	.13	.08
VII. Your Characteristics	.27	.29	.40	.33	.35	—	.43	.18	.08
Subtotal[a]	.92	.81	.86	.76	.68	.42	—	.12	.02
VI. Preference Between Two Activities	.12	.12	.10	.08	.13	.14	.14	—	.22
VIII. Preference in the World of Work	.00	−.05	−.03	−.01	.02	.06	−.01	.25	—

Note: Figures above the diagonal are based on sample of 9,467 women; those below, on sample of 9,484 men.
[a] Subtotal "Like" percentage is calculated on all items in Parts I through V and Part VII.

total percentages for the GRS combined group. (Note that, as stated earlier, the Subtotal involves only the six parts of the inventory scored in a Like/Indifferent/Dislike or Yes/?/No format.) In general, the women in the occupational samples have somewhat higher average "Like" response percentages than do the men in the sample group who are in the same occupations.

The occupational samples retained from the 1985 edition tend to have higher "Like" response percentages (ranging from 29.9 for male Geologists to 43.1 for female Ministers) than the occupational groups collected for the 1994 revision (ranging from 23.6 for male Farmers to 37.6 for female Ministers). The issue of varying "Like" percentages over time is discussed in greater detail in Chapter 2. Since the occupational groups' "Like," "Indifferent," and "Dislike" percentages probably differ partially as a function of the characteristics of the people in the group and partially as a function of the time during which the data were collected, making occupational comparisons is probably unwarranted.

"Like" Percentage Correlations

The correlations among the "Like" percent indexes for the eight parts of the inventory as well as the subtotals for the six similar parts are given in Table 9.2; the correlations for women are above the diagonal, and the correlations for men are below the diagonal. (The correlations for the "Indifferent" and "Dislike" percent indexes, not shown in this table, are similar in pattern to those for the "Like" percent index.) Correlations among the first five parts of the inventory, all of which contain only Like/Indifferent/Dislike items, are fairly high, indicating a fair consistency in the number of "Like" responses given for the various parts. Part VII (Your Characteristics), which requires Yes/?/No responses, correlates moderately with the first five parts and with the Subtotal.

The correlations of Parts VI and VIII with the other parts are much smaller. In Part VI (Preference Between Two Activities) and Part VIII (Preference in the World of Work), the respondent can choose either the item on the left or the item on the right or can choose the equal sign in the middle to indicate that the items are equal in attraction. While this forced-choice format diminishes any tendency for response set, it also makes statistical analysis more difficult because the individual's response depends on a combination of attraction or aversion to the two choices. However, the left and right choices in Parts VI and VIII do not reflect a systematic arrangement of items or two poles of a psychological characteristic: if the alternatives in this part were realigned in new item combinations, activities formerly rejected by particular respondents might be selected, and vice versa. Based on this pattern of correlations, the composition of the Subtotal score was considered more accurate if Parts VI and VIII were not included.

Occasionally, extremely high "Like" percentage scores on other parts of the inventory will be accompanied by high "=" percentage scores on the two parts with the preference items. This pattern often reflects the response set of an individual who is unwilling to reject anything. The "Like," "Indifferent," and "Dislike" percentages for Parts VI and VIII are presented on the Profile, along with scores for the other six parts, to provide counselors and clients with complete information.

Correlations between the Subtotal and each of the parts reflect, to some extent, the number of items in each section. For example, the longest section of the inventory is Part I (Occupations), with 135 items; this part has the highest correlation with the Subtotal. The correlations between the parts of the inventory (see Table 9.2) might indicate a tendency for people to adopt the same response set over the various parts, though this tendency is not particularly pronounced. As demonstrated earlier by Figures 4.1 through 4.3, the most important determinant of response is item content. It is not possible to determine what percentage of the variation in response can be attributed to response set, but it is clearly less than the amount attributable to item content. These figures do indicate that people differ in the number of items to which they respond "Like," "Indifferent," and "Dislike" and that they are consistent over a variety of inventory parts.

The Infrequent Responses Index

The Infrequent Responses (IR) index is used to identify invalid or highly unusual Profiles, answer sheets that may have been marked incorrectly, and clients with androgynous or atypical interests. To develop the IR index, the item-response percentages of the GRSs were analyzed to locate items that were chosen infrequently. Since one important criterion in selecting items for the *Strong* was that their percentages of endorsements of "Like" were neither extremely high nor extremely low, not many of the items that survived the item screening were selected infrequently by the total GRS. When the female and male GRSs were separated, however, several items showed a "Like" response rate of 6 percent or less; these items became the IR indexes, with a specific index for each gender.

The IR indexes include 11 items for females and 14 for males. Table 9.3 shows the response distributions for the GRSs as well as the distribution for samples of female and male college students. In the female GRS, less than 1 percent of the 9,467 women gave more than 4 infrequent responses, so for women, 4 infrequent responses were established as the acceptable threshold number of atypical responses. For the 181 female college students, less than 1 percent gave more than 4 infrequent responses. In the male GRS, less than 1 percent of the 9,484 men gave more than 6 infrequent responses, so for men, 6 infrequent responses were established as the acceptable threshold number of atypical responses. For the 82 male college students, less than 2 percent gave more than 6 infrequent responses. (The proportion probably would have been smaller had there been a larger sample of male college students, since there were only 2 responses beyond the cutoff point.)

The item weights are assigned so that any respondent who selects more than the threshold number of infrequent responses will receive a low score on the index; if the respondent marks more atypical responses than most people do, the score becomes negative. An inverse-weighting technique was employed to simplify the use of the index by counselors and other users: in practice, each respondent is given a constant on this IR index (5 for females, 7 for males), and 1 point is subtracted from this constant for each infrequent response selected. (Note from Table 9.3 that the IR scale does not make use of 0 because it would be difficult to interpret, since it is neither a positive nor a negative number.) The result is printed on the Profile as the IR score: the highest possible score is 5 for women and 7 for men, and the lowest possible score is –7 for women and –8 for men.

The counselor needs only to remember that if the IR index number is preceded by a negative sign, there is likely to be a problem with the results. Almost anyone who chooses more of these responses than 99 percent of the GRS has given an inordinately large number of infrequent responses, and such results should be scrutinized carefully to make certain that no problems occurred during administration or scoring of the inventory.

Although the IR can indicate the presence of an invalid or highly unusual Profile, it cannot specify which of many possible circumstances is responsible. The respondent may have been confused by some aspect of the *Strong:* In one case successfully flagged by the IR index, the respondent skipped a number when marking the answer sheet and answered the remainder of the items in the wrong spaces. In another case, a job applicant was irritated that she

Table 9.3 Score Distributions on the Female and Male Infrequent Responses Indexes

# of Infrequent Responses	Score	1994 General Reference Sample[a]			1993 College Sample[b]		
		Frequency	Cumulative Percent	Percent	Frequency	Cumulative Percent	Percent
Female Samples on the Female Index							
0	5	7,048	74.4	74.4	116	61.7	61.7
1	4	1,537	16.2	90.7	48	25.5	87.2
2	3	517	5.5	96.1	12	6.4	93.6
3	2	203	2.1	98.3	9	4.8	98.4
4	1	79	0.8	99.1	2	1.1	99.5
5	−1	52	0.5	99.7	0	0.0	99.5
6	−2	10	0.1	99.8	1	0.5	100.0
7	−3	11	0.1	99.9	0	0.0	100.0
8	−4	4	0.0	99.9	0	0.0	100.0
9	−5	4	0.0	100.0	0	0.0	100.0
10	−6	0	0.0	100.0	0	0.0	100.0
11	−7	2	0.0	100.0	0	0.0	100.0
Male Samples on the Male Index							
0	7	6,796	71.7	71.7	44	53.7	53.7
1	6	1,626	17.1	88.8	21	25.6	79.3
2	5	511	5.4	94.2	4	4.9	84.1
3	4	255	2.7	96.9	5	6.1	90.2
4	3	99	1.0	97.9	4	4.9	95.1
5	2	78	0.8	98.7	2	2.4	97.6
6	1	45	0.5	99.2	0	0.0	97.6
7	−1	31	0.3	99.5	0	0.0	97.6
8	−2	10	0.1	99.7	1	1.2	98.8
9	−3	15	0.2	99.8	0	0.0	98.8
10	−4	7	0.1	99.9	1	1.2	100.0
11	−5	4	0.0	99.9	0	0.0	100.0
12	−6	5	0.1	100.0	0	0.0	100.0
13	−7	0	0.0	100.0	0	0.0	100.0
14	−8	2	0.0	100.0	0	0.0	100.0

[a] For the female General Reference Sample, N = 9,467; for the male General Reference Sample, N = 9,484.
[b] For the female college sample, N = 181; for the male college sample, N = 82. The college samples were formed by combining the three college groups used in studying the test-retest reliability of the 1994 scales (see Chapter 5). The frequencies listed were taken from the first testing.

was forced to take the inventory, so she filled in the answer sheet randomly. In still another case, an individual tried to fool the system—"just to see what would happen," he said—by marking choices reflecting the exact opposite of his true feelings. Other cases of a negative IR index reflect that, because the items are chosen separately by gender, the respondent may have somewhat androgynous interests; that in itself is useful information. Occasionally, a negative IR index simply indicates that the respondent has unique interests. Each case of a negative IR should be checked on its own merits.

CHAPTER 10

General Strategies for Interpreting the Strong

This chapter shows how the *Strong* can be used in a general career-counseling or career development program and suggests a strategy for interpreting the *Strong* Profile. Although the *Strong* can be used with confidence with a variety of clients, the interpretation strategy presented here represents, by necessity, a general or "typical" sequence of suggested steps; the chapters that follow discuss how this strategy can be altered or refined to deal with particular problems or to take into account the needs of clients from specific populations. In each of these chapters, case studies illustrate the process of interpretation in relevant situations. ◆

Effect of Interpreting the Strong

Studies have demonstrated the effectiveness of test interpretation in general as a component of the career-counseling process (Goodyear, 1990). A goal of most career counselors is to have clients engage in career exploration behaviors. In addition to the specific and concrete information that may be gained from such activity, counselors hope that their clients will develop or expand their educational or career options.

To test some of these assumptions, Randahl, Hansen, and Haverkamp (1993) tracked students for one year after they had received a one-hour group interpretation of the *Strong*. The researchers compared the career exploration behaviors of these students with those of a group of students who had not taken the *Strong*. As predicted, those who had received an interpretation engaged in significantly more career exploration behaviors than did the contrast group. In particular, students who had an interpretation were significantly more likely than were those in the contrast group to have talked to family members, advisors, professors, and persons in careers; to have read about careers; and to have used computerized career exploration programs and other services of the career development center. Furthermore, 90.6 percent of the students said that they were satisfied or very satisfied with the interpretation of the *Strong*.

Cooper (1986) compared the effects of vocational counseling, in both individual and group settings, on personal and career indecision. One of the three sessions in each treatment method was devoted to interpreting the *Strong*. Although he did not find any differences between the individual and group treatments, both yielded a decrease in personal indecisiveness.

Slaney and Lewis (1986) studied the effects of two career interventions for 34 reentry women who were undecided about their careers. One intervention consisted of administering the Vocational Card Sort; the other, of simply administering the *Strong* and then having the women read an interpretive report of their results. Both treatments resulted in less career indecision; there were no differences between the two groups on this or other outcome measures.

Shahnasarian and Peterson (1988) examined the effects of providing a videotaped cognitive structuring intervention prior to a computer-assisted career guidance (CACG) intervention. Although they did not use the *Strong*, the videotape consisted of a ten-minute presentation of the six occupational environments described by Holland (1985) that form the basis for the General Occupational Themes (GOTs). The results showed that the addition of the videotape led to better adoption and retention of the six-theme model. The clients who viewed the videotape also became more alike in the number of occupations they were considering: those with fewer career alternatives added some options, and those with more alternatives eliminated some. Most of the clients in this group arrived at three to five career alternatives as a result of the combined videotape and CACG intervention. Unfortunately, this experiment did not include a test of the effects of the videotape alone. However, the researchers concluded that the cognitive structuring provided by the videotape may have "helped the subjects perceive relationships among occupations more clearly, thus enabling them to better formulate and evaluate options." Research is needed to determine whether the GOTs on the *Strong* could provide a similar structure.

What is most striking about these studies is not their positive results but the fact that such results were achieved after such a minimal interpretation of the *Strong*. In two of these studies, the entire intervention with the *Strong* consisted of administration of the inventory followed by a one-hour interpretive session. In the other study, the intervention consisted of a ten-minute videotape on the Holland model. Yet these minimal interventions produced increased career exploration, decreased indecisiveness, and increased cognitive understanding of the structure of careers. Goodyear (1990) observed a similar phenomenon in his review of the effects of test interpretation in general (i.e., not just the *Strong*) in career counseling. He concluded that clients who received a test interpretation experienced greater gains (on the various outcome measures employed in the studies) than did those in the control groups, despite what appeared to be minimal or "unadorned" interpretations. In many cases, the clients simply received reports of their test results. These findings, along with those reported above, suggest that more comprehensive and individualized interpretations—of the *Strong* or any other instrument—might produce even more pronounced effects.

Although interpreting test scores is unquestionably beneficial, it should not be performed in isolation or divorced from other components of career counseling, such as searching for career information or decision making. Other relevant information about the client must be integrated with the test results; according to Anastasi (1990, p. 258): "The context in which the individual is now living and was reared needs to be considered in interpreting *any* test score for *anyone*, for *any* purpose" (her emphasis). For example, in career counseling integrating information about the client's family and home life into the counseling process is important. Information about the client's financial needs is also often an important factor to consider.

A Career-Counseling Sequence

The *Strong Interest Inventory* is one tool that can be used effectively in the process of career counseling. The main reasons for using the *Strong* in career counseling are to:

▲ objectively identify the client's interests,

▲ provide a framework for organizing the client's interests into general and specific categories within the world of work, and

▲ help the client identify potentially relevant occupations that may not have been previously considered.

To afford the client the full benefit of the *Strong*, counselors must understand the material presented in this guide and know when to consult it, have the skills necessary to interpret the patterns of scores on the Profile, be able to communicate those interpretations to the client, and know the limits of the inventory, particularly with younger clients. The psychometric information presented in the preceding chapters, in conjunction with the more practical guidelines and case studies offered here and in the chapters and appendixes that follow, provide the foundation for an understanding of the complexity of the *Strong* and its many virtues and applications.

Additional insight can be gained by consulting the *Strong* support materials, such as interpretive reports, and the professional literature.

If the role of the *Strong* in the career-counseling process is to be properly understood, this process itself should be examined. Although the details vary from one counseling model to another, a fairly typical career-counseling sequence is presented here. This sequence is summarized in Figure 10.1, shown on page 184.

Step 1. Initiate the counseling relationship; develop rapport with the client and encourage an atmosphere of trust to facilitate the client's self-exploration.

Step 2. Identify and clarify the broad outlines of the client's career problems or concerns.

Step 3. With the client, identify alternative solutions to these problems and concerns and establish mutually agreed-upon counseling goals—for example:

- identify the causes of career dissatisfaction or uncertainty and list possible solutions;
- confirm or disconfirm a previously made choice;
- develop a list of educational or job options;
- evaluate the options in terms of how well the client's interests, work values, and abilities match the requirements of the various job options;
- narrow down the number of reasonable options; or
- expand the number of options the client has previously considered.

Step 4. Begin the self-exploration process by determining the adequacy and extent of the client's present knowledge regarding self and the world of work; ascertain how self-aware the client is in terms of interests, values, and abilities; determine whether any pertinent test scores are already available.

Step 5. Determine what additional information you and the client will need to complete the self-exploration.

Step 6. Explain methods for obtaining self-information (e.g., assessment instruments, examining past experiences and behavior, observing others).

Step 7. Discuss the client's beliefs or feelings about the entire career-counseling process. Focus on any concerns or skepticism the client may have about increasing self-awareness or test taking in general. Begin to demystify tests; for example, stress that tests "cannot tell you what you should do" or "measure how successful you will be in a particular job." Make the point that tests do not provide answers but rather suggest promising possibilities for exploration.

Step 8. Identify the tests and inventories that measure the factors about which the client needs more information and those that are relevant to the client's goals. Clients are often confused about what they can learn from an inventory. A frequent misconception is that interest inventories measure intelligence, abilities, or aptitudes. For each test or inventory that might be used, explain what it measures (and, often, what it does not measure) and how that information will fit into the self-exploration process. Emphasize that both you and the client will participate in interpreting the results.

Step 9. Together with the client, select the battery of tests, inventories, and other data-gathering techniques likely to produce the most useful information. A client who has been directly engaged in selecting the assessment instruments is less likely to discredit the resulting information than is a client who has merely been assigned to take a test.

Step 10. Prepare a brief record of all the important discoveries and decisions made while going through Steps 1 through 9, for use in the posttesting interview.

Step 11. Administer the inventories with clear instructions about the manner in which the client should respond to the various types of items. For example, clients taking the *Strong* should be told to focus strictly on their like or dislike of each activity or occupation listed; they should not be concerned with past success (or failure) in pursuing that activity or the likelihood of future success.

Step 12. With the client's *Strong* Profile in hand, preview the results in preparation for the interpretation interview. Before talking with the client about her or his results, determine whether the Profile scores are valid or whether they present problems of interpretation. A glance at the Snapshot (first page of the Profile) can quickly indicate whether you are dealing with a flat or depressed Profile. Begin to formulate hypotheses about the client's interests and about apparent inconsistencies in the results. (Detailed suggestions for what to look for in this preinterview review are offered in the next section and outlined in Figure 10.2.)

Step 13. Interpret the *Strong* with the client and develop additional hypotheses to explain his or her scores. (A procedure for interpreting the Profile is given in a later section of this chapter and is outlined in Figure 10.3.)

Step 14. Evaluate with the client the hypotheses generated in Step 13 and integrate the new information with other data (e.g., information about the client's abilities, job experience, and/or scores from other tests). For example, Hammer and Kummerow (1992) show how the results of the *Myers-Briggs Type Indicator* (MBTI®) can be integrated with the *Strong* to expand the client's self-understanding.

Step 15. Once some career alternatives congruent with the client's interests have been identified, discuss how to gather information about related occupations, jobs, educational alternatives, and leisure or recreational activities. Discuss specific exploration activities, such as searching a career library or the local public library, going on informational interviews, or volunteering. The client should be encouraged to learn more about educational and job-entry requirements, current and projected openings in the job market, income potential, working conditions, and other special considerations. If the *Strong* Interpretive Report is being used along with the Profile, some of this information will be included for several of the occupations on which the client scored highest. The *Occupational Outlook Handbook* (published by the U.S. Department of Labor) is a valuable source of additional information. Other resources include literature published by trade or professional organizations and people currently or previously employed in particular occupations. These activities may lead to a "short list" of the options the client believes are most important to consider.

Step 16. Help the client decide among the alternatives that have been identified. This decision should incorporate all the pertinent information about self and the world of work the client has identified. Some clients will decide to reduce their alternatives to a few possibilities at this point. The counselor should help the client develop a strategy for selecting among the possibilities in the future. Many clients have little experience in decision making; the work done in selecting an alternative or a small set of alternatives can provide a valuable lesson in decision making.

Step 17. Help the client develop an action plan and a time line for implementing the decisions she or he has made.

Step 18. Review the steps of the counseling sequence to reinforce what has been learned and help the client develop confidence and self-reliance in the process of career exploration.

Step 19. Discuss with the client the fact that career development is a lifelong activity. Point out that reconfirmation of known interests, at some point in the future, is as valuable as the initial discovery of new interests. Many clients appreciate a comparison of *Strong* inventories taken within a year or two of each other and may find taking the *Strong* again during periods of career transition or dissatisfaction particularly illuminating.

Figure 10.1 A Career-Counseling Sequence

Step 1. Develop rapport.
Step 2. Identify the problem.
Step 3. Establish counseling goals.
Step 4. Assess client's knowledge of self and world of work.
Step 5. Determine what additional information is needed.
Step 6. Decide methods for increasing self-knowledge.
Step 7. Discuss client's expectations of career counseling.
Step 8. Identify whether instruments can help increase knowledge of self and world of work.
Step 9. If so, mutually agree on what inventories to use.
Step 10. Record discoveries and hypotheses so that you can refer to them later.
Step 11. Administer instruments.
Step 12. Preview *Strong* results before interpretation.
Step 13. Interpret the *Strong*.
Step 14. Integrate other information with *Strong* results, including abilities.
Step 15. Develop career exploration plan.
Step 16. Help client develop a decision-making strategy.
Step 17. Help client develop an action plan and time line.
Step 18. Review and reinforce the career exploration process.
Step 19. Emphasize that career development is a lifelong activity.

Orienting the Client to Administration of the Strong

As the steps in the counseling sequence illustrate, the *Strong* should be administered in the context of career planning. A client should not simply be asked to sit down and begin marking an answer sheet. An orientation to testing is required, the character and extent of which will vary according to the situation. For example, the counselor might perceive that a client has an unusual amount of skepticism or apprehension or a high degree of competitiveness (e.g., among students seeking entrance to medical school) that must be addressed before an inventory can be administered.

At a minimum, clients should be told that the inventory is designed to help people make occupational decisions by identifying patterns in their likes and dislikes and by showing how these patterns compare with those of people in a wide range of occupations. Consider saying something such as the following:

> *This inventory is used to help you understand your interests in a general way and to show some kinds of activities and work in which you might be comfortable. The item booklet lists many jobs, activities, school subjects, and so forth, and you are asked to show your liking or disliking for each. Your answers will be compared by computer with the answers given by people already working in a wide range of jobs, and your scores will show how similar or dissimilar your interests are to the interests of these people. Since this is not a test of your abilities but an inventory of your interests, your results will be far less useful if you try to imagine what answers will make you look "good" or "bad."*

The amount of additional information offered to the client will vary with the circumstances. If appropriate, consider giving the following explanation:

- ▲ *When you are deciding on your answers, don't worry about how well you could perform a job or activity. Instead, ask yourself simply how much you would like or dislike that activity. If you have no strong feelings either way, mark "Indifferent." Do not try to analyze your responses too much.*
- ▲ *The inventory cannot "tell you what you should be" or solve your problems; it can only give you information that will help you understand yourself.*
- ▲ *The results will help you organize your interests into patterns and help you explore your occupational inclinations, leisure interests, preferred work environment, and types of people with whom you are comfortable working.*

When administering the *Strong* (see Chapter 3), be alert for any possibility that the client does not understand the instructions. This is more likely to occur with younger clients or those for whom English is a second language. For example, some clients may "jokingly" suggest that their lack of skills or education in certain areas will affect their responses ("I won't have to worry about any jobs that need math. I'm not any good at that"). Encourage such people to respond to the items in terms of their interests only: *If you would enjoy designing buildings, say so; don't worry about the math that might be needed.*

Preparing for Interpretation of the Profile: A Checklist

The information on the Profile is designed so that the interpretation moves from the general—the General Occupational Scales (GOTs) and the Basic Interest Scales (BISs)—to the specific—the Occupational Scales (OSs) and the Personal Style Scales. Depending on the individual client, some parts of the Profile may be used more than others.

Ideally, counselors should study the Profile before the client arrives for the interview. With preparation, the interpretation will be easier and more accurate. Especially until familiarity is acquired with the *Strong* and the new Profile, careful preparation is warranted. After becoming familiar with the *Strong* and understanding how its scales relate to one another, the time needed for this review is minimal.

The checklist (condensed in Figure 10.2) offers guidelines for preinterview preparation, along with references to the chapters where complete interpretive information can be found. Before sitting down with the client, follow these steps:

Step 1. Verify the validity of the Profile, by first checking the client's total number of responses (at the bottom of page 6 of the Profile).

Because the inventory has 317 items, the number reported here should be close to this figure. Generally, the scoring procedures will not be notably affected by a few missing responses. However, as a rule of thumb, consider that at least 300 of the items should be answered for a Profile to be considered valid. If the client has made fewer than 300 responses, a warning is printed on the Profile. When this occurs, there are several options to consider. If the answer sheet is available, examine it for light pencil marks; in some cases simply making heavier pencil marks and then rescoring (via the computer) solves the problem.

When several responses are omitted in sequence, it usually is because the person overlooked an entire block of questions in the booklet. Retesting the client immediately may be the best option. If the omitted responses are scattered on the answer sheet, see if they form a pattern. Do all the missing responses reflect similar occupations? If so, the client may have a gap in his or her knowledge about occupations in this area. Or perhaps a group of occupations or other items were not answered because of cultural differences in the meaning of certain items. Questioning the client will probably reveal which of these hypotheses is correct. Retesting is not advised until the necessary knowledge has been acquired.

Step 2. As a second check on Profile validity, examine the infrequent responses (page 6 of the Profile). This index is a measure of the number of highly unusual responses given by the client; the figure reported will be negative if the person picked an unusually high number of atypical responses (see Chapter 9). Should this occur, check the answer sheet and/or interview the client. Until a reasonable explanation has been found, treat the Profile with caution. Usually, some specific explanation emerges (e.g., the person inadvertently skipped a number on the answer sheet and therefore incorrectly marked some of the following responses, or the person failed to take the task seriously and filled in the answer sheet randomly).

Note that a negative number does not necessarily indicate an invalid Profile. In some cases, it is an accurate reflection of a client's idiosyncratic interest pattern. For example, one woman had a negative number because she responded "Like" to a number of activities to which most women respond "Dislike" (e.g., "Machinist," "Military drill," and "Machine shop supervisor"). Thus, her infrequent responses were an accurate reflection of her interests in the military and in automotive mechanics. She had worked for years on an army base, owned a pickup truck that she repaired herself, and made repairs for her friends at work as well.

Step 3. Check the Administrative Indexes (at the bottom of page 6 of the Profile). The response percentages for the inventory's eight parts indicate the general distribution of the client's responses for each section of items. For the five parts of the booklet that use this format, these responses indicate how responses were distributed over the "Like," "Indifferent," and "Dislike" choices; one part of the booklet uses the responses "Yes," "?," and "No." Percentages for the other two sections show how responses were distributed over the left, right, or middle choices. Average response percentages for each section of items can be found in Table 9.1 in Chapter 9. Moderate deviations from these averages are rarely troublesome, however, since scoring techniques take

Figure 10.2 Preinterpretation Checklist

- ▲ Determine the validity of the Profile by checking the total number of responses, the number of infrequent responses, and the Administrative Indexes.
- ▲ Examine the overall pattern of scores on the Snapshot (page 1); identify special challenges for interpretation (see Chapter 11).
- ▲ Examine the GOTs and BISs in detail (page 2); look for patterns as well as inconsistencies.
- ▲ Examine the OSs (pages 3–5).
- ▲ Look for inconsistencies between OSs and GOTs and BISs.
- ▲ Check scores on opposite-gender OSs.
- ▲ Develop a preliminary Theme code and begin identifying related occupations.
- ▲ Examine the Personal Style Scales (page 6).
- ▲ Develop hypotheses for discussion with the client.

Note: Page numbers above refer to pages of the Profile.

into account substantial individual response differences. Extreme response percentages can be clinically useful, although in practice they have been found to be subject to occasional overinterpretation. If they do indicate problems, the remainder of the Profile is suspect (see Chapter 11).

Step 4. Turn to the Snapshot and examine the overall pattern of the client's highest scores on each of the three main scales: the GOTs, BISs, and OSs. The Snapshot lists the client's scores on the GOTs, five highest BISs, and ten highest OSs. Although the Snapshot is useful as a summary of results, it has the limitations of all summaries. During the preinterpretation review of the Profile and during the interpretation interview itself, be sure to highlight for the client any specific information from any of the scales that has not been captured in the summary.

A quick glance at the Snapshot will reveal whether or not the client's Profile is flat. For each of the three sections of scores on the Snapshot, if all scores are below average (or mid-range for the OSs), a special explanation is printed in the space below the title of the section. This text acknowledges the pattern of low scores and offers some explanations (see Chapter 11 for an explanation of flat Profiles).

Step 5. Turn to page 2 of the Profile and identify the high scores on the GOTs and on all 25 BISs. Look for scores on each of these sets of scales that confirm or disconfirm the overall pattern observed on the Snapshot page.

Step 6. Turn to pages 3, 4, and 5 of the Profile and examine the pattern of scores on all the OSs, paying particular attention to those scores above 40. These are plotted with a dot in one of the three right-hand columns labeled "Similar Interests" and represent occupations for which the client's interests are similar to those of people of the client's gender in those occupations. Look for clusters of interests in these high scores. The organization of Occupational Scales by Theme helps in identifying clusters.

Step 7. Compare the results on page 2 with those of the OSs on pages 3 to 5 to identify any inconsistencies between the GOTs and the BISs on the one hand and the OSs on the other. Inconsistencies may suggest that nonoccupational interests are being tapped by the first two sets of scales. The *Strong* measures several types of interests: avocational as well as vocational, preferred living or work environments, and types of people with whom one is comfortable. If there are high scores on the GOTs or BISs but no high scores among the OSs in the corresponding Themes, the GOTs and BISs may be measuring nonoccupational interests (see Chapter 11).

Step 8. Also on pages 3 to 5, note high scores on opposite-gender OSs and see how well they fit into the emerging Profile pattern (see Chapter 17).

Step 9. Using the OSs on which the client scored above mid-range (i.e., 40 and above) and/or the Theme code or codes that describe the pattern of the client's interests, begin to identify occupations not on the Profile that show similar interests. Appendix A contains each occupation on the *Strong* with a list of related occupations; occupations are listed by Theme code in Appendix B.

Step 10. Check the Personal Style Scales (page 6 of the Profile). Determine how the scores on these scales fit into the pattern of interests that has emerged from the other *Strong* scales (these issues are taken up in a later section of this chapter).

Step 11. On the basis of this review, develop hypotheses about the client's interests that can be tested with his or her help during the interpretation interview. For example, does the client's pattern of interests reflect a clear focus of interests or lack of development of interests?

Interpreting the Strong Profile

Having reviewed the Profile and developed hypotheses or identified questions to discuss with the client,

Figure 10.3 Steps in Interpreting the *Strong*

Preparation
- **Step 1.** Review the purpose of the *Strong*—to measure interests, not abilities.
- **Step 2.** Emphasize exploration of general interests and life-style as well as specific occupational interests.
- **Step 3.** Discuss the client's reaction to taking the *Strong*.
- **Step 4.** Emphasize that the client will need to determine how accurately the scores reflect his or her interests.

Interpretation
- **Step 5.** Briefly explain Holland's theory.
- **Step 6.** Define each Theme and its related BISs.
- **Step 7.** Explain any diametrically opposed interests.
- **Step 8.** Interpret the OSs.
- **Step 9.** Examine the client's scores on the opposite gender–normed OSs.
- **Step 10.** Interpret the four Personal Style Scales.

Exploration
- **Step 11.** Develop a Theme code.
- **Step 12.** Use the code to generalize to other occupations beyond the Profile.

the counselor can begin the interpretation session. Figure 10.3 illustrates a sequence of steps that has generally been found useful in interpreting the *Strong*, whether with individual clients or in group settings. (Although this basic model can be applied to both situations, there are differences that are discussed in a later section.) The steps shown in the figure and elaborated below can be seen as part of a three-part model:

▲ preparation,
▲ interpretation, and
▲ exploration.

Preparation

Step 1. Begin with a review of the purpose of the *Strong* and its use in career counseling. The points made here are similar to those presented to the client when the *Strong* was administered; however, they are important enough to bear repeating. Consider stressing the following points:

- *The* Strong *is a measure of* interests, *not abilities.*
- *The* Strong *is not a crystal ball—it can only provide you with information. It is up to you to make appropriate use of your results.*
- *This inventory will provide you with a great deal of useful information, but other information about your abilities, your previous experiences, and your motivation should also be considered.*
- *Career planning is not a passive activity. You need to take the initiative in planning or redirecting your career.*
- *Career planning is a lifelong activity, not the work of interpreting a single inventory in a single interview. The information you get from this inventory should be used with common sense, in long-range planning, now and in the years to come; it should not be used to make one-time decisions about the immediate future.*

Step 2. Explain that the *Strong* can help in the exploration of a person's general interests and life-style as well as specific occupational interests. It may be helpful to mention that, because of the various sets of items, five major types of interests can be examined: vocational interests, avocational interests, interests in types of environments, interests in types of people, and interests in types of tasks.

Step 3. Ask how the client perceived the *Strong* while filling out the answer sheet. (Was the process interesting? Frustrating?) Find out what the client's mood was on the day of the testing. Any extreme feelings at the time of testing may be reflected in the Profile scores and Administrative Indexes, and retesting may be indicated.

Step 4. Make clear that, although the meaning of the scales will be explained, the client will need to determine how accurately the scores reflect his or her interests. Consider saying something such as,

When you review your results, think about why you scored the way you did. Think about your past work experiences, the interests of your friends or family, what you do in your spare time, and the school subjects you liked or disliked and how they might have influenced your responses.

Interpretation

Note: Experience with the Snapshot has demonstrated that counselors use it in different ways. Some go over the entire Snapshot first, using it to explain the different sections of the *Strong*, to provide a simplified overview of results, and to provide a cognitive map for a more detailed interpretation. Others begin their interpretations with page 2 of the Profile (focusing on the GOTs and BISs), proceed through pages 3 through 6, and then return to the Snapshot, using it to review or sum up the client's overall results.

Step 5. Give a brief explanation of Holland's theory (see Chapter 5). Explain that people can be described as falling into one or more of six different occupational types and that the world of work can also be divided into these categories. Understanding Your Results on the *Strong* (on the back of the Profile) contains a hexagon and information about the six Themes that can be used to help the client understand his or her similarities and differences. The hexagon and definitions printed on the *Strong* worksheet also can be used to illustrate the explanation and to clarify how the six types relate to one another (i.e., neighboring types are somewhat alike; diametrically opposed types are quite different).

Step 6. Define each Theme and its related BISs in greater detail. To provide visual cues during this step, it may be helpful to use Understanding Your Results on the *Strong* (on the back of the Profile); the GOT and BIS sections on the Snapshot that include brief definitions of each Theme and of the five highest BISs; page 2 of the Profile, where both the GOTs (and their definitions) and the BISs are listed; or the *Strong* worksheet.

When examining the client's scores, it may be helpful to emphasize those Themes or BISs on which she or he scored "High Interest" or "Very High Interest." In addition, it may be helpful to identify scores on the Themes and BISs that are in the "Very Little Interest" range and to discuss how these are part of a larger pattern of likes and dislikes or how they support the pattern seen in the high scores.

Step 7. If the respondent has diametrically opposed interests (scores of "High Interest" or "Very High Interest" on opposite corners of the hexagon), inquire about the possibility of conflicting feelings or confusion about vocational choices. Help the client to develop strategies for satisfying the conflicting interests (see Chapter 11).

Step 8. Discuss the OSs (pages 3 through 5 of the Profile). Proceed through the Profile in R-I-A-S-E-C order, or begin with the Themes that contain the highest scores (i.e., 40 or higher). In either case, examine the Theme codes that appear to the left of the scale name for these OSs. Look for a pattern in these codes. It can also be helpful to identify OS scores of "Very Little Interest" and to discuss how these are part of a larger pattern.

Step 9. Examine the client's scores on the opposite gender–normed OSs for confirmation of the interest patterns that have already been identified (see Chapter 17).

Step 10. Discuss the client's scores on each of the four Personal Style Scales (page 6 of the Profile). Scores on these scales can add significant insights to the interpretation of the other results and can confirm or help to refine information from the other scales. The client's response percentages to each section of the *Strong* (see the Administrative Indexes section at the bottom of page 6) can also be discussed. However, this information is generally not of much interest to clients unless they have extreme response percentages.

Exploration

Step 11. Develop a Theme code or codes that summarize the results across all three sets of scales. The easiest and most efficient way to do this is to look again at the Snapshot. In the first section of the Snapshot, a Theme code is provided based on the client's highest scores on the GOTs (unless the client has no scores of "Average Interest" or above on the GOTs). Review the client's scores on the BISs and the OSs on the Snapshot and develop a code for each of those sections as well (additional suggestions for how to develop codes are found in later sections of this chapter). Make sure to incorporate any additional information about the client's interests that may not be represented on this summary. If codes from the different sets of scales do not converge, the GOTs and BISs may be tapping the client's nonoccupational interests, a possibility that can then be explored.

Step 12. Using the Theme code or codes developed in Step 11, identify further occupational possibilities related to the client's scores on the OSs on the Profile. (See Appendix B for additional occupations coded by Theme.) The *Strong* Interpretive Report, Professional Report, and worksheet also contain related occupations.

Be sure to involve the client in all phases of the interpretation. While the counselor can explain the meaning of the scales and how they relate to one another, only the client can explain how she or he satisfies the interests identified and how they fit into her or his overall life-style.

Adapting the Sequence for Interpreting the Strong in Groups

Although clients generally express more overall satisfaction with individual interpretations (Goodyear, 1990), funding limitations, large caseloads, and limits on interview time may make group interpretations more practical, particularly in organizational settings. Some modifications of the preceding interpretive sequence can be made when using the *Strong* in a group setting. Group interpretations have been shown to be as or more effective than individual interpretations (Oliver & Spokane, 1988). After summarizing the results of numerous studies, these researchers found that the most effective mode of delivery of career counseling was career classes. The mean score averaged across the outcome measures used in the various studies for clients who participated in career classes was over two standard deviations greater than the mean for the control groups, who did not receive career counseling. The effectiveness of this approach may have been due to the multiple sessions typical of career classes or because clients could compare results with their peers and work as a group to solve career problems.

Most of the modifications for interpreting the *Strong* in groups occur in the interpretation and exploration sections of the sequence. For example, once the six Themes have been introduced in Step 5, clients can be asked to discuss the Themes among themselves with the goal of having each person identify the Theme that best describes him or her. This exercise is even more effective when group members know one another and can question or give feedback to each other about their Themes. A variation on this exercise that works well in large groups is to divide the members into six groups based on their highest GOT score. Using interpretive booklets, reports, and examples from their own experience, each group prepares and presents their Theme to the rest of the group. Similar procedures can be adapted for interpreting the Personal Style Scales in Step 10.

Although it was developed for the 1985 *Strong*, additional suggestions for conducting group interpretations can be found in *Using the Strong in Organizations* (Hirsh, 1986). This binder provides an explicit script for use by the workshop or class leader as well as many exercises that can foster interaction and peer learning. It also contains reproducible masters that can be used as handouts or made into overheads. Despite its name, the accompanying materials have been used effectively in high school and college settings. New publications are also now under development to aid in conducting professional group interpretations.

Looking for Patterns in the Three Main Scale Types

The steps described earlier and outlined in Figure 10.3 provide a general sequence of activities for interpreting the Profile with the client and for beginning the process of career exploration and decision making. What follows are more in-depth suggestions for interpreting the main scale types and for integrating the results. The focus here is on using the different scales to develop a Theme code that summarizes the client's pattern of interests and offers a springboard for further career exploration. The procedure is to develop a code for each of the three main scale types, then compare the three codes.

In recognition of the importance of using codes in career exploration, a one- to three-letter code based on the GOTs is printed in the first section of the Snapshot, directly below the ranking of the GOTs. This code consists of the first letter of each of the top three GOTs (although a code is not printed if all GOTs are below "Average Interest"). A code is also provided on the *Strong* Professional Report, which is derived from the client's high scores on the professional occupations that form a subset of the OSs. For counselors who are unfamiliar with procedures for coding and the various ways in which codes can be derived from a Profile, the following resources are available: Brew (1987), Hirsh and Vessey (1987), and Levin (1991). Although these publications were prepared to accompany the 1985 *Strong*, the coding procedure remains the same.

The General Occupational Themes

When interpreting the GOTs, a useful approach is to use the Theme code provided on the Snapshot (1) to summarize the pattern of the client's general interests and (2) to serve as a bridge to the larger world of work. The code emphasizes Themes with interpretive comments "High Interest" or "Very High Interest." These interpretive comments compare the client's score to the General Reference Sample, composed of people of the same gender as the client, drawn from a wide variety of occupations.

The Snapshot expedites the identification of these Themes, since the client's Theme scores are ranked by interpretive comment. If two or more GOT scores are accorded the same interpretive comment (e.g., "High Interest"), the Themes are ranked by score. To facilitate coding, the first letter of each Theme is printed to the left of each Theme name; the Theme code is identified in the text below the Themes. For example, if the Profile has a checkmark in the "Very High Interest" box after the E Theme and another in the box indicating "High Interest" after the I Theme, and no other scores above "Average Interest," then the GOT code EI will be printed for this client. Later on, this code can be transferred to the *Strong* worksheet if needed.

Before proceeding, it may also help to mention those Themes at the other end of the continuum with checkmarks in the "Very Little Interest" box. These results suggest areas that do not characterize the client's interests. Such scores often accent those Themes on which the client showed "High Interest" by way of contrast. For example, a counselor might say: *"You showed little interest in the Realistic area, which tends to confirm your high interest in the Social Themes—you really do like to work with people more than with tools or machines."*

The Basic Interest Scales

The next step in helping the client to identify a pattern in his or her interests is to look at the BISs in the same manner. The BISs on which the client has "Very High Interest" or "High Interest" usually will cluster in one or two of the RIASEC areas. The Snapshot may again provide an efficient means of identifying the BIS code, since the five BISs on which the client scored highest are ranked by interpretive comment. The Theme code for each of the BISs is printed to the left of the scale name. Examine these scales and help the client determine an appropriate one-, two-, or three-letter code that summarizes the client's high BISs.

Since the *Strong* has 25 BISs but only 5 are summarized on the Snapshot, page 2 of the Profile should also be examined to make sure that the code is consistent with the information from *all* the BISs. In some cases, this review may result in additional letters being added to the code. For example, if all five of the BISs listed on the Snapshot have checkmarks in the "High Interest" or "Very High Interest" boxes, and all are from the Investigative Theme, then I is the first letter of the code. But if an examination of all 25 of the BISs on page 2 of the Profile reveals a number of other BISs with scores above 50 clustered in the Enterprising Themes, then E can be added to the code. How many letters are added to the code (up to a generally agreed-upon maximum of three) is a matter for the counselor's judgment.

The Occupational Scales

The next step in the process of identifying the client's pattern of interests is to study the results on the OSs, looking for scores that indicate similarity between the client and people in particular occupations. The ten OSs on which the client scored highest are ranked on the Snapshot by interpretive comment. Each of these occupations has a Theme code of one to three letters representing the interests characteristic of people of the client's gender in that occupation. All ten occupations on the Snapshot may point immediately to a Theme code that identifies the client's pattern of interests. For example, all ten may contain the letters A, S, or E, indicating Artistic, Social, and Enterprising interests.

If the client has many high scores and diverse interests, however, the top ten ranked on the Snapshot may not adequately summarize his or her interests. Review pages 3 through 5 of the Profile with the client to determine how well the ten scales on the Snapshot summarize her or his occupational interests. Another cluster of occupations with somewhat lower scores may suggest that another letter be added to the code. For example, the codes for the ten highest occupations listed on the Snapshot may all indicate that the client's interests lie in occupations in the Artistic and Social areas. Examination of all the OSs, however, may reveal another cluster of scales in the "Similar" ranges suggesting interests in the Investigative Theme. In this case, a code with the letters ASI in some combination offers avenues for further exploration.

When examining the codes of the OSs on which the client's scores indicate a similarity of interests, do not be too exacting. Look for codes that have the same letter(s). The exact order of the letters is not as important as identifying the overall pattern (a point that should be made explicitly and repeatedly with some clients). Try at this point to be as inclusive as possible. For example, a client may score high on Psychologist, which has a code of IA, and on the male Technical Writer scale, which has a code of AI. This indicates a pattern of interest in the Artistic and Investigative areas that may be worth exploring if confirmed by other scores. In this case, the client should be encouraged to explore occupations coded I, A, IA, and AI.

Because of the great number of OSs (and, to a lesser extent, BISs) and due to the complexity of some individuals' interests, a code that summarizes the information across all three scale types will not always be immediately apparent. It is important here, as in all phases of the interpretation, to listen closely to how the client responds to information about his or her scores on the various scales. Results that touch a chord in the client or have some degree of emotional saliency are worth exploring further. These reactions, as well as the counselor's own experience in interpreting the *Strong*, can help resolve any close calls.

Table 10.1 Selected Items from the Mathematician Scales Illustrating How a Theme Code Suggests Day-to-Day Likes and Dislikes

Item	GOT Code	Response
Astronomer	I	Like
Chemist	I	Like
Doing research work	I	Like
Interviewing prospects in selling	E	Dislike
Advertising executive	E	Dislike
Public relations director	E	Dislike

Note: The first letter of the code of the male and female Mathematician OSs is I.

Once a Theme code based on the OSs has been derived, it can be used not only to help the client identify related occupations but also to further the client's understanding about the world of work. There are at least three ways to use the OS code as a teaching tool. First, the code, along with the sample items for the GOTs (see Chapter 5), can be used to demonstrate that the items that make up an OS reflect both the likes *and dislikes* of people in a given occupation. For example, the female and male Mathematician scales both have I (Investigative) as the first letter of their codes, indicating that investigative items are weighted as "Likes" on this scale. The sample items for the Investigative Theme shown in Chapter 5 can be discussed with the client to illustrate what kind of occupations or day-to-day activities are associated with Investigative interests. However, because the Mathematician scales are Investigative, items that represent the Theme that is diametrically opposed on the hexagon—Enterprising—are weighted as "Dislikes." Table 10.1 illustrates how the Investigative and Enterprising Themes are both represented in the item content of the Mathematician scale and scored in the "Like" and "Dislike" directions, respectively.

Second, the codes can also be used to draw attention to similarities between occupations. For example, Medical Illustrator and Technical

Writer are both coded Artistic-Investigative-Realistic (AIR). People interested in science and creative self-expression, along with some interests in the Realistic area, may find that either of these occupations would satisfy their interests, although their particular talents and abilities would have to be considered as well. Other examples of OSs with identical codes are Accountant, Banker, and female Small Business Owner. All three of these occupations are coded CE, indicating that people in these occupations tend to share Conventional and Enterprising interests. Such commonalities can be used to help clients understand that many occupations can satisfy their interests.

Third, the codes can also be used to draw attention to the differences that can separate closely related occupations. For example, Advertising Executive is coded AE, while Marketing Executive is coded EA. Although these are similar occupations, executives working in advertising are more interested in the Artistic components of the job, while marketing executives focus more on the business side. If the Theme code developed for the client contains both A and E, then both of these occupations, along with any others with A and E in the code that can be identified from other sources, should be added to the client's list of possibilities. After collecting information about options and beginning to narrow down choices, the client may find it useful to draw finer distinctions between the occupations represented by the different order of the letters in their codes.

Integrating the Three Codes

Now that each set of scales has been coded, counselor and client can work together to identify an overall pattern. This process may be as simple as glancing at the Snapshot and observing that all of the highest-scored scales point to the same Theme or Themes. Profiles on which the high scores on the GOTs, BISs, and OSs all have the same or similar codes are called "consistent Profiles." These Profiles are the most straightforward to interpret, since the client's general and specific interests are in line with his or her occupational interests. Other Profiles, however, may show inconsistencies between the three sets of scales. Such inconsistencies may indicate that the client's vocational and leisure interests differ (see Chapter 11).

Be prepared, however, for the client who wants to focus on only one or two OSs. While this desire is perfectly appropriate and should be discussed, it is important to point out the underlying Themes, indicating how these particular occupations fit into a larger picture and encouraging the client to think about related occupations not on the Profile.

Using the Theme Codes to Generalize to Other Occupations

Once information from the three Theme codes has been derived and integrated, the next step is to use this information to identify those potential occupations for career exploration that are not immediately suggested by the *Strong*. Use of the code can help the client understand where people with his or her particular range of interests, or code type, tend to settle in the occupational world. Skillful generalization beyond the Profile will maximize the number of opportunities the client might actively consider. Maximizing options is especially important for clients with few high scores, since it allows for the identification of additional occupations that may fit the client's interests. For clients with many high scores, generalizing beyond the *Strong* results can make it easier to see overall trends in interests and to understand the diversity of interests.

For both kinds of clients, the code can serve as a cognitive map to help them negotiate their way through the world of work. In fact, one resource for helping clients identify additional occupations having the same code, the *Strong* worksheet, employs a map metaphor. Other sources of related occupations include Appendixes A and B of this guide, the *Strong* Interpretive Report, the *Strong* Professional Report, and the *Dictionary of Holland Occupational Codes* (Gottfredson & Holland, 1989). With the use of these various listings, the client can assemble a wide range of potential occupations to consider.

For example, if the client scores high on a Social-Enterprising (SE) OS such as Community Service Organization Director, she or he might want to consider occupations such as Camp Director, Social Worker, Community Relations Director, or Volunteer Services Director, all of which are listed in conjunction with Community Service Organization Director in Appendix A. The client might also consider the additional SE-type occupations listed in Appendix B, such as Juvenile Parole Officer, Labor Arbitrator, Mental Health Worker, and Vocational Counselor.

No interest inventory can provide scales that will measure the respondent's interests in every occupation or school major. Thus, generalizing the OSs to additional occupations and majors of the same type can greatly expand the usefulness of the instrument. In particular, clients should be encouraged to consider relevant occupations they may not have considered before, because of either lack of exposure, misconceptions about those occupations, or preconceptions that the occupations are not open to them on grounds of gender, social class, ethnic background, or physical capacity.

Using the Personal Style Scales

The four Personal Style Scales (page 6 of the Profile) are the Work Style scale, the Learning Environment scale, the Leadership Style scale, and the Risk Taking/Adventure scale. Descriptions of these scales are found in Chapter 8. These scales have been standardized so that the mean score on each is 50, with a standard deviation of 10. Each scale is represented as a continuum with anchors at the poles reflecting the items that comprise the scale.

The Personal Style Scales have a variety of uses in career counseling, including helping clients:

▲ refine their choices based on information about their personal style,
▲ identify the style they will feel most comfortable using when working in their chosen career,
▲ increase job satisfaction,
▲ choose rewarding leisure activities,
▲ determine how alternatives for further learning or training may fit with their learning style,
▲ identify their interest in assuming a particular leadership style, and
▲ identify how much risk they are willing to take in choosing or changing careers.

Scores on the Personal Style Scales, either alone or in conjunction with other *Strong* scales, can point toward areas of occupational interest. For example, a score toward the takes chances pole of the Risk Taking/Adventure scale may lead the client to consider specific occupations for which risk is inherent, such as jobs in law enforcement or the military. Scores on the Personal Style Scales can also support or reinforce scores on other *Strong* scales. For example, a score toward the works with people pole on the Work Style scale would provide additional motivation for a client with a high score on the Sales Basic Interest Scale to pursue a career in sales.

Another use of the Personal Style Scales is to help clients focus on how they might prefer to go about doing their jobs within the general area of interest they have chosen. Although there are differences in interests *between* occupational groups, there are differences *within* occupations as well (DeWitt, 1980). For example, while a client may exhibit a high score for Accountant, a range of specialties exist within the occupation that could satisfy those interests (e.g., tax accounting, auditing, or consultation). Accounting firms vary in size from one-person operations to giant multinationals. For instance, a client scoring toward the works with people pole of the Work Style scale, toward the academic pole of the Learning Environment scale, toward the takes chances pole of the Risk Taking/Adventure scale, and toward the directs others pole of the Leadership Style scale might prefer a position as an accountant in which she or he could manage a staff of accountants doing high-level consulting work with high-tech or start-up firms.

Work Style Scale

The Work Style scale can be useful in helping clients select occupational alternatives or improve satisfaction with their current job. Those scoring above 50 on this scale have an interest in working with others, generally on teams or in groups. They may believe that goals and tasks are better accomplished whenever people can work together toward a common goal. Those scoring below 50 prefer to work alone with ideas, data, or things. They believe that their best work is done when they can be alone and are able to concentrate for long periods on one complicated task.

Although the Work Style scale is a successor to the Introversion-Extroversion scale from the 1985 *Strong*, it should be noted that, like its predecessor, this scale is not a general measure of extroversion; it taps the more narrow domain of preferred amount of interaction with others in a work setting. The difference can be demonstrated by examining correlations between the old Introversion-Extroversion scale with the Extraversion-Introversion scale of the *Myers-Briggs Type Indicator*. Studies reporting the relationship between these two scales show correlations ranging between .33 and .47 (Hammer &

Kummerow, 1992; Myers & McCaulley, 1985), suggesting that the scales are measuring some common characteristics, but that each is also tapping something the other is not. The *Strong* scale is work-oriented, whereas the MBTI scale has a broader purpose, being designed to reflect a more general orientation to the external world, not just to the work environment.

Learning Environment Scale

Much of career counseling revolves around the amount and kind of education or training the client decides or needs to pursue. The Learning Environment scale provides an indication of the kind of learning environment or approach to education and training the client may prefer. It is particularly useful when counseling high school students about choice of college, major, or job training program; when counseling college students who are dissatisfied with their current selection of courses or who are considering graduate school; and when working with adults in career transition who are considering additional education or training.

Briefly, clients scoring toward the practical pole prefer learning opportunities in which they can deal with real problems and learn to solve them in concrete ways. They are probably more interested in practical and applied problems and see education as a means to an end. They may find the thought of further education or training more palatable when their scores are interpreted to them in this way.

Those scoring toward the academic pole of the Learning Environment scale will probably feel more comfortable learning in a "typical" liberal arts, or arts and sciences, university program. They tend to pursue learning for its own sake. People with scores of 55 or above on this scale should be encouraged to pursue some kind of postgraduate work. Experience suggests that many people with high scores who do not continue their education later wish they had. Some of these clients have been castigated by family or friends for their academic interests and are relieved to hear the positive interpretation of their scores on this scale. For those with very high scores, the issue is not whether they will further their education but how to arrange their lives so they can do so for as long as they feel they need to.

When interpreting this scale, the counselor must stress to the client that it is *not* a measure of *abilities;* it is simply a measure of interest in academic pursuits. Some people with scores toward the academic pole of this scale will not do particularly well at the university level, although they probably will enjoy the experience. Some scoring toward the practical pole will go on to earn advanced degrees, although they usually will report that they have enrolled in a particular program to help them achieve a specific goal.

Leadership Style Scale

Scores on the Leadership Style scale indicate a liking or a disliking of activities that are associated with a leadership style that can be characterized by active, directive, take-charge behaviors. Those who score toward the directs others pole of this scale are often outspoken in their views and opinions; those scoring toward the leads by example pole may be reluctant to assume active leadership roles that require them to be directive. These people may become leaders when nominated or championed by others rather than when they themselves seek the position, or they may lead by example, drawing others to follow by their performance, energy, or particular talent.

When interpreting this scale, the counselor must emphasize that the Leadership Style scale does *not* measure one's interest in becoming a leader per se, nor does it suggest any competencies in exercising leadership or the likelihood of achieving a leadership position. The scale is simply a measure of liking or disliking a particular leadership style. It does not mean that a client will adopt this style when or if she or he in fact assumes a leadership position. Some people with scores toward the directs others pole of this scale may not be particularly effective leaders in some contexts. Some scoring toward the leads by example pole may become very effective "behind the scenes" leaders or leaders of self-managed work teams. Furthermore, cultural orientations, which are not picked up by this scale, may influence leadership style choices.

Risk Taking/Adventure Scale

As suggested earlier, results on the Risk Taking/Adventure scale, either alone or in conjunction with other *Strong* scales, may point the client toward or away from specific occupations that match his or her proclivities regarding risk and adventure. Those scoring toward the takes chances pole may choose jobs in which their willingness to take risks is put to the test. Although the items on this scale primarily suggest physical risks, those scoring toward the takes chances pole may also enjoy or be willing to take other kinds of risks, such as financial risks. These people may enjoy work in sales or investments. Those whose scoring indicates a dislike for risk taking or adventure would probably be unlikely to select or even consider occupations that involved physical, financial, or social risks.

The results of this scale may also be used to suggest how a client might respond to activities or decisions in the career-counseling process itself. Those scoring toward the takes chances pole may jump at the first attractive opportunity that presents itself or be willing to consider major shifts in career or occupation. Those scoring toward the plays it safe pole may be very reluctant to make changes without having completed comprehensive career research and having given careful consideration to all of their options. Young people tend to score higher on the Risk Taking/Adventure scale than do older people, as discussed in Chapter 8.

Using the Strong to Explore Developmental Issues

The GOTs and BISs are measures of interests that may be vocational (career, job), avocational (leisure, recreational), or environmental (work settings) and may also reflect the client's preferences for types of people (co-workers, friends, significant others). Because these scales measure broad interests, scores on them can be used to examine broader developmental issues such as balancing work and leisure or appreciating the importance of major transitions (e.g., from work to retirement). The Personal Style Scales can also be useful in looking at developmental or life-style issues.

The desired counseling outcome is an integration of various life roles that helps the client identify a preferred overall life-style, not simply make a career selection. For example, a client whose score indicates a "High Interest" on the Nature BIS may be interested in:

- working in occupations with interests in nature such as animal husbandry, biology, farming, forestry, veterinary medicine, or vocational agriculture education;
- pursuing leisure activities such as camping, canoeing, or rock climbing;
- living in a rural area or small community rather than in a city; or
- associating with people who like to spend time outdoors.

This client should spend some time exploring all these aspects of his or her score on the Nature scale and think about what kind of life-style might allow an integration of these various interests.

The interests of some people are focused on just one or two areas; their preferred work tasks, play activities, environments, and associates all reflect these dominant interests. Other people's inclinations are more diverse but nonetheless offer enough overlap to allow an integration of their interests. Yet another group of people has interests so diverse that their lives become compartmentalized to accommodate the various roles they assume. High and low scores on the GOTs and BISs can help clients judge how well their interests match their life-styles. During the counseling process, negative affect (e.g., tension, dissatisfaction, irritation, stress, conflict) may be attributed to involvement in jobs, careers, schools, work or personal relationships, or other situations that are in opposition to the client's interests (high scores) and aversions (low scores).

Conclusion

This chapter has provided a general career-counseling sequence and shown how the *Strong* can play an integral part in this process. The effectiveness of the *Strong* will be enhanced if the client is properly prepared for administration, and if the counselor is well versed in the interpretive process. The three-step model presented here—preparation, interpretation, exploration—provides an overview and summary of this process and can be used to further a client's career exploration and decision making.

References

Anastasi, A. (1990). Diversity and flexibility. *Counseling Psychologist, 18*(2), 258–261.

Brew, S. (1987). *Career development guide for use with the Strong Interest Inventory.* Palo Alto, CA: Consulting Psychologists Press.

Cooper, S. E. (1986). The effects of group and individual vocational counseling on career indecision and personal indecisiveness. *Journal of College Student Personnel, 27,* 39–42.

DeWitt, D. W. (1980). An analysis of within occupation interest groupings of women and men in occupations representative of the Holland typology. *Dissertation Abstracts International, 40,* 6197A–6198A. (University Microfilms.)

Goodyear, R. K. (1990). Research on the effects of test interpretation. A review. *Counseling Psychologist, 18*(2), 240–257.

Gottfredson, G. D., & Holland, J. L. (1989). *Dictionary of Holland occupational codes* (2nd ed.). Odessa, FL: Psychological Assessment Resources.

Hammer, A. L., & Kummerow, J. K. (1992). *Strong + MBTI career development guide.* Palo Alto, CA: Consulting Psychologists Press.

Hirsh, S. K. (1986). *Using the Strong in organizations.* Palo Alto, CA: Consulting Psychologists Press.

Hirsh, S. K., & Vessey, T. (1987). *Introduction to the Strong in organizational settings.* Palo Alto, CA: Consulting Psychologists Press.

Holland, J. L. (1985). *Making vocational choices: A theory of vocational personalities and work environments* (2nd ed.). Englewood Cliffs, NJ: Prentice-Hall.

Levin, A. (1991). *Introduction to the Strong for career counselors.* Palo Alto, CA: Consulting Psychologists Press.

Myers, I. B., & McCaulley, M. H. (1985). *Manual: A guide to the development and use of the Myers-Briggs Type Indicator.* Palo Alto, CA: Consulting Psychologists Press.

Oliver, L., & Spokane, A. (1988). Career intervention outcome: What contributes to client gain? *Journal of Counseling Psychology, 35,* 447.

Randahl, G. J., Hansen, J. C., & Haverkamp, B. (1993). Instrumental behaviors following test administration and interpretation: Exploration validity of the Strong Interest Inventory. *Journal of Counseling and Development, 71,* 435–439.

Shahnasarian, M., & Peterson, G. W. (1988). The effect of a prior cognitive structuring intervention with computer-assisted career guidance. *Computers in Human Behavior, 4,* 125–131.

Slaney, R. B., & Lewis, E. T. (1986). Effects of career exploration on career undecided reentry women: An intervention and follow-up study. *Journal of Vocational Behavior, 28,* 97–109.

CHAPTER 11

Challenges in Interpreting the Strong

The preceding chapter outlined a general strategy for interpreting the *Strong* Profile for various prototypical clients. As every counselor knows, however, no client fits the general model exactly. The purpose of this chapter is to suggest useful strategies for those clients whose Profiles offer special interpretive challenges.

The challenges most often encountered in interpretation are those presented by clients whose Profiles indicate the following:

▲ low scores on most or all of the scales (flat Profiles),

▲ many high scores with no discernible pattern,

▲ diverse interests,

▲ diametrically opposed interests,

▲ discrepancies between the scores on different types of scales, and

▲ extreme scores on some of the Personal Style Scales. ◆

Flat Profiles

Flat Profiles are those with scores primarily in the "Average Interest" range on the General Occupational Themes (GOTs) and Basic Interest Scales (BISs) and that show little differentiation from one Occupational Scale (OS) to the next. This definition is not precise, however, since researchers have defined differentiation in various ways. For the purposes of this chapter, flat Profiles include those on which there may be a few high scores scattered about, usually on the OSs. The important characteristic is the lack of noticeable or meaningful differentiation, which makes interpretation a challenge. Even for Profiles that contain a few high scores, the hypotheses discussed in the following sections should be considered and when appropriate discussed with the client. Another kind of Profile that falls under this rubric is defined by Hansen (1992) as the *depressed* Profile, similar to a flat Profile but with scores on the GOTs and BISs generally *below* average. Since the features of these two Profiles are so similar and since they present the same kind challenge to the counselor, they are both referred to here as *flat*.

Although this definition of a flat Profile is fairly general, the program used to score the answer sheet and print a Profile for the client requires a precise definition, since the program must identify "flat" scores within each section of scales and print explanatory text in the appropriate section. The *Strong* Snapshot provides a summary of the client's highest scores on the three main types of scales (i.e., the GOTs, the BISs, and the OSs). Within each section is a ranking of the client's top scores. To the left of the ranking is printed explanatory text about the meaning of the scales in that section. In addition, for the GOT section, the client's Theme code, determined by the GOT scores, is printed immediately below the ranking of the GOTs. Using the decision rules that follow, the program determines whether or not the scores in that section constitute a flat set of scores and then prints the appropriate explanatory text.

1. For the GOTs, the flat Profile text is printed whenever there are no GOTs of "Average Interest" or above. There is also no GOT code computed or printed since a code based on a highest score of "Little Interest" would probably be more misleading than helpful.

   The General Occupational Themes describe interests in six very broad areas, including interest in work and leisure activities, kinds of people, and work settings. Your interests in each area are shown at the right in rank order.

   Your results here may *mean that your interests are very specific and are not represented by these six Themes. Also, you may not be clear right now about your general interests or you may need more information about the world of work. Think about why your results came out this way. Your interests may be reflected on the other* Strong *scales.*

2. For the BISs, the following flat Profile text is printed whenever there are no BISs of "Average Interest" or above:

   The Basic Interest Scales measure your interests in 25 specific areas or activities. The 5 areas in which you show the most interest are listed at the right in rank order. Your results on all 25 Basic Interest Scales are found on page 2.

   Your results may *mean that you have specific interests not measured by these scales or that you are unclear about your interests at this time. You may want to spend time thinking about activities you like.*

3. For the OSs, the following flat Profile text is printed whenever there are no same-gender OSs with scores of 30 or greater.

   The Occupational Scales measure how similar your interests are to the interests of people who are satisfied working in those occupations. The 10 scales on which you scored highest are listed at the right in rank order. Your results on all 211 Occupational Scales are found on pages 3, 4, and 5. The letters to the left of each scale identify the Theme or Themes that best describe the interests of people working in that occupation.

   Your results suggest that you do not have much in common with the people in the occupations found on the Strong. *This* may *mean that you have occupational interests not measured by the* Strong, *you cannot define your occupational interests right now, or you need more knowledge of or experience in the work world. Think about why you may have scored the way you did. Also give some thought to activities that you like that could be linked to particular occupations.*

Note that on the Snapshot, "flat" is determined independently for each section of scales. The flat Profile text may appear in one or two of the sections but not in the other, or it may appear in all three. No single summary statement designates an *overall* flat Profile (although a branch of the Interpretive Report does address flat Profiles). An overall flat Profile will be immediately obvious from the Snapshot if all three sections are flat. Since the Snapshot shows the highest of the client's scores, a flat Snapshot means a flat Profile. Also note that, on the basis of the cut scores used to print the flat Profile text, some Profiles may have many low scores and appear undifferentiated even though they do not have the flat Profile text. For those Profiles, the hypotheses discussed in the following sections should also be considered.

A flat Profile will result when the client says "Like" to very few of the items on the inventory. Table 11.1 lists reasons why this might occur. An overall "Like" response rate of roughly 15 to 20 percent or less will often yield such a Profile. Because scores on the GOTs and the BISs are keyed to "Like" responses, a person responding "Like" to few items cannot have high scores on *any* of these scales. To see if the response rate might be affecting the Profile, check the client's overall "Like" response rate for those items answered in the Like/Indifferent/Dislike format and in the Yes/?/No format (found in the Subtotal row in the Administrative Indexes box on page 6 of the Profile). Although the response percentages for the various item sections vary, the average "Like" response rate for the sections represented by the subtotal is about 32 percent, with a standard deviation of about 12; the percentage is slightly lower for men, slightly higher for women.

Hansen (1992) estimated that a flat Profile occurs with only about 3 percent of adult Profiles and 6 percent of adolescent Profiles. Pinkney's (1985) review of the literature found occurrences of 10 to 20 percent in the few studies that addressed this issue, although it is not clear that these studies employed the same definition of "flat."

Table 11.1 Possible Reasons for Flat Profiles

Narrow or well-defined interests
Little knowledge of the world of work
Cultural differences
Altered mood
Chronic indecision
Unwillingness to make a commitment
Unwillingness to work
A pervasive "Indifferent" or "Dislike" style
Low self-esteem
Lack of vocational identity; role conflict
Family or peer pressure

There are a number of reasons a client may have a low "Like" response rate and therefore a flat Profile (see Table 11.1). Each of these reasons should be explored with the client during the interpretation of a flat Profile. Although flat Profiles are more difficult to interpret than are typical well-differentiated Profiles, they do contain useful information. By using the strategies elaborated here, these Profiles can help counselors and clients to understand interest patterns and determine appropriate career planning.

Narrow Interests

A flat Profile can indicate narrow, well-defined interests. Clients with flat Profiles may have several scores in the "Average Interest" range on the GOTs and BISs or one or two scores near 40 on the OSs that coincide with their specific interests. Often, these clients need only be asked a few questions before they begin to talk freely about a passionate interest. They are often so devoted to this subject that they are indifferent to almost everything else. The challenge for the counselor is to help these clients identify specific jobs or work environments in which their interests can be expressed or to help them identify and work through blocks (e.g., a lack of opportunities or the need for training) that are keeping them from reaching their goals. Clients with narrow interests are not likely to remain blocked after a discussion of their options and time spent exploring career resources. Occasionally, such clients have difficulty finding a paying job that offers opportunities for expression of their interests, particularly if financial or other constraints are involved. In this case, counseling focuses on helping the client decide how to be self-supporting or support a family while pursuing his or her interests during leisure time.

Client 1. A case of a 38-year-old woman illustrates a number of these issues. Client 1's *Strong* Snapshot shows that she had "Little Interest" or "Very Little Interest" on all six of the GOTs (see Figure 11.1). The Enterprising and Artistic Themes were the highest of these low scores. The BIS section of the Snapshot shows her five highest BISs in rank order; she has "Average Interest" on four of the five scales. These BISs fall primarily into the Enterprising Theme (Sales and Merchandising) and Artistic Theme (Art and Culinary Arts), which confirms the pattern noted in the GOTs. Six of her top ten OSs also have Enterprising in the code.

Despite these low scores on the GOTs and the BISs, Client 1 quickly identified with the EA Theme pattern that emerged. She described herself as having a strong interest in a specialized area of apparel design and manufacturing. She has three degrees, an associate degree in fashion merchandising from a highly respected fashion institute, another in textile marketing and development, and a bachelor's degree in apparel and textiles. She had entered a nursing program out of high school but did not enjoy it and consequently began her studies in the textile field.

Consistent with her score on the Learning Environment scale (29), all of these educational and training experiences were in settings where practical, hands-on learning was emphasized. Client 1 interpreted the OSs in the Artistic Theme on which she scored in the mid-range or similar range as reflecting her interest in the design aspects of textiles. When she left high school she had also thought of being a paralegal (44). And, she said that she could see herself having her own business someday (her score on the Small Business Owner scale was 37). After receiving her bachelor's degree, she worked for four years in a textile manufacturing company. When Client 1 and her husband decided to move to another part of the country, she took a job that allowed her to work in an Enterprising-Artistic environment. Although she is satisfied with her current job, she would eventually like to return to textiles or apparel design or manufacturing. She believes that she needs additional, highly specialized training in a particular skill to do

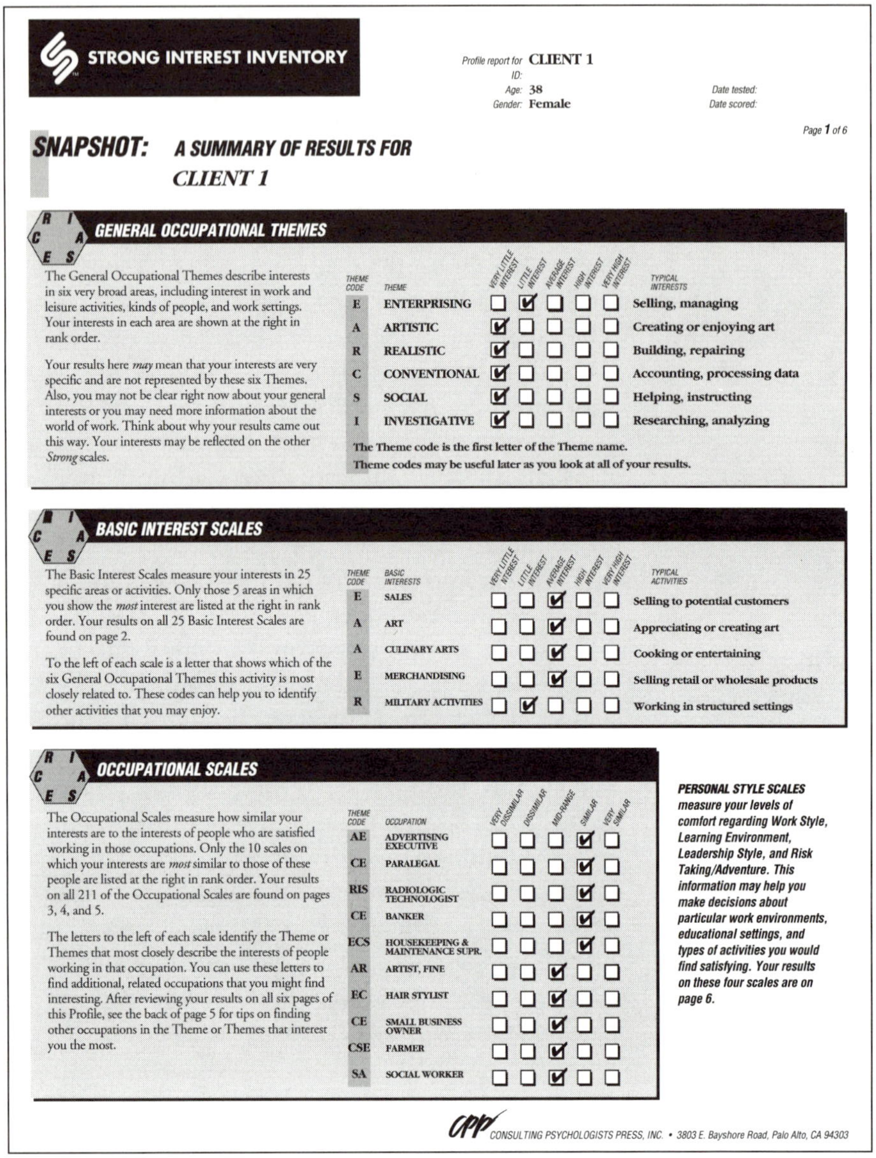

STRONG INTEREST INVENTORY

Profile report for CLIENT 1
ID:
Age: 38
Gender: Female

Date tested:
Date scored:

Page 1 of 6

SNAPSHOT: A SUMMARY OF RESULTS FOR CLIENT 1

GENERAL OCCUPATIONAL THEMES

The General Occupational Themes describe interests in six very broad areas, including interest in work and leisure activities, kinds of people, and work settings. Your interests in each area are shown at the right in rank order.

Your results here *may* mean that your interests are very specific and are not represented by these six Themes. Also, you may not be clear right now about your general interests or you may need more information about the world of work. Think about why your results came out this way. Your interests may be reflected on the other *Strong* scales.

Theme Code	Theme	Very Little Interest	Little Interest	Average Interest	High Interest	Very High Interest	Typical Interests
E	ENTERPRISING		✓				Selling, managing
A	ARTISTIC	✓					Creating or enjoying art
R	REALISTIC	✓					Building, repairing
C	CONVENTIONAL	✓					Accounting, processing data
S	SOCIAL	✓					Helping, instructing
I	INVESTIGATIVE	✓					Researching, analyzing

The Theme code is the first letter of the Theme name.
Theme codes may be useful later as you look at all of your results.

BASIC INTEREST SCALES

The Basic Interest Scales measure your interests in 25 specific areas or activities. Only those 5 areas in which you show the *most* interest are listed at the right in rank order. Your results on all 25 Basic Interest Scales are found on page 2.

To the left of each scale is a letter that shows which of the six General Occupational Themes this activity is most closely related to. These codes can help you to identify other activities that you may enjoy.

Theme Code	Basic Interests	Very Little Interest	Little Interest	Average Interest	High Interest	Very High Interest	Typical Activities
E	SALES			✓			Selling to potential customers
A	ART			✓			Appreciating or creating art
A	CULINARY ARTS			✓			Cooking or entertaining
E	MERCHANDISING			✓			Selling retail or wholesale products
R	MILITARY ACTIVITIES		✓				Working in structured settings

OCCUPATIONAL SCALES

The Occupational Scales measure how similar your interests are to the interests of people who are satisfied working in those occupations. Only the 10 scales on which your interests are *most* similar to those of these people are listed at the right in rank order. Your results on all 211 of the Occupational Scales are found on pages 3, 4, and 5.

The letters to the left of each scale identify the Theme or Themes that most closely describe the interests of people working in that occupation. You can use these letters to find additional, related occupations that you might find interesting. After reviewing your results on all six pages of this Profile, see the back of page 5 for tips on finding other occupations in the Theme or Themes that interest you the most.

Theme Code	Occupation	Very Dissimilar	Dissimilar	Mid-Range	Similar	Very Similar
AE	ADVERTISING EXECUTIVE				✓	
CE	PARALEGAL				✓	
RIS	RADIOLOGIC TECHNOLOGIST				✓	
CE	BANKER				✓	
ECS	HOUSEKEEPING & MAINTENANCE SUPR.				✓	
AR	ARTIST, FINE			✓		
EC	HAIR STYLIST			✓		
CE	SMALL BUSINESS OWNER			✓		
CSE	FARMER			✓		
SA	SOCIAL WORKER			✓		

***PERSONAL STYLE SCALES** measure your levels of comfort regarding Work Style, Learning Environment, Leadership Style, and Risk Taking/Adventure. This information may help you make decisions about particular work environments, educational settings, and types of activities you would find satisfying. Your results on these four scales are on page 6.*

CPP CONSULTING PSYCHOLOGISTS PRESS, INC. • 3803 E. Bayshore Road, Palo Alto, CA 94303

Figure 11.1 Snapshot for Client 1, Showing a Flat Profile

so, but also acknowledges that she doesn't "need another degree." She plans to take some courses part-time toward certification in this area.

This case illustrates how a Profile that is essentially flat can be interpreted using the highest of the low scores. An interest pattern emerged that made sense to the client and confirmed her very focused interests.

Lack of Knowledge

A flat Profile can mean that the respondent is not very knowledgeable about the world of work. Lack of information about occupations, and perhaps about other aspects of the world in general, can lead to a reluctance to say "Like" to unfamiliar items, resulting in a low "Like" response rate. Or such reluctance can lead to a normal number of "Like" responses but result in scale scores that do not cluster in a definable pattern. In either case, career counseling should proceed with the hypothesis that the respondent has simply not reached a stage of life in which a definable pattern of interests has emerged.

Such clients need to engage in a variety of career exploration activities (e.g., browsing through career literature; reading books on careers or on making career decisions; or discussing jobs with parents, teachers, and friends who do have work experience). If feasible, they also can serve as volunteers or work at part-time jobs to gain vocational experience. Or they might consider taking general survey courses at a college or community college, perhaps through an evening school. The counselor can brainstorm with the client various ways to gain more knowledge and experience. Once such clients have expanded their awareness of the world of work, they often find it useful to retake the *Strong*.

Cultural Differences

Language or cultural differences can yield a flat Profile. The client may be unfamiliar with various items and thus be reluctant to respond definitively to them. Or cultural pressures may inhibit the client from saying "Like." (See Chapter 15 for a discussion of using the *Strong* with these clients.)

Mood

The respondent's mood at the time of completing the *Strong* can influence the level and differentiation of his or her scores. If the respondent has had an especially difficult day and is then asked to sit down after work or school and take the inventory, the result may be a flat Profile. One client, after a grueling day of job interviews, was asked to take the *Strong* and to do it quickly, which yielded predictably discouraging results. A better approach would have been to defer the testing to a time that would be more conducive and more convenient to the client. Mood can also be a factor contributing to flat Profiles among outplacement clients to whom the *Strong* is administered too soon after losing a job. These clients need some time to deal with the emotional issues surrounding the loss of their jobs before being asked to express their interests.

Not Wanting to Commit

Some people who are in the midst of contemplating career changes may be undecided, and a flat Profile may reflect their unreadiness or unwillingness to make a commitment either to change or to accept the status quo. In these cases, low scores on the GOTs and BISs may reflect a temporary state, one that could be characterized as a "call for help" in the face of an excruciating quandary. Their current situation can also result in a score toward the plays it safe pole of the Risk Taking/Adventure Personal Style scale. Discussing the results of this scale can help to bring the reasons for the client's indecision to the forefront for discussion. Once the client's ambivalence has been addressed, the OS portion of the Profile is likely to be useful in identifying his or her interest patterns.

Indecisiveness

While some clients may have flat Profiles because they are temporarily undecided, others will exhibit flat Profiles because they are what has been characterized as *chronically indecisive*. Differentiating between developmental indecision and chronic indecision can be useful in planning an intervention strategy with the client. A developmentally undecided client lacks the knowledge about self and about the world of work that is necessary to make a decision. A chronically undecided client, in contrast, is unable to decide because of anxiety, a shifting self-perception, unrealistic expectations, or a tendency to expect external sources to assist in making the decisions.

The inability or unwillingness of these clients to make decisions or to act on a decision is pervasive, extending beyond the workplace into their personal relationships. The underlying reasons for such chronic gridlock will probably need to be addressed before specific career issues can be resolved. Hammer and Kummerow (1992) discuss how using the *Myers-Briggs Type Indicator* (MBTI) to focus on personality development can be helpful in counseling these clients.

Practitioners have observed that children growing up in alcohol-related dysfunctional families may experience chronic career indecision that is a function of anxiety, identity confusion, and a tendency toward an external locus of control. Like other chronically undecided clients, adult children of alcoholics tend to take a succession of unrelated entry-level positions or jobs that represent general underemployment (Schumrum & Hartman, 1988).

Not Wanting to Work

Some people have flat Profiles simply because they do not want to work. For many people, holding a job is strictly a necessity, and a flat Profile reflects their basic apathy or antipathy toward work. This effect will be apparent in low scores on the GOTs and BISs and sometimes on the OSs as well. Obviously, such an attitude must be respected, although the reasons such a client would agree to take the inventory should be explored; what seems to be apathy toward work may be symptomatic of an underlying issue.

A Pervasive Negative Style

Routinely saying "Dislike" or "Indifferent" may reflect a pervasive attitude toward life; for some clients, personal identity may be defined more by what they dislike than by what they like. Younger students who exhibit this pattern may be rebellious or may be suffering from depression. Engaging these clients in a discussion of their *low* scores can be a useful way to help them think about what they want to do, or at least not do. When confronted with high "Indifferent" or "Dislike" response percentages, discussions with the client should be directed toward distinguishing whether his or her few high scores reflect clearly defined interests with an indifference to everything else, a general indifference toward life and/or work, or a conscious response style indicating a lack of motivation to respond to items on the inventory.

Low Self-Esteem

Flat Profiles can also be a sign of low self-esteem. Ohlde (1979) found that students with high and medium levels of self-esteem had Profiles that were significantly more differentiated than those of low-self-esteem students. The high- and medium-self-esteem students also had significantly more scores in the "Similar" to "Very Similar" range on the OSs and more high scores on the BISs than did the low-self-esteem students. The students with high and medium levels of self-esteem also responded more often with "Like" responses, while students with low self-esteem were more likely to show a high percentage of "Dislike" responses, which can result in a flat Profile. Robbins (1987) also found a moderate correlation (.22, $p < .05$) between self-esteem and the existence of a differentiated Profile. Career exploration can also be affected by low self-esteem. Miller (1982) found that students who responded "Yes" to more of the items in the Your Characteristics section of the *Strong* were more likely to engage in career exploration. A low response percentage in this section has been identified as a possible indicator of low self-esteem (Hansen, 1992).

Clients who exhibit low self-esteem may not be able to respond meaningfully and reliably to what they like and dislike until they have established a coherent and positive sense of self. Career counseling with these clients may need to focus first on increasing self-esteem. Once this is accomplished, these students may benefit from retaking the *Strong*.

Undeveloped Vocational Identity

Clients who have little sense of themselves as "workers," who have little idea about what they can do, or who are in conflict about the role they wish to assume may exhibit flat Profiles. These are often people who have recently returned to the paid work force after a long hiatus, such as women who remained in the home while their children were young. These women may be experiencing a role conflict, trying to learn or integrate new roles or struggling to develop a vocational identity. They need support for trying out new roles and encouragement for engaging in career exploration. They may also need help identifying how their current skills can be transferred to jobs or careers in which they are interested.

External Pressures

Students who are unable to choose a major because of intense pressure from family or peers may exhibit flat Profiles. Once the source of pressure has been identified and addressed and some time spent exploring developmental issues of independence and identity, such students often find retaking the *Strong* to be a valuable experience.

Other Strategies for Interpreting Flat Profiles

Hansen (1992) and Pinkney (1985) offer suggestions for interpreting flat Profiles that involve making within-Profile comparisons of scores rather than relying on the traditional comparisons with the occupational norm or general reference groups. Hansen (1992) suggests using the highest of the client's scores as the focus of interpretation. This interpretation should be conducted keeping in mind all the possible sources of a flat Profile enumerated earlier. In taking this approach, consider beginning with a statement such as, *"Rather than comparing your scores to those of other people, let's simply look at your areas of greatest interest, which are the areas in which your highest scores occur."*

When interpreting the GOTs and BISs, focus first on any scores in the "Average Interest" range. Since these sets of scales are composed of items keyed to "Like" responses, an interpretive comment in the "Average Interest" range suggests that the client responded "Like" to about half of the items. Discussing the meaning of these scales will often elicit some positive responses to elements of the Theme descriptions. These responses can then be used as a bridge into the world of work. When discussing the GOTs, it can be helpful to use the table on the back of page 2 of the Profile, which lists additional characteristics of people with interests in each of the areas.

The client may respond positively to something in this table, which can then become a focus for a discussion of his or her interests. There are also additional information and examples of the GOTs and the BISs on the *Strong* worksheet and contained in other support material for the *Strong*.

When interpreting the OSs, begin with the highest of the mid-range scores, those from 35 to 39. Start with any OS scores of 39; identify the scales and determine how well they fit with any "Average Interest" scores on the GOTs and BISs. Next, go to OS scores of 38, then 37. Be careful, however, not to assume, or convey to the client, that a score of 39 is significantly higher than one of 38 or 37. The goal of this process is simply to identify a discernible pattern in the client's interests by evaluating the OS scores in the context of the highest of the low GOTs and BISs. Typically, a number of possible options that fit with the rest of the Profile will emerge from this process, and the interpretation can proceed. Once a Theme code has been identified, however tentatively, it can be used to generalize to related occupations not on the Profile in the usual manner. The client may discover some related occupations that pique his or her interest.

When adopting this procedure, close attention must be paid to how much sense the scores on the OSs make in conjunction with the rest of the Profile. Clinical judgment and feedback from the client may be necessary to determine whether the high OS scores form a reasonable pattern of interests. It is important to gauge the client's reaction to tentative suggestions of patterns, because a collection of scores that appears random to the counselor may make perfect sense to the client. Hansen (1984) presents the Profile of a client who had no OS scores above 40; examination of the highest of the mid-range OS scores nevertheless revealed a pattern of Realistic occupations. This finding was consistent with the client's highest Theme, which was Realistic, on which he scored average, and with the only two BISs on which he scored above average, those being Agriculture and Nature. The client agreed that the Profile fit his interests, and the occupation he ultimately took up was ranching.

Although interpreting flat Profiles using this approach can reveal a clear pattern of interests, thereby laying a foundation for the client's career exploration, probably the best advice for interpreting a flat Profile is to not overinterpret it. Discussing with the client those hypotheses (described earlier and summarized in Table 11.1) that seem most likely will sometimes indicate that the client needs to become involved in personal or career development. With these clients, discussions about identity or independence may take precedence over, or at least be as important as, a focused discussion of career alternatives. When these issues have been dealt with, re-testing with the *Strong* often proves interesting and useful.

Another approach to use when confronted with a flat Profile is to turn to other sources of information. Although career counseling should always involve multiple sources of information, it is especially important when dealing with clients who have flat Profiles. Two other assessment instruments, the *Career Beliefs Inventory* (CBI) and the *Myers-Briggs Type Indicator*, may be particularly useful with such clients.

The CBI (Krumboltz, 1991) measures 25 beliefs that may be hindering or blocking career exploration or decision making and may be influencing the client exhibiting a flat Profile. For example, one CBI scale measures the client's belief that his or her career decision is influenced by others, while another taps how important the approval of others is to the client. Interpreting the client's scores on these two scales can point to external pressures that may affect how the client responds to the *Strong* items. This discussion may be the first step in helping the client challenge her or his beliefs. The MBTI can be used in a number of ways. First, the MBTI Career Report (Hammer & Macdaid, 1992) provides a list of careers congruent with the client's personality preferences. Many clients with flat Profiles on the *Strong* are nonetheless able to identify personality preferences that can be linked to occupations they can explore further. The MBTI can also be used to provide a larger context in which to view the client's *Strong* Profile. Hammer and Kummerow (1992) have developed a model showing how to relate scores on the two instruments and offer suggestions for interventions based on the overall pattern of scores on both.

Elevated Profiles

Another interpretive challenge is the elevated Profile, which shows a large number of high scores on the GOTs, BISs, and OSs. Such a Profile usually results from a person responding "Like" to many—more than 55 percent—of the inventory items (compared with an average "Like" response rate of about 32 percent). High "Like" response rates have a greater effect on the GOT and BIS scores than on the OS scores, since scores on these scales increase strictly as a function of "Like" responses, while OS scores increase as a function of both "Likes" *and* "Dislikes." Possible reasons for elevated Profiles are summarized in Table 11.2 and discussed in the following sections.

Fear of Appearing Negative

Some clients believe that saying "Dislike" reflects negatively on their personality, character, or values. This may be an extreme case of the adage "If you can't say anything nice about someone, don't say anything at all," applied in this case to career choice. Conveying to clients prior to administration of the *Strong* that the inventory compares their likes and dislikes to those of people working in a variety of occupations may reduce the likelihood of such a response set.

Trying to Please Everyone

Some clients who respond "Like" to a large number of items may be signaling a desire to please everyone. A client receiving strong conflicting messages from family or peers about what they "should be" may respond "Like" to almost everything as insurance against displeasing anyone. In other cases, many high scores reflect a combination of the client's own interests and the client's guesses about what others might like to see. When dealing with such clients, the external pressures must first be identified and then issues of independence and identity addressed. It is useful to have them review their high scores and select those that best reflect their own interests, as opposed to what others want for them. At this point, some clients can easily classify their *Strong* results as "theirs" and "mine."

Note the similarity here to the client described in the section on flat Profiles who says "Dislike" to everything. Saying "Like" to everything and saying "Dislike" to everything sometimes represent opposite sides of the same coin. Either strategy can serve as a protection against alienating family or peers. The one avoids opening up; the other resists being pinned down.

Desire to Keep Options Open

Other clients hesitate to say "Dislike" because they have a strong desire or need to keep all of their options open for as long as possible. This hesitancy sometimes indicates a difficulty in making commitments or choices that extends beyond the career area and into interpersonal or other areas of the client's life. Hammer and Kummerow (1992) show how this tendency can be a function of personality development and provide some suggestions for how to address it using the results of the *Myers-Briggs Type Indicator* along with the *Strong*.

Table 11.2 Possible Reasons for Elevated Profiles

Equating "Dislike" with being negative
Trying to please everyone
Having a desire to keep all options open
Resisting being pinned down
Having true diversity of interests
Having multipotential interests and abilities

Diversity of Interests

An elevated Profile may reflect a true diversity of interests. People with a wide range of interests will score high on many of the GOTs (Gaeddert & Hansen, 1993) and BISs. They may also have a large number of scores in the "Similar" and "Very Similar" categories on the OSs. These scores will most likely occur in occupations across several of the Theme types rather than being concentrated in one or two.

Mulitpotentialed Clients

A subset of clients with diverse interests (and elevated Profiles) not only have a wide range of interests but also demonstrate multiple abilities that may allow them to succeed in many different occupations. These clients have been referred to as "multipotentialed" (Pask-McCartney & Salomone, 1988; Super, 1953).

Client 2. The Profile for one multipotentialed client showed "Average Interest" or above on all six GOTs, with Artistic being "Very High Interest" and Social and Investigative being "High Interest." His Snapshot showed that all the top five BISs (Writing, Art, Science, Social Service, and Music/Dramatics) were in the "Very High Interest" range. An examination of page 2 of the Profile showed that all but one of the 25 BISs were "Average Interest" or above. Client 2 also showed scores of "Similar" or above on 47 of the

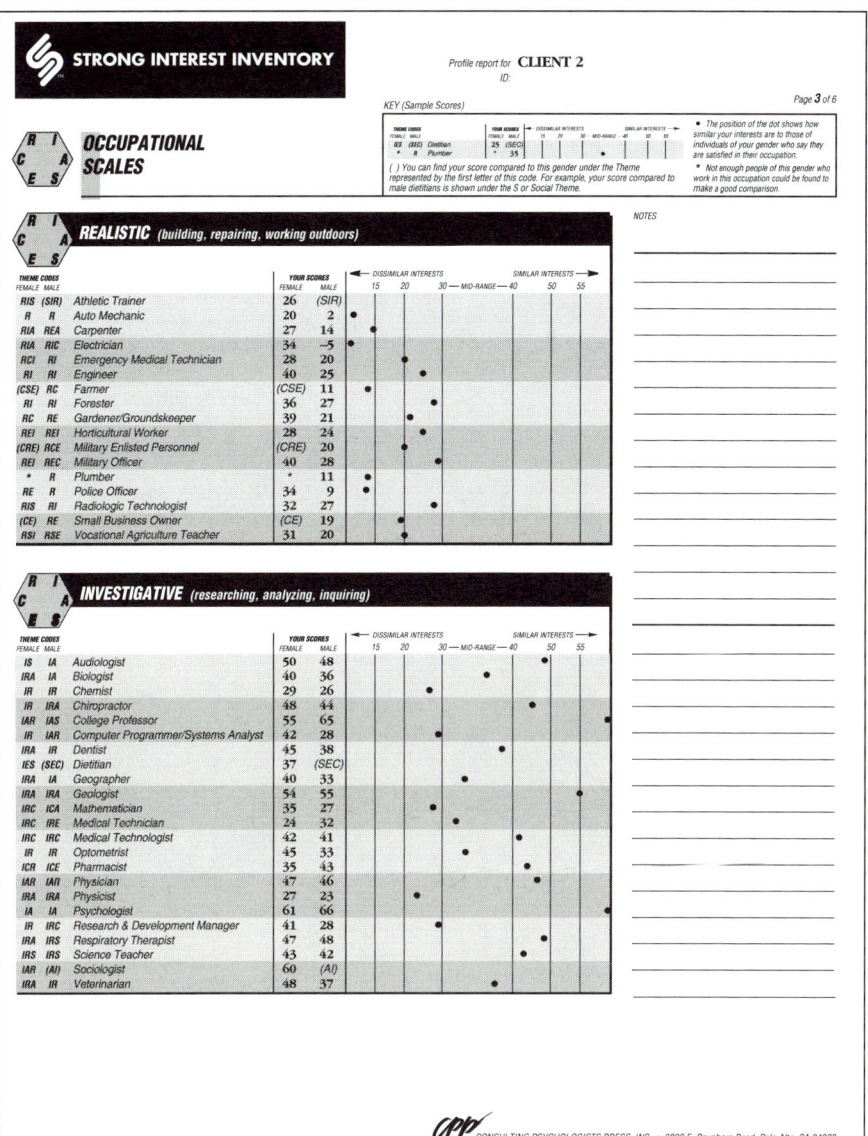

Figure 11.2 Realistic, Investigative, Artistic, and Social Occupational Scales for Client 2, Showing an Elevated Profile. (Client 2's scores on the Artistic and Social Occupational Scales are shown on Page 206.)

OSs. As can be seen in Figure 11.2, most of these scores were on OSs that fall within the Investigative, Artistic, and Social Themes, consistent with his GOT and BIS scores.

Client 2 had received an undergraduate degree in psychology and a master's degree in physics. Although interested in science and physics in general, he did not enjoy day-to-day work in this field (his score on the Physicist OS was 23). He decided to return to psychology by pursuing a law degree, with plans to train as a client advocate in mental health. However, since he did not pass the bar, he took a job as a contract specialist dealing in intellectual property for a high-technology firm. Client 2 found this work challenging and interesting but decided after a few years that he did not want to be a lawyer and considered returning to graduate school in psychology.

This client's high scores on the Artistic scales reflect the fact that he is a published poet, jazz musician, and symphony composer. His occupational history, which included many years of education, is consistent with his very high score (67) on the Learning Environment scale. His Risk Taking/Adventure score (55) also indicates a willingness to take risks, borne out by his frequent career changes. Given Client 2's dissatisfaction with his current job in a high-tech firm, it is interesting to note that his lowest BIS score was on Computer Activities. His "Very High Interest" score on the Artistic GOT, as well as his many high BIS and OS scores within the Artistic Theme, indicate his strong interest in this

Figure 11.2 (continued) Artistic and Social Occupational Scales for Client 2

STRONG INTEREST INVENTORY
Profile report for CLIENT 2
Page 4 of 6

OCCUPATIONAL SCALES (continued)

ARTISTIC (creating or enjoying art, drama, music, writing)

Theme Codes Female	Male	Occupation	Your Scores Female	Male
AE	AE	Advertising Executive	28	47
ARI	ARI	Architect	41	46
ARI	A	Artist, Commercial	48	49
AR	A	Artist, Fine	39	37
ASE	AS	Art Teacher	37	56
AE	AE	Broadcaster	47	48
AES	AES	Corporate Trainer	48	44
ASE	ASE	English Teacher	56	59
(EA)	AE	Interior Decorator	(EA)	31
A	A	Lawyer	53	53
A	A	Librarian	57	59
AIR	AIR	Medical Illustrator	42	47
A	A	Musician	55	57
ARE	ARE	Photographer	49	46
AER	ASE	Public Administrator	45	49
AE	AE	Public Relations Director	35	47
A	A	Reporter	59	61
(IAR)	AI	Sociologist	(IAR)	63
AIR	AI	Technical Writer	60	58
A	AI	Translator	60	51

SOCIAL (helping, instructing, caregiving)

Theme Codes Female	Male	Occupation	Your Scores Female	Male
(RIS)	SIR	Athletic Trainer	(RIS)	17
S	*	Child Care Provider	41	*
SE	SE	Community Service Organization Director	30	42
(IES)	SEC	Dietitian	(IES)	41
S	S	Elementary School Teacher	35	51
SAE	SA	Foreign Language Teacher	41	47
SE	SE	High School Counselor	52	52
SE	*	Home Economics Teacher	33	*
SAR	SA	Minister	46	54
SCE	SCE	Nurse, LPN	26	38
SI	SAI	Nurse, RN	51	53
SAR	SA	Occupational Therapist	56	61
SE	SE	Parks and Recreation Coordinator	37	36
SRC	SR	Physical Education Teacher	18	27
SIR	SIR	Physical Therapist	42	46
SEA	SEC	School Administrator	35	41
SEA	SEA	Social Science Teacher	51	53
SA	SA	Social Worker	56	63
SE	SEA	Special Education Teacher	29	49
SA	SA	Speech Pathologist	49	57

area. Client 2 recognized, however, that he preferred to express his Artistic interests in his leisure time and that he had a strong desire to work in a field where he could be of service to others. His consideration of a doctoral program in psychology was reinforced by the fact that his four highest OS scores were for Psychologist, College Professor, Social Worker, and Sociologist.

Strategies for Interpreting Elevated Profiles

Elevated Profiles are somewhat easier to interpret than are flat Profiles, although diverse interests and multipotentiality present the client with difficult decisions. The first step is to use the highest of the client's many high scores. For example, it may be useful to begin with the two to three highest GOTs, the six to eight highest BISs, and all of the "Very Similar" OSs. If necessary, scores on the remaining GOTs and BISs can be examined to determine how they fit the pattern that emerges from the higher scores. Reviewing the Snapshot is particularly useful in these cases since it provides an immediate summary of the client's highest scores.

Summary Theme codes can be developed for the GOTs, BISs, and OSs using the highest ranking scores within each of these sets of scales. As noted in the discussion of flat Profiles, when appropriate, the computer program that produces the Profile computes a code for the GOTs, which is printed on the Snapshot directly below the ranked list of GOTs. In some cases, these codes will all point to the same interest area or areas, thus simplifying the interpretation. In such instances, the client can observe that his or her many interests all center around an interest in two or three of the Themes. When such a consistent pattern can be identified, the client may realize that the specific occupation chosen is less important than making sure that this occupation offers the opportunity to express the identified pattern of interests.

If the elevated Profile represents a client with a true diversity of interests, counseling may involve helping the individual identify different approaches to accommodating this diversity. Suggestions might include:

▲ changing occupations frequently,
▲ pursuing a job that entails contact with people who have highly diverse interests,
▲ pursuing a job that incorporates constant variety and change,
▲ taking up several different hobbies and leisure activities, and
▲ cultivating friends with interests in a wide range of activities.

For example, one client with an elevated Profile and diverse interests left her high-level position in a large bank to pursue a career as an outplacement counselor. After appropriate training, she chose a firm that allowed her to work with individuals at all organizational levels from a wide variety of industries. She was very happy with her new career because she felt that it satisfied her desire for constant change and diversity (Hammer & Kummerow, 1992).

Some clients with diverse interests find that their particular abilities or talents guide them in one direction or another. Integrating the results of interest and ability assessments can be useful in counseling these clients. Multipotentialed clients, however, have the capacity for satisfaction and success in any of several occupations and may find it difficult to make career decisions that could limit their options. Such clients can benefit from examining each occupational possibility separately, discussing the advantages and disadvantages of each and receiving feedback throughout the process. The more multifaceted or complex an individual, the more difficult it can be for that person to define "who I am." For some multipotentialed clients, delaying occupational choice and thus retaining their options may be a valid decision (Pask-McCartney & Salomone, 1988).

Diametrically Opposed Interests

Profiles on which the client has high scores on GOTs that are directly opposite one another on the hexagon (Realistic and Social, Investigative and Enterprising, and Artistic and Conventional) can also prove challenging for a number of reasons. First, clients with such an interest pattern may have conflicting feelings about their current job or their long-term career plans. Second, these clients may already have sensed the difficulty in finding positions that can satisfy opposed interests.

These clients' confusion or conflicts may become evident when their GOT results are first described, and they react with frustration to what appear to be contradictory descriptions for their highest scoring Themes. They can be helped by acknowledging the oppositional forces of their interests and the difficulty they may have encountered in attempting to accommodate their interests in the workplace. They can be encouraged to view unusual combinations of interests as a potential asset.

Clients with opposing interests may have discovered that there are not as many jobs available for their consideration as there are for those whose interests are adjacent on the hexagon. For example, a person with Artistic-Conventional interests will have fewer occupations to choose from than will someone with an Investigative-Realistic pattern. In fact, the *Dictionary of Holland Occupational Codes* lists *no* occupations for which the first two letters of the code are AC or CA (Gottfredson & Holland, 1989). This does not mean that there are no career options for people with this code (see the example that follows for how this interest pattern can be expressed in an occupation), only that with the particular procedure used for coding occupations, none were found whose tasks directly reflected this combination of interests.

Some people deal with the tension inherent in having such opposed interests by:

▲ choosing one area of interest for their vocational focus and the other for their avocational focus,
▲ performing job activities associated with one Theme while working in an environment that reflects the diametrically opposed Theme,
▲ creating or molding a job to fit their unusual combination of interests,
▲ periodically changing jobs or careers, or
▲ becoming a temporary worker.

Some clients compartmentalize their lives to accommodate their diverse interests, spending their leisure time with people whose interests are very different from those of their work colleagues. These people often do not talk about their work with their friends, and their colleagues at work may be surprised to learn how they spend their leisure time.

Others with opposed interests find satisfaction in performing job activities associated with one Theme while working in an environment that reflects the diametrically opposed Theme. For example, a person with Artistic-Conventional interests may work as an accountant for an organization such as an art gallery, theater, or orchestra. The organization will likely consider itself fortunate to have an accountant who takes such a keen interest in its larger mission. A person with Investigative-Enterprising interests may conduct research in a business setting. For one whose primary pattern is Enterprising-Investigative, a career as manager of a research and development department might offer an opportunity to express his or her opposite interests.

Still other individuals succeed by creating or molding a job to fit their unusual combination of interests. For example, a researcher with both Enterprising and Investigative interests may conduct financial research on the performance of businesses, work for a market-research firm, or start a small business based on his or her expertise in a technical field.

Some people satisfy their diverse interests by periodically changing jobs or careers. They may work intently for periods at one career and then switch to another that satisfies their opposite interest, perhaps repeating this pattern a number of times in their occupational life.

A creative way to satisfy diametrically opposed interests that more and more people are taking advantage of is to build a career as a temporary employee. Traditionally, temporary positions have tended to be for clerical workers and administrative assistants, but this strategy is now open to workers in many occupational areas and at all employment levels. There are even temporary CEOs. In times of recessionary pressure, firms have come to rely on contract workers at the managerial and even executive levels. A number of firms now specialize in placing temporary executives such as chief financial officers or marketing executives, who may work part-time with one or more firms for a number of years.

Inconsistencies Among the Types of Strong Scales

Some Profiles offer a challenge because they exhibit seemingly inconsistent scores on different sets of scales. For example, a client may score high on the Mathematics BIS but indicate little interest on the Mathematician OS. Or the client may score high on one or two of the BISs in the Realistic Theme yet have a score of "Average Interest" or below on the Theme itself.

Such conflicting scores offer an opportunity to discuss the all-encompassing nature of occupations and to emphasize that interest in one particular activity is not sufficient for a person to enjoy all aspects of the environment surrounding that activity or the day-to-day tasks of those working in that occupation. An intense interest in mathematics is only one element in the interests of professional mathematicians; artists are unique in ways other than their interest in artistic activities; people in social service settings stand apart on factors other than "service-to-humanity" concerns. Thus, patterns of scores that appear inconsistent are, in fact, an asset because they force the counselor and client to fully understand the meaning of the scales, which in turn leads to more accurate interpretation.

Inconsistencies Between the General Occupational Themes and the Basic Interest Scales

Inconsistencies can occur between clients' scores on the GOTs and BISs that fall within the same Theme. The BISs represent clusters of more specific interests that fall within the broader GOTs. However, no effort was made during the development of the two sets of scales to guarantee that all of the items on the R Theme, for example, also appear on the Realistic BISs—Agriculture, Nature, Military Activities, Athletics, and Mechanical Activities. Conversely, the items that appear on the Realistic BISs do not all appear on the R Theme. Although most of the items on a given Theme will appear on that Theme's associated BISs, they generally will be distributed across them.

The items that make up the Themes measure general interests in occupations. The BISs offer additional information about what the client *likes to do*. Clients often have no difficulty making a distinction between who they are and what they like to do. Consequently, it is possible for a client to say "Like" to all the items within a particular Theme, resulting in "Very High Interest" on that scale, without also having high scores on any of the BISs within that Theme. In such cases the "Very High Interest" Theme score is an expression of a person's general orientation—an expression of *who she or he is*.

Discrepancies between scores on the GOTs and BISs often reflect either diverse or well-defined interest patterns. For example, a client with diverse interests exhibited "High Interest" on the following BISs: Medical Science (Investigative); Medical Service (Social); Athletics (Realistic); and Music/Dramatics, Art, and Writing (Artistic). Her corresponding scores on the I, S, R, and A GOTs were not "High Interest," however, and were thus inconsistent with her scores on the BISs. This pattern suggested that she was interested in the specific activities indicated by her BIS scores but did not have a general interest in any of the broader areas represented by the Themes. In fact, she worked as a medical researcher, which satisfied her interests in medical science and medical service, but did not have a general interest in science or social service that might characterize high scores on the Investigative and Social GOTs, respectively. Likewise, her interests in the Realistic area were focused on enjoying sports (golf, skiing, tennis, swimming, and racquetball) both as a participant and as a spectator, but she had no interest in other areas reflected in the Realistic Theme, such as mechanical activities or military activities. Her artistic interests were expressed by attending artistic performances and concerts.

Clients with well-defined interests who exhibit inconsistencies between the GOTs and BISs have scores of "High Interest" on a limited number of scales and scores of "Average Interest" or even "Little Interest" on related scales. One such client scored "Average Interest" on the I Theme but "High Interest" on the Mathematics BIS, which is coded I. During the interpretation, he questioned this apparent inconsistency. Discussion revealed that the client had a bachelor's degree in economics, worked as a computer consultant, and spent his leisure time developing accounting software. Thus, his work and leisure life were barely distinguishable from one another.

He had only a passing interest in other Investigative activities, such as science or medicine (his scores on Science and Medical Science were both "Average Interest"). He was not particularly interested in general Investigative topics, environments, or people but rather chose to concentrate on a narrow area within the Investigative Theme.

Inconsistencies Between the GOTs and BISs, and the OSs

Another inconsistency that presents a challenge for interpretation occurs when a client scores high on either, or both, the GOTs and the BISs and low on the corresponding OSs. For example, inconsistencies can occur when there are contrasting scores on the Investigative GOT and the Mathematician OS; the Realistic Theme and the Farmer OS (for males); the Social Theme and Parks and Recreation Coordinator.

Inconsistencies can also occur between BISs and OSs. From his research on the relationships between the BISs and OSs, Johnson (1972) reported that approximately half of all Profiles exhibit one or more apparent inconsistencies between the BISs and OSs. For example, a client may have highly contrasting scores on pairs of scales that are obviously related, such as Art and Fine Artist, Mathematics and Mathematician, and Military Activities and Military Officer. Because Profiles with such contrasts occur often, counselors must understand the implications of the inconsistencies and learn how to explain them to clients.

Properly interpreted, inconsistencies can give the client (and counselor) considerable insight into what the scores on each scale type mean. Although contrasting results can initially be confusing, they provide excellent examples of the effects of the different strategies used to construct the GOTs and the BISs and OSs. Since the item content of the GOTs and BISs is homogeneous, high scores can be earned only by responding "Like" to those items. But the interests and aversions of people in particular occupations involve more than one dimension. Thus, high scores on the heterogeneous OSs can be earned only by having the interests *as well as* the aversions of people in those occupations. For example, an interest in Realistic activities is only one aspect of farming, athletics is only one interest of recreation leaders, and military

Table 11.3 A Sample of Items Weighted Positively and Negatively on the Male Mathematician Scale

Items Weighted Positively	Items Weighted Negatively
Astronomer	Advertising executive
Geometry	Athletic director
Author of technical books	Employment manager
Physics	Public relations director
Doing research work	Working regular hours
Teaching adults	Manager, Chamber of Commerce
Scientific research worker	Auto racer
Meeting and directing people	Statistician
Designer, electronic equipment	Public relations director
College professor	Interviewing clients

activities represent only one aspect of the interests of officers in the armed services. To score high on one of these OSs, one must resemble the members of that occupation in a variety of ways.

For example, consider the differences between the Mathematics BIS and the Mathematician OS. The BISs reflect the respondent's answers to items directly concerned with certain well-defined areas of activity; the score on the Mathematics BIS, for example, is based on responses to only eleven items, all heavily mathematical in nature. The "Like" responses for these items are all weighted positively, the "Dislike" responses negatively; thus, the only way an individual can score high on this scale is by indicating "Like" to most of the items, and the only way to score low is by indicating "Dislike" to most of the same items.

By contrast, the OSs are much more heterogeneous in content. The male Mathematician OS includes 45 items covering a wide range of subjects and activities. Each item was included because mathematicians responded differently to it than did the men in the General Reference Sample. There was no attempt to screen the items intuitively for any special type of content. (The female Mathematician scale was analogously constructed.) The heterogeneity of the item content of the OSs is illustrated in Table 11.3, which shows a sample of both positively and negatively weighted items from the male Mathematician OS.

Both the number and the diversity of the items emphasize the many ways male mathematicians differ from other men. This scale is also interesting because it has about an equal number of items weighted positively and negatively. Consequently, one way of scoring high on the Mathematician scale, or "looking like a mathematician," is to answer "Dislike" to all the negatively weighted items, and thus to share the aversions of mathematicians—a way of expressing communality of interests that may not be obvious to clients. An analogous explanation holds for other pairs of scales for which apparent inconsistencies can occur (e.g., Agriculture—Farmer; Art—Fine Artist; or Social Service—Social Worker).

The explanation is always the same: the BIS in question is homogeneous in content (i.e., the items are related to one another and thus measure a single interest factor), and a high score can be earned only by indicating a preference for the activities subsumed by the items. The OSs, by contrast, are heterogeneous, and a high score can be earned in many different ways (e.g., reporting the same pattern of likes, the same pattern of dislikes, or a pattern of some likes and some dislikes, compared with people in the indicated occupation).

A conflict between the GOTs and BISs and related OSs can occur in either direction, with scales from either set being high and those from the other set being low. The most frequent occurrence will show a high GOT or BIS score with a low related OS. When this occurs, it means that the client has general interests in a broad area (GOTs) and/or in more specific activities within that area (BISs) but does *not* share the specific likes and *dislikes* of people employed in that occupation. The more general interests may find expression in avocational interests, but the person may not enjoy working in that occupation day after day.

The reverse pattern can also be true—high scores on an OS but low scores on the related GOT or BIS. This pattern indicates that the person has fairly narrow or well-defined interests in a particular occupation that do not extend to other aspects of the Theme measured by the GOT or BIS. For example, a client whose entire career has been spent researching a specialized area in mathematics may score high on the Mathematician OS but average or low on the Mathematics BIS and/or the Investigative Theme. Such inconsistencies may be observed in conjunction with some flat Profiles, as described in a preceding section.

When inconsistencies occur, the OSs are the best predictors of *occupational* choice, whereas scores on the other scales may be better predictors of how one spends leisure time. One client, for example, had "High Interest" in the Realistic Theme and on three BISs within that Theme: Agriculture, Nature, and Mechanical Activities. However, he had low scores on all the R-Theme OSs. His Realistic interests were an expression of his preference for an outdoor leisure environment, which included activities such as camping, hiking, and gardening. His occupation as a researcher fell within the Investigative Theme.

Inconsistencies as Indications of Possible Faking

Occasionally, when the *Strong* is taken as part of an entrance or placement procedure, inconsistencies between various types of scales suggest an attempt to exaggerate or fake an interest in some area. Most people answer the items honestly, even in highly competitive selection situations (Campbell, 1971). But respondents can deliberately affect their Profile scores, especially on the BISs, since the item content of these scales is homogeneous and, consequently, more obvious than the item content of the OSs.

One client, for example, took the *Strong* as part of a leadership training workshop. His BIS scores in the Enterprising area seem to fit the Profile of someone interested in assuming management roles. However, he scored low on all the OSs involved with management or administration. His high A-Theme scores were actually more congruent with his current occupation as a journalist. When asked about his high scores on Public Speaking, Law/Politics, and Organizational Management, he indicated that he had exaggerated his interest in those areas to look more like the other participants in the workshop. Once this response pattern had been acknowledged, attention could be focused on the client's OS scores. Because of their heterogeneous nature, the OSs are less susceptible to attempts by clients to influence results and therefore can be used as the basis for interpretation.

Challenges Involving the Personal Style Scales

The client's results on the four Personal Style Scales (i.e., Work Style, Learning Environment, Leadership Style, and Risk Taking/Adventure) also occasionally provide interpretive challenges.

Although interpretation of the Work Style scale is generally straightforward, Profiles with extreme scores toward either pole (say, two standard deviations from the mean) may present a challenge. One might hypothesize that the person with an extreme score toward the works with people pole may demand a lot of interaction with the counselor, who may find it difficult to progress systematically through any preferred counseling sequence. When interpreting the Profile of a person with an extreme score toward the works with ideas/data/things pole, the counselor may have to work harder to engage the client. With these clients it may be necessary to slow down and allow enough time for the client to internally process his or her responses or reactions. The client may prefer to have some time alone to process his or her results before discussing them with the counselor. These clients may also experience some difficulty initiating or engaging in informational or job interviews and may need extra coaching in presenting their strengths and skills to the interviewers. These speculations about extreme scores on this scale need to be tested by researchers.

The Learning Environment scale will probably offer fewer interpretive challenges than the Academic Comfort scale from the 1985 *Strong*, which it replaced and which was too often confused with abilities. Problem are less likely to arise with the new scale, both because of the name change and because of how the scale was constructed and normed (see Chapter 8). However, a client scoring far toward the practical pole of the Learning Environment scale who is considering a highly academic undergraduate program or graduate or professional education may present a challenge. It is important when discussing the client's plans to avoid any suggestion that the client might not succeed in a different environment. Interpretation should focus instead on helping the client to identify and understand the kind of learning environment that she or he finds most interesting and the difficulties that might ensue from remaining for an extended time in a different environment.

With respect to the Leadership Style scale, an interpretive challenge may occur when a client who is already in a leadership position or who wishes to assume such a position scores toward the leads by example pole. In this case, the client needs to understand that this scale measures a liking or disliking for a particular kind of leadership *style*. It does not directly measure an interest in assuming leadership positions, and it most certainly does not tap any leadership *abilities*.

People with scores toward the leads by example pole can and do become successful leaders. However, they probably will not be comfortable assuming the directive, take-charge, outgoing approach characteristic of those scoring toward the directs others pole. They probably will exhibit a more quiet, collaborative approach, preferring to do their job well and thus lead by example. They may also be more inclined to pursue the leadership of specific projects in which their expertise can be helpful or to assume a more team-oriented, inclusive leadership style. Note, however, that some people who are successful managers or on a management track who score toward the leads by example pole may be relieved when their score is interpreted to them, since it explains some of the job dissatisfaction they may be experiencing. For one manager who scored near this pole, the interpretation of his results, along with other *Strong* scores, motivated him to switch to a professional rather than a managerial track within his organization.

Clients with extreme scores on the Risk Taking/Adventure scale (more than one and one-half standard deviations from the mean of 50) may present challenges not so much in interpreting the Profile but in what they choose to do, or not do, with the information from the interpretation. Those with scores toward the takes chances pole may be ready to jump at the first opportunity. The challenge with such clients is to help them slow down enough to perform the necessary research and to give careful consideration to the information from their Profile, so that they can make an informed decision.

Clinical experience suggests that those scoring far toward the plays it safe pole may have trouble taking the final step toward career exploration. In fact, their dissatisfaction with their current situation may reach intolerable levels before they are willing to move to a new career. In counseling, these individuals often ask for assurances from the counselor that the risk will be worth it. Counseling with clients who are reluctant to take risks can focus on helping them clarify the exact nature of the risks involved and develop contingency plans to deal with the risks. An interesting approach that has been suggested in working with such clients is to help them identify the risks involved in *not* changing (Perosa & Perosa, 1984).

Some clients will have scores more than one standard deviation above the mean (toward the right pole) on all four Personal Style Scales. Such a pattern indicates a high degree of interest in working with people, learning in an academic environment, adopting an outgoing and directive leadership style, and taking risks. All the sales representatives in one organization had such a pattern. Each of these individuals had earned a master's degree and had worked in a variety of positions before entering sales. They all very much enjoyed the extensive personal contact with a wide variety of people that was a primary aspect of their job; they also were motivated by the risk involved in working on commission. The challenge presented by individuals with such a pattern is very similar to that of clients with elevated Profiles; in fact, such a pattern of scores on the Personal Style Scales often accompanies an elevated Profile.

Other clients have scores more than one standard deviation below the mean (toward the left pole) on all four of the Personal Style Scales. For many such clients, this pattern does not present a particular problem but simply indicates a preference for working alone, liking a practical learning environment, disliking a directive leadership style, and preferring to play it safe. For other clients, however, such a pattern suggests limited social or vocational experience or a lack of self-confidence. These hypotheses should be explored with the client, especially when they occur in the context of a flat Profile.

References

Campbell, D. P. (1971). *Handbook for the Strong Vocational Interest Blank.* Stanford, CA: Stanford University Press.

Gaeddert, D., & Hansen, J. C. (1993). Development of a measure of interest diversity. *Journal of Career Assessment, 1*(3), 294–308.

Gottfredson, G. D., & Holland, J. L. (1989). *Dictionary of Holland occupational codes* (2nd ed.). Odessa, FL: Psychological Assessment Resources.

Hammer, A. L., & Kummerow, J. K. (1992). *Strong + MBTI career development guide.* Palo Alto, CA: Consulting Psychologists Press.

Hammer, A. L., & Macdaid, G. P. (1992). *MBTI career report.* Palo Alto, CA: Consulting Psychologists Press.

Hansen, J. C. (1984). *User's guide for the SVIB-SCII.* Stanford, CA: Stanford University Press.

Hansen, J. C. (1992). *User's guide for the Strong Interest Inventory.* (rev. ed.). Stanford, CA: Stanford University Press.

Johnson, R. W. (1972). Contradictory scores on the Strong-Vocational Interest Blank. *Journal of Counseling Psychology, 19*, 487–490.

Krumboltz, J. D. (1991). *Manual for the Career Beliefs Inventory.* Palo Alto, CA: Consulting Psychologists Press.

Miller, M. F. (1982, September). Interest pattern structure and personality characteristics of clients who seek career information. *Vocational Guidance Quarterly*, pp. 28–35.

Ohlde, C. D. (1979). Relationship between self-esteem and response style. *Journal of Counseling Psychology, 26*, 455–458.

Pask-McCartney, C., & Salomone, P. R. (1988). Difficult cases in career counseling: III: The multipotentialed client. *The Career Development Quarterly, 36*, 231–240.

Perosa, S. L., & Perosa, L. M. (1984). The mid-career crisis in relation to Super's career and Erikson's adult development theory. *International Journal of Aging and Human Development, 20*, 53–68.

Pinkney, J. W. (1985). A card sort interpretive strategy for flat profiles on the Strong-Campbell Interest Inventory. *Vocational Guidance Quarterly, 33*(4), 331–339.

Robbins, S. R. (1987). Predicting change in career indecision from a self-psychology perspective. *The Career Development Quarterly, 35*, 288–296.

Schumrum, T., & Hartman, B. W. (1988). Adult children of alcoholics and chronic career indecision. *The Career Development Quarterly, 37*, 118–126.

Super, D. E. (1953). A theory of vocational development. *American Psychologist, 8*(5), 185–190.

CHAPTER 12

Using the Strong with Adults

The *Strong* can be used to help adults with career issues that can arise throughout the adult life span, from choosing a first career to planning for retirement. *Strong* results might be particularly useful for:

▲ choosing an occupation requiring vocational or technical training;

▲ choosing a professional career;

▲ planning for career development;

▲ changing careers in mid-life (voluntarily or not);

▲ reassessing major life roles;

▲ training, retraining, or returning to school; and

▲ planning for retirement.

Each of these uses of the *Strong* is discussed here, including how the new scales, updated occupational samples, and other features of the 1994 *Strong* can be useful in working with adults. ◆

Vocational/Technical Career Exploration

Of the 109 occupations currently represented by the 211 *Strong* Occupational Scales (OSs), about one-third do not require a four-year college degree for entry (see Table 12.1). There are another nine occupations (e.g., Buyer) for which a four-year degree may be necessary for certain positions or in particular organizations; for others, a certificate from a vocational or technical school or a degree from a two-year college is sufficient to obtain an entry-level position. So, up to 40 percent of the occupations on the *Strong* offer options for those who do not wish to pursue a four-year college degree.

In addition to the vocational/technical OSs found on the Profile, the complete lists of OSs in Appendixes A and B can assist clients in identifying a full range of potential occupations. The list of related occupations provided for each scale in Appendix A can be matched with the occupations on the Profile for which a client scored in the "Similar" range to generate an extensive list of options. For example, one woman had interests similar to those of Emergency Medical Technician (coded RCI), Radiologic Technologist (RIS), Respiratory Therapist (IRA), and Medical Technician (IRC). A list of 19 additional vocational occupations has been extracted from Appendix A for the client to consider (see Table 12.2). In addition, Appendix B in the guide, or the *Strong Career Finder*, can be consulted to identify more vocational occupations with R, I, RI, and IR codes. If desired, the search could also be extended to occupations with combinations of I, R, A, and C to generate even more options.

Even client interest in occupations that do typically require a college degree can be generalized to vocational/technical occupations not requiring that level of education. This can be done by using the Theme codes and a resource such as the *Strong Career Finder*, or, for a more extensive listing, the *Dictionary*

Table 12.1 Occupations on the *Strong* Not Requiring a Four-Year College Degree for Entry

Agribusiness Manager
Auto Mechanic
Bookkeeper
Carpenter
Chef
Child Care Provider
Credit Manager
Dental Assistant
Dental Hygienist
Electrician
Emergency Medical Technician
Farmer
Flight Attendant
Florist
Food Service Manager
Gardener/Groundskeeper
Hair Stylist
Horticultural Worker
Housekeeping & Maintenance Supervisor
Life Insurance Agent
Medical Records Technician
Medical Technician
Military Enlisted Personnel
Nurse, LPN
Optician
Paralegal
Photographer
Plumber
Police Officer
Purchasing Agent
Radiologic Technologist
Realtor
Respiratory Therapist
Restaurant Manager
Secretary
Small Business Owner
Store Manager
Travel Agent

of Holland Occupational Codes (DHOC) (Gottfredson & Holland, 1989). For example, a client who scores high on the Chemist scale may not wish to pursue an advanced degree. He or she may, however, use the Theme code for Chemist—IR—to identify other occupations with Investigative and Realistic interests that require less educational preparation. A search of the *DHOC* for occupations coded IR that do not generally require a college degree but that appear to be related to chemistry yields such occupational titles as Scientific Helper (IRS), Chemical Preparer (IRE), and Laboratory Assistant (IRC). Further alternatives could be identified by searching for occupations coded RI. In addition, many other IR and RI occupations with less direct links to chemistry may prove interesting to IR clients.

How Theme codes can be used to identify career options is illustrated by the case of an installation technician whose job at a major communications firm was eliminated due to technological changes ("Pac Bell," 1990). This man's *Strong* results indicated "Very High Interest" on the Realistic Theme as well as "High Interest" on the Artistic and Investigative Themes. Although his Artistic and Investigative results were not related to his former job, he realized these scores reflected his avocational interests and thus had relevance for future job satisfaction. With the aid of a counselor, this client was able to identify a new job within the company that combined his various interests—providing technical support to an account executive in the marketing department.

Career Development in Organizations

Facilitating employee career development is a major task for human resource professionals in business, government, and other organizations. Career development includes:

▲ career planning to facilitate the development of talented employees or to support internal recruitment programs,

▲ mid-career counseling to choose between management and technical career paths, and

▲ counseling for "plateaued" employees (those who feel they have reached the limit of upward movement in their organization) who may be considering lateral or downward transfers within the organization or movement out of the organization.

Table 12.2 Example of Using Appendix A to Identify Additional Vocational Occupations

Emergency Medical Technician	Radiologic Technologist	Respiratory Therapist	Medical Technician
Ambulance attendant	Health physicist	Cardiopulmonary technician	Blood bank technician
Paramedic	Mammography technician	Home care coordinator	Blood and plasma
Physician assistant	Nuclear medical technician	Neonatal care coordinator	laboratory assistant
Medical assistant	Radiation therapist		Cytotechnician
	Ultrasound technologist		Hematology technician
	X-ray technician		Medical technologist
			Serology technician

Because assessment of interests and skills is a vital part of any career development program, the *Strong* can be used in each of these situations.

Career Planning

Career planning in large organizations must deal, at least to some extent, with the forces that are moving career development away from defining advancement solely as a promotion (Mirvis, 1993). Gutteridge, Leibowitz, and Shore (1993) go so far as to label moving up the corporate ladder an "obsolete" criterion for career development. The rapid development of a global economy is one force behind such change. More and more employees and managers must learn to operate in a global business environment vastly different from the corporate culture they have known. Demographic forces are also at work, with an increasing portion of the population now in a position to seek career advancement. At the same time, in an effort to be more responsive, many large employers are paring down their managerial ranks to create less hierarchical organizations. These forces have had an impact on career development practices, including a need for in-house counseling, training, and recruitment programs; dual career tracks; and programs for dealing with career plateauing.

Over 83 percent of companies participating in a nationwide survey said that they planned to increase their training during the 1990s. They estimated that 58 percent of training expenditures would be spent on in-house programs, 28 percent on outside consultants, and 14 percent on college programs (Mirvis, 1993). In-house programs include individual career counseling as well as workshops and classes. Research has demonstrated that classes have a markedly greater effect on client outcomes than do other kinds of career-counseling services, a finding likely attributable to the fact that classes involve a greater number of sessions (Oliver & Spokane, 1988). Although individual career counseling was the most effective in terms of the number of hours required, career classes and workshops were the most effective in terms of the number of clients reached. The superiority of career classes suggests that they may be worth the investment for many organizations. Another study, however, suggests that few organizations seem aware of this advantage: only 34 percent of the firms surveyed were using career planning workshops or classes (Gutteridge et al., 1993).

Information about employee skills and personality preferences is part of many career development programs. Some organizations use the *Strong* in seminars designed to help employees develop plans to achieve their career goals. For example, one workshop offered as part of an in-house career planning program at a major public utility used both the *Strong* and *Myers-Briggs Type Indicator* (MBTI) ("*Strong* and MBTI Help," 1993). Participants in this workshop first identified their top ten skills and the situations in which they used those skills effectively. They then linked these skills to their *Strong* and MBTI results. Using the *Strong* Organizational Specialty Report and the Individual Summary Report (both developed for the 1985 *Strong*) along with custom worksheets developed by Margaret Bradley, the utility's senior training specialist, they identified jobs within the company that fit their skills and interests. The 1985 *Strong* Leisure Report was also used to identify how they might achieve a better balance between personal and professional activities (Hammer, 1990).

Some large companies use the *Strong* in conjunction with in-house recruitment and development programs. In one organization, for example, Theme codes were assigned to all the jobs ("Data Base," 1989). Employees who took the *Strong* as part of a career development program and had their results interpreted by a trained professional could enter into a computer their occupational codes and desired level in the organization. The computer then provided them with information about all jobs in the organization with matching codes at that level.

Choosing Between Managerial and Technical Careers

Until recently, in many organizations the only way for a technical worker to advance was to be promoted into management and then follow the standard management development path. Dr. Raymond Hill, who collected the data for the *Strong's* Research and Development (R & D) Manager scale has referred to this practice as "liquidating technical talent" ("*Strong* Assists," 1989). In a major workforce study, over 70 percent of the firms surveyed said that keeping the skills of their employees current was a somewhat serious or very serious issue (Mirvis, 1993). To avoid this pitfall, many corporations have begun providing dual career tracks—one for those wishing to advance through the ranks of management and one for those with technical expertise who seek increased responsibility or technical knowledge.

Career development along a technical track can be accomplished in a number of ways, including financial rewards for new inventions or products and opportunities for technical experts to expand their knowledge or keep abreast of new technical developments by attending conferences or other educational programs. Such changes have helped ensure that organizations retain employees who are informed about fast-changing technology. Managers in these organizations have realized that productivity gains can be achieved not only by training managers but also by encouraging individual contributions from highly motivated technical employees.

The *Strong* can be used to help technical employees determine whether they might prefer a managerial or a technical track. The Research & Development Manager scales (one scale each for female and male R & D managers) within the Investigative Theme will probably be most helpful. A high score by a technical employee on one or both of these scales indicates that his or her likes and dislikes are similar to those of managers with technical training who supervise or manage primarily technical employees.

If a technical employee does not score above midrange on one or both of the Research & Development Manager scales, this result suggests that the employee might be more satisfied pursuing advancement along a technical path rather than a management track. High scores on the following *Strong* scales would provide additional support for a technical track: the Realistic Theme; the Investigative Theme; and the Mechanical Activities, Science, Mathematics, Medical Science, Computer Activities, or Data Management Basic Interest Scales (BISs).

When considering this decision, clients should be encouraged to examine their scores on both the female and male Research & Development Manager scales, because the technical disciplines represented in the two samples are somewhat different. The women's sample contains relatively more technical managers from the life sciences; in the men's sample engineers comprise the majority of managers. Counselors should familiarize themselves with the descriptions of these samples (see Appendix A) and choose the scale that provides the best comparison for a given client.

Some employees with technical training who are considering a managerial track might be interested in general management positions involving responsibility for broad-based projects and supervision of many different kinds of employees, not just technical workers. Support for this direction would be evidenced by high scores on the Enterprising General Occupational Theme (GOT) and on some of the BISs within that Theme, particularly the Organizational Management scale. Note that people in general management positions in technically driven organizations, however, may have high scores on some of the scales in the Investigative or Realistic areas, as do technical employees. The latter, however, will generally not exhibit a high score on the Enterprising Theme.

To briefly digress, the combination of Investigative and Enterprising interests found in general managers in technical fields is noteworthy from the point of view of Holland's theory because these two Themes are diametrically opposed on the hexagon. Holland hypothesized that such opposing interests often result in internal conflict about which interests to pursue or lead to job dissatisfaction since it is difficult to find jobs combining both themes. Becoming a technical manager, or a general manager in a technical organization, could offer a viable solution in the case of diametrically opposed interests. (Other occupations that could offer outlets for these two hypothetically opposed interests include Business professor, Financial planner, and Software manager.)

To illustrate how the *Strong* may be useful in helping clients decide between technical and management careers, consider the case of a very productive research scientist with a large industrial manufacturing firm. His good work was noticed by his supervisors, who "rewarded" him by starting him on a management track. Although his performance was satisfactory as head of a small research team, his evaluations suffered when he was put in charge of an entire department. He resented the time spent on administrative tasks and missed working in the lab. Eventually he decided to participate in the company's career development program, which included administration of the *Strong*.

His *Strong* results showed high scores on the Investigative Theme, the Science and Mathematics BISs, and on numerous I-Theme OSs (e.g., Geologist, Biologist, Chemist, Physicist, Mathematician, and College Professor). These scores all supported his interest in a career as a research scientist. Furthermore, his low score on the R & D Manager scale, along with low scores on scales in all the Enterprising areas, helped him understand his increased dissatisfaction as he moved into a management track. As he examined his Profile, he realized that his position as a manager did not adequately allow him to satisfy his scientific interests. He concluded that a return to the lab would be a better solution to his dissatisfaction than would be a mid-career change to a new occupation.

Three of the Personal Style Scales may also be useful for career development counseling with technical professionals. One of these scales, Leadership Style, can be used to determine whether or not the client is interested in taking an outgoing, directive approach to leading that might be more typical of a person in a general management position, particularly in a large organization, than it would of a researcher who may provide scientific leadership in a specific area. Another scale, Work Style, may also be useful with those scoring toward the works with ideas/data/things pole, suggesting that such people prefer a technical track; those scoring toward the works with people pole may find more opportunities to express their interests in supervisory or management positions. A third scale, Learning Environment, may also be useful, since it is particularly important for those developing along a technical track to continually improve or update their technical knowledge and skills. Those scoring toward the academic pole will be interested in learning for its own sake and in keeping up with the latest developments in their field. A technical person scoring toward the practical pole may be better suited for implementing—or managing the implementation of—new ideas, products, or services created by others.

Career Plateauing

As stated earlier, in the economic environment of the 1990s, career development can no longer be equated with moving up in an organization (Gutteridge et al., 1993). As a consequence, more people are reaching "plateaus" in their careers and are doing so at a younger age than ever before. A plateau is reached when an employee has gone as far as she or he can go in an organization. Because of limited opportunities for advancement, this employee has nothing to look forward to but years of performing the same tasks over and over. Unless addressed through human resource planning, plateauing can be detrimental to both the individual and the organization. The employee's motivation and satisfaction deteriorate, while the organization suffers lower productivity and a dearth of employees able to keep the organization vital and growing.

Some organizations deal with career plateauing by structuring rewards for lateral, or even downward, movement in the organization. Rewards may include monetary incentives in the form of raises similar to those accompanying promotions, opportunities to learn new skills or to lead temporary project teams or task forces, responsibility for high-profile projects, or the chance to work in an area more congruent with one's interests (Hall, 1986). Such efforts, sometimes referred to as job enrichment programs, seek to enhance the impact of an individual's contribution to the organization and benefit both the organization and the individual.

The *Strong* can be useful in helping employees who have reached a plateau to identify alternative activities, projects, or entire career paths that fit their interests. These interests can then be matched with opportunities within the organization or can be used to identify alternatives outside the organization that might provide a better match for the employees' interests. The following case illustrates a client who reached a plateau and was unable to find satisfactory alternative opportunities within the organization.

Client 1. Upon receiving her doctorate, Client 1 (see Figure 12.1), a psychologist, took a position with a consulting firm whose specialty was assessment for

STRONG INTEREST INVENTORY

Profile report for CLIENT 1
ID:
Age:
Gender: Female
Date tested:
Date scored:

Page 1 of 6

SNAPSHOT: A SUMMARY OF RESULTS FOR CLIENT 1

GENERAL OCCUPATIONAL THEMES

The General Occupational Themes describe interests in six very broad areas, including interest in work and leisure activities, kinds of people, and work settings. Your interests in each area are shown at the right in rank order. Note that each Theme has a code, represented by the first letter of the Theme name.

You can use your Theme code, printed below your results, to identify school subjects, part-time jobs, college majors, leisure activities, or careers that you might find interesting. See the back of this Profile for suggestions on how to use your Theme code.

Theme Code	Theme	Very Little Interest	Little Interest	Average Interest	High Interest	Very High Interest	Typical Interests
C	CONVENTIONAL				✓		Accounting, processing data
S	SOCIAL			✓			Helping, instructing
E	ENTERPRISING			✓			Selling, managing
I	INVESTIGATIVE			✓			Researching, analyzing
R	REALISTIC		✓				Building, repairing
A	ARTISTIC	✓					Creating or enjoying art

Your Theme code is CSE—(see explanation at left).
You might explore occupations with codes that contain any combination of these letters.

BASIC INTEREST SCALES

The Basic Interest Scales measure your interests in 25 specific areas or activities. Only those 5 areas in which you show the *most* interest are listed at the right in rank order. Your results on all 25 Basic Interest Scales are found on page 2.

To the left of each scale is a letter that shows which of the six General Occupational Themes this activity is most closely related to. These codes can help you to identify other activities that you may enjoy.

Theme Code	Basic Interests	Very Little Interest	Little Interest	Average Interest	High Interest	Very High Interest	Typical Activities
E	PUBLIC SPEAKING					✓	Persuading or influencing people
E	SOCIAL SERVICE				✓		Helping people
E	LAW/POLITICS				✓		Discussing laws and public policies
C	OFFICE SERVICES				✓		Performing clerical and office tasks
E	ORGANIZATIONAL MANAGEMENT				✓		Managing or supervising others

OCCUPATIONAL SCALES

The Occupational Scales measure how similar your interests are to the interests of people who are satisfied working in those occupations. Only the 10 scales on which your interests are *most* similar to those of these people are listed at the right in rank order. Your results on all 211 of the Occupational Scales are found on pages 3, 4, and 5.

The letters to the left of each scale identify the Theme or Themes that most closely describe the interests of people working in that occupation. You can use these letters to find additional, related occupations that you might find interesting. After reviewing your results on all six pages of this Profile, see the back of page 5 for tips on finding other occupations in the Theme or Themes that interest you the most.

Theme Code	Occupation	Very Dissimilar	Dissimilar	Mid-Range	Similar	Very Similar
EAS	HUMAN RESOURCES DIRECTOR					✓
AES	CORPORATE TRAINER					✓
A	LAWYER					✓
EA	MARKETING EXECUTIVE					✓
SEA	SCHOOL ADMINISTRATOR					✓
CE	PARALEGAL					✓
AER	PUBLIC ADMINISTRATOR					✓
AE	PUBLIC RELATIONS DIRECTOR				✓	
A	LIBRARIAN				✓	
SEA	SOCIAL SCIENCE TEACHER				✓	

***PERSONAL STYLE SCALES** measure your levels of comfort regarding Work Style, Learning Environment, Leadership Style, and Risk Taking/Adventure. This information may help you make decisions about particular work environments, educational settings, and types of activities you would find satisfying. Your results on these four scales are on page 6.*

CPP CONSULTING PSYCHOLOGISTS PRESS, INC. • 3803 E. Bayshore Road, Palo Alto, CA 94303

Figure 12.1 Snapshot for Client 1, a Small Business Owner

selection and management development. This position allowed her to pursue her interests in applied psychology. For the first few years she enjoyed her duties, which primarily involved conducting and writing formal psychological assessments. One of the reasons she enjoyed this job was that she was able to learn many new skills. After four or five years, however, she began to feel that she was doing the same thing over and over and was not learning anything new. Her motivation, both initially and subsequently, was consistent with her score on the Learning Environment scale (60), which indicated that she enjoyed learning for its own sake. Client 1 discussed her dissatisfaction with her employer, and they decided that she could experiment with some other tasks in the firm, such as training and conducting workshops. When it became clear, however, that these activities were not valued and reinforced, she realized that she had reached a plateau in her career and began to consider other options, such as opening her own business.

Client 1's scores on the GOTs, BISs, and OSs all showed a high degree of interest in activities and occupations related to public speaking, training, human resources, and social service. Her score of 33 (mid-range) on the Psychologist scale also helped confirm her decision to leave her job. Another pattern of results confirmed her interest in running a business: her scores of "Similar" on the Small Business Owner scale and "High Interest" on the Organizational Management and Office Services scales, the similarity of her interests to quite a few of the OSs in the Conventional Theme, and her scores toward the right poles of the Work Style and Leadership Style

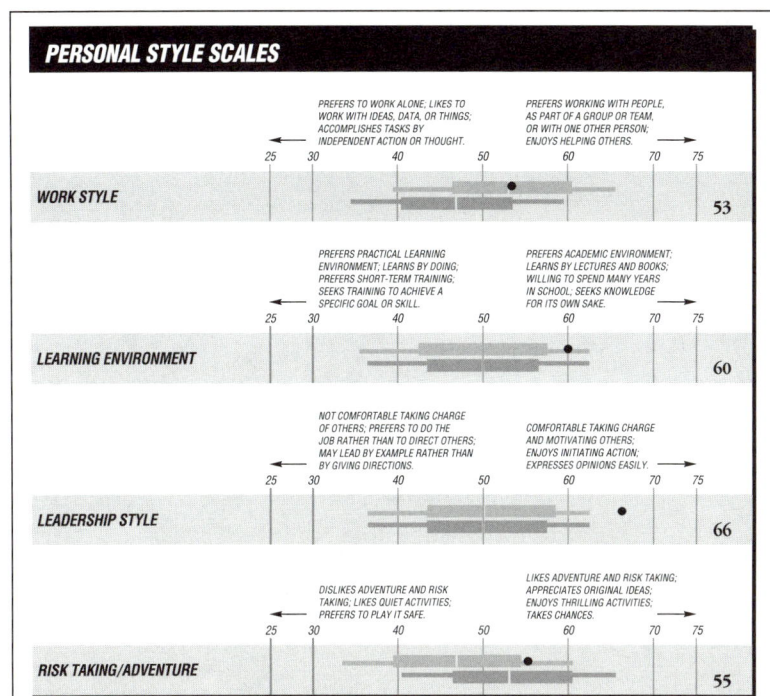

Figure 12.1 (continued) Personal Style Scales for Client 1, a Small Business Owner

scales. Her score on the Risk Taking/Adventure scale suggested that although she was somewhat interested in taking risks, she probably would not jump precipitously into a new area. After carefully researching the financial implications of running a small business, she did successfully open her own training and consulting firm.

Career Change

Although issues of career change are related to issues of career development, it is useful to discuss the former separately. Career change is often more dramatic than career development since it can involve relocation, family issues, and financial concerns. The following issues associated with career change can be addressed with use of the *Strong*:

▲ the reasons why people seek to change careers,
▲ the limitations of congruence between interests and work as a career change goal,
▲ obstacles typically encountered by those seeking a career change,
▲ differentiating between career and job dissatisfaction, and
▲ career change as part of a larger life-style reassessment.

Reasons for Career Change

Although individuals have a multitude of reasons for changing careers (see Table 12.3), research has suggested that an important, if not *the* most important, reason is the desire to find a job that is more congruent with their interests (Perosa & Perosa, 1984; Thomas, 1980). Gottfredson (1979), using a nationally representative sample of employed men, found that those who were employed in jobs congruent with their aspirations rose from 43 percent at age 16 to 84 percent at age 28. (As Gottfredson points out, however, such congruence can be achieved through either a change in jobs or a change in aspirations.) These findings suggest that the *Strong* can be useful to career changers, both to help them initially choose careers that are good matches for their interests and to help them make an informed change when they decide to do so. Voluminous research and extensive professional practice have demonstrated the value of this approach in helping career clients.

Limitations of Congruence

Counselors should not, however, view congruence as the exclusive goal of career counseling. Although a basic tenet of career theory and practice, this principle—if taken too far or too literally—may influence the client to adopt an "if only I can find the 'right' job, then everything will be all right" perspective and to assume too passive a role in the career search process. Current career theories acknowledge the inherent limitations of the congruency approach and emphasize the need to go beyond a simplistic matching of people with jobs.

It is important to recognize that individuals can also mold or shape their jobs to fit their personal style (Nicholson & West, 1989). Chartrand (1991) notes that counselors should help clients realize that they can proactively shape their jobs to achieve a better match with their interests. For example, a person who scores toward the works with people pole on the Work Style scale might seek out more opportunities to join teams or work groups. Others whose *Strong* results do not closely match the interests of their immediate peers might volunteer for new tasks or accept responsibilities that are not directly related to their job descriptions but that offer an opportunity to work on a project more in line with their interests. Entirely new jobs can be, and have been, created in this manner as organizations have realized the benefits of letting employees work at tasks in which they have a high degree of interest.

It is also possible to achieve career satisfaction, and success, in a job by *not* "fitting in." This scenario can occur when an employee's personal characteristics complement, rather than match, those of others already in the occupation. Such employees can bring important new perspectives or skills to a job. To succeed, however, these "misfits" may need to work harder to carve out a place for themselves—for example, by finding a group of supportive colleagues, by altering the tasks they perform, or perhaps by arranging to do some work at home. When interpreting the *Strong*, counselors should not focus exclusively on congruence as a career goal but may need to help clients see that there are other options, including adapting the job to fit his or her interests and contributing by being different.

Obstacles to Career Change

Although the desire for a better match between interests and job duties is the primary motivation for most career changers, a number of circumstances, real or perceived, can prevent or delay such changes. The *Strong* can be used to help clients overcome some of these obstacles (see Table 12.4).

The primary obstacles for some career changers are their own beliefs about themselves and about the world of work. Inappropriate belief structures can,

Table 12.3 Reasons for a Making a Career Change

Find a job more congruent with values and interests.

Find a way to express formerly denied or undervalued aspects of self.

Reassess major life roles.

Gain more time for recreation.

Become more active after dependent children leave home.

Seek a lost dream.

Turn a hobby into a career.

Accommodate health problems.

Reduce stress or the effects of burnout.

Find another job after being laid off or fired.

Fulfill a desire to relocate.

Make more money.

Gain prestige or status.

Gain greater security.

in turn, lead to unrealistic vocational aspirations (Salomone & McKenna, 1982). To help identify how a client's beliefs might influence a career decision, counselors can use the *Career Beliefs Inventory* (CBI) (Krumboltz, 1991) in conjunction with the *Strong*. The CBI consists of 25 scales, each of which identifies a belief that may prevent an individual from achieving his or her career goals or taking action toward those goals. For example, one CBI scale distinguishes between a belief that it is better not to try if failure is possible and a belief that it is better to try hard despite possible failure. Although the CBI manual suggests using the instrument at the beginning of career counseling (Krumboltz, 1991), it is often useful with clients *after* they have taken the *Strong*, identified a clear pattern of interests, but then become blocked in career exploration.

Lack of finances can be a major obstacle to mid-career change (Neapolitan, 1980). Many career changers face the possibility of a significant loss of income; in addition, the costs of retraining or further education can be prohibitive. Social conditions, such as high unemployment rates or technological change within a given industry, can also increase the risks associated with career change. The Risk Taking/Adventure scale of the *Strong* can be useful in helping clients identify how much risk they are willing to undertake in a career change. Although not designed to identify specific risks, results of the Risk Taking/

Table 12.4 Obstacles to a Career Change
Beliefs
Financial problems (possible reduction in salary)
Dependent children
Cost or time involved in education
Unwillingness to take risks
Doubts about skills or abilities
Unwillingness to relocate to a new geographic area
Limited ability to see self in a new role

Adventure scale can provide a stimulus to discuss the client's feelings regarding risk. Those with scores toward the plays it safe pole often prefer a "play it safe" approach to the world. ("Play it safe" is an item on the scale that, if endorsed, will move the client's score toward the plays it safe pole.) In fact, the career dissatisfaction of those with extreme scores toward the plays it safe pole may have to reach intolerable levels before they are willing to move to a new career. In counseling, these individuals often ask for assurances from the counselor that the risk will be worth it. For others with less extreme scores, their feelings about risk may not necessarily prevent them from taking a chance, but any major steps will need to be carefully researched and considered.

Sometimes people are deterred from making a career change because of doubts about their ability to succeed in a new area (Vaitenas & Wiener, 1977). Some doubt their abilities because they are unfamiliar with alternative occupations in which their present skills could be used (Frederickson, Macy, & Vicker, 1978). For example, a teacher who claimed she would "quit teaching today" if she could be assured "smashing success" in her dream occupation as a lawyer hesitated to pursue her ambitions when she realized such assurances were not forthcoming (Perosa & Perosa, 1987).

Counseling interventions with clients who are reluctant to take risks may focus on helping them clarify the exact nature of the risks involved and to develop contingency plans to deal with the risks. Perosa and Perosa (1984) suggest that counselors encourage and help such clients identify the risks involved in *not* changing. *Strong* results from the OSs can be useful in helping such clients discover realistic alternatives that match their interests. In addition, understanding that their interests are similar to those of others satisfactorily employed in a given occupation can diminish the perception of risk and help these clients move toward personal change.

Career Dissatisfaction or Job Dissatisfaction?

When counseling potential career changers, it is important that the counselor probe in some detail about the source of the dissatisfaction that has prompted the client to consider a change. In some cases, the problem may be that the person is dissatisfied with specific facets of his or her current job, rather than dissatisfied with his or her career. (The person's current career may be congruent with his or her interests.) Job dissatisfaction can arise as a result of, for example, the desire for a better salary, poor relationships with co-workers or a boss, or geographic location. A client who is dissatisfied for these reasons may be disappointed when *Strong* results confirm his or her current career choice. However, such a client's Profile may also offer clues about how to change the job environment to achieve greater satisfaction without making a major career change.

The solution to job satisfaction may be as simple as a transfer down the hall or to a different division, or it may involve greater specialization. For example, a tax accountant was dissatisfied with her job, although her scores on the Accountant and other OSs confirmed that her interests were similar to those of her colleagues. However, since this client's Work Style scale indicated a strong preference toward working with people and she had a high score on the Investigative Theme, she decided to explore different subspecialties within the field of accounting, such as financial planning and consultation. Discussion of her *Strong* results led her to consider working for a consulting firm, where she would be more likely to find opportunities to satisfy her interests in working with others while using her financial and analytical skills.

Life-Style Issues

As suggested in Table 12.3, people's reasons for changing careers are often intertwined with broader issues or concerns about life-style. Increasingly, careers are viewed as a combination of work and leisure activities that evolve throughout one's life (McDaniels, 1984). In one study of career changers, about half of the subjects indicated they changed careers because of a desire for more balance in their lives: 26 percent said they wanted to spend more time with their families, while 23 percent wanted more time for recreation (Thomas, 1980).

Research has shown that clients are most satisfied when counseling helps resolve both vocational and personal problems (Nevo, 1990). For clients who are reassessing their career in relation to their life-style, administering the *Salience Inventory* (Nevill & Super, 1986a) and *Values Scale* (Nevill & Super, 1986b) in conjunction with the *Strong* may be useful. The *Salience Inventory* measures the client's investment in five possible roles: worker, homemaker, student, citizen, and leisurite. A client who is moving away from a primary concentration on work can identify other roles in which to invest time and energy. The *Values Scale* is scored for 21 values, each of which could be used to evaluate occupational or leisure alternatives identified by the *Strong*. Use of these instruments with the *Strong* can expand career counseling into what might be called "life-style" counseling.

Career change and the consideration of alternative life-styles is sometimes motivated by a desire to avoid burnout or "workaholic" patterns. Although people of any of the six vocational types can experience burnout, those with a high score on the Investigative Theme may be particularly prone to overwork. These individuals may spend so many hours on the job that they have no time left for leisure pursuits (Hansen, 1988). A counselor's suggestion that they make a special effort to incorporate family, friends, and leisure into their routine can help clients with high interest in the Investigative area to feel better understood and also motivate them to achieve a greater balance between work and play.

When using the *Strong* to help clients explore a more balanced life-style, it may help to recognize that leisure activities can either complement or supplement vocational interests (Hansen, 1990). Complementary leisure activities are those that satisfy the same basic interests as do the person's work activities, as is often the case with the Investigative types described earlier. Supplementary leisure activities, in contrast, are those that offer opportunities to do something entirely different or to expand one's experience. Career counseling around life-style issues often involves helping clients identify supplementary leisure activities.

The GOTs and the BISs may be helpful for those seeking a change that would permit them to achieve a better balance in their life roles. Clients often feel relieved when they see a high score on a BIS that captures a particular avocational or leisure interest. This confirmation is sometimes all the prompting they need to pursue their interest further.

Outplacement

Growth of the outplacement industry has mirrored changes in the American economy, as more workers find themselves forced to change jobs. Whereas outplacement services were once the exclusive province of high-level executives, many corporations now make such services available to all employees leaving the company, primarily in the form of group workshops. A large-scale survey showed that over half of the companies that downsized offered outplacement services (Mirvis, 1993). Although some programs are limited to helping former employees prepare resumes, most provide some kind of self-assessment measure designed to help the employee identify occupational alternatives. Many outplacement firms use the *Strong* to assess the interests of such clients.

The majority of individuals who use outplacement services do so because they are leaving an organization involuntarily. Employees undergoing forced career changes are likely to experience shock or disbelief and high levels of frustration, anxiety, or depression as they deal with losing their jobs (Perosa & Perosa, 1987). For this reason, it is important to offer vocational counseling as well as some personal counseling. In consideration of the client's emotional state at the beginning of the outplacement process, the counselor should carefully time administration of the *Strong* or any other self-assessment measure. This planning decreases the likelihood that a negative mood or self-doubts resulting from the job loss will "contaminate" the client's responses to the *Strong*. Most counselors deal with this situation by first allowing time for the client to deal with the shock of being unemployed. It is important not to wait too long, however, since most outplacement clients are eager to take concrete steps toward finding a new job and view taking an interest inventory as one such step.

A flat or depressed Profile, or a low "Like" response percentage in the "Your Characteristics" section of the *Strong*, may be an indication that the client's mood may have negatively influenced her or his responses. When the outplacement client's "Like" response percentage is below about 30 percent, the counselor should be aware of the possibility that the *Strong* may have been administered prematurely. In this case, dealing with the client's feelings about being released and then readministering the instrument may be necessary.

After taking the *Strong*, either in a group workshop or counseling setting, clients can identify the job skills necessary for those occupations on the Profile for which they scored high. They can then determine their transferable skills and prepare a career plan that utilizes those skills. For example, at one outplacement program conducted by a large bank, the *Strong* confirmed the interests of a man who had served as a bank branch manager until his position was terminated. What he had enjoyed most about the job was using his computer skills to research new business development possibilities; this interest, along with his *Strong* scores, prompted him to apply these skills by forming his own software company ("Wells Fargo," 1991).

The *Strong* Professional Report, first published in 1993 and revised in 1994, is used in outplacement for clients at the managerial or professional level (Hammer, 1993). This report is designed for people seeking jobs that typically require a four-year college degree for entry. These clients could be those who already have a bachelor's or advanced degree and who want a position that will utilize their education, or clients who are willing to acquire the necessary education. The report lists the client's scores for all of the professional occupations. In addition, the client's scores are used to compute a professional Occupational Scales code that in turn provides (1) a list of additional professional occupations not found on the *Strong* and (2) a description of how an individual of that vocational type might behave in an organization, including information on management style, contributions to an organization, and preferred working environment.

Many outplacement clients, especially those who are taking advantage of early retirement programs, view their termination as an opportunity, provided they are not facing a financial crisis. Unemployment may provide a chance to spend more time with their families, engage in leisure activities, begin second careers, return to school, or even start their own businesses. The desire to start a business currently is so pervasive that many firms have special outplacement services designed to help clients with this interest analyze the feasibility of their ideas and prepare business plans.

The *Strong* can be a useful tool in helping clients decide whether or not to pursue a career as an entrepreneur. Scores on the Enterprising GOT, on some of the BISs within that Theme, and on the Small Business Owner OS would be expected to be high among entrepreneurs. The results on the Risk Taking/Adventure scale can provide a valuable springboard for discussion of risks involved in starting out on one's own. The Work Style scale can help clients identify potential obstacles to starting their own business. Those who prefer to work with ideas, data, or things may actually enjoy the long, solitary struggle that is often part of starting a business, although their work style may keep them from making the marketing efforts needed to succeed. Those scoring toward the works with people pole, in contrast, may become frustrated by their lack of contact with others; these individuals will have to make the effort to establish an active network of friends or colleagues with whom they can discuss their business.

Training and Education

The *Strong* can be used to help adults identify training opportunities congruent with their interests. Such opportunities could involve retraining for outplaced employees, advanced technical training to keep up with changes in a fast growing field, or management training to broaden or refine managerial skills. For people whose jobs have been eliminated due to technological changes or other economic developments, the *Strong* may be helpful in identifying retraining programs congruent with the person's interests and preferred learning style. Conveying to such clients that retraining does not necessarily mean moving away from one's field of interest can be comforting. The Learning Environment scale can help clients identify the most appropriate learning environment for further vocational training.

Recognizing the value of workers who can keep up with changes in a global economy, some corporations and government agencies have created in-house training programs that range from basic skill-building courses to advanced workshops for professional employees. Other companies contract with established educational institutions to provide training. Universities alone drew over 38,000 managers to advanced education courses in 1992; recent estimates suggest that corporations now budget about $30 billion a year for training activities, of which about $6 billion is spent on training managers (Fuchsberg, 1993).

Regardless of where the training takes place, those who provide the instruction need to accommodate the wide variety of learning styles characteristic of adult learners (Gutteridge et al., 1993). The Learning Environment scale can be useful in helping individuals choose among educational options as well as in helping educators tailor programs to the individuals' preferred learning environments. Those individuals with high scores toward the academic pole of this scale would be expected to prefer a learning environment in which the theoretical underpinnings of the field are presented along with the latest research and that use a lecture or independent reading format. These kinds of students would also probably enjoy the opportunity to discuss and debate current topics of interest. A university setting might provide such an environment. A client scoring toward the practical pole, in contrast, would probably prefer an applied program, such as one that offers on-the-job training.

It is also possible, however, that learners scoring toward opposite poles of the Learning Environment scale will choose the same general learning environment, although they will probably do so for different reasons, and may pursue different paths within that environment. For example, suppose two mid-career managers with different scores on the Learning Environment scale enrolled in the same MBA program. The manager with the score toward the academic pole might be interested in the theory of organizations and pursue an organizational behavior track, with the possibility of continuing on for a doctorate later. The manager with the score toward the practical pole might have elected to pursue an MBA because this credential would improve chances for advancement. Thus, interpretation of the *Strong* must take into account the goals and objectives of the individuals.

MBA students provide a good example of how the *Strong* may be useful in training and educational settings. Many of these students are adults who have returned to school after experience in the workforce. The typical MBA student, according to surveys at two major business schools, is 27 years old and has worked for two to seven years before entering the program ("Wharton," 1991). A number of programs administer the *Strong* (and the MBTI) to all students near the beginning of their program to help them plan their course work and identify the kind of industries in which they may be interested in working. A group Profile prepared for one MBA class, using the 1985 version of the *Strong*, showed that the students' three highest Themes were Enterprising, Artistic, and Investigative. The highest BISs were Adventure, Business Management, Mathematics, Law/Politics, Public Speaking, and Athletics. Two of the highest OSs were Investments Manager and Marketing Executive ("Wharton," 1991).

Strong results can be used during individual placement interviews with MBAs and other students to help them make the best job match. For example, one MBA student who took the 1985 *Strong* scored low on the Academic Comfort scale and the Investigative Theme and had other scores that indicated a liking for structure and organization. He accepted a position with a fast-growing biotechnology firm where he had to work closely with scientists and physicians (who tend to score high on the Investigative Theme and on scales indicating a dislike of structure). Although the potential mismatch between his interests and chosen work environment was pointed out at a placement interview before he left the MBA program, he persisted on pursuing this job. Within three months he had experienced the mismatch for himself and within another three months had moved to a more traditional firm. Even this man's decision-making process was consistent with his *Strong* results: individuals who score low on Academic Comfort characteristically prefer to learn through experience ("Stanford," 1991).

A twenty-year longitudinal study of the career progress of male MBA students from a prestigious business school, using an early version of the *Strong Vocational Interest Blanks (SVIB)*, found that on average, half of those graduating with MBAs had more than one employer within the first five years. The researchers observed a steady movement out of large companies and into small businesses. Those who moved into small businesses tended to hold more positions overall and to have scored lower on the Personnel Director scale than did those who became general managers in large corporations. Those who were earning the highest compensation after twenty years had scored higher on the *SVIB* scales of Managerial Orientation and Sales Manager and lower on the Engineer scale. High scores on the Sales Manager scale were also related to self-perception of success after twenty years (Harrell & Harrell, 1984). This study is evidence that occupational behavior can be predicted from *Strong* results even over a twenty-year period.

Retirement

The *Strong* can be useful in helping adult clients plan for retirement. Research has shown that those who begin retirement planning as early as mid-career are more likely to have a smooth transition into retirement than are those who have neglected to identify their leisure options (Kragie, Gerstein, & Lichtman, 1989). The *Strong* is well suited to helping clients investigate retirement options, since it includes a section of items that asks people to indicate their liking for various activities such as golf, skiing, and art galleries. Research shows that leisure activities can be predicted by *Strong* scores for these items (Cairo, 1979; Varca & Shaffer, 1982). Leisure or avocational interests can also be directly suggested by scores on the GOTs and the BISs. The suggestions in the *Strong* Leisure Report are based on clients' scores for these scales.

For some, retirement is a chance to change directions—to engage in those activities or pursue those interests that have been neglected or put off for many years. For others, retirement activities are a continuation of their vocational interests but with the opportunity to work autonomously at their own pace. As discussed in the outplacement section, the *Strong* can be used to identify supplementary interests (those that offer opportunities to do something entirely different) or complementary interests (those that satisfy the same basic interests as the person's work activities did) (Hansen, 1990).

Client 2. The case of Client 2, a 71-year-old retired architect, illustrates how both supplementary and complementary interests can be combined in retirement planning. Client 2 had originally attended music school but then became an architect because he was not able to support a family as a musician. He enjoyed his work and had a successful career lasting 40 years. Upon retiring, however, he was undecided as to how he wanted to spend his time and so consulted a counselor specializing in retirement counseling. His results (shown in Figure 12.2) showed "Very High Interest" in the Artistic GOT as well on the Music/Dramatics, Art, Applied Arts, and Social Service BISs. He also showed "High Interest" in the Social GOT and the Religious Activities BIS.

Although his scores on most of the OSs in the Artistic Theme were "Similar" or above, Client 2 was most struck by his score on the Musician scale. He had maintained his interest in music and played trombone in a neighborhood group. It was not without some sense of wondering "what if" (he had pursued his original training) that Client 2 decided to focus his energy in retirement on mastering his instrument. In addition, he used his results on the other *Strong* scales to plan his retirement so that he could pursue these other interests: working with a church group to help others, reading literature, and attending symphony concerts.

Conclusion

The *Strong* has proved useful with a wide variety of adult career concerns, including career development, career change, retraining, and retirement. Although these applications have been extensive, research with adults has lagged behind. Compared with studies of college students, relatively few studies of the effects of career counseling on adults have been published in the professional literature (Oliver & Spokane, 1988). More outcome studies are needed to demonstrate the most effective methods of using the *Strong* with adults in various circumstances.

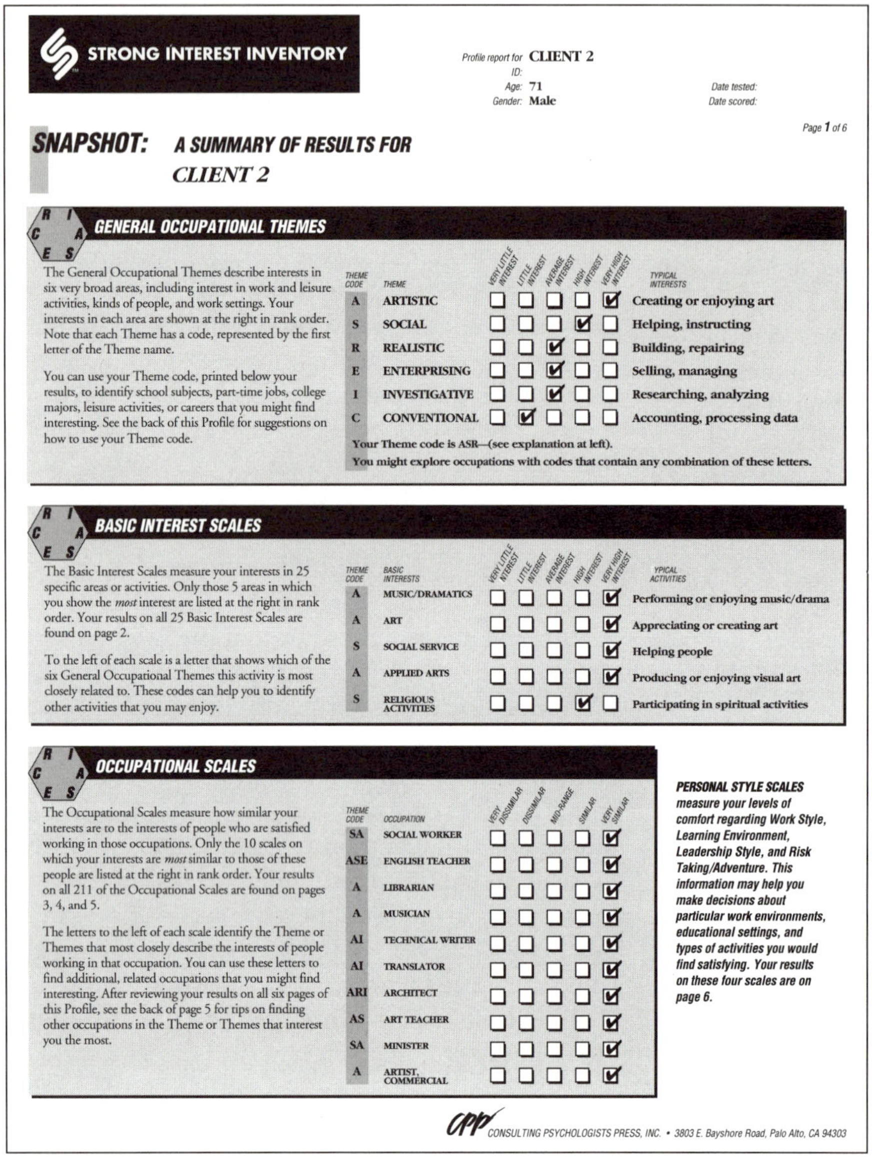

STRONG INTEREST INVENTORY

Profile report for CLIENT 2
ID:
Age: 71
Gender: Male
Date tested:
Date scored:

Page 1 of 6

SNAPSHOT: A SUMMARY OF RESULTS FOR CLIENT 2

GENERAL OCCUPATIONAL THEMES

The General Occupational Themes describe interests in six very broad areas, including interest in work and leisure activities, kinds of people, and work settings. Your interests in each area are shown at the right in rank order. Note that each Theme has a code, represented by the first letter of the Theme name.

You can use your Theme code, printed below your results, to identify school subjects, part-time jobs, college majors, leisure activities, or careers that you might find interesting. See the back of this Profile for suggestions on how to use your Theme code.

Theme Code	Theme	Very Little Interest	Little Interest	Average Interest	High Interest	Very High Interest	Typical Interests
A	ARTISTIC	☐	☐	☐	☐	☑	Creating or enjoying art
S	SOCIAL	☐	☐	☐	☑	☐	Helping, instructing
R	REALISTIC	☐	☐	☑	☐	☐	Building, repairing
E	ENTERPRISING	☐	☐	☑	☐	☐	Selling, managing
I	INVESTIGATIVE	☐	☐	☑	☐	☐	Researching, analyzing
C	CONVENTIONAL	☐	☑	☐	☐	☐	Accounting, processing data

Your Theme code is ASR—(see explanation at left).
You might explore occupations with codes that contain any combination of these letters.

BASIC INTEREST SCALES

The Basic Interest Scales measure your interests in 25 specific areas or activities. Only those 5 areas in which you show the *most* interest are listed at the right in rank order. Your results on all 25 Basic Interest Scales are found on page 2.

To the left of each scale is a letter that shows which of the six General Occupational Themes this activity is most closely related to. These codes can help you to identify other activities that you may enjoy.

Theme Code	Basic Interests	Very Little Interest	Little Interest	Average Interest	High Interest	Very High Interest	Typical Activities
A	MUSIC/DRAMATICS	☐	☐	☐	☐	☑	Performing or enjoying music/drama
A	ART	☐	☐	☐	☐	☑	Appreciating or creating art
S	SOCIAL SERVICE	☐	☐	☐	☐	☑	Helping people
A	APPLIED ARTS	☐	☐	☐	☐	☑	Producing or enjoying visual art
S	RELIGIOUS ACTIVITIES	☐	☐	☐	☑	☐	Participating in spiritual activities

OCCUPATIONAL SCALES

The Occupational Scales measure how similar your interests are to the interests of people who are satisfied working in those occupations. Only the 10 scales on which your interests are *most* similar to those of these people are listed at the right in rank order. Your results on all 211 of the Occupational Scales are found on pages 3, 4, and 5.

The letters to the left of each scale identify the Theme or Themes that most closely describe the interests of people working in that occupation. You can use these letters to find additional, related occupations that you might find interesting. After reviewing your results on all six pages of this Profile, see the back of page 5 for tips on finding other occupations in the Theme or Themes that interest you the most.

Theme Code	Occupation	Very Dissimilar	Dissimilar	Mid-Range	Similar	Very Similar
SA	SOCIAL WORKER	☐	☐	☐	☐	☑
ASE	ENGLISH TEACHER	☐	☐	☐	☐	☑
A	LIBRARIAN	☐	☐	☐	☐	☑
A	MUSICIAN	☐	☐	☐	☐	☑
AI	TECHNICAL WRITER	☐	☐	☐	☐	☑
AI	TRANSLATOR	☐	☐	☐	☐	☑
ARI	ARCHITECT	☐	☐	☐	☐	☑
AS	ART TEACHER	☐	☐	☐	☐	☑
SA	MINISTER	☐	☐	☐	☐	☑
A	ARTIST, COMMERCIAL	☐	☐	☐	☐	☑

***PERSONAL STYLE SCALES** measure your levels of comfort regarding Work Style, Learning Environment, Leadership Style, and Risk Taking/Adventure. This information may help you make decisions about particular work environments, educational settings, and types of activities you would find satisfying. Your results on these four scales are on page 6.*

CPP CONSULTING PSYCHOLOGISTS PRESS, INC. • 3803 E. Bayshore Road, Palo Alto, CA 94303

Figure 12.2 Snapshot for Client 2, a Retired Architect

References

Cairo, P. C. (1979). The validity of the Holland Basic Interest Scales of the Strong Vocational Interest Blank: Leisure activities versus occupational membership as criteria. *Journal of Vocational Behavior, 15*, 68–77.

Chartrand, J. M. (1991). The evolution of trait-and-factor career counseling: A person x environment fit approach. *Journal of Counseling and Development, 69*, 518–524.

Data base links employees' interests to real jobs. (1989, Spring). *Strong Forum, 6*(1), 2.

Frederickson, R. H., Macy, F. U., & Vicker, D. (1978). Barriers to adult career change. *Personnel and Guidance Journal, 57*, 166–169.

Fuchsberg, G. (1993, September 10). Taking control. *Wall Street Journal*, pp. R1–R4.

Gottfredson, G. D., & Holland, J. L. (1989). *Dictionary of Holland occupational codes* (2nd ed.). Odessa, FL: Psychological Assessment Resources.

Gottfredson, L. S. (1979). Aspiration-job match: Age trends in a large, nationally representative sample of young white men. *Journal of Counseling Psychology, 26*(4), 319–328.

Gutteridge, T. G., Leibowitz, Z. B., & Shore, J. E. (1993). *Organizational career development. Benchmarks for building a world-class workforce.* San Francisco: Jossey-Bass.

Hall, D. T. (1986). Breaking career routines: Midcareer choice and identity development. In D. T. Hall (Ed.), *Career development in organizations* (pp. 120–159). San Francisco: Jossey-Bass.

Hammer A. L. (Ed.). (1990). *Strong Interest Inventory topical reports manual.* Palo Alto, CA: Consulting Psychologists Press.

Hammer, A. L. (1993). *Strong Interest Inventory Professional Report guide*. Palo Alto, CA: Consulting Psychologists Press.

Hansen, J. C. (1988). *Leisure topical report for the Strong Interest Inventory*. Palo Alto, CA: Consulting Psychologists Press.

Hansen, J. C. (1990). *Leisure Report*. In A. L. Hammer (Ed.), *Strong Interest Inventory topical reports manual* (pp. 3–4). Palo Alto, CA: Consulting Psychologists Press.

Harrell, T. W., & Harrell, M. S. (1984). *Stanford MBA careers: A 20 year longitudinal study* (Research paper No. 723). Graduate School of Business, Stanford University.

Kragie, E. R., Gerstein, M., & Lichtman, M. (1989). Do Americans plan for retirement? *The Career Development Quarterly, 37*, 232–239.

Krumboltz, J. D. (1991). *Manual for the Career Beliefs Inventory*. Palo Alto, CA: Consulting Psychologists Press.

McDaniels, C. (1984). Work and leisure in the career span. In N. C. Gysbers & Associates (Eds.), *Designing careers* (pp. 558–590). San Francisco: Jossey-Bass.

Mirvis, P. H. (Ed.). (1993). *Building the competitive workforce: Investing in human capital for corporate success*. New York: Wiley.

Neapolitan, J. (1980). Occupational change in mid-career: An exploratory investigation. *Journal of Vocational Behavior, 16*, 212–225.

Nevill, D. D., & Super, D. E. (1986a). *The Salience Inventory*. Palo Alto, CA: Consulting Psychologists Press.

Nevill, D. D., & Super, D. E. (1986b). *The Values Scale*. Palo Alto, CA: Consulting Psychologists Press.

Nevo, O. (1990). Career counseling from the counselee perspective: Analysis of feedback questionnaires. *The Career Development Quarterly, 38*, 314–324.

Nicholson, N., & West, M. (1989). Transitions, work histories, and careers. In M. B. Arthur, D. T. Hall, & B. S. Lawrence (Eds.), *Handbook of career theory* (pp. 181–201). Cambridge, England: Cambridge University Press.

Oliver, L., & Spokane, A. (1988). Career intervention outcome: What contributes to client gain? *Journal of Counseling Psychology, 35*, 447.

Pac Bell uses the *Strong* and MBTI for career growth and team building. (1990, Spring). *Strong Forum, 7*(1), 2.

Perosa, S. L., & Perosa, L. M. (1984). The mid-career crisis in relation to Super's career and Erikson's adult development theory. *International Journal of Aging and Human Development, 20*, 53–68.

Perosa, S. L., & Perosa, L. M. (1987). Strategies for counseling midcareer changers: A conceptual framework. *Journal of Counseling and Development, 65*, 558–561.

Salomone, P. R., & McKenna, P. (1982). Difficult career counseling cases: 1—Unrealistic vocational aspirations. *Personnel and Guidance Journal, 60*, 283–286.

Stanford uses the *Strong* and MBTI to help MBAs successfully market themselves. (1991, Fall). *Strong Forum, 8*(2), 1–2.

Strong assists high-tech employees. (1989, Spring). *Strong Forum, 6*(1), 1–2.

Strong and MBTI help revitalize employees. (1993, Spring). *Strong Forum, 10*(1), 1, 5.

Thomas, L. E. (1980). A typology of mid-life career changers. *Journal of Vocational Behavior, 16*, 173–182.

Vaitenas, R., & Wiener, Y. (1977). Developmental, emotional, and interest factors in voluntary mid-career change. *Journal of Vocational Behavior, 11*, 291–304.

Varca, P. E., & Shaffer, G. S. (1982). Holland's theory: Stability of avocational interests. *Journal of Vocational Behavior, 21*, 288–298.

Wells Fargo helps employees change careers. (1991, Spring). *Strong Forum, 8*(1), 1.

Wharton helps future leaders make the best career decisions. (1991, Fall). *Strong Forum, 8*(2), 2.

CHAPTER 13

Using the Strong with College Students

The *Strong Interest Inventory* is one of the most widely used inventories (of any kind) in college settings (Watkins, Campbell, & McGregor, 1988). College students are a diverse population—they vary widely in age, personal background, and work history—so the *Strong* can be useful in clarifying a number of issues that commonly surface while an individual attends college.

The primary uses of the *Strong* in a college, community college, or university setting are to help students choose a major and to aid the career planning of those students who have already declared a major. Using the *Strong* for these purposes can occur in any of several contexts: individual counseling, group counseling, career-planning workshops or classes, or as part of career placement services. This chapter discusses these primary uses of the *Strong* and also addresses its use with students who desire to change majors, with graduate students, and in helping students select extracurricular activities congruent with their interests. ◆

Why Students Take the Strong

When choosing a college major, or when planning for a job or career after college, students often take interest inventories (Johnson & Hoese, 1988) such as the *Strong* to help them:

▲ explore a range of alternatives,

▲ narrow choices to a few possibilities,

▲ suggest new options they have not thought of before, or

▲ confirm a choice they have already made.

It has been demonstrated (Randahl, Hansen, & Haverkamp, 1993) that receiving an interpretation of the *Strong* can lead to important career exploration behaviors. Specifically, the *Strong* helps students expand their alternatives by comparing their responses to those of people satisfactorily employed in 109 different occupations. Also, the Theme codes associated with the Basic Interest Scales (BISs) and each of the Occupational Scales (OSs) can be used to identify many additional occupations, school subjects, or college majors congruent with a student's interests. The *Strong* worksheet, *Career Exploration: A Journey of Discovery*, can also help students generate additional options and alternatives for consideration. For more about this worksheet, see Chapter 3.

While some students benefit from additional options, others already perceive a wide range of choices and need help narrowing their options, creating an action plan, or making decisions.

An interpretation of the *Strong* that focuses on general patterns and addresses the similarities among seemingly different occupations can help accomplish this goal. Understanding general patterns can help students identify the interests that underlie what at first may seem a diverse collection of scores and then help them identify how best to express their primary interests. For example, one client with scores of "Similar" or above on many Social OSs realized that what was really important to him was a job that allowed him to help others in some way. Once he understood his primary motivation, it was easier for him to select among the many options.

Yet other students who take the *Strong* are already clear about their interests and may even have tentatively chosen a college major or an occupation. Even in these cases, the *Strong* has proved useful in suggesting options that the student has not previously considered. Some of these students also find it helpful to discuss their test results with a counselor and thus confirm their choice (Campbell, 1990). In one study, 23 percent of the students seeking career counseling were looking for confirmation of choices they had already made (Nevo, 1990).

Although the *Strong* can help students meet the career goals mentioned previously, some students arrive with goals or expectations that cannot be met. When asked for their reason for seeking help, they say they want to take "that test that will tell me what I should be." These students need to understand the nature of the career-counseling process, the purposes of the *Strong*, and what it can and cannot do. In these cases, it is particularly important to follow the preadministration and preinterpretation instructions outlined in Chapter 10.

When Students Should Take the Strong

To maximize the benefits to students of using the *Strong*, the inventory must be administered fairly early in the student's college experience. This can make it easier for students to engage in early advisory and planning activities. Some colleges administer the *Strong* to every student during freshman orientation and then keep the results on file until the students participate in career-planning activities, such as classes or workshops, that are offered later. For example, one college ("*Strong* Integral," 1988) uses the *Strong* in its four-phase career-counseling program that includes (1) administration of the *Strong* to every student at orientation followed by group interpretations during the first semester, (2) career luncheons with college administrators, (3) career exploration of occupations in which the students are interested, and (4) a workshop on resume writing and interviewing.

There are other advantages to large-scale early administration of the *Strong*. Administration of the inventory is more efficient when all students can be tested at once. Some colleges even mail copies of the *Strong* Item Booklet/Answer Sheet to students before they arrive on campus as part of an orientation packet. Large-scale administration also provides a valuable database for future institutional research. For example, data on the interests of incoming students can be aggregated and compared over the years. Such information can be used to alert college administrators to changes in student interests and help them plan offerings for extracurricular activities, campus or community services, and courses. This method also encourages students to think about majors and careers early in their college experience. This helps lower the incidence of students who arrive at the career center just before, or sometimes after, they are required to declare a major. This technique also provides a means to introduce students to the college's counseling, or career-counseling, services, since it is usually the staff of these centers who administer the *Strong* and notify students about how they can receive feedback on their results.

Using the Strong to Choose a Major

All of the *Strong* scales—the General Occupational Themes (GOTs), BISs, OSs, and Personal Style Scales—can be used to help students choose a college major. In some cases, this decision will mean first choosing a general area of study to explore. For others, the results may point directly to a specific major. The value of using the *Strong* to help students choose a major was illustrated by E. K. Strong, Jr., himself, who offered the following anecdote about his son's use of the inventory:

> What really convinced me emotionally that we had something [valuable in the inventory] was a personal experience. My son had been an indifferent student

in college and had no idea what he wanted to do vocationally. He took my test and came out with [a score showing a similarity to] Physician, an occupation he had never considered entering. Well, he went to medical school, got straight A's throughout, and has been a dedicated and successful physician ever since (Consulting Psychologists Press, 1963).

Using the GOTs

The GOT results may be particularly useful when counseling or advising first-year students and can reduce some of the anxiety associated with beginning college. The Themes, and their relationship on the hexagon, provide a cognitive map that can help these students make sense of what is often a confusing web of options. Research has demonstrated the benefits of helping students acquire a general cognitive framework for exploring interests. In one study (Shahnasarian & Peterson, 1988), a video that interpreted the six Themes was shown to a group of students to help them identify more alternatives for consideration. A cognitive schema such as the one offered by the six Themes can also sensitize students to information in their environment as well as help them encode and retrieve information (Peterson, Sampson, & Reardon, 1991).

Recognizing that students, especially those at large universities, can sometimes feel overwhelmed by the college environment and thus have difficulty choosing a major, the staff at one university decided to take the idea of a cognitive map literally (Jacoby, Rue, & Allen, 1984). Student development staff from a number of different campus offices collaborated in designing six attractive, colorful "UMaps," one for each of the six Themes. Each map outlined campus resources and opportunities keyed to that Theme, including academic programs, career possibilities, internship and volunteer opportunities, campus organizations, and recreational activities. The authors pointed out that such maps can be used successfully in recruitment, orientation programs, academic advising, and career counseling.

The GOTs can be used to help those students who are not yet prepared to select a specific major to understand their general interests. These students will often be those whose knowledge of or experience in the world of work is relatively limited. The interests of such students may still be developing. Information about their general interests, derived from the GOTs, can help them direct their attention to areas in which further exploration would be most profitable and in which they will be most likely to find a good match.

The process of interpretation should focus on helping students establish a Theme code. Once a code has been identified, students can be given suggestions for courses or campus activities that would be expected to appeal to individuals with that code. General survey courses related to an individual's highest Theme area might be particularly helpful.

Using the BISs

Once a general area of interest has been identified from the GOTs, the students' results on the BISs can help to clarify areas that should be explored. In this way, colleges or departments can be identified to provide at least a temporary "home" for those students not ready to declare a major. The BISs can also be useful in helping students identify extracurricular activities they might find interesting and that might lead to additional options for majors. This use of the BISs is described in "Using the *Strong* to Identify Extracurricular Activities" later in this chapter.

Using the OSs

Although the OSs were designed to identify the similarity of students' interests to those of working adults, research has shown that these scales also are effective in helping students select college majors that match their interests (Hansen & Swanson, 1983; Hansen & Tan, 1992; Sackett & Hansen, 1991). When counseling students about choosing a college major, it is important to realize that OSs provide both direct and indirect links between occupations and college majors. A direct link occurs when the OS points directly to a college major of a similar name; an indirect link occurs when the OS is very broad, so that a number of different majors could lead to work in that occupation. By pointing out indirect links, counselors can convey to students that there are many paths to a particular job or career, thus ameliorating the anxiety of students who feel great pressure, imposed from others or by themselves, to choose the "right" major. A few OSs are so broad, however, that additional information is needed to link them to a major. For example, for a student scoring high on the College Professor scale, other scales would have to be used to identify the content area of interest. Examples of both direct and indirect links are shown in Table 13.1.

Table 13.1 Examples of Direct and Indirect Links Between *Strong* Occupational Scales and College Majors

Examples of Direct Links		Examples of Indirect Links	
Occupational Scale	Major	Occupational Scale	Major
Psychologist	Psychology	Physician	Biology
Small Business Owner	Business	Artist, Fine	Art history
Engineer	Mechanical engineering	Technical Writer	English
Translator	Modern languages	Human Resources Director	Business

Using the Learning Environment Scale

The Learning Environment (LE) scale results can be particularly helpful to college students who are choosing a major. Although there is considerable variation within majors, some areas of study are by their nature concerned with theory and abstractions (e.g., literature, philosophy), while others focus on the practical application of ideas or tools (e.g., business, engineering). Scores on the LE scale may also help students identify which courses they would find most satisfying; courses heavy in reading, lectures, and writing may be more appealing for those students scoring toward the academic pole of this scale, while students who score toward the practical pole may prefer labs or other courses in which they can learn by doing. Scores on the Learning Environment scale may also be useful to graduate students, who must decide whether to pursue an academic career in their field or to look for a job in business or some other applied area where they can put their knowledge to work.

Accuracy of the Strong to Predict Choice of Majors

Concurrent and Predictive Validities

In one study (Hansen & Swanson, 1983), the *Strong* was administered to first-year students at orientation; these students were also asked if they had decided on a major. Among those who had already chosen a major, 64 percent of females and 61 percent of males scored above 40 on the OS most closely related to their major. Four years later, those students who remained in school took the *Strong* again and were again asked to report their college major. As seniors, 73 percent of females and 76 percent of males scored above 40 on the OS most closely related to their major. As expected, the agreement between college major and OS was greater when the students were seniors than when they were first-year students, which reinforces the value of experience in developing and clarifying interests. For those students who had majored in a subject *not* directly found on the *Strong* (for example, a major in art history, which was matched to such OSs as Fine Artist or Commercial Artist), the percentages of those scoring above 40 were even higher: 82 percent for female and 94 percent for male first-year students.

While this evidence of concurrent validity is impressive, the researchers also examined the predictive validity of the OSs. This is important, since the *Strong* is used to help students plan ahead. To address the question of predictive validity, the results of the *Strong* administered during orientation were matched with the students' college majors four years later. The scores on the OSs accurately predicted the students' majors for 57 percent of the female and for 53 percent of the male students. These prediction ratios are noteworthy for a four-year period, especially when considering the general instability of interests among the college-age population.

Another study of the validity of the *Strong* for predicting college majors (Hansen & Tan, 1992) showed similar results. The students' OSs above 40 (the lower boundary of the "Similar" interest category) successfully matched the college major for 79 percent of the female and for 83 percent of the male students. The majority (68 percent) of the students were in their first or second year; as with the previous study, accuracy would be expected to be higher among seniors.

Although the concurrent and predictive validities demonstrated in these studies are impressive, their significance is further enhanced with the realization that the direct matches of OS names with college majors constitutes rigorous and stringent criteria for agreement between OS results and choice of college majors. When these criteria are relaxed and indirect matches are counted as well, the agreement percentages rise substantially. For example, in the study by Hansen and Tan (1992) described previously, the concurrent validity of the *Strong* was virtually 100 percent for males when indirect matches were counted. When reviewing the data from their study, Hansen and Swanson (1983, p. 198) concluded that the *Strong* was "particularly successful at predicting major fields when free of the restriction of one-to-one matching with available Occupational Scales." This is important, since no inventory can provide a direct match for all possible majors; extrapolations beyond the Profile will always be needed. These studies provide convincing evidence that the validity of the *Strong* is such that it can be used with confidence in helping students choose a college major.

Factors That Affect Accuracy of Prediction

The long-term predictive accuracy of the *Strong* is affected by various factors that the counselor should consider when helping students choose majors. These factors include preferences in learning environments, satisfaction with early choice of major, self-concept, occupational stereotypes, and elevated profile results.

Swanson and Hansen (1985) found that students' scores on the Academic Comfort scale moderated the predictive value of the *Strong* for college major choices: those students who were more comfortable in the academic environment where the study was conducted were more likely to choose majors predicted by their Profile than were those students who scored low on Academic Comfort. This study should be replicated using the new Learning Environment scale, which replaced the Academic Comfort scale on the 1994 *Strong*.

Another study (Hansen & Swanson, 1983) found that the correlation between the *Strong* results and choice of a college major is greater for students who are satisfied with their initial choice of major than for those who are not satisfied.

Wallace and Walker (1990) found that there was significantly more congruence between *Strong* results and choices of major for students who have a high self-concept than for students whose self-concept was low; these results were not affected by the students' gender or ethnic group.

Although occupational stereotypes have not yet been the subject of research on correlation between *Strong* results and the choice of a college major, it is a factor that counselors should consider when interpreting the inventory. For example, a student may be considering nursing as a career, thinking that it would provide a good opportunity for expression of his or her Social interests. However, an examination of the Theme code for that occupation shows that the codes for Registered Nurse are SI for women and SAI for men. These codes indicate that in addition to Social interests, Investigative interests are also characteristic of successfully employed male and female nurses, and that Artistic interests are also characteristic of male nurses. Some nursing programs may even emphasize Investigative interests over Social. With this information, the student can consider whether his or her level of interest in Investigative topics is sufficient to sustain a long period of educational training.

Another factor in predicting the correlation between *Strong* results and the college major selected is whether the student has elevated Profile results. Some students have difficulty choosing a major (or sticking to one they have already chosen) because they see so many possibilities and cannot decide among them. Nevo (1990) found that 34 percent of the clients requesting career counseling in a college counseling center did so because they were unable to choose from among the many fields that interested them; these students often have elevated Profile results. When asked, they often articulated the combination of excitement and anxiety that they feel in confronting so many opportunities. Some of these clients feel that any decision they make will severely limit their potential and force them to give up something valuable. Counseling with such clients often involves helping them integrate their multiple interests creatively, either within a career or between career and avocational activities. (For more information on interpreting elevated Profiles, see Chapter 11.)

Client 1. The case of a male college student illustrates how the *Strong* can be used to help students choose a college major and encourage exploration. Client 1's Snapshot is shown in Figure 13.1. He scored in the "Average Interest" range on four of the six General Occupational Themes, with scores on the Investigative, Realistic, and Conventional Themes all close to one another. The BIS in which he showed highest interest is the Athletics scale, which reflects the fact that all of his hobbies are sports-related and that he is a member of the varsity swim team at his university. His other high BISs show interests in activities in the

Figure 13.1 Snapshot for Client 1, a College Student Choosing a Major

STRONG INTEREST INVENTORY

Profile report for CLIENT 1
ID:
Age: 20
Gender: Male
Date tested:
Date scored:

Page 1 of 6

SNAPSHOT: A SUMMARY OF RESULTS FOR CLIENT 1

GENERAL OCCUPATIONAL THEMES

The General Occupational Themes describe interests in six very broad areas, including interest in work and leisure activities, kinds of people, and work settings. Your interests in each area are shown at the right in rank order. Note that each Theme has a code, represented by the first letter of the Theme name.

You can use your Theme code, printed below your results, to identify school subjects, part-time jobs, college majors, leisure activities, or careers that you might find interesting. See the back of this Profile for suggestions on how to use your Theme code.

Theme Code	Theme	Very Little Interest	Little Interest	Average Interest	High Interest	Very High Interest	Typical Interests
I	INVESTIGATIVE			✓			Researching, analyzing
R	REALISTIC			✓			Building, repairing
C	CONVENTIONAL			✓			Accounting, processing data
A	ARTISTIC			✓			Creating or enjoying art
S	SOCIAL		✓				Helping, instructing
E	ENTERPRISING		✓				Selling, managing

Your Theme code is IRC—(see explanation at left).
You might explore occupations with codes that contain any combination of these letters.

BASIC INTEREST SCALES

The Basic Interest Scales measure your interests in 25 specific areas or activities. Only those 5 areas in which you show the *most* interest are listed at the right in rank order. Your results on all 25 Basic Interest Scales are found on page 2.

To the left of each scale is a letter that shows which of the six General Occupational Themes this activity is most closely related to. These codes can help you to identify other activities that you may enjoy.

Theme Code	Basic Interests	Very Little Interest	Little Interest	Average Interest	High Interest	Very High Interest	Ypical Activities
R	ATHLETICS					✓	Playing or watching sports
I	MATHEMATICS					✓	Working with numbers or statistics
I	MEDICAL SCIENCE				✓		Working in medicine or biology
R	MECHANICAL ACTIVITIES			✓			Working with tools and equipment
A	APPLIED ARTS			✓			Producing or enjoying visual art

OCCUPATIONAL SCALES

The Occupational Scales measure how similar your interests are to the interests of people who are satisfied working in those occupations. Only the 10 scales on which your interests are *most* similar to those of these people are listed at the right in rank order. Your results on all 211 of the Occupational Scales are found on pages 3, 4, and 5.

The letters to the left of each scale identify the Theme or Themes that most closely describe the interests of people working in that occupation. You can use these letters to find additional, related occupations that you might find interesting. After reviewing your results on all six pages of this Profile, see the back of page 5 for tips on finding other occupations in the Theme or Themes that interest you the most.

Theme Code	Occupation	Very Dissimilar	Dissimilar	Mid-Range	Similar	Very Similar
RI	ENGINEER					✓
RI	RADIOLOGIC TECHNOLOGIST					✓
IR	DENTIST				✓	
R	PLUMBER				✓	
CI	ACTUARY				✓	
IR	OPTOMETRIST				✓	
CE	ACCOUNTANT				✓	
IR	CHEMIST				✓	
R	AUTO MECHANIC				✓	
RIC	ELECTRICIAN				✓	

***PERSONAL STYLE SCALES** measure your levels of comfort regarding Work Style, Learning Environment, Leadership Style, and Risk Taking/Adventure. This information may help you make decisions about particular work environments, educational settings, and types of activities you would find satisfying. Your results on these four scales are on page 6.*

CPP CONSULTING PSYCHOLOGISTS PRESS, INC. • 3803 E. Bayshore Road, Palo Alto, CA 94303

Investigative area (Mathematics and Medical Science), the Realistic area (Mechanical Activities), and Artistic area (Applied Arts).

His interests in the Investigative and Realistic BISs are consistent with his scores on the GOTs. This pattern is further confirmed by his results on the Occupational Scales. His Snapshot shows ten OSs in the "Similar" range or above, six of which are coded RI or IR. With these results in hand and armed with the knowledge that he had always done well in math and science in high school, he decided to first explore a major in engineering. This field would also be consistent with his score of 35 on the Work Style scale, which is toward the works with ideas/data/things pole.

After discussing some possibilities with engineering majors and professors, taking some survey courses, and examining the course requirements for different engineering specialties, he settled on civil engineering. He believed that this specialty would allow him the opportunity to work with his hands (reflected in his scores on the OSs of Plumber, Auto Mechanic, and Electrician, and in his Mechanical Activities BIS) and to pursue his interest in science and math (Chemist OS and Mathematics BIS, respectively). From what he had learned about civil engineering, he liked the fact that he would be working in a field where the results were concrete and immediately observable. He believed that other engineering fields, such as electrical engineering, were too abstract or theoretical for his liking. This attitude is consistent with his score of 45 on the Learning Environment scale, which is toward the practical pole.

Although he believed that civil engineering was a good choice and he was excited about taking courses in that major, he was also intrigued by the scores on the *Strong* that reflected an interest in medicine (Medical Science BIS, Radiologic Technologist and Dentist OSs). He admitted that he had some interest in this area but wasn't sure how it might be realized, since he was not interested in being a physician (his score on the male Physician scale was 32). He decided to explore this area further with a goal of identifying possible careers or majors where his interest in engineering and medicine might be combined. So, although he had made a choice that was consistent with his interest pattern and with which he was satisfied, he remained open to further exploration.

Using the *Strong* to Choose a Career

The *Strong* can be used with students who have already chosen a major and are successfully completing a course of study but who need help in their career exploration and planning. *Strong* results can help students explore career alternatives or consider options for postgraduate education or training.

Using the OSs

The OSs provide the most direct source of information about occupations that students might find interesting. Students' responses are compared with those of both men and women who are satisfactorily employed in 109 occupations. Research on the predictive validity of the OSs indicates that there is substantial relationship between high scores on the OSs and the eventual occupation entered (Hansen & Campbell, 1985). Depending on how the match between OSs and occupational titles is defined, between 50 percent and 60 percent of all college students enter occupations that are predictable from their *Strong* scores. For example, Spokane (1979) examined the concurrent and predictive validity of the *Strong* for college women and men who completed the inventory, first during orientation and again in their senior year; they were also asked for their occupational preferences as seniors. High scores on the OSs (above 40) predicted occupational preferences for 55 percent of the female and 62 percent of the male students almost four years later. Concurrent validity was demonstrated by the finding that OS scores from the seniors matched occupational preferences for 68 percent of females and 88 percent of males. Furthermore, students whose occupational preferences were consistent with their OS scores four years earlier were more satisfied with their choices.

Another example is provided by a study of graduate students in a counseling psychology program (Betz & Taylor, 1982); 89 percent of these students had a score of "Similar" or above on the Psychologist scale. While this result demonstrated the overall concurrent validity of the *Strong* for this group, the authors also suggested that the results could be used in a more refined way: they found that scores on the Investigative Theme indicated which of the students were more likely to be strongly interested in research, either in addition to or instead of counseling practice. Although the validity estimates for the *Strong* reported in this guide (Chapter 7) and elsewhere indicated that the inventory can be used with confidence to help students choose postgraduate careers, it is important to note that a study by Dolliver and Kunce (1973) suggested that the level of predictive accuracy reported in such longitudinal studies probably underestimates the true predictive accuracy of the scales.

Using Consistency Across Scales

When helping students in career planning, it is important to consider the pattern of scores across the entire Profile. If the scores on the GOTs, BISs, and OSs all point toward the same field, or even the same specific occupation, students should be strongly encouraged to direct their exploration efforts toward that area first.

Johnson and Johansson (1972) have shown that consistency between scores on the BISs and the OSs leads to greater predictive accuracy. A student with a high score on one of the sales-related OSs (e.g., Realtor or Life Insurance Agent) and a high score on the Sales BIS is more likely to choose sales work than is a student with equally high scores on these same OSs but a low or moderate score on the Sales BIS. Students with the latter pattern of scores are more likely to choose a people-oriented but non-sales occupation such as Public Relations Director.

In some cases, there may be discrepancies between scores on the GOTs and BISs, scales that use homogeneous items and scoring (i.e., they are all scored positively for "Like" responses), and the OSs, which are composed of heterogeneous items and are scored positively for both "Like" and "Dislike" responses. In such cases, students' career exploration should be guided primarily by the OSs, which generally demonstrate better predictive validity. However, these discrepancies also provide valuable information and need to be integrated into the interpretation; they often point to leisure or avocational interests that help round out the picture of the student's overall interests. See Chapter 11 for more information about how to interpret Profiles with such inconsistencies.

Using the Personal Style Scales

The Personal Style Scales results can be useful with students choosing a career. The results of the Work Style scale can help students identify their interest in working either with people or with ideas/data/things. Those whose scores indicate that they prefer to deal with concepts and data also like to work alone. Students who score this way may need quiet to concentrate on their studies and may feel that too much contact with others is distracting. Those scoring toward the works with people pole may gravitate toward education or other "service" careers such as psychology. A student who is highly people oriented may seek out opportunities to work in groups or on teams.

The Leadership Style scale can also help students make decisions about career opportunities. Individuals who score toward the directs others pole may focus on jobs that will eventually allow them to function as supervisors or team leaders. Those who score toward the leads by example pole may enjoy working on projects but not leading. They may feel more comfortable pursuing positions in which they work alone or in small groups and do not have responsibility for giving directions to others.

Scores on the Risk Taking/Adventure scale are generally inversely correlated with age. Many students view their time in college as an opportunity to try new things, and this results in higher scores on this scale than those generally obtained by adults. For this reason, high scores should not be overinterpreted. Students scoring toward the takes chances pole of this scale may approach the task of choosing a career with a sense of "nothing ventured, nothing gained." Those scoring toward the plays it safe pole may approach their decision more cautiously, wanting to research their alternatives carefully.

Using Additional Sources of Information

As with any client, it is important that *Strong* results be integrated with other information—aptitudes, work experience, extracurricular activities—when helping a student with career planning (Lowman, 1991). Valuable information to incorporate into career counseling includes how well the students like and perform in specific courses, both within and outside their majors. Four or more years of college provide many opportunities for students to discover and express their interests, and provide detailed performance data in the form of grades. Work experience also needs to be considered, including part-time or summer jobs, volunteer work, and work associated with extracurricular activities. Students sometimes need help seeing how their extracurricular interests and the skills they may have used or acquired when engaging in extracurricular activities transfer to the world of work. The *Strong* worksheet, *Career Exploration: A Journey of Discovery*, can help students identify sources of additional information and begin to recognize interest patterns in this information.

Additionally, integrating information about the client's personality, values, and beliefs with the *Strong* results can provide a much deeper understanding of what careers and work environments the client is likely to find satisfying and rewarding. Using the *Strong* with the *Myers-Briggs Type Indicator* has been shown to be particularly useful (Hammer & Kummerow, 1992). Use of these two instruments together can suggest additional options for clients in career counseling and can help confirm particular areas that warrant further exploration. Other instruments that have been used along with the *Strong* by career counselors include the *Career Beliefs Inventory* (Krumboltz, 1991) and the *Values Scale* (Nevill & Super, 1986).

Client 2. The case of a middle-aged student returning to school illustrates how the *Strong* can be used to clarify career choices. Client 2, a 47-year-old man, was employed as a truck driver. He attended college when he was in his twenties but dropped out after two years because he did not know what he wanted to do with a college degree. He traveled around the country for several years, then married and settled

Figure 13.2 Snapshot for Client 2, a College Student Choosing a Career

STRONG INTEREST INVENTORY

Profile report for **CLIENT 2**
ID:
Age: **47**
Gender: **Male**

Date tested:
Date scored:

Page **1** of 6

SNAPSHOT: A SUMMARY OF RESULTS FOR *CLIENT 2*

GENERAL OCCUPATIONAL THEMES

The General Occupational Themes describe interests in six very broad areas, including interest in work and leisure activities, kinds of people, and work settings. Your interests in each area are shown at the right in rank order. Note that each Theme has a code, represented by the first letter of the Theme name.

You can use your Theme code, printed below your results, to identify school subjects, part-time jobs, college majors, leisure activities, or careers that you might find interesting. See the back of the Profile for suggestions on how to use your Theme code.

THEME CODE	THEME	VERY LITTLE INTEREST	LITTLE INTEREST	AVERAGE INTEREST	HIGH INTEREST	VERY HIGH INTEREST	TYPICAL INTERESTS
I	INVESTIGATIVE			✓			Researching, analyzing
R	REALISTIC			✓			Building, repairing
A	ARTISTIC			✓			Creating or enjoying art
C	CONVENTIONAL			✓			Accounting, processing data
E	ENTERPRISING	✓					Selling, managing
S	SOCIAL	✓					Helping, instructing

Your Theme code is IRA—(see explanation at left).
You might explore occupations with codes that contain any combination of these letters.

BASIC INTEREST SCALES

The Basic Interest Scales measure your interests in 25 specific areas or activities. Only those 5 areas in which you show the *most* interest are listed at the right in rank order. Your results on all 25 Basic Interest Scales are found on page 2.

To the left of each scale is a letter that shows which of the six General Occupational Themes this activity is most closely related to. These codes can help you to identify other activities that you may enjoy.

THEME CODE	BASIC INTERESTS	VERY LITTLE INTEREST	LITTLE INTEREST	AVERAGE INTEREST	HIGH INTEREST	VERY HIGH INTEREST	YPICAL ACTIVITIES
I	MATHEMATICS					✓	Working with numbers or statistics
R	NATURE					✓	Appreciating nature
R	AGRICULTURE				✓		Working outdoors
I	SCIENCE				✓		Conducting scientific research
R	MECHANICAL ACTIVITIES			✓			Working with tools and equipment

OCCUPATIONAL SCALES

The Occupational Scales measure how similar your interests are to the interests of people who are satisfied working in those occupations. Only the 10 scales on which your interests are most similar to those of these people are listed at the right in rank order. Your results on all 211 of the Occupational Scales are found on pages 3, 4, and 5.

The letters to the left of each scale identify the Theme or Themes that most closely describe the interests of people working in that occupation. You can use these letters to find additional, related occupations that you might find interesting. After reviewing your results on all six pages of this Profile, see the back of page 5 for tips on finding other occupations in the Theme or Themes that interest you the most.

THEME CODE	OCCUPATION	VERY DISSIMILAR	DISSIMILAR	MID-RANGE	SIMILAR	VERY SIMILAR
RI	FORESTER					✓
RI	ENGINEER					✓
IRA	GEOLOGIST					✓
IA	GEOGRAPHER					✓
IA	BIOLOGIST					✓
IR	CHEMIST					✓
ICA	MATHEMATICIAN					✓
IAR	COMPUTER PROGR./ SYSTEMS ANALYST					✓
IAS	COLLEGE PROFESSOR					✓
IRA	PHYSICIST				✓	

***PERSONAL STYLE SCALES** measure your levels of comfort regarding Work Style, Learning Environment, Leadership Style, and Risk Taking/Adventure. This information may help you make decisions about particular work environments, educational settings, and types of activities you would find satisfying. Your results on these four scales are on page 6.*

CPP CONSULTING PSYCHOLOGISTS PRESS, INC. • 3803 E. Bayshore Road, Palo Alto, CA 94303

in a rural area, where he was employed in various jobs, including logger and truck driver. He spent most of his leisure time reading (particularly history), earning his pilot's license, and designing and building a house with his wife. When the house was completed after many years, he began to look for other ways to spend his leisure time and thought about returning to school, although he was not sure what he wanted to study.

His GOT results (Figure 13.2) indicated "Average Interest" in Realistic, Investigative, Artistic, and Conventional areas, suggesting that there were some things about each of these he liked. His top five BISs showed a combination of outdoor interests as well as interests in math, science, and computers. His top ten OSs showed a consistent pattern of high similarity with those in occupations that are coded both Investigative and Realistic and with some Artistic occupations as well. He quickly confirmed his outdoor interests; he had lived in small towns or rural areas all his life. He was intrigued by the possibility of combining these interests with some kind of scientific occupation. To test this idea, he enrolled part-time in a community college and took introductory math and science courses. He liked these courses so much and did so well in them (somewhat to his surprise) that he approached his supervisor and asked for a semester-long leave of absence so he could take a full course load that included calculus, engineering, and computer programming.

His results on the Personal Style Scales helped round out the picture. His Work Style scale score (24) indicated a clear interest in working independently on projects that do not require much people contact. His Leadership Style score (25) confirmed this task orientation. His Learning Environment scale score of 51 suggested that an academic environment was a good match for his interests. His Risk Taking/Adventure score fell in the middle of the scale but tended toward the plays it safe pole. When asked how this score fit with the fact that he is a licensed pilot with an interest in small, experimental aircraft, he said that flying held low risk for a knowledgeable pilot. He saw a connection, however, between his Risk Taking/Adventure score and his desire to move cautiously into a new career; he was concerned about his chances of finding a new job that matched his interests, given his age and desire to stay in the same geographic location.

Client 2 chose civil engineering as his major, and he did extremely well. He completed the course work while working part-time as a county surveyor.

Using the Strong to Change a Major

Some students decide on a college major early. They know what they want to be at a young age and enter college with a major already decided. The results of one study suggest that Investigative types are more likely to choose majors early (Spokane, Malett, & Vance, 1978). While for some students an early decision may help focus their efforts, for others it may prove premature. One study showed that within a five-semester period, 58 percent of students changed majors (Spokane et al., 1978). Which students persist and which change majors may depend on how well informed they are about the world of work and about their interests when making their initial choices. In the Spokane study, those students whose *Strong* results were consistent with their choices of major were the least likely to change.

There are several reasons students might seek to change majors. Students whose choices were based on only the most general information or even on stereotypes about an occupation may have discovered that the day-to-day realities did not live up to their idealized preconceptions. Or they may have found that their interests or motivation were not sustained. Others may have become discouraged when they found that they must compete, perhaps for the first time, with students whose abilities in their chosen field equaled or exceeded their own.

Family pressures can be another reason students select a major early and later desire to change. When this occurs, discussions about *Strong* scores can open communication between parents and students, so that students can make decisions suited to their own interests and goals rather than those of their parents. *Strong* results present parents with specific information about the student's interests—information that may not have surfaced in earlier discussions—and they provide the student with an opportunity to explain personal feelings in ways that might not be possible otherwise. See Chapter 1 for specific examples of how *Strong* results helped open a dialogue between students and parents.

Using the Strong to Counsel Graduate Students

A number of doubts or concerns may prompt graduate students to request academic advising or career counseling. Concerns include:

▲ whether to continue with the graduate program or quit and get a job,
▲ whether to transfer to another institution,
▲ whether to choose a different dissertation topic,
▲ whether to switch to a different subspecialty, and
▲ how to deal with stress or burnout.

Acquiring an advanced degree can be a long and arduous task. At some point, many graduate students express doubts about whether they want to complete their program. For some, dissatisfaction is driven by financial concerns; they may have family responsibilities that make it difficult to remain in school. Or they may become dissatisfied with their life as a student when they see friends earning attractive salaries or getting a start on their careers. For others, doubts may be symptoms of stress or burnout, especially if they have gone directly from high school to college and then immediately to graduate school. After twenty or so years of schooling without a break, they may simply need a temporary respite. In other cases, however, the issues are akin to those faced by working adults. For graduate students, therefore, it may be instructive to use the *Strong* results to distinguish between job dissatisfaction and career dissatisfaction.

Job Dissatisfaction

In the context of graduate school, *job* dissatisfaction means that specific sources of dissatisfaction can be identified, although the student's interest in the general area he or she has chosen remains high. Dissatisfaction may arise from various sources: for example, the student may have chosen the wrong subspecialty, dissertation topic, thesis advisor, or school.

Using the GOTs and BISs

Graduate students who are experiencing job dissatisfaction will often have a high score on the OSs most directly related to their major. In fact, they may have a consistent pattern across all three main sets of *Strong* scales (i.e., the GOTs, BISs, and OSs) that suggests that their choice is indeed consistent with their interests. Some students may be disappointed when their *Strong* results confirm their interest in their chosen field: acutely aware of their feelings of dissatisfaction, they are frustrated that the results have not provided an "answer." When this occurs, the counselor can engage the student in a process designed to uncover the sources of dissatisfaction and help him or her develop strategies to alleviate the problem.

Using the OSs

Occasionally, students who experience job dissatisfaction show "Average Interest" or "Little Interest" in the GOTs or BISs associated with their area, while at the same time scoring "Similar" or above on the OSs related to their chosen profession. This pattern may occur because of the different methods used for selecting items and for scoring the different sets of *Strong* scales. When completing the *Strong* Item Booklet/Answer Sheet, dissatisfied students may have responded "Dislike" to items they perceived as related to their areas of study. These "Dislike" responses may result in low scores on the GOTs and BISs because these are homogeneous scales. However, because the OSs have a much more heterogeneous item content and are scored positively for both "Like" and "Dislike" responses, it is much less likely that the OSs would reflect the dissatisfaction to the same degree. These differences between the scores on the sets of scales provide valuable insight, since they are evidence of the extent of a student's dissatisfaction and can be discussed with the student. Sources of dissatisfaction can be identified and subjected to problem solving.

Using the Personal Style Scales

The Personal Style Scales may also help pinpoint some of the sources of dissatisfaction and suggest courses of action. Students' results on the Learning Environment scale may reveal a discrepancy between their preferred learning style and the educational environment in which they find themselves. Although there are important exceptions (e.g., programs in applied science or highly technical fields), many graduate students probably score toward the academic pole of the Learning Environment scale. Some students, however, particularly those who are returning to school after having already worked in the field, may tend more toward the practical pole of this scale. Identifying such a discrepancy may guide these students to consider options other than staying the course or quitting altogether: perhaps finding a more applied program, or one that combines full-time work with night or weekend courses, would increase their level of satisfaction.

The Work Style scale can also be useful in suggesting ways to ameliorate a student's dissatisfaction. Graduate students who score toward the works with people pole of this scale, in particular, may find that they work better when they can intersperse periods of solitary work on their research with social activities. Those with scores toward the works with ideas/data/things pole may need to arrange their schedules so that they have long periods of uninterrupted time to concentrate on their academic work.

Career Dissatisfaction

In other cases, however, career dissatisfaction explains a graduate student's unhappiness. *Career* dissatisfaction in graduate students is more far-reaching, reflecting a dislike of the major field of study itself. Graduate students may have discovered through intensive work in the field that they can no longer sustain their interest or motivation. They may maintain a general interest in the area but have come to realize that they do not really like the day-to-day situations and challenges that they will encounter if they pursue an occupation in that field.

Strong results that point to *career* dissatisfaction among graduate students are those in which scores on all the scales related to the student's area of study are low, or in which one or more of the GOTs or BISs related to the student's major are high, but scores on the OSs related to the major are low. The latter pattern may suggest that the student maintains a general interest in the area but is not interested in the work routinely done by those in the occupation or in the work environment typical of the occupation. Students whose results point to career dissatisfaction need help identifying alternative fields or occupations.

Using the Strong to Identify Extracurricular Activities

In addition to helping students choose majors and careers, the *Strong* can also be useful in helping students identify what kinds of extracurricular activities they might find interesting or revitalizing. Involvement in campus groups can, in turn, provide a means for students to explore and get experience in various activities that can help them further develop their interests. At first, students may not recognize that their interests in leisure activities can lead to career possibilities or help them develop transferable skills.

Involvement in campus life outside the classroom can provide other benefits as well. For example, it can reduce a student's likelihood of failing or dropping out; students who are integrated into the fabric of campus life may find the support necessary to help them through the inevitable stressful episodes of the college experience. Participating in leisure activities also provides a break from the rigors of academics and can refresh and reenergize students, which in turn may help improve academic performance. For example, one psychology graduate student who scored high on the Nature BIS arranged her schedule so she would have time for walks and long hikes; this provided the break that she needed to keep focused on her studies.

The Leadership Style scale, one of the Personal Style Scales, can be particularly useful in helping students select extracurricular activities that match their interests. The Leadership Style scale measures an interest in assuming a leadership or supervisory role that is characterized by taking charge and directing others. A student scoring toward the directs others pole on this scale may be encouraged to seek leadership positions in campus activities or courses where she or he can learn more about leadership. Those scoring toward the leads by example pole may not be interested in assuming campus leadership positions; they are more likely to want to work independently to accomplish tasks on their own rather than through others. Experimenting with a particular leadership style while in college can ultimately help students make satisfying career choices.

Conclusion

The *Strong* is used extensively with college students because it has proved successful in helping them choose a major, plan for a job or career after college, change majors, choose among postgraduate training or education, and select extracurricular activities that they might find interesting. It has been shown to be useful in helping graduate students make decisions about their course of study and identifying sources of dissatisfaction. The research on using the *Strong* with students demonstrates that the inventory can be used with confidence for these purposes. Overall, the studies mentioned in this chapter support Strong's original proposition that interests measured during college are strongly predictive of choice of college major and occupational choice.

References

Betz, N. E., & Taylor, K. M. (1982). Concurrent validity of the Strong-Campbell Interest Inventory for graduate students in counseling. *Journal of Counseling Psychology, 29*(6), 626–635.

Campbell, V. L. (1990). A model for using tests in counseling. In C. E. Watkins & V. L. Campbell (Eds.), *Testing in Counseling Practice.* Hillsdale, NJ: Erlbaum.

Consulting Psychologists Press. (1963). *1963–1964 Catalogue of Psychological Tests and Services.* Palo Alto, CA: Author.

Dolliver, R. H., & Kunce, J. E. (1973). Who drops out of an SVIB follow-up study? *Journal of Counseling Psychology, 20,* 188–189.

Hammer, A. L., & Kummerow, J. K. (1992). *Strong + MBTI career development guide.* Palo Alto, CA: Consulting Psychologists Press.

Hansen, J. C., & Campbell, D. P. (1985). *Manual for the Strong Interest Inventory* (4th ed.). Stanford, CA: Stanford University Press.

Hansen, J. C., & Swanson, J. L. (1983). Stability of interests and the predictive and concurrent validity of the 1981 SCII for college majors. *Journal of Counseling Psychology, 30,* 194–201.

Hansen, J. C., & Tan, R. N. (1992). Concurrent validity of the 1985 Strong Interest Inventory for college major selection. *Measurement and Evaluation in Counseling and Development, 25,* 53–57.

Jacoby, B., Rue, P., & Allen, K. T. (1984, March). UMaps: A person-environment approach to helping students make critical choices. *Personnel and Guidance Journal,* pp. 426–428.

Johnson, R. W., & Hoese, J. (1988). Career planning concerns of SCII clients. *The Career Development Quarterly, 30,* 251–258.

Johnson, R. W., & Johansson, C. B. (1972). Moderating effects of basic interests on predictive validity of SVIB occupational scales. *Proceedings of the 80th Annual Convention of the American Psychological Association* (pp. 589–590).

Krumboltz, J. D. (1991). *Manual for the Career Beliefs Inventory.* Palo Alto, CA: Consulting Psychologists Press.

Lowman, R. L. (1991). *The clinical practice of career assessment.* Washington, DC: American Psychological Association.

Nevill, D. D., & Super, D. E. (1986). *The Values Scale.* Palo Alto, CA: Consulting Psychologists Press.

Nevo, O. (1990). Career counseling from the counselee perspective: Analysis of feedback questionnaires. *The Career Development Quarterly, 38,* 314–324.

Peterson, G. W., Sampson, J. P., & Reardon, R. C. (1991). *Career development and services: A cognitive approach.* Pacific Grove, CA: Brooks/Cole.

Randahl, G. J., Hansen, J. C., & Haverkamp, B. (1993). Instrumental behaviors following test administration and interpretation: Exploration validity of the Strong Interest Inventory. *Journal of Counseling and Development, 71,* 435–439.

Sackett, S., & Hansen, J. C. (1991). *Career development concerns of student-athletes.* Paper presented at the meeting of the American Association of Counseling and Development, Reno, NV.

Shahnasarian, M., & Peterson, G. W. (1988). The effect of a prior cognitive structuring intervention with computer-assisted career guidance. *Computers in Human Behavior, 4,* 125–131.

Spokane, A. R. (1979). Occupational preference and the validity of the Strong-Campbell Interest Inventory for college women and men. *Journal of Counseling Psychology, 26,* 312–318.

Spokane, A. R., Malett, S. D., & Vance, F. L. (1978). Consistent curricular choice and congruence of subsequent changes. *Journal of Vocational Behavior, 13,* 45–53.,

Strong integral to structured counseling program. (1988, Fall). *Strong Forum, 5*(1), 3.

Swanson, J. L., & Hansen, J. C. (1985). The relationship of the construct of academic comfort to educational level, performance, aspiration, and prediction of college major choices. *Journal of Vocational Behavior, 26,* 1–12.

Wallace, G. R., & Walker, S. P. (1990). Self-concept, vocational interests, and choice of academic major in college students. *College Student Journal, 23*(4), 361–367.

Watkins, C. E., Campbell, V. L., & McGregor, P. (1988). Counseling psychologists' uses of and opinions about psychological tests: A contemporary perspective. *Counseling Psychologist, 16*(3), 476–486.

CHAPTER 14

Using the Strong with High School Students

Robbie M. Kaplan

High school students need guidance to identify potential occupations and college majors. These choices are likely to have a greater impact on their lives than will most other decisions they make. Students should have access to relevant occupational information, professional advice, and the best possible data about themselves when making such decisions. Students' interests have been found to be a major determinant of both occupational choice and college major (Scharf, 1970; Thomas, Morrill, & Miller, 1970). The *Strong* has proved to be beneficial for long-range educational and career planning purposes and was designed specifically for these situations.

The *Strong* is usually offered to eleventh- or twelfth-graders (i.e., sixteen-, seventeen-, and eighteen-year-olds). It is a useful tool for students beginning the process of career exploration, because it enables them to learn about themselves by clarifying and confirming their interests and by comparing their interests—their likes and dislikes—with the interests of individuals who report that they are satisfactorily employed in a wide range of occupations. Many high schools use the *Strong* with all students; others find it is especially effective with those who need help in selecting a course of study, academic goals, or future occupation. In addition, the *Strong* is appropriate for high school students who are undecided about whether they want to go to college (Spitzer & Levinson, 1988). It is also effective with students who already have made firm decisions but who could use the reassurance of seeing their choices confirmed or benefit from discovering new options for exploration. *Strong* results can be helpful for students in ninth or tenth grade as they select their academic courses and begin to explore the world of work.

This chapter begins with some general comments about age and reading level and provides suggestions about how to administer and interpret the *Strong* when working with high school students. The second half of the chapter examines specific situations in which the *Strong* is especially useful with high school students. ◆

Age and Reading Level

Some counselors are concerned about whether the *Strong* might be less appropriate for teenagers than it is for adults. Although interests may be transitory during the teenage years, they begin to solidify for most students at age seventeen or eighteen. The reliability of vocational interest measurement tends to increase as age increases (Zarrella & Schuerger, 1990); nevertheless, by the eighth grade there is considerable stability in the configuration of an individual's Profile (Hansen & Stocco, 1980; Strong, 1943).

Remarkable levels of interest stability have been found among people tested over a twelve-year interval—first as college freshmen and later as working adults (Swanson & Hansen, 1988). High school seniors are close in age to college freshmen and should have comparable levels of interest stability. A study of the interests of high school and college students (Hansen & Stocco, 1980) demonstrated the effect of age on test-retest reliabilities. Although Basic Interest Scale (BIS) median three-year test-retest correlations were lower for high school students ($r = .56$) than for adults ($r = .82$), the correlations were nonetheless high enough to warrant the use of the BISs with young adults. Counselors should be aware that, especially with high school students, some scores are likely to change over a three-year period.

The level of scores on most of the BISs tends to increase slightly in individuals from the age of fifteen into adulthood. Teenagers tend to mark "Like" to a smaller number of items than adults do; this is probably a reflection of their limited exposure to a wide range of occupational activities. Students also tend to choose "Indifferent" more often, undoubtedly for the same reason. As their experience expands, so does the number of their likes.

The *Strong* Item Booklet/Answer Sheet is written at the eighth-grade reading level to ensure that the less-skilled readers among the ninth- and tenth-graders can understand it.

Administration and Interpretation

In the high school setting, the *Strong* can be administered to individuals or in groups, the latter being more common because of time and resource constraints. In either case, potential administration problems include:

▲ lack of experience in completing computer answer sheets,

▲ the uncommon routine of writing names in reverse order, and

▲ unfamiliarity with different occupations and subjects.

To make sure that students complete the Item Booklet/Answer Sheet accurately, counselors should carefully monitor the entire administration process and provide clear instructions for both completing the demographic information on page 2 and filling in the ovals on pages 2 through 5 on the Item Booklet/Answer Sheet. For students who are unfamiliar with some items—for example, occupations in Part I (e.g., "Rancher," "Astronomer," or "Civil Engineer") or school subjects in Part II (e.g., "Botany," "Calculus," or "Physiology")—offering definitions or explanations for the items is helpful. This kind of assistance reduces guesswork and enables students to more accurately estimate their preferences or aversions to the items, thus yielding more meaningful Profile scores.

High school counselors can interpret Profile results one on one, in small groups of three to four, or in large groups ranging from ten to fifty. Most counselors offer follow-up one-on-one counseling to students who are interested in learning more about their interests and options. Students can understand their results better if they participate in the interpretation of their *Strong* results. For example, the counselor can read aloud descriptions of the General Occupational Themes (GOTs) and BISs and encourage students to indicate which characteristics best describe them. The counselor and students can then pull together accurate Theme descriptions to identify areas for exploration.

Students can broaden their base of potential careers by using their identified GOTs to locate additional careers in the *Dictionary of Holland Occupational Codes* (Gottfredson & Holland, 1989), which lists and organizes occupations included in the *Dictionary of Occupational Titles* (1991). Another useful resource for occupation information is the *Occupational Outlook Handbook* (1994). Computerized guidance systems provide lists and narratives of additional occupations based on *Strong* results; particularly useful are the *Guidance Information System (GIS)* (1993) and the *Discover* (1993) program.

Parents are rarely involved in *Strong* interpretations but are often sent a letter offering the option to discuss their child's results with a counselor over the phone or in person. Enclosing such a letter and *Strong* results with report cards is one way to involve parents successfully.

Administration of the *Strong* can be integrated into the curriculum as part of a career unit or class segment. Career units usually comprise four to eight class periods (45 to 60 minutes each). A sample unit may include *Strong* administration (along with other assessment inventories); interpretation of test results; career discussion/research; and resume, application, and job search skills.

Career workshops also work well as part of English or life skills/preparation classes, usually consisting of four to six class periods. A sample unit may include *Strong* administration (along with other assessment inventories), overview of the career planning process, interpretation, and occupational research. Some workshops culminate with students researching an occupation of interest; conducting exploratory interviews; and writing a paper, either as a class requirement or for extra credit.

Holding career-day events also provides students with the opportunity to explore the world of work. Such events may feature individual presentations or panel discussions that provide information about a wide range of occupations. These programs may be considered optional, although attendance can be increased by scheduling them during required class periods. Holding career programs after administering the *Strong* allows counselors to poll students about their inventory results and to invite parent and community speakers to represent the most requested occupations. However, offering a career day prior to administering the *Strong* also has advantages; this approach gives the students a better basis for expressing their career interests.

When to Use the Strong with High School Students

Situations in which *Strong* results are particularly useful for high school students include:

- identifying or confirming career/college major choices,
- exploring career options with non–college bound students,
- working with at-risk students, and
- assessing educational goals.

Each of these uses of the *Strong* is discussed here.

Identifying and Confirming Career/College Major Choices

College-bound eleventh- and twelfth-grade students need to establish areas of interest and to make a tentative selection of their college major. *Strong* interpretations that focus on identifying characteristics and patterns in the GOTs and BISs can help students visualize how their interests relate to specific vocations. Students can then use this information to research colleges that offer programs in line with their interests. Students' inventory results can provide options they might not otherwise consider. For example, a student told his counselor he wanted to attend the U.S. Military Academy at West Point. Since his father was a retired military officer and he himself had grown up in a military environment, the student felt this was a natural career choice for him. While his counselor was investigating procedures for enrolling in the military academy, the student took the *Strong*. His results indicated he was an Artistic type and would have had a difficult time with the inflexibility of this educational environment. The student confirmed these results and, after a discussion about his options, decided to attend the Fashion Institute for a year. He took an interior design course, loved it, and began an apprenticeship with an architectural firm in San Francisco. His instructor and the architectural firm were so impressed with him that he was sent to school in Germany through their architectural program ("High School Students Test," 1990).

The *Strong* is helpful both in confirming career or college major choices that have already been made (Hansen & Swanson, 1983) and in redirecting students who have made less-than-optimal choices about postsecondary education, occupations, or college majors. The following cases illustrate these uses of the *Strong*.

Client 1. Client 1 is a seventeen-year-old twelfth-grader who wants to pursue a career in the entertainment field. He has a learning disability in math. His Profile, although fairly flat on the GOTs and BISs, does show a consistent pattern of interests on the Occupational Scales (OSs). (See Chapter 11 for a discussion of flat and depressed Profiles.)

Figure 14.1 Snapshot and Administrative Indexes for Client 1, Confirming a High School Student's Choice of College Major

STRONG INTEREST INVENTORY

Profile report for CLIENT 1
ID:
Age: 17
Gender: Male
Date tested:
Date scored:

Page 1 of 6

SNAPSHOT: A SUMMARY OF RESULTS FOR CLIENT 1

GENERAL OCCUPATIONAL THEMES

The General Occupational Themes describe interests in six very broad areas, including interest in work and leisure activities, kinds of people, and work settings. Your interests in each area are shown at the right in rank order. Note that each Theme has a code, represented by the first letter of the Theme name.

You can use your Theme code, printed below your results, to identify school subjects, part-time jobs, college majors, leisure activities, or careers that you might find interesting. See the back of the Profile for suggestions on how to use your Theme code.

Theme Code	Theme	Very Little Interest	Little Interest	Average Interest	High Interest	Very High Interest	Typical Interests
E	ENTERPRISING	☐	☐	☑	☐	☐	Selling, managing
A	ARTISTIC	☐	☐	☑	☐	☐	Creating or enjoying art
C	CONVENTIONAL	☐	☐	☑	☐	☐	Accounting, processing data
S	SOCIAL	☐	☑	☐	☐	☐	Helping, instructing
I	INVESTIGATIVE	☐	☑	☐	☐	☐	Researching, analyzing
R	REALISTIC	☑	☐	☐	☐	☐	Building, repairing

Your Theme code is EAC—(see explanation at left).
You might explore occupations with codes that contain any combination of these letters.

BASIC INTEREST SCALES

The Basic Interest Scales measure your interests in 25 specific areas or activities. Only those 5 areas in which you show the *most* interest are listed at the right in rank order. Your results on all 25 Basic Interest Scales are found on page 2.

To the left of each scale is a letter that shows which of the six General Occupational Themes this activity is most closely related to. These codes can help you to identify other activities that you may enjoy.

Theme Code	Basic Interests	Very Little Interest	Little Interest	Average Interest	High Interest	Very High Interest	Typical Activities
A	WRITING	☐	☐	☐	☑	☐	Reading or writing
E	MERCHANDISING	☐	☐	☑	☐	☐	Selling retail or wholesale products
A	MUSIC/DRAMATICS	☐	☐	☑	☐	☐	Performing or enjoying music/drama
E	LAW/POLITICS	☐	☐	☑	☐	☐	Discussing law and public policies
E	SALES	☐	☐	☑	☐	☐	Selling to potential customers

OCCUPATIONAL SCALES

The Occupational Scales measure how similar your interests are to the interests of people who are satisfied working in those occupations. Only the 10 scales on which your interests are *most* similar to those of these people are listed at the right in rank order. Your results on all 211 of the Occupational Scales are found on pages 3, 4, and 5.

The letters to the left of each scale identify the Theme or Themes that most closely describe the interests of people working in that occupation. You can use these letters to find additional, related occupations that you might find interesting. After reviewing your results on all six pages of this Profile, see the back of page 5 for tips on finding other occupations in the Theme or Themes that interest you the most.

Theme Code	Occupation	Very Dissimilar	Dissimilar	Mid-Range	Similar	Very Similar
AE	PUBLIC RELATIONS DIRECTOR	☐	☐	☐	☐	☑
AE	BROADCASTER	☐	☐	☐	☐	☑
A	LAWYER	☐	☐	☐	☐	☑
CA	PARALEGAL	☐	☐	☐	☐	☑
AE	ADVERTISING EXECUTIVE	☐	☐	☐	☐	☑
SA	SOCIAL WORKER	☐	☐	☐	☐	☑
A	REPORTER	☐	☐	☐	☑	☐
A	LIBRARIAN	☐	☐	☐	☑	☐
EAS	FLIGHT ATTENDANT	☐	☐	☐	☑	☐
AI	TRANSLATOR	☐	☐	☐	☑	☐

***PERSONAL STYLE SCALES** measure your levels of comfort regarding Work Style, Learning Environment, Leadership Style, and Risk Taking/Adventure. This information may help you make decisions about particular work environments, educational settings, and types of activities you would find satisfying. Your results on these four scales are on page 6.*

CPP CONSULTING PSYCHOLOGISTS PRESS, INC. • 3803 E. Bayshore Road, Palo Alto, CA 94303

SUMMARY OF ITEM RESPONSES

ADMINISTRATIVE INDEXES *(response percentages)*

OCCUPATIONS	13 % L	44 % I	43 % D
SCHOOL SUBJECTS	21 L	41 I	38 D
ACTIVITIES	33 L	2 I	65 D
LEISURE ACTIVITIES	31 L	14 I	55 D
TYPES OF PEOPLE	30 L	15 I	55 D
CHARACTERISTICS	25 Y	8 ?	67 N
SUBTOTAL	21 %	30 %	49 %
PREFERENCES: ACTIVITIES	34 L	33 =	33 R
PREFERENCES: WORK	50 L	17 =	33 R

The subtotal of his Administrative Indexes shows a response rate of 21 percent "Like," 30 percent "Indifferent," and 49 percent "Dislike." Although he dislikes most math and science subjects because they are abstract and difficult for him, the percentages of "Dislike" for School Subjects (38 percent) is not as high as those found in Activities (65 percent) and Leisure Activities (55 percent). He feels these results are indicative of his well-defined interests and that his results reflect what he enjoys (Figure 14.1).

Client 1's highest Themes are Enterprising ("Average Interest") and Artistic ("Average Interest"); he feels these descriptions are accurate. Among his high BISs are Writing ("High Interest"), and Music/Dramatics ("Average Interest"). These BIS scores tie in with his current assignment as entertainment editor of the school newspaper and his interest in and ability to play the piano. He feels the descriptions of Law/Politics ("Average Interest") and Merchandising ("Average Interest") fit him but disagrees with his

STRONG INTEREST INVENTORY

Profile report for CLIENT 2
ID:
Age: 17
Gender: Female
Date tested:
Date scored:

Page 1 *of* 6

SNAPSHOT: ***A SUMMARY OF RESULTS FOR CLIENT 2***

GENERAL OCCUPATIONAL THEMES

The General Occupational Themes describe interests in six very broad areas, including interest in work and leisure activities, kinds of people, and work settings. Your interests in each area are shown at the right in rank order. Note that each Theme has a code, represented by the first letter of the Theme name.

You can use your Theme code, printed below your results, to identify school subjects, part-time jobs, college majors, leisure activities, or careers that you might find interesting. See the back of the Profile for suggestions on how to use your Theme code.

THEME CODE	THEME	VERY LITTLE INTEREST	LITTLE INTEREST	AVERAGE INTEREST	HIGH INTEREST	VERY HIGH INTEREST	TYPICAL INTERESTS
E	ENTERPRISING	☐	☐	☑	☐	☐	Selling, managing
I	INVESTIGATIVE	☐	☐	☑	☐	☐	Researching, analyzing
A	ARTISTIC	☐	☑	☐	☐	☐	Creating or enjoying art
S	SOCIAL	☐	☑	☐	☐	☐	Helping, instructing
C	CONVENTIONAL	☐	☑	☐	☐	☐	Accounting, processing data
R	REALISTIC	☐	☑	☐	☐	☐	Building, repairing

Your Theme code is EI—(see explanation at left).
You might explore occupations with codes that contain any combination of these letters.

BASIC INTEREST SCALES

The Basic Interest Scales measure your interests in 25 specific areas or activities. Only those 5 areas in which you show the *most* interest are listed at the right in rank order. Your results on all 25 Basic Interest Scales are found on page 2.

To the left of each scale is a letter that shows which of the six General Occupational Themes this activity is most closely related to. These codes can help you to identify other activities that you may enjoy.

THEME CODE	BASIC INTERESTS	VERY LITTLE INTEREST	LITTLE INTEREST	AVERAGE INTEREST	HIGH INTEREST	VERY HIGH INTEREST	TYPICAL ACTIVITIES
E	MERCHANDISING	☐	☐	☐	☑	☐	Selling retail or wholesale products
E	SALES	☐	☐	☐	☑	☐	Selling to potential customers
R	ATHLETICS	☐	☐	☑	☐	☐	Playing or watching sports
A	MUSIC/DRAMATICS	☐	☐	☑	☐	☐	Performing or enjoying music/drama
S	TEACHING	☐	☐	☑	☐	☐	Instructing young people

OCCUPATIONAL SCALES

The Occupational Scales measure how similar your interests are to the interests of people who are satisfied working in those occupations. Only the 10 scales on which your interests are most similar to those of these people are listed at the right in rank order. Your results on all 211 of the Occupational Scales are found on pages 3, 4, and 5.

The letters to the left of each scale identify the Theme or Themes that most closely describe the interests of people working in that occupation. You can use these letters to find additional, related occupations that you might find interesting. After reviewing your results on all six pages of this Profile, see the back of page 5 for tips on finding other occupations in the Theme or Themes that interest you the most.

THEME CODE	OCCUPATION	VERY DISSIMILAR	DISSIMILAR	MID-RANGE	SIMILAR	VERY SIMILAR
EAS	FLIGHT ATTENDANT	☐	☐	☐	☐	☑
EC	BUYER	☐	☐	☐	☐	☑
AE	ADVERTISING EXECUTIVE	☐	☐	☐	☑	☐
CA	LIFE INSURANCE AGENT	☐	☐	☐	☑	☐
SA	SOCIAL WORKER	☐	☐	☐	☑	☐
ECA	STORE MANAGER	☐	☐	☐	☑	☐
EAS	HUMAN RESOURCES DIRECTOR	☐	☐	☐	☑	☐
SE	COMMUNITY SERV. ORGANIZATION DIR.	☐	☐	☐	☑	☐
ECR	OPTICIAN	☐	☐	☐	☑	☐
CE	PARALEGAL	☐	☐	☐	☑	☐

***PERSONAL STYLE SCALES** measure your levels of comfort regarding Work Style, Learning Environment, Leadership Style, and Risk Taking/Adventure. This information may help you make decisions about particular work environments, educational settings, and types of activities you would find satisfying. Your results on these four scales are on page 6.*

CPP CONSULTING PSYCHOLOGISTS PRESS, INC. • 3803 E. Bayshore Road, Palo Alto, CA 94303

Figure 14.2 Snapshot for Client 2, a High School Student Reconsidering Her Choice of College Major

score in Sales ("Average Interest") because he dislikes rejection. The largest concentration of occupations to which he has similar interests appear in the A Theme: Public Relations Director, Broadcaster, Advertising Executive, and Reporter, and all are occupations that Client 1 would like to explore. College majors for the A Theme include broadcasting, mass communications, journalism, creative writing, advertising, and public relations. This client's *Strong* results confirmed his plans to pursue a major in communications.

Client 2. Client 2, a seventeen-year-old twelfth-grader, had already decided on a college major and occupation. She applied to four colleges and planned to major in psychology or Spanish and become a clinical psychologist. She selected these majors after taking a psychology class and because although she does not enjoy it, she studied Spanish for five years and feels it would be an asset when applying for jobs. This student was a member of the National Honor Society and successfully completed advanced placement and honors courses; nonetheless, Client 2 confided that she misses classes and spends little time studying. She explained that she is going to college for social reasons and has purposely chosen colleges with relaxed academic environments that will not require her to work hard.

Client 2's highest Theme (Figure 14.2) is Enterprising ("Average Interest"). Her counselor contrasted this Theme with the Theme codes for Psychologist (IA) and Clinical Psychologist (SIA) from the *Dictionary of Holland Occupational Codes*. Her score for the Investigative Theme is "Average Interest," and for Artistic and Social it is "Little Interest." Client 2's score on the *Strong* female Psychologist OS (25) confirmed that she would probably not like the day-to-day work of a psychologist. Her highest BISs are Merchandising ("High Interest"), Sales ("High Interest"), and Athletics ("Average Interest"). Athletics play an important part in this client's life, and the idea of selling or marketing a service or product, particularly in the sports area, sounds appealing. When Client 2 and her counselor researched the Clinical Psychologist occupation, they discovered a doctoral degree is often required. Since she plans to pursue only a bachelor's degree, the client is redirecting her career focus and exploring Enterprising majors such as business administration, retail merchandising, and marketing.

Exploring Career Options with Non–College Bound Students

Non–college bound students have an immediate need for definitive information to establish areas of interest and identify potential occupations to enter the workplace. The Occupational Scales and their corresponding Theme codes can be beneficial to these students, providing them with specific occupations as well as Theme clusters to expand their occupational choices. Students can then research and explore these occupations through a variety of career/vocational sources. For example, one twelfth-grader who was having difficulty in his English, math, and science classes had scores of "High Interest" on the Artistic and Enterprising Themes. Since he also had "Similar" interest scores for occupations with A and AE Themes, his counselor suggested that he investigate Artistic and Enterprising careers. He found a part-time job at an art supply store, loved the environment, and was able to move into a full-time job when he graduated from high school. His future goal is to get on-the-job training and progress into store management.

In another example, a twelfth-grader with a history of failing grades was not planning to attend college. Although he had scores of "Average Interest" in the Enterprising and Social Themes, he had a cluster of "Similar" interest scores on the Realistic OSs. These occupations—including Farmer, Gardener/Groundskeeper, and Plumber—appealed to him because he liked to build, work with his hands, and be outdoors. His BIS scores indicated an interest in agriculture. He was enrolled in a job-site program that concentrated on bricklaying and carpentry; the counselor recommended that he explore his interests as revealed by the *Strong* by participating in the horticultural program. His preference for practical learning was consistent with his Learning Environment (LE) score of 26. An apprenticeship program would provide this student with the opportunity to earn while learning a vocation. He has been counseled to apply himself to his course work so he would be eligible to enter a state apprenticeship program.

Working with At-Risk Students

Counseling at-risk students presents a unique set of challenges. These students have grown up in circumstances that have hindered their educational progress and limited their exposure to a wide range of occupations. They are often nontraditional learners whose approach to learning makes it difficult for them to adjust to traditional school settings. Many of these students have not experienced successes, educationally or otherwise, that have allowed them to develop confidence and self-esteem; thus, they may need extra encouragement to believe in themselves and their abilities. Counselors can help these students see that they can choose between diverse opportunities and careers and can help them make informed decisions about their future.

The *Strong* can help counselors make a difference in these students' lives. For example, a student who was being hospitalized for depression scored "High Interest" on the Artistic and Social Themes. When the counselor identified some careers that she might find interesting, the student turned to her therapist and said, "I guess now I have a reason to go on" ("High School Students Turn," 1993).

Interpretation sessions with at-risk students are most effective when conducted in small groups of two to four. An opening discussion of what the students dream about doing in the future and what subjects they would like to know more about can make them more receptive to learning about their results. In addition, by carefully reviewing their Profiles prior to interpretation, counselors can identify any potential areas of interest, no matter how slight, that can help to stimulate students' enthusiasm for the exploration process.

Since depressed and flat Profiles are common among this population, it is generally most effective

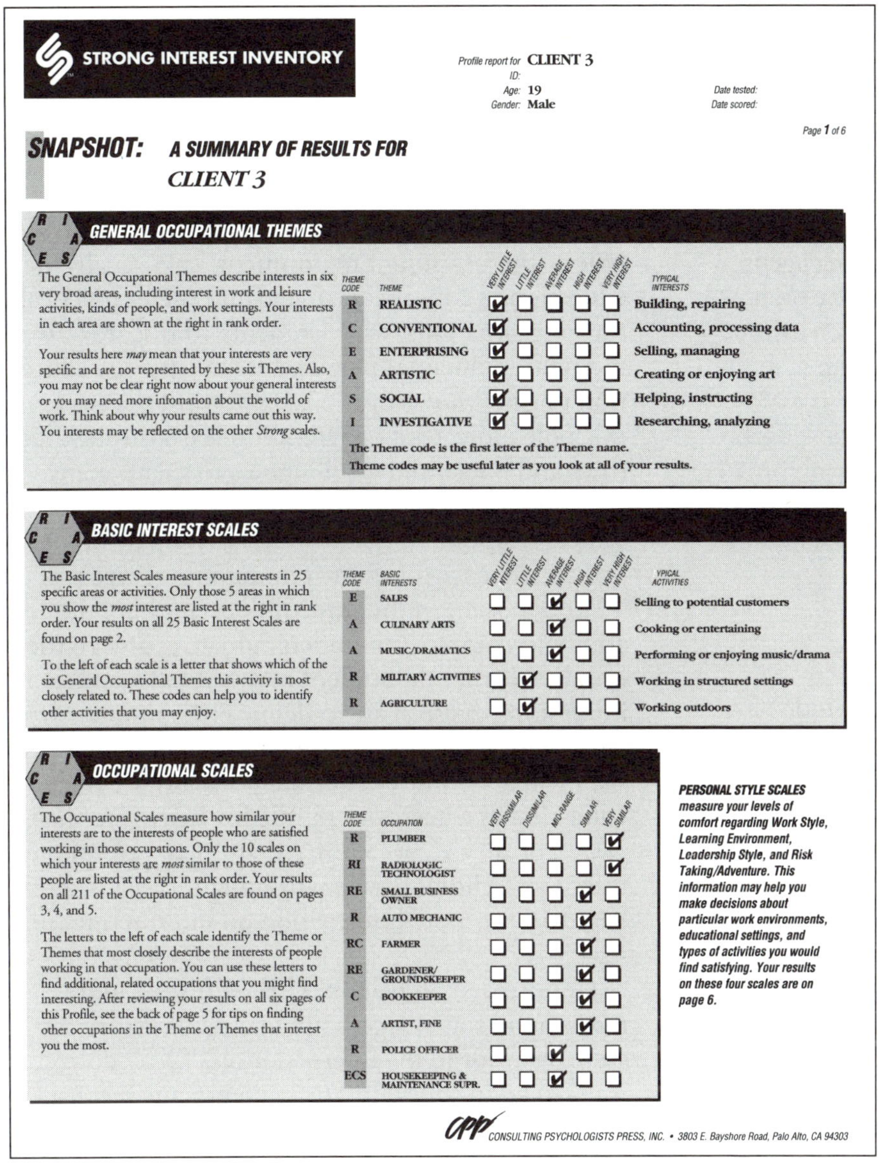
STRONG INTEREST INVENTORY

Profile report for CLIENT 3
ID:
Age: 19
Gender: Male
Date tested:
Date scored:

Page 1 of 6

SNAPSHOT: A SUMMARY OF RESULTS FOR CLIENT 3

GENERAL OCCUPATIONAL THEMES

The General Occupational Themes describe interests in six very broad areas, including interest in work and leisure activities, kinds of people, and work settings. Your interests in each area are shown at the right in rank order.

Your results here *may* mean that your interests are very specific and are not represented by these six Themes. Also, you may not be clear right now about your general interests or you may need more infomation about the world of work. Think about why your results came out this way. You interests may be reflected on the other *Strong* scales.

Theme Code	Theme	Very Little Interest	Little Interest	Average Interest	High Interest	Very High Interest	Typical Interests
R	REALISTIC	✓					Building, repairing
C	CONVENTIONAL	✓					Accounting, processing data
E	ENTERPRISING	✓					Selling, managing
A	ARTISTIC	✓					Creating or enjoying art
S	SOCIAL	✓					Helping, instructing
I	INVESTIGATIVE	✓					Researching, analyzing

The Theme code is the first letter of the Theme name.
Theme codes may be useful later as you look at all of your results.

BASIC INTEREST SCALES

The Basic Interest Scales measure your interests in 25 specific areas or activities. Only those 5 areas in which you show the *most* interest are listed at the right in rank order. Your results on all 25 Basic Interest Scales are found on page 2.

To the left of each scale is a letter that shows which of the six General Occupational Themes this activity is most closely related to. These codes can help you to identify other activities that you may enjoy.

Theme Code	Basic Interests	Very Little Interest	Little Interest	Average Interest	High Interest	Very High Interest	Ypical Activities
E	SALES			✓			Selling to potential customers
A	CULINARY ARTS			✓			Cooking or entertaining
A	MUSIC/DRAMATICS			✓			Performing or enjoying music/drama
R	MILITARY ACTIVITIES		✓				Working in structured settings
R	AGRICULTURE		✓				Working outdoors

OCCUPATIONAL SCALES

The Occupational Scales measure how similar your interests are to the interests of people who are satisfied working in those occupations. Only the 10 scales on which your interests are *most* similar to those of these people are listed at the right in rank order. Your results on all 211 of the Occupational Scales are found on pages 3, 4, and 5.

The letters to the left of each scale identify the Theme or Themes that most closely describe the interests of people working in that occupation. You can use these letters to find additional, related occupations that you might find interesting. After reviewing your results on all six pages of this Profile, see the back of page 5 for tips on finding other occupations in the Theme or Themes that interest you the most.

Theme Code	Occupation	Very Dissimilar	Dissimilar	Mid-Range	Similar	Very Similar
R	PLUMBER					✓
RI	RADIOLOGIC TECHNOLOGIST					✓
RE	SMALL BUSINESS OWNER				✓	
R	AUTO MECHANIC				✓	
RC	FARMER				✓	
RE	GARDENER/ GROUNDSKEEPER				✓	
C	BOOKKEEPER				✓	
A	ARTIST, FINE				✓	
R	POLICE OFFICER			✓		
ECS	HOUSEKEEPING & MAINTENANCE SUPR.			✓		

***PERSONAL STYLE SCALES** measure your levels of comfort regarding Work Style, Learning Environment, Leadership Style, and Risk Taking/Adventure. This information may help you make decisions about particular work environments, educational settings, and types of activities you would find satisfying. Your results on these four scales are on page 6.*

CPP CONSULTING PSYCHOLOGISTS PRESS, INC. • 3803 E. Bayshore Road, Palo Alto, CA 94303

Figure 14.3 Snapshot for Client 3, a High School Student Entering the Workforce

to work with the highest GOTs and BISs, even if the highest are "Little Interest" or "Very Little Interest." The counselor can read aloud the Theme descriptions and have students identify the characteristics that best fit them. Any areas of interest can then be tied to potential jobs or careers. The counselor needs to provide specific guidelines for the next steps students can take to explore these job or career opportunities; the *Strong* worksheet, *Career Exploration: A Journey of Discovery,* may be helpful in leading students through the steps of exploration. The counselor can also suggest that students visit the library and use books, manuals, directories, and handbooks to research jobs or careers and can encourage students to conduct exploratory interviews.

Client 3. Client 3, a nineteen-year-old student, has struggled through school, repeating both eleventh and twelfth grades. His Profile showed that he responded "Like" to only 5 percent of the *Strong* items, resulting in depressed scores of "Very Little Interest" on all six of the GOTs (Figure 14.3). He was bored with school and considered music his only interest. His highest Themes were Realistic ("Very Little Interest") and Conventional ("Very Little Interest"); his highest BISs were Sales, Culinary Arts, and Music/Dramatics—he showed "Average Interest" in all three. He felt this description fit him well.

When asked what he would like to be doing, Client 3 responded that he could see himself repairing or configuring stereos, which was consistent with his highest Theme score, Realistic. Seven of his highest scores on the OSs were in the Realistic Theme. With help from his counselor, Client 3 brainstormed ways to tie his interests together, such as repairing or selling musical instruments or stereos (numerous repair occupations are coded R) or representing musicians as a booking agent. His counselor also offered practical advice on how to conduct exploratory interviews, research careers, and test out his choices (e.g., by working in a music store). To gain self-esteem as well as experience in the world of work, Client 3 took a job after school as a grocery store clerk. This job provided him with enough income while he explored the training he would need for the jobs he had identified.

Assessing Educational Goals

The *Strong* can be useful when assessing students' educational goals, whether they are planning post-secondary education or training. Counselors may find it helpful to combine a discussion of high school students' *Strong* results with a discussion of their academic records. This approach provides a more comprehensive assessment and can motivate students to improve academically or to redirect their course of study toward more appropriate college majors and career goals.

For example, one student scored "High Interest" in the Investigative Theme and "Very High Interest" in the BISs of Science and Mathematics. He expressed a strong desire to major in science in college. However, he had difficulty passing chemistry, and his parents, in frustration, threatened not to send him to college unless his grades improved. His counselor reviewed the educational requirements for his identified occupations, which led to a discussion about whether he could be successful as a chemist if he were doing poorly in high school chemistry. The counselor discussed why his grade was not higher and recommended strategies that could help him improve his academic record.

The Learning Environment scale can also provide useful information that can help students assess their academic goals. This scale predicts how students approach the job of being a student and their preference for either an academic or practical learning environment. It is important to stress that this scale is not an indication of how intelligent students are, how well they will do, or what grades they will get—it does not predict academic success or failure, and *it is not a measure of ability.*

Students who score toward the left (practical) pole of the Learning Environment scale usually view education as a means to an end and prefer practical learning situations, while students who score toward the right (academic) pole of this scale pursue education to gain knowledge. A score toward the academic pole indicates a preference to learn through lectures and books and a willingness to spend many years in school; a score toward the practical pole indicates an orientation toward learning by doing and a preference for short-term training. A score of 40 does not mean the student does not have the ability to complete an undergraduate degree; rather, it indicates that the student may not have sufficient interest to persist in an academic environment. Students with scores toward the practical pole who persist in an academic environment usually see their education as a necessary hurdle for entry into their career, or they view college chiefly as an extension of their high school social environment. (See Chapters 8 and 10 for more information on interpreting this scale.)

Counselors can help make the LE scale more meaningful for college-bound students if they ask students prior to the interpretation, "Why do you want to go to college?" The students' answers usually describe their preferences for learning and can help them understand their motivation for attending college. For example, one student with an LE score of 37 stated that he wanted to attend college to meet new people and be independent; he never mentioned a desire to learn. Another student, a National Honor Society member with a Learning Environment score of 41, stated she wanted to attend college to prepare for a career. She confided that she persevered in advanced placement classes, although she found them difficult, not to broaden her knowledge but to enhance her academic record. She felt this would make her more likely to gain admittance to the college of her choice. The LE scale helped both these students understand how they would approach being college students.

Conclusion

The *Strong* provides a useful starting point for high school students to begin researching, exploring, and expanding career options. Although the *Strong* has been widely used with high school students, research has lagged with this population. More long-term studies should be done in these areas: following high school students through college and career to determine their satisfaction with their chosen college majors and occupations, identifying which scales (GOTs, BISs, or OSs) are most useful in interpreting the Profiles of high school students, and verifying that the Learning Environment scale is a helpful predictor in selecting postsecondary education.

References

Dictionary of occupational titles. (1991). Washington, DC: U.S. Department of Labor.

Discover. (1993). Iowa City, IA: American College Testing.

Gottfredson, G. D., & Holland, J. L. (1989). *Dictionary of Holland occupational codes* (2nd ed.). Odessa, FL: Psychological Assessment Resources.

Guidance Information System. (1993). Cambridge, MA: Riverside Publishing, a Houghton Mifflin Company.

Hansen, J. C., & Stocco, J. L. (1980). Stability of vocational interests of adolescents and young adults. *Measurements and Evaluation in Guidance, 13,* 173–178.

Hansen, J. C., & Swanson, J. L. (1983). Stability of interests and the predictive and concurrent validity of the 1981 SCII for college majors. *Journal of Counseling Psychology, 30,* 194–201.

High school students test their dreams. (1990, Spring). *Strong Forum, 7*(1), 3.

High school students turn to the Strong for career direction. (1993, Spring). *Strong Forum, 10*(1), 3, 5.

Occupational outlook handbook. (1994). Washington, DC: U.S. Department of Labor.

Scharf, R. (1970). Relative importance of interest and ability in vocational decision-making. *Journal of Counseling Psychology, 17,* 258–262.

Spitzer, D., & Levinson, E. M. (1988). A review of 10 vocational interest inventories and recommendations for selection, interpretation, and use by school psychologists. *School Psychology Review, 17*(4), 673–692.

Strong, E. K., Jr. (1943). *Vocational interests of men and women.* Stanford, CA: Stanford University Press.

Swanson, J. L., & Hansen, J. C. (1988). Stability of vocational interests over 4-year, 8-year, and 12-year intervals. *Journal of Vocational Behavior, 33,* 185–202.

Thomas, L. E., Morrill, W. H., & Miller, C. D. (1970). Educational interests and achievement. *Vocational Guidance Quarterly, 18,* 199–202.

Zarrella, K. L., & Schuerger, J. M. (1990). Review of the temporal stability of occupational interest inventories. *Psychological Reports, 66,* 1067–1074.

CHAPTER 15

Cross-Cultural Use of the Strong

Nadya A. Fouad, Lenore W. Harmon, & Jo-Ida C. Hansen

Since the civil rights movements of the 1960s there have been demands for psychological tests and inventories that are culturally fair and unbiased (Anastasi, 1988; Hansen, 1984; Tittle & Zytowski, 1978; Walsh & Betz, 1990; Zytowski & Borgen, 1983). Clearly, the underlying questions "Do interest inventories work for ethnic group members?" and "Are interest inventory scales developed for European Americans valid for members of racial and ethnic minority groups?" are important to every counselor who works with racial and ethnic minority group members. The literature indicates that, in general, the *Strong* can be used with ethnic minority group members, and data collected from racial and ethnic group members as part of the 1994 revision indicate that there are few differences between racial and ethnic group members and white members of occupational groups. However, cultural variables do affect vocational assessment (Fouad, 1993), and counselors working with racial and ethnic minority group clients should consider the client's culture when interpreting the *Strong*.

This chapter (1) discusses use of the *Strong* with culturally diverse clients, (2) reviews cross-cultural research on the *Strong*, and (3) presents the data collected on racial and ethnic minority group members who participated in research for the 1994 revision. The data presented at the end of this chapter are an important first step in giving counselors definitive answers to questions of how culture affects interest inventories. ◆

Cross-Cultural Counseling Use of the Strong

Racial and ethnic minority clients who approach career counseling for help in making career decisions often have the same concerns as do white clients but may also have concerns unique to their cultural background. Cultural values and background can influence the concerns these clients bring to career counseling, modify how they view the inventory and the test-taking procedure, or affect their use of information provided by the *Strong*. For these reasons, it is important for counselors to help clients place their interest information in a cultural context.

Variables to consider include:

- the client's language and facility with English,
- the client's familiarity with interest inventories and use of the *Strong* in career counseling,
- influence of significant family members in the client's decision-making process,
- influence of environmental barriers (such as racism or discrimination) on the client's consideration of various careers, and
- culturally stereotypic interests that may or may not be an accurate reflection of the client's interests.

These variables are discussed in the following section. Note that this discussion focuses on use of the *Strong* with culturally diverse clients and is not meant to be an exhaustive discussion of cross-cultural counseling. Readers are strongly encouraged to consult Sue and Sue (1990) or Leong (in press) for more in-depth material about respective racial and ethnic groups.

Culturally Appropriate Career Counseling

Fouad and Bingham (in press) discuss a culturally appropriate career-counseling model in which sensitivity to the client's culture is a part of every step, from developing rapport to helping clients identify their concerns to developing culturally appropriate goals and interventions. The career-counseling sequence described in Chapter 10, then, may need adjustment when working with clients who are not white. While not meant to be exhaustive or to address counseling issues with separate groups of racial and ethnic minority clients, this discussion highlights some of the primary modifications that may be necessary in culturally appropriate career counseling.

Modifying the Career-Counseling Sequence

Cultural sensitivity is a critical step in establishing rapport (Step 1 in the career-counseling sequence). Acknowledging and valuing cultural differences and communicating an appreciation of a client's cultural background are important components in this process. Step 2 in the career-counseling sequence is problem identification. Approaching this step from a culturally appropriate perspective means being aware that clients may have issues that are culturally specific or that result from their interaction with the white culture (e.g., racism or discrimination). Clients may need encouragement to discuss these problems or may need extra support if they are struggling to make a career choice that is different from what is traditionally expected of them. Counseling goals (Step 3) should include those relevant to cultural issues as well as those most commonly considered in career counseling.

Fouad and Bingham (in press) include an additional step in their model that directly addresses whether clients have specific cultural issues to bring into career counseling. In order to help clients understand such cultural influences, counselors can use a checklist, an interview, or a genogram or can ask clients to draw the impact of culture on their choices. This step can also be used with white clients who are exploring the influence of gender-role stereotyping on their choices.

Assessment of the client's knowledge of self and the world of work and interventions to increase that knowledge (Steps 4 through 6) can be affected by the client's cultural background. For example, for some cultures an emphasis on self-exploration may be considered inappropriate, while for other cultures it may be important to consider exploration of self-knowledge in relation to others (e.g., "How are your work values the same as your family's?"). Information about the world of work may be very limited for some cultures or may be stereotyped by race or gender.

Steps 15 through 17 of the career-counseling sequence are to develop a career exploration plan, a decision-making strategy and action plan, and a time line for accomplishment of various tasks. However, for many clients this approach may be too linear. Latino/Hispanic clients, for example, prefer a less linear approach to career counseling; while they may smile and seem agreeable in the counseling session, they may have no intention of following such an action plan.

As mentioned earlier, several factors may be of specific concern in using the *Strong* with clients from culturally diverse backgrounds. These are highlighted in the following sections.

Language

The *Strong* is written in standard English, with a reading level falling between eighth and ninth grade. If the client has limited English-speaking facility, the counselor and client may decide that a translation of the *Strong* would be appropriate. Until translations of the 1994 *Strong* are available, counselors may choose to administer one of the translations of the 1985 *Strong*. The Spanish version is the most commonly used translation in the United States. Counselors using this version often ask which type of Spanish is used in the translation—whether it is more typical, for example, of Mexico or Cuba. The translation is considered to be fairly standard Spanish and is relatively free of idiomatic expressions that would characterize one country or another.

Familiarity with Assessment Procedures and Career Counseling

Career counselors using interest inventories often assume that clients are familiar with interest inventories and assessment procedures. This assumption may not be true, particularly for clients who have not been exposed to the educational system in the United States. The *Strong* may appear intimidating, threatening, or confusing if a client is not knowledgeable about attitude surveys and does not understand the concept that "there is no right or wrong answer." The counselor's responsibility, then, is to assess the client's familiarity with assessment procedures before administering the *Strong* and to demystify the assessment process if necessary. In order to reduce any potential threat, the term *test* has been eliminated from the 1994 Item Booklet/Answer Sheet, instructions, and report of results.

It is equally important to assess the client's familiarity with the role of the *Strong* in career counseling. Some clients, no matter what their culture, may be very familiar with the *Strong* (and even come for career counseling asking for "that test that tells me what to be"), while others may be unfamiliar with it. Nevertheless, cultural background can influence expectations of career counseling, as well as the most effective method for presenting *Strong* results. For example, Asian clients, who often expect a counselor to be an expert and authority figure, may be unwilling to challenge the request to take the *Strong*, even if they do not understand why they are taking it (Leong & Gim, in press). Counselors need to set appropriate expectations for counseling and to explain fully the usefulness of the results.

African-American clients may not trust the assessment process (Gibbs, 1990) and may be suspicious of *Strong* results. Counselors may need to address their concerns directly and point out that the *Strong* results can help them explore options they might not otherwise consider. It may also help to point out that the ethnicity data collected in 1992 and 1993 on the updated occupational samples indicate that only 31 items (slightly less than 10 percent) differentiated African-American males from the male General Reference Sample (GRS), and 26 items differentiated African-American females from the female General Reference Sample. For example, Table 15.3 (later in this chapter) indicates that both African-American males and females liked religious items more than did the combined GRSs, while African-American men in the updated occupational groups disliked outdoors items, and African-American women disliked agriculture and outdoors items more than the combined GRSs did. Table 15.4 (later in this chapter) demonstrates that those differences appear on very few of the Basic Interest Scales (BISs) or General Occupational Themes (GOTs). These data should give African Americans confidence that their interests are similar to the interests of the individuals used in constructing the *Strong* scales.

Family Influences

Many racial and ethnic group members in the United States place high cultural values on group or collective goals and strong emphasis on family input into career decision making. Such a value system may mean greater spousal involvement when considering a job opportunity, or it may mean that career decisions are made in close consultation with a client's parents. Since the latter case, in particular, is not typical of dominant culture norms, counselors need to be careful not to label their clients as "enmeshed" or "dependent" when it occurs. For example, an Asian-American client with strong traditional values may choose an occupation that her family deems appropriate, even if her interests seem to fit better with another occupational area. Her counselor needs to focus on helping her make the most appropriate decision—one that incorporates her cultural and familial values—not the most independent decision.

Environmental Barriers

Incorporating the client's cultural context in career counseling may also involve acknowledging external barriers the client perceives. For example, one client who had immigrated to the United States from Vietnam as a teenager felt that he had reached the glass ceiling (an invisible barrier to advancement for women and minority group members) in an engineering firm due to his ethnicity. His supervisors told him he had the technical skills needed to succeed in his job but that he did not speak up enough in meetings, and he subsequently was passed up for promotions. He attended assertiveness workshops on the recommendation of his supervisors but felt that assertive or aggressive behavior at work was in conflict with his cultural values. This client's *Strong* scores were highest on the Investigative and Realistic GOTs. He scored "Similar" to men in the Engineering occupation but wanted to find a career more congruent with his cultural values. His results also indicated an interest in medical occupations. With the counselor's help he decided to become a surgeon, a career he felt would be a good fit with his things-oriented interests as well as his medical interests and one in which he thought he would be less likely to hit the glass ceiling or experience cultural conflicts.

Stereotypical Interests

Use of the *Strong* with culturally diverse populations can be most complex when a client's results are "stereotypical" for members of that culture. For example, African-American clients may indicate interests in occupations typical of the Enterprising and Social Themes (Carter & Swanson, 1990), while Asian-American clients may indicate interests in the Investigative or Realistic Themes. The counselor needs to consider whether these results are a true reflection of these clients' interests or whether they are an indication of the clients' perception of occupational opportunities available to them. Looking at the results of the Work Style scale, which shows a preference for working with people or with ideas/data/things, can help the counselor clarify whether the client's Social Theme interests are genuine.

Client 1. Client 1, a young woman who immigrated from Hong Kong, had been trained as an underwriter (an Enterprising and Conventional occupation) but gave up her job to relocate elsewhere in the United States with her husband. She wanted to use the opportunity to seek further schooling and a change of career. Her *Strong* results, shown in Figure 15.1, indicate her highest interests were in the Artistic, Investigative, and Realistic Themes. Her scores on the Basic Interest Scales are consistent with her results on the Themes, as shown in the Snapshot. Although she was similar to women in some Investigative occupations as well as those in the Artistic area, she was satisfied as an underwriter and was not opposed to seeking another occupation in this general area. She also was intrigued by some R- and I-coded occupations and wanted to explore them as well.

In this case, the stereotypical results for Asian Americans (Realistic and Investigative) were only partially an accurate picture of the client's interests; her highest interests were Artistic. Leong and Gim (in press) note that for many Asian-American clients, expressed interests may be a more accurate reflection than inventoried interests. Thus, counselors are encouraged to ask clients to talk about what they like in addition to using the *Strong* to help clients explore options. After reviewing her *Strong* results, this client considered returning to school to be an architect, but she decided instead to take another job as an underwriter, at least for a while. Her family obligations precluded further training, the pay as an underwriter was acceptable, and she would be flexible to move with her husband when they decided to relocate in the future.

Review of Research on Cross-Cultural Interests

Cross-cultural use of the *Strong* falls into three major categories: use of the English version with U.S. racial and ethnic minorities, use of the English version in other countries, and translation and use in other languages. Use of the *Strong* with these groups is predicated on the assumption that it is valid to use the instrument with populations other than majority culture clients (analysis of data collected for the 1994 *Strong* revision supports this assumption).

Ward and Bingham (1993) questioned whether it is appropriate to use the *Strong* with various ethnic groups, whether there is research support for its use, and whether there are any special precautions or considerations needed in using the *Strong* with ethnic minority clients. The following sections address their first two questions; the final section of the chapter deals with their third question.

Use with U.S. Racial and Ethnic Minorities

Studies comparing the interest structure of whites with that of African Americans, American Indians, and Latinos/Hispanics indicate reasonable correspondence of all groups to Holland's hexagonal model

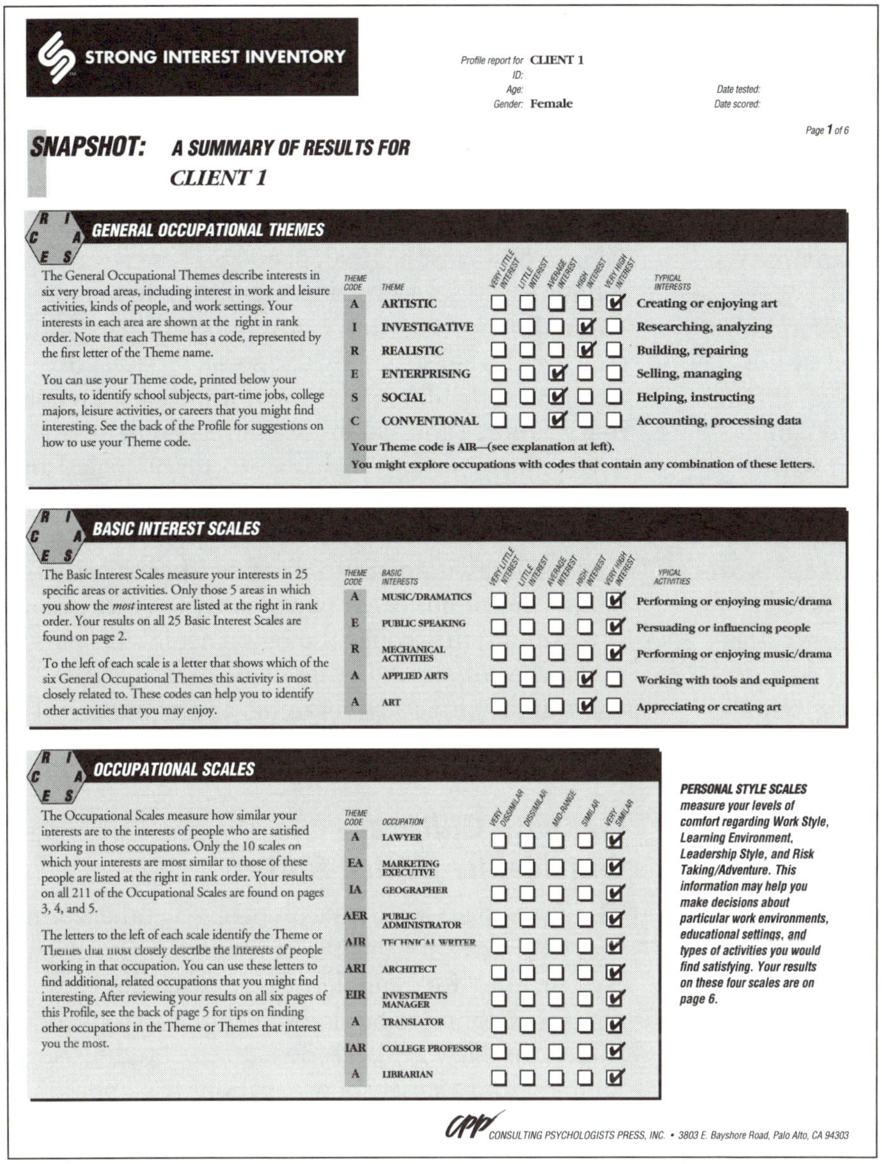

STRONG INTEREST INVENTORY

Profile report for CLIENT 1
ID:
Age:
Gender: Female

Date tested:
Date scored:

Page 1 of 6

SNAPSHOT: A SUMMARY OF RESULTS FOR CLIENT 1

GENERAL OCCUPATIONAL THEMES

The General Occupational Themes describe interests in six very broad areas, including interest in work and leisure activities, kinds of people, and work settings. Your interests in each area are shown at the right in rank order. Note that each Theme has a code, represented by the first letter of the Theme name.

You can use your Theme code, printed below your results, to identify school subjects, part-time jobs, college majors, leisure activities, or careers that you might find interesting. See the back of the Profile for suggestions on how to use your Theme code.

THEME CODE	THEME	VERY LITTLE INTEREST	LITTLE INTEREST	AVERAGE INTEREST	HIGH INTEREST	VERY HIGH INTEREST	TYPICAL INTERESTS
A	ARTISTIC					✓	Creating or enjoying art
I	INVESTIGATIVE				✓		Researching, analyzing
R	REALISTIC				✓		Building, repairing
E	ENTERPRISING			✓			Selling, managing
S	SOCIAL			✓			Helping, instructing
C	CONVENTIONAL			✓			Accounting, processing data

Your Theme code is AIR—(see explanation at left).
You might explore occupations with codes that contain any combination of these letters.

BASIC INTEREST SCALES

The Basic Interest Scales measure your interests in 25 specific areas or activities. Only those 5 areas in which you show the *most* interest are listed at the right in rank order. Your results on all 25 Basic Interest Scales are found on page 2.

To the left of each scale is a letter that shows which of the six General Occupational Themes this activity is most closely related to. These codes can help you to identify other activities that you may enjoy.

THEME CODE	BASIC INTERESTS	VERY LITTLE INTEREST	LITTLE INTEREST	AVERAGE INTEREST	HIGH INTEREST	VERY HIGH INTEREST	YPICAL ACTIVITIES
A	MUSIC/DRAMATICS					✓	Performing or enjoying music/drama
E	PUBLIC SPEAKING					✓	Persuading or influencing people
R	MECHANICAL ACTIVITIES					✓	Performing or enjoying music/drama
A	APPLIED ARTS				✓		Working with tools and equipment
A	ART				✓		Appreciating or creating art

OCCUPATIONAL SCALES

The Occupational Scales measure how similar your interests are to the interests of people who are satisfied working in those occupations. Only the 10 scales on which your interests are most similar to those of these people are listed at the right in rank order. Your results on all 211 of the Occupational Scales are found on pages 3, 4, and 5.

The letters to the left of each scale identify the Theme or Themes that most closely describe the interests of people working in that occupation. You can use these letters to find additional, related occupations that you might find interesting. After reviewing your results on all six pages of this Profile, see the back of page 5 for tips on finding other occupations in the Theme or Themes that interest you the most.

THEME CODE	OCCUPATION	VERY DISSIMILAR	DISSIMILAR	MID-RANGE	SIMILAR	VERY SIMILAR
A	LAWYER					✓
EA	MARKETING EXECUTIVE					✓
IA	GEOGRAPHER					✓
AER	PUBLIC ADMINISTRATOR					✓
AIR	TECHNICAL WRITER					✓
ARI	ARCHITECT					✓
EIR	INVESTMENTS MANAGER					✓
A	TRANSLATOR					✓
IAR	COLLEGE PROFESSOR					✓
A	LIBRARIAN					✓

***PERSONAL STYLE SCALES** measure your levels of comfort regarding Work Style, Learning Environment, Leadership Style, and Risk Taking/Adventure. This information may help you make decisions about particular work environments, educational settings, and types of activities you would find satisfying. Your results on these four scales are on page 6.*

CPP CONSULTING PSYCHOLOGISTS PRESS, INC. • 3803 E. Bayshore Road, Palo Alto, CA 94303

Figure 15.1 Snapshot for Client 1, an Asian-American Female

(Doughtie, Chang, Alston, Wakefield, & Yom, 1976; Fouad, Cudeck, & Hansen, 1984; Harrington & O'Shea, 1980; Lamb, 1978; Scott & Anadon, 1980). Swanson (1992) found the same order of interests as postulated by Holland for African-American college students but did not find support for the calculus assumption, which proposes that themes are equidistant. She found that scores for African Americans demonstrated that the Realistic and Investigative Themes were relatively closer, the Artistic Theme was farther apart, and the Social, Enterprising, and Conventional Themes were closer together than theoretically predicted by Holland (1985). Fouad et al. (1984), using Latino/Hispanic high school and community college students, also found support for Holland's (1985) model.

Perhaps because large differences in the structure of interests of various racial groups have not been found, few studies have been conducted on the predictive validity of interest inventories for minorities. Haviland and Hansen (1987) found that the *Strong* predicted majors for American Indian college students, and a study by Borgen and Harper (1973) and another by Whetstone and Hayles (1975) found that the *Strong* predicted membership in career groups for African Americans as well as it did for whites. A study by Hines (1983), in contrast, showed poor predictive validity for the 1974 *Strong* for African Americans who were predominantly lower-income students at an urban college.

Studies comparing mean profiles of interests for ethnic minorities and whites also offer conflicting conclusions. A comparison of the interests of Latino/Hispanic and white college students found no significant differences on the GOTs (Montoya & DeBlassie, 1985). A study comparing the interests of African-American and white female and male college students found that the former tended to have stronger interests in Social, Enterprising, and Conventional areas while the latter had stronger interests in the Realistic area (Yura, 1986).

Another study, using a sample of American Indian students, focused on interests as measured by the 1981 Occupational Scales (OSs) (Gawhega, 1982). The American Indian female students had significantly different scores from those of white female students on only 4 of 81 OSs, while the American Indian male students differed from white male students on only 5 of 81 scales. This difference approximates the number of significant differences (i.e., 3 for each gender) that one might expect by chance, leading the author to conclude that the *Strong* demonstrated functional utility for both cultural groups.

A review of studies using the *Strong* with American Indians by Hansen (1987) concluded that, although the data were somewhat conflicting, American Indian women tended to score higher on the Realistic Theme than did white women, and American Indian men tended to score higher on the Conventional Theme than did white men. Hansen also noted fewer differences between American Indian and white college students than high school students.

Research comparing the interests of whites and Asian Americans has revealed gender differences as well as between-group differences. Sue and Kirk (1972) found that Chinese-American males and females tended to have more Investigative and Conventional Theme interests than did white males and females, and Chinese-American females had higher interests in domestic activities than did white females. In another study, Japanese-American male students were found to have higher interests in Realistic and Investigative Theme areas than did white male students, and Japanese-American female students had higher Conventional and Investigative Theme interests than did white female students. Unlike the Chinese-American women, Japanese-American women did not have higher domestic activities interests (Sue & Kirk, 1973).

Two reviews of the validity literature on the *Strong* for minorities cited the need for more research. Arbona (1990) reviewed the literature of career counseling with Latinos/Hispanics, concluding that "Hispanic students' view of the world of work is similar to the view held by the majority culture" and also calling for large-scale studies with better sampling to clarify this issue. The second review, which looked specifically at the validity of the *Strong* with African Americans, concluded that "little evidence exists for the psychometric validity of the *Strong* with blacks" (Carter & Swanson, 1990, p. 206). These researchers found that African Americans tended to have more Social, Enterprising, and Conventional Theme interests (e.g., higher scores in sales, social service, business, and verbal-linguistic areas), while whites tended to have more Realistic, Investigative, and Artistic Theme interests (e.g., higher scores for biological and physical sciences, technical and skilled trades, and aesthetic-cultural occupations). These differences could reflect within-group characteristics or participants' perceptions of the opportunity to enter various occupations; they could also reflect actual occupational choices, which in turn could indicate differences in the formation, meaning, and expression of interests.

Use with Cultures Outside the United States

The *Strong* has been used with people in other countries who are reasonably fluent in English. The interest structures, for example, of U.S. psychology students were found to be almost identical to those of students in New Zealand (Bull, 1975). Studies using samples from a variety of occupations (e.g., police officers, engineers, artists, psychologists, and physicians) in several countries (e.g., Germany, Mexico, Austria, Switzerland, Scotland, Australia, Canada, Great Britain, New Zealand, South Africa, and Pakistan) supported the conclusion that the interests of people in a particular occupation are extremely similar across cultures (Fouad & Hansen, 1987; Fouad, Hansen, & Arias, 1989; Lonner, 1968; Lonner & Adams, 1972; Shah, 1971; Strong, 1943).

Hansen (1987), discussing international use of the *Strong*, concluded that item-level differences seemed to disappear at the scale and Profile levels. International use of the *Strong* has been investigated by Fouad, Hansen, and colleagues (Fouad & Dancer, 1992a, 1992b; Fouad & Hansen, 1987; Fouad, Hansen, & Arias, 1986, 1989), whose work has given limited support to the use of interest inventories with validated translations across national boundaries. The authors found, for example, a greater similarity between Mexican and U.S.

engineers than between Mexican and U.S. lawyers, but they found that the response of Mexican student lawyers were similar to those of U.S. professional lawyers, indicating the cross-cultural use of the *Strong* for both occupational groups. The authors also found that differences between engineering groups tended to be avocational, with Mexican engineers indicating greater breadth of interests than U.S. engineers. The authors' findings, noted earlier, of the similarity of interests across cultures also provided evidence of the effective use of the *Strong* across cultures. However, Fouad and Hansen (1987) cautioned that factors influencing career choice vary greatly across cultures, and much more research on the transferability of the *Strong* is needed before it may be used without caution across national boundaries.

Translations of the Strong

The 1985 *Strong* was translated into Spanish by the publisher, using a three-step process. First, a translation was prepared by a university professor of Spanish; then the original translation was reviewed, corrected, and modified by a bilingual person whose native language was Spanish. Finally, the revised translation was forwarded to another professor of Spanish for final review.

In addition, a back translation, or translation from Spanish back into English, was completed, and the two English versions of the *Strong* (i.e., original and back-translated) were compared for discrepancies. Only 8 out of the 325 items did not have identical wording (e.g., Debates [Spanish] for Arguments [English]). These 8 items were modified for the 1985 Spanish version to reflect more accurately the English meaning.

Field testing involved bilingual high school and community college students from eleven schools in the states of California, New Mexico, and Washington (Hansen & Fouad, 1984). Most of the subjects were of Mexican heritage; a small number were of Cuban, Puerto Rican, Central American, and South American descent. Each person completed both the Spanish and English versions. Correlations between scale scores on the Spanish and English forms were high (median for GOTs = .85, for BISs = .84, and for OSs = .83); scores between the Spanish and English OS Profiles correlated .92 with each other.

Another study (Fouad, Cudeck, & Hansen, 1984), which extended the work of Hansen and Fouad on the accuracy of the Spanish translation, provides evidence of the divergent and convergent validity of the English and Spanish GOTs as well as evidence that the psychological constructs of the two forms are similar. A confirmatory factor analysis showed that a model that postulated two method factors and six trait factors, with a hexagonal pattern hypothesized among the trait factors, appeared to fit the data. The method factors (two forms of the inventory) were very similar, producing a correlation of .79. The correlations among the trait factors (the six GOTs) formed a perfect circumplex, supporting Holland's model of the structure of interests.

The 1985 *Strong* also has been translated into French Canadian (Chevrier, 1979) for use in Canada. Two separate Hebrew translations were prepared and were then merged into one form; the merged form was back-translated to check the accuracy of the translation. A version of the *Strong* is available in Italian. The wording of the *Strong* items also was adapted for use in Great Britain (M. Cook, personal communication, 1982). For example, the American English version used Auto Racer, Business Teacher, and Realtor, while the British version used Racing Driver, Commerce Teacher, and Estate Agent.

A translated version of the 1985 *Strong* is also in use in Iceland (Konrads, 1987), and a large project is under way to validate the 1985 *Strong* for use in Australia (E. Care & F. Naylor, personal communication, 1987, 1994). Additional research translations have been done in Swedish, Bahamian, German, Icelandic, Portuguese, and Taiwanese, but are not available for commercial use as of this writing. With the increase in global communication, it is anticipated that work will continue on translations and validation of those translations. Translations of the 1994 *Strong* will be undertaken in the future.

Data Collected in 1992–1993 for Racial and Ethnic Minority Groups

For the first time, more than 55,000 individuals who filled out the research version of the *Strong* were asked voluntarily to indicate their ethnicity on the Item Booklet/Answer Sheet. While some individuals may have chosen not to report their ethnicity, approximately 3,000 racial and ethnic group members did respond to this option, providing a unique opportunity to analyze the inventory for ethnic group differences. Racial and ethnic data can be used to describe differences in interests across minority groups and to clarify whether systematic differences exist in interest patterns across groups. These data can also be used to investigate differences among ethnic groups within a particular occupation—for example, to determine whether African-American librarians differ from other librarians.

This section begins with a description of the characteristics of minority group members of occupational groups. Then preliminary analyses of differences between interests of minority group members and the GRS are presented; finally, within-group analyses are examined for the four occupational groups that had enough ethnic minority group members to permit such analyses.

Demographic Characteristics

Table 15.1 shows the sample sizes and other demographic information for the four largest racial and ethnic groups, together numbering 2,445. These groups were African Americans, Latinos/Hispanics, Asians, and American Indians. An additional 531 minority group members responded but were not members of one of these groups. They either belonged to smaller groups (e.g., Alaskan natives) or identified with two or more ethnic minority groups.

The demographic information presented here is not representative of all members of these ethnic minority groups and should not be used to generalize beyond a description of the groups from which the data was collected. It is important to remember that the major thrust of the data collection was to obtain responses from members of 50 occupational groups who met the criteria of satisfaction, number of years in the occupation, and minimum age of 25, and who performed typical tasks for that occupation. In most cases, it was not possible to determine a member's ethnicity from the group list used to identify occupational group members (e.g., lists of members of the American Bar Association used to identify lawyers). Accordingly, it was not possible to determine whether ethnic minority group members' response rates were proportional to their representation in the occupational sample.

Table 15.1 indicates that mean ages for racial and ethnic group participants fell between 38 and 44. Average numbers of years in the occupation fell between 11 and 16. Almost all American Indians and African Americans were born in the United States. Among Asians, 10.5 percent were born in China, 9.9 percent in the Philippines, 9.3 percent in India, and 7.3 percent in Japan; of these groups, 75.8 percent had been in the United States for more than 10 years and 89.7 percent had spoken English for more than 10 years. Among Latinos/Hispanics, 34.8 percent were born in Latin America, 85.7 percent had been in the United States for more than 10 years, and 90.2 percent had spoken English for more than 10 years.

The educational levels for each of the four groups were relatively high, with over 85 percent of all groups completing some schooling beyond high school, and 42 to 89 percent achieving at least a bachelor's degree. The four minority groups were widely distributed over the occupational groups. American Indians were found in 28 occupational groups of females and 29 occupational groups of males. Since the number of American Indians was small relative to the number of occupational groups, most occupational groups contained fewer than five American Indians. Asians were found in 45 occupational groups of females and 45 occupational groups of males. Even though the total number of Asians surveyed was 795, the majority of occupational groups contained seven or fewer Asians. African Americans were found in 46 occupational groups of females and 45 occupational groups of males. Although African-American respondents constituted the largest of the four racial and ethnic groups, the majority of occupational groups had fewer than six African Americans. Latinos/Hispanics were found in 48 occupational groups of females and 45 occupational groups of males, with the majority of occupational groups containing five or fewer Latinos/Hispanics.

While most occupational groups had relatively small numbers of racial and ethnic group members, 67 percent of the 49 male occupational groups had at least 5 percent ethnic minority representation: 49 percent contained from 5 to 9 percent minorities, and 18 percent had 10 percent minorities. For the 49 female occupational groups, the comparable percentages were 71, 53, and 18 percent. Several occupations had more than 5 percent specific ethnic minority group members, and several had more than 10 percent specific ethnic minority group members, as shown in Table 15.2. Table 15.2 also indicates that nine male occupational groups and nine female occupational groups contained at least one ethnic minority group that made up 5 percent or more of the total. The percentages ranged from 5 percent of the

Table 15.1 Sample Sizes and Demographic Data for the Four Largest Racial and Ethnic Groups in the *Strong* Sample

Sample Size and Demographic Data	Ethnicity and Gender							
	African American		American Indian		Asian		Latino(a)/Hispanic	
	Female	Male	Female	Male	Female	Male	Female	Male
Sample Size	437	368	81	78	402	393	314	372
Mean Age	42.6	43.6	41.9	42.6	38.5	42.2	38.7	40.1
Age Range	25–84	26–79	26–63	25–63	25–64	25–74	25–68	25–70
Mean Years in Occupation	15.8	16.2	13.8	15.5	12.0	15.0	11.5	14.5
Median Educational Level	BA/BS	BA/BS	AA	BA/BS	Master	Master	BA/BS	BA/BS
% Completing Educational Level								
Some High School	0.5	0.0	1.4	0.0	0.0	0.0	0.3	0.3
High School	2.8	2.0	13.5	5.1	0.8	1.0	4.2	3.0
Trade/Technical	3.3	2.0	9.4	6.4	0.8	1.0	2.6	4.1
Some College	13.6	13.8	21.6	14.1	5.5	6.7	11.9	13.3
Associate Degree (AA)	7.7	10.5	12.2	12.8	3.5	5.7	6.4	10.8
College Degree (BA/BS)	23.9	33.3	20.3	25.6	37.4	29.7	32.2	32.6
Graduate/Professional	48.2	38.4	21.3	36.0	52.0	55.9	42.4	35.9
% Speaking English								
11–20 Years	0.2	0.3	0.0	0.0	12.4	12.5	10.8	9.4
20+ years	98.2	98.1	98.8	97.4	81.3	80.9	83.5	87.1
% Living in U.S.								
11–20 years	2.5	4.1	0.0	0.0	20.9	18.8	15.2	11.6
20+ years	97.0	94.3	100.0	98.7	65.4	67.9	75.9	83.3

Note: This table does not include data on members of smaller ethnic groups (e.g., Alaskan natives), people who identify with two or more ethnic groups, and people who did not indicate their ethnicity.

male Paralegal group (African American) to 15.3 percent of the female Translator group (Latina/Hispanic).

While it is satisfying to see that ethnic minority group members were members of most of the 50 occupational groups sampled for the 1994 *Strong*, the fact that they were so well distributed across the groups makes it difficult to assess differences across ethnic groups within the same occupation. It is important to remember, as stated earlier, that all ethnicity data collected were voluntarily reported by the individuals, and thus the figures in each occupational group may underestimate minority representation in that group.

Between-Group Racial and Ethnic Differences

Differences between racial and ethnic groups and whites may appear in racial and ethnic groups' responses to individual items, in a pattern of interests on the GOTs or BISs, and/or in differences on the OSs. Group differences in any of these areas may have counseling implications for the use of the *Strong* with racial and ethnic groups.

Between-Group Item Differences

One way to answer the question "Does ethnicity affect *Strong* results?" is to determine systematic

Table 15.2 Occupational Samples with > 10% Combined Ethnic Membership and Specific Ethnic Groups That Compose ≥ 5% of an Occupational Sample

Occupational Samples with > 10% Combined Ethnic Membership	Gender	Specific Ethnic Groups That Compose ≥ 5% of an Occupational Sample
Auto Mechanic	Female	
Child Care Provider	Female	African American (8.5%), Latina/Hispanic (5.2%)
Dentist	Female	Asian (9.1%)
Engineer	Female	Asian (7.9%)
Engineer	Male	
Flight Attendant	Female	
Flight Attendant (27.3%)	Male	Asian (13.3%), African American (5.7%)
Housekeeping & Maintenance Supervisor	Female	African American (8.7%)
Housekeeping & Maintenance Supervisor (22.5%)	Male	African American (13.2%), Latino/Hispanic (5.2%)
Medical Records Technician	Male	African American (5.7%)
Occupational Therapist	Male	
Paralegal	Male	African American (5.0%)
Physicist	Female	Asian (8.7%)
Physicist	Male	Asian (7.7%)
Police Officer	Female	Latina/Hispanic (6.1%)
Police Officer	Male	Latino/Hispanic (6.3%)
Radiologic Technologist	Male	Latino/Hispanic (6.8%)
Translator (25.0%)	Female	Latina/Hispanic (15.3%), Asian (5.2%)
Translator (22.1%)	Male	Latino/Hispanic (13.0%)
___a	Female	Actuary: Asian (5.2%)
___a	Male	Chemist: Asian (5.6%)
___a	Female	School Administrator: African American (7.3%)

Note: Numbers in parentheses in the left column indicate those occupations in which more than 20 percent of the members of the occupation belong to ethnic minority groups. Numbers in parentheses in the right column indicate the percent of members of an occupational group who belong to a particular ethnic group.

a Occupational sample did not have a combined ethnic membership greater than 10 percent, but did have an individual ethnic group that comprised 5 percent or more of the sample.

differences in responses to items on the inventory that exist among minority group members. To examine the differences between ethnic group members and whites, the item responses of the four largest ethnic minority groups were examined separately by gender and minority group. These responses were compared with the item responses of the male and female GRSs. In each case, items were found that distinguished the eight resulting groups (male and female for each of the minority groups). Using a 16 percent difference in response percentages between the ethnic group and the GRS resulted in the numbers of items and item characteristics indicated in Table 15.3. Although they are not enough to build scales, the responses give some information about the minority members in the sample—for example:

▲ Interest in religious items appears to differentiate African Americans, and to a lesser extent American Indians, from the GRS.

▲ All groups, with the exception of American Indians, indicate that they like to communicate with people from other cultures more than do members of the GRS.

Table 15.3 Response Differences Between Ethnic Sample and General Reference Sample by Gender

			Items Differentiating Ethnic Sample from GRS				
Ethnic Group	Gender	Sample Size	N Items[a]	N Likes	Examples	N Dislikes	Examples
African American	Female	437	26	14	Religious leader	12	Rancher
							Nature study
African American	Male	368	31	21	Religious people	10	Camping
					Fashion model		Skiing
American Indian	Female	81	23	8	Nurse	15	Sculptor
					Religious music		
American Indian	Male	78	5	5	Physically sick people	0	
					Work in which you move from place to place vs. Work in which you live in one place[b]		
Asian	Female	402	5	5	Designer, electronic equipment	0	
Asian	Male	393	12	12	Clothes designer	0	
					Bilingual teacher		
Latina/Hispanic	Female	314	6	6	Modern languages	0	
Latino/Hispanic	Male	372	7	6	Ancient languages	1	Going to a play vs. Going to a dance[c]

[a] Figures in this column indicate the total number of items on which members of a particular ethnic group responded in a way significantly different from the General Reference Sample. The cutoff used was a minimum 16% difference in response to an item.
[b] American Indian males responded that they like work in which you move from place to place more than the GRS does.
[c] Latino/Hispanic males responded that they like going to a play less than the GRS does and like going to a dance more than the GRS does.

- American Indians, but not African Americans, have a greater interest in the outdoors than do members of the GRS.
- Latinos/Hispanics, and to a lesser extent Asians, are more interested in language than are members of the GRS. Note, however, that many of the Latinos/Hispanics are from the Translator occupational groups, and these interests may reflect their occupational interests rather than interests characteristic of ethnic group members.
- Asian, African-American, and Latino/Hispanic males indicate that they like living in a city more than males in the GRS. Latina/Hispanic females also like living in a city more than the females in the GRS, but American Indian females like it less than the female GRS.

While these results are intriguing and may help counselors interpret interest patterns for some racial and ethnic minority clients, it is important to point out that at most only 31 items (i.e., less than 10 percent) differentiated a minority group from the GRS. This finding helps keep in perspective the relative similarity among racial and ethnic groups in responding to the 317 items on the revised *Strong*. It is also important to note that it is unknown whether these differences are typical of the cultural groups, since these data were collected for information about vocational interests of an occupational group, rather than the vocational interests of all racial and ethnic group members.

Between-Group Scale Differences

A second way to examine the data is to determine if the item differences just described affect scale means for members of racial and ethnic groups. In other words, is a greater interest in religious items or in items related to nature reflected in higher mean scores on the relevant GOTs or BISs?

Table 15.4 shows the means for each male and female GRS and male and female racial and ethnic groups on the GOTs, BISs, and Personal Style Scales. Differences between racial and ethnic groups and

GRSs that were greater than one-half standard deviation are noted. Racial and ethnic groups were remarkably similar on the GOTs and BISs. Many of the differences noted at the item level were not reflected in differences on the BISs, and none of the items were reflected in differences on the GOTs.

Only two BISs differed by 5 points or more for all racial and ethnic groups. African Americans demonstrated the item differences noted earlier with higher means on the Religious Activities BIS for both males and females and lower means for females on the Nature BIS than did the GRS. Also, on the Learning Environment Personal Style Scale, American Indian females demonstrated a 7-point difference from the GRS (43.0 versus 50.0). This latter score probably reflects the fact that American Indian females whose highest educational level was high school had lower scores on Learning Environment than did females in the GRS whose highest educational level was high school (30.6 versus 37.3).

Within-Occupation Racial and Ethnic Differences

The third way that racial and ethnic group differences may be examined is to investigate differences between racial and ethnic group members and whites within the same occupation. This analysis can be done by examining whether the same items differentiate occupational group members from the GRS and by examining whether ethnic group members within the group differ from the GRS on any of the scales.

Within-Group Item Differences

Four occupational groups contained approximately 50 or more members of one ethnic minority group: Asian male Flight Attendants, African-American male and female Housekeeping & Maintenance Supervisors, and Latina/Hispanic female Translators. These small samples were used to conduct an exploratory analysis to determine whether distinctive characteristics could differentiate the occupational groups. Experimental scales were constructed by differentiating the item responses of each ethnic minority group with the appropriate GRS. Item responses for all the remaining members of the occupational group were also compared with the appropriate male or female GRS. Then the items that differentiated the ethnic minority group from the GRS were compared with the items that differentiated the rest of that occupational group from the GRS.

Analysis revealed a substantial overlap in the items separating minority groups and the rest of their occupational groups from the GRS. Table 15.5 on page 270 shows that for three occupations, roughly half of the items from each set were overlapping. Another way to state this result is to say that the ethnic groups in three occupations were differentiated from the GRS in ways similar (50% of the items) to all other groups in those occupations. One group—the African-American male Housekeeping & Maintenance Supervisors—was differentiated from the GRS on one-third of the items in ways similar to others in the occupation. Table 15.6 on page 271 gives examples of overlapping and nonoverlapping items for the two groups in each occupation.

Some of the unique items that differentiated the ethnic minority group but not the rest of the occupational group were items that differentiated the whole ethnic minority group from the GRS. Note that, as shown in Table 15.6, an interest in the religious items "Religious music" and "Young people's religious group" differentiated African-American male and female Housekeeping & Maintenance Supervisors but not other Housekeeping & Maintenance Supervisors from the GRS, indicating that those interests appear at the item level, in the BISs, and in the OSs. Table 15.6 lists the ten items that most differentiate minority group members in each of the four occupational groups and compares them with the ten most-differentiating items for all the other remaining members of the four occupational groups.

It is important to remember that these scales were only experimental, as they were based on groups of ethnic minority members that were too small to build dependable scales. Under these conditions, the item overlap is quite striking. Although the overlap was far from complete among ethnic group members and other members of the same occupational group, comparisons across occupational groups showed no overlap at all. In fact, there is little question that the items selected characterized people in different occupational groups. The comparisons of Asian male Flight Attendants with other male Flight Attendants and Latina/Hispanic female Translators with other female Translators showed the most overlap.

As already noted, African Americans expressed greater interest in religious activities in the comparisons between African-American male and female Housekeeping & Maintenance Supervisors and the rest of the Housekeeping & Maintenance Supervisors in the *Strong* occupational sample.

Table 15.4 Means and Standard Deviations on General Occupational Themes, Basic Interest Scales, and Personal Style Scales for Females and Males in the General Reference Sample, Whites, and Specific Racial and Ethnic Groups

Scale	Mean/S.D.	African American Female	African American Male	American Indian Female	American Indian Male	Asian Female	Asian Male	Latino(a)/Hispanic Female	Latino(a)/Hispanic Male	White Female	White Male	GRS Female	GRS Male
General Occupational Theme													
Realistic	Mean	44.1	51.1	46.3	53.7	48.3	53.5	45.3	52.9	46.5	53.5	46.7	53.3
	S.D.	8.5	9.7	9.5	10.3	9.6	9.8	8.5	9.7	8.9	9.8	9.1	9.8
Investigative	Mean	46.4	50.3	46.3	49.1	52.2	54.8	47.7	50.7	49.0	51.3	49.0	51.0
	S.D.	10.3	10.7	10.0	10.2	9.9	9.1	10.1	10.0	10.1	9.9	10.3	10.0
Artistic	Mean	52.1	48.3	49.0	45.9	54.0	48.9	54.6	48.9	52.8	47.0	52.6	47.4
	S.D.	9.6	10.0	9.1	9.9	8.7	9.5	8.9	9.8	9.4	9.8	9.4	10.0
Social	Mean	54.8	52.7	50.5	50.1	50.7	50.0	51.7	49.8	51.5	48.5	51.3	48.7
	S.D.	10.0	10.3	10.6	10.6	9.8	9.3	10.0	9.4	10.0	9.8	10.1	9.7
Enterprising	Mean	52.6	52.2	48.9	51.0	51.8	50.9	50.3	49.8	50.1	49.3	50.4	49.6
	S.D.	10.0	10.9	9.6	10.9	10.0	10.4	10.0	9.9	9.7	10.1	9.8	10.1
Conventional	Mean	52.2	52.4	53.6	49.6	51.8	51.0	48.8	49.6	50.4	49.4	50.6	49.4
	S.D.	10.8	10.1	11.0	9.4	10.1	9.3	10.2	9.4	10.6	9.4	10.5	9.5
Basic Interest Scale													
Agriculture	Mean	43.4	47.0	49.7	54.3	46.2	49.7	46.0	49.6	48.4	52.2	48.3	51.8
	S.D.	8.1	8.5	10.0	9.6	8.5	8.7	9.3	9.3	10.0	9.9	10.0	9.9
Applied Art	Mean	47.9	48.4	47.8	47.4	53.6	51.1	51.3	49.7	50.9	48.9	50.9	49.1
	S.D.	10.3	10.2	10.7	10.4	9.3	9.6	9.4	9.8	10.0	10.0	10.1	9.9
Art	Mean	51.5	47.7	50.4	45.9	55.1	49.3	55.0	48.9	53.0	46.7	52.8	47.2
	S.D.	9.3	9.4	9.6	10.1	8.2	9.4	8.6	9.4	9.3	9.9	9.3	9.9
Athletics	Mean	47.1	55.1	47.2	51.8	46.4	52.8	46.6	54.0	47.2	53.0	47.2	52.8
	S.D.	8.6	8.6	8.4	9.8	8.4	9.2	8.4	9.8	9.1	10.0	9.1	10.0
Computer Activities	Mean	52.9	53.7	52.8	51.1	51.8	52.4	49.1	51.6	49.8	50.1	49.9	50.1
	S.D.	11.1	10.1	11.5	9.9	10.1	9.0	11.0	9.8	10.5	9.6	10.4	9.7
Culinary Arts	Mean	52.6	48.5	53.1	48.3	54.0	48.4	53.8	48.2	53.4	46.4	53.4	46.5
	S.D.	8.9	10.0	8.0	9.4	8.7	9.6	8.6	9.3	9.0	9.7	8.9	9.7

267

Table 15.4 Means and Standard Deviations on General Occupational Themes, Basic Interest Scales, and Personal Style Scales for Females and Males in the General Reference Sample, Whites, and Specific Racial and Ethnic Groups (continued)

Scale	Mean/S.D.	African American Female	African American Male	American Indian Female	American Indian Male	Asian Female	Asian Male	Latino(a)/Hispanic Female	Latino(a)/Hispanic Male	White Female	White Male	GRS Female	GRS Male
Basic Interest Scale (continued)													
Data Management	Mean	50.0	53.0	50.2	49.3	51.2	52.6	47.3	50.1	48.9	51.0	49.2	50.8
	S.D.	9.9	9.4	10.0	9.2	9.3	9.5	9.6	9.7	10.2	10.0	10.1	9.9
Law/Politics	Mean	49.5	54.1	44.8	52.0	47.5	50.0	49.1	51.6	48.3	51.7	48.3	51.7
	S.D.	9.9	10.1	8.7	9.2	9.2	9.3	10.0	9.7	9.8	9.8	9.8	9.8
Mathematics	Mean	48.0	51.2	48.4	49.2	52.4	54.3	46.8	50.2	48.7	51.5	48.8	51.2
	S.D.	9.8	9.7	9.4	8.7	9.7	9.1	10.0	9.7	10.0	9.7	10.0	9.8
Mechanical Activities	Mean	45.7	52.7	46.5	52.9	49.5	54.6	45.5	53.3	46.5	53.4	46.8	53.2
	S.D.	8.4	9.8	8.7	10.5	9.4	9.7	8.3	9.7	8.7	9.9	8.9	10.0
Medical Science	Mean	47.7	50.9	47.9	50.5	51.0	52.9	48.6	50.6	49.8	50.8	49.7	50.6
	S.D.	10.5	10.5	10.0	11.3	9.9	9.7	9.9	9.6	9.9	9.8	10.0	9.9
Medical Service	Mean	51.1	51.9	53.1	52.5	50.8	51.1	50.2	50.8	50.8	48.8	50.6	48.9
	S.D.	10.3	10.7	11.8	10.8	10.1	10.0	10.4	9.5	10.5	9.7	10.5	9.7
Merchandising	Mean	52.7	51.3	49.0	49.8	52.9	50.9	51.1	49.4	50.7	48.8	50.9	49.1
	S.D.	9.8	10.1	9.3	10.6	9.8	10.3	10.1	9.8	9.9	10.0	10.0	9.9
Military Activities	Mean	49.2	56.8	50.1	55.5	47.4	52.6	47.5	53.9	47.2	52.7	47.4	52.9
	S.D.	9.1	12.4	9.4	10.9	7.8	10.4	8.0	11.7	7.5	10.9	7.7	11.0
Music/Dramatics	Mean	53.4	50.2	49.2	46.0	54.1	49.5	55.1	50.4	52.7	47.2	52.4	47.6
	S.D.	9.4	9.8	8.6	10.0	8.9	9.8	9.6	9.5	9.5	9.8	9.6	9.9
Nature	Mean	43.3	45.3	48.6	52.1	49.0	49.4	47.8	48.1	50.5	50.4	50.1	49.9
	S.D.	10.2	10.5	11.2	9.5	9.7	9.6	9.9	9.6	10.0	9.9	10.2	9.9
Office Services	Mean	54.4	51.5	55.7	49.4	51.5	49.1	50.7	49.1	51.7	48.0	51.8	48.2
	S.D.	11.1	9.9	11.5	9.6	10.2	8.7	10.3	8.9	10.7	8.7	10.8	8.8
Organizational Management	Mean	51.6	53.3	49.8	51.0	50.2	50.8	49.4	50.1	49.3	50.3	49.4	50.6
	S.D.	9.0	9.7	8.7	9.5	9.4	9.4	9.6	9.6	9.3	9.7	9.9	10.1
Public Speaking	Mean	51.5	54.2	45.6	52.0	47.1	49.1	49.6	51.1	48.6	51.0	48.7	51.2
	S.D.	9.5	9.8	8.7	10.4	9.0	9.4	9.6	9.6	9.7	9.9	9.8	10.0

Table 15.4 Means and Standard Deviations on General Occupational Themes, Basic Interest Scales, and Personal Style Scales for Females and Males in the General Reference Sample, Whites, and Specific Racial and Ethnic Groups (continued)

		African American		American Indian		Asian		Latino(a)/Hispanic		White		GRS	
Scale	Mean/S.D.	Female	Male	Female	Male	Female	Male	Female	Male	Female	Male	Female	Male
Basic Interest Scale (continued)													
Religious Activities	Mean	56.8	55.1	52.5	50.1	48.0	48.9	50.1	50.3	50.0	49.7	50.1	49.8
	S.D.	9.2	9.9	11.0	10.0	9.7	10.0	9.9	9.9	9.8	10.2	9.9	10.2
Sales	Mean	51.3	52.1	48.7	52.1	50.6	51.3	49.2	50.4	48.6	50.4	49.2	50.8
	S.D.	9.7	10.1	9.1	10.7	10.0	9.7	9.5	9.9	9.1	10.3	9.4	10.5
Science	Mean	46.5	50.9	47.0	49.7	51.7	54.7	47.5	51.2	48.7	51.5	48.8	51.2
	S.D.	9.4	10.5	10.1	9.6	9.8	9.0	9.4	9.5	9.6	9.9	9.9	10.0
Social Service	Mean	54.7	51.6	50.5	48.7	51.5	49.1	53.4	49.8	52.5	47.4	52.2	47.8
	S.D.	10.0	10.2	10.0	10.1	9.6	9.3	9.6	9.2	9.8	9.6	9.9	9.6
Teaching	Mean	51.5	51.6	46.8	50.1	49.7	50.3	49.8	49.9	50.5	49.8	50.2	49.8
	S.D.	9.8	9.5	10.7	10.6	9.3	8.8	9.9	9.3	9.9	9.8	10.0	9.9
Writing	Mean	51.6	48.0	48.0	47.1	51.3	47.9	52.1	47.8	51.9	48.0	51.7	48.3
	S.D.	9.6	9.9	9.3	9.9	9.2	9.1	9.0	10.0	9.6	10.0	9.6	10.1
Personal Style Scale													
Leadership Style	Mean	52.8	53.7	48.4	52.1	48.0	48.0	51.2	50.9	50.1	49.9	50.1	50.0
	S.D.	9.5	9.7	9.3	9.3	9.4	9.7	9.3	8.9	10.0	10.0	10.0	10.0
Learning Environment	Mean	48.9	48.8	43.0	47.2	50.2	49.8	50.4	49.3	50.4	50.0	50.0	50.0
	S.D.	9.6	8.9	10.2	8.7	9.2	8.4	9.9	9.5	10.3	9.4	10.4	9.5
Risk Taking/Adventure	Mean	44.1	50.9	45.5	55.2	46.5	51.0	47.5	54.0	46.8	53.4	46.9	53.1
	S.D.	9.1	9.2	10.5	8.6	9.8	9.6	9.4	9.2	9.8	9.3	9.7	9.4
Work Style	Mean	56.2	51.3	52.8	49.5	51.3	46.4	54.7	48.8	53.3	46.5	53.1	46.9
	S.D.	8.1	9.2	8.9	9.4	9.2	8.6	9.3	8.4	9.4	9.5	9.6	9.4

Table 15.5 Overlap in Items Differentiating Occupational Groups—Specific Ethnic Group Members and All Other Members of the Occupation—from the GRS

Occupational Scale	Gender	Ethnicity	N Items Differentiating Group from GRS	Minimum % Cutoff	N Items Overlap[a]
Flight Attendant	Male	Asian	62	22	32
		Non-Asian	61	18	
Housekeeping & Maintenance Supervisor	Female	African American	62	25	27
		Non-African American	65	16	
Housekeeping & Maintenance Supervisor	Male	African American	62	21	19
		Non-African American	39	14	
Translator	Female	Latina/Hispanic	61	16	31
		Non-Latina/Hispanic	59	16	

[a] The Ns shown here indicate that ethnic group members within an occupation are quite similar to all others in that occupation in terms of the items that differentiate them from the GRS.

Does this imply the need for a separate scale for African-American Housekeeping & Maintenance Supervisors? Probably not, since the religious items that differentiated the African-American Housekeeping & Maintenance Supervisors from the GRS were items that differentiated the larger group of African Americans from the GRS. Thus, an African-American Housekeeping & Maintenance Supervisors scale might incorporate cultural values that do not differentiate African-American Housekeeping & Maintenance Supervisors from African Americans in other occupations.

On the basis of this analysis it was possible to generalize from these four groups to other ethnic groups in other occupations and conclude that ethnic minority group members within an occupation are quite similar to others in that occupation *in terms of the items that differentiate them* from the GRS. Of course, this conclusion does not negate the fact that important cultural differences exist among members of different ethnic minority groups that must be taken into account in counseling. It simply suggests that counselors can confidently use with all ethnic groups the OSs that were developed with primarily white occupational groups. Such use can be advocated because the interests that differentiate people within occupations seem to be stronger than their ethnic interests in many cases. When the ethnic interests appear to be stronger, they appear to be quite specific.

Within-Group Profile Differences

Although there were only four groups with large enough sample sizes (samples of 50 or more minority group members) to do the analyses just reported, a number of other occupational groups contained approximately 30 or more members of ethnic minority groups. This number was considered sufficient to calculate a mean Profile. Such Profiles were calculated for all the ethnic minority group members in four occupational groups as well as for the rest of the members of their occupational groups: Latino/Hispanic male police officers, Asian female dentists, African-American female librarians, and African-American female school administrators. The mean profiles for each group's GOTs and BISs are in Figures 15.2 through 15.5, with differences greater than 5 points (half a standard deviation) between the ethnic group members and the rest of the group indicated. Figure 15.5 also contains OSs and Personal Style Scales for African-American female school administrators.

Table 15.6 Top Ten Items Listed in Rank Order Differentiating Occupational Groups—Specific Ethnic Group Members and All Other Members of the Occupation—from the GRS

Male Flight Attendants

	Asians	All Others
1.	Flight attendant	Flight attendant
2.	Fashion model	Fashion model
3.	Professional dancer	Working regular hours (−)
4.	Waiter/Waitress	Waiter/Waitress
5.	Artist's model	Artist's model
6.	Clothes designer	Clothes designer
7.	College professor (−)	Experimenting with new grooming preparations (+) vs. Experimenting with new office equipment
8.	Dance teacher	TV announcer
9.	Interior decorator	Acting
10.	Shopping for the latest fashions	Actor/Actress

Female Translators

	Latinas/Hispanics	All Others
1.	Foreign correspondent	Foreign correspondent
2.	Modern languages	Modern languages
3.	Foreign service officer	Foreign service officer
4.	Can communicate easily with people of different cultures	Bilingual teacher
5.	Music and arts events (+) vs. Athletic events	Editor
6.	Ancient languages	Ancient languages
7.	Magazines about art or music	Free-lance writer
8.	Checking printed material for errors	Checking printed material for errors
9.	Attending lectures	Working regular hours (−)
10.	Physical education director vs. Free-lance writer (+)	Physical education director vs. Free-lance writer (+)

Male Housekeeping & Maintenance Supervisors

	African Americans	All Others
1.	Housekeeper	Housekeeper
2.	Skiing (−)	Geometry (−)
3.	Physical education director (+) vs. Free-lance writer	College professor (−)
4.	Drilling in a military company	Doing a job yourself vs. Telling somebody else to do the job (+)
5.	Religious music	Buyer of merchandise
6.	Military drill	Factory manager
7.	Hotel manager	Hotel manager
8.	Boxing	Civil service employee
9.	Employment manager	Employment manager
10.	Young people's religious group	Security guard

Female Housekeeping & Maintenance Supervisors

	African Americans	All Others
1.	Housekeeper	Housekeeper
2.	Religious music	College professor (−)
3.	Hotel manager	Hotel manager
4.	Skiing (−)	Doing a job yourself vs. Telling somebody else to do the job (+)
5.	Employment manager	Hospital records clerk
6.	Airline pilot vs. Airline ticket agent (+)	Security guard
7.	Religious people	Nonconformists (−)
8.	Zoology (−)	Working full time (+) vs. Working part time
9.	Young people's religious groups	Customer service representative
10.	Doing your own laundry work	Factory manager

Note: Items followed by (−) would be scored negatively. On items that involve a choice between two activities, a plus sign (+) indicates the activity that the particular group liked more than the GRS did.

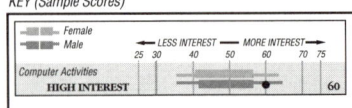
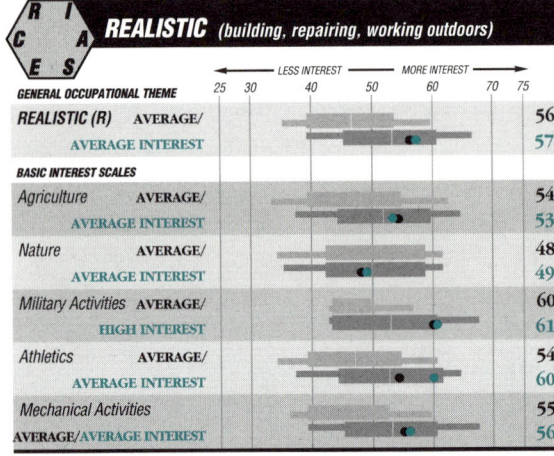
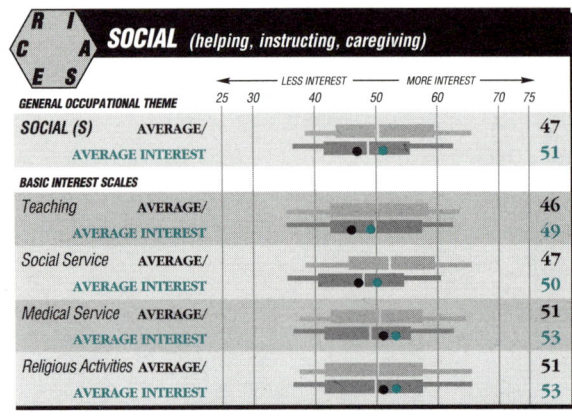
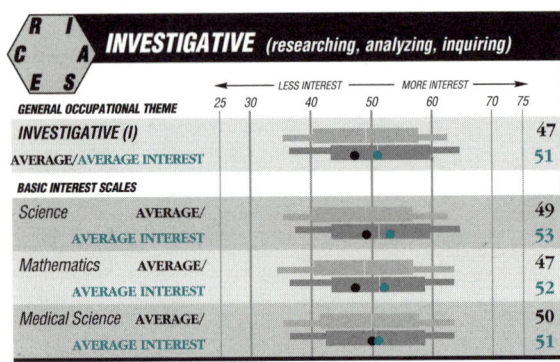
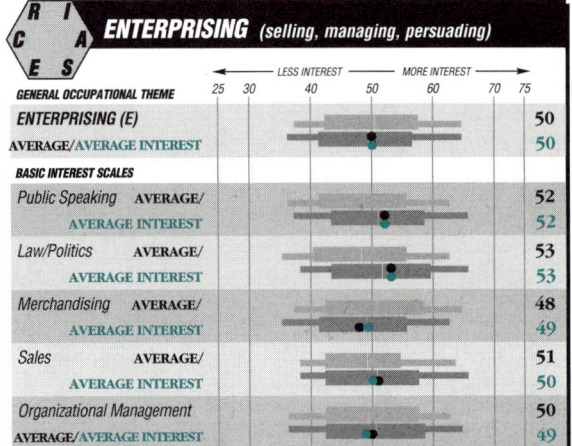
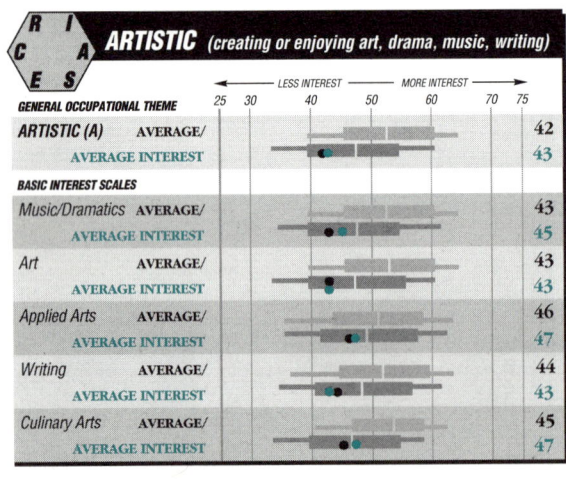
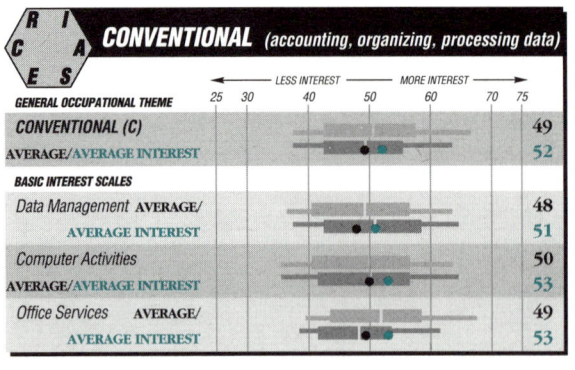

Figure 15.2 Scores on the GOTs and BISs of Latino/Hispanic Male Police Officers and Scores of All Other Male Police Officers in the *Strong* Occupational Sample

Note: Latino/Hispanic male police officers' scores are shown in blue; scores of non-Latino/Hispanic male police officers are shown in black.

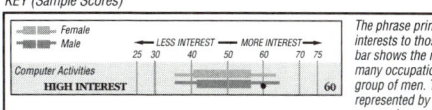
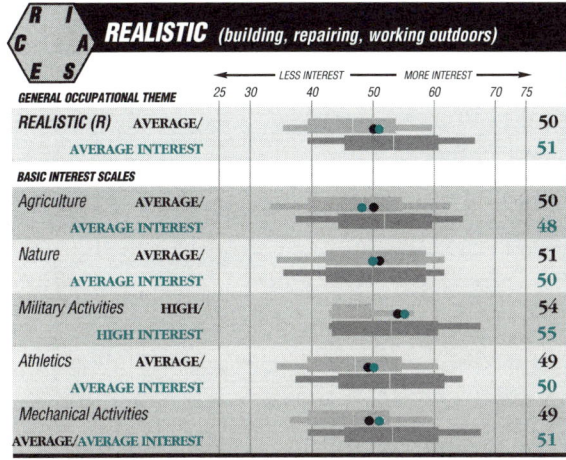
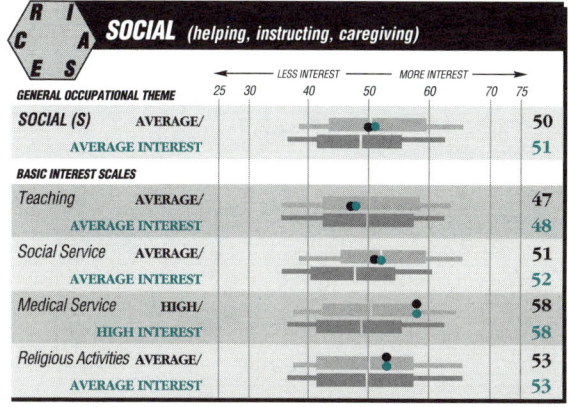
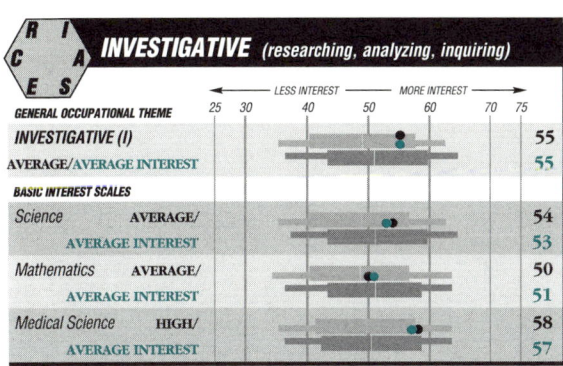
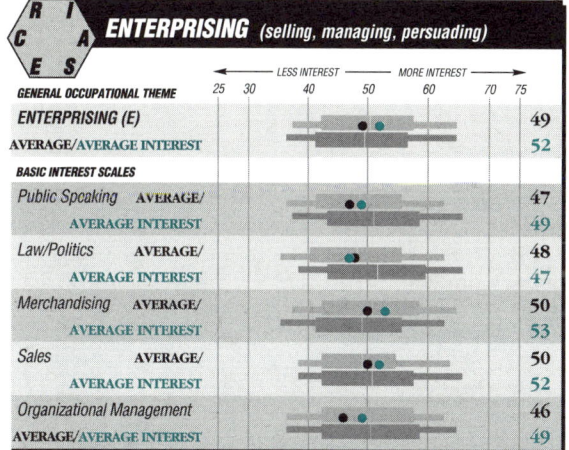
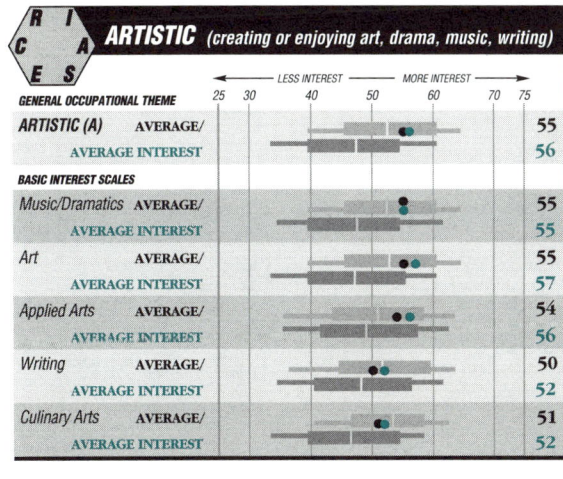
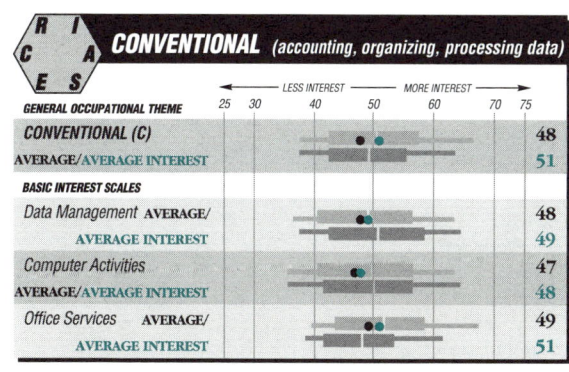

Figure 15.3 Scores on the GOTs and BISs of Asian Female Dentists and Scores of All Other Female Dentists in the *Strong* Occupational Sample

Note: Asian female dentists' scores are shown in blue; scores of non-Asian female dentists are shown in black.

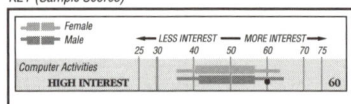
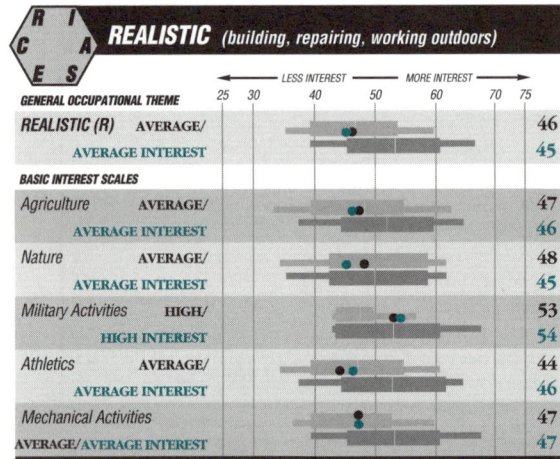
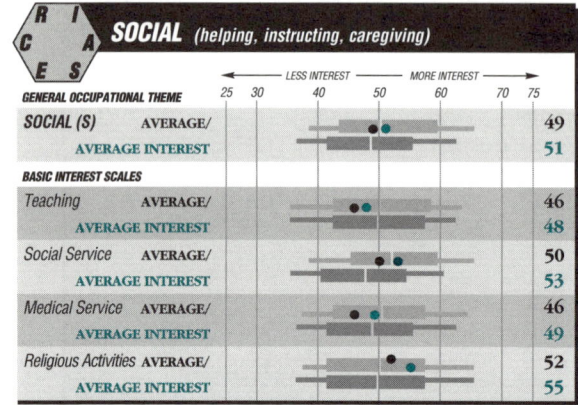
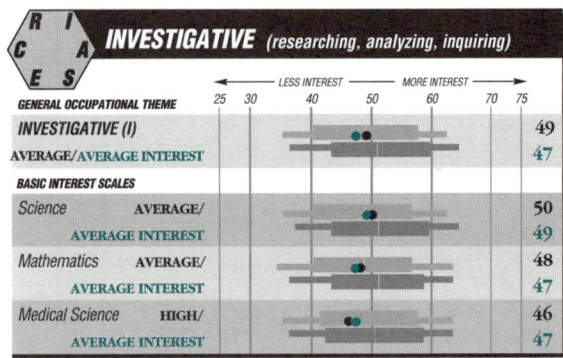
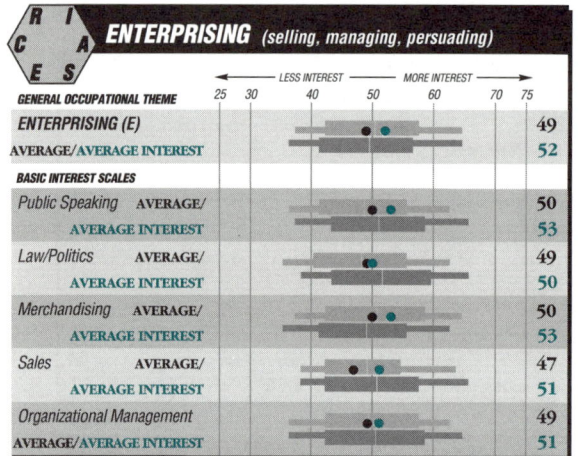
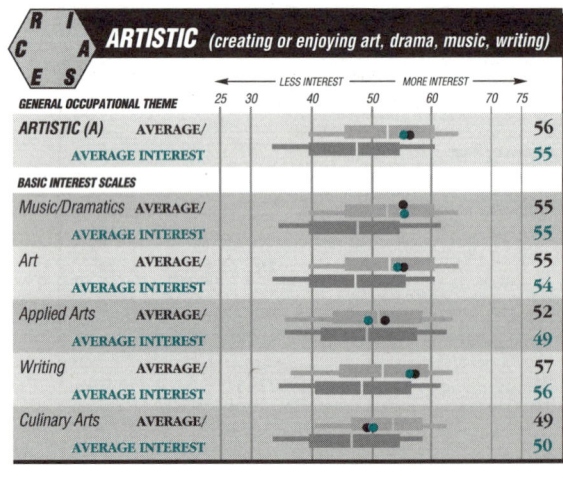
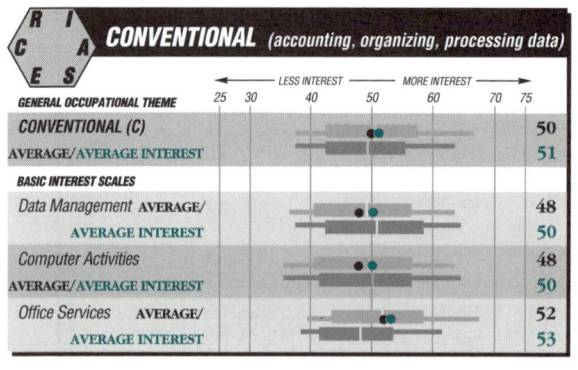

Figure 15.4 Scores on the GOTs and BISs of African-American Female Librarians and Scores of All Other Female Librarians in the *Strong* Occupational Sample

Note: African-American female librarians' scores are shown in blue; scores of non–African American female librarians are shown in black.

Latino/Hispanic male police officers (Figure 15.2, page 272) were similar to other male police officers on all but two GOTs and BISs. They indicated more interest in athletics and mathematics than the rest of the police officers in the occupational group. These interests were also reflected in their scores of "Similar" on the female Optometrist OS, female Physical Education Teacher, and male Elementary School Teacher. They differed from male police officers on 31 other scales, but all were scales on which both groups were dissimilar or in the mid-range. They scored 48.2 on their own scale, while the rest of the group scored 50.1 on their own scale.

Asian female dentists (Figure 15.3, page 273) were similar to other female dentists on all the GOTs and BISs and differed on only two OSs: female Florist and female Veterinarian. However, scores for both groups were in the mid-range on these scales. Asian female dentists scored 48 on their own scale, while the rest of the group scored 50.7.

African-American female librarians (Figure 15.4) were similar to all other female librarians on all GOTs and BISs except the Nature BIS, where their scores showed less interest. OS differences were found on 22 scales, but all the differences were in the "Dissimilar" range and thus would not be considered vocationally relevant. African-American female librarians scored 5 points lower on their own scale (45.6 versus 50.6) and on the male and female Technical Writer OSs, though all were in the "Similar" range, and thus African-American librarians would still be considered to be similar to librarians or technical writers.

As shown in Figure 15.5 (pages 277–279), African-American female school administrators were similar to all other female school administrators on all the GOTs and BISs, except that they had lower mean scores on the Nature BIS and higher mean scores on the Religious Activities BIS. Note that all OS scores plotted in Figure 15.5 are those on the female scales only. African-American female school administrators scored 5 points different from the rest of the occupational group on 17 scales, but both groups scored "Dissimilar" on these scales; they scored 50.20 on their own scale, while the larger group scored 50.22 on the School Administrator scale.

Figure 15.5 shows, for African-American female school administrators, just how similar the Profiles for ethnic group members and the rest of an occupational group are despite the fact that the ethnic minority group is very small. In this case the N is 30. Neither African-American nor other female school administrators have any Occupational Scale mean scores that fall in the "Similar" range for occupations in the Realistic or Investigative Themes. Both groups, however, do have scores in the "Similar" range for three occupations in the Artistic Theme: Corporate Trainer, Lawyer, and Librarian. Both groups also had scores that fall near 40 (the boundary between "Mid-range" and "Similar" on the Profile) on the Artistic occupations Broadcaster and Public Administrator.

In the Social Theme, both groups have scores in the "Similar" range for four occupations: Community Service Organization Director, High School Counselor, School Administrator, and Social Science Teacher. On the Occupational Scale for Social Worker, African-American female school administrators fall into the "Similar" range while the rest of the female school administrators fall just below that range. Only one scale among the Occupational Scales in the Enterprising Theme has a score in the "Similar" range for both groups: Human Resources Director. Among Conventional Occupational Scales, Paralegal and Small Business Owner scores for both groups fall near 40. Scores of both groups are very similar on all four Personal Style Scales.

Conclusions and Future Needs

Taken all together, the data indicate that the *Strong* may be used with confidence with racial and ethnic group members. Item differences are few and quite specific, they seldom affect the GOTs or BISs, and racial and ethnic minority members of an occupation are very similar to other members of their occupational group. Where differences occur, they do not affect the similarity of racial and ethnic group members to others within the occupation and thus appear to have little vocational relevance.

Future research is clearly needed to substantiate these findings, and while these data indicate that results do not differ across cultural groups, as discussed in the first part of this chapter, culture must be incorporated as a variable when interpreting the inventory to clients. Future research also needs to focus on the way that different racial and ethnic group members perceive the structure of interests and the world of work. The results of such research will help counselors in their interpretation of the *Strong* to clients who are members of racial and ethnic groups.

References

Anastasi, A. (1988). *Psychological testing* (6th ed.). New York: Macmillan.

Arbona, C. (1990). Career counseling research and Hispanics: A review of the literature. *Counseling Psychologist, 18*, 300–323.

Borgen, F. H., & Harper, G. T. (1973). Predictive validity of measured vocational interests with black and white college men. *Measurement and Evaluation in Guidance, 6*, 19–27.

Bull, P. E. (1975). Structure of occupational interests in New Zealand and America on Holland's typology. *Journal of Counseling Psychology, 22*, 554–556.

Carter, R. T., & Swanson, J. L. (1990). The validity of the Strong Interest Inventory with black Americans: A review of the literature. *Journal of Vocational Behavior, 36*, 195–209.

Chevrier, J. M. (Trans. and Ed.). (1979). *Test de préférences professionnelles Strong-Campbell manuel* [French translation of D. P. Campbell, *Manual for the Strong-Campbell Interest Inventory*]. Montreal: Institut de Recherches Psychologiques.

Doughtie, E. B., Chang, W. C., Alston, H. L., Wakefield, J. A., Jr., & Yom, B. L. (1976). Black-white differences on the Vocational Preference Inventory. *Journal of Vocational Behavior, 8*, 41–44.

Fouad, N. A. (1993). Cross-cultural vocational assessment. *The Career Development Quarterly, 42*, 4–13.

Fouad, N. A., & Bingham, R. P. (in press). Career counseling with racial/ethnic minorities. In W. B. Walsh & S. H. Osipow (Eds.), *Handbook of vocational psychology* (2nd ed.). Hillsdale, NJ: Erlbaum.

Fouad, N. A., Cudeck, R., & Hansen, J. C. (1984). Convergent validity of the Spanish and English forms of the SCII for bilingual Hispanic high school students. *Journal of Counseling Psychology, 31*, 33–48.

Fouad, N. A., & Dancer, L. S. (1992a). Cross-cultural structure of interests. *Journal of Vocational Behavior, 40*, 129–143.

Fouad, N. A., & Dancer, L. S. (1992b). Comments on the universality of Holland's theory. *Journal of Vocational Behavior, 40*, 220–228.

Fouad, N. A., & Hansen, J. C. (1987). Cross-cultural predictive accuracy of the Strong-Campbell Interest Inventory. *Measurement and Evaluation in Counseling and Development, 20*, 3–10.

Fouad, N. A., Hansen, J. C., & Arias, F. G. (1986). Multiple discriminant analyses of cross-cultural similarity of vocational interests of lawyers and engineers. *Journal of Vocational Behavior, 28*, 85–96.

Fouad, N. A., Hansen, J. C., & Arias, F. G. (1989). Cross-cultural similarity of vocational interests of professional engineers. *Journal of Vocational Behavior, 34*, 88–99.

Gawhega, A. (1982). An assessment and comparison of Native American students with non-Indian students relative to vocational aspirations. *Dissertation Abstracts International, 43*(10), 3301A (University Microfilms No. 83, 04859).

Gibbs, J. T. (1990). Mental health issues of black adolescents: Implications for policy and practice. In A. R. Stiffman & L. E. Davis (Eds.), *Ethnic issues in adolescent mental health* (pp. 21–52). Newbury Park, CA: Sage.

Hansen, J. C. (1984). The measurement of vocational interests: Issues and future directions. In R. B. Lent & S. D. Brown (Eds.), *Handbook of counseling psychology* (pp. 99–136). New York: Wiley.

Hansen, J. C. (1987). Cross-cultural research on vocational interests. *Measurement and Evaluation in Counseling and Development, 19*, 163–176.

Hansen, J. C., & Fouad, N. A. (1984). Translation and validation of the Spanish form of the Strong-Campbell Interest Inventory. *Measurement and Evaluation in Guidance, 16*, 192–197.

Harrington, T. F., & O'Shea, A. J. (1980). Applicability of Holland's (1973) model of vocational development with Spanish-speaking clients. *Journal of Counseling Psychology, 27*, 246–251.

Haviland, M., & Hansen, J. C. (1987). Criterion validity of the Strong-Campbell Interest Inventory for American Indian college students. *Measurement and Evaluation in Counseling and Development, 19*, 196–201.

Hines, H. (1983). The Strong-Campbell Interest Inventory: A study of its validity with a sample of black college students. *Dissertation Abstracts International, 45*(06), 1901B (University Microfilms No. 84-19, 502).

Holland, J. L. (1985). *Making vocational choices* (2nd ed.). Englewood Cliffs, NJ: Prentice-Hall.

Konrads, S. (1987, November). *Cross-cultural validation of the Lawyer and Engineer Scales for linguistically equivalent forms of the Strong Campbell Interest Inventory.* Doctoral Dissertation. University of Minnesota, Minneapolis.

Lamb, R. R. (1978). Validity of the ACT Interest Inventory for minority group members. In C. K. Tittle & D. G. Zytowski, *Sex-fair interest measurement: Research and implications* (pp. 113–119). Washington, DC: National Institute of Education.

Leong, F. T. L. (Ed.). (in press). *Career development and vocational behavior of racial and ethnic minorities.* Hillsdale, NJ: Erlbaum.

Leong, F. T. L., & Gim, R. H. C. (in press). Career assessment and intervention for Asian Americans. In F. T. L. Leong (Ed.), *Career development and vocational behavior of racial and ethnic minorities.* Hillsdale, NJ: Erlbaum.

Lonner, W. J. (1968). The SVIB visits German, Austrian, and Swiss psychologists. *American Psychologist, 23*, 164–179.

Lonner, W. J., & Adams, H. L. (1972). Interest patterns of psychologists in nine western nations. *Journal of Applied Psychology, 56*, 146–151.

Montoya, H., & DeBlassie, R. (1985). Strong-Campbell Interest Inventory comparisons between Hispanic and Anglo college students: A research note. *Hispanic Journal of Behavioral Science, 3*, 285–289.

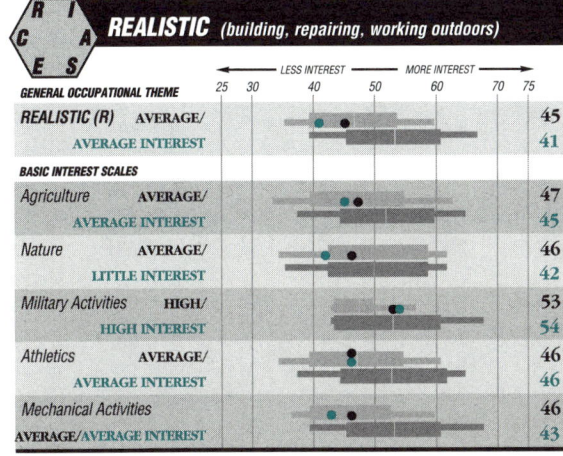
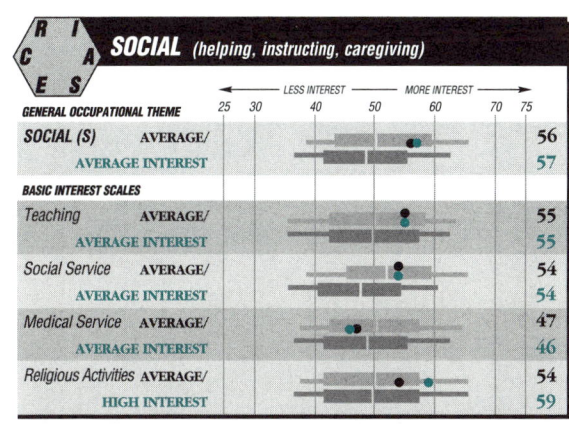
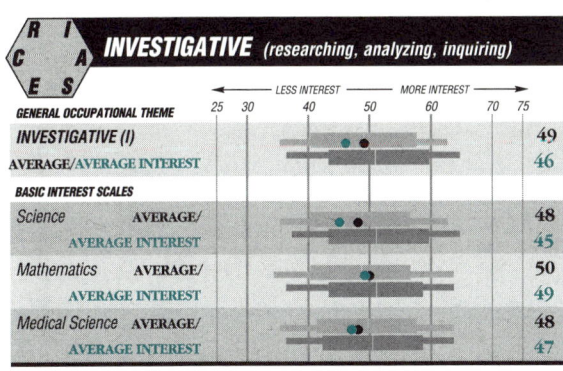
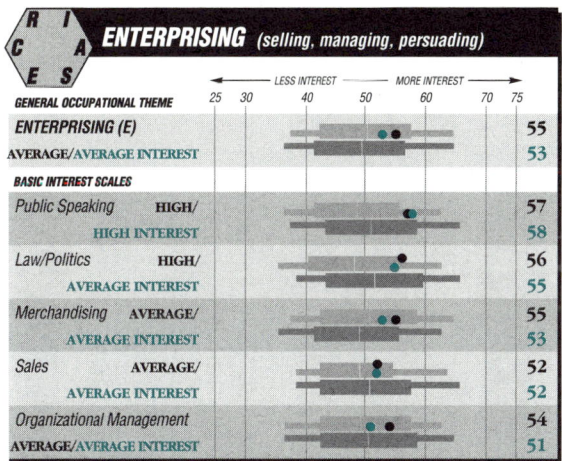
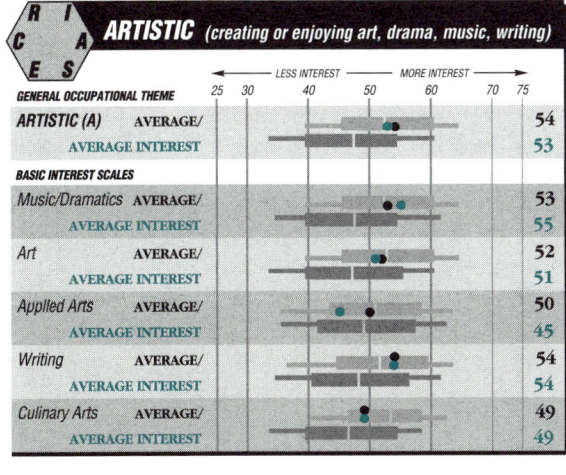
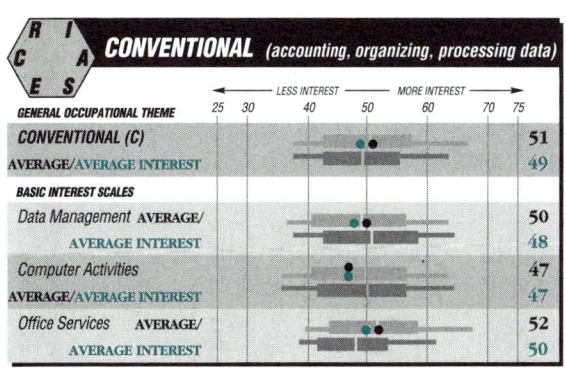

Figure 15.5 Profile Scores of African-American Female School Administrators and Scores of All Other Female School Administrators in the *Strong* Occupational Sample (figure continues on pages 278–279)

Note: African-American female school administrators' scores are shown in blue; scores of non–African American female school administrators are shown in black.

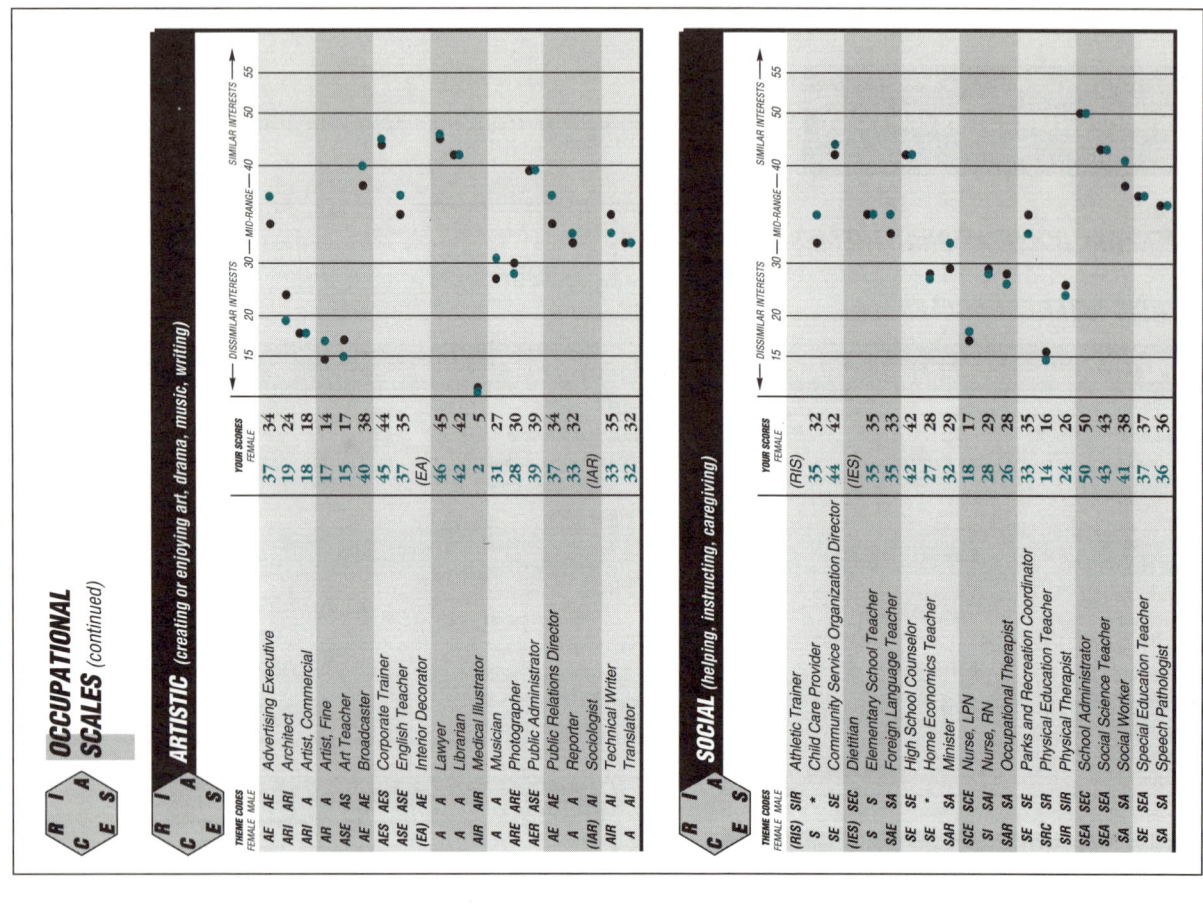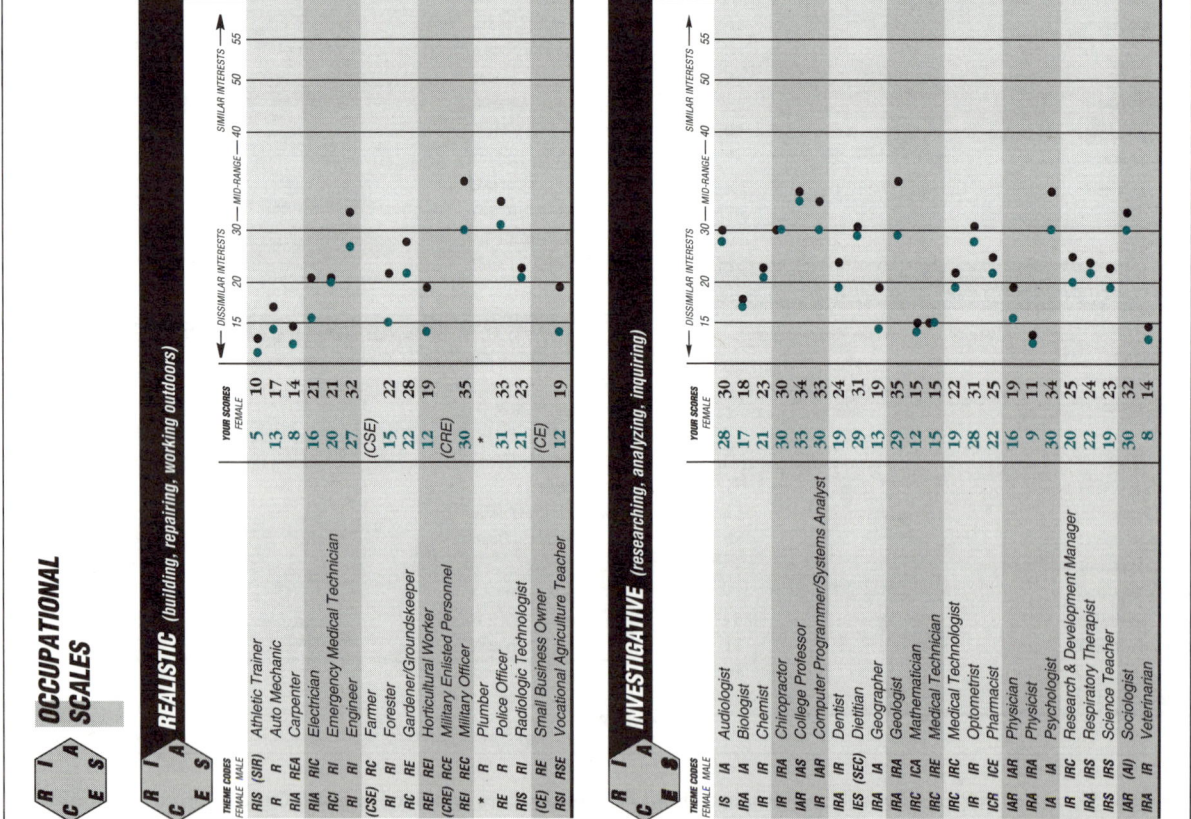

Figure 15.5 Profile Scores of African-American Female School Administrators and scores of All Other School Administrators (continued)

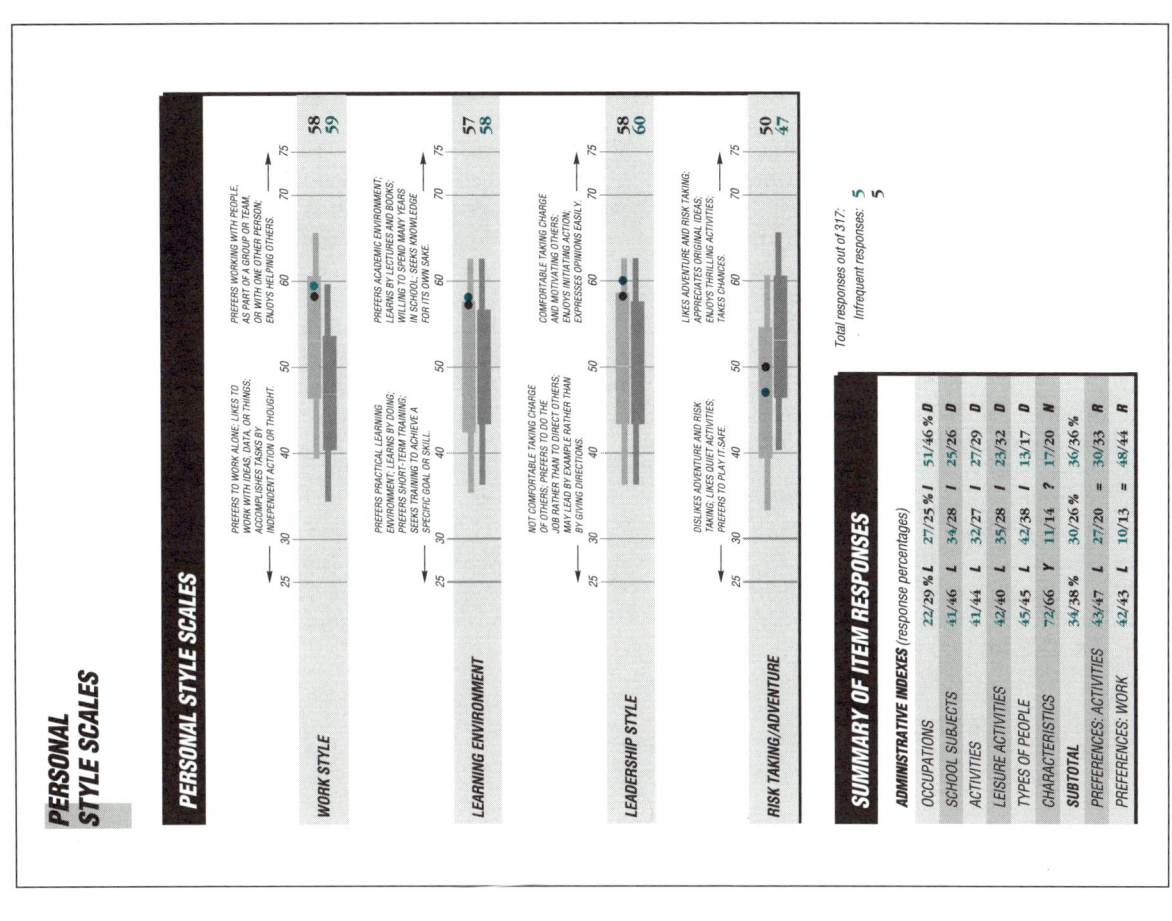
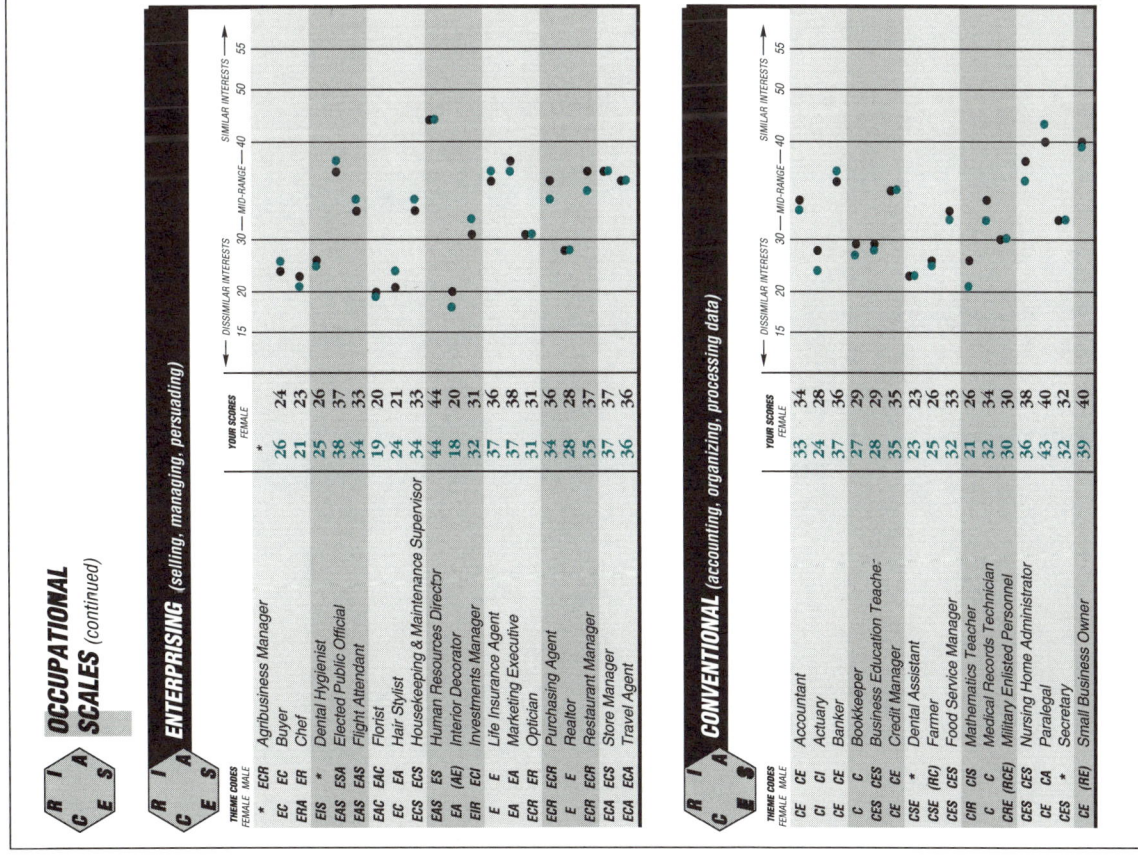

Figure 15.5 Profile Scores of African-American Female School Administrators and Other School Administrators (continued)

Scott, T. B., & Anadon, M. (1980). A comparison of the vocational interest profiles of Native American and Caucasian college-bound students. *Measurement and Evaluation in Guidance, 13*, 35–42.

Shah, I. (1971). A cross-cultural comparative study of vocational interests. *Dissertation Abstracts International, 31*(8-B), 5049.

Strong, E. K., Jr. (1943). Vocational interests of men and women. Stanford, CA: Stanford University Press.

Sue, D. W., & Kirk, B. A. (1972). Psychological characteristics of Chinese American students. *Journal of Counseling Psychology, 19*, 471–478.

Sue, D. W., & Kirk, B. A. (1973). Differential characteristics of Japanese American and Chinese American college students. *Journal of Counseling Psychology, 20*, 142–148.

Sue, D. W., & Sue, D. (1990). *Counseling the culturally different: Theory and practice* (2nd ed.). New York: Wiley Interscience.

Swanson, J. L. (1992). The structure of vocational interests for African-American college students. *Journal of Vocational Behavior, 40*, 144–157.

Tittle, C. K., & Zytowski, D. G. (Eds.). (1978). *Sex-fair interest measurement: Research and implications*. Washington, DC: National Institute of Education.

Walsh, W. B., & Betz, N. E. (1990). *Tests and assessment* (2nd ed.). Englewood Cliffs, NJ: Prentice-Hall.

Ward, C. M., & Bingham, R. P. (1993). Career assessment of ethnic minority women. *Journal of Career Assessment, 1*, 246–257.

Whetstone, R. D., & Hayles, V. R. (1975). The SVIB and black college men. *Measurement and Evaluation in Guidance, 12*, 105–109.

Yura, C. A. (1986). An investigation of black college students and white college students on the Strong-Campbell Interest Inventory. *Dissertation Abstracts International, 46*(09), 2572A (University Microfilms No. 85-23, 756).

Zytowski, D. G., & Borgen, F. H. (1983). Assessment. In W. B. Walsh & S. H. Osipow (Eds.), *Handbook of vocational psychology: Vol. 2. Applications* (pp. 5–45). Hillsdale, NJ: Erlbaum.

CHAPTER 16

Using the Strong with People Who Have Disabilities

Diane W. DeWitt

The *Strong* can be used with adults who have a wide range of physical, psychological, intellectual, and neurological disabilities. Public Law 101-336, the Americans with Disabilities Act of 1990 (ADA), defines disability as any "mental or physical impairment that substantially limits one or more of the major life activities," such as working, walking, or hearing (Mancuso, 1990). According to the ADA, people are regarded as having a disability based on the limitations from the impairment, not on whether or not they are taking medication or some form of treatment to reduce the negative effects of their condition. Disability may involve more than one condition, and sometimes each condition when considered alone would not constitute a disability.

Becoming a full workforce participant is the eventual goal of many of the approximately 43 million adults with disabilities in the United States who experience a 64 percent to 70 percent unemployment rate (Pape & Tarvydas, 1993). Obtaining vocational counseling, taking vocational tests, and making job-related decisions are aspects of achieving this goal. In recent years, more widespread use of the *Strong* to measure the interests of adults with disabilities has contributed to helping them find satisfying roles in the workforce.

Counselors can use the *Strong* with adults who have disabilities to achieve a variety of counseling objectives. It can be used to learn about the vocational and leisure interests of adults who have disabilities. It can be used to help adults with disabilities enter the workforce, select training programs, compete for reentry or transitional positions, or participate in vocational rehabilitation evaluation. The *Strong* can also be useful for employers when they need to accommodate the changed capacities of current employees whose abilities have been affected by an accident, occupational injury, sudden illness, or chronic condition.

Situations in which the *Strong* can be used effectively with adults who have disabilities are discussed in this chapter, following a general discussion about administration and interpretation of the inventory with clients who have disabilities. The chapter concludes with a brief review of literature focusing on the vocational interests of adults who have disabilities. ◆

Administration

The *Strong* can be administered to all clients who have disabilities except those who have reading, cognitive processing, intellectual, or neurological impairments that result in not understanding or not being able to respond to the inventory. According to Holvey and others (1986), reading level is the main restriction for use of the *Strong*. Conditions that may preclude use of the inventory include moderate to severe mental retardation (Jagger, Neukrug, & McAuliffe, 1992) as well as certain developmental and learning disabilities, such as severe dyslexia or autism. The minimum requirements for taking the *Strong* are that clients be able to:

- understand the inventory items,
- develop answers on their own, and
- write their answers with a pencil, speak their answers, point out their answers to a test proctor, or enter their answers using a keyboard.

Administration and interpretation of the *Strong* with clients who have disabilities need not differ significantly from the procedures described for adults who do not have disabilities. However, when administering the inventory to adults with disabilities, it may be necessary to accommodate for individual functional limitations. According to Nester (1993), "carefully thought-out test accommodation can be successful in preserving the reliability and validity of tests" such as the *Strong*. In addition, she emphasizes the importance of complying fully with federal antidiscrimination regulations when testing people with disabilities for employment and postsecondary school admission.

Before administering the *Strong*, the administrator must be certain that the physical facilities meet basic ADA accessibility criteria. For example, the testing area should be accessible to both wheelchairs and walking aids. The lighting should be excellent. The workstation and chair should be ergonomically safe and sturdy. The testing area should be free of distractions such as "waiting room" music or people talking nearby.

All testing materials should be suited to the individual. For example, clients with hand and upper limb impairments (e.g., arthritis or carpal tunnel syndrome) may need a special pencil holder that allows them to grip a regular-sized pencil, or they may prefer to use a keyboard data entry system. For those who cannot write or use a keyboard, the test administrator can fill in the answers following the verbal responses of the client. For those with limited vision, the text can be enlarged with a photocopier, or it can be read aloud by the administrator.

Individualization is key to accommodating the needs of clients with disabilities. Counselors need to work with each client, asking questions as appropriate, to enable his or her full participation. It is important to remember that, whenever possible, most adults with disabilities like to be able to "do it by themselves"; if they are unable to do so, the counselor can modify the test environment or procedures to suit the client's particular needs. One important modification in test procedure is elimination of any pressure to complete the inventory within a required time period (Nester, 1993). This is particularly important for those who have a disability such as major depression or mental illness or whose hands are weak or injured. In addition, clients with back pain or other orthopedic problems can be allowed to both stand and/or walk about at intervals.

Even clients with multiple disabilities can be successfully accommodated so that they can take the *Strong*. For example, one client had lower back pain caused by an automobile accident, had a long-standing anxiety disorder that was under treatment, and had recently undergone surgery for carpal tunnel syndrome. During test taking he was restless, and his pencil markings were too light to be scored by electronic means. The following modifications were made to his testing procedure: he was allowed to take breaks and was told to take all the time he needed, and a clerical worker darkened his answers so the inventory could be scored. In addition, he was closely observed during the test; this observation period provided additional data to be used in interpreting his inventory results. Although these adaptations meant extra work for the administrator, they made it possible for the client to take the *Strong*.

Often cues regarding rehabilitation potential can be identified by observing test-taking approaches. For example, measuring the extra time a client who has a disability needs to complete the inventory can be of diagnostic value, because it may indicate the pace at which that individual will be able to perform other similar tasks at home, school, and work. Observing the frequency with which a client needs to take a break from the test can also provide information about that person's work behaviors as well as indicate potential problems in the accuracy of inventory results.

Interpretation

When interpreting the inventory, it is advisable to ask the client whether the testing procedure interfered with his or her answers. Asking focused but open-ended questions about whether the individual found the inventory interesting or was able to maintain concentration can elicit information about any test-taking problems. When interpreting *Strong* results for a client who has a disability, standard procedures can be followed (see Chapter 10). Neubert, Danehey, and Taymans (1990) found that it is especially important to emphasize how vocational choices can be expanded when discussing results with clients who have been accustomed to experiencing limitations stemming from their disabilities.

Pacing the interpretation to match the client's rate of comprehension is also important. For example, it may be helpful to discuss results over two or three sessions, thus giving clients more time to assimilate their results. Clients can also be given assignments (e.g., reading, making job-site visits, or cross-referencing *Strong* results with other vocational information) during this time to enrich the exploration process.

Situations in Which the Strong Is Useful with Workers Who Have Disabilities

Specific situations in which the *Strong* can be useful with adults with disabilities include:

▲ on-the-job evaluation,
▲ determining reasonable accommodation, and
▲ exploring options for those entering the workforce or changing careers.

Each of these situations is discussed in the following sections.

On-the-Job Evaluation and Accommodation

According to the ADA, it is the employer's responsibility to determine how to help an employee who manifests behaviors that are unusual or interfere with job performance and to accommodate him or her in the event of disability. This may mean making a series of decisions, including whether or not the person has a disability, whether or not the person is in a suitable occupation, and whether or not the current job will continue to be the best placement. Employers can use the *Strong* (along with other assessment tools) to identify the special needs of employees with disabilities and to make decisions about their placement.

When an employee with a disability must be accommodated on the job, it is important to examine the degree of fit between that individual's current position, capacities, and inclinations (Mancuso, 1990). To do this, interest information from the *Strong* can be used to develop a personalized return-to-work action plan. For example, certain responsibilities (e.g., visiting customers outside the office or lifting supplies heavier than 5 pounds) might be eliminated from the client's job description. Every effort can be made to incorporate in the job aspects that are consistent with the employee's interests, as indicated by the *Strong*. Thus, if the employee who could no longer visit customers outside the office had high interest in activities related to the Enterprising General Occupational Theme (GOT), she or he could be involved in sales activities that did not require travel, such as telemarketing.

Client 1. Client 1 was a scientist who developed a mental illness (psychosis) that occasionally interfered dramatically with his ability to carry out his tasks. In particular, because he was not taking his prescribed medication, he developed some bizarre behaviors related to auditory hallucinations. It became immediately necessary to modify his current work assignment, including the cessation of all responsibilities that involved travel. During this temporary hiatus from his usual assignments, he underwent a comprehensive evaluation.

His *Strong* results confirmed the suitability of his current position. His score of 62 ("High Interest") on the Investigative Theme of the GOTs as well as his score of 61 on the Learning Environment scale and his score of 40 on the Work Style scale were characteristic of the Profile of a scientist. His Risk Taking/Adventure score (64) clearly confirmed his enthusiasm about the field work that was an essential aspect of his job. In addition, he had scores that showed high similarity on a series of I-Theme Occupational Scales (OSs), including the one in which he was originally trained, Chemist. He also had high scores for College Professor, Dentist, Audiologist,

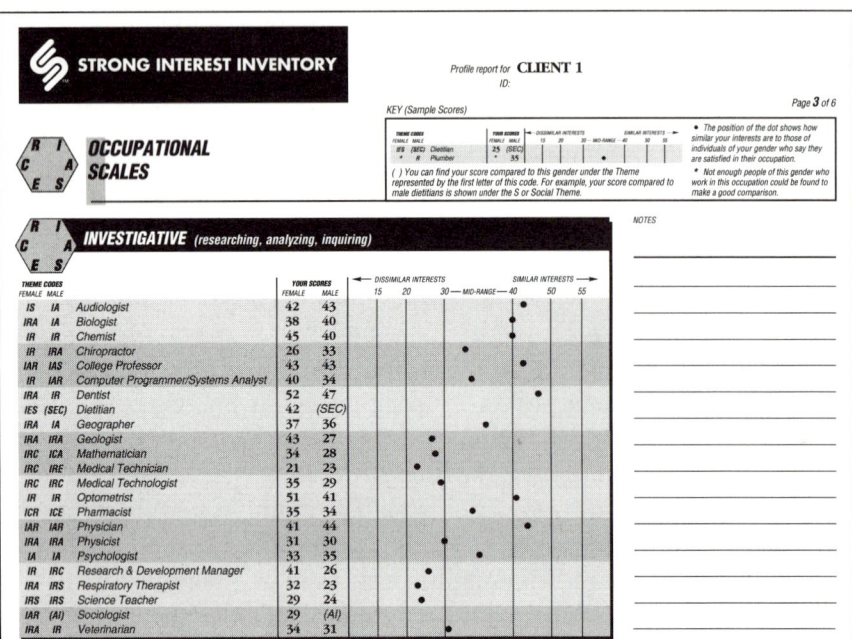

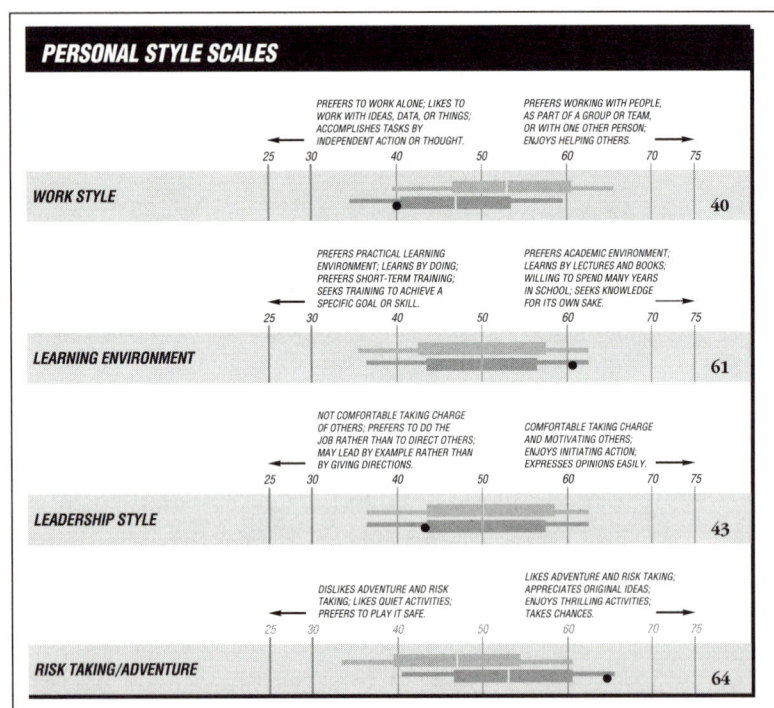

Figure 16.1 Investigative Occupational Scales and Personal Style Scales for Client 1, a Scientist Reassessing His Work Duties

Technical Writer, Optometrist, and Physician. Client 1's scores on the Investigative OSs and the Personal Style Scales are shown in Figure 16.1.

Client 1 believed that his Profile results supported his decision to remain in science. He also wanted to remain in his current job. His employer decided to accommodate this client's disability so that he could remain employed as a scientist. For example, he was given permission to take "mental" breaks whenever he felt the need, he was given ample time off for treatment, and he traveled for work only when he had a special release from his psychiatrist.

Job/Career Planning

Making important career or job decisions that involve entering the workforce or changing occupations can be stressful for anyone. For individuals with disabilities, this process may be associated with an even greater degree of urgency and anxiety. And for those who have developmental or learning disabilities (i.e., learning slowly or below their expected age level), this confusion can be especially accentuated. Without reliable, criterion-referenced feedback about their interests and information about occupations that match those interests, individuals with disabilities often seek vocational direction in a scattered and ineffective manner. They often enter the wrong occupation.

The *Strong* provides focused and individualized feedback that can help alleviate confusion caused by disability and provide clients with a broader range of options to explore. The *Strong* can be particularly helpful when disability renders a previous occupation no longer suitable. Studies of clients in a rehabilitation setting who had a variety of disabilities (e.g., orthopedic impairment, learning disabilities, mental illness, substance abuse, mental retardation, and epilepsy) confirmed that such clients are, in fact, able to accurately indicate their vocational interests during testing (Janikowski et al., 1990, 1992).

Client 2. Client 2, who was being treated for depression following a divorce, reported life-long learning problems. Although she had completed four years of college and worked as a certified public accountant (CPA) for six years, she was slow and often confused. She reported many instances of being misunderstood at work because her disability was not apparent or easy to explain, and she was often mistakenly seen as having a negative or "lazy" attitude. She had been fired several times.

On the *Strong,* her OS scores for Accountant were 20 (female) and 7 (male), suggesting that the career of CPA was not a suitable occupation for her. Her Conventional score was 43, which showed only "Average Interest" in this Theme, compared to the high interest she showed in the Investigative and Realistic Themes. Her Holland code was IRA.

This client felt her *Strong* results offered her many choices that were more appropriate to her needs. She immediately began to explore a long list of prospective occupations: Engineer, Computer Programmer/Systems Analyst, Radiologic Technologist, Medical Technologist, Chemist, Physical Therapist, Respiratory Therapist, Pharmacist, Optometrist, Dentist, and Occupational Therapist. All but two of these occupations are in the Realistic and Investigative Themes (Figure 16.2, page 286).

Client 2 planned to leave her job as a CPA and find work in an internship or as a volunteer in a medical service role as a transitional placement before retraining in a medical service occupation. Her high scores on the Medical Service and Medical Science Basic Interest Scales (BISs), combined with her high scores on several Occupational Scales in the medical field, indicated the appropriateness of this decision. She informed the court during her marriage dissolution settlement conference that she would be able to retrain within a reasonable period of time and reenter the workforce in an occupation that matched her interests and abilities. She was optimistic that she would soon be self-supporting.

Reducing Stereotypical Vocational Choices

Unfortunately, rehabilitation counseling does not always result in the most accurate placement of clients with disabilities. Such workers are often placed in work roles that have been traditionally regarded as suitable (e.g., janitorial work for adults with mental retardation) rather than in jobs that match their unique strengths and limitations. More recently it has been recognized that placing adults with disabilities in transitional or "light duty" positions can provide them with on-site training and allow them to prove their abilities to both themselves and their employers. The *Strong* can be used to help clients examine a full range of options and to make the most appropriate choices.

For example, a 30-year-old man, although a college graduate, had never been a member of the workforce as a result of a personality disorder and bouts of anxious depression. His *Strong* results revealed Social interests and high similarity on the OSs for Elementary School Teacher, Special Education Teacher, and the female OS for Child Care Provider, but little similarity on the OSs for College Professor and High School Counselor. These results encouraged him to consider a job teaching children, even though his family and friends viewed this vocational choice as inappropriate for a college-educated man. He decided to select a career path that is nontraditional for men and is happy working in a

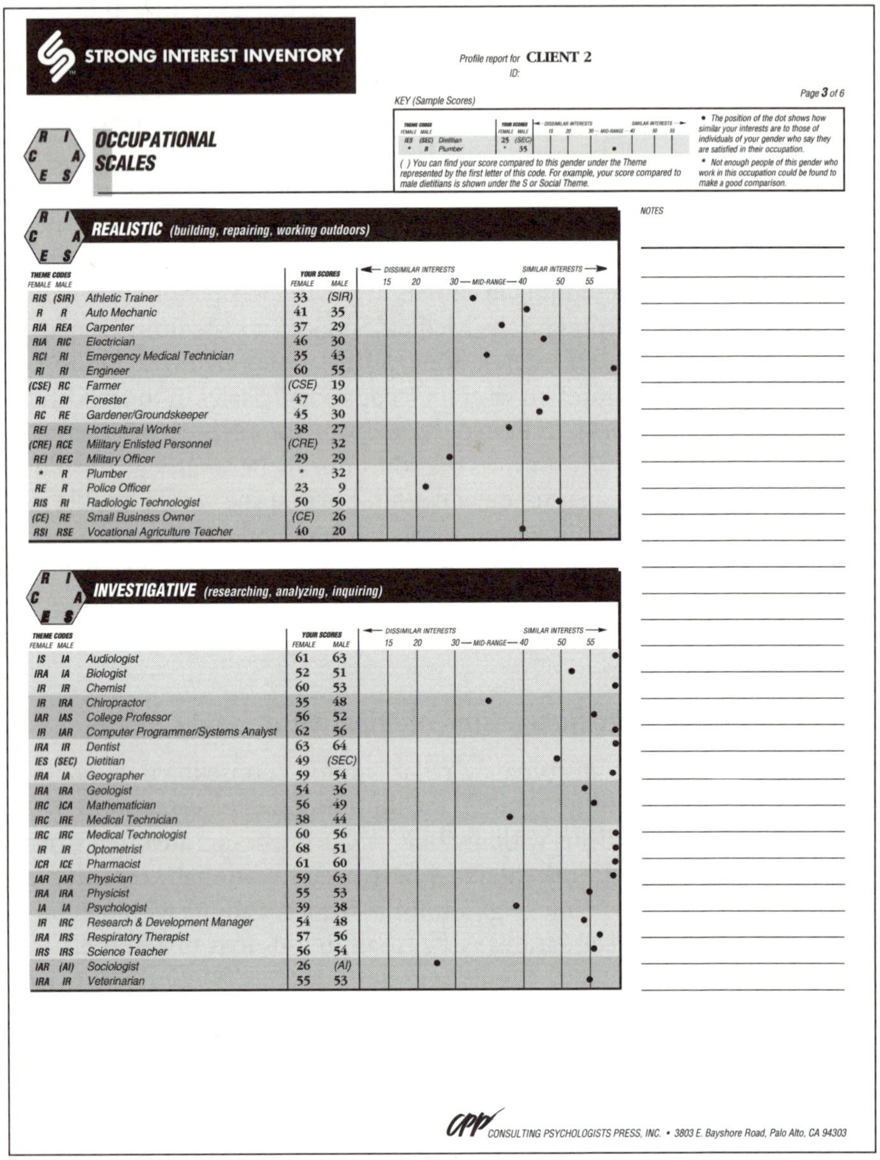

STRONG INTEREST INVENTORY

Profile report for CLIENT 2
ID:

Page 3 of 6

KEY (Sample Scores)

THEME CODES FEMALE	THEME CODES MALE		YOUR SCORES FEMALE	YOUR SCORES MALE
IES	(SEC)	Dietitian	25	(SEC)
*	R	Plumber	*	35

( ) You can find your score compared to this gender under the Theme represented by the first letter of this code. For example, your score compared to male dietitians is shown under the S or Social Theme.

• The position of the dot shows how similar your interests are to those of individuals of your gender who say they are satisfied in their occupation.

* Not enough people of this gender who work in this occupation could be found to make a good comparison.

OCCUPATIONAL SCALES

REALISTIC (building, repairing, working outdoors)

← DISSIMILAR INTERESTS 15 20 30 — MID-RANGE — 40 50 55 SIMILAR INTERESTS →

THEME CODES FEMALE	THEME CODES MALE		YOUR SCORES FEMALE	YOUR SCORES MALE
RIS	(SIR)	Athletic Trainer	33	(SIR)
R	R	Auto Mechanic	41	35
RIA	REA	Carpenter	37	29
RIA	RIC	Electrician	46	30
RCI	RI	Emergency Medical Technician	35	43
RI	RI	Engineer	60	55
(CSE)	RC	Farmer	(CSE)	19
RI	RI	Forester	47	30
RC	RE	Gardener/Groundskeeper	45	30
REI	REI	Horticultural Worker	38	27
(CRE)	RCE	Military Enlisted Personnel	(CRE)	32
REI	REC	Military Officer	29	29
*	R	Plumber	*	32
RE	R	Police Officer	23	9
RIS	RI	Radiologic Technologist	50	50
(CE)	RE	Small Business Owner	(CE)	26
RSI	RSE	Vocational Agriculture Teacher	40	20

INVESTIGATIVE (researching, analyzing, inquiring)

← DISSIMILAR INTERESTS 15 20 30 — MID-RANGE — 40 50 55 SIMILAR INTERESTS →

THEME CODES FEMALE	THEME CODES MALE		YOUR SCORES FEMALE	YOUR SCORES MALE
IS	IA	Audiologist	61	63
IRA	IA	Biologist	52	51
IR	IR	Chemist	60	53
IR	IRA	Chiropractor	35	48
IAR	IAS	College Professor	56	52
IR	IAR	Computer Programmer/Systems Analyst	62	56
IRA	IR	Dentist	63	64
IES	(SEC)	Dietitian	49	(SEC)
IRA	IA	Geographer	59	54
IRA	IRA	Geologist	54	36
IRC	ICA	Mathematician	56	49
IRC	IRE	Medical Technician	38	44
IRC	IRC	Medical Technologist	60	56
IR	IR	Optometrist	68	51
ICR	ICE	Pharmacist	61	60
IAR	IAR	Physician	59	63
IRA	IRA	Physicist	55	53
IA	IA	Psychologist	39	38
IR	IRC	Research & Development Manager	54	48
IRA	IRS	Respiratory Therapist	57	56
IRS	IRS	Science Teacher	56	54
IAR	(AI)	Sociologist	26	(AI)
IRA	IR	Veterinarian	55	53

NOTES

CPP CONSULTING PSYCHOLOGISTS PRESS, INC. • 3803 E. Bayshore Road, Palo Alto, CA 94303

Figure 16.2 Realistic and Investigative Occupational Scales for Client 2, an Accountant Seeking a Career Change

transitional training program at a Montessori preschool. His internship performance is outstanding.

Improving the Vocational Counseling Process

Inclusion of the *Strong* can improve the process of vocational counseling and lead to more comprehensive and appropriate outcomes. However, counselors need to be aware that this process may require additional time and discussion with clients who have disabilities. It is important for these clients to thoroughly review their *Strong* results with the counselor without feeling pressured to come to any immediate decisions. Since they may exhibit dependent behavior when it comes to decision making, these clients should be given as much time as they need to assimilate what they have learned from the *Strong*, examine their options, and incorporate them in decision making.

Counselors also need to be aware that even with the advantages of career assessment, clients with disabilities may face compounding problems as a result of environmental factors. A combination of disability, financial, emotional, and family factors may necessitate extra counseling attention. At times, this may mean putting forth extra effort to convince a client to explore the *Strong* recommendations; at other times it may mean providing creative but closely related occupational alternatives.

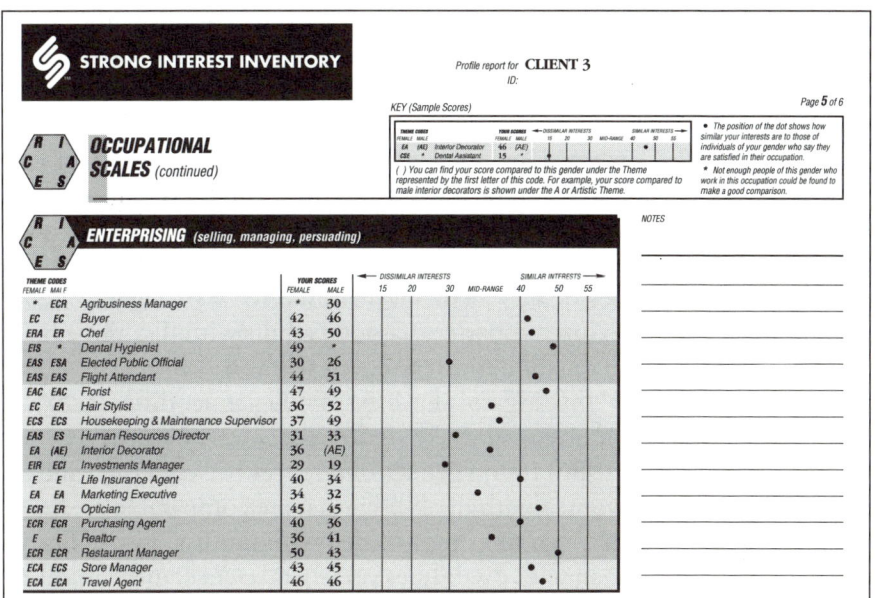

Figure 16.3 Enterprising Occupational Scales for Client 3, a Flight Attendant Changing Careers Due to Disability

Facilitating Work Reentry

The process of rehabilitation is ongoing and can take a variety of forms. Sometimes the client may temporarily have a full disability; at other times, the person may either have a partial disability or be fully restored. Clients also differ in how soon they are able to work again and how they choose to reenter the workforce. The *Strong* can be useful in helping clients in each of these situations to make a smooth workforce reentry.

Shanes-Hernandez, interviewed in the *Strong Forum*, ("*Strong* Integral," 1989) provides an example of how the *Strong* can be used in the rehabilitation of patients who have a mental illness that results in a temporary disability while receiving hospital treatment. The *Strong* results were used as part of discharge planning to help clients find transitional job placement or agency referrals for further vocational services. Since clients who have psychiatric disabilities often find it particularly difficult to get placements even after appropriate occupations have been identified, the *Strong* results increased the confidence of these clients in their work choices and helped them to persevere in their job search.

Client 3. Client 3 is a flight attendant with more than 25 years' experience who developed a disability of upper limb nerve problems that resulted in multiple surgeries, a pain syndrome, depression, and unemployment. When she took the *Strong* and discovered numerous high scores on medical service OSs, such as Radiologic Technologist, Optometrist, Audiologist, Physical Therapist, Nurse, Dietitian, and Dental Hygienist, she was convinced the inventory "knew something," because she had briefly been a nurse prior to becoming a flight attendant.

Client 3's highest GOT score was Enterprising and she showed "High Interest" in the Merchandising and Sales BISs. She also had high scores on several E-Theme OSs (Figure 16.3). This pattern of scores enabled Client 3 to identify a new set of alternatives for a range of OSs: Interior Decorator, Community Service Organization Director, Buyer, Chef, Corporate Trainer, Public Relations Director, Florist, Restaurant Manager, Store Manager, and Purchasing Agent. Interestingly, both her Travel Agent and Flight Attendant scores were elevated, further confirming her results, since she still wanted to be a flight attendant, although she could not remain in that career due to her disability. In order for this client to train for and enter a new occupation that did not require upper limb strength, she needed to have conviction about her choices; in fact, she was able to state assertively that she had made good choices because they matched her measured interests on the *Strong*. She enrolled in a Retail and Wholesale Sales Manager certificate program that will eventually lead to a position as a Buyer.

Research on the Vocational Interests of People Who Have Disabilities

A growing number of researchers have investigated the interest patterns of individuals with disabilities, both to learn about the vocational interests of various subgroups of people who have disabilities and to determine how to best incorporate these findings into the vocational counseling process. The results of some studies emphasize the similarities between adults who have disabilities and adults who do not have disabilities (Brookings & Bolton, 1986; Holvey et al., 1986; Jagger et al., 1992; Roessler & Bolton, 1985; Rohe & Athelstan, 1985). Other data suggest that the vocational development of adults with disabilities differs from that of adults without disabilities as a result of (1) delays in development, (2) negative self-concept, (3) impaired decision-making ability, and (4) limited aspirations (Curnow, 1989; Farrugia, 1983; Fraser et al., 1985; Rohe & Athelstan, 1982; "*Strong* Helps People," 1992).

Neubert and others (1990) investigated the relationship between vocational interests and specific outcome variables, such as success at placement in job tryouts and employment, for 69 young people with mild disabilities, such as dyslexia and other learning disabilities. This study indicated that knowing the vocational interests of an adult with disabilities is valuable in more accurately placing that person. Another study provided evidence that mature adults who have disabilities perform much better when they are employed in occupations that match their vocational interests. Jagger and others (1992) found that 97 people who had physical and psychiatric disabilities and were "successfully rehabilitated" had patterns of vocational interests (interest patterns could be described using the Holland typology) that matched their work roles—results that are similar to those found with people without disabilities. The authors suggest that combining recommendations derived from the *Strong* results with other vocational assessment information could assist in decision making and lead to better predictions of job satisfaction for individuals with disabilities.

Brookings and Bolton (1986) found that the interests of people with intellectual disabilities (3 percent), emotional disabilities (26 percent), and physical disabilities (71 percent) could be individually differentiated. Their interest patterns closely corresponded with those of adults without disabilities and college students reported in studies completed over the last four decades. These interest patterns had a generally low correlation with age, educational level, and measured intelligence level and could be measured with accuracy as long as the individual being assessed was able to understand and respond to the inventory items. In a separate study, personality factors were found to be strongly related to interest patterns among adults with disabilities in rehabilitation programs (Bolton, 1986).

Investigators have examined gender differences among adults with disabilities. Holvey and others (1986) found gender differences between men and women with disabilities that are comparable to those between men and women without disabilities. The men with disabilities preferred science, mechanical, and outdoor areas, whereas the women with disabilities preferred business, interpersonal service, and verbal, time perspective, and computational areas. Roessler and Bolton (1985) also found gender differences in their group data, which they attributed to differences in acculturation. These findings should be kept in mind when using the *Strong* so that inventory results do not limit the exploratory stage of career decision making, thus reducing consideration of potentially appropriate nontraditional occupational choices.

Although it is not a central concern of their study, Neubert and others (1990) also noted gender-based and stereotypical interests among a group of adults with disabilities whose primary diagnosis was either learning disability (53.6 percent) or mental retardation (46.6 percent). They cite three other studies with similar findings for adults with other types of disabilities: hearing impairments; trainable mental retardation; and nonspecified physical, emotional, and intellectual disabilities.

Fraser and others (1985) investigated the interests of patients with epilepsy. The women tended to have interests like women in the general sample, but the men's interests differed from men in the general sample when the patient had a history of early onset or a history of major motor seizures. Men with early-onset epilepsy had unusually low Investigative interests (GOT scores), and male patients with major seizure disorders had exceptionally low Academic Comfort scores. (The Academic Comfort scale has been deleted and the Learning Environment scale has been added to the 1994 *Strong*.) These findings lead Fraser and others to conclude that men with more serious impairments may be at greater risk for making poor vocational choices and therefore would benefit from a more supportive and extensive exploratory intervention.

Rohe and others (Rohe & Athelstan, 1982; "*Strong* Helps People," 1992) studied the vocational interests of adults with spinal cord injuries, both before and after injury, by asking about preinjury interests using a recall method. In general, they found that inventory results were as useful with this population as they were with adults without disabilities. The patients with spinal cord injuries tended to be more introverted and had more pronounced Realistic interests but lower Social interests. This indicated a preference for work that was practical and concrete, required use of their hands, or was performed outdoors and a dislike for work that put them in a helping or service role. The researchers also concluded that these patients might not feel understood by the medical technical service people around them in the hospital and clinic.

Rohe and Athelstan (1985) found no change in vocational interests before or after the spinal cord injury that could be explained by the impact of injury or the subsequent onset of disability. For example, scores on the Academic Comfort scale increased by 1.8 points, Realistic and Investigative scores were higher, and Social and Enterprising scores were lower. These postinjury changes resembled those of persons without disabilities and appeared to be a function of aging rather than a result of injury. Thus, it was concluded that the choices of individuals with disabilities can be regarded as stable and can provide continuity for such people, even in the face of changes in physical or mental capacity. Rohe, interviewed in the *Strong Forum* ("*Strong* Helps People," 1992), reports that the *Strong* can be useful in confirming such individuals' psychological identity at a critical time in their lives. The inventory can reassure these individuals about the continuity of their interests.

Conclusion

The ADA mandate is that essentially all Americans with disabilities have access to public services, public accommodations, transportation and telecommunications services, and employment (Jones, 1992). Use of the *Strong* can contribute to the accomplishment of this objective by helping to provide individuals with disabilities full access to psychological and vocational services, career counseling, vocational testing, and related opportunities and options available to those without disabilities.

References

Americans with Disabilities Act of 1990, Public Law 101-336, title 42, United States Code, Section 12101.

Bolton, B. (1986). Canonical relationships between vocational interests and personality of adult handicapped persons. *Rehabilitation Psychology, 31*(3), 169–182.

Brookings, J. B., & Bolton, B. (1986). Vocational interest dimensions of adult handicapped persons. *Measurement and Evaluation in Counseling and Development, 18*(4), 168–175.

Curnow, T. C. (1989). Vocational development of persons with disabilities. *The Career Development Quarterly, 37*, 269–278.

Farrugia, D. (1983). A study of vocational interests and attitudes of hearing impaired clients. *Journal of Rehabilitation of the Deaf, 17*(1), 107.

Fraser, R. T., Trejo, W. R., Temkin, N. R., Clemmons, D. C., & Dodrill, C. B. (1985). Accessing vocational interests of those with epilepsy. *Rehabilitation Psychology, 30*(1), 29–33.

Holvey, J. M., Partridge, E. D., & Wagner, E. E. (1986). Sex differences in vocational interests among rehabilitation clients. *Journal of Applied Rehabilitation Counseling, 17*(4), 51–53.

Jagger, L., Neukrug, E., & McAuliffe, G. (1992). Congruence between personality traits and chosen occupation as a predictor of job satisfaction for people with disabilities. *Rehabilitation Counseling Bulletin, 36*(1), 54–60.

Janikowski, T. P., Bordieri, J. E., & Musgrave, J. (1992). The impact of vocational evaluation on client self-estimated aptitudes and interests. *Rehabilitation Counseling Bulletin, 36*(2), 70–83.

Janikowski, T. P., Bordieri, J. E., Shelton, D., & Musgrave, J. (1990). Convergent and discriminate validity of microcomputer evaluation screening and assessment (MESA) interest survey. *Rehabilitation Bulletin, 34*(2), 139–148.

Jones, N. L. (1992). The Americans with Disabilities Act (ADA): An overview of major provisions. CRS Report for Congress, Congressional Research Service, Library of Congress, July 27, 1990, updated March 18, 1992.

Mancuso, L. L. (1990). Reasonable accommodation for workers with psychiatric disabilities. *Psychosocial Rehabilitation Journal, 14*(2), 3–19.

Nester, M. A. (1993). Psychometric testing and reasonable accommodations for persons with disabilities. *Rehabilitation Psychology, 38*(2), 75–85.

Neubert, D. A., Danehey, A. J., & Taymans, J. M. (1990). Vocational interest, job tryouts, and employment outcomes of individuals with mild disabilities in a time-limited transition program. *Vocational Evaluation and Work Adjustment Bulletin, 23*(1), 17–23.

Pape, D. A., & Tarvydas, V. M. (1993). Responsible and responsive rehabilitation consultation on the A.D.A.: The importance of training for psychologists. *Rehabilitation Psychology, 38*(2), 117–131.

Roessler, R., & Bolton, B. (1985). Vocational interests and occupations of rehabilitation clients. *Vocational Evaluation and Work Adjustment Bulletin, 18*(1), 16–20.

Rohe, D. E., & Athelstan, G. P. (1982). Vocational interests of persons with spinal cord injury. *Journal of Counseling Psychology, 29*(3), 283–291.

Rohe, D. E., & Athelstan, G. P. (1985). Change in vocational interests after spinal cord injury. *Rehabilitation Psychology, 30*(3), 131–143.

Strong helps people cope with spinal cord injury. (1992, Fall). *Strong Forum, 9*(2), 1, 3.

Strong integral to treatment plan. (1989, Spring). *Strong Forum, 6*(1), 3, 4.

CHAPTER 17

The Importance of Gender in Interpreting the Strong

The issue of gender differences is an important consideration in career counseling, as even a brief perusal of the career literature will demonstrate. There has been increased recognition and discussion of women's career development in the literature covering career development itself, organizations, counseling, and industrial/organizational psychology in the past 20 years. While this guide is not the forum for a review of these contributions, users of the *Strong* need to understand how gender differences are handled on the inventory.

This chapter presents a brief history of how gender differences have been handled in previous versions of the *Strong*, followed by a description of how they are treated on the 1994 Profile. Strategies for interpreting the Profile for men and women using opposite-gender scales are presented, and issues in interpreting the *Strong* with women are discussed. The purpose of these sections is to illustrate how the information on the Profile can be used to help expand clients' career options. The latter part of the chapter presents technical material on the differences between men's and women's interests, including a description of the nature of these differences at both the item and scale levels on the 1994 *Strong*. ◆

Historical Perspective

Beginning with the men's form published in 1927 and the women's in 1933, the interests of women and men were analyzed separately on the *Strong*. Two reasons may be cited for E. K. Strong's decision to make that enduring distinction. First, the item responses of women and men were different in the 1930s. Second, the employment patterns of women and men differed markedly, not only in the large number of women in the homemaker-mother role but also in the radically different distribution of the genders in most occupations. Given these two factors, the provision of a single inventory seemed inappropriate.

This system worked fairly well for nearly four decades. Still, E. K. Strong himself was always eager for people to undertake research on the women's form. The counseling profession, however, never really settled upon a philosophy for handling the two forms. Some counselors, for example, used the men's form with career-oriented women. The dual system was cumbersome for researchers too; for instance, when testing a group of 20 women and 20 men, the investigator was forced to choose among giving everybody one form, eliminating one gender from the sample, or using two different forms with two small subsamples.

More profound concerns began to emerge in the 1960s. As attention focused on the inequalities of gender roles, and as pressures increased on institutions and programs that were continuing to separate the genders artificially, the necessity and wisdom of two separate forms were questioned more often and more vigorously.

One of the main goals in developing the 1974 *Strong*, the version on which the female and male forms were combined, and in conducting each revision of the inventory since then, was to help eliminate any differential treatment of the genders in career measurement and counseling. Efforts along these lines, in addition to eliminating the separate-gender forms of the inventory, have included removing gender-role bias from the items, norming the General Occupational Themes (GOTs) and Basic Interest Scales (BISs) on samples containing both males and females, and seeking occupational samples for Occupational Scales (OSs) for both men and women.

Considerable attention has been given over the years to eliminating gender-role bias in the selection and wording of items. Although a recent article on the impact of feminist critiques on testing and assessment (Lewis & Wild, 1991) cited the 1985 *Strong* as a successful assessment tool from this perspective, all the items proposed for the 1994 revision were again reviewed by an independent consultant, and some refinements were made.

Types of Gender Differences

To a large degree, the gender differences in interests of females and males are of two kinds. One involves *cultural* differences, which appear in almost every sample examined. These differences are documented at both the item level and scale-score levels and appear for almost all occupations and samples. Other gender differences are specific to a particular occupation; these are *occupationally related* differences, which remain even after the cultural differences are removed. Such differences can be identified by comparing the item content of female- and male-normed OSs. For example, male pharmacists as a group have more interest in Enterprising activities than do female pharmacists; thus, the male Pharmacist scale includes items such as "Retailer," "Sales manager," "Buying merchandise for a store," and "Displaying merchandise in a store" (all weighted positively) that are not on the female Pharmacist scale.

Representing Gender Differences on the Strong

Given that gender differences exist for some items and scales on the *Strong*, the question of how to treat them on the Profile arose. Two approaches were possible: (1) score each person only on scales developed for his or her own gender or (2) score each person on all scales, regardless of the individual's gender.

One of the goals in the ongoing development of the *Strong* has been to encourage clients to explore a wide range of occupations, including those that may previously have been dominated by one gender. Thus, the solution to the dilemma posed by gender differences has been to report as much information as possible to clients so that they, along with their counselors, can choose the most appropriate comparison. Therefore, the information on the Profile includes:

▲ interpretive comments on the GOTs and BISs that compare the client's scores with the scores of other individuals of the same gender and a graphic plotting of those scores;

▲ a graphic device, the box-and-whisker graph, that shows approximately how the client's scores on the GOTs, BISs, and Personal Style Scales compare with those of other persons of the same gender but can also demonstrate how the person scored compared with persons of the opposite gender;

▲ standard scores on the GOTs, BISs, and the Personal Style Scales that are based on a comparison of the client's responses with those of the combined General Reference Sample (GRS), which includes over 18,000 women and men;

▲ scores on all available OSs—those based on same- as well as opposite-gender occupational samples;

▲ a graphic plotting of the client's scores on the same-gender OSs; and

▲ a summary and graphic display on the *Strong* Snapshot of how the client's highest scores on the GOTs, BISs, and Occupational Scales compare with those of persons of the same gender.

This approach offers each individual who takes the *Strong* the maximum amount of information possible and encourages each person at least to ponder the similarity, or lack of it, between his or her interests and those of men and women in a wide range of occupations. This strategy should help clients, both male and female, to expand their options. Counselors and researchers have recognized that the availability of same-gender, opposite-gender, and combined norms on the *Strong* makes it possible for the inventory to meet this goal (Betz, 1993). As Betz pointed out, the mere fact that there *are* OSs for both men and women for most of the occupations communicates the appropriateness of these occupations for both genders.

The drawback of this all-inclusive approach, however, is the amount of information that appears on the Profile. The method chosen to effectively organize clients' results is to highlight those scores that are the most meaningful for interpretation—the scores based on same-gender comparisons. Because these scores are plotted graphically on all pages of the Profile and are also those on which the interpretive comments are based, clients can easily focus on key results. This solution resolves the dilemma of providing the maximum number of scores to each individual while at the same time emphasizing those scores that are normed in the most technically accurate manner and are the most predictive.

For the 1994 revision, another aid developed to organize the information is the Snapshot, which provides a convenient summary of a client's scores on the GOTs, BISs, and OSs. This first page of the Profile provides an efficient tool for helping the client focus on the most important information and an overall pattern, if any. A detailed description of the Snapshot and the other five pages of the Profile is provided in Chapter 3.

It is worth noting here that the box-and-whisker graphs used for the GOTs, BISs, and Personal Style Scales can be used to explore the relationship of the client's scores to those of both women and men. The upper boxes indicate the middle 50 percent of the scores of the female GRS, and the lower boxes show the middle 50 percent of scores of the male GRS. The thinner lines, or "whiskers," that extend from each end of the boxes define the middle 80 percent of the scores, and the vertical space in the middle marks the mean score for that gender. The client's score is plotted with a black dot on the graph for that client's gender. Because the graphs for females and males are adjacent and use the same number line, it also is easy to see how the client's score compares to the opposite-gender norms by simply observing where the dot would fall if it were moved vertically onto the graph for the other gender (either up to the women's graph or down to the men's graph).

A numerical score is also provided on the Profile for the GOTs, BISs, and Personal Style Scales. This score is based on a comparison of the respondent with the average score for the combined female and male GRSs. (For a more detailed description of how the combined group was formed, refer to Chapter 5.)

Using Gender Differences in Interpretation

How can information about gender differences be used when interpreting a client's *Strong* results? It is important for counselors to become familiar with interpretive challenges associated with the provision of both same- and opposite-gender scores on the scales and with special issues that can arise in interpreting the *Strong* with women.

As is demonstrated later in the technical section of this chapter, women and men, *on the average*, report somewhat different interests at both the item level and the scale level. This fact must be handled carefully, however, when working with any single individual, for she or he easily can fall outside the average; the existence of average differences does not justify limiting the options of either gender.

Interpreting the Strong Using Opposite-Gender Scales

For any client, the same gender–normed OSs continue to be the most valid and most reliable, but OSs normed for the opposite gender can also be interpreted, though counselors should do so cautiously. The basic strategy for interpreting these scales is to use them for confirmation or refutation of patterns that emerge from an interpretation of the Profile. With this approach, the absolute values of individual scale scores become less important. The following three examples identify circumstances in which interpreting opposite-gender scores can be useful.

Example #1. A client scores high on a same-gender scale but even higher on the corresponding opposite-gender scale.

In this case, a high score on an opposite-gender scale may be used to confirm an interest in a particular occupation. The consistency in level of scores on the two scales (both in the "Very Similar" range) is more important than the differences between the scores. The client need not be concerned about the absolute values of the two scores. Thus, although one client, a female, scored 56 on the female-normed Fine Artist scale and 60 on the male-normed Fine Artist scale, the counselor need not dwell on the 4-point difference but rather should appreciate the confirmation of her interest in the area of fine art.

Example #2. A client scores high on an opposite-gender scale but low on the corresponding same-gender scale for the same occupation.

High scores on opposite-gender scales can be used to suggest occupational interests if the high score fits in with an existing pattern of interests. For example, one female client scored high on the male-normed Elementary School Teacher scale but low on the female-normed Elementary School Teacher scale. The procedure to use with such a case is to examine the scores on other OSs related to teaching and education (e.g., Foreign Language Teacher, Social Science Teacher, Special Education Teacher) to assess the presence of a pattern of interests. However, in the past, the career direction of men and women within elementary education differed; males were more likely to enter administration and females to continue as classroom teachers. So, if this same client who scored high on the male Elementary School Teacher scale also had high scores on the School Administrator scale, she might want to consider educational administration. In general, the pattern of other scores may reflect what aspects of an occupation a client may find appealing.

For other occupations, such as banking or pharmacy, women and men traditionally have entered different areas within the occupation. (Note the point made earlier that the interests of male pharmacists suggest that they are more interested in retail management than are women pharmacists.) These, as well as other, occupational groups are made up of individuals of various ages and some—perhaps those who entered their occupation decades ago—may still play traditional roles. These traditional patterns can provide added insight into discrepancies in scores on female- and male-normed scales representing the same occupation.

Example #3. A client scores high on an opposite gender–normed scale for which there is no same gender–normed scale.

This pattern can occur for women who score high on the Plumber and Agribusiness Manager scales and for men who score high on the Dental Assistant, Dental Hygienist, Secretary, Child Care Provider, and Home Economics Teacher scales. For example, a male client scored high on the female-normed Secretary scale. This score was supported by his high scores on scales such as the Conventional Theme, the Office Services BIS, and other C-Theme female-normed OSs such as Dental Assistant (CSE) and Military Enlisted Personnel (CRE). This consistent pattern of interests across the three sets of scales provides support for choosing occupations such as secretary or administrative assistant.

Even when other-gender scores do not add a lot of information about the similarity or dissimilarity of a person's interests to those of people in various occupations beyond that provided by same-gender scores (Apostal, 1986), clients are often curious about their scores on the opposite-gender OSs. Interpreting these scores occasionally provides clients with a richer understanding of their *Strong* results.

Interpreting the Strong with Women

Women have been entering the workforce in great numbers over the past decade or so. One survey estimated that by the year 2000 women will account for about 47 percent of employed persons, up from 33 percent in 1960 (Mirvis, 1993). Women are entering the workforce at different ages and at different stages of their lives than is typical for men. Women are also seeking additional education and training and thus are older than the typical college student (18 to 24) when beginning their college education. The number of women aged 25 to 34 enrolled in college grew by 50 percent from 1975 to 1987, while the number doubled for those 35 and older (Saveri, 1991).

These demographic trends suggest the relevance of understanding differences in the career development patterns of women and men and the impact these differences can have on career theory and on the career planning and exploration of individuals.

Some researchers have described women's career development as similar to but more complex than men's (Hackett & Lonborg, 1993). Support for the complexity theory has been found in at least two occupations: engineer and public administrator (Gaeddert & Hansen, 1993). The women in this study demonstrated more diversity of interests than did men on a composite diversity of interest index calculated by summing the diversity scores from five separate measures. The percentage of women in the high-diversity group was about two and a half times that of men. There are two implications of this finding, if it is replicated with other occupational groups. One is that women may be more satisfied in work environments in which their diverse interests can be accommodated. The other is that women may bring a broader viewpoint or outlook to work tasks.

When considering career options, women have tended to choose occupations traditionally viewed as "female," primarily those associated with the Social and Conventional Themes, in part because they often underestimate and therefore underuse their abilities in other areas (Betz, Heesacker, & Shuttleworth, 1990). Despite the instructions on the Item Booklet/Answer Sheet to consider interests, not abilities, when responding to *Strong* items, research on the 1981 *Strong* (Lapan, Boggs, & Morrill, 1989) suggested that the responses of some women and men on the Realistic and Investigative Themes in particular may be related to self-estimates of ability or expectations of personal effectiveness. In this study, women's scores on the R and I Themes were lower than those of men, which was a function of the fact that the women perceived themselves as less effective in these areas.

A recent study by Hansen, Collins, Swanson, and Fouad (1993) of the 1985 *Strong* showed that in a multidimensional scaling analysis the members of the Men-in-General and Women-in-General groups differed in the way their interests were structured. Women did not distinguish between Realistic and Investigative Themes as much as men did. The authors point out that this finding may be related to the fact that women usually have less experience in these areas. They also found that social interests were more central and salient for women than for men.

There is some evidence, however, that these trends may be changing. One study (Betz et al., 1990) reports an increase in women choosing (1) careers in which the number of female and male employees is approximately equal, and (2) careers that employ far more men than women. The study also found a tendency for college women to choose careers based on their interests rather than on stereotypes. The pattern of avoidance by men of female-dominated areas, however, seems to continue.

Many theorists currently consider it too limiting to regard career as a distinct component of life-style and to treat career development as a linear advancement. Because of the multiple roles that women and men play, the concept of career must be broadened to include life-style issues and a balance among various roles (Marshall, 1989; McDaniels, 1984; McDaniels & Gysbers, 1992). The problem of balancing multiple roles was considered to be a priority among a sample of women managers studied by Marshall. This research indicated the importance of recognizing diversity among career paths and the need for more flexible work environments to accommodate the varying demands of careers, relationships, family, and self. Many women (and men) are finding the flexibility they are seeking within entrepreneurial ventures; many new businesses created to serve the needs of women and older people in recent years have been founded by women. The addition of the Small Business Owner OS to the 1994 *Strong* can help more women consider this option.

Identifying Occupational Stereotypes

Counselors need to be alert to the possibility that a female client's career goals, expectations, and perhaps some of her *Strong* scores may reflect occupational stereotypes based on gender roles. For example, Betz (1993) pointed out that college women with high scores on the S Theme or on the BISs within the S Theme should be questioned further about the source of their interest. The client and counselor can explore to what extent social interests reflect a woman's perception of traditional career paths for a woman as opposed to legitimate motivating interests for a career in this area. In *some* cases, high scores in the social area reflect limited exposure to women working in traditionally male-oriented occupations, little opportunity to identify with successful career women, or limited perceptions about what constitutes an acceptable career path for a woman. Social interests should not be emphasized over interests in other Themes that may also be high, or even those in the mid-range. According to Betz, the restricted range of vocational experience demonstrated by some college women or by women returning to the workforce need not restrict options.

Some women have recently reentered the workforce after a hiatus of working as homemakers for many years. The *Strong* can be useful in helping these women identify job and career alternatives. Some of these women exhibit low vocational self-confidence. Others may not have had much exposure to positions other than that of homemaker. Both kinds of women *may* show flat or depressed Profiles or, as just discussed, high scores only on scales within the S Theme. These women may have rarely thought of themselves as having a "career" and may have little identification with successful career women.

Expanding Career Options

The OSs can be particularly useful in helping women with limited vocational knowledge or experience expand their options, whether they are women entering the workforce for the first time or those reentering after a long pause. Any scores on the OSs in the "Similar" or above range (or even in the mid-range for those with flat Profiles) can be used to help clients start thinking about careers. When their high OS scores are interpreted as indicating a similarity of interests to women working in those occupations, these women can begin to identify with successful career women. Such clients may need to engage in extensive career exploration and may benefit from retaking the *Strong* after they have had time to explore the world of work through reading in a career library or informational interviewing. Interpretation of scores on the male OSs can also help break down stereotypes by showing these women that their interests are similar to those of men working in those occupations. Counselors can use same-gender, opposite-gender, and combined norms on the *Strong* to assist in breaking down stereotypes (Betz, 1993).

Client 1. The case of Client 1, a 48-year-old woman who worked as a homemaker for 18 years, illustrates how the OSs can help expand career options for women reentering the workforce. After completing a bachelor's degree in English, this woman worked in a library for a few years before leaving to raise her children. When she decided to return to the workforce, she was not sure that she again wanted to work in a library, and so sought career counseling.

As shown in Figure 17.1, this woman had no GOTs above average and only three BISs above average: Applied Arts, Art, and Mechanical Activities. Her results on the OSs showed that her interests were "Very Similar" to those of female librarians (53) and female architects (62) and "Similar" to those of people in six other occupations with codes that contain the Artistic Theme. Although a few other OS scores within other Themes were in the "Similar" range, it was her score on the Architect scale that surprised her, both because of its magnitude and because she had never considered becoming an architect. The possibility of following such a career path raised many issues for her because she had not been considering the possibility of returning to school or of entering a demanding profession. After discussion, however, she began to explore the opportunities at a local college, where she eventually enrolled in a master's program in architecture and did very well.

Using Additional Assessments with the Strong

A number of practitioners have suggested that in career counseling with women it is important to include additional assessments along with interest inventories (Hackett & Lonborg, 1993). The instruments that make up the Career-Development Assessment and Counseling (C-DAC) battery (Super, Osborne, Walsh, Brown, & Niles, 1992) have been suggested as particularly useful: the *Salience Inventory* (Nevill & Super, 1986a), the *Values Scale* (Nevill & Super, 1986b), the *Adult Career Concerns Inventory* (Super, Thompson, & Lindeman, 1988), and the *Career Development Inventory* (Thompson, Lindeman, Super, Jordaan, & Myers, 1981). Niles and Usher (1993) give an example of how the results of the *Strong* can be integrated with some of these other inventories to enhance the client's self-understanding and career exploration.

Two other instruments should also be considered as part of a career battery. One is the *Career Beliefs Inventory* (Krumboltz, 1991), which can be used to help identify beliefs that may hinder or block career exploration. The other is the *Myers-Briggs Type Indicator* (Hammer & Macdaid, 1992; Myers & McCaulley, 1985), which can be used to provide a broader perspective for the individual and thus may be useful for looking at career issues in a larger context.

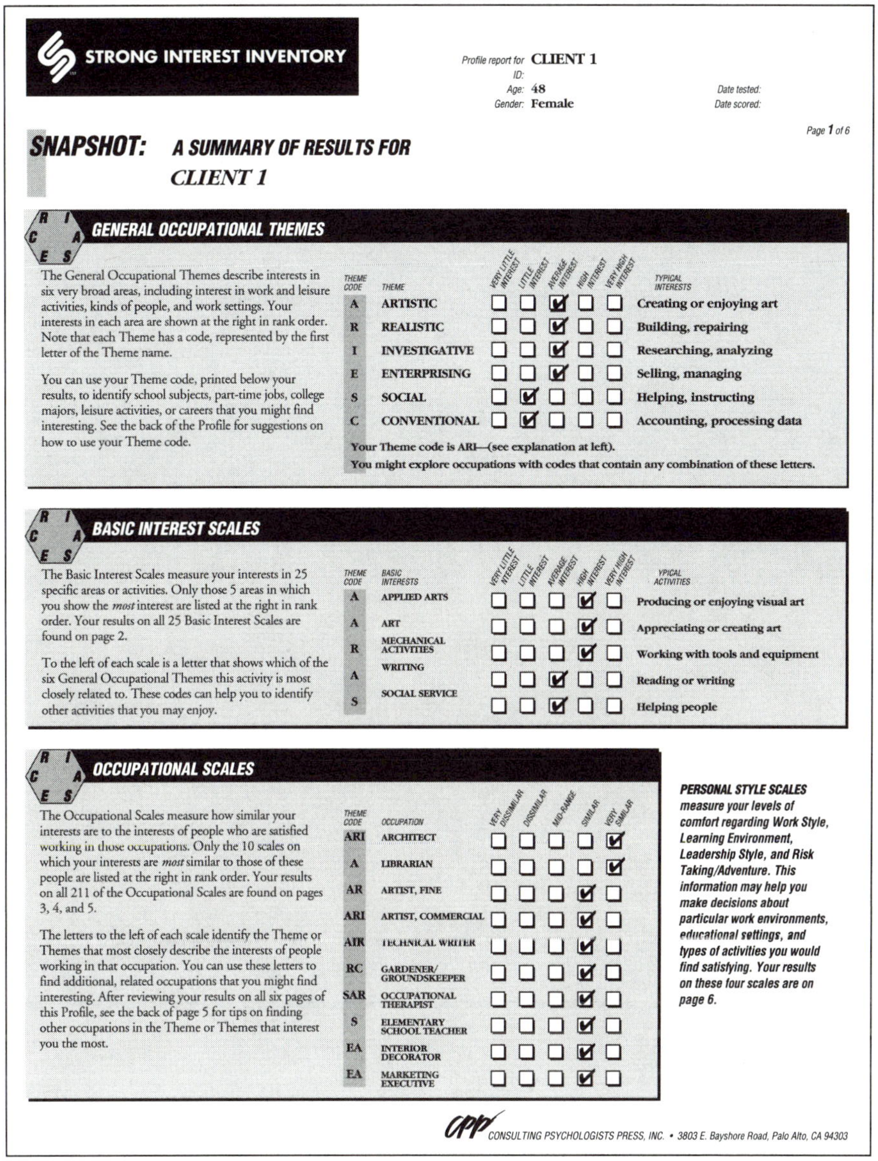

STRONG INTEREST INVENTORY

Profile report for CLIENT 1
ID:
Age: 48
Gender: Female
Date tested:
Date scored:

Page 1 of 6

SNAPSHOT: A SUMMARY OF RESULTS FOR CLIENT 1

GENERAL OCCUPATIONAL THEMES

The General Occupational Themes describe interests in six very broad areas, including interest in work and leisure activities, kinds of people, and work settings. Your interests in each area are shown at the right in rank order. Note that each Theme has a code, represented by the first letter of the Theme name.

You can use your Theme code, printed below your results, to identify school subjects, part-time jobs, college majors, leisure activities, or careers that you might find interesting. See the back of the Profile for suggestions on how to use your Theme code.

Theme Code	Theme	Very Little Interest	Little Interest	Average Interest	High Interest	Very High Interest	Typical Interests
A	ARTISTIC			✓			Creating or enjoying art
R	REALISTIC			✓			Building, repairing
I	INVESTIGATIVE			✓			Researching, analyzing
E	ENTERPRISING			✓			Selling, managing
S	SOCIAL		✓				Helping, instructing
C	CONVENTIONAL		✓				Accounting, processing data

Your Theme code is ARI—(see explanation at left).
You might explore occupations with codes that contain any combination of these letters.

BASIC INTEREST SCALES

The Basic Interest Scales measure your interests in 25 specific areas or activities. Only those 5 areas in which you show the *most* interest are listed at the right in rank order. Your results on all 25 Basic Interest Scales are found on page 2.

To the left of each scale is a letter that shows which of the six General Occupational Themes this activity is most closely related to. These codes can help you to identify other activities that you may enjoy.

Theme Code	Basic Interests	Very Little Interest	Little Interest	Average Interest	High Interest	Very High Interest	Typical Activities
A	APPLIED ARTS				✓		Producing or enjoying visual art
A	ART				✓		Appreciating or creating art
R	MECHANICAL ACTIVITIES				✓		Working with tools and equipment
A	WRITING			✓			Reading or writing
S	SOCIAL SERVICE			✓			Helping people

OCCUPATIONAL SCALES

The Occupational Scales measure how similar your interests are to the interests of people who are satisfied working in those occupations. Only the 10 scales on which your interests are *most* similar to those of these people are listed at the right in rank order. Your results on all 211 of the Occupational Scales are found on pages 3, 4, and 5.

The letters to the left of each scale identify the Theme or Themes that most closely describe the interests of people working in that occupation. You can use these letters to find additional, related occupations that you might find interesting. After reviewing your results on all six pages of this Profile, see the back of page 5 for tips on finding other occupations in the Theme or Themes that interest you the most.

Theme Code	Occupation	Very Dissimilar	Dissimilar	Mid-Range	Similar	Very Similar
ARI	ARCHITECT					✓
A	LIBRARIAN					✓
AR	ARTIST, FINE				✓	
ARI	ARTIST, COMMERCIAL				✓	
AIR	TECHNICAL WRITER				✓	
RC	GARDENER/GROUNDSKEEPER				✓	
SAR	OCCUPATIONAL THERAPIST				✓	
S	ELEMENTARY SCHOOL TEACHER				✓	
EA	INTERIOR DECORATOR				✓	
EA	MARKETING EXECUTIVE				✓	

PERSONAL STYLE SCALES *measure your levels of comfort regarding Work Style, Learning Environment, Leadership Style, and Risk Taking/Adventure. This information may help you make decisions about particular work environments, educational settings, and types of activities you would find satisfying. Your results on these four scales are on page 6.*

CPP CONSULTING PSYCHOLOGISTS PRESS, INC. • 3803 E. Bayshore Road, Palo Alto, CA 94303

Figure 17.1 Snapshot for Client 1, a Woman Reentering the Workforce

The Nature of the Differences Between Women's and Men's Interests

The following sections describe in more detail the differences between the interests of women and men at the item and scale levels. They also describe the analyses used to identify and comprehend these differences.

Gender Differences at the Item Level

The research version of the *Strong* used to collect data for the 1994 inventory contained 379 items. Analysis of these items revealed that 97 of them differentiated between women and men in the GRSs by 16 percent or more. Thus, in comparing response percentages between the two GRSs, there were enough relatively large differences between women and men that, had this been a goal, a separate scale could have been built that differentiated the interests of females from males.

The first item that would have appeared on such a scale would have been "Decorating a room with flowers," which showed the largest difference between females and males (50 percent). The last item chosen for such a scale would have been "Thrilling, dangerous activities vs. Quiet, safe activities," which differentiated the genders at the 16 percent level. It

Table 17.1 Item Response Comparisons to the Item "Operating Machinery" for Five Pairs of Female and Male Samples

Sample	Response	Response Percentage		Percentage Difference
		Female	Male	
Men- and Women-in-General (1938, 1946)	"Like"	27	54	−27
(N = 500 women and 500 men)	"Indifferent"	34	26	8
	"Dislike"	39	20	19
Men- and Women-in-General (1969)	"Like"	26	42	−16
(N = 1,000 women and 1,000 men)	"Indifferent"	32	34	−2
	"Dislike"	42	24	18
Men- and Women-in-General (1974)	"Like"	23	47	−24
(N = 300 women and 300 men)	"Indifferent"	36	34	2
	"Dislike"	41	19	22
Men- and Women-in-General (1985)	"Like"	22	45	−23
(N = 300 women and 300 men)	"Indifferent"	39	35	4
	"Dislike"	39	20	19
General Reference Samples (1994)	"Like"	18	37	−19
(N = 9,467 women and 9,484 men)	"Indifferent"	34	37	−3
	"Dislike"	48	26	22

is probably unnecessary to specify how each gender answered these questions. Most readers will be able to predict very accurately which gender responded "Like" to which of these items because some behaviors and attitudes continue to be more prevalent for one gender.

Even when the overall rate of endorsement for some items changes over time, the differences between the way women and men respond persist. For example, for the item "Operating machinery" shown in Table 17.1, the percentages of both females and males who respond "Like" have generally decreased over the years, while the differences between the responses of women and men, shown in the last column of the table, have remained fairly constant.

Figure 17.2 shows how a number of occupational groups responded to the item "Operating machinery." The distribution of average percentage of "Like" responses for occupations covers the whole range, but the distributions for female and male occupational samples differ somewhat, with the female samples having lower endorsement rates than the male samples. However, the high- and low-scoring occupational groups shown in the figure reveal that there is some overlap between the high-scoring and low-scoring groups of females and males despite the fact that the percentage of "Like" responses differs for females and males in the same occupations.

Although the 1994 female-male differences are obvious when looking at the last column of Table

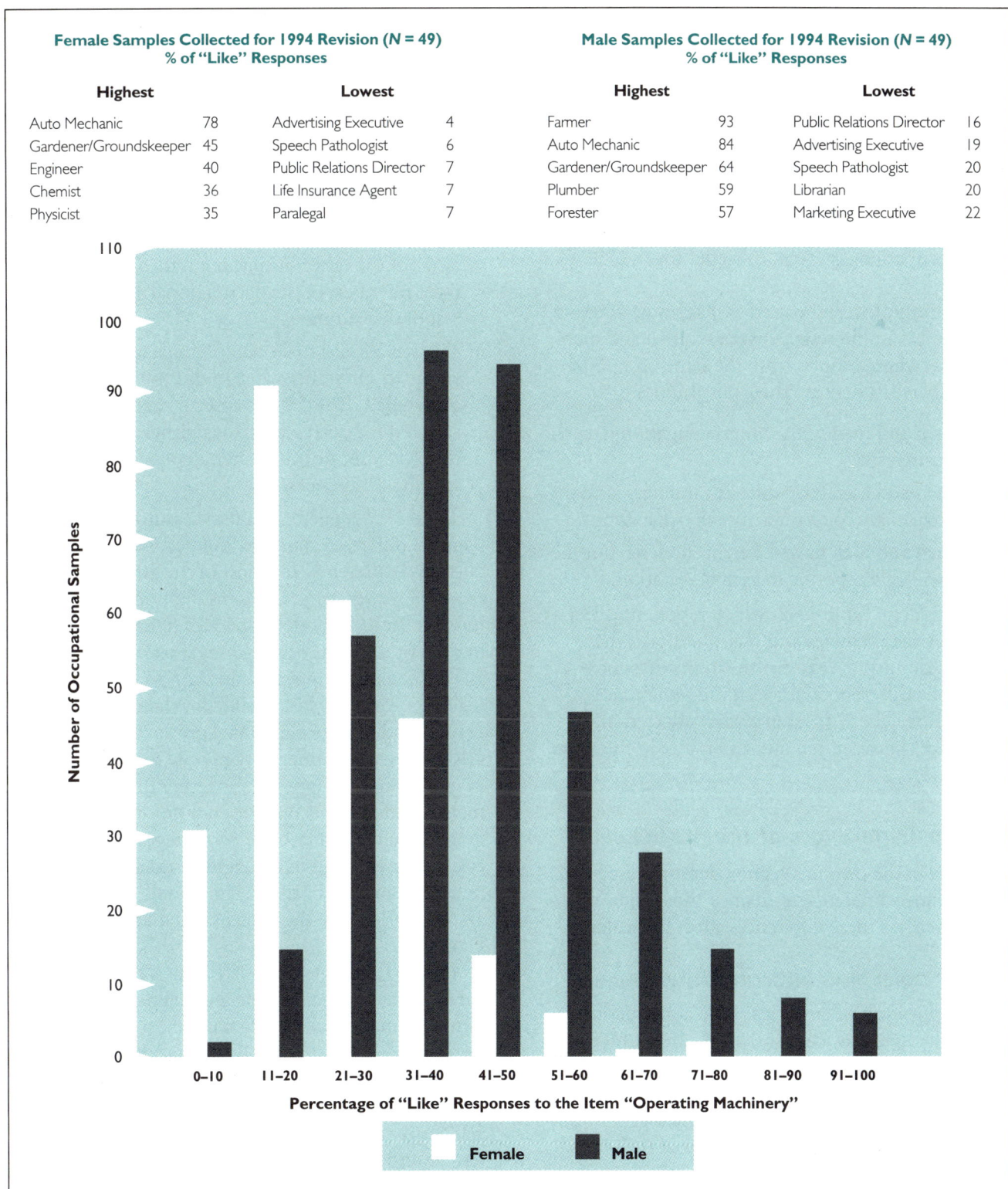

Figure 17.2 Percentage of "Like" Responses to the Item "Operating Machinery" for 621 Occupational Samples Collected over the History of the *Strong*

Note: The 621 occupational samples collected over the history of the *Strong* include 253 female samples and 368 male samples.

17.1, where the female GRS is compared with the male GRS, one might expect such differences to disappear when women and men in the same occupation are compared. Table 17.2 shows the items—ten favored by women and ten by men—with the largest gender differences in "Like" responses between women and men in the GRSs. For each of these twenty items, the table also shows the percentage of "Like" responses for women and men in eight occupational groups collected for the 1994 revision.

These samples can be used to determine whether the contrasts in interests between women and men disappear when samples from the same occupation are compared. There are three possibilities:

1. Women and men in the same occupation have the same interests.
2. Women and men have different interests, and the differences are constant across all occupations.
3. Women and men have different interests, but the differences are specific to each occupation.

The data in Table 17.2, which represent differences between females and males, support the third possibility, at least for the items that show the largest differences between the female and male GRSs. These differences are reflected in the differences between females and males in the same occupation.

Gender Differences at the Scale Level

The data in the previous section demonstrated that some gender differences remain at the item level. How, then, do these differences affect the scales?

Gender Differences in Occupational Scales

The implication of empirical scale construction is that the items selected for an OS are a function of the popularity of the item both in the occupational group and in the GRS for that gender. Thus, there are several possible ways in which gender differences may affect the composition of the scales. On any given item, these possibilities include the following:

1. The female and male occupational groups responded similarly, and so did the GRSs. In this case, the item would be selected (or not selected) depending on whether the occupational groups answered in the same way or differently than the GRSs for both scales.
2. The female and male occupational groups responded differently, but the female and male GRSs responded similarly to one another. In this case, an item could be selected for one OS and not the other.
3. The female and male occupational groups responded similarly, but the female and male GRSs responded differently from one another. In this case, an item could be selected for one scale and not the other, even though the female and male members of the occupational group responded similarly.
4. The female and male occupational groups responded differently, and so did the female and male GRSs. In this case, an item could be selected for both scales, for neither scale, or for one scale but not the other, depending on the specific differences.

Table 17.2 suggests that females and males in the General Reference Samples and occupational groups answered differently for most of the 20 items listed there. However, these 20 items did not appear on most of the 16 OSs developed for females and males in each of the eight occupations shown in the table. In fact, the items appeared on only 33 of the 320 scales on which it was possible for them to show up. Female and male occupational groups and the two GRSs responded differently in only the ten instances in which an item appeared on either the female or the male scale for an occupation, but not on both scales for the occupation (see the percentages marked with either F or M), and in the eight instances in which an item appeared on both the female and male scales for an occupation (see the percentages marked with both F and M).

Table 17.3 (pages 302–304) shows the means and correlations between female and male scales for the same occupations for the female and male General Reference Samples. Table 17.4 (page 305) summarizes some comparisons between the correlations in Table 17.3 and comparable correlations based on the 1985 *Strong*. In general, the correlations between the female and male Occupational Scales are higher for both females and males in 1994. It may be that selecting fewer items per scale increased the similarity of the Occupational Scales. (See Chapter 7 for a more detailed discussion of the process of selecting items for the scales.) It is clear from the content of the scales that some items appear on both the female and male scales for the same occupation and that the proportion of those items differs by scale.

Table 17.2 Items Showing Large Difference Between Women and Men in the Same Occupations (Percentage Difference Between the Two Genders in "Like" or "Dislike" Responses to Designated Items)

					Occupation					
Item	GRS	Accountant	Credit Manager	Elementary School Teacher	Farmer	Physical Therapist	Physicist	Police Officer	Social Worker	Average of the 9 Samples
Favored by Women										
"Decorating a room with flowers"	50.1	47.8	57.7	48.5	59.9	50.7	38.4	47.1	46.3	49.6
"Interior decorator"	39.8	47.1	44.4	41.0	52.6	39.6	26.9	46.5 M	39.4	41.9
"Looking at things in a clothing store"	38.9	40.3	40.0	44.9	50.9	41.5	30.2	40.6	37.1	40.5
"Shopping for the latest fashions"	38.6	40.4	41.5	52.0	54.8	43.2	36.1	44.2	38.4	43.2
"Clothes designer"	37.8	38.6	35.3	36.4	50.7	37.9	36.4	40.5	34.7	38.7
"Florist"	36.9	35.7	41.6	31.6	49.4	37.2	32.3	41.2	35.0	37.9
"Dance teacher"	30.8	35.3	35.2	27.7	35.9	35.7	21.9	36.8	28.9	32.0
"Beauty and haircare consultant"	30.3	36.9	38.5	36.9	61.5 F	31.1	11.2 F	35.5	28.0	34.4
"Planning a large party"	30.0	31.2	36.6	33.5	35.2	27.2	19.0	26.1	28.5	29.7
"Trying new cooking recipes"	27.3	38.3	25.0	29.0	46.8	23.6	25.7	25.1	22.5	29.3
Favored by Men										
"Popular mechanics magazines"	41.3	39.7	42.7	46.3	60.8	53.2	28.6	43.4	45.1	44.6
"Being responsible for earning money to support the family vs. Being responsible for caring for children"	35.2	40.0	41.7	37.4 FM	66.0 F	44.2	28.2	23.1	31.1	38.5
"Boxing"	31.2	37.2	36.3	32.7	34.1	40.7	17.3	36.0 FM	32.0	33.1
"Sports pages in the newspaper"	30.8	41.7 M	46.5	40.4	37.6	38.2	24.8	17.4	32.2	34.4
"Military officer"	28.8	26.3	35.4	28.2	24.0	27.1	23.7	19.6 FM	24.1	26.4
"Auto racer"	27.2	36.1	30.1	38.1	40.3	34.0	21.3	10.7 FM	27.3	29.5
"Enjoy tinkering with small hand tools"	25.8	27.1	28.8	37.1	49.9	28.7	16.6	29.7	26.9	30.1
"Music and arts events vs. Athletic events"	25.1	39.3 FM	39.4 M	25.7	42.7	28.9 F	15.7 M	17.9 FM	22.7	28.6
"Mechanical engineer"	24.7	23.3	34.2	32.3	44.8	31.3	8.9 FM	22.2	22.1 FM	27.1
"Machinist"	24.6	20.0	32.8	33.0	51.3 M	35.5	12.0 F	26.4	19.5	28.3

Note: The occupations in this table were selected from among those sampled for this revision to parallel those selected for a similar analysis completed for the 1985 Strong (see Table 7.3 in Hansen & Campbell, 1985). The letter "F" indicates that the item appears on the female scale; the letter "M" indicates that the item appears on the male scale.

Table 17.3 Mean Scores on and Correlations Between the 102 Pairs of Women's and Men's Occupational Scales

Occupational Scale	Female GRS				Male GRS			
	Correlation Between F and M Scales	Mean Score on Female Scale	Mean Score on Male Scale	Mean Difference	Correlation Between F and M Scales	Mean Score on Male Scale	Mean Score on Female Scale	Mean Difference
Accountant	.92	32	26	6	.92	31	34	−3
Actuary	.92	30	25	5	.91	30	35	−5
Advertising Executive	.87	31	37	−6	.85	30	27	3
Architect	.89	24	29	−5	.88	26	26	0
Artist, Commercial	.94	17	25	8	.94	16	12	−4
Artist, Fine	.92	17	24	−7	.93	18	15	3
Art Teacher	.92	12	28	16	.91	16	6	−10
Athletic Trainer	.88	16	15	1	.88	19	22	−3
Audiologist	.72	36	39	−3	.74	39	31	8
Auto Mechanic	.74	23	19	4	.83	25	34	−9
Banker	.80	36	31	5	.76	35	34	1
Biologist	.94	23	25	−2	.93	25	27	−2
Bookkeeper	.85	30	27	3	.84	30	32	−2
Broadcaster	.93	32	34	−2	.93	29	30	−1
Business Education Teacher	.94	26	35	−9	.93	31	24	7
Buyer	.93	19	26	7	.94	24	15	−9
Carpenter	.84	20	18	2	.88	24	30	−6
Chef	.82	26	33	7	.82	26	20	−6
Chemist	.96	28	24	4	.97	28	35	−7
Chiropractor	.85	30	32	−2	.87	30	32	−2
College Professor	.89	31	34	−3	.90	34	34	0
Community Service Organization Director	.82	36	34	2	.82	34	35	−1
Computer Programmer/ Systems Analyst	.87	35	28	7	.84	30	41	−11
Corporate Trainer	.89	33	39	−6	.89	38	32	6
Credit Manager	.72	35	34	1	.75	37	35	2
Dentist	.93	29	27	2	.93	30	31	−1
Dietitian	.67	30	37	−7	.70	30	29	1
Elected Public Official	.95	26	25	1	.95	27	27	0
Electrician	.75	25	11	−14	.79	24	34	10
Elementary School Teacher	.74	32	36	−4	.72	31	22	9
Emergency Medical Technician	.90	26	25	1	.89	30	30	0
Engineer	.94	33	27	6	.95	35	41	−6
English Teacher	.97	25	32	−7	.97	24	19	5
Farmer	.74	30	25	5	.79	29	30	−1

Table 17.3 Mean Scores on and Correlations Between the 102 Pairs of Women's and Men's Occupational Scales (continued)

Occupational Scale	Female GRS				Male GRS			
	Correlation Between F and M Scales	Mean Score on Female Scale	Mean Score on Male Scale	Mean Difference	Correlation Between F and M Scales	Mean Score on Male Scale	Mean Score on Female Scale	Mean Difference
Flight Attendant	.89	34	44	−10	.86	35	28	7
Florist	.90	21	30	−9	.88	23	13	10
Food Service Manager	.72	33	36	−3	.75	32	30	2
Foreign Language Teacher	.93	25	35	−10	.94	27	17	10
Forester	.87	29	25	4	.85	32	37	−5
Gardener/Groundskeeper	.71	35	31	4	.76	32	41	−9
Geographer	.75	34	24	10	.69	24	41	−17
Geologist	.87	24	18	6	.85	23	33	−10
Hair Stylist	.63	25	36	−11	.61	26	19	7
High School Counselor	.96	30	32	−2	.97	28	27	1
Horticultural Worker	.92	26	22	4	.93	22	27	−5
Housekeeping & Maintenance Supervisor	.86	33	34	−1	.85	35	33	2
Human Resources Director	.95	33	34	−1	.95	35	31	4
Interior Decorator	.80	18	35	−17	.76	23	11	12
Investments Manager	.73	28	24	4	.77	30	35	−5
Lawyer	.95	34	35	1	.95	35	35	0
Librarian	.89	35	42	−7	.91	32	29	3
Life Insurance Agent	.94	29	26	3	.95	28	31	−3
Marketing Executive	.79	32	34	−2	.76	32	34	−2
Mathematician	.91	16	12	4	.91	15	25	−10
Mathematics Teacher	.96	24	18	6	.96	23	27	−4
Medical Illustrator	.82	12	21	−9	.79	11	13	−2
Medical Records Technician	.80	37	42	−5	.73	36	35	1
Medical Technician	.82	24	23	1	.83	28	26	2
Medical Technologist	.94	27	26	1	.94	30	31	−1
Military Enlisted Personnel	.90	32	25	7	.91	32	36	−4
Military Officer	.90	32	24	8	.91	32	40	−8
Minister	.95	20	32	−12	.96	28	16	12
Musician	.93	25	38	13	.94	29	17	−12
Nurse, LPN	.92	22	33	−11	.91	28	16	12
Nurse, RN	.87	33	37	−4	.86	31	28	3
Nursing Home Administrator	.85	34	40	6	.86	37	32	−5
Occupational Therapist	.90	32	38	−6	.90	33	27	6
Optician	.86	32	27	5	.88	30	33	−3

Table 17.3 Mean Scores on and Correlations Between the 102 Pairs of Women's and Men's Occupational Scales (continued)

Occupational Scale	Female GRS				Male GRS			
	Correlation Between F and M Scales	Mean Score on Female Scale	Mean Score on Male Scale	Mean Difference	Correlation Between F and M Scales	Mean Score on Male Scale	Mean Score on Female Scale	Mean Difference
Optometrist	.89	34	24	10	.88	29	39	−10
Paralegal	.73	37	36	1	.70	34	33	1
Parks and Recreation Coordinator	.92	35	36	−1	.93	38	38	0
Pharmacist	.85	32	35	−3	.83	35	33	2
Photographer	.87	29	29	0	.86	27	29	−2
Physical Education Teacher	.87	19	14	5	.87	18	27	−9
Physical Therapist	.88	30	32	−2	.88	32	29	3
Physician	.91	23	25	−2	.90	25	27	−2
Physicist	.96	15	16	1	.95	19	24	5
Police Officer	.67	33	22	11	.76	29	40	−11
Psychologist	.95	28	29	−1	.95	27	27	0
Public Administrator	.97	28	30	−2	.97	30	30	0
Public Relations Director	.95	23	32	−9	.95	27	21	6
Purchasing Agent	.93	31	30	−1	.93	32	33	1
Radiologic Technologist	.88	33	34	−1	.88	35	31	4
Realtor	.94	19	28	−9	.94	29	21	8
Reporter	.93	25	30	−5	.93	26	24	2
Research & Development Manager	.95	25	19	6	.94	27	32	−5
Respiratory Therapist	.95	30	28	2	.94	29	33	−4
Restaurant Manager	.92	30	30	0	.92	28	30	−2
School Administrator	.94	34	32	2	.95	32	35	−3
Science Teacher	.96	23	24	−1	.96	28	25	3
Small Business Owner	.63	40	29	11	.61	35	40	−5
Social Science Teacher	.93	33	33	0	.94	33	33	0
Social Worker	.89	33	36	−3	.89	29	27	2
Sociologist	.96	24	29	−5	.96	27	24	3
Special Education Teacher	.92	32	39	−7	.92	32	24	8
Speech Pathologist	.87	34	41	−7	.89	33	25	8
Store Manager	.96	31	30	1	.96	28	28	0
Technical Writer	.94	33	38	−5	.95	31	28	3
Translator	.83	29	38	−9	.87	31	23	8
Travel Agent	.92	31	36	−5	.92	32	30	2
Veterinarian	.95	24	25	1	.94	28	28	0
Vocational Agriculture Teacher	.84	23	20	−3	.87	24	26	2

Table 17.4 Summary of Correlations Between Scores on Female and Male Scales for the Female and Male General Reference Samples (1994) and Women-in-General and Men-in-General (1985)

Sample	Median	Middle 50%	Range
Female GRS (1994)	.90	.84–.94	.63–.97
Women-in-General (1985)	.85	.79–.90	.26–.95
Male GRS (1994)	.91	.84–.94	.61–.97
Men-in-General (1985)	.84	.75–.90	.08–.95

Note: The 1985 data are summarized from Hansen & Campbell (1985), Table 7.6, pp. 84–85.

Table 17.5 (page 306) shows that for the most highly and least highly correlated pairs of scales the percentage of overlapping items differs. For scales with higher correlations between female and male scales, the percentage of overlapping items on the scales is higher. However, the correlation does not appear to be completely a function of the overlap because correlation coefficients in the .60 to .63 range have quite different proportions of overlapping items on the scales.

Only ten OSs of the 102 pairs listed in Table 17.3 show a difference of 10 standard score points (1 standard deviation) or more between females and males in the GRSs. Table 17.6 (page 307) lists these differences; note that males score higher on three of the four female scales and females score higher on five of the six male scales. Considerably fewer of the 1994 scales have mean differences this large between females and males compared with those on the 1985 *Strong*.

The Feasibility of Combined-Gender Scales

A number of efforts have been made over the last two decades to examine the feasibility of replacing the separate gender–normed OSs with combined-gender (unisex) scales (Campbell & Hansen, 1981; Hansen, 1976; Johansson & Harmon, 1972; Webber & Harmon, 1978). In general, these studies have suggested that the differences warrant maintaining separate scales. Previous research has also suggested that combined-gender scales sometimes produce higher overlap between some occupational groups and the in-general group.

The data collected for the 1994 revision, however, suggest fewer gender differences in the 1994 OSs than there have been in the past, probably as a result of different scale construction procedures as well as some modest convergence in male and female interests over the years. However, since differences in the scales have not been eradicated and single-gender scales are being maintained, a careful study of Table 17.3 is recommended so that the user can recognize those scales for which there are differences.

Single-Gender Scales

Only seven of the 109 occupations represented on the Profile do not have OSs for both women and men. (Remember, however, that every person taking the *Strong* is scored on all scales.) Seven scales represent occupational groups for which it was possible only to collect samples of workers of one gender who fit the criteria for the *Strong* sample. (See Chapter 7 for a discussion of these criteria.) These groups are Agribusiness Manager (male only), Child Care Provider (female only), Dental Assistant (female), Dental Hygienist (female), Home Economics Teacher (female), Plumber (male), and Secretary (female). Although an effort was made to obtain suitable samples for both females and males for all occupations, the effort was not always successful. However, it has been possible to collect both male and female samples from many occupations historically associated with only one gender (e.g., Auto Mechanic, Electrician, Nurse, Forester, and Farmer).

Gender Differences in the GOTs, BISs, and Personal Style Scales

Although the GOTs were normed on the combined GRS of over 18,000 adults, men and women score differently on some of the scales. The two areas in which the differences are largest are the R Theme and the A Theme. Males in the GRS scored about 7 points higher than females on the Realistic GOT,

Table 17.5 Overlapping Items in Most and Least Highly Correlated Female and Male Occupational Scales

Occupational Scale	Correlation		N Items on Scale		N Overlapping Items	Percent Items on Scale	
	Female	Male	Female	Male		Female	Male
English Teacher	.97	.97	60	51	43	72	84
Public Administrator	.97	.97	54	48	40	74	83
Chemist	.96	.97	53	48	39	74	81
High School Counselor	.96	.97	51	50	39	77	78
Hair Stylist	.63	.61	43	45	21	49	47
Small Business Owner	.63	.61	27	40	16	59	40
Dietitian	.67	.70	40	46	19	48	41
Police Officer	.67	.76	45	48	28	62	58
Geographer	.75	.69	50	45	24	48	53

Note: Correlations are based on scores of the female and male General Reference Samples (*N* = 9,467 women; *N* = 9,484 men).

while females in the GRS scored about 5 points higher than males on the Artistic GOT.

There are also differences between the scores of men and women on some of the BISs. As shown in Chapter 6, those BISs on which men in the GRS scored 5 or more points higher than women were Military Activities, Athletics, and Mechanical Activities. BISs on which women in the GRS scored at least 5 points or higher than men included Art and Culinary Arts. These findings replicate and help pinpoint the pattern observed on the GOTs, for which the primary differences were in the R and A Themes.

Two of the four Personal Style Scales, the Work Style and Risk Taking/Adventure scales, show gender differences. (There were no gender differences on the Leadership Style or Learning Environment scales.) Women, on average, tended to score more toward the works with people pole of the Work Style scale, while men tended to score more toward the works with ideas/data/things pole. On the Risk Taking/Adventure scale, men tended to score more toward the takes chances pole, while women tended to score more toward the plays it safe pole. While these results may appear to reflect stereotypical gender differences, scores on these two scales can help clients explore their own unique styles in relationship to traditionally perceived male-female differences. (See Chapter 8 for a detailed discussion of the Personal Style Scales.)

Conclusion

Women and men, on the average, continue to respond differently to about one-quarter to one-third of the inventory items. This difference is large enough to warrant separately normed GOTs, BISs, and Personal Style Scales. Women and men in the same occupations also respond differently to a number of items on the *Strong*. However, the impact of gender differences on the OSs may be less than previously thought because the items on which there are large differences do not often appear on the Occupational Scales. The 1994 *Strong* continues to offer separate OSs for women and men in the same occupation because for some occupations the female and male scales do not correlate very highly. Additional research is needed to determine whether separate scales for women and men should be maintained on future versions of the inventory.

The differences between interests of women and men that are evident have been accounted for by including information on the Profile that allows women and men to compare their scores with those of over 9,000 women, over 9,000 men, and the entire GRS, which combines the men's and women's data. The client, along with his or her counselor, can select the most valid comparison, although same-gender comparisons will generally be the most predictive. The inclusion of all this

Table 17.6 Occupational Scales with Score Differences ≥ 10 Between Females and Males in the General Reference Samples

Occupational Scale	Absolute Difference	Gender Scoring Higher
Female		
Auto Mechanic	11	Male
Carpenter	10	Male
Geologist	10	Male
Speech Pathologist	10	Female
Male		
Art Teacher	12	Female
Electrician	12	Male
Interior Decorator	12	Female
Librarian	10	Female
Medical Illustrator	10	Female
Hair Stylist	10	Female

information may lead clients to consider occupations that they previously ignored, thinking these fields were open only to members of the opposite gender. Barriers based on gender differences are now falling, and virtually all occupations are open to qualified people of either gender. It is important that the counselor challenge perceived barriers that may be leading the client to rule out certain occupations.

References

Apostal, R. A. (1986). Interpretable and noninterpretable female-male score differences on selected Strong-Campbell Interest Inventory Occupational Scales. *Psychological Reports, 58,* 899–902.

Betz, N. E. (1993). Issues in the use of ability and interest measures with women. *Journal of Career Assessment, 1*(3), 217–232.

Betz, N. E., Heesacker, R. S., & Shuttleworth, C. (1990). Moderators of the congruence and realism of major and occupational plans in college students: A replication and extension. *Journal of Counseling Psychology, 37*(3), 269–276.

Campbell, D. P., & Hansen, J. C. (1981). *Manual for the SVIB-SCII* (3rd ed.). Stanford, CA: Stanford University Press.

Gaeddert, D., & Hansen, J. C. (1993). Development of a measure of interest diversity. *Journal of Career Assessment, 1*(3), 294–308.

Hackett, G., & Lonborg, S. D. (1993). Career assessment for women: Trends and issues. *Journal of Career Assessment, 1*(3), 197–216.

Hammer, A. L., & Macdaid, G. P. (1992). *MBTI Career Report manual.* Palo Alto, CA: Consulting Psychologists Press.

Hansen, J. C. (1976). Exploring new directions for SCII occupational scale construction. *Journal of Vocational Behavior, 9,* 147–160.

Hansen, J. C., & Campbell, D. P. (1985). *Manual for the Strong Interest Inventory* (4th ed). Stanford, CA: Stanford University Press.

Hansen, J. C., Collins, R. C., Swanson, J. L., & Fouad, N. A. (1993). Gender differences in the structure of interests. *Journal of Vocational Behavior, 42,* 200–211.

Johansson, C. B., & Harmon, L. W. (1972). Strong Vocational Interest Blank: One form or two? *Journal of Counseling Psychology, 19,* 404–410.

Krumboltz, J. D. (1991). *Manual for the Career Beliefs Inventory.* Palo Alto, CA: Consulting Psychologists Press.

Lapan, R. T., Boggs, K. R., & Morrill, W. H. (1989). Self-efficacy as a mediator of Investigative and Realistic General Occupational Themes on the Strong-Campbell Interest Inventory. *Journal of Counseling Psychology, 36*(2), 176–182.

Lewis, M., & Wild, C. L. (1991). The impact of feminist critique on tests, assessment, and methodology. *Psychology of Women Quarterly, 15,* 581–596.

Marshall, J. (1989). Re-visioning career concepts: A feminist invitation. In M. B. Arthur, D. T. Hall, & B. S. Lawrence (Eds.), *Handbook of career theory* (pp. 275–291). Cambridge, England: Cambridge University Press.

McDaniels, C. (1984). Work and leisure in the career span. In N. C. Gysbers & Associates (Eds.), *Designing careers* (pp. 558–590). San Francisco: Jossey-Bass.

McDaniels, C., & Gysbers, N. C. (1992). *Counseling for career development.* San Francisco: Jossey-Bass.

Mirvis, P. H. (Ed.). (1993). *Building the competitive workforce: Investing in human capital for corporate success.* New York: Wiley.

Myers, I. B., & McCaulley, M. H. (1985). *Manual: A guide to the development and use of the Myers-Briggs Type Indicator.* Palo Alto, CA: Consulting Psychologists Press.

Nevill, D. D., & Super, D. E. (1986a). *The Salience Inventory.* Palo Alto, CA: Consulting Psychologists Press.

Nevill, D. D., & Super, D. E. (1986b). *The Values Scale.* Palo Alto, CA: Consulting Psychologists Press.

Niles, S. G., & Usher, C. G. (1993). Applying the career-development assessment and counseling model to the case of Rosie. *The Career Development Quarterly, 42*(1), 61–66.

Saveri, A. (1991). The realignment of workers and work in the 1990s. In J. K. Kummerow (Ed.), *New directions in career planning and the workplace: Practical strategies for counselors* (pp. 117–153). Palo Alto, CA: Consulting Psychologists Press.

Super, D. E., Osborne, W. L., Walsh, D. J., Brown, S. D., & Niles, S. G. (1992). Developmental career assessment and counseling: The C-DAC model. *Journal of Counseling and Development, 71*(1), 74–80.

Super, D. E., Thompson, A. S., & Lindeman, R. H. (1988). *Manual for the Adult Career Concerns Inventory.* Palo Alto, CA: Consulting Psychologists Press.

Thompson, A. S., Lindeman, R. H., Super, D. E., Jordaan, J. P., & Myers, R. A. (1981). *Manual for the Career Development Inventory.* Palo Alto, CA: Consulting Psychologists Press.

Webber, P. L., & Harmon, L. W. (1978). The reliability and concurrent validity of three types of occupational scales for two occupational groups: Some evidence bearing on handling sex differences in interest scale construction. In C. K. Tittle & D. G. Zytowski (Eds.), *Sex-fair interest measurement: Research and implications.* Washington, DC: National Institute of Education, Department of Health, Education, and Welfare.

APPENDIX A

Occupational Scales Samples, DOT Codes, and Related Job Titles

The samples described in this appendix are those used to develop the current *Strong Interest Inventory* Occupational Scales (OSs). For each, the column headed "*N*" indicates the number of people in the norm group that was used to construct the scale. "Year Tested" indicates the year in which the members of that occupational sample took the *Strong Interest Inventory.* "Mean Age" provides the average age of the people in the sample, and "Mean Years Experience" provides the average numbers of years the people in the sample have worked in the occupation.

The column labeled "Composition" indicates the sources for the people who make up each occupational sample. This column also provides selected demographic data about the occupations. Among the demographic data are educational background, typical work activities, areas of specialization, and types of businesses or institutions in which participants are employed.

The column labeled "DOT Code and Description" offers, for each occupation, synopses of the information presented in the *Dictionary of Occupational Titles* (DOT). The description begins with the three-digit DOT code most appropriate for that sample. These three digits will help your client locate related occupations in the *Dictionary of Occupational Titles.* The first digit indicates within which of nine very broad categories the occupation fits:

0/1 Professional, technical, and managerial occupations
2   Clerical and sales occupations
3   Service occupations
4   Agricultural, fishery, forestry, and related occupations
5   Processing occupations
6   Machine trades occupations
7   Bench work occupations
8   Structural work occupations
9   Miscellaneous occupations

The second digit indicates a more specific division of work within the nine broad categories, and the third digit locates a particular occupation within that division. The information presented under "Composition" and "DOT Code and Description" will help you to aid your client in identifying the responsibilities, job tasks, work environments, and skills entailed in each of the occupations on the Profile.

The last column, "Related Occupations," is a list of jobs related to each of the Occupational Scale samples. This list, along with the occupations suggested in Appendix B, will help you to broaden your client's career exploration beyond the *Strong* Profile to find other occupations appropriate for his or her consideration.

Description of the Strong Occupational Scales

Sample/Scale	N	Year Tested	Mean Age	Mean Years Exper.	Composition	DOT Code and Description	Related Occupations
Accountant (Female)	383	1992	36.7	11.0	Members of American Institute of Certified Public Accountants. 73% completed bachelor's degree, 25% master's or professional degree. 12% were sole practitioners, 30% worked for accounting firm, 44% worked for business/industry, 7% worked for government.	160. Compiles and analyzes financial information to prepare entries into accounts and for financial reports. Designs new systems or utilizes or modifies existing systems to provide records of assets, liabilities, and transactions of establishment. Maintains accounts and records or supervises subordinates in such bookkeeping activities as recording disbursements, expenses, or tax payments or in maintenance of accounting controls over inventories, purchases. Audits contracts, orders, and vouchers and prepares reports that substantiate individual transactions before their settlement. May work independently for a fee, as a member of an accounting firm, or for a corporation.	Auditor Budget accountant City auditor Controller Cost accountant County auditor Internal auditor Property accountant Systems accountant
Accountant (Male)	881	1992	42.1	17.4	See women's sample above. 64% completed bachelor's degree, 32% master's or professional degree. 13% were sole practitioners, 34% worked for accounting firm, 41% worked for business/industry, 5% worked for government.		
Actuary (Female)	642	1992	36.4	12.8	Members of American Academy of Actuaries. 70% completed bachelor's degree, 28% master's or professional degree.	020. Applies knowledge of mathematics, statistics, and principles of finance and business to problems in insurance, annuities, and pensions. Determines mortality, accident, sickness, disability, and retirement rates. Constructs probability tables regarding fire, natural disasters, and unemployment, based on analysis of statistical data and other pertinent information. Designs or reviews insurance and pension plans and calculates premiums. Ascertains premium rates required and cash reserves and liabilities necessary to ensure payment of future benefits. Determines equitable basis for distributing surplus earnings under participating contracts in mutual companies. May specialize in one type of insurance.	Applied mathematician Economist Financial analyst Operations-research analyst Rate analyst Rate engineer Risk manager Statistician Value engineer
Actuary (Male)	593	1992	42.0	18.0	See women's sample above. 62% completed bachelor's degree, 33% master's or professional degree.		

Description of the *Strong* Occupational Scales

Sample/Scale	N	Year Tested	Mean Age	Mean Years Exper.	Composition	DOT Code and Description	Related Occupations
Advertising Executive (Female)	205	1992	36.3	12.1	From commercially compiled national listing. 70% completed bachelor's degree, 14% master's or professional degree. 84% worked for full-service advertising agency; 7% for small, specialized agency; 4% for direct marketing agency; 4% were self-employed.	164. Plans or assists in planning advertising programs to promote sale of company's products; consults with company officials, sales department, and advertising agency to develop promotional plans. Prepares advertising brochures and manuals for publication. Reviews and proofreads layout and copy before advertisement or brochure is printed. May write copy, do layout work, prepare sales kits, set up displays, or write sales outlines for use by sales staff, or direct other workers performing these duties.	Ad agency manager Advertising manager Advertising promotions manager Advertising sales manager Creative director Display manager Media director Radio advertising director
Advertising Executive (Male)	348	1992	47.0	21.7	See women's sample above. 63% completed bachelor's degree, 14% master's or professional degree. 75% worked for full-service advertising agency; 11% for small, specialized agency; 2% for direct marketing agency; 9% were self-employed.		
Agribusiness Manager (Male)	297	1972	43.4	16.0	Grain elevator managers (22%), implement dealers (21%), farm supply managers (21%), dairy processing plant managers (20%), nursery managers (16%).	180. Nursery manager: grows plants for sale to trade or retail customers; determines type and quantity to be grown. Selects and purchases seed, nutrients, and disease-control chemicals. Directs and coordinates workers planting, raising, and cutting plants for sale. 529. Dairy processing manager: supervises and coordinates production of dairy products. Directs workers in receiving and testing milk and in operations such as pasteurizing and storing dairy products. 529. Grain elevator manager: supervises and coordinates unloading, loading, storing, inspection, cleaning, and blending of grain for milling and shipment. *624/272. Implement dealer and farm service supply manager: sells and repairs implements used on farms, such as cultivators, harvesting machines, plows, tractors, and weeders. *Both of these codes describe the tasks done by people in this occupation.	Cooperative manager Dairy processing manager Elevator manager Farm implement dealer Farm supply manager Grain buyer Nursery manager

Description of the *Strong* Occupational Scales

Sample/Scale	N	Year Tested	Mean Age	Mean Years Exper.	Composition	DOT Code and Description	Related Occupations
Architect (Female)	603	1993	39.3	14.4	Members of American Institute of Architects. 40% completed bachelor's degree, 56% master's or professional degree. Areas of specialization included public/institutional (34%), commercial (29%), residential (24%), industrial (2%).	001. Researches, plans, and designs building projects for clients, including private residences and office and public buildings, and organizes services for construction. Consults with client to determine size and space requirements and provides information regarding cost, design, materials, equipment, and estimated building time. Plans layout of project; integrates structural, mechanical, and ornamental elements into unified design. Prepares sketches of proposed project for client. Writes specifications and prepares scale and full-size drawings and other contract documents for use of building contractors and crafts people.	Architectural drafter Designer Evaluating architect Landscape architect Landscape drafter Marine architect Principal architect Technical architect Urban designer
Architect (Male)	560	1993	47.2	22.8	See women's sample above. 48% completed bachelor's degree, 43% master's or professional degree. Areas of specialization included public/institutional (41%), commercial (34%), residential (12%), industrial (4%).		
Artist, Commercial (Female)	222	1983	33.9	9.8	Artists working for agencies and studios listed in *The Creative Black Book*, national directory of art services, as well as national sample of artists listed in *Bell Yellow Pages*. 3% had high school diploma, 20% had some art courses not leading to degree in art, 8% completed associate degree in art, 54% bachelor's, 8% master's. 33% were freelance artists, 22% were employed by advertising agency, 19% by studio. Major activities included illustration (17%), graphic design (13%), administration (8%), keylining (7%), layout (7%), combination (38%).	141. Designs artwork to promote public consumption of materials, products, or services. Designs artwork for books, magazines, newspapers, television, or packaging. Determines arrangement of material; prepares illustrations and sketches for client; gives instruction to people who prepare final layout. May select type or draw lettering.	Art director Cartoonist Cinematographer Clothes designer Color expert Display designer Fashion artist Furniture designer Graphic designer Illustrator Mechanical artist Medical illustrator Photograph retoucher Production artist Publication designer Set illustrator or designer
Artist, Commercial (Male)	206	1979	38.8	15.6	See women's sample. 27% had taken art courses not leading to degree, 47% completed bachelor's degree, 6% master's. 39% were freelance artists, 23% were employed by studio, 10% by advertising agency, 15% by combination of employers.		

Description of the *Strong* Occupational Scales

Sample/Scale	N	Year Tested	Mean Age	Mean Years Exper.	Composition	DOT Code and Description	Related Occupations
Artist, Fine (Female)	247	1979	44.4	17.0	Selected from *Who's Who in American Art.* 18% had taken art courses not leading to degree, 25% completed bachelor's degree, 42% master's. 58% were freelance artists, 15% were employed by educational institutions, 22% by combination of employers.	144. Creates artworks whose primary purpose is to be viewed for aesthetic content. Conceives and develops works of art; selects the theme, subject matter, medium, and manner of execution. May paint a variety of original subject material using watercolors, oils, acrylics, tempera, or other paint medium. May create artwork on stone, metal, wood, or other material, using various tools, procedures, and processes to etch, engrave, carve, paint, or draw. May design and construct three-dimensional artworks.	Filmmaker Glassblower Metalsmith Painter Photographer Potter Printmaker Sculptor Weaver
Artist, Fine (Male)	213	1979	43.5	20.5	See women's sample above. 13% had taken art courses not leading to degree, 15% completed bachelor's degree, 55% master's. 39% were freelance artists, 39% were employed by educational institutions, 15% by combination of employers.		
Art Teacher (Female)	360	1981	39.0	11.2	Members of National Art Association, secondary division. All were secondary school teachers. 41% completed bachelor's degree, 58% master's. 79% of sample spent minimum of 50% of time teaching; other activities included lesson preparation, grading, and administrative functions. Main areas of art included general, painting and drawing, sculpture, ceramics, print making, and weaving.	149. Teaches courses such as drawing, color, weaving, crafts, sculpture, and painting. Instructs students through lectures, demonstrations, and audiovisual aids. Prepares course objectives and teaching outline and evaluates student progress. Selects books and art supplies. Keeps attendance records and maintains discipline. Participates in faculty and professional meetings, conferences, and teacher-training workshops. Performs related duties such as sponsoring special activities or student organizations.	Art therapist Crafts instructor Design instructor Drawing teacher Graphic arts teacher Industrial design instructor
Art Teacher (Male)	303	1978	40.2	14.9	See women's sample above. All were secondary school teachers. 15% completed bachelor's degree, 64% master's, 19% doctorate.		

Description of the Strong Occupational Scales

Sample/Scale	N	Year Tested	Mean Age	Mean Years Exper.	Composition	DOT Code and Description	Related Occupations
Athletic Trainer (Female)	242	1983	29.3	5.9	National sample of certified athletic trainers from National Athletic Trainers Association. 25% completed bachelor's degree, 73% master's, 2% doctorate. Employers included four-year colleges (59%), high schools (22%), two-year colleges (5%), professional athletic teams (1%), other (12%). 7% specialized in particular sport. Major activities included evaluation and treatment of injuries (39%), covering practices and games (29%), combination (27%).	153. Evaluates physical condition and advises and treats professional and amateur athletes to maintain maximum physical fitness for participation in athletic competition. Prescribes routine and corrective exercises to strengthen muscles. Recommends special diets to build up health and help athletes maintain a healthy weight. Gives massages to relieve soreness, strains, and bruises. Administers first aid to injured players. Treats chronic minor injuries and related disabilities to maintain athletes' performance. May give heat and diathermy treatments as prescribed by health service.	Physical fitness teacher Physical therapist Sports medicine coordinator
Athletic Trainer (Male)	250	1983	32.5	9.4	See women's sample above. 30% completed bachelor's degree, 68% master's, 1% doctorate. Employers included four-year colleges (59%), high schools (16%), professional athletic teams (9%), two-year colleges (5%), combination (2%). 21% specialized in particular sport. Major activities included evaluation and treatment of injuries (48%), covering practices and games (24%), combination (25%).		
Audiologist (Female)	509	1993	36.6	11.1	Audiologist members of American Speech-Language-Hearing Association. 92% completed master's degree, 7% doctorate. 27% worked in hospital, 23% in physician's office, 13% in school, 13% in audiologist's or speech-language pathologist's office (including self-employment), 7% in college or university, 7% in some other health care facility, balance in research, industrial, and other settings.	076. Determines hearing impairment and implements habilitation and rehabilitation services for patient. Administers and interprets variety of tests to determine type and degree of hearing impairment, site of damage, and effects on comprehension and speech. Evaluates test results and works with teachers, speech pathologists, and families to determine communication problems related to disability. May conduct research on auditory systems or design and develop clinical procedures and apparatus.	Hearing-test technician Speech and hearing specialist Speech therapist Speech pathologist Voice pathologist

Description of the *Strong* Occupational Scales

Sample/Scale	N	Year Tested	Mean Age	Mean Years Exper.	Composition	DOT Code and Description	Related Occupations
Audiologist (Male)	426	1993	43.3	16.8	See women's sample. 69% completed master's degree, 30% doctorate. 18% worked in hospital, 17% in physician's office, 6% in school, 26% in audiologist's or speech-language pathologist's office (including self-employment), 15% in college or university, balance in research, industrial, and other settings.		
Auto Mechanic (Female)	165	1993	34.5	10.7	List of automobile mechanics certified by National Institute for Automotive Service Excellence and commercially compiled list of automobile repair establishments. 18% had a high school diploma; 17% had attended trade technical school in addition, 40% had some college or associate degree, 13% completed bachelor's degree, 4% master's. 44% worked in independent repair shop, 20% in car dealership, 8% in tire dealership, 7% in specialty repair shop, 7% in fleet repair shop, balance in service stations, body shops, machine shops, and government agencies.	620. Repairs and overhauls automotive vehicles. Examines vehicle and discusses with customer or automotive service estimator the nature and extent of damage or malfunction. Plans work procedure using charts, technical manuals, and experience. Removes and disassembles mechanical units, such as engine, transmission, or differential, and inspects parts for wear, using micrometers, calipers, and thickness gauges. Repairs, overhauls, rebuilds, or replaces parts. Rewires ignition system, lights, and instrument panel. Realigns and adjusts brakes. Mends damaged body and fenders. Installs and repairs accessories.	Automotive body repairer Diesel, truck, or bus mechanic Motorcycle mechanic Automotive painter or customizer Automotive repair service estimator
Auto Mechanic (Male)	561	1993	38.7	18.0	See women's sample above. 22% had high school diploma, 29% had attended trade/technical school in addition, 31% had some college or associate degree, 5% completed bachelor's degree, 2% master's. 46% worked in car dealership, 23% in independent repair shop, 7% in tire dealership, balance in specialty repair shops, fleet repair shops, service stations, body shops, machine shops, and government agencies.		

Description of the *Strong* Occupational Scales

Sample/Scale	N	Year Tested	Mean Age	Mean Years Exper.	Composition	DOT Code and Description	Related Occupations
Banker (Female)	283	1992	43.1	17.7	From commercially compiled national listing. 25% had high school diploma or had attended trade/technical school in addition, 45% had some college or associate degree, 19% completed bachelor's degree, 9% master's or professional degree. Major activities included administration/supervision, customer contact, and planning/policy development.	186. Directs bank's monetary programs, transactions, and security measures in accordance with banking principles and legislation. Coordinates program activities and evaluates operating practices to ensure efficient operations. Oversees receipt, disbursement, and expenditure of money. Directs safekeeping and control of assets and securities. Approves loans and participates as member of committees concerned with lending and customer service functions. Directs accounting for assets. Reviews financial and operating statements and presents reports and recommendations to bank officials or board committees. Maintains financial and community business affiliations.	Bank controller Bank officer Cashier Credit union manager Loan officer Operations officer Teller Treasurer Trust officer
Banker (Male)	264	1992	44.8	19.5	See women's sample above. 5% had high school diploma or had attended trade/technical school in addition, 17% had some college or associate degree, 54% completed bachelor's degree, 21% master's or professional degree. Major activities included administration/supervision, customer contact, and planning/policy development.		
Biologist (Female)	282	1992	46.8	17.9	Members of American Institute of Biological Sciences. 28% had master's degree, 71% doctorate. 53% worked in four-year colleges and universities, 8% in community colleges, 11% in federal government agencies, 8% in industry, 5% in schools, 5% in other nonprofit organizations. Major activities included teaching/training, technical writing, administration, basic research, and consulting.	041. Studies origin, relationship, development, anatomy, functions, and other basic principles of plant and animal life. May specialize in research centering around a particular plant, animal, or aspect of biology. May prepare environmental impact reports. May teach college courses.	Anatomist Aquatic biologist Bacteriologist Biochemist Biomedical researcher Botanist Ecologist Entomologist Geneticist Microbiologist Oceanographer Ornithologist Physiologist Plant pathologist Zoologist
Biologist (Male)	757	1992	50.0	22.1	See women's sample above. 15% had master's degree, 85% doctorate. 59% worked in four-year colleges and universities, 5% in community colleges, 9% in federal government agencies, 6% in industry, 4% in schools, 6% in other nonprofit organizations. Major activities included teaching/training, technical writing, basic research, administration, applied research, and consulting.		

Description of the *Strong* Occupational Scales

Sample/Scale	N	Year Tested	Mean Age	Mean Years Exper.	Composition	DOT Code and Description	Related Occupations
Bookkeeper (Female)	243	1993	45.7	19.0	From commercially compiled listing of firms that employ bookkeepers. 14% had high school diploma, 49% some college or associate degree, 27% completed bachelor's degree, 7% master's or professional degree. 68% were self-employed or worked for their own firm, 17% were employed by accounting firm, balance by variety of organizations.	210. Keeps records of financial transactions of an establishment using computer and calculator. Verifies, allocates, and posts transactions to subsidiary accounts in journals or computer files from sales slips, invoices, receipts, and computer printouts. Summarizes details in separate ledgers or computer files and transfers data to general ledger. Reconciles and balances accounts. May compile reports on accounts payable and receivable, profit and loss, cash receipts, and expenditures to show statistics pertinent to operation of business.	Accountant Accounting clerk Audit clerk Credit clerk Medical records clerk Night auditor Statistical clerk Teller
Bookkeeper (Male)	116	1993	51.2	23.6	See women's sample above. 2% had high school diploma, 21% some college or associate degree, 58% completed bachelor's degree, 17% master's or professional degree, 2% doctorate. 45% were self-employed or worked for their own firm, 40% were employed by accounting firm, balance by variety of organizations.		
Broadcaster (Female)	220	1983	32.4	7.8	Sample collected from stations listed in *Broadcasting Yearbook* and from responses to ads in *Inside Radio* and *Radio and Records*. Also members of American Women in Radio and Television, Inc. 23% had high school diploma, 57% completed bachelor's degree, 9% master's. 84% were employed by commercial station, 15% by public station. 56% were department heads. Major activities included on-the-air broadcasting (28%), programming (13%), sales (9%), research (7%), news gathering and reporting (6%), combination (26%), other (general management, production, and copyrighting functions, 9%).	159. Announces radio and television programs to audience. Memorizes script, reads, or ad-libs to identify stations; introduces and closes shows; and announces station breaks, commercials, or public service information. Cues worker to transmit program from network central station according to schedule. May describe public event or interview guest or moderate panel or discussion show. May keep daily program log. May be designated according to media or type of program.	Anchor Announcer Assignment editor Continuity director Disc jockey General manager Local announcer Music director Network announcer News director Operations director Promotions director Reporter Sports director Television announcer Traffic director

Description of the *Strong* Occupational Scales

Sample/Scale	N	Year Tested	Mean Age	Mean Years Exper.	Composition	DOT Code and Description	Related Occupations
Broadcaster (Male)	213	1983	34.2	12.8	See women's sample. 26% had high school diploma, 53% completed bachelor's degree, 7% master's. All were radio broadcasters; 85% were employed by commercial station. 65% were department heads. Major activities included on-the-air broadcasting (30%), programming (21%), management and administration (8%), news gathering and writing (4%), sales (3%), combination (25%), other (3%).		
Business Education Teacher (Female)	576	1993	45.1	18.1	Members of National Business Education Association. 28% completed bachelor's degree, 64% master's or professional degree, 8% doctorate. 56% were employed in public schools, 30% in colleges or universities, 6% in private or parochial schools.	091. Instructs students through lectures, demonstrations, and audiovisual aids. Prepares course objectives and teaching outline, assigns lessons, and corrects homework. Administers tests to evaluate students' progress. Keeps attendance records and maintains discipline. Participates in faculty and professional meetings, conferences, and teacher-training workshops. Performs related duties such as sponsoring special activities or student organizations. Teaches courses such as typing, business law, bookkeeping, accounting, shorthand, merchandising, word processing, or office management.	Accounting teacher Bookkeeping instructor Business law teacher Merchandising instructor Typing teacher
Business Education Teacher (Male)	545	1993	47.5	21.5	See women's sample above. 16% completed bachelor's degree, 61% master's or professional degree, 22% doctorate. 52% were employed in public schools, 36% in colleges or universities, 7% in private or parochial schools.		
Buyer (Female)	214	1983	35.4	8.8	Names from *Salesmen's Guide to Women's and Children's Wear Buyers* and *Salesmen's Guide to Men's and Boys' Wear Buyers*. 33% had high school diploma, 11% completed associate degree, 48% bachelor's. 46% were employed by department stores, 29% by specialty shops, 10% by chains. 81% bought for more than one department.	162. Purchases merchandise for resale. Selects and orders merchandise from showings of manufacturing representatives, basing selection on nature of clientele, demand for specific merchandise, and experience as buyer. Authorizes payment of invoices or return of merchandise. May conduct staff meetings with selling personnel to introduce new merchandise. May price items for resale.	Assistant buyer Children's buyer Men's buyer Women's buyer

Description of the *Strong* Occupational Scales

Sample/Scale	N	Year Tested	Mean Age	Mean Years Exper.	Composition	DOT Code and Description	Related Occupations
Buyer (Male)	219	1983	36.9	10.8	See women's sample. 25% had high school diploma, 8% completed associate degree, 60% bachelor's, 7% master's. 40% were employed by department stores, 25% by specialty shops, 18% by chains. 96% bought for more than one department.		
Carpenter (Female)	97	1984	31.4	4.7	Members of United Brotherhood of Carpenters and Joiners of America, and participants in Women in Trades Conference. 46% had high school diploma, 6% completed associate degree, 33% bachelor's, 8% master's. 39% were final-year apprentices, 34% were at journey level. 26% did mainly rough carpenter work, 5% finish, 64% combination. 36% of sample specialized in particular area of carpentry. 91% of sample spent minimum of 50% of time doing manual labor. Other activities included reading blueprints, communicating with contractors, problem solving, and administrative functions.	860. Constructs, erects, installs, and repairs structures and fixtures of wood, plywood, and wallboard, using carpenter's hand tools and power tools, and conforming to local building codes. Studies blueprints, sketches, or building plans for information pertaining to type of material required and dimensions of structure or fixture to be fabricated. Selects specified type of materials, prepares layout, marks cutting and assembly lines on materials, and fastens them together. Verifies trueness of structures and erects framework for structures.	Acoustical carpenter Apprentice carpenter Boatbuilder Cabinetmaker Carpentry repairer Contractor Finish carpenter Form builder Joiner Journey carpenter Maintenance carpenter Mold carpenter Rough carpenter
Carpenter (Male)	199	1983	27.3	4.6	Members of United Brotherhood of Carpenters and Joiners of America. 73% had high school diploma, 7% completed associate degree, 8% bachelor's, 2% other. 82% were final-year apprentices, 15% were at journey level. 18% did mainly rough carpentry, 21% finish, 53% combination. 30% of sample specialized in particular area of carpentry. 62% of sample spent minimum of 75% of time doing manual labor. Other activities included reading blueprints, communicating with contractors, problem solving, and administrative functions.		

Description of the *Strong* Occupational Scales

Sample/Scale	N	Year Tested	Mean Age	Mean Years Exper.	Composition	DOT Code and Description	Related Occupations
Chef (Female)	106	1984	31.8	6.8	Members of American Culinary Federation, Inc., and graduates of Johnson and Wales College in Providence, RI, and of Culinary Institute, Hyde Park, NY. 6% had high school diploma, 14% attended trade or vocational school, 58% completed associate degree, 12% bachelor's, 1% master's. 21% were employed by restaurants, 16% by hotels, 11% by private clubs, 6% by catering services, 5% by educational institutions, 25% by combination, remainder by resorts, hospitals, or institutional firms. Major activities were food preparation (42%), supervision and training (15%), planning menus (3%), combination (33%).	313. Supervises, coordinates, and participates in activities of cooks and other kitchen personnel engaged in preparing and cooking foods in a hotel, restaurant, or other eating establishment. Estimates food consumption and purchases food stuffs and kitchen supplies. Selects, develops, and cooks recipes. May employ, train, or discharge workers. May plan menus.	Banquet chef Chef saucer Chef tournant Cook Corporate chef Executive chef Food production manager Garde manger chef Pantry chef Pastry chef Sous chef
Chef (Male)	296	1983	37.4	14.0	Members of American Culinary Federation, Inc. 17% had high school diploma, 33% attended technical or vocational school, 22% completed associate degree, 10% bachelor's, 3% master's. 25% were employed by restaurants, 21% by private clubs, 15% by hotels, 18% by combination, remainder by resorts, hospitals, educational institutions, caterers, industrial firms, or other. Major activities included supervision and training (30%), food preparation (22%), ordering food (3%), combination (40%).		
Chemist (Female)	271	1993	41.2	14.8	Members of American Chemical Society. 41% completed master's or professional degree, 59% doctorate. Major activities included teaching/training, management/supervision, applied research, and basic research. 47% were employed by business/industry, 30% by educational institutions, 12% by government agencies.	022. Conducts research, analysis, synthesis, and experiments on substances for product and process development, quantitative and qualitative analysis, improvement of methods, and development of knowledge. Devises new equipment, formulas, methods, and processes for solution of technical problems. May teach college courses.	Assayer Biochemist Clinical chemist Food chemist Forensic researcher Immunochemist Organic chemist Pharmaceutical chemist

Description of the *Strong* Occupational Scales

Sample/Scale	N	Year Tested	Mean Age	Mean Years Exper.	Composition	DOT Code and Description	Related Occupations
Chemist (Male)	304	1993	48.1	20.6	See women's sample. 26% completed master's or professional degree, 74% doctorate. Major activities included teaching/training, management/supervision, applied research, and basic research. 59% were employed by business/industry, 22% by educational institutions, 7% by government agencies.		
Child Care Provider (Female)	349	1993	41.1	12.6	From lists of licensed child day care establishments in California, Texas, and Maryland. 9% had high school diploma, 40% some college or associate degree, 30% completed bachelor's degree, 14% master's, 2% doctorate.	092. Day care center director: directs activities of preschool, day care center, or other child development facility to provide instruction and care for children. Prepares budget, authorizes purchases, interviews and hires staff, and reviews facility to ensure conformance to state and local regulations. Confers with parents regarding facility activities and policies. Confers with staff concerning child behavior and learning problems. 359. Nursery school attendant: cares for group of children and attends to their basic needs. Organizes and leads activities that stimulate the children's physical, emotional, intellectual, and social growth. Plans and leads recreational activities and participates with or instructs children in games, reading, and arts and crafts. Maintains discipline. May serve meals and/or refreshments. 355. Child care attendant: attends to personal needs of disabled children while in school to receive specialized academic and physical training. Secures children in equipment. Monitors children using life support equipment. Helps children perform physical activities, such as boarding buses, using prosthetic devices, eating, etc.	Camp counselor Camp director Children's tutor Elementary school teacher Kindergarten teacher Nanny Preschool teacher Teacher's aide

Description of the Strong Occupational Scales

Sample/Scale	N	Year Tested	Mean Age	Mean Years Exper.	Composition	DOT Code and Description	Related Occupations
Chiropractor (Female)	212	1979	42.8	14.3	Rosters obtained from American Chiropractic Association, International Chiropractors Association, and *Digest of Chiropractic Economics*. 90% were self-employed or in partnerships; 10% were employed by clinics, educational institutions, or combination.	079. Diagnoses and treats muscular and skeletal conditions of the spinal column and other body joints to prevent disease and correct abnormalities of the human body believed to be caused by interference with the nervous system. Examines to determine nature and extent of disorder using x-ray machines and other instruments. Manipulates spine or other involved areas.	Acupuncturist Chiropractic assistant Osteopath
Chiropractor (Male)	230	1982	38.7	11.7	Members of American Chiropractic Association. 90% were self-employed or in partnerships; 10% were employed by clinics, educational institutions, or combination. 88% of sample spent minimum of 50% of time in diagnosis or treatment of patients.		
College Professor (Female)	400	1972	49.0	17.0	From college catalog faculty listings; mix sought with respect to academic area, type of institution, and location; criteria of selection included high academic rank and level of education. 1% completed less than master's degree, 22% master's, 77% doctorate or equivalent. Academic disciplines included business and law (9%); linguistics (8%); mathematics (7%); physical sciences (12%); biomedical sciences (10%); medical services (10%); social services and education (10%); social sciences (10%); art, music, and literature (13%); miscellaneous (12%).	090. Conducts college or university classes for undergraduate or graduate students. Prepares and delivers lectures, compiles bibliographies of specialized materials, and stimulates discussions. Compiles, administers, and grades examinations or assigns this work to others. Directs research of others. Conducts research in particular field of knowledge and publishes findings in professional journals. Performs related duties such as advising students and working with student organizations. Serves on faculty committees; provides professional consulting services to government and industry.	Dean Department chair Instructor

Description of the Strong Occupational Scales

Sample/Scale	N	Year Tested	Mean Age	Mean Years Exper.	Composition	DOT Code and Description	Related Occupations
College Professor (Male)	229	1983	43.5	13.2	Nationwide sample from mail list company of college and university professors. 19% completed master's degree, 79% doctorate. 42% were employed by public universities, 21% by private universities, 16% by private four-year colleges, 14% by public four-year colleges. Titles included full professor (38%), associate professor (39%), assistant professor (23%). Academic disciplines included social sciences (23%), physical sciences (16%), biomedical sciences (15%), art and literature (13%), social service and education (11%). Major activities included teaching (23%), research (12%), administration (7%), class preparation (7%), publishing (2%), combination (45%). 37% held administrative as well as academic appointment.		
Community Service Organization Director (Female)	418	1993	38.3	11.6	Listings obtained from Association of Professional Directors of YWCAs and YMCAs in United States; directors of agencies listed in United Way Directory of Human Services in Greenwich, CT; Denver, CO; Honolulu, HI; Des Moines, IA; Phoenix and Mesa, AZ; Columbus and Cincinnati, OH; Houston, TX; and Miami, FL. 4% had high school diploma, 14% some college or associate degree, 58% completed bachelor's degree, 22% master's or professional degree, 2% doctorate. Major activities included administration/supervision, member and community contact, budget planning, program planning, and fund raising.	187. Directs, organizes, and coordinates program activities of non-profit agency to provide specialized human services. Consults with co-operating agencies to coordinate efforts. Reviews and prepares budgets and reports. Prepares and releases reports, studies, and publications to promote public understanding and support for programs. Recruits and trains staff or volunteers. Represents organization in the community. May be involved in fund raising and public speaking activities and the development of training or educational material pertinent to the organization and its programming.	Camp director Community outreach worker Community relations director Educational program director Recreation facility manager Social welfare administrator Social worker Volunteer services director

Description of the *Strong* Occupational Scales

Sample/Scale	N	Year Tested	Mean Age	Mean Years Exper.	Composition	DOT Code and Description	Related Occupations
Community Service Organization Director (Male)	390	1993	41.6	16.4	See women's sample. 4% had some college or associate degree, 62% completed bachelor's degree, 30% master's or professional degree, 3% doctorate. Major activities included administration/supervision, member and community contact, budget planning, program planning, and fund raising.		
Computer Programmer/ Systems Analyst (Female)	248	1993	38.6	11.8	Responses to advertisement in *Dr. Dobbs Journal*, Members of Association for Computing Machinery and employees of Apple Computer Corporation in San Francisco Bay Area. 4% had some college or associate degree, 40% completed bachelor's degree, 42% master's or professional degree, 13% doctorate. Major activities included teaching/training, programming, testing and maintaining software, customer support and problem diagnosis, writing manuals, and systems analysis. 35% worked in for-profit computer or software company, 27% in for-profit company not solely devoted to computers or software, 18% in educational institutions, 7% in government agencies, 7% in other nonprofit organizations, 5% were self-employed.	030. Computer programmer: plans, develops, tests, and writes computer programs, applying knowledge of programming techniques and computer systems. Confers with supervisor and users to resolve questions of program intent, data input, and output requirements. Observes test runs and corrects program errors. Analyzes, reviews, and rewrites programs to increase operating efficiency or to adapt program to new requirements. 012. Systems analyst: analyzes user requirements, procedures, and problems to automate processing or to improve existing computer system. Confers with personnel of units involved to analyze current operational procedures, identify problems, and learn requirements. Writes detailed description of user needs, program functions, and steps required to develop or modify computer program.	Business programmer Computer scientist Data processor Data processing manager Engineering programmer Information scientist Manager of information systems Process control programmer Programmer-analyst Scientific programmer Software manager Systems manager Technical consultant Technical support analyst

Description of the *Strong* Occupational Scales

Sample/Scale	N	Year Tested	Mean Age	Mean Years Exper.	Composition	DOT Code and Description	Related Occupations
Computer Programmer/ Systems Analyst (Male)	483	1993	38.7	13.9	See women's sample. 11% had some college or associate degree, 38% completed bachelor's degree, 36% master's or professional degree, 15% doctorate. Major activities included teaching/training, programming, testing and maintaining software, customer support and problem diagnosis, writing manuals, and systems analysis. 43% worked in for-profit computer or software company, 29% in for-profit company not solely devoted to computers or software, 10% in educational institutions, 3% in government agencies, 3% in other nonprofit organizations, 9% were self-employed.		
Corporate Trainer (Female)	226	1993	42.1	11.9	Members of American Society for Training and Development. 2% had high school diploma, 6% some college or associate degree, 33% completed bachelor's degree, 51% master's, 8% doctorate. Major activities included instruction, instructional design, needs analysis, and administration/ supervision. 53% worked in business/ industry, 14% were self-employed or in partnership, 9% worked in government agency, balance in educational, medical, and other non-profit organizations.	166. Develops and conducts training programs for employees. Confers with management to gain knowledge of work situation requiring training for employees to understand changes in policies, procedures, regulations, and technologies. Formulates teaching outline and determines instruction methods, using knowledge of specified training needs and the effectiveness of such methods as individualized training, group instruction, lectures, conferences, and workshops. Selects or develops teaching aids such as computer tutorials, training manuals, demonstration models, and multimedia aids. Conducts training sessions on specified areas such as new employee orientation, use of computers and software, sales techniques, health and safety, and leadership development. Tests trainees to measure progress and evaluate effectiveness of training.	Career development director Education and training manager Human resources director Teacher Technical training coordinator Training instructor Training representative Training specialist
Corporate Trainer (Male)	232	1993	46.6	16.8	See women's sample above. 1% had high school diploma, 7% some college or associate degree, 26% completed bachelor's degree, 51% master's, 14% doctorate. Major activities included instruction, instructional design, needs analysis, and administration/ supervision. 56% worked in business/ industry, 15% were self-employed or in partnership, 8% worked in government agency, balance in educational, medical, and other nonprofit organizations.		

Description of the *Strong* Occupational Scales

Sample/Scale	N	Year Tested	Mean Age	Mean Years Exper.	Composition	DOT Code and Description	Related Occupations
Credit Manager (Female)	322	1993	39.2	12.3	Members of National Association of Credit Management. 21% had high school diploma or had attended trade/technical school in addition, 48% some college or associate degree, 23% completed bachelor's degree, 4% completed master's or professional degree. Major activities included collection, customer relations, establishing credit policy, management/supervision, teaching/training others.	168. Manages credit and collection department of commercial house, department store, hotel, or similar institution. Investigates financial standing and reputation of prospective customer accounts. Supervises collection of bad accounts and worthless checks. Keeps records of collection. May submit delinquent account to agency or attorney for collection.	Credit analyst Credit counselor Finance manager Loan officer
Credit Manager (Male)	454	1993	45.2	18.4	See women's sample above. 3% had high school diploma, 21% some college or associate degree, 58% completed bachelor's degree, 16% master's or professional degree. Major activities included collection, customer relations, management/supervision, establishing credit policy, teaching/training others.		
Dental Assistant (Female)	215	1979	32.8	8.7	Members of American Dental Association, and write-in responses to articles in *The Explorer*, publication of National Association of Dental Assistants. 30% had high school diploma, 16% completed associate degree, 45% had certificates in dental assisting. 76% were employed by private clinics, 14% by educational institutions.	079. Assists dentist during examination and treatment of patients. Prepares patients and materials, sterilizes instruments, and sets up instrument trays. Takes and records medical and dental histories and vital signs of patients. Exposes dental diagnostic x-rays. Pours, trims, and polishes study casts. Instructs patients in oral hygiene and plaque control programs. Assists dentist during dental procedures. May perform office support duties and may clean patients' teeth.	Chairside dental assistant Dental office manager Dental secretary Dental surgical assistant Orthodontics technician

Description of the *Strong* Occupational Scales

Sample/Scale	N	Year Tested	Mean Age	Mean Years Exper.	Composition	DOT Code and Description	Related Occupations
Dental Hygienist (Female)	236	1982	32.6	9.7	Members of National Dental Hygiene Association. All were licensed hygienists. 56% completed associate degree, 32% bachelor's, 3% master's. 90% worked for private dental office. 93% spent minimum of 50% of time working in preventive dentistry.	078. Performs dental prophylactic treatment and instructs groups and individuals. Removes calcareous deposits, accretions, and stains from teeth by using dental instruments. Examines patient for signs of disease and charts condition of disease and decay for treatment by dentist. Lectures community organizations regarding oral hygiene. May expose and develop x-ray film, apply solutions to aid in arresting dental decay, prepare filling material, and sterilize instruments.	Community health dental hygienist Oral hygienist Public school dental hygienist
Dentist (Female)	365	1993	36.7	9.8	Members of American Dental Association. 72% were in private practice, 18% were employed by private practitioners, balance were employed by public and private organizations.	072. Diagnoses and treats disease, injuries, and malformations of teeth and gums and related oral structures. Examines patient using x-rays, mirrors, explorers, and other diagnostic procedures and instruments. Cleans, fills, extracts, and replaces teeth using dental appliances, medications, and surgical implements. Provides preventive dental services to patients.	Endodontist Oral pathologist Oral surgeon Orthodontist Pediatric dentist Periodontist Prosthetic dentist Public health dentist
Dentist (Male)	416	1993	45.2	18.5	See women's sample above. 89% were in private practice, 7% were employed by government agencies, 4% were employed by private practitioners.		
Dietitian (Female)	208	1983	37.9	11.4	Obtained with assistance of American Dietetic Association; all were practicing, technician registered dietitians. 51% completed bachelor's degree, 45% master's, 3% doctorate. 31% were employed by hospitals, 16% by government, 15% by educational institutions, 14% were self-employed, 5% were employed by business/industry, 12% combination. Major activities included administration/management (28%), teaching (24%), consulting (22%), combination (17%), other (8%).	077. Plans and directs food service program in hospitals, schools, and restaurants. Plans menus and diets, providing required food and nutrients to feed individuals and groups. Directs workers engaged in food preparation. Purchases or requisitions food, equipment, and supplies. Maintains and analyzes records to determine improved methods for purchasing and using food, equipment, and supplies. Instructs individuals and groups in nutrition. Consults with physicians and other health care professionals to determine nutritional needs of medical patients.	Clinical dietitian Community dietitian Dietetic technician Food scientist Nutrition education coordinator Nutritionist Pediatric dietitian Public health dietitian Renal dietitian Research dietitian Therapeutic dietitian

Description of the *Strong* Occupational Scales

Sample/Scale	N	Year Tested	Mean Age	Mean Years Exper.	Composition	DOT Code and Description	Related Occupations
Dietitian (Male)	108	1983	34.1	7.8	See women's sample. 50% completed bachelor's degree, 33% master's, 14% doctorate. 24% were employed by hospitals, 18% by government, 13% by educational institutions, 7% by military, 5% were self-employed, 2% were employed by business/industry, 9% other, 22% combination. Major activities included administration and management (54%), teaching (16%), consulting (11%), combination (16%).		
Elected Public Official (Female)	224	1978	48.2	6.3	Selected from rosters provided by National Women's Education Fund, including state legislators, statewide constitutional officeholders, and members of House of Representatives; and from list of city and county officials from *Women in Public Office: Biographical Directory and Statistical Analysis*. 23% had high school diploma, 39% completed bachelor's degree, 16% master's. 39% were employed in other occupations while they held office.	188. Holds elected public office in legislative bodies such as Congress, state legislatures, county commissions, and city councils. Involved in legislative action of the government. Listens to lobbyists and determines budget for the government.	Attorney general City council member County commissioner Governor Legislator Mayor Representative Senator
Elected Public Official (Male)	208	1979	46.3	8.6	Members of 93rd U.S. Congress, tested by R. Willow. Others selected from *State Elective Officials and the Legislatures*, published by Council of State Governments. 20% had high school diploma, 30% completed bachelor's degree, 26% law degree, 13% master's, 6% doctorate. 67% were employed in other occupations while they held office.		

Description of the *Strong* Occupational Scales

Sample/Scale	N	Year Tested	Mean Age	Mean Years Exper.	Composition	DOT Code and Description	Related Occupations
Electrician (Female)	60	1984	29.2	4.4	Members of International Brotherhood of Electrical Workers and numerous women's organizations. 33% had high school diploma, 18% completed electrical apprenticeship, 13% had certificate from vocational school, 7% completed associate degree, 25% bachelor's. 77% were employed as construction electricians, 8% maintenance electricians, 8% other, 7% combination. 83% of sample spent minimum of 50% of time doing manual labor. Other activities included reading blueprints, communication with contractors, problem solving, and administrative functions. 57% of sample were third- or fourth-year apprentices, 32% were at journey level.	824. Plans layout and installs and repairs wiring, electrical fixtures, apparatus, and control equipment. Plans new or modified installations to minimize waste of materials, to provide access for future maintenance, and to avoid unsightly, hazardous, and unreliable wiring. Checks that new or modified installations are consistent with specifications and local electrical codes. Prepares sketches showing location of wiring or follows diagrams and blueprints, ensuring that concealed wiring is in future walls, ceilings, and flooring. Measures, bends, cuts, threads, assembles, and installs electrical conduit. Pulls wire through conduit, splices wires, and connects wiring to lighting fixtures and power equipment. Installs controls and distribution apparatus. Connects power cable to equipment and installs grounding leads.	Airplane electrician Apprentice electrician Automotive electrician Electrical installation supervisor Electrical repairer Estimator Inspector Journey electrician Line maintainer Line repairer Powerhouse electrician Streetlight supervisor Wireperson
Electrician (Male)	260	1984	34.6	13.2	Members of International Brotherhood of Electrical Workers. 22% had high school diploma, 46% completed electrical apprenticeship, 14% had certificate from vocational school, 8% completed associate degree, 7% bachelor's. 88% were employed as construction electricians, 4% maintenance electricians, 5% other, 4% combination. 79% of sample spent minimum of 50% of time doing manual labor. Other activities included reading blueprints, communicating with contractors, problem solving, and administrative functions. 31% of sample were third- or fourth-year apprentices, 61% were at journey level.		

Description of the Strong Occupational Scales

Sample/Scale	N	Year Tested	Mean Age	Mean Years Exper.	Composition	DOT Code and Description	Related Occupations
Elementary School Teacher (Female)	241	1993	43.9	16.8	From commercially compiled national listing. 43% completed bachelor's degree, 54% master's. 86% were employed in public schools.	092. Teaches elementary school students academic, social, and motor skills. Prepares course objectives and outline following curricular guidelines of the state and school. Lectures, demonstrates, and uses audiovisual teaching aids to present subject matter. Evaluates student progress. Assigns lessons, corrects papers, and hears oral presentations. Counsels students when adjustment and academic behavior problems arise. Discusses problems with parents and suggests remedial action. Keeps attendance and grade records as required by school board.	Children's tutor Day care worker Kindergarten teacher Nursery school teacher Preschool teacher Remedial teacher Teacher's aide
Elementary School Teacher (Male)	220	1993	43.0	18.0	See women's sample above. 47% completed bachelor's degree, 49% master's, 2% doctorate. 86% were employed in public schools.		
Emergency Medical Technician (Female)	207	1983	37.2	5.7	Members of National Association of Emergency Medical Technicians. 13% had high school diploma, 6% attended vocational school, 36% had some college, 8% completed associate degree, 19% bachelor's, 2% master's. Employers included community and municipal services, such as police and fire departments (45%), private ambulance companies (24%), hospitals (20%), combination (6%), other (4%). 74% spent minimum of 50% of time giving emergency medical care; other activities included driving ambulance, determining nature of injuries, and taking training courses.	079. Administers first aid treatment to and transports sick or injured persons to medical facility, working as a member of emergency medical team. Determines nature and extent of illness or injury, or magnitude of catastrophe, to establish first aid procedures to be followed or the need for additional assistance, basing decisions on statements of persons involved, examination of victim, and knowledge of emergency medical practice. Communicates with professional medical personnel at emergency treatment facility to obtain instructions regarding further treatment and to arrange for reception of victims at treatment facility.	Ambulance attendant Medical assistant Paramedic Physician assistant

Description of the *Strong* Occupational Scales

Sample/Scale	N	Year Tested	Mean Age	Mean Years Exper.	Composition	DOT Code and Description	Related Occupations
Emergency Medical Technician (Male)	241	1983	33.8	7.1	See women's sample. 10% had high school diploma, 16% attended vocational school, 24% had some college, 15% completed associate degree, 22% bachelor's. Employers included community and municipal services, such as police and fire departments (55%), hospitals (18%), private ambulance companies (17%), combination (3%), other (6%). 50% of sample spent minimum of 50% of time giving emergency medical care; other activities included driving ambulance, determining nature of injuries, and taking training courses.		
Engineer (Female)	254	1993	32.1	7.8	Membership lists of American Society of Civil Engineers, American Society of Mechanical Engineers, Institute of Electrical and Electronics Engineers, and Institute of Industrial Engineers. 65% completed bachelor's degree, 30% master's, 5% doctorate. 43% were employed by business/industrial firms, 14% by engineering firms, 14% by government agencies, 9% by public utilities, 4% were self-employed or in partnership.	003. Electrical engineer: conducts research, design, and developmental activities concerned with electrical components, products, and systems. 005. Civil engineer: plans, designs, and constructs structures such as roads, buildings, and airfields. 007. Mechanical engineer: applies principles of physics and engineering for the use of mechanical and heat power. 008. Chemical engineer: applies principles of chemistry, physics, and mathematics to manufacturing. All engineering specialties may function in one or more activities, such as research, development, design, production, consulting, administration, management, teaching, technical writing, or technical sales or service.	Aeronautical engineer Biomedical engineer Chemical engineer Civil engineer Electrical engineer Geophysicist Industrial engineer Marine engineer Mechanical engineer Metallurgist Mineral engineer Nuclear engineer Product engineer
Engineer (Male)	512	1993	43.0	18.3	See women's sample above. 2% had less than bachelor's degree, 56% completed bachelor's degree, 31% master's, 2% professional degree, 9% doctorate. 30% were employed by business/industrial firms, 29% by engineering firms, 16% by government agencies, 5% by public utilities, 9% were self-employed or in partnership.		

Description of the *Strong* Occupational Scales

Sample/Scale	N	Year Tested	Mean Age	Mean Years Exper.	Composition	DOT Code and Description	Related Occupations
English Teacher (Female)	303	1982	39.1	11.0	National sample, members of National Council of Teachers of English, Secondary Section. All secondary school English teachers. 39% completed bachelor's degree, 57% master's. 48% taught mainly literature, 35% writing, 12% grammar. 81% spent minimum of 40% of time teaching; other activities included lesson preparation, grading, and meetings.	091. Teaches courses in composition, literature, grammar, poetry, creative writing, and speech. Instructs students through lectures, demonstrations, and audiovisual aids. Prepares course objectives and course outlines. Assigns lessons and corrects homework. Administers tests to evaluate students' progress. Keeps attendance records and maintains discipline. Participates in faculty and professional meetings, conferences, and teacher-training workshops. Performs related duties such as sponsoring special activities or student organizations.	Literature teacher Publications advisor Speech teacher Writing teacher
English Teacher (Male)	222	1982	39.1	14.6	See women's sample above. 29% completed bachelor's degree, 68% master's, 3% doctorate. 49% taught mainly literature, 29% writing, 16% grammar. 87% spent minimum of 40% of time teaching; other activities included lesson preparation, grading, and meetings.		
Farmer (Female)	92	1992	51.0	26.7	Lists provided by Texas Farm Bureau, Iowa Farm Bureau, American Agri-women, and responses to mailings to members of National Farmers Organization and article in their newsletter. 37% had high school diploma, 11% attended trade/technical school in addition, 22% some college or associate degree, 23% completed bachelor's degree, 4% master's or professional degree. Major activities included record keeping, business/financial planning, purchasing, marketing/customer contact, supervision, and machinery operation.	421. Manages a tract of land devoted to production of plants and animals. Raises various kinds of crops and livestock according to market conditions, weather, and size and location of farm. Selects and purchases seed, fertilizer, farm machinery, livestock, and feed and assumes responsibility for sale of crop and livestock products. May hire or direct workers engaged in various farm duties, depending on the size and nature of the farm.	Animal breeder Dairy farmer Field crop farmer Grain farmer Livestock farmer Poultry farmer Rancher Tree farmer Vegetable farmer Vine-fruit farmer

Description of the *Strong* Occupational Scales

Sample/Scale	N	Year Tested	Mean Age	Mean Years Exper.	Composition	DOT Code and Description	Related Occupations
Farmer (Male)	152	1992	51.2	28.4	Lists provided by Texas Farm Bureau, Iowa Farm Bureau, and responses to mailings to members of National Farmers Organization and article in their newsletter. 38% had high school diploma, 11% attended trade/technical school in addition, 20% some college or associate degree, 24% completed bachelor's degree, 3% master's. Major activities included purchasing, business/financial planning, machinery operation, record keeping, marketing/customer contact, crop planning/scheduling, and supervision.		
Flight Attendant (Female)	553	1992	38.5	14.4	Members of Association of Flight Attendants. 15% had high school diploma or had attended trade/technical school in addition, 47% some college or associate degree, 34% completed bachelor's degree, 2% master's.	352. Provides variety of personal services for safety and comfort of airline passengers during flight. Explains use of safety equipment such as seat belts, oxygen masks, and life jackets. Serves previously prepared meals and beverages. Verifies tickets and directs passengers to their seats. Prepares reports showing place of departure and destination, passenger ticket numbers, and meal and beverage inventories.	Bus attendant Cabin attendant In-flight service coordinator Passenger service representative Purser Train attendant
Flight Attendant (Male)	412	1992	36.5	11.3	See women's sample above. 6% had high school diploma or had attended trade/technical school in addition, 38% some college or associate degree, 50% completed bachelor's degree, 5% master's.		
Florist (Female)	211	1983	40.4	11.3	Retail members of Society of American Florists listed in *Who's Who in Floriculture*. 18% had high school diploma, 9% attended vocational school, 35% had some college, 9% completed associate degree, 21% bachelor's. 84% worked in family-owned florist shop; 91% of shops employed less than 10 people. 93% were single florist shops, 7% part of chain. 79% bought all inventory from supplier, 2% had greenhouse, 18% obtained inventory from combination. Major activities included designing arrangements (25%), taking inventory (17%), customer contact (13%), combination (44%).	142. Designs and fashions live, cut, dried, or artificial floral arrangements for events. Confers with client regarding price and type of arrangement desired. Plans arrangements according to client's requirements and costs, using knowledge of design and properties of materials, or selects appropriate standard design pattern. Selects and arranges flora and foliage necessary for arrangement. May instruct or direct other workers.	Floral arranger Floral designer Greenhouse florist Retail florist Wholesale florist

Description of the Strong Occupational Scales

Sample/Scale	N	Year Tested	Mean Age	Mean Years Exper.	Composition	DOT Code and Description	Related Occupations
Florist (Male)	207	1983	40.2	15.8	See women's sample. 6% had high school diploma, 35% had attended some college, 9% completed associate degree, 36% bachelor's. 84% worked in family-owned florist shop; 72% of shops employed less than 10 people. 79% were single florist shops, 21% part of chain. 63% bought all inventory from supplier, 6% had greenhouse, 31% obtained inventory from combination of two. Major activities included designing arrangements (23%), taking inventory (18%), customer contact (11%), combination (41%).		
Food Service Manager (Female)	180	1984	40.6	9.9	Members of Hospital, Institution, and Educational Food Service Society. 33% had high school diploma, 27% completed associate degree, 17% bachelor's, 5% master's, 18% other. 88% were employed by hospitals or nursing homes, 5% by educational institutions. Major activities included personnel management (23%), customer contact (6%), record keeping and financial planning (5%), combination (55%).	187. Coordinates food service activities of hotels, restaurants, or other institutional establishments or at social functions. Estimates food and beverage costs and requisitions or purchases supplies. Confers with food preparation and other personnel to plan menus and related activities, such as dining room and banquet operations. Directs hiring and assignment of personnel. Investigates and resolves food quality and service complaints.	Banquet manager Cafeteria/lunchroom manager Caterer Catering manager Coffee shop manager Commissary production supervisor Dietitian Food and beverage manager Food production manager Food service supervisor Industrial cafeteria manager
Food Service Manager (Male)	116	1984	36.4	10.7	See women's sample above. 22% had high school diploma, 5% certificate from vocational-technical institution, 7% completed associate degree, 30% bachelor's, 32% master's, 1% doctorate. 53% were employed by hospitals or nursing homes, 20% by educational institutions, 19% other. Major activities included personnel management (24%), purchasing and inventory (6%), customer contact (3%), record keeping and financial planning (3%), combination (56%).		

Description of the Strong Occupational Scales

Sample/Scale	N	Year Tested	Mean Age	Mean Years Exper.	Composition	DOT Code and Description	Related Occupations
Foreign Language Teacher (Female)	315	1978	37.5	11.6	Members of American Council on the Teaching of Foreign Languages. 35% completed bachelor's degree, 64% master's. 91% were employed by secondary schools.	091. Instructs students through lectures, demonstrations, and audio-visual aids. Prepares course objectives and course outlines, assigns lessons, and corrects homework. Administers tests to evaluate students' progress. Keeps attendance records and maintains discipline. Participates in faculty and professional meetings, conferences, and teacher-training workshops. Performs related duties such as sponsoring special activities or student organizations. Teaches courses in grammar, reading, and speaking of various languages plus cultural customs, history, geography, and literature.	Interpreter Translator
Foreign Language Teacher (Male)	251	1979	38.8	13.4	See women's sample above. 25% completed bachelor's degree, 71% master's. 92% were employed by secondary schools.		
Forester (Female)	438	1993	35.5	11.2	Members of American Society of Foresters. 4% completed associate degree, 56% bachelor's, 33% master's, 6% doctorate. 55% were employed by federal government; 18% by state, regional, or local government; 13% by industry; 8% were self-employed or employed by consulting firm. 59% were engaged in forest resource/ecosystem management. Balance were spread over variety of specializations.	040. Manages and develops forest lands and their resources for economic and recreational purposes. Maps forest areas, estimates standing timber and future growth, and manages timber sales. Conducts research on cutting and removing timber, with minimum waste and damage, and on methods of processing wood for various uses. Directs suppression of forest fires and conducts fire-prevention programs. Plans campsites and recreation centers and directs construction and maintenance of cabins, fences, and roads.	Fire ranger Forest ecologist Forest geneticist Forestry economist Land use manager Range manager Research forester Silviculturist Soil conservationist Timber forester Tree planter Urban forester
Forester (Male)	921	1993	47.0	21.7	See women's sample above. 2% completed associate degree, 59% bachelor's, 26% master's, 11% doctorate. 27% were employed by federal government; 24% by state, regional, or local government; 23% by industry; 18% were self-employed or employed by consulting firm. 61% were engaged in forest resource/ecosystem management. Balance were spread over variety of specializations.		

Description of the Strong Occupational Scales

Sample/Scale	N	Year Tested	Mean Age	Mean Years Exper.	Composition	DOT Code and Description	Related Occupations
Gardener/ Groundskeeper (Female)	94	1992	39.8	11.3	Members of Professional Grounds Management Society and from commercially compiled national listing of gardening firms. 20% had high school diploma or had attended trade/ technical school in addition, 34% some college or associate degree, 31% completed bachelor's degree, 10% master's, 1% professional degree.	406. Maintains grounds of industrial, commercial, or public property. Plants, fertilizes and waters lawn, shrubs, trees, and flowers. Cuts lawns, trims and edges around walks, and prunes trees and shrubbery. Sprays herbicides and insecticides. Shovels snow from walks and driveways and spreads salt. Uses various hand and power tools. May make minor equipment repair.	Cemetery worker Farmer Forest conservation worker Greenhouse worker Greenskeeper Horticultural worker Horticulturist Landscape specialist Nursery worker Tree surgeon Tree trimmer
Gardener/ Groundskeeper (Male)	362	1992	40.1	16.7	See women's sample above. 13% had high school diploma or had attended trade/technical school in addition, 35% some college or associate degree, 42% completed bachelor's degree, 8% master's.	408. Plans and executes small-scale landscaping operations and maintains grounds and landscape of private and business residences. Prepares and grades terrain, applying fertilizers, seeding and sodding lawns, and transplanting shrubs and plants, using manual and power tools and equipment. Mows and trims lawns. Cleans grounds. 301. Yard worker: plants, transplants, fertilizes, sprays pesticides, prunes, cultivates, and waters flowers, shrubbery, lawn, and trees. Seeds and mows lawns, rakes leaves, and keeps grounds free of debris. May divide time between several homes, working on hourly or daily basis.	
Geographer (Female)	195	1979	38.3	11.3	Members of Association of American Geographers. 15% completed bachelor's degree, 43% master's, 40% doctorate. 54% were employed by educational institutions, 26% by government, 10% by private industry; major activities included teaching (41%), research/field work (22%), administration (11%), combination (15%). Areas of specialization included physical/environmental (26%), urban/economic (24%), cultural (18%).	029. Studies nature and use of earth's surface. Conducts research on physical and climatic aspects of area or region, making observations of landforms, climates, soils, plants, and animals. Acts as consultant on subjects such as economic exploitation of regions and determination of ethnic and natural boundaries between nations. May use surveying equipment or construct maps, graphs, and diagrams. May teach college courses.	Cartographer Community developer Environmental planner Land surveyor Marine surveyor Photogrammetrist Topographical drafter Urban planner

Description of the *Strong* Occupational Scales

Sample/Scale	N	Year Tested	Mean Age	Mean Years Exper.	Composition	DOT Code and Description	Related Occupations
Geographer (Male)	277	1979	40.7	14.9	See women's sample. 3% completed bachelor's degree, 14% master's, 81% doctorate. 81% were employed by educational institutions, 11% by government. Major activities included teaching (51%), administration (15%), research/field work (13%), combination (20%). Areas of specialization included urban/economic (26%), physical/environmental (24%), cultural (16%).		
Geologist (Female)	212	1979	35.4	9.9	From *Geological Society of America Directory*. 23% completed bachelor's degree, 47% master's, 30% doctorate. 36% were employed by government, 27% by educational institutions, 26% by private industry. Major activities were research and exploration (59%), teaching (13%), combination (12%).	024. Studies composition, structure, and history of earth's crust. Examines rocks, minerals, and fossils to identify sequence of processes affecting development of earth. Helps to locate mineral, geothermal, and petroleum deposits and underwater resources. Studies ocean bottom. Applies geological knowledge to engineering problems encountered on construction projects. Prepares reports and maps and interprets research data. May teach college courses.	Earth science teacher Forest geologist Hydrologist Marine geologist Mineralogist Paleontologist Petroleum geologist Prospector Seismologist Soils engineer
Geologist (Male)	242	1979	39.4	15.0	See women's sample above. 12% completed bachelor's degree, 36% master's, 52% doctorate. 39% were employed by educational institutions, 30% by private industry, 24% by government. Major activities included research and exploration (41%), teaching (22%), administration (12%), combination (18%).		
Hair Stylist (Female)	181	1984	35.3	13.6	From listings of state licensing boards of Alaska, Georgia, Illinois, Iowa, Michigan, Minnesota, South Dakota, Utah, Wisconsin, as well as national sampling from *Bell Telephone Yellow Pages*. 3% had high school diploma, 91% attended school of cosmetology, 1% completed associate degree, 4% other. Major activities included hairdressing (72%), management (6%), combination (20%).	332. Provides beauty services for customers. Suggests hair styles according to physical features of patron and current styles, or from instructions of patron. Analyzes hair to determine condition and treatment. Shampoos hair and massages scalp and styles hair with clippers, scissors, and razors. Provides other hair- and scalp-conditioning treatments. May also shape and polish nails, remove unwanted hair, or shape eyebrows.	Barber Beautician Cosmetologist Make-up artist Salon manager

Description of the Strong Occupational Scales

Sample/Scale	N	Year Tested	Mean Age	Mean Years Exper.	Composition	DOT Code and Description	Related Occupations
Hair Stylist (Male)	195	1984	37.0	14.6	See women's sample. 6% had high school diploma, 82% attended school of cosmetology, 3% completed associate degree, 4% bachelor's. Major activities included hairdressing (62%), management (17%), teaching (2%), combination (15%).		
High School Counselor (Female)	208	1982	42.3	10.3	High school guidance counselors, all members of American Association for Counseling and Development. 89% completed master's degree, 1% Ph.D., 1% Ed.D. Average of 49% of workday was spent counseling students. Major areas of counseling included crisis and personal counseling (27%), class scheduling (16%), graduation requirements (10%), pre-college/vocational school counseling (7%), career counseling (7%), combination (30%).	045. Counsels individuals and provides group educational and vocational guidance services. Collects and organizes information about individuals through records, tests, interviews, and professional sources to appraise their interests, aptitudes, abilities, and personality characteristics for vocational and educational planning. Compiles and studies occupational, educational, and economic information to aid counselees in making and carrying out objectives. Assists individuals to understand and overcome social and emotional problems. Engages in research and follow-up activities to evaluate counseling techniques. May teach classes.	Counseling services director Counselor Dean of guidance Education coordinator Guidance counselor Psychologist School psychologist Vocational counselor
High School Counselor (Male)	266	1982	42.3	12.5	See women's sample above. 2% completed bachelor's degree, 79% master's, 6% Ph.D., 5% Ed.D. Average of 48% of work day was spent counseling students. Major areas of counseling included class scheduling (20%), crisis and personal counseling (18%), pre-college/vocational school counseling (11%), career counseling (10%), graduation requirements (8%), combination (31%).		
Home Economics Teacher (Female)	312	1979	38.3	12.3	Members of American Home Economist Association. 51% completed bachelor's degree, 47% master's. 86% were employed by elementary or secondary schools.	*091/096. Teaches courses in food, sewing, budgeting, child care, and homemaking. Prepares course objectives and outline, administers tests, assigns lessons, and corrects homework. Keeps attendance records and maintains discipline. Participates in faculty and professional meetings. May sponsor student organizations.	Consumer services consultant Extension service agent 4-H club agent Home economist Home-extension agent Home-service director

*Both of these codes describe the tasks done by people in this occupation.

Description of the Strong Occupational Scales

Sample/Scale	N	Year Tested	Mean Age	Mean Years Exper.	Composition	DOT Code and Description	Related Occupations
Horticultural Worker (Female)	155	1983	31.5	6.7	Nationwide sample from catalog of *American Association of Nurserymen*. 28% had high school diploma, 12% certificate from vocational-technical institution, 12% completed associate degree, 36% bachelor's, 4% master's. Employers included retailers and landscapers combined (28%); wholesalers only (25%); wholesalers, retailers, and landscapers combined (19%); retailers only (11%); wholesalers and retailers combined (6%); landscapers only (5%), other (5%). 44% were in place of employment specializing in area of horticulture. Major activities included customer service (35%), care of plants (18%), administrative functions (9%), soil preparation (6%), combination (26%).	405. Plants, cultivates, and harvests horticulture specialties such as flowers and shrubs and performs related duties in environmental systems. Hauls and spreads topsoil, fertilizer, and peat moss to condition land. Sows seeds and plants cuttings. Determines nutrient and moisture requirements and detects and identifies germ and pest infestations. Applies herbicides, fungicides, and pesticides to destroy undesirable growth and pests. Reads and interprets sensing indicators and regulates humidity, ventilation, and carbon dioxide systems to control environmental conditions. Pollinates, prunes, and transplants plants to ensure development of marketable products. May work with customers, selling or providing horticultural information.	Horticulturist Greenhouse laborer Greenhouse manager Landscaper Nursery laborer Propagator
Horticultural Worker (Male)	208	1983	32.9	10.4	See women's sample above. 17% had high school diploma, 10% certificate from vocational-technical institution, 9% completed associate degree, 55% bachelor's, 5% master's. Employers included wholesalers only (29%); retailers and landscapers combined (22%); landscapers only (12%); wholesalers, retailers, and landscapers combined (12%); retailers only (7%); wholesalers and retailers combined (7%); wholesalers and landscapers combined (5%); other (6%). 53% were in place of employment specializing in area of horticulture. Major activities included customer service (20%), administrative functions (17%), care of plants (16%), soil preparation (10%), combination (30%).		

Description of the Strong Occupational Scales

Sample/Scale	N	Year Tested	Mean Age	Mean Years Exper.	Composition	DOT Code and Description	Related Occupations
Housekeeping & Maintenance Supervisor (Female)	577	1993	45.6	14.3	Members of National Executive Housekeepers Association. 27% had high school diploma, 9% attended trade/technical school in addition, 41% some college or associate degree, 10% completed bachelor's degree, 2% master's. 40% worked in hospitals, 25% in nursing/convalescent homes, 15% in hotels, 6% in educational institutions. Major activities included administration/supervision, training, customer contact, staff meetings, policy/procedure planning, and purchasing.	187. Directs institutional housekeeping program to ensure clean, orderly, and attractive condition of establishment. Establishes standards and procedures for work of housekeeping staff. Inspects and evaluates physical condition of establishment and submits to management recommendations for painting or repairs. Organizes and directs departmental training programs, resolves personnel problems, and hires new employees. Writes activities and personnel reports for review.	Athletic equipment custodian Building services manager Caretaker Custodian Executive housekeeper Home housekeeper Janitorial services manager Laundry services manager Property services manager
Housekeeping & Maintenance Supervisor (Male)	569	1993	43.2	15.0	See women's sample above. 9% had high school diploma, 6% attended trade/technical school in addition, 44% some college or associate degree, 29% bachelor's, 6% master's. 51% worked in hospitals, 14% in nursing/convalescent homes, 6% in hotels, 14% in educational institutions. Major activities included administration/supervision, training, customer contact, staff meetings, policy/procedure planning, and purchasing.		
Human Resources Director (Female)	445	1992	41.4	12.5	Members of Society for Human Resource Management. 2% had high school diploma, 16% some college or associate degree, 44% completed bachelor's degree, 37% master's or professional degree, 1% doctorate. 58% were employed by business/industry, 24% by nonprofit organizations, 5% by educational institutions, 5% by government, 2% by consulting firms, 7% other. Major activities included administration/supervision, benefits/compensation administration, teaching/training, and employee recruitment.	166. Plans and carries out policies relating to all phases of personnel activities. Organizes recruitment, selection, and training procedures. Confers with company and union officials to establish pensions and insurance plans, workers' compensation policies, and similar functions. Studies personnel records and supervisors' reports for information such as educational background to determine personnel suitable for promotions or transfers. May act as liaison between management and labor.	Benefits manager Career development director Compensation manager Education and training manager Employee relations manager Employment manager Industrial relations director Job analyst Personnel director Placement director

Description of the Strong Occupational Scales

Sample/Scale	N	Year Tested	Mean Age	Mean Years Exper.	Composition	DOT Code and Description	Related Occupations
Human Resources Director (Male)	496	1992	46.4	18.6	See women's sample. 4% had some college or associate degree, 48% completed bachelor's degree, 44% master's or professional degree, 3% doctorate. 68% were employed by business/industry, 13% by non-profit organizations, 8% by government, 5% by educational institutions, 3% by consulting firms, 2% other. Major activities included administration/supervision, benefits/compensation administration, teaching/training, and employee recruitment.		
Interior Decorator (Female)	222	1982	40.4	14.9	Names supplied by American Society of Interior Designers. 65% completed bachelor's degree, 9% master's, 13% graduated from professional school of interior design. 59% were self-employed or in partnership, 18% were employed by retail store, 4% by architectural firm. 34% specialized in residential design. Major activities included preparation of presentations for clients (32%), administrative functions (12%), conferring with clients and contractors (5%), combination (45%).	142. Plans, designs, and furnishes interior environment of residential, commercial, or industrial buildings. Confers with client to determine needs and preferences, available budget, and function of space to plan the interior. Devises harmonious color scheme and sketches plans of rooms, showing arrangement of furniture and accessories. Estimates cost. Selects and purchases decorative and functional material and accessories or creates original designs for furnishings to conform with decorative scheme.	Color director Environmental planner Facilities planner Interior architect Interior designer Set decorator Space planner
Interior Decorator (Male)	214	1982	41.6	16.5	See women's sample above. 58% completed bachelor's degree, 11% master's, 14% graduated from professional school of interior design. 57% were self-employed or in partnership, 15% were employed by retail store, 4% by architectural firm, 9% worked for more than one employer. 27% specialized in residential design, 22% in commercial design. Major activities included preparation of presentations for clients (32%), administrative functions (15%), conferring with clients and contractors (6%), combination (36%).		

Description of the Strong Occupational Scales

Sample/Scale	N	Year Tested	Mean Age	Mean Years Exper.	Composition	DOT Code and Description	Related Occupations
Investments Manager (Female)	212	1982	34.8	9.7	Members of Financial Analysts Federation. 44% completed bachelor's degree, 46% master's, 1% doctorate, 3% other. 47% considered themselves financial analysts, 38% money managers, 15% investment managers. Employers included commercial banks (30%), corporations (19%), money management firms (18%), investment banks (9%), brokerage firms (6%), government (4%), self-employed (4%), other (8%). Major activities included managing funds and portfolios (29%), research and analysis (15%), consulting (12%), investing (11%), combination (24%), other (4%).	020. Financial analyst: conducts statistical analyses of information affecting investment programs of public, industrial, and financial institutions. 186. Investment fund manager: trades securities and provides securities investment and counseling services for a bank and its customers. 251. Stockbroker: buys and sells stocks and bonds for individuals and organizations as representatives of stockbrokerage firm. 160. Investment analyst: analyzes financial information to forecast economic conditions. Gathers and analyzes company financial data. Recommends investment timing to company or to clients.	Bond analyst Commodity analyst Financial advisor/ planner Financial analyst Investment analyst Investment fund manager Money manager Portfolio manager Security analyst Stockbroker
Investments Manager (Male)	212	1982	40.9	15.4	See women's sample above. 26% completed bachelor's degree, 68% master's, 4% doctorate. 42% considered themselves financial analysts, 38% money managers, 20% investment managers. Employers included commercial banks (26%), corporations (23%), money management firms (21%), brokerage firms (9%), investment banks (8%), other (7%). Major activities included managing funds and portfolios (29%), investing (12%), research and analysis (10%), consulting (8%), administration (8%), selling (6%), combination (22%), other (4%).		

Description of the *Strong* Occupational Scales

Sample/Scale	N	Year Tested	Mean Age	Mean Years Exper.	Composition	DOT Code and Description	Related Occupations
Lawyer (Female)	551	1992	38.0	9.5	Members of American Bar Association. 36% devoted most time to business law, 22% to litigation, 10% to general practice, 8% to family/divorce, 8% to government, 6% to labor and employment, 3% to criminal law. 20% worked in law firm employing 10–99 lawyers, 17% in law firm employing 2–9 lawyers, 14% in law firm employing 100 or more lawyers, 15% in corporate law department, 12% in government agency, 11% were sole practitioners.	110. Conducts criminal and civil lawsuits, draws up legal documents, advises clients of legal rights, and practices other phases of law. Gathers evidence to initiate legal action. Represents clients in court or before quasi-judicial or administrative agencies of government. May act as trustee, guardian, or executor. May teach college courses in law.	Corporate lawyer Criminal lawyer District attorney Government attorney Patent lawyer Probate lawyer Real estate lawyer Tax attorney Trial attorney
Lawyer (Male)	418	1992	45.0	17.7	See women's sample above. 35% devoted most time to business law, 26% to litigation, 14% to general practice, 6% to government, 5% to labor and employment, 3% to family/divorce, 3% to criminal law. 24% worked in law firm employing 2–9 lawyers, 18% in law firm employing 10–99 lawyers, 14% in law firm employing 100 or more lawyers, 13% in corporate law department, 8% in government agency, 15% were sole practitioners.		
Librarian (Female)	1,187	1992	44.9	16.4	Librarian members of American Library Association and Special Libraries Association. 92% completed master's degree, 3% professional degree, 5% doctorate. 33% worked in four-year college or university library, 29% in public library, 12% in school library, 11% in library of for-profit organization, 5% in library of nonprofit organization (nongovernment).	100. Maintains library collection of books, periodicals, documents, films, recordings, and other materials and helps groups and individuals to locate and obtain materials. Explains use of reference sources. Describes or demonstrates procedures for searching catalog files and shelf collections to obtain materials. Performs variety of duties to maintain reference and circulation materials, such as copying authors' names and book titles on catalog cards. May select, order, catalog, or classify materials. May answer correspondence on special subjects.	Acquisitions librarian Audiovisual librarian Bibliographer Bookmobile librarian Branch librarian Catalog librarian Children's librarian Circulation librarian Medical librarian Reference librarian

Description of the *Strong* Occupational Scales

Sample/Scale	N	Year Tested	Mean Age	Mean Years Exper.	Composition	DOT Code and Description	Related Occupations
Librarian (Male)	355	1992	45.4	17.6	See women's sample. 78% completed master's degree, 7% professional degree, 14% doctorate. 45% worked in four-year college or university library, 30% in public library, 6% in library of for-profit organization, 5% for U.S. government.		
Life Insurance Agent (Female)	265	1992	44.2	11.4	Members of National Association of Life Underwriters. 13% had high school diploma or had attended trade/technical school in addition, 36% some college or associate degree, 33% completed bachelor's degree, 17% master's or professional degree.	250. Selects and sells all types of life insurance based on client's present insurance and government benefits to establish plan for financial security. Calls on policyholders to keep insurance plan up to date and to advise client concerning life insurance pensions, taxation, and family financing. Suggests method of premium payments and settlement option. May require knowledge of law, accounting, taxation, or government benefits.	Insurance broker Life insurance underwriter Pension specialist
Life Insurance Agent (Male)	294	1992	45.8	16.2	See women's sample above. 5% had high school diploma or had attended trade/technical school in addition, 26% some college or associate degree, 50% completed bachelor's degree, 16% master's or professional degree.		
Marketing Executive (Female)	298	1992	39.5	12.6	Members of American Marketing Association. 4% had some college or associate degree, 36% completed bachelor's degree, 47% master's. Major activities included research/analysis, administration/planning, communications, and direct marketing/sales/customer contact.	050. Researches market conditions to determine potential sales of products or services; establishes research methodology and designs format for data gathering such as surveys, polls, or questionnaires. Analyzes data on customers and competitors to determine future trends. Prepares reports of findings. 163. Plans and administers sales policies and programs. Directs workers engaged in preparing promotional correspondence. Confers with department heads to formulate plans for soliciting business. Plans and prepares advertising and arranges for publicity.	Data collection manager Marketing analyst Marketing promotion director Media research director Sales manager
Marketing Executive (Male)	349	1992	45.5	17.8	See women's sample above. 4% had some college or associate degree, 25% completed bachelor's degree, 50% master's. Major activities included research/analysis, administration/planning, communications, and direct marketing/sales/customer contact.		

Description of the *Strong* Occupational Scales

Sample/Scale	N	Year Tested	Mean Age	Mean Years Exper.	Composition	DOT Code and Description	Related Occupations
Mathematician (Female)	213	1982	41.1	14.9	Names from combined membership list of Mathematical Association of America and Society for Industrial and Applied Mathematics. All completed doctorate. 93% were employed by colleges or universities, 3% by business/industry, 1% by government. 29% considered themselves theoretical mathematicians, 22% applied, 48% combination. 81% identified primary job function as teacher, 8% researcher, 2% statistician, 2% computer scientist. Major activities included teaching (74%), research (5%), combination (15%).	020. Conducts research in fundamental mathematics and in application of mathematical techniques to science management and other fields or solves or directs solutions to problems by mathematical methods. Conducts research in such branches of mathematics as algebra, geometry, and number theory. Conceives and develops ideas for application of mathematics to a wide variety of fields. Performs computations and applies methods of numerical analysis to solve problems in support of mathematical, scientific, or industrial research activity. May teach college courses.	Actuary Applied mathematician Computer application engineer Engineer analyst Operation research analyst Statistician
Mathematician (Male)	270	1982	41.7	16.4	See women's sample above. All completed doctorate. 95% were employed by colleges or universities, 2% by business/industry, 1% by government. 32% considered themselves theoretical mathematicians, 23% applied mathematicians, 44% combination. 68% identified primary job function as teacher, 14% researcher, 4% computer scientist, 2% statistician. Major activities included teaching (67%), research (10%), combination (14%).		
Mathematics Teacher (Female)	245	1982	37.7	11.9	National sample, *National Science Teachers Association, U.S. Registry.* 40% completed bachelor's degree, 59% master's. 43% taught mainly algebra, 20% geometry, 14% basic math; other areas included trigonometry, calculus, computer science, and analytic geometry. All were high school teachers; 98% taught more than one grade. 92% spent minimum of 40% of time teaching; other activities included lesson preparation, grading, administrative functions. 22% also were involved in advising other school activities relating to math, such as math club.	091. Teaches courses such as algebra, geometry, arithmetic, and computer science. Instructs students through lectures, demonstrations, and audiovisual aids. Prepares course objectives and course outlines, assigns lessons, and corrects homework. Administers tests to evaluate students' progress. Keeps attendance records and maintains discipline. Participates in faculty and professional meetings, conferences, and teacher-training workshops. Performs related duties such as sponsoring special activities or student organizations.	Algebra teacher Arithmetic teacher Calculus teacher Computer science teacher Geometry teacher Statistics teacher Trigonometry teacher

Description of the Strong Occupational Scales

Sample/Scale	N	Year Tested	Mean Age	Mean Years Exper.	Composition	DOT Code and Description	Related Occupations
Mathematics Teacher (Male)	226	1982	39.1	14.0	See women's sample. 31% completed bachelor's degree, 64% master's. 42% taught mainly algebra, 19% geometry, 10% basic math, 7% computer science, 4% trigonometry, 4% calculus, 10% combination. All were high school teachers; 96% taught more than one grade. 91% spent minimum of 40% of time teaching; other activities included lesson preparation, grading, administrative functions. 20% also were involved in advising other school activities related to math, such as math club.		
Medical Illustrator (Female)	99	1984	37.2	11.0	Members of Association of Medical Illustrators. 40% completed bachelor's degree, 52% master's. 44% were self-employed, 26% were employed by medical centers, 14% by teaching institutions, 5% other, 9% combination. 78% of those not self-employed also did freelance work. 34% specialized in particular medical field. 76% spent minimum of 50% of time illustrating; other activities included consulting, research, and administrative functions.	141. Makes sketches and constructs tridimensional models to illustrate surgical and medical research procedures, anatomical and pathological specimens, and unusual clinical disorders. Develops drawings, paintings, diagrams, and models illustrating medical findings for use in publications, exhibits, consultation, research, or teaching activities. Devises visual aids to assist in interpreting research programs. May specialize in illustrations in a particular medical field.	Audiovisual resource person Biocommunication graphic artist Medical graphic technician Medical sculptor Scientific illustrator
Medical Illustrator (Male)	61	1984	41.9	16.2	See women's sample above. 20% completed bachelor's degree, 63% master's, 12% doctorate. 15% were self-employed, 31% were employed by medical centers, 28% by teaching institutions, 20% other, 7% combination. 83% of those not self-employed also did freelance work. 38% specialized in particular medical field. 58% spent minimum of 50% of time illustrating; other activities included consulting, research, and administrative functions.		

Occupational Scales Samples, DOT Codes, and Related Job Titles **347**

Description of the *Strong* Occupational Scales

Sample/Scale	N	Year Tested	Mean Age	Mean Years Exper.	Composition	DOT Code and Description	Related Occupations
Medical Records Technician (Female)	395	1992	40.9	14.3	Members of American Health Information Management Association. 8% had high school diploma or had attended trade/technical school in addition, 45% some college or associate degree, 37% completed bachelor's degree, 9% master's. 71% were employed by hospitals. Most time was devoted to areas of clinical coding/classification, computerized health data, quality assurance and case management, and medicolegal issues.	079. Compiles and maintains medical records of patients to document patient condition and treatment. Reviews records for completeness and to abstract and code clinical data such as diseases, procedures, and therapies, using standard classification systems. Compiles medical care and census data for statistical reports on diseases treated, surgery performed, and use of hospital facilities in response to inquiries from law firms, insurance companies, and government agencies. Maintains and uses variety of health record indexes and storage and retrieval systems. Operates computer to process, store, and retrieve health information.	Data manager Insurance clerk Medical records administrator Medical secretary Medical transcriptionist Medical writer
Medical Records Technician (Male)	247	1992	40.3	12.9	See women's sample above. 1% attended trade/technical school, 20% some college or associate degree, 49% completed bachelor's degree, 26% master's, 2% professional degree, 2% doctorate. 66% were employed by hospitals. Most time was devoted to areas of computerized health data, clinical coding/classification, medicolegal issues, and quality assurance/case management.		
Medical Technician (Female)	259	1982	43.3	21.2	Certified members of Association of American Medical Technologists. 83% had some college courses and/or training in medical technology, 11% completed bachelor's degree, 2% master's degree. 50% were employed by hospital laboratory, 9% by clinic of 5 physicians or less, 7% by clinic of more than 5, 7% by independent clinic lab, 6% by health agency, 6% by military, 14% other. Specialties included clinical chemistry (8%), hematology (7%), blood bank (6%), combination (38%), no specialty (25%), other (8%). Major activities included conducting lab tests (46%), supervisory functions (7%), administrative functions (7%), specimen preparation (4%), combination (33%).	078. Performs routine tests in medical laboratory for use in treatment and diagnosis of disease. Prepares tissue samples, takes blood samples, and executes such laboratory tests as urinalysis and blood counts. Makes quantitative and qualitative chemical and biological analyses of body specimens, under supervision of medical technologist.	Blood bank technician Blood and plasma laboratory assistant Cytotechnician Hematology technician Medical technologist Serology technician

Description of the *Strong* Occupational Scales

Sample/Scale	N	Year Tested	Mean Age	Mean Years Exper.	Composition	DOT Code and Description	Related Occupations
Medical Technician (Male)	233	1982	44.6	22.1	See women's sample. 75% had some college and/or training in medical technology, 17% completed bachelor's degree, 5% master's. 54% were employed by hospital laboratory, 13% by independent clinic lab, 9% by military, 5% by clinic of more than 5 physicians, 4% by clinic of less than 5, 3% by health agency, 13% other. Specialties included clinical chemistry (7%), cystology (5%), hematology (5%), combination (38%), no specialty (21%), other (15%). Major activities included conducting lab tests (30%), supervisory functions (16%), administration (18%), combination (30%).		
Medical Technologist (Female)	266	1984	37.9	13.7	Members of American Society for Medical Technology. 88% completed bachelor's degree, 12% master's. 68% were employed by hospital laboratory, 9% by independent clinic lab, 5% by clinic, 3% by government, 2% by research institution, 2% by physicians, 10% other, 2% combination. Specializations included clinical chemistry (18%), hematology (17%), blood bank (10%), microbiology (9%), other (7%), combination (25%), no specialization (13%). Major activities included conducting lab tests (44%), administrative functions (11%), supervising lab workers (8%), analyzing results (2%), combination (31%).	078. Performs and analyzes chemical and bacteriologic tests to provide data for use in disease diagnosis, treatment, and prevention. Receives specimens from laboratory and makes quantitative and qualitative chemical analyses. Cultivates, isolates, and identifies bacteria, parasites, and other microorganisms. Cuts, stains, and mounts tissue sections for study by pathologist. Performs blood tests and transfusions, studies morphology of blood, prepares vaccines and serums, groups or types blood, and cross-matches that of donor and recipient to ascertain compatibility. May calibrate and use equipment designed to measure glandular or other bodily activities.	Blood bank technologist Chemistry technologist Cytotechnologist Hematology technologist Histologist Laboratory technologist Medical technician Nuclear medical technologist Serology technologist Tissue technologist

Description of the *Strong* Occupational Scales

Sample/Scale	N	Year Tested	Mean Age	Mean Years Exper.	Composition	DOT Code and Description	Related Occupations
Medical Technologist (Male)	206	1984	37.0	12.4	See women's sample. 93% completed bachelor's degree, 7% master's. 68% were employed by hospital laboratory, 8% by independent clinic lab, 4% by clinic, 8% other, 5% combination. Specializations included clinical chemistry (18%), hematology (8%), microbiology (6%), blood bank (3%), other (15%), combination (20%), no specialty (28%). Major activities included conducting lab tests (41%), administrative functions (22%), supervising lab workers (10%), analyzing results (2%), combination (24%).		
Military Enlisted Personnel (Female)	838	1984	29.7	8.1	Roster of enlistees (Air Force, Army, Marine, Navy) provided by Defense Manpower Data Center, Department of Defense. 66% had high school diploma, 12% degree or certificate from vocational-technical institution, 12% completed associate degree, 7% bachelor's, 2% master's.	378. Provides technical support for the operation of military overland vehicles, aircraft, and vessels. Repairs and maintains equipment and transportation vehicles. Aids in transportation of military personnel, mail, and freight. May aid officers in navigation of vessels or aircraft depending upon branch of service. May prepare weapons or artillery and participate in drills and operations concerned with protecting the nation and maintaining order during civil unrest. May be trained in any number of jobs paralleling civilian occupations.	Aircraft mechanic Amphibian crew member Boatswain Boiler technician Communication systems operator Counterintelligence agent Disaster specialist Drafter Electronic technician Map editor Reconnaissance crew member Ship crew member Sonar operator Survival specialist Teletype technician Weather forecaster Yeoman
Military Enlisted Personnel (Male)	817	1984	33.2	13.4	See women's sample above. 66% had high school diploma, 13% degree or certificate from vocational-technical institution, 15% completed associate degree, 3% bachelor's, 3% master's.		

Description of the Strong Occupational Scales

Sample/Scale	N	Year Tested	Mean Age	Mean Years Exper.	Composition	DOT Code and Description	Related Occupations
Military Officer (Female)	801	1979	32.2	8.6	Roster of commissioned officers (Air Force, Army, Navy) provided by Defense Manpower Data Center, Department of Defense. 57% completed bachelor's degree, 38% master's.	196. Air Force officer: pilots jets to transport passengers, mail, and freight. May pilot combat aircraft or experimental aircraft. Uses navigation instruments to locate position and course of aircraft. 197. Navy officer: operates, manages, and pilots vessels. Performs technical supervision of marine operations. Has administrative and technical responsibility for operation, maintenance, and safety of vessels. Supervises activities of ship's crew. Army officer: directs personnel in preparing weapons, equipment, and artillery for movement and combat operations. Organizes unit operations when deployed in field. Prepares unit reports and schedules.	Air traffic controller Captain Commander Communications officer Fighter pilot Intelligence officer Military weapons analyst Navigator Supply officer
Military Officer (Male)	899	1979	37.3	14.0	See women's sample above. 41% completed bachelor's degree, 43% master's.		
Minister (Female)	250	1977	34.8	5.8	Collected with cooperation of Midwest Career Development Center. 6% completed bachelor of divinity degree, 78% master of divinity, 6% doctor of divinity. 95% were employed by churches. 90% served as pastors, 4% as chaplains. 42% were Methodist, 14% Church of Christ, 19% other.	120. Conducts religious worship and performs other spiritual functions associated with beliefs and practices of religious faith. Provides spiritual and moral guidance and assistance to members. Prepares and delivers sermons and leads worship services. Interprets doctrines of religion. Instructs people who are to become members of the faith. Counsels those in spiritual need and comforts bereaved. Oversees religious education program. May write articles for publication and engage in interfaith, community, civic, educational, or recreational activities sponsored by or related to interests of denomination.	Assistant pastor Campus pastor Chaplain Hospital chaplain Missionary Pastor Youth director
Minister (Male)	255	1982	41.1	14.1	See women's sample above. Members of United Presbyterian Church, Episcopalian Church Center, Lutheran Church of America, American Lutheran Church. 3% completed bachelor of divinity degree, 88% master of divinity, 8% doctor of divinity. 59% were Lutheran, 24% Episcopal, 17% Presbyterian. 93% were employed by churches. 89% served as pastors, 2% as chaplains. Hours spent equally in conducting services, counseling, teaching, and administrative functions.		

Description of the *Strong* Occupational Scales

Sample/Scale	N	Year Tested	Mean Age	Mean Years Exper.	Composition	DOT Code and Description	Related Occupations
Musician (Female)	209	1979	35.4	14.4	Members of musicians' unions in Milwaukee, San Francisco, Fort Worth, Atlanta, St. Louis, Denver, and Minneapolis; and from national write-in response to articles in musicians' publications. Data collected with assistance of L. Harmon. 23% had high school diploma, 40% completed bachelor's degree, 24% master's. 94% had private instruction averaging 13 years. 22% were employed in other occupations simultaneously.	152. Plays one or more musical instruments in recital, in accompaniment, or as a member of orchestra, band, or other musical group to entertain. Plays music either reading score or by memory, manipulating keys, bow, valves, string, or percussion devices. May improvise or transpose music. May compose or arrange music.	Arranger Composer Conductor Music teacher Orchestrator Singer Sound producer Stage manager
Musician (Male)	230	1979	34.2	16.3	See women's sample above. 34% had high school diploma, 30% completed bachelor's degree, 14% master's. 86% had private instruction averaging 8 years. 31% were employed in other occupations simultaneously.		
Nurse, Licensed Practical (Female)	228	1983	41.4	11.7	Members of National Federation of Licensed Practical Nurses. 12% had high school diploma, 80% attended vocational-technical school, 3% completed associate degree. 61% were employed by hospitals, 14% by nursing homes, 4% by clinics, 4% by industry, 5% combination. 58% specialized in one area of nursing; specialties included psychiatric nursing, intensive care, orthopedics, pediatrics, and metabolics. 94% spent minimum of 50% of time doing applied nursing.	079 Provides prescribed medical treatment or personal care services to ill, injured, convalescent, or disabled persons in hospitals, clinics, or similar settings. Takes and records temperature, blood pressure, and pulse. Dresses wounds and gives alcohol rubs and massages. Administers specified medications. Assembles and uses such equipment as catheters, tracheotomy tubes, and oxygen suppliers. Performs routine laboratory work such as urinalysis. Sterilizes equipment and supplies. Records food and fluid intake and output. Bathes, dresses, and assists patients in walking and turning.	Chiropractic assistant Dialysis technician Emergency medical technician Medical records clerk Nurse's aide Optometric assistant Orderly Orthopedic technician Orthoptist Podiatric assistant Practical nurse Psychiatric aide Respiratory therapist Surgical technician

Description of the *Strong* Occupational Scales

Sample/Scale	N	Year Tested	Mean Age	Mean Years Exper.	Composition	DOT Code and Description	Related Occupations
Nurse, Licensed Practical (Male)	128	1983	38.5	10.8	Members of National Federation of Licensed Practical Nurses, and names selected from list of state associations and state boards of examiners. 8% had high school diploma, 88% certificate from vocational-technical school, 4% completed associate degree. 77% were employed by hospitals, 8% by private homes, 4% by clinics, 4% by nursing homes, 4% combination, 4% other. 62% specialized in particular area of nursing, including psychiatric nursing, intensive care, pediatrics, orthopedics, and geriatrics. 96% spent minimum of 50% of time doing applied nursing.		
Nurse, Registered (Female)	885	1992	44.6	19.2	Members of American Nurses Association. 3% had high school diploma, 20% some college or associate degree, 32% completed bachelor's degree, 34% master's, 7% doctorate. 63% were employed by hospitals, 15% by schools of nursing, 6% by physician's offices or ambulatory care clinics, 4% by home health agencies, 4% by public health agencies, 3% by nursing homes.	075. Performs acts requiring substantial specialized judgment and skill in observation, care, and counsel of ill, injured, or infirm persons and in promotion of health and prevention of illness. Administers medication; prepares equipment; assists physician; and takes temperature, pulse, blood pressure, and other vital signs. May teach nursing courses.	Anesthetic nurse Community health nurse General duty nurse Head nurse Mental health nurse Midwife Nurse practitioner Occupational health nurse Oncology nurse Private duty nurse Psychiatric nurse Public health nurse School nurse Surgical nurse
Nurse, Registered (Male)	704	1992	41.2	14.0	See women's sample above. 1% had high school diploma, 22% some college or associate degree, 35% completed bachelor's degree, 37% master's, 2% professional degree, 4% doctorate. 73% were employed by hospitals, 6% by schools of nursing, 6% by physician's offices or ambulatory care clinics, 4% by home health agencies, 3% by military, 3% were self-employed.		

Description of the Strong Occupational Scales

Sample/Scale	N	Year Tested	Mean Age	Mean Years Exper.	Composition	DOT Code and Description	Related Occupations
Nursing Home Administrator (Female)	238	1993	47.2	15.2	From commercially compiled national listing. 6% had high school diploma or had attended trade/technical school in addition, 32% some college or associate degree, 35% completed bachelor's degree, 19% master's, 5% professional degree. Major activities included administration/supervision/management, contact with residents/families, government and regulatory compliance/liaison.	187. Directs administration of home. Develops programs and services. Administers fiscal operations such as budget planning. Directs hiring and training of personnel. Directs and coordinates activities of medical, nursing, and service staffs. Develops policies and procedures.	Health care administrator Hospital administrator Institution director Sheltered workshop director
Nursing Home Administrator (Male)	306	1993	44.3	14.2	See women's sample above. 2% had high school diploma, 10% some college or associate degree, 47% completed bachelor's degree, 35% master's, 2% professional degree, 3% doctorate. Major activities included administration/supervision/management, contact with residents/families, government and regulatory compliance/liaison.		
Occupational Therapist (Female)	328	1992	39.5	13.8	Members of American Occupational Therapy Association. 66% completed bachelor's degree, 31% master's or professional degree, 1% doctorate. 45% were employed by hospitals and clinics, 20% by educational institutions, 16% were self-employed or in private practice, 9% were employed by nursing homes.	076. Plans, organizes, and participates in medically oriented occupational programs in hospitals or similar institutions to rehabilitate patients who are physically or mentally ill. Uses creative and manual arts; recreational, educational, and social activities; prevocational evaluations; and training in everyday activities such as personal care and homemaking to help patients regain functioning or adjust to disabilities. Consults with other members of rehabilitation team to coordinate therapeutic activities for individual patients.	Art therapist Corrective therapist Music therapist Occupational therapy aide Pediatric therapist Recreational therapist Rehabilitation therapist Vocational evaluator
Occupational Therapist (Male)	388	1992	40.4	14.1	See women's sample above. 53% completed bachelor's degree, 42% master's or professional degree, 4% doctorate. 46% were employed by hospitals and clinics, 17% by educational institutions, 17% were self-employed or in private practice, 6% were employed by nursing homes.		

Description of the *Strong* Occupational Scales

Sample/Scale	N	Year Tested	Mean Age	Mean Years Exper.	Composition	DOT Code and Description	Related Occupations
Optician (Female)	258	1982	36.0	9.9	Members of Opticians Association of America. 25% had high school diploma, 9% attended vocational-technical school, 43% had some college, 12% completed associate degree, 8% bachelor's, 2% master's. 55% learned dispensing skills on job, 8% in school, 4% as apprentices, 33% combination. Employers included retail optical stores (44%), self-owned optical stores (36%), ophthalmologists (10%), department stores (7%). Major activities included combination of determining style and size of lens, adjusting glasses, and writing work orders. No one who spent more than 25% of time attending to administrative details was included in sample.	716. Designs, fits, and adapts lenses and frames using written optical prescription. Analyzes prescription in conjunction with client's vocational and avocational visual requirements. Recommends specific lenses for safety and efficiency. Assists clients in selecting frames according to style and color, coordinating frames with facial and eye measurements and optical prescriptions. Measures client's bridge and eye size, temple length, vertex distance, pupillary distance, and optical centers of eyes. Prepares work order and instructions for grinding lenses and fabricating spectacles. Verifies exactness of finished lens spectacles. Adjusts frames and lens position to fit client. Instructs client on adapting and wearing spectacles and procedures for their care. Sells optical goods.	Contact lens molder Contact lens technician Ophthalmic technician Optical model maker Optical technician Plastic eye technician Precision lens technician
Optician (Male)	213	1981	37.8	15.2	See women's sample above. 19% had high school diploma, 7% attended vocational-technical school, 43% had some college, 13% completed associate degree, 15% bachelor's, 1% master's. 52% learned dispensing skills on job, 10% in school, 4% as apprentices, 2% in military, 31% combination. Employers included retail optical stores (38%), self-owned optical stores (35%), ophthalmologists (16%), hospitals (2%), department stores (2%). Major activities included combination of determining style and size of lens, fitting and adjusting lens, and analyzing prescriptions. No one who spent more than 25% of time attending to administrative details was included in sample.		

Description of the *Strong* Occupational Scales

Sample/Scale	N	Year Tested	Mean Age	Mean Years Exper.	Composition	DOT Code and Description	Related Occupations
Optometrist (Female)	191	1979	38.0	11.8	Members of American Optometric Association. 60% were self-employed or in partnership, 11% were employed by clinics or hospitals, 13% combination. 75% reported private practice as major activity.	079. Examines eyes and prescribes corrective lenses or procedures. Examines patient for visual pathology or ocular manifestations of systemic diseases and refers those with pathological condition to medical practitioner. May specialize in prescribing and fitting contact lenses or other visual aids and administering visual training and eye exercises.	Ophthalmologist Optician Optometric assistant Pediatric optometrist
Optometrist (Male)	220	1979	39.7	14.2	See women's sample above. 83% were self-employed or in partnership. 93% reported private practice as major activity.		
Paralegal (Female)	488	1993	37.7	9.9	Members of National Federation of Paralegal Associations. 5% had high school diploma or had attended trade/technical school in addition, 39% some college or associate degree, 48% completed bachelor's degree, 6% master's. 73% were employed in private law firm, 19% in corporate law department, 3% in government agency, 4% other.	119. Researches law, investigates facts, and prepares documents to assist lawyer. Researches and analyzes law sources such as statutes, legal articles, and legal codes to prepare legal documents such as briefs, pleadings, wills, and contracts for review, approval, and use by attorney. Investigates facts and law of case to determine causes of action and prepare case accordingly. Files pleadings with court. Prepares affidavits and maintains document file. Delivers or directs delivery of subpoenas to witnesses and parties to action. May supervise other law office employees, act as arbitrator between disputing parties, or serve as law librarian for firm.	Law clerk Legal assistant
Paralegal (Male)	120	1993	38.2	8.2	See women's sample above. 2% attended trade/technical school, 34% some college or associate degree, 48% completed bachelor's degree, 13% master's, 2% professional degree. 62% were employed in private law firm, 11% in corporate law department, 6% in court system, 4% in government agency, 17% other.		
Parks and Recreation Coordinator (Female)	714	1993	37.1	13.0	Members of National Recreation Park Association. 4% had some college or associate degree, 60% completed bachelor's degree, 28% master's, 5% doctorate. 65% were employed by government, 16% by health care facility, 8% by educational institution, 8% by other nonprofit institutions. Major activities included administration, community/public contact, and education/training.	195. Conducts recreation activities with assigned groups in public department or volunteer agency. Organizes, promotes, and develops interest in activities such as arts and crafts, sports, music, dramatics, camping, and hobbies. Cooperates with other staff in conducting community events and works with neighborhood groups to determine recreational interests and needs of all ages.	Camp director Community center director Leisure service supervisor Park manager Recreational therapist Recreation leader Resort manager Youth activities director

Description of the Strong Occupational Scales

Sample/Scale	N	Year Tested	Mean Age	Mean Years Exper.	Composition	DOT Code and Description	Related Occupations
Parks and Recreation Coordinator (Male)	900	1993	42.9	18.3	See women's sample. 5% had some college or associate degree, 51% completed bachelor's degree, 35% master's, 8% doctorate. 84% were employed by government, 8% by educational institution. Major activities included administration, community/public contact, and education/training.		
Pharmacist (Female)	321	1992	36.0	11.9	Members of American Pharmaceutical Association. 65% completed bachelor's degree, 8% master's, 23% professional degree, 4% doctorate. 28% were employed by chain pharmacies, 24% by hospital pharmacies, 17% by independent pharmacies, 5% by grocery/discount store pharmacies. Major activities included dispensing, consultation with other health professionals, administration/supervision/management, and patient counseling.	074. Compounds and dispenses prescribed medications following professional standards and legal requirements. Reviews issued prescriptions to assure accuracy and determine formulas and ingredients needed. Weighs, measures, and mixes drugs with correct quantity and composition. Stores and preserves vaccines, serums, and other drugs subject to deterioration. May assay medications to determine identity, purity, and strength. May participate in store management activities.	Hospital pharmacist Pharmacy helper Pharmacy manager Research pharmacist
Pharmacist (Male)	370	1992	45.7	21.5	See women's sample above. 62% completed bachelor's degree, 12% master's, 21% professional degree, 5% doctorate. 33% were employed by independent pharmacies, 19% by hospital pharmacies, 12% by chain pharmacies, 7% by grocery/discount store pharmacies, 6% by educational institutions. Major activities included dispensing, consultation with other health professionals, and administration/supervision/management.		

Description of the *Strong* Occupational Scales

Sample/Scale	N	Year Tested	Mean Age	Mean Years Exper.	Composition	DOT Code and Description	Related Occupations
Photographer (Female)	249	1978	36.9	10.9	Members of Professional Photographers of America, National Press Photographers Association, and Society of Photographers in Communication. 21% had high school diploma, 38% completed bachelor's degree, 13% master's. 35% received training on job, 23% from photography courses not leading to degree, 14% from degree courses, 28% combination. 51% were self-employed or in partnerships; remainder were employed by studios, businesses, newspapers, magazines, or combination.	143. Photographs persons, motion picture sets, merchandise, exteriors and interiors, machinery, and fashions. Arranges equipment such as lighting, screens, and shades and moves objects to obtain desired effects. Sets camera for correct angle and distance and adjusts lens for focus. Mixes solutions and chemicals used in developing films. Enlarges and prints pictures. Has knowledge of function of various cameras, lenses, films, accessories, and related technology.	Audiovisual producer Biological photographer Camera operator Industrial photographer Medical photographer Motion picture photographer Photo editor Photojournalist Portrait photographer Scientific photographer Travel photographer Video technician
Photographer (Male)	161	1978	38.9	15.1	See women's sample above. 24% had high school diploma, 10% completed associate degree, 31% bachelor's. 44% received training on job, 15% from photography courses not leading to degree, 20% from degree courses, 22% from combination. 56% were self-employed or in partnerships; 14% were employed by newspapers or magazines, remainder by studios, businesses, or combination.		
Physical Education Teacher (Female)	291	1979	36.6	13.1	Members of American Alliance for Health, Physical Education, and Recreation. 47% completed bachelor's degree, 52% master's. 84% were employed by secondary schools.	099. Instructs students in physical education activities in educational institutions. Teaches individual and team sports. Plans physical education program to promote the development of students' physical attributes and social skills. Instructs individuals or groups in calisthenics, gymnastics, or corrective exercises. Determines type and level of difficulty of exercises and appropriate movements. Organizes, leads, and referees indoor and outdoor games.	Aquatic director Athletic director Coach Dance instructor Exercise instructor Recreational therapist Team manager Umpire/referee
Physical Education Teacher (Male)	219	1979	38.5	14.2	See women's sample above. 18% completed bachelor's degree, 76% master's. 81% were employed by secondary schools.		

Description of the Strong Occupational Scales

Sample/Scale	N	Year Tested	Mean Age	Mean Years Exper.	Composition	DOT Code and Description	Related Occupations
Physical Therapist (Female)	715	1992	36.5	12.8	Members of American Physical Therapy Association. 63% completed bachelor's degree, 32% master's or professional degree, 3% doctorate. 36% worked in hospitals, 23% in private offices, 14% in educational institutions, 10% in home health agencies, 8% in extended care facilities or nursing homes.	076. Plans and administers medically prescribed physical therapy treatment for patients with disabilities, disorders, and injuries in order to relieve pain, develop or restore function, and maintain maximum performance. Uses physical means such as exercise, massage, heat, water, light, and electricity to assist in treatment. Applies diagnostic and prognostic muscle, joint, nerve, and functional ability tests. Directs and aids patients in active and passive exercises, muscle reeducation, and using pulleys and weights, steps, and inclined surfaces. Directs patients in care and use of wheelchairs, braces, canes, crutches, and prosthetic and orthotic devices.	Athletic trainer Home health physical therapist Pediatric physical therapist Physical therapy aide Physical therapy assistant Rehabilitation coordinator Research physical therapist
Physical Therapist (Male)	543	1992	40.1	15.3	See women's sample above. 61% completed bachelor's degree, 35% master's or professional degree, 3% doctorate. 45% worked in private offices, 28% in hospitals, 7% in extended care facilities or nursing homes, 6% in home health agencies, 6% in educational institutions.		
Physician (Female)	211	1982	38.8	9.4	National sample from mail list company, and members of American College of Physicians. 26% practiced medicine in small private clinics (less than 5 physicians), 14% in public hospitals, 11% in private hospitals, 8% in HMO clinics, 6% for government, 3% in large private clinics (more than 5 physicians), 19% other, 10% combination. Specialties included general/family practitioner, internist, pediatrician, anesthesiologist, gynecologist/obstetrician, neurologist, pathologist, radiologist, dermatologist, allergist, medical researcher, and college professor. Major activities included patient consultation and examination (33%), diagnosis and treatment (13%), research (8%), surgery (2%), other (7%), combination (31%).	070. Diagnoses and treats diseases and disorders of the human body. Examines patients, using all types of medical equipment, instruments, and tests, following standard medical procedures. Analyzes test and physical exam results to diagnose condition and determine treatment. Advises patients concerning diet, exercise, and hygiene methods for disease prevention. Performs surgery, prescribes medication, and may engage in research to aid in control and cure of disease.	Allergist Anesthesiologist Cardiologist Dermatologist Emergency room physician Family practitioner Internist Neurologist Nurse practitioner Obstetrician Ophthalmologist Pathologist Pediatrician Physician assistant Psychiatrist Radiologist Research physician Surgeon

Description of the Strong Occupational Scales

Sample/Scale	N	Year Tested	Mean Age	Mean Years Exper.	Composition	DOT Code and Description	Related Occupations
Physician (Male)	272	1982	40.9	10.8	See women's sample. 33% practiced medicine in small private clinics (less than 5 physicians), 13% in private hospitals, 12% in large private clinics (more than 5 physicians), 10% in public hospitals, 8% other, 12% combination. Specialties included general/family practitioner, cardiologist, internist, pediatrician, urologist, pathologist, radiologist, otolaryngologist, anesthesiologist, gynecologist/obstetrician, dermatologist, surgeon, medical researcher, and college professor. Major activities included patient consultation and examination (32%), diagnosis and treatment (19%), research (9%), surgery (5%), combination (26%).		
Physicist (Female)	348	1992	43.3	15.8	Members of American Physical Society. All had doctorate. 53% were employed by four-year colleges and universities, 16% by national laboratories, 13% by private industry, 13% by two-year colleges, 7% by government agencies.	023. Conducts research into phases of physical phenomena. Develops theories and laws on basis of observation and experiments and develops methods to apply laws and theories of physics to industry, medicine, and other fields. Performs experiments with lasers, betatrons, telescopes, mass spectrometers, electron microscopes, and other equipment to observe structure and properties of matter. May specialize in an area of physics and may teach college courses.	Astrophysicist Biophysicist Geophysicist Medical physicist Nuclear physicist Plasma physicist Solid-state physicist Theoretical physicist
Physicist (Male)	483	1992	47.1	19.7	See women's sample above. All had doctorate. 42% were employed by four-year colleges and universities, 22% by private industry, 18% by national laboratories, 7% by government agencies, 5% were self-employed.		

Description of the *Strong* Occupational Scales

Sample/Scale	N	Year Tested	Mean Age	Mean Years Exper.	Composition	DOT Code and Description	Related Occupations
Plumber (Male)	96	1993	45.9	24.6	From commercially compiled national listing. 2% had less than high school diploma, 23% high school diploma, 15% attended trade/technical school in addition, 46% some college or associate degree, 6% completed bachelor's degree.	862. Assembles, installs, and repairs pipes, fittings, and fixtures of heating, water, and drainage systems, according to specifications and plumbing codes. Studies building plans to determine work aids and sequence of installations. Inspects structure to ascertain obstructions to be avoided to prevent weakening of structure resulting from installation of pipe. Locates and marks position of pipe and pipe connections in walls and floors and cuts openings in walls and floors to satisfactorily accommodate them. Cuts, threads, bends, and joins pipe for adequate installation. Assembles and installs valves, pipe fittings, and pipes. Fills pipe system and reads pressure gauges to determine leakage. Installs, repairs, and maintains plumbing and plumbing fixtures.	Boilermaker Electrician Elevator installer Heating, air-conditioning, refrigeration mechanic Industrial machinery repairer Millwright Sheet-metal worker Stationary engineer
Police Officer (Female)	116	1993	37.4	11.6	Attendees at meeting of International Association of Women Police, members of United Federation of Police Officers, Texas Police Association, and Cal Cops. 8% had high school diploma, 47% some college or associate degree, 29% completed bachelor's degree, 15% master's.	375. Patrols assigned beat to control traffic, prevent crime or disturbance of peace, and arrest violators. Reports to scene of accident, renders first aid to injured, and investigates causes and results of accidents. Writes and files daily activity report with superior officer.	Accident-prevention squad Constable Deputy Detective Highway Patrol officer Narcotics investigator Sheriff Special agent Vice detective
Police Officer (Male)	484	1993	40.7	15.3	Members of United Federation of Police Officers, Texas Police Association, and Cal Cops. 10% had high school diploma, 48% some college or associate degree, 28% completed bachelor's degree, 8% master's.		

Description of the Strong Occupational Scales

Sample/Scale	N	Year Tested	Mean Age	Mean Years Exper.	Composition	DOT Code and Description	Related Occupations
Psychologist (Female)	287	1981	40.1	10.4	National sample of members of American Psychological Association. All completed doctorate degree. 46% were employed by educational institutions, 23% were self-employed or in partnership, 10% were employed by government, 2% by private industry, 14% combination, 5% other. Most frequent specialties included clinical (44%), counseling (10%), developmental (7%), educational (6%), experimental (5%), social (4%), plus industrial/organizational.	045. Collects, interprets, and applies scientific data to human and animal behavior and mental processes, formulates hypotheses and experimental designs, and analyzes results using statistics. Writes papers describing research. May provide therapy and counseling for groups or individuals. Investigates processes of learning and growth and human interrelationships. May apply psychological techniques to personnel administration and management. May teach college courses in field of specialization.	Clinical psychologist Counseling psychologist Developmental psychologist Educational psychologist Engineering psychologist Experimental psychologist Industrial-organizational psychologist School psychologist Social psychologist Vocational psychologist
Psychologist (Male)	318	1981	41.0	13.0	See women's sample above. All completed doctorate degree. 51% were employed by educational institutions, 16% were self-employed or in partnership, 15% were employed by government, 3% by private industry, 9% combination, 6% other. Most frequent specialties included clinical (38%), experimental (9%), counseling (9%), social (4%), industrial/organizational (4%), educational (4%), plus developmental and personality.		
Public Administrator (Female)	201	1979	37.7	9.0	Members of American Society for Public Administration. 22% completed bachelor's degree, 65% master's. 69% were employed by government agencies, 11% by educational institutions.	188. Manages federal, state, local, and international government activities as well as government-owned-and-operated business and educational institutions. Directs and coordinates activities, programs, and services. Develops and administers budget. Prepares and releases reports and studies. Represents agency at meetings. Evaluates programs.	Affirmative action coordinator City manager Community organization director Correctional agency director County administrator Economic development director Employment service director Hospital administrator Management analyst Public works commissioner Zoning director
Public Administrator (Male)	216	1979	38.0	11.7	See women's sample above. 17% completed bachelor's degree, 73% master's. 82% were employed by government agencies, 5% by educational institutions.		

Description of the Strong Occupational Scales

Sample/Scale	N	Year Tested	Mean Age	Mean Years Exper.	Composition	DOT Code and Description	Related Occupations
Public Relations Director (Female)	403	1992	38.8	12.4	Members of Public Relations Society of America. 5% had some college or associate degree, 66% completed bachelor's degree, 28% master's, 1% doctorate. 23% were employed in business/industry, 13% in public relations or consulting firms, 13% were self-employed, 12% were employed in educational institutions, 7% in health/medical institutions, 7% in government agencies, 16% in other nonprofit organizations. Major activities included writing/editing, administration/supervision, internal consultation, and media relations.	165. Plans and promotes programs designed to create and maintain favorable public image for an individual, group, or organization. Plans and directs development and communication of information designed to inform, develop credibility, and promote goodwill and a positive public image. Prepares and distributes fact sheets, news releases, photographs, and videotapes to media representatives. Purchases advertising time and space.	Audiovisual communications manager Communications specialist Community relations director Employee communications manager Fundraising director Information services director Lobbyist Marketing director Media relations director Municipal community consultant Public affairs manager Sales/service promoter Sports information director
Public Relations Director (Male)	291	1992	47.0	20.6	See women's sample above. 4% had some college or associate degree, 55% completed bachelor's degree, 35% master's, 2% professional degree, 4% doctorate. 27% were employed in business/industry, 19% in public relations or consulting firms, 14% were self-employed, 10% were employed in educational institutions, 9% in government agencies, 16% in other nonprofit organizations. Major activities included writing/editing, administration/supervision, internal consultation, and media relations.		

Description of the *Strong* Occupational Scales

Sample/Scale	N	Year Tested	Mean Age	Mean Years Exper.	Composition	DOT Code and Description	Related Occupations
Purchasing Agent (Female)	247	1983	38.3	7.8	Members of National Institute of Governmental Purchasing, members of National Association, and write-in responses to articles in purchasing publications. 15% had high school diploma, 50% had attended some college, 7% completed associate degree, 21% bachelor's, 2% master's. 33% saw themselves as senior buyer, 31% as chief purchasing officer, 7% as assistant purchasing officer, 7% as supervisory buyer, 7% as junior buyer. Sample consisted of purchasers and buyers for industrial, commercial, and utility firms, educational institutions, and government agencies.	Coordinates activities involved with the purchasing of equipment and supplies necessary for operation of an organization such as an industrial establishment, public utility, or government unit. Interviews vendors to obtain information relative to products' price and to determine ability of vendor to produce product or service and to meet delivery date. Prepares purchase orders and keeps records pertaining to costs of delivery, product performance, and inventories. Discusses defects of purchased goods with quality control personnel to determine source of trouble and takes corrective action.	Contract specialist Field contractor Finance and purchasing director Subcontract administrator
Purchasing Agent (Male)	224	1979	41.2	11.2	See women's sample above. 27% had some college education, 44% completed bachelor's degree, 18% master's.		
Radiologic Technologist (Female)	543	1993	38.2	15.0	From American Registry of Radiologic Technologists. All were registered technologists. 32% attended trade/technical school in addition to high school, 48% had some college or associate degree, 14% completed bachelor's degree, 1% master's. 77% were employed in hospitals or clinics, 20% in private offices. Specialty areas included radiography (46%), mammography (13%), magnetic resonance (10%), computed tomography (8%), nuclear medicine (7%).	078. Operates radiologic equipment to produce x-rays of patients for diagnostic and therapeutic purposes. Administers drugs or chemical mixtures orally to render organs opaque. Develops film in accordance with photographic techniques. Assists in treating diseased or affected areas of body under supervision of physician by exposing area to specified concentration of x-rays for prescribed periods of time. May assist in therapy requiring application of radium or radioactive isotopes.	Health physicist Mammography technician Nuclear medical technician Radiation therapist Ultrasound technologist X-ray technician

Description of the Strong Occupational Scales

Sample/Scale	N	Year Tested	Mean Age	Mean Years Exper.	Composition	DOT Code and Description	Related Occupations
Radiologic Technologist (Male)	430	1993	39.1	14.6	See women's sample. All were registered technologists. 14% attended trade/technical school in addition to high school, 56% had some college or associate degree, 20% completed bachelor's degree, 5% master's, 1% professional degree. 82% were employed in hospitals or clinics, 9% in private offices. Specialty areas included radiography (40%), administration (12%), computed tomography (11%), magnetic resonance (11%), cardiovascular-interventional (10%), radiation therapy (7%).		
Realtor (Female)	209	1977	44.3	8.3	Members of Women's Council of Realtors. 64% had high school diploma, 26% completed bachelor's degree. 55% were employed by real estate firms, 36% were self-employed or in partnerships. Sales specialty areas included residential (64%), combination of residential and commercial (30%).	250. Rents, buys, and sells properties for clients on commission basis. Reviews trade journals to keep informed of market conditions and property values. Interviews prospective clients and accompanies prospects to property sites. Quotes purchase price and discusses conditions of sale or terms of lease. Draws up real estate contracts such as deeds and negotiates loans on property.	Building consultant Fee appraiser Real estate sales agent Residence leasing agent
Realtor (Male)	208	1983	41.7	8.9	National sample, members of National Association of Realtors. 25% had high school diploma, 11% completed associate degree, 47% bachelor's, 12% master's, 2% doctorate. 45% were self-employed or in partnerships, 46% were employed by real estate firms. Sales specialty areas included residential (48%), commercial (5%), combination of residential and commercial (40%). Major activities included obtaining listings (9%), learning about properties (6%), showing properties (6%), arranging details of transaction (6%), combination (59%).		

Description of the *Strong* Occupational Scales

Sample/Scale	N	Year Tested	Mean Age	Mean Years Exper.	Composition	DOT Code and Description	Related Occupations
Reporter (Female)	207	1979	38.0	10.7	From *Alphabetized Directory of American Journalists*. All those selected indicated "reporter" or "writer" as job title. Also members of National Federation of Press Women. 15% had high school diploma, 69% completed bachelor's degree, 14% master's.	131. Collects and analyzes facts about newsworthy events by interview, investigation, or observation and writes news stories. Takes notes and reads publicity releases, copies of speeches, or similar materials. Researches and verifies information to facilitate writing of stories. Refers stories to supervising editor for approval. Receives and evaluates news tips and suggestions for future stories. Monitors police and fire radio communications to obtain news story leads.	Bureau chief Business writer City editor Columnist Copy editor Court reporter Editorial writer Fashion editor Food editor Investigative reporter News editor Outdoor writer Sportswriter
Reporter (Male)	208	1979	35.3	11.9	See women's sample above. All of those selected indicated "reporter" or "writer" as job title. 14% had high school diploma, 72% completed bachelor's degree, 12% master's.		
Research & Development Manager (Female)	201	1983	37.7	5.4	National sample from Hugo Dunhill Mailing Lists, Inc. file on women R & D managers, and from nine U.S. Navy laboratories. 45% completed bachelor's degree, 30% master's, 25% doctorate. Educational background by general area was 45% life sciences, 34% physical sciences, 11% mathematics and computer sciences, 10% engineering. Management level included lower (34%), middle (43%), upper (18%), vice president (5%). Collected by R. Hill, University of Michigan.	189. Directs and coordinates activities concerned with research and development of new concepts and ideas and basic data on and applications for organization's products, services, or ideologies. Plans and formulates aspects of research and development proposals. Reviews and analyzes proposals submitted to determine if benefits derived and possible applications justify expenditures. Develops and implements procedures for monitoring approved projects.	Manufacturing engineer Marketing research and analysis director Product development manager Product research director
Research & Development Manager (Male)	215	1983	44.8	10.9	From R & D departments of a broad range of scientific and engineering-based firms. 38% completed bachelor's degree, 31% master's, 31% doctorate. Educational background by general area was 57% engineering, 27% physical sciences, 10% life sciences, 6% mathematics and computer science. Management included lower (11%), middle (45%), upper (39%), vice president (5%). Collected by R. Hill, University of Michigan.		

Description of the Strong Occupational Scales

Sample/Scale	N	Year Tested	Mean Age	Mean Years Exper.	Composition	DOT Code and Description	Related Occupations
Respiratory Therapist (Female)	216	1983	33.0	7.1	Members of American Association for Respiratory Therapy. All were staff therapists. 4% had certificate from vocational school, 7% had some college, 56% completed associate degree, 33% bachelor's. 94% were employed by hospitals: 53% in intensive care, 16% in respiratory therapy unit, 22% other. Major activities included implementation of treatment programs (51%), emergency care (11%), giving instruction (5%), pulmonary lab work (4%), combination (23%). 88% were registered or certified therapists. 34% specialized in area of pulmonary care, including newborn intensive care, pulmonary rehabilitation, critical care, and geriatric care.	076. Administers respiratory therapy and life support to patients with deficiencies and abnormalities of cardiopulmonary system, under supervision of physician and by prescription. Operates breathing devices, performs bronchopulmonary drainage, and assists patients in breathing exercises. Monitors patients' physiological responses to therapy as well as equipment function. Maintains patients' charts. Consults with physician in the event of adverse reaction.	Cardiopulmonary technician Home care coordinator Neonatal care coordinator
Respiratory Therapist (Male)	206	1983	31.8	7.4	See women's sample above. 3% had certificate from vocational school, 9% had some college, 49% completed associate degree, 34% bachelor's. 86% were employed by hospitals: 54% in intensive care, 15% in respiratory therapy unit, 18% in other. Major activities included implementation of treatment programs (43%), administrative duties (9%), emergency care (7%), pulmonary lab work (6%), giving instruction (4%), combination (28%). 92% were registered or certified therapists. 42% specialized in area of pulmonary care, including newborn intensive care, pulmonary rehabilitation, critical care, and geriatric care.		

Description of the *Strong* Occupational Scales

Sample/Scale	N	Year Tested	Mean Age	Mean Years Exper.	Composition	DOT Code and Description	Related Occupations
Restaurant Manager (Female)	152	1984	37.4	10.0	Members of National Restaurant Association, and national sampling from *Bell Yellow Pages*. 24% had high school diploma, 27% had some college, 9% completed associate degree, 31% bachelor's, 6% master's. 37% were restaurant owners, 63% held management positions. Major activities included customer contact (26%), personnel management (17%), record keeping and financial planning (9%), combination (41%).	319. Supervises employees engaged in serving food; trains workers; oversees kitchen; hires personnel; keeps records and requisitions supplies and equipment. May direct preparation of food and beverages and plan menus. Coordinates work of employees to promote efficiency.	Cafeteria manager Caterer Chef Club manager Convention manager Deli manager Fast-food manager Flight kitchen manager Food services director Hotel manager Innkeeper Resort manager
Restaurant Manager (Male)	192	1984	38.8	14.3	See women's sample above. 18% had high school diploma, 26% had some college, 10% completed associate degree, 43% bachelor's, 3% master's. 49% were restaurant owners, 41% held management positions. Major activities included customer contact (25%), personnel management (23%), record keeping and financial planning (11%), combination (38%).		
School Administrator (Female)	347	1992	48.6	22.3	Members of American Association of School Administrators. 42% completed master's degree, 8% professional degree, 49% doctorate. 43% worked in public schools, 36% in public school district office, 4% in county office of education, 3% in state office of education, 1% in private or parochial schools.	099. School superintendent: administers affairs of school system under direction of board of education. Directs school budget and determines amount of school bond issues required to finance educational program. Interprets programs and policies of school system to individuals, groups, and agencies.	Assistant principal Assistant superintendent Career education director County school administrator Curriculum director Dean of students Principal School district administrator Superintendent Vocational education administrator
School Administrator (Male)	314	1992	61.2	32.3	See women's sample above. 30% completed master's degree, 7% professional degree, 62% doctorate. 43% worked in public schools, 31% in public school district office, 4% in county office of education, 3% in state office of education.	Principal: directs and coordinates educational, administrative, and counseling activities of primary or secondary school. Develops, coordinates, and evaluates educational program to ensure conformance to state and school board standards. Confers with teachers, students, and parents. Plans budget. Interviews, hires, and evaluates teachers.	

Description of the Strong Occupational Scales

Sample/Scale	N	Year Tested	Mean Age	Mean Years Exper.	Composition	DOT Code and Description	Related Occupations
Science Teacher (Female)	213	1983	38.7	12.3	National sample, *National Science Teachers Association, U.S. Registry*. 32% completed bachelor's degree, 65% master's. All were high school teachers; 84% taught more than one grade. 55% taught primarily biology, 16% chemistry, 9% general science, 5% physics, 14% mixed. Other subjects included physiology, environmental science, geology, astronomy, and botany. 92% of sample spent minimum of 40% of time teaching. Other activities included lesson preparation, grading, meetings, conferences. 28% were involved in other school activities relating to subject taught.	091. Instructs students through lectures, demonstrations, and audiovisual aids. Prepares course objectives and course outline. Assigns and corrects homework. Administers tests to evaluate students' progress. Keeps attendance records and maintains discipline. Participates in faculty and professional meetings, conferences, and teacher-training workshops. Performs related duties such as sponsoring special activities or student organizations. Teaches courses such as chemistry, biology, physiology, physics, geology, general science, and health.	Astronomy teacher Biology teacher Chemistry teacher Earth science teacher General science teacher Geology teacher Health teacher Physics teacher Physiology teacher
Science Teacher (Male)	237	1983	39.5	14.7	See women's sample above. 30% completed bachelor's degree, 66% master's, 2% doctorate, 3% other. All were high school teachers; 89% taught more than one grade. 45% taught primarily biology, 18% chemistry, 12% general science, 9% physics, 14% mixed. Other subjects included physiology, environmental science, geology, astronomy, and botany. 96% of sample spent minimum of 40% of time teaching. Other activities included lesson preparation, grading, meetings, conferences. 17% were involved in other school activities relating to subject taught.		

Description of the *Strong* Occupational Scales

Sample/Scale	N	Year Tested	Mean Age	Mean Years Exper.	Composition	DOT Code and Description	Related Occupations
Secretary (Female)	269	1983	40.7	17.0	National sample, members of Professional Secretaries International. 52% had high school diploma, 12% attended secretarial school, 16% business school, 8% completed associate degree, 8% bachelor's. 33% were employed by manufacturing firms, 9% by private business, 6% by hospitals, 51% other (casinos, trade associations, publishers, chemical research industries). Specialties included corporate secretary (15%), medical (6%), public relations (3%), education (3%), technical (2%), legal (2%), other (7%), no specialty (45%), combination (18%). 75% spent less than 50% of time typing (the mode was 25%). Other activities included dictation, transcription, filing, maintenance of records, correspondence, supervisory functions, and research.	201. Schedules appointments, gives information to callers, take dictation, and otherwise relieves officials of clerical work and administrative and business detail. Composes and types routing correspondence. Schedules appointments. Greets visitors, ascertains nature of business, and conducts visitors to appropriate person. May arrange travel schedule and reservations. May compile and type statistical reports.	Administrative assistant Clerk-typist Data entry clerk Executive secretary Financial secretary Legal secretary Medical secretary Office manager Personal secretary Receptionist School secretary Social secretary Stenographer Word processor
Small Business Owner (Female)	206	1993	45.6	16.3	Members of National Small Business United, members of National Federation of Independent Businesses in Illinois, and from commercially compiled national listing. 16% had high school diploma, 8% attended trade/technical school in addition, 28% had some college or associate degree, 21% completed bachelor's degree, 15% master's, 3% professional degree, 2% doctorate. Major activities included customer service, management/supervision, and marketing/sales.	185. Owns and manages a business engaged in selling goods or providing services. Performs the following duties personally or supervises employees performing these duties: plans and prepares work schedules and assigns employees to specific duties. Formulates pricing policies for profitability. Coordinates sales and service promotion activities and prepares merchandise displays and advertising copy. Sells merchandise or provides services of the business. Takes inventories and reconciles cash with sales receipts, keeps operating records, or prepares requisitions to replenish merchandise. Interviews, hires, and trains employees. May answer customer complaints or inquiries.	Business consultant Contractor Customer services manager Department store manager Wholesaler

Description of the Strong Occupational Scales

Sample/Scale	N	Year Tested	Mean Age	Mean Years Exper.	Composition	DOT Code and Description	Related Occupations
Small Business Owner (Male)	398	1993	47.8	22.8	See women's sample. 12% had high school diploma, 6% attended trade/technical school in addition, 28% had some college or associate degree, 36% completed bachelor's degree, 8% master's, 4% professional degree, 1% doctorate. Major activities included customer service, management/supervision, and marketing/sales.		
Social Science Teacher (Female)	230	1983	39.8	11.9	National sample, National Science Teachers Association, U.S. Registry. 39% completed bachelor's degree, 58% master's, 1% doctorate. All were high school teachers; 86% taught more than one grade. 54% taught primarily history, 12% government/civics, 6% psychology, 4% geography, 3% economics, 10% mixed. Other areas were marriage and family, area studies, energy/ecology, and ethics. 86% spent minimum of 40% of time teaching. Other activities were lesson preparation, grading, and meetings/conferences. 22% were involved in other school activities relating to subject taught.	091. Teaches courses such as American studies, career exploration, economics, geography, government, civics, history, and political science. Instructs students through lectures, demonstrations, and audiovisual aids. Prepares course objectives and course outline. Assigns lessons and corrects homework. Administers tests to evaluate students' progress. Keeps attendance records and maintains discipline. Participates in faculty and professional meetings. Performs related duties such as sponsoring special activities or student organizations.	American studies teacher Career development teacher Criminology teacher Economics teacher Geography teacher Government/civics teacher History teacher Political science teacher Psychology teacher Sociology teacher
Social Science Teacher (Male)	224	1983	39.2	14.1	See women's sample above. 27% completed bachelor's degree, 68% master's, 4% doctorate. All were high school teachers; 81% taught more than one grade. 56% taught primarily history, 16% government/civics, 5% economics, 4% psychology, 3% geography, 10% mixed. Other areas were marriage and family area studies, energy/ecology, ethics. 91% spent minimum of 40% of time teaching. Other activities were lesson preparation, grading, and meetings/conferences. 9% were involved in other school activities relating to subject taught.		

Description of the *Strong* Occupational Scales

Sample/Scale	N	Year Tested	Mean Age	Mean Years Exper.	Composition	DOT Code and Description	Related Occupations
Social Worker (Female)	488	1992	44.4	15.4	Members of National Association of Social Workers. 3% completed bachelor's dgree, 88% master's, 4% professional degree, 4% doctorate. 41% were employed by private, nonprofit organization, 29% by government, 21% were in private practice, 8% worked for commercial or for-profit organization. Areas of specialization included mental health (38%), child and family (25%), health and medical (15%), aging/gerontology (7%).	195. Performs social service functions in a public or volunteer social welfare agency. Counsels and aids individuals and families requesting assistance of social service agency. Interviews clients with problems such as personal and family adjustment, finances, or physical or mental impairments to determine nature and degree of problem. Counsels clients individually or in groups regarding plans for meeting needs and assists clients to mobilize their inner capacities and environmental resources to improve social functioning. Helps clients to modify attitudes and patterns of behavior by increasing understanding. Refers clients to community resources and other agencies when appropriate.	Camp director Case aide Caseworker Child welfare caseworker Community organization worker Family caseworker Field director Group worker Management aide Marriage counselor Medical social worker Parole officer Probation officer Program aide Psychiatric social worker School social worker Social welfare administrator
Social Worker (Male)	458	1992	45.8	18.4	See women's sample above. 2% completed bachelor's degree, 81% master's, 8% professional degree, 8% doctorate. 38% were employed by government, 38% by private, nonprofit organization, 17% were in private practice, 7% worked for commercial or for-profit organization. Areas of specialization included mental health (46%), child and family (25%), health and medical (7%), substance abuse (7%).		
Sociologist (Female)	210	1974	42.2	11.2	Members of American Sociological Association; all had doctorate. Major activities included teaching (48%), research (15%), administration (9%), combination (24%).	054. Conducts research into development, structure, and behavior of groups of people and patterns of culture and social organization that have arisen out of group life in society. Collects and analyzes data concerning social phenomena. May teach college courses and may specialize in research areas such as criminology, social problems, or social ecology.	Criminologist Demographer Industrial sociologist Medical sociologist Research sociologist Rural sociologist Social research analyst Urban sociologist
Sociologist (Male)	212	1974	40.3	11.4	See women's sample above. Major activities included teaching (45%), research (17%), administration (15%), combination (21%).		

Description of the Strong Occupational Scales

Sample/Scale	N	Year Tested	Mean Age	Mean Years Exper.	Composition	DOT Code and Description	Related Occupations
Special Education Teacher (Female)	263	1993	42.0	15.3	From commercially compiled national listing. 29% completed bachelor's degree, 69% master's, 1% professional degree. 96% worked in public schools, 2% in public school district office. Areas of specialization included learning disabilities (46%), gifted and talented (12%), mental retardation (7%), behavioral disorders (5%).	094. Teaches students with disabilities, adapting techniques and methods of instruction to meet individual needs of students. Plans curriculum and prepares other materials, considering factors such as individual needs, abilities, learning levels, and physical disabilities. Confers with staff to develop programs that maximize students' potentials. Instructs students. Prepares course objectives and course outlines, assigns lessons, and corrects homework. Administers tests to evaluate students' progress. Keeps attendance records and maintains discipline. Participates in faculty and professional meetings, conferences, and teacher-training workshops. Performs related duties such as sponsoring special activities and student organizations.	Educational therapist Teacher of gifted and talented Teacher of people with emotional disabilities Teacher of people with learning disabilities Teacher of people with physical disabilities
Special Education Teacher (Male)	221	1993	42.9	17.1	See women's sample above. 33% had bachelor's degree, 66% master's, 1% professional degree, 1% doctorate. 96% worked in public schools. Areas of specialization included learning disabilities (40%), mental retardation (18%), behavioral disorders (13%), gifted and talented (10%).		
Speech Pathologist (Female)	425	1992	39.3	13.4	Speech pathologist members of American Speech-Language-Hearing Association. 93% completed master's degree, 1% professional degree, 5% doctorate. 55% were employed by elementary or secondary schools, 15% by hospitals, 6% by residential health care facilities, 6% by colleges and universities, 6% by speech-language pathologist or audiologist offices.	076. Diagnoses, treats, and performs research related to speech and language problems. Treats language and speech impairments such as aphasia, stuttering, and articulatory problems of organic and nonorganic etiology. Plans, directs, or conducts remedial programs designed to restore or improve communicative efficiency. Provides counseling and guidance to individuals with speech and language disabilities. Diagnoses and evaluates these speech and hearing problems in relationship to educational, medical, social, and psychological factors.	Audiologist Hearing-test technician Interpreter for people with impaired hearing Oral myologist Speech clinician Speech consultant Speech correctionist Speech and hearing specialist Speech therapist
Speech Pathologist (Male)	334	1992	46.6	19.8	See women's sample above. 64% completed master's degree, 36% doctorate. 33% were employed by elementary or secondary schools, 23% by hospitals, 18% by colleges and universities, 7% by residential health care facilities, 7% by speech-language pathologist or audiologist offices.		

Description of the Strong Occupational Scales

Sample/Scale	N	Year Tested	Mean Age	Mean Years Exper.	Composition	DOT Code and Description	Related Occupations
Store Manager (Female)	176	1984	36.8	9.8	Obtained with assistance of National Retail Merchants Association, Minnesota Retail Merchants Association, and through national *Bell Yellow Pages*. 50% had high school diploma, 3% vocational-technical certificate, 9% completed associate degree, 33% bachelor's, 2% master's. Types of merchandise included clothing (32%), jewelry (7%), combination (57%, including food, hardware, and other). Major activities included financial records and planning (15%), personnel management (13%), inventory control (9%), customer service (8%), merchandise presentation (5%), other (12%), combination (34%).	185. Directs and coordinates activities of stores. Develops and implements policies and procedures for store. Negotiates or approves contracts with suppliers of merchandise, security, or maintenance. Reviews operating and financial statements. Confers with administrative personnel. Conducts supervisory staff meetings. Prepares budgets and reports on operations. Supervises and trains workers. Coordinates sales promotions. May perform sales, inventory, or stocking activities as needed.	Advertising manager Buyer/purchasing director Credit manager General merchandiser Personnel manager Retail sales manager
Store Manager (Male)	238	1984	39.1	15.5	See women's sample above. 23% had high school diploma, 16% had some college, 7% completed associate degree, 46% bachelor's, 4% master's. Types of merchandise included clothing (36%), combination (54%, including jewelry, hardware, food, and other). Major activities included financial records and planning (13%), inventory control (11%), personnel management (9%), administrative functions (6%), merchandise presentation (5%), customer service (5%), combination (47%).		

Description of the Strong Occupational Scales

Sample/Scale	N	Year Tested	Mean Age	Mean Years Exper.	Composition	DOT Code and Description	Related Occupations
Technical Writer (Female)	350	1992	39.2	8.8	Members of Society for Technical Communication. 11% had some college or associate degree, 55% completed bachelor's degree, 30% master's, 3% doctorate. 60% were employed by business/industry, 13% by consulting firms, 13% were self-employed, 6% were employed by educational institutions, 5% by government agencies. Areas of specialization included product documentation (69%), on-line documentation (5%), technical reports (9%).	131. Develops, writes, and edits material for reports, manuals, briefs, proposals, instructional books, catalogs, and related technical and administrative publications concerned with work methods and procedures and installation, operation, and maintenance of machinery and other equipment. Observes production and experimental activities to determine operating procedures and details. Interviews production and engineering personnel and reads journals and reports to be familiar with product technologies and production methods. Reviews data relative to operation, maintenance, and service of equipment	Advertising and public relations writer Computer publications editor On-line documentation writer Science reporter/correspondent Science writer Scientific copy editor Scientific editor Scientific indexer Software editor Technical editor Technical writing instructor
Technical Writer (Male)	274	1992	42.6	12.2	See women's sample above. 15% had some college or associate degree, 51% completed bachelor's degree, 26% master's, 5% doctorate. 69% were employed by business/industry, 7% by consulting firms, 15% were self-employed, 3% were employed by educational institutions, 3% by government agencies. Areas of specialization were product documentation (74%), on-line documentation (8%), technical reports (6%), promotional writing (6%).		
Translator (Female)	475	1993	43.1	13.0	Members of American Translators Association. 2% attended trade/technical school, 11% some college or associate degree, 36% completed bachelor's degree, 38% master's, 2% professional degree, 10% doctorate. 58% were self-employed, 12% worked in business/industry, 9% in educational institutions, 9% in government, 3% in translation firms, 3% in international organizations.	137. Translates documents and other material from one language to another. Reads and rewrites material in specified language or languages, following established rules in semantics and syntax. May specialize in particular type of material, such as news or scientific reports, and may be identified according to language translated.	Editor Foreign language teacher Interpreter Linguist Translation director

Description of the *Strong* Occupational Scales

Sample/Scale	N	Year Tested	Mean Age	Mean Years Exper.	Composition	DOT Code and Description	Related Occupations
Translator (Male)	238	1993	48.2	16.2	See women's sample. 10% had some college or associate degree, 27% completed bachelor's degree, 37% master's, 7% professional degree, 18% doctorate. 59% were self-employed, 12% worked in business/industry, 10% in educational institutions, 10% in government, 3% in translation firms, 3% in international organizations.		
Travel Agent (Female)	264	1983	41.4	11.7	Members of American Society of Travel Agents. 30% had high school diploma, 15% certificate from travel school, 5% certificate from vocational school not related to travel, 9% completed associate degree, 34% bachelor's, 3% master's. 9% made primarily commercial bookings, 23% leisure, 68% combination. 32% were members of Institute of Certified Travel Agents. Major activities included administrative functions (25%), reservations (16%), advising clients (11%), traveling (3%), combination (42%).	252. Plans itineraries and arranges accommodations and other travel services for customers of travel agency. Converses with customers to determine destination, mode of transportation, travel dates, financial considerations, and accommodations required. Plans or describes and sells itinerary package tours. Gives customers brochures concerning travel. Computes cost of travel and accommodations, books customers on transportation carrier, and makes hotel reservations. Tickets passengers and collects payment. May specialize in foreign or domestic service. May act as wholesaler and assemble tour packages.	Airline reservation agent Ticket agent Tour operator Traffic agent Travel clerk Travel counselor
Travel Agent (Male)	214	1983	41.8	13.4	See women's sample above. 16% had high school diploma, 8% certificate from travel school, 2% certificate from vocational school not related to travel, 6% completed associate degree, 49% bachelor's, 13% master's, 5% other. 11% made primarily commercial bookings, 20% leisure, 69% combination. 20% were members of Institute of Certified Travel Agents. Major activities included administrative functions (37%), reservations (12%), advising clients (10%), traveling (2%), combination (38%).		

Description of the Strong Occupational Scales

Sample/Scale	N	Year Tested	Mean Age	Mean Years Exper.	Composition	DOT Code and Description	Related Occupations
Veterinarian (Female)	459	1992	35.5	9.4	Members of American Veterinary Association. All had DVM degree, 4% had additional doctorate. 45% were employees in private practice, 34% were in own private practice, 11% worked in educational institutions, 5% in government agencies, 3% in industry. 53% specialized in small animals, 10% in large animals.	073. Diagnoses and treats diseases and disorders of animals. Examines animals for the nature of the disease or injury. Inoculates against disease. Performs autopsies. Advises owners on care and breeding of animals. Engages either in general practice, treating various animal species, or in specialty, restricting practice to pets or to a single species.	Equine veterinarian Feline veterinarian Laboratory-animal veterinarian Large-animal veterinarian Livestock inspector Research veterinarian Small-animal veterinarian Veterinary anesthesiologist Veterinary assistant Veterinary microbiologist Zoo veterinarian
Veterinarian (Male)	327	1992	43.6	17.3	See women's sample. All had DVM degree, 7% had additional doctorate. 75% had own private practice, 13% were employees in private practice, 13% worked in educational institutions, 6% in government, 2% in industry. 72% specialized in small animals, 9% in large animals.		
Vocational Agriculture Teacher (Female)	135	1982	31.1	5.8	Collected with assistance of National Vocational Agriculture Teacher's Association, Inc., and names from *Agriculture Teachers' Directory*. 3% completed associate degree, 53% bachelor's, 36% master's, 7% other. 59% were employed by high schools, 14% by vocational-technical institutions, 8% by junior or community colleges, 4% by colleges or universities. 76% spent minimum of 40% of time in classroom instruction. Other activities included lesson preparation, assignment evaluation, administrative functions, and outdoor instruction.	091. Teaches courses in agriculture, horticulture, farm management, equipment maintenance and repair, crop judging, production, agricultural supplies, and services. Prepares teaching outline for course of study, assigns lessons, and corrects homework. Administers tests to evaluate students' progress. Keeps attendance records and maintains discipline. Participates in faculty and professional meetings, conferences, and teacher-training workshops. Performs related duties such as sponsoring special activities and student organizations.	Agribusiness teacher Agricultural education instructor Agricultural mechanics teacher Animal husbandry teacher Farm-management instructor Forestry instructor Horticulture instructor Landscaping instructor Vocational training instructor
Vocational Agriculture Teacher (Male)	239	1982	37.6	11.7	See women's sample above. 38% completed bachelor's degree, 49% master's. 69% were employed by high schools, 10% by colleges or universities, 9% by vocational institutions, 7% by junior or community colleges. 75% spent minimum of 40% of time in classroom instruction. Other activities included lesson preparation, assignment evaluation, administrative functions, and outdoor instruction.		

APPENDIX B

Occupations and Their Theme Codes

The list of occupations that follows is designed for use with the *Strong* Profile. It can be used to help individuals identify their interest patterns and to expand their career options. Each occupation in the list has been assigned a code indicating the General Occupational Theme or Themes (GOTs) that most strongly characterize it. For example, the occupation Geologist has the code IRA, indicating that the Investigative, Realistic, and Artistic Themes, in that order, describe people in that occupation. The occupations are listed in the order of the six GOTs—R, I, A, S, E, C—according to their Theme code. For some of the occupations on this list, the Theme code is different for women and men, reflecting the fact that the interests of women and men employed in these occupations differ.

This list includes all the occupations on the *Strong* Profile and many other occupations derived from various sources. Many of the Theme codes were derived by testing people in that occupation to see on which Themes they scored highest. Other Theme codes were derived by asking people of known code types which occupations they liked. A few Theme codes were derived from other published sources.

This list is organized into three columns. The one-, two-, or three-letter Theme codes for each occupation are found in the first column. The second column contains the names of the occupations, which are listed alphabetically within Theme code category. The third column identifies the gender or genders to which the codes in the first column apply. There are four kinds of entries in the third column:

▲ An entry of "(F, M)" indicates that both women and men in that occupation share the same code.

▲ A single letter—"(F)" or "(M)"—indicates that data are available only for that gender in that occupation.

▲ A single letter, followed by a letter and another code, indicates that women and men in that occupation have different Theme codes. For example, the entry

    RE   Small Business Owner   (M; F = CE)

means that men who are small business owners tend to have Realistic and Enterprising interests, while women who are small business owners tend to have Conventional and Enterprising interests. Occupations such as this one are also cross-referenced, meaning that for this example there is another entry in the table:

    CE   Small Business Owner   (F; M = RE)

▲ A blank in the third column indicates that the data available on these occupations were not classified separately by gender.

When working with an individual's Profile, use this appendix to help expand the client's options. To do this, use the section of the list that corresponds to the individual's Theme code. The easiest way to begin might be to use the Theme code that is printed in the General Occupational Themes section of the client's *Strong* Snapshot. You may also derive a code from the Basic Interest Scales, the Occupational Scales, or any combination of scales. (See Chapter 10 for more information on deriving and using Theme codes for clients.)

For example, if the person showed "Average Interest" or above on the Enterprising, Social, and Conventional Themes, then his or her Theme code is ESC. Now find those sections of the list with the E, S, and C Themes in the first column. To make sure that the client considers all possible options, at least at first, it helps to scan the list for occupations that are characterized by the client's Theme code in any of its various combinations—in this case, ECS, ESC, SEC, SCE, CES, CSE, ES, EC, CE, CS, SE, SC, E, S, and C. The occupations derived from this list can then become the initial focus of the client's career exploration.

These Theme codes should be used as guidelines, not dictates. The codes were assigned on the basis of the best available statistics, and they usually accord well with common sense. They are based on averages, however, and should be treated as such. Clearly, not all people in any one occupation are alike or share the same interests, and many people who are contentedly employed have Theme codes other than the one listed for their occupation. Nonetheless, the Theme codes of people working together are usually similar.

Realistic Occupations and Theme Codes

Theme Code	Occupation	Gender Codes
R	Air Force Enlisted Personnel	(M; F = C)
R	Air Force Officer	(F, M)
R	Auto Mechanic	(F, M)
R	Charter Bus Driver	(F, M)
R	Correctional Officer	(F, M)
R	Forest Ranger	(M)
R	Metro Bus Driver	(F, M)
R	Painter	(F, M)
R	Plumber	(M)
R	Police Officer	(M; F = RE)
R	Rancher	(M)
R	Telephone Technician	(M)
R	Tool-and-Die Maker	(M)
R	Union Leader	
RI	Cartographer	(F, M)
RI	Civil Engineer	(F, M)
RI	Emergency Medical Technician	(M; F = RCI)
RI	Engineer	(F, M)
RI	Forester	(F, M)
RI	Machinist	(M)
RI	Mechanical Engineer	(F, M)
RI	Navy Officer	(F; M = RIC)
RI	Petroleum Engineer	(M)
RI	Pilot	(M; F = ERI)
RI	Radiologic Technologist	(M; F = RIS)
RIA	Carpenter	(F; M = REA)
RIA	Electrician	(F; M = RIC)
RIS	Appraiser	
RIS	Arc Welder	
RIS	Athletic Trainer	(F; M = SIR)
RIS	Radiologic Technologist	(F; M = RI)
RIE	Alteration Tailor	
RIE	Electronics Engineer	
RIE	Facilities Planner	
RIE	Wine Maker	
RIC	Electrician	(M; F = RIA)
RIC	Electronics Assembler and Tester	
RIC	Navy Officer	(M; F = RI)
RIC	Optical Engineer	
RS	Industrial Arts Teacher	(M)
RSI	Cabinetmaker	(M)
RSI	Marine Corps Officer	(F; M = RSE)
RSI	Special Agent, Customs	
RSI	Vocational Agriculture Teacher	(F; M = RSE)
RSE	Athletic Director	(F; M = E)
RSE	Audio-Video Repairer	
RSE	County Sheriff	(M)
RSE	Dog Groomer	
RSE	Highway Patrol Officer	(M; F = RCE)
RSE	Marine Corps Officer	(M; F = RSI)
RSE	Vocational Agriculture Teacher	(M; F = RSI)
RSC	City or State Employee	(M; F = SC)
RSC	Silversmith	
RE	Baker	(M; F = CE)
RE	Building Contractor	(M)
RE	Gardener/Groundskeeper	(M; F = RC)
RE	Police Officer	(F; M = R)
RE	Professional Athlete	(F; M = ER)
RE	Secret Service Agent	(M; F = ER)
RE	Small Business Owner	(M; F = CE)
REI	Aircraft Sales Representative	
REI	Environmental Project Manager	
REI	Horticultural Worker	(F, M)
REI	Military Officer	(F; M = REC)
REI	Production Planner	
REI	Safety Engineer, Mines	
REA	Carpenter	(M; F = RIA)
REA	Marine Service Manager	
RES	Animal Trainer	
RES	Fire Fighter	
REC	Jeweler	
REC	Military Officer	(M; F = REI)
REC	Orchard Manager	
RC	Army Officer	(F, M)
RC	Drafting Technician	(M; F = AR)
RC	Farmer	(M; F = CSE)
RC	Gardener/Groundskeeper	(F; M = RE)
RC	Instrument Assembler	(F, M)
RC	Marine Corps Enlisted Personnel	(M; F = CRS)
RC	Navy Enlisted Personnel	(F, M)
RC	Prison Warden	(M)
RCI	Emergency Medical Technician	(F; M = RI)
RCI	Furniture Restorer	
RCI	Software Technician	
RCS	Machine Shop Supervisor	(M)
RCS	Research Assistant	
RCE	Highway Patrol Officer	(F; M = RSE)
RCE	Interstate Bus Driver	(M; F = R)
RCE	Military Enlisted Personnel	(M; F = CRE)

Investigative Occupations and Theme Codes

Theme Code	Occupation	Gender Codes
I	Electronics Designer	(M)
I	Electronics Technician	(F; M = IR)
I	Internist	(F, M)
I	Scientific Researcher	(F, M)
I	Social Scientist	(M; F = AI)
I	Statistician	(F, M)
IR	Animal Science Professor	(M)
IR	Astronaut	
IR	Chemical Engineer	(F, M)
IR	Chemist	(F, M)
IR	Chiropractor	(F; M = IRA)
IR	Computer Programmer/ Systems Analyst	(F; M = IAR)
IR	Dentist	(M; F = IRA)
IR	Electrical Engineer	(F, M)
IR	Electronics Technician	(M; F = I)
IR	Experimental Psychologist	(F; M = IA)
IR	Inventor	(M; F = IA)
IR	Laboratory Technician	(F, M)
IR	Medical Researcher	(F; M = IA)
IR	Obstetrician	(F, M)
IR	Optometrist	(F, M)
IR	Pathologist	(F, M)
IR	Research & Development Manager	(F; M = IRC)
IR	Surgeon	(F, M)
IR	Veterinarian	(M; F = IRA)
IRA	Biologist	(F; M = IA)
IRA	Chiropractor	(M; F = IR)
IRA	Dentist	(F; M = IR)
IRA	Geographer	(F; M = IA)
IRA	Geologist	(F, M)
IRA	Physicist	(F, M)
IRA	Respiratory Therapist	(F; M = IRS)
IRA	Veterinarian	(F; M = IR)
IRS	Anesthesiologist	
IRS	Biochemist	
IRS	Curator	
IRS	Entomologist	
IRS	Geneticist	
IRS	Meteorologist	
IRS	Neurologist	
IRS	Osteopath	(M)
IRS	Respiratory Therapist	(M; F = IRA)
IRS	Science Teacher	(F, M)
IRS	Zoo Laboratory Assistant	
IRE	Archeologist	
IRE	Chief Credit Analyst	
IRE	Food Scientist	(M)
IRE	Medical Technician	(M; F = IRC)
IRC	Integrated Circuit Layout Designer	
IRC	Mathematician	(F; M = ICA)
IRC	Medical Technician	(F; M = IRE)
IRC	Medical Technologist	(F, M)
IRC	Research & Development Manager	(M; F = IR)
IA	Astronomer	(M)
IA	Audiologist	(M; F = IS)
IA	Biologist	(M; F = IRA)
IA	Clinical Psychologist	(F, M)
IA	Economist	(M)
IA	Experimental Psychologist	(M; F = IR)
IA	Geographer	(M; F = IRA)
IA	Inventor	(F; M = IR)
IA	Language Interpreter	(F, M)
IA	Medical Researcher	(M; F = IR)
IA	Psychologist	(F, M)
IA	Scientific Illustrator	(F)
IAR	College Professor	(F; M = IAS)
IAR	Computer Programmer/ Systems Analyst	(M; F = IR)
IAR	Physician	(F, M)
IAR	Sociologist	(F; M = AI)
IAS	Art Appraiser	
IAS	College Professor	(M; F = IAR)
IAS	Counseling Psychologist	(F, M)
IAS	Pediatrician	(M; F = IS)
IAS	Psychiatrist	(F, M)
IS	Audiologist	(F; M = IA)
IS	Educational Psychologist	(M; F = ISA)
IS	Pediatrician	(F; M = IAS)
ISR	Cardiopulmonary Technologist	
ISR	Paleontologist	
ISA	Educational Psychologist	(F; M = IS)
ISA	Physician Assistant	
ISE	Photographic Engineer	
ISC	Bursar	
ISC	Dialysis Technician	
IER	Project Engineer	
IER	Laboratory Supervisor	
IEA	Land Surveyor	
IEA	Quality Control Director	
IES	Dietitian	(F; M = SEC)
IES	Occupational Analyst	
IEC	Fire Protection Engineer	
IC	Computer Operator	(M; F = C)
ICR	Navigator	
ICR	Pharmacist	(F; M = ICE)
ICA	Mathematician	(M; F = IRC)
ICE	Pharmacist	(M; F = ICR)

Artistic Occupations and Theme Codes

Theme Code	Occupation	Gender Codes
A	Artist, Commercial	(M; F = ARI)
A	Artist, Fine	(M; F = AR)
A	Art Museum Director	(F, M)
A	Author	(F, M)
A	Entertainer	(F, M)
A	Lawyer	(F, M)
A	Librarian	(F, M)
A	Musician	(F, M)
A	Opera Singer	(F, M)
A	Poet	(F, M)
A	Reporter	(F, M)
A	Translator	(F; M = AI)
AR	Artist, Fine	(F; M = A)
AR	Drafting Technician	(F; M = RC)
AR	Landscape Gardener	(M; F = AI)
ARI	Architect	(F, M)
ARI	Artist, Commercial	(F; M = A)
ARI	Model Maker	
ARS	Stage Technician	
ARE	Cake Decorator	
ARE	Photographer	(F, M)
AI	Anthropologist	
AI	Ballet Dancer	(F; M = AE)
AI	Landscape Gardener	(F; M = AR)
AI	Social Scientist	(F; M = I)
AI	Sociologist	(M; F = IAR)
AI	Technical Writer	(M; F = AIR)
AI	Translator	(M; F = A)
AIR	Landscape Architect	
AIR	Medical Illustrator	(F, M)
AIR	Sculptor	(M; F = AER)
AIR	Technical Writer	(F; M = AI)
AIS	Orchestra Conductor	
AIS	Paper and Prints Restorer	
AIE	Cryptanalyst	
AIE	Motion Pictures Set Designer	
AS	Art Teacher	(M; F = ASE)
AS	Music Teacher	(M; F = SA)
AS	Optical Effects Layout Person	
AS	Public Administrator	(M; F = A)
AS	Singing Messenger	
AS	Writing Teacher	(F, M)
ASR	Exhibit Builder	
ASR	Painting Restorer	
ASI	Dance Therapist	
ASI	Exhibit Artist	
ASI	Television Technician	
ASE	Art Teacher	(F; M = AS)
ASE	Composer	
ASE	English Teacher	(F, M)
ASE	Pastry Chef	
ASE	Playwright	
ASE	Public Administrator	(M; F = AER)
ASC	Police Artist	
AE	Advertising Executive	(F, M)
AE	Ballet Dancer	(F; M = AI)
AE	Broadcaster	(F, M)
AE	Children's Clothes Designer	(F)
AE	Costume Designer	(F)
AE	Fashion Model	(F)
AE	Illustrator	(F)
AE	Interior Decorator	(M; F = EA)
AE	Public Relations Director	(F, M)
AER	Amusement Park Entertainer	
AER	Equestrian	
AER	Makeup Artist	
AER	Public Administrator	(F; M = ASE)
AER	Sculptor	(F; M = AIR)
AEI	Arranger	
AEI	Package Designer	
AEI	Puppeteer	
AEI	Screen Writer	
AES	Account Executive	
AES	Choreographer	
AES	Copy Writer	
AES	Corporate Trainer	(F, M)
AES	Creative Director	
AES	Editor	
AES	Industrial Designer	
AES	Wedding Consultant	
AEC	Photojournalist	
ACS	Graphologist	

Social Occupations and Theme Codes

Theme Code	Occupation	Gender Codes
S	Child Care Provider	(F)
S	Elementary School Teacher	(F, M)
S	Guidance Counselor	(F, M)
S	Public Health Nurse	(F, M)
SR	Medication Aide	
SR	Physical Education Teacher	(M; F = SRC)
SRI	Home Health Technician	
SRI	Stock Control Clerk	
SRE	Agricultural Extension Agent	(M)
SRE	Animal Keeper	
SRE	Orderly	
SRE	Recreation Leader	(F; M = SE)
SRC	Job Development Specialist	
SRC	Mail Carrier	
SRC	Physical Education Teacher	(F; M = SR)
SI	Cardiac Monitor Technician	
SI	Nurse, RN	(F; M = SAI)
SI	Student Personnel Worker	(M)
SIR	Athletic Trainer	(M; F = RIS)
SIR	Orientation Therapist for Persons with Visual Disabilities	
SIR	Physical Therapist	(F, M)
SIR	Podiatrist	
SIA	School Psychologist	(F, M)
SIE	Correctional Agency Director	
SIE	Head Nurse	
SIE	Medical Records Administrator	
SIE	Nursing Instructor	
SIE	Psychiatric Technician	
SIE	School Nurse	
SIC	Index Editor	
SA	Foreign Language Teacher	(M; F = SAE)
SA	Mental Health Worker	(M; F = SE)
SA	Minister	(M; F = SAR)
SA	Music Teacher	(F; M = AS)
SA	Occupational Therapist	(M; F = SAR)
SA	Social Worker	(F, M)
SA	Speech Pathologist	(F, M)
SA	Writer, Children's Books	(F)
SAR	Minister	(F; M = SA)
SAR	Occupational Therapist	(F; M = SA)
SAI	Nurse, RN	(M; F = SI)
SAE	Foreign Language Teacher	(F; M = SA)
SAE	Food & Drug Inspector	
SE	Community Service Organization Director	(F, M)
SE	Football Coach	(M)
SE	High School Counselor	(F, M)
SE	Home Economics Teacher	(F)
SE	Juvenile Parole Officer	(M)
SE	Labor Arbitrator	(M)
SE	Mental Health Worker	(F; M = SA)
SE	Parks and Recreation Coordinator	(F, M)
SE	Recreation Leader	(M; F = SRE)
SE	Special Education Teacher	(F; M = SEA)
SE	Vocational Counselor	(F)
SER	Department Store Manager	
SER	Fast Food Services Manager	
SER	Hospital Administrator	
SER	School Superintendent	
SEI	Loan Officer	
SEI	Radio and TV Producer	
SEA	Dean of Students	
SEA	Occupational Therapy Aide	
SEA	School Administrator	(F; M = SEC)
SEA	Social Science Teacher	(F, M)
SEA	Special Education Teacher	(M; F = SE)
SEC	Dietitian	(M; F = IES)
SEC	Disk Jockey	
SEC	Employment Interviewer	
SEC	Political Scientist	
SEC	School Administrator	(M; F = SEA)
SEC	Security Guard	
SC	Airline Ticket Agent	
SC	City or State Employee	(F; M = RSC)
SCI	Packaging Engineer	
SCI	Preparole Counseling Aide	
SCE	Educational Consultant	
SCE	Eligibility Worker	
SCE	Interpreter for Persons with Hearing Disabilities	
SCE	Nurse, LPN	(F, M)
SCE	Rehabilitation Counselor	(M)
SCE	Stunt Performer	
SCE	Taxicab Coordinator	

Enterprising Occupations and Theme Codes

Theme Code	Occupation	Gender Codes
E	Athletic Director	(M; F = RSE)
E	Chamber of Commerce Executive	(M; F = EC)
E	Foreign Correspondent	(F)
E	Funeral Director	(M; F = ECS)
E	Life Insurance Agent	(F, M)
E	Personnel Director	(F; M = ES)
E	Realtor	(F, M)
E	Retailer	(F, M)
E	Sports Reporter	(M)
E	Traveling Salesperson	(M)
ER	Auctioneer	(M)
ER	Chef	(M; F = ERA)
ER	Dance Teacher	(F)
ER	Nursery Manager	(M)
ER	Optician	(M; F = ECR)
ER	Pest Controller	(M; F = CE)
ER	Professional Athlete	(M; F = RE)
ER	Secret Service Agent	(F; M = RE)
ERI	Pilot	(F; M = RI)
ERA	Chef	(F; M = ER)
ERA	Park Superintendent	
ERA	Stockbroker	(F; M = EC)
ERS	Bellhop	
ERS	Ski Patroller	
ERS	Warehouse Supervisor	
EI	Computer Salesperson	(M; F = ES)
EIR	Foreign Exchange Trader	
EIR	Industrial Engineer	
EIR	Investments Manager	(F; M = ECI)
EIR	Motorcycle Racer	
EIA	Communications Consultant	
EIS	Controller	
EIS	Dental Hygienist	(F)
EIS	Training and Education Manager	
EIC	Chief Bank Examiner	
EIC	Industrial Health Engineer	
EA	Hair Stylist	(M; F = EC)
EA	Interior Decorator	(F; M = AE)
EA	Marketing Executive	(F, M)
EA	Professional Dancer	(F)
EAS	Elected Public Official	(F; M = ESA)
EAS	Flight Attendant	(F, M)
EAS	Housing Manager	
EAS	Human Resources Director	(F; M = ES)
EAC	Florist	(F, M)

Theme Code	Occupation	Gender Codes
ES	Computer Salesperson	(F; M = EI)
ES	County Extension Agent	(M)
ES	Human Resources Director	(M; F = EAS)
ES	Industrial Salesperson	(M)
ES	Occupational Health Nurse	(F)
ES	Personnel Director	(M; F = E)
ES	Sales Manager	(F, M)
ES	TV Announcer	(F, M)
ESR	Airport Manager	
ESR	Financial Planner	
ESR	Museum Director	
ESR	University Business Manager	
ESR	Urban Planner	
ESI	Estate Planner	
ESI	Lifeguard	
ESI	Securities Trader	
ESA	College Admissions Director	
ESA	Elected Public Official	(M; F = EAS)
ESA	Head Waiter/Head Waitress	
ESA	Lobbyist	
ESC	Employment Manager	(M; F = CSE)
ESC	Media Director	
ESC	Receptionist	(F)
ESC	Travel Bureau Manager	(M; F = ECS)
EC	Appliance Salesperson	(M)
EC	Buyer	(F, M)
EC	Chamber of Commerce Executive	(F; M = E)
EC	Corporation Executive	
EC	Hair Stylist	(F; M = EA)
EC	Launderer	(M)
EC	Manufacturer	(M)
EC	Office Manager	(M; F = C)
EC	Retail Clerk	(F; M = ECS)
EC	Stockbroker	(M; F = ERA)
EC	Wholesaler	(M)
ECR	Agribusiness Manager	(M)
ECR	Factory Manager	(M)
ECR	Farm Supply Manager	(M)
ECR	Optician	(F; M = ER)
ECR	Purchasing Agent	(F, M)
ECR	Restaurant Manager	(F, M)
ECI	Investments Manager	(M; F = EIR)
ECA	Store Manager	(F; M = ECS)
ECA	Travel Agent	(F, M)
ECS	Auto Sales Dealer	(M)
ECS	Funeral Director	(F; M = E)
ECS	Hotel Manager	(F, M)
ECS	Housekeeping & Maintenance Supervisor	(F, M)
ECS	Retail Clerk	(M; F = EC)
ECS	Store Manager	(M; F = ECA)
ECS	Travel Agency Manager	(F; M = ESC)

Conventional Occupations and Theme Codes

Theme Code	Occupation	Gender Codes
C	Air Force Enlisted Personnel	(F; M = R)
C	Bank Cashier	(F; M = CS)
C	Bookkeeper	(F, M)
C	Computer Operator	(F; M = IC)
C	Hospital Records Clerk	(F)
C	Hospital Secretary	(F)
C	IRS Tax Auditor	(F, M)
C	Medical Records Technician	(F, M)
C	Office Clerk	(F, M)
C	Office Manager	(F; M = EC)
C	Printer	(M)
C	Production Manager	(M)
C	Proofreader	(F)
CR	Army Enlisted Personnel	(M; F = CRS)
CR	Sewing Machine Operator	(F, M)
CR	Telephone Operator	(F; M = CER)
CRI	Business Programmer	
CRI	Fire Protection Engineering Technician	
CRS	Army Enlisted Personnel	(F; M = CR)
CRS	Crew Scheduler	
CRS	Data Processing Control Clerk	
CRS	Highway Maintenance Worker	
CRS	Marine Corps Enlisted Personnel	(F; M = RC)
CRS	Sound Cutter	
CRS	Stock Transfer Clerk	
CRE	Army Noncommissioned Officer	(F, M)
CRE	Electrologist	
CRE	Garment Inspector	
CRE	Military Enlisted Personnel	(F; M = RCE)
CI	Actuary	(F, M)
CIR	Mathematics Teacher	(F; M = CIS)
CIS	Mathematics Teacher	(M; F = CIR)
CIS	Polygraph Examiner	
CIE	Building Inspector	
CA	Paralegal	(M; F = CE)
CS	Bank Cashier	(M; F = C)
CS	Dietary Assistant	(F)
CS	Surveillance System Monitor	

Theme Code	Occupation	Gender Codes
CSR	Collection Clerk	
CSR	Food and Beverage Controller	
CSI	Editorial Assistant	
CSI	Financial Analyst	
CSE	County Welfare Worker	(M)
CSE	Dental Assistant	(F)
CSE	Dietitian	(M; F = ISR)
CSE	Employment Manager	(F; M = ESC)
CSE	Executive Housekeeper	(F, M)
CSE	Farmer	(F; M = RC)
CSE	Systems Accountant	
CSE	Title Examiner	
CSE	Underwriter	
CE	Accountant	(M, F)
CE	Administrative Assistant	(F)
CE	Baker	(F; M = RE)
CE	Banker	(F, M)
CE	Certified Public Accountant	(F, M)
CE	Courtroom Stenographer	(F)
CE	Credit Manager	(F, M)
CE	Department Store Clerk	(F, M)
CE	IRS Agent	(F, M)
CE	Office Worker	(F)
CE	Paralegal	(F; M = CA)
CE	Pest Controller	(F; M = ER)
CE	Small Business Owner	(F; M = RE)
CE	Tax Preparer	
CER	Animated Cartoon Painter	
CER	Budget Analyst	
CER	Dairy Processing Manager	(M)
CER	Grain Elevator Manager	(M)
CER	Procurement Engineer	
CER	Ski Tow Operator	
CER	Telephone Operator	(M; F = CR)
CEI	Customs Inspector	
CES	Business Education Teacher	(F, M)
CES	Cost Accountant	
CES	Food Service Manager	(F, M)
CES	Nursing Home Administrator	(F, M)
CES	Script Reader	
CES	Secretary	(F)
CES	Usher	

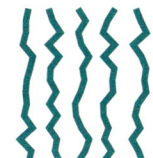

Index

Academic Comfort scale. *See under* Special Scales (1985 *Strong*)
ADA. *See* Americans with Disabilities Act (ADA; 1990)
Adams, H. L., 260
Administration, 30, 282
  emotions during test, 188, 201, 202
  orientation, 184–185
  reevaluation, 24, 188, 202
  with students, 232, 246–247
Administrative Indexes, 186, 188, 201
  changes in 1994 version, 20–21, 22
  description, 2–3, 29
  Infrequent Responses index, 20–21, 22, 179–180, 186
  "Like," "Indifferent," "Dislike" percent indexes, 21, 29, 175–179
  Total Responses index, 20–21, 22, 175
Adult Career Concerns Inventory (Super et al.), 296
Adults, 23–24
  career exploration
    change in career, 221–224
    within organizations, 216–221
    outplacement, 224–225
    retirement, 225, 227, 228
    training, 217, 225–227, 294
    vocational/technical areas, 215–216, 217, 218–219
  interpretation, 20, 157, 194
Age groups, 4, 109, 245, 246
  guidelines for use, 23–24
  in racial and ethnic sample, 262, 263
Allen, K. T., 233
Alston, H. L., 258–259
Americans with Disabilities Act (ADA; 1990), 281, 282, 283, 289
Anadon, M., 258–259
Anastasi, A., 255
Answer sheet. *See* Item Booklet/Answer Sheet
Apostal, R. A., 294
Arbona, C., 260
Arias, F. G., 260–261
Artistic (A) Theme, 47, 305
  changes in 1994 version, 16–18
  and Personal Style Scales, 74, 158, 163–164
  See also General Occupational Themes (GOTs)
Assessment tools, 3, 181–183, 257, 296
Athelstan, G. P., 288, 289

Basic Interest Scales (BISs), 2, 23, 24
  applications
    at-risk students, 250–252
    college students, 232, 233, 237–238
    counseling, 78–80
    high school students, 246
  changes in 1994 version, 12–13, 18, 20, 21–22, 75, 82–83
  cultural differences, 257
    between groups, 263–266, 267–269
    within groups, 266, 270–275, 277–279
  defined, 70–78
  gender differences, 292–296, 297, 302, 306
  interpretation, 186–192, 195
    elevated Profiles, 203–207
    flat Profiles, 197–203
    inconsistent scores, 208–211
    preinterpretation, 186–187
  relationship
    to BISs, 73–74
    to GOT scales, 53, 69, 70–78, 83, 86–87
    to OSs, 91, 105, 106–107
    to Personal Style Scales, 164, 165
    to Profile, 21–22, 27, 28, 79
  reliability, 82–85, 88–90
  scale construction, 12–13, 80–83
  validity, 85, 91–104, 153
Betz, N. E., 237, 255, 293, 295–296
Bias, 3
  gender, 291–292
  occupational stereotypes, 235, 240, 285–286, 295–296
  people with disabilities, 285–286
  racial and ethnic groups, 258
Bigley, S. E., 151, 152
Bingham, R. P., 256, 258
Boggs, K. R., 295
Bolton, B., 288
Bordieri, J. E., 285
Borgen, F. H., 80, 81, 83, 112, 160, 162, 255, 259
Bradley, M., 217
Brandt, J. E., 151, 152
Brew, S., 190
Brookings, J. B., 288
Brown, S. D., 296

385

CACG. *See* Computers, assistance in career guidance
Cairo, P. C., 80, 227
California Psychological Inventory, 30
Campbell, D. P., 6, 9, 34, 40, 43, 44, 53, 58, 59, 80, 81, 83, 84, 91, 112, 121, 151, 156, 160, 162, 211, 237, 305
Campbell, V. L., 231, 232
Care, E., 261
Career Beliefs Inventory (CBI; Krumboltz), 222, 238, 296
Career counseling. *See* Counseling
Career-Development Assessment and Counseling (C-DAC) battery, 296
Career Development Inventory (Thompson et al.), 296
Career exploration. *See* Exploration, career
Carter, R. T., 258, 260
CBI. *See Career Beliefs Inventory* (CBI; Krumboltz)
Chang, W. C., 258–259
Chartrand, J. M., 53, 222
Chevier, J. M., 261
Choices. *See* Decision making
Clark, K. E., 81
Clemmons, D. C., 288–289
Cohen, J., 147
Cole, N. S., 53
College students, 84–85, 294
  choices
    academic major, 232–237, 240
    activities, 233, 242
    career, 237–240
    counseling, 240–242
  guidelines for use, 23–24, 231–232
  interpretation
    GOT scales, 51
    Personal Style Scales, 20, 157, 158, 194
  See also Educational level
Collins, R. C., 295
Computers
  assistance in career guidance, 182, 246, 282
  data collection, 11, 35, 110–111
  scoring by, 25, 30
  See also Scoring
Concurrent validity, 91, 234, 237–238
  of BISs, 91, 92–104
  of GOT scales, 59, 63
  of OSs, 15, 16, 112, 114–121, 130, 147–148
  See also Validity
Consulting Psychologists Press, 232–233
Conventional (C) Theme, 49–50, 295
  and BISs, 77–78
  changes in 1994 version, 13, 16–18
  and Personal Style Scales, 159, 163–164
  See also General Occupational Themes (GOTs)
Cook, M., 261
Cooper, S. E., 181
Counseling, 28, 160
  applications, 3–8
    at-risk students, 250–252
    college students, 232, 238–242
    high school students, 246–247
    life-style issues, 195, 223–224
    limits, 24
    people with disabilities, 285–287
    with support materials, 238–240
  cultural appropriateness, 255–258
  gender differences, 293–296
  interpretation, 181–183
    BIS scores, 78–80
    GOT scores, 51, 60–62, 65–67

Counseling (continued)
    Personal Style Scales, 187, 193–195
    preinterpretation, 183, 185–187
    Profile, 2, 26, 29, 187–192
    Theme codes, 121–130, 189, 192–193
    unpredictable scales, 153–154
  orientation, 184–185
  sequence, 182–184, 256
  See also Interpretation
Creaser, J. W., 16, 153
Crites, J. O., 3
Cross-Cultural use. *See* Racial and ethnic groups
Cudeck, R., 6, 258–259
Curnow, T. C., 288

Dancer, L. S., 260
Danehey, A. J., 283, 288
"Data Base Links Employees' Interests to Real Jobs," 217–218
Data collection, 9–10, 11
  gender in, 36–40, 41
  item selection, 33–42
  for racial and ethnic groups, 261–279
DeBlassie, R., 260
Decision making, 3–5, 256
  and elevated Profiles, 203–207, 212, 235
  and flat Profiles, 197–203, 212, 224–225, 296
  and inconsistent scores, 208–211
  and opposite interest scores, 207–208
  and OSs, 105–106
  for people with disabilities, 285, 286, 288–289
  and Personal Style Scales, 211–212
  after testing, 181–182, 184, 189
  See also Counseling
DeWitt, D. W., 193
Dictionary of Holland Occupational Codes (Gottfredson & Holland), 192, 207, 215–216
Dictionary of Occupational Titles (DOT), 24, 246
Disabilities, people with, 281–282
  applications, 283–287
  interpretation, 283
  vocational interests, 285, 288–289
Discover, 246
"Dislike" response percentages, 25, 29, 42, 186
  for BISs, 79, 177
  changes in 1994 version, 11, 16, 17, 21, 111–113, 120, 178
  for GOT scales, 50, 177
  interpretation, 175–179
  item selection, 33–35
  for OSs, 106, 111–113, 120
  for Profiles, 29, 204
Dissatisfaction
  with careers, 221–224, 240–242
  with jobs, 5, 44, 183
  plateauing, 216, 217, 219–221
Dodrill, C. B., 288–289
Dolliver, R. H., 151, 152, 237
Douce, L. A., 156, 160
Doughtie, E. B., 258–259
Dunnette, M. D., 147

Eastes, S., 80, 81, 83, 162
Educational level
  and job training, 217, 225–227, 294
  in racial and ethnic sample, 262, 263
  reading level, 23–24, 245, 246, 282
  and validity of Personal Style Scales, 20, 156, 158, 166, 167, 171–172
  See also College students; High school students

Edwards Personal Preference Schedule (EPPS), 59
Elster, R. S., 147
Enhanced Guide for Occupational Exploration, The (Maze & Mayall), 108
Enterprising (E) Theme, 48–49
   and BISs, 74, 75–77
   changes in 1994 version, 16–18
   and Personal Style Scales, 75, 76, 77, 156, 163–164
   See also General Occupational Themes (GOTs)
EPPS. See *Edwards Personal Preference Schedule (EPPS)*
Evaluation on the job, 283–284
Exploration
   of college majors, 232–237, 240, 247–253
   of life issues, 4, 195, 223–224
   self-exploration, 4, 44, 183, 184
Exploration, career, 109
   career change, 221–224
   for college students, 237–240
   and flat Profiles, 200–201, 296
   for high school students, 247–253
   within organizations, 216–221
   outplacement, 224–225
   for people with disabilities, 283–289
   retirement, 225, 227, 228
   after test taking, 181–182, 183
   training, 217, 225–227, 294
   vocational identity, 80, 202
   vocational/technical jobs, 215–219
   for women, 294–296

Faking, 211
Farrugia, D., 288
Fouad, N. A., 6, 255, 256, 258–259, 260–261, 295
Foxworth, C. L., 21
Frank, A. C., 16, 153
Fraser, R. T., 288–289
Frederickson, R. H., 223
Fuchsberg, G., 226

Gaeddert, D., 204, 295
Gawhega, A., 260
Gender differences, 291–292
   in BISs, 292–296, 297, 306
   in counseling, 293–296
   in data collection, 35–40, 41
   in GOT scales, 59, 292–296, 297, 305–306
   interpretation, 293–296
   at item level, 297–300, 301
   in OSs, 292–296, 297, 300–307
   in Personal Style Scales, 20, 156, 159, 160, 162, 292–296, 297, 305–306
   on Profile, 160, 162
   at scale level, 300–306, 307
General Occupational Themes (GOTs), 2, 7, 55, 232
   applications
      at-risk students, 250–252
      client age, 23, 24
      college students, 233, 237–238, 241
   changes in 1994 version, 11–12, 21–22
   cultural differences, 257
      between groups, 263–266, 267–269
      within groups, 266, 270–275, 277–279
   gender differences, 59, 292–296, 297, 302, 305–306
   history and theory, 43–53
   interpretation, 51, 60–62, 65–67, 186–192
      life roles, 195
      opposite interest scores, 207–208

General Occupational Themes (continued)
   on Profile, 21–22, 28
      addition of in 1970s, 51–53
      elevated scores, 203–207
      flat scores, 197–203
      Snapshot summary, 26, 27
   relationship
      to BISs, 69, 70–80, 83, 86–87
      to OSs, 105, 106–107, 121–130
      to Personal Style Scales, 163–164
   reliability, 53–58
   scale construction, 11–12, 50–55
   validity, 58–67
   See also Holland's Themes; RIASEC Themes
General Reference Samples (GRSs), 28, 55, 56, 161–167
   cultural differences, 257, 266, 270–275, 277–279
   development, 11, 40–42, 110–111
   gender differences, 292–293
   See also Data collection; Samples
Gerstein, M., 227
Gibbs, J. T., 257
Gim, R. H. C., 257, 258
GIS. See *Guidance Information System (GIS)*
Glass, G. V., 148
Goodyear, R. K., 181, 182, 189
Gottfredson, G. D., 44, 192, 207, 215–216, 246
Gottfredson, L. S., 221
Groups
   interpretation of *Strong* results for, 189
   research on interests of, 6, 7
   See also Age groups; Occupational groups
Guidance Information System (GIS), 246
Gutteridge, T. G., 217, 219, 226
Gysbers, N. C., 295

Hackett, G., 294–295, 296
Hageseth, J. A., 7
Hall, D. T., 219
Hammer, A. L., 20, 184, 193–194, 201, 203, 204, 207, 217, 225, 296
Handbook for the Strong Vocational Interest Blank (Campbell, D. P.), 81, 91
Hanlon, R. J., 6
Hansen, J. C., 4, 6, 9, 23, 34, 40, 43, 44, 53, 58, 59, 80, 84, 91, 112, 121, 130, 151, 152, 153, 156, 160, 181, 197, 198, 202, 203, 204, 224, 227, 231, 233, 234, 235, 237, 246, 247, 255, 258–261, 295, 305
Harmon, L. W., 112, 151, 305
Harper, G. T., 259
Harrell, M. S., 227
Harrell, T. W., 227
Harrington, T. F., 258–259
Hartman, B. W., 201
Haverkamp, B., 153, 181, 231
Haviland, M., 259
Hayles, V. R., 259
Heesacker, R. S., 295
High school students, 84–85
   administration of *Strong* to, 23–24, 246–247
   choosing careers and college majors, 247–253
   interpretation, 246–247
      GOT scales, 51
      Personal Style Scales, 158, 194
   See also Educational level
"High School Students Test Their Dreams," 247
"High School Students Turn to the Strong for Career Direction," 250

Hill, R., 218
Hines, H., 259
Hirsh, S. K., 189, 190
Hoese, J., 231
Holland, J. L., 43–44, 52, 53, 54, 58, 106, 163, 182, 192, 207, 215–216, 246, 259
Holland's Themes, 44–50
　See also General Occupational Themes (GOTs); *individual themes*
Holland's theory, 11, 15, 27, 51
　assumptions, 43–44
　history, 52–53
　and Personal Style Scales, 163–164
　See also General Occupational Themes (GOTs)
Holvey, J. M., 282, 288
Hood, A. B., 151, 152
Hutchins, E. B., 6

"Indifferent" response percentages, 25, 42, 246
　changes in 1994 version, 21, 112–113, 120, 178
　for GOT scales, 50
　interpretation, 175–179, 186
　item selection, 33–35
　for OSs, 112–113, 120
　for Profiles, 29
Infrequent Responses (IR) index, 186
　changes in 1994 version, 20–21, 22
　interpretation and use, 179–180
Interest inventories, 1, 255
　applications, 3–8, 231
　effectiveness, 33, 150, 183
Internal consistency reliability, 237–238
　of BISs, 82–83
　of GOT scales, 11, 53–54
　of Personal Style Scales, 164, 166
　See also Reliability
Interpretation
　challenges, 197–212
　　elevated scores, 192, 203–207, 212, 235
　　flat scores, 183, 186, 192, 197–203, 212, 224–225, 296
　　gender differences, 293–296
　　inconsistent scores, 208–211
　　opposite interests scores, 188, 192, 207–208
　counseling sequence, 182–184, 256
　generalization using Theme codes, 121–130, 189, 192–193
　group, 189
　orientation, 184–185
　sections of Profile
　　Administrative Indexes, 175–180
　　BISs, 186–192, 195
　　GOT scales, 51, 60–62, 65–67, 186–192, 195
　　OSs, 106–107, 186–193
　　Personal Style Scales, 155–161, 187, 193–195, 211–212
　strategies, 181–195
　with various populations
　　at-risk students, 250–252
　　career changers, 221–223
　　college students, 233
　　culturally diverse, 255–258
　　high school students, 246–247
　　people with disabilities, 282–287
　　retirees, 225, 227, 228
　　women, 294–295
　See also Counseling
Introversion–Extroversion Scale. See under Special Scales (1985 *Strong*)

Investigative (I) Theme, 46, 295
　and BISs, 72–73, 74
　changes in 1994 version, 13, 16–18, 75
　and Personal Style Scales, 156, 158, 159, 163–164
　See also General Occupational Themes (GOTs)
Irvin, J. A., 151, 152
Item Booklet/Answer Sheet, 33
　changes in 1994 version, 9–10, 21, 75
　guidelines for use, 2, 25, 30, 246
　reading level, 23–24, 246
Items, 2, 30
　changes in 1994 version, 10–11
　interpretive use of, 35–42
　reading level, 23–24, 245, 246
　sections, 25–26
　selection, 10–11, 33–35, 108
　See also Responses

Jacobs, M., 16, 153
Jacoby, B., 233
Jagger, L., 282, 288
Janikowski, T. P., 285
Job accommodation, 283–284
Job design, 7–8
Job dissatisfaction, 5, 44, 183
　career dissatisfaction vs., 221–224, 240–242
　plateauing, 216, 217, 219–221
Job selection, 4–5
Joahnsson, C. B., 43, 53, 80, 81, 83, 91, 153, 160, 162, 305
Johnson, R. W., 91, 153, 209, 231
Jones, N. L., 289
Jordaan, J. P., 296
Journal of Educational Psychology, 150

Kirk, B. A., 16, 153, 260
Kivlighan, D. M., Jr., 7
Konrads, S., 261
Korben, D., 59
Kragie, E. R., 227
Krumboltz, J. D., 203, 222, 238, 296
Kummerow, J. K., 184, 193–194, 201, 203, 204, 207
Kunce, J. E., 151, 237

Lamb, R. R., 258–259
Language
　item changes, 10–11, 75
　and limited English-speaking clients, 24, 185
　and reading level, 23–24, 245, 246
　translations, 6, 30–31, 256–257, 261
Lapan, R. T., 295
Leadership Style scale, 238, 242
　and BISs, 74, 75, 76, 77
　interpretation, 156, 159–160, 193, 194, 212
　scale construction, 18–20, 161–164, 165
　See also Personal Style Scales
Learning Environment scale, 234, 241, 252
　and BISs, 75, 76, 77
　interpretation, 156, 158–159, 193, 194, 211–212
　scale construction, 18–20, 161–164, 165
　See also Personal Style Scales
Leibowitz, Z. B., 217, 219, 226
Leisure activities, 8, 44, 80, 193, 233, 242
Leong, F. T. L., 256, 257, 258
Levin, A., 190

Levinson, E. M., 245
Lewis, E. T., 181
Lewis, M., 292
Lichtman, M., 227
"Like" response percentages, 25, 42, 246
  for BISs, 79
  changes in 1994 version, 11, 16, 21, 111–113, 120, 178
  gender differences in, 297–300
  for GOT scales, 50
  interpretation, 175–179, 186
  item selection, 33–35
  for occupational groups, 36–40, 41
  for OSs, 111–113, 120
  for Profiles, 29
    elevated scores, 204
    flat scores, 198–204, 224–225
Limited English-speaking clients, 24, 185, 256–257
Lindeman, R. H., 296
Lonborg, S. D., 294–295, 296
Lonner, W. J., 6, 260
Lowman, R. L., 238

Macdaid, G. P., 203, 296
Macy, F. U., 223
Making Vocational Choices: A Theory of Careers (Holland), 43
Malett, S. D., 240
Mancuso, L. L., 281, 283
Manual for the Strong-Campbell Interest Inventory (Campbell, D. P.; 1974), 81
Marshall, J., 295
Mayall, D., 108
Maze, M., 108
MBTI. See *Myers-Briggs Type Indicator* (MBTI)
McArthur, C., 151, 152
McAuliffe, G., 282, 288
McCaulley, M. H., 193–194, 296
McDaniels, C., 223, 295
McGovern, T. V., 7
McGregor, P., 231
McKenna, P., 222
Men-in-General (1985 *Strong*), 11, 111, 295
  See also General Reference Samples (GRSs)
Miller, C. D., 245
Miller, M. F., 202
Miller, M. J., 21
Minnesota Multiphasic Personality Inventory (MMPI), 151
Minnesota Vocational Interest Inventory (Clark), 81
Mirvis, P. H., 217, 218, 224, 294
MMPI. See *Minnesota Multiphasic Personality Inventory (MMPI)*
Montoya, H., 260
Morrill, W. H., 245, 295
Most, R., 1
Musgrave, J., 285
Myers-Briggs Type Indicator (MBTI)
  integration with *Strong*, 30, 184, 193–194, 201, 204, 217, 296
  use with college students, 226, 238
Myers, I. B., 193–194, 296
Myers, R. A., 296

Naylor, F., 261
Neapolitan, J., 222
Nester, M. A., 282
Neubert, D. A., 283, 288
Neukrug, E., 282, 288
Nevill, D. D., 224, 238

Nevo, O., 224, 232, 235
Nicholson, N., 222
Niles, S. G., 296
Norms, 3, 6, 24
  BISs, 83, 84, 85
  GOT scales, 55
  OSs, 120
  Personal Style Scales, 162

Occupational groups, 5–6, 44
  differences between, 177–178
  item responses for, 35–40, 41
  in OS construction, 108–113, 120
  in racial and ethnic sample, 262–263, 264
  and validity of Personal Style Scales, 166, 168–170
Occupational Outlook Handbook (U.S. Department of Labor), 184, 246
Occupational Scales (OSs), 2, 23, 42, 215
  applications, 105–106
    college students, 232–234, 237–238, 241
    high school students, 250
  changes in 1994 version, 9–10, 11, 13–18, 19, 21–22
  cultural differences
    between groups, 263–266, 267–269
    within groups, 266, 270–275, 277–279
  derivation of Theme codes, 121–130
  gender differences, 292–296, 297
  interpretation, 106–107, 186–193
    elevated scores, 203–207
    flat scores, 197–203
    inconsistent scores, 208–211
    unpredictable scales, 153–154
  relationship
    to BISs, 78, 80, 91, 105, 106–107
    to GOT scales, 53, 105, 106–107, 121–130
  reliability, 112, 114–121, 130, 131–146, 153
  as reported on Profile, 21–22, 26–29
  scale characteristics, 114–130
  scale construction, 13–18, 19, 40, 107–113, 120
  validity, 15, 16, 109, 112, 114–121, 130, 147–153
Ohlde, C. D., 202
Oliver, L., 189, 217, 227
Organizations, career development in, 216
  career tracks, 218–219
  planning, 217–218
  plateaus, 219–221
Osborne, W. L., 296
O'Shea, A. J., 258–259
Outplacement, 224–225

"Pac Bell Uses the *Strong* and MBTI for Career Growth and Team Building," 216
Pape, D. A., 281
Partridge, E. D., 282, 288
Pask-McCartney, C., 204, 207
Percent overlap, 114–120, 130, 147–149
Perosa, L. M., 212, 221, 223, 224
Perosa, S. L., 212, 221, 223, 224
Personal Style Scales, 2–3, 70
  applications, 193, 238, 241
  content, 155–161
  cultural differences
    between groups, 263–266, 267–269
    within groups, 275
  gender differences, 292–296, 297, 302, 306–307

Personal Style Scales (continued)
  interpretation, 155–161, 186–187
    challenges, 211–212
    strategies, 193–195
  introduction of in 1994, 13, 18, 19, 20, 21–22, 160
  on Profile, 21–22, 28, 29
  relationship
    to BISs, 164, 165
    to GOT scales, 163–164
  reliability, 164, 166, 167
  scale construction, 18–20, 161–164, 165
  validity, 20, 156, 158, 166–172, 185–186
  See also individual scales
Peterson, G. W., 182, 233
Peterson, R. A., 80, 81, 83, 160, 162
Pinkney, J. W., 198, 202
Plateau, career, 216, 217, 219–221
Predictive validity, 91, 149, 259–260
  of BISs, 153
  for career choice by college students, 237–238
  for choice of major, 234–237
  of OSs, 109, 149–153
  of SCII, 151–152
  of SVIB, 151–152, 226–227
  See also Validity
Prediger, D. J., 26
Profile, 188, 201
  BIS scores on, 21–22, 27–28, 79
  changes in 1994 version, 17, 18, 19, 21–22, 26–27
  description, 2–5, 26–29, 292–293
  and gender differences, 160, 162
  GOT scores on, 21–22, 26–28, 197–207
  interpretation, 2, 185–192
    elevated scores, 192, 203–207, 212, 235
    flat scores, 183, 186, 192, 197–203, 212, 224–225, 296
    inconsistent scores, 208–211
    Snapshot, 186–187, 190–192, 198–203
  OS scores on, 21–22, 26–29, 197–207
  Personal Style Scales on, 21–22, 28, 29
  reliability, 246
  of SVIB, 51–52
  validity, 185–186
Public Law 101–336 (ADA), 281, 282, 283, 289

Racial and ethnic groups, 201
  counseling, 255–258
  data collection, 261–279
  demographic characteristics, 262–263
  item responses, 226, 270
  occupational samples, 266–275
  scale differences, 265–266, 270–275
  research, 6–7, 258–261
    future needs, 261, 275
Randahl, G. J., 153, 181, 231
Reading level, 23–24, 245, 246, 282
Realistic (R) Theme, 45–46
  and BISs, 70–72
  changes in 1994 version, 13, 16–18
  gender differences in, 295, 305
  and Personal Style Scales, 156, 159, 163–164
  See also General Occupational Themes (GOTs)
Reardon, R. C., 233
Reliability, 6, 237–238
  of BISs, 82–85, 88–90
  changes in 1994 version, 11–12
  of GOT scales, 11, 53–58
  of high school students' results, 246

Reliability (continued)
  of items, 35, 40
  of OSs, 15, 16, 112, 114–121, 130, 131–146, 153
  of Personal Style Scales, 164, 166, 167
  of SVIB, 51–52
  See also Internal consistency reliability; Test-retest reliability
Responses, 22, 33
  to sampling, 109–110
  by sections, 25–26
  See also Administrative Indexes; "Dislike" response percentages; "Indifferent" response percentages; "Like" response percentages
Retirement, 225, 227, 228
RIASEC Themes, 58, 156, 157
  changes in 1994 version, 15, 16–18, 19
  theory, 44
  use of Theme codes for OSs, 121–130
  See also General Occupational Themes (GOTs); *individual themes*
Risk Taking/Adventure scale, 76, 201, 302
  interpretation, 156, 160–161, 193, 194–195, 212
  scale construction, 18–20, 161, 162–164, 165
  See also Personal Style Scales
Robbins, S. R., 202
Roessler, R., 288
Rohe, D. E., 288, 289
Rounds, J. B., 53, 58, 164
Rue, P., 233

Sackett, S., 233
Salience Inventory (Nevill & Super), 224, 296
Salomone, P. R., 204, 207, 222
Samples, 108–113, 120
  See also Data collection; General Reference Samples (GRSs); Occupational groups
Sampson, J. P., 233
Saveri, A., 294
Scharf, R., 245
Schuerger, J. M., 246
Schumrum, T., 201
Scoring, 2, 25, 30, 32, 183, 192
  See also Computers
Scott, T. B., 258–259
Self-exploration, 4, 44, 183, 184
Shaffer, G. S., 59, 227
Shah, I., 6, 260
Shahnasarian, M., 182, 233
Shelton, D., 285
Shore, J. E., 217, 219, 226
Shuttleworth, C., 295
SII. See Strong Interest Inventory (1985); *Strong Interest Inventory* (1994)
Slaney, R. B., 181
Smith, M. L., 148
Social (S) Theme, 47–48
  and BISs, 74–75
  changes in 1994 version, 13, 16–18
  gender differences in, 295, 296
  and Personal Style Scales, 75, 156, 163–164
  See also General Occupational Themes (GOTs)
Special Scales (1985 *Strong*)
  Academic Comfort, 18, 19, 20, 158, 211, 235
  Introversion-Extroversion, 18, 19, 159, 193
Spitzer, D., 245
Spokane, A., 53, 151–152, 189, 217, 227, 237, 240
"Stanford Uses the *Strong* and MBTI to Help MBAs Successfully Market Themselves," 226
Stauffer, E., 6

Stocco, J., 23, 84, 246
"*Strong* Assists High-Tech Employees," 218
Strong-Campbell Interest Inventory
   predictive validity, 151–152
Strong, E. K., Jr., 1, 40, 43, 51–52, 105, 107, 150, 152, 232–233, 246, 260, 291
"*Strong* Helps People Cope with Spinal Cord Injury," 288, 289
"*Strong* Integral to Structured Counseling Program," 232
Strong Interest Inventory (1985), 217
   comparison with 1994 version, 9–10, 25, 26
      Administrative Indexes, 20–21, 22
      BISs, 12–13, 18, 21–22, 75, 82–83
      GOT scales, 11–12, 21–22
      items, 10–11, 75
      OSs, 9–10, 11, 13–18, 19, 21–22, 107, 108, 121
   Men-in-General, 11, 111, 295
   Profile, 21–22
   Special Scales, 18, 19, 20, 158, 159, 193, 211, 235
   Women-in-General, 11, 111, 295
Strong Interest Inventory (1994)
   applications, 3–8
      adults, 215–228
      age groups, 4, 23–24, 245, 246
      college students, 231–242
      for decision making, 3–4
      groups, 6, 7, 189
      guidelines, 23–24
      high school students, 245–253
      limits, 24
      people with disabilities, 281–289
      racial and ethnic groups, 255–279
   assumptions and capabilities, 2–3
   changes from earlier versions, 9–10, 25, 26
      addition of Personal Style Scales, 13, 18, 19, 20, 21–22, 160
      Administrative Indexes, 20–21, 22
      BISs, 12–13, 18, 20, 21–22, 70, 75, 82–83
      GOT scales, 11–12, 21–22
      items, 10–11, 75
      OSs, 9–10, 11, 13–18, 19, 21–22, 107, 108, 121
      reference sample, 11
      sampling of racial and ethnic groups, 6–7, 261–263
   content
      Administrative Indexes, 175–180
      BISs, 69–104
      GOT scales, 43–68
      items, 33–42
      OSs, 105–154
      Personal Style Scales, 155–172
   gender-normed scales, 291–292
   history of, 1–2, 52–53
   integration with MBTI, 30, 184, 193–194, 201, 204, 217, 296
   interpretation
      challenges, 197–212
      gender differences, 291–307
      results, 29–30
      strategies, 181–195
   materials, 24–29
   purpose, 2–3, 187–188
   support materials, 30, 32, 184, 192, 231, 251
   translations, 6, 30–31, 256–257, 261
   See also individual scales
"*Strong* and MBTI Help Revitalize Employees," 217
Strong Vocational Interest Blanks (SVIB), 1–2, 81
   reliability, 51–52
   validity, 51–52, 151–152, 226–227

Students. *See* College students; High school students
Sue, D., 256
Sue, D. W., 256, 260
Super, D. E., 204, 224, 238, 296
SVIB. *See Strong Vocational Interest Blanks (SVIB)*
Swanson, J. L., 23, 130, 151, 152, 153, 233, 234, 235, 246, 247, 258, 259, 260, 295

Tan, R. N., 153, 233, 234–235
Tarvydas, V. M., 281
Taylor, K. M., 237
Taymans, J. M., 283, 288
Temkin, N. R., 288–289
Terman, L., 2
Test-retest reliability
   of BISs, 83–85, 88–90
   of GOT scales, 12, 54–58
   of OSs, 112, 121, 130, 131–146
   of Personal Style Scales, 164, 166, 167
   See also Reliability
Tests. *See* Assessment tools; *names of specific tests*
Themes. *See* General Occupational Themes (GOTs); RIASEC Themes
Thomas, L. E., 221, 223–224, 245
Thompson, A. S., 296
Thurstone, L. L., 52
Tilton, J. W., 130, 147, 148
Tilton's overlap. *See* Percent overlap
Tipton, R. M., 7
Tittle, C. K., 255
Total Responses (TR) index, 20–21, 22, 175
Tracey, T. J., 53, 58, 164
Translations, 6, 30–31, 256–257, 261
Trejo, W. R., 288–289

Usher, C. G., 296
Usher, M. C., 112
Using the Strong in Organizations (Hirsh), 189
Utz, P., 59

Vaitenas, R., 223
Validity, 6, 22, 23, 28, 35
   of BISs, 85, 91–104, 153
   and choice of career by college students, 237–238
   and choice of major by college students, 234–237
   of GOT scales, 58–67
   for minority populations, 260–261
   of OSs, 15, 16, 109, 112, 114–121, 130, 147–153
   of Personal Style Scales, 20, 156, 158, 166–172, 185–186
   of Profile, 185–186
   of *SVIB*, 51–52, 151–152, 226–227
   See also Predictive validity
Values Scale (Nevill & Super), 224, 238, 296
Vance, F. L., 240
Varca, P. E., 59, 227
Vessey, T., 190
Vicker, D., 223
Vocational Interests of Men and Women (Strong), 2
Vocational Preference Inventory (VPI; Holland*)*, 54, 58–59

Wagner, E. E., 282, 288
Wakefield, J. A., Jr., 258–259
Walker, S. P., 235
Wallace, G. R., 235
Walsh, D. J., 296
Walsh, W. B., 53, 255
Ward, C. M., 258

Watkins, C. E., 231
Webber, P. L., 305
"Wells Fargo Helps Employees Change Careers," 225
West, M., 222
"Wharton Helps Future Leaders Make the Best Career Decisions," 226
Whetstone, R. D., 259
Whitney, D. R., 53
Wiener, Y., 223
Wild, C. L., 292
Williams, P. A., 16, 153
Women. *See* Gender differences
Women-in-General (1985 *Strong*), 11, 111, 295
  See also General Reference Samples (GRSs)

Work Style scale, 26, 241, 302
  and BISs, 74, 75, 76, 77
  interpretation, 156–158, 193–194, 211
  scale construction, 18–20, 161–164, 165
  See also Personal Style Scales

Yom, B. L., 258–259
Yura, C. A., 260

Zarella, K. L., 246
Zytowski, D. G., 255

PROFILE
ITEM BOOKLET & ANSWER SHEET

STRONG INTEREST INVENTORY™

SAMPLE

DO NOT FOLD, STAPLE, OR SEPARATE THE PAGES OF THIS BOOKLET

CONSULTING PSYCHOLOGISTS PRESS, INC. • Palo Alto, California

8508

MARKING INSTRUCTIONS

This item booklet will be electronically scanned by a computer. To help ensure that your responses are scanned accurately, follow the marking instructions below.
- Use a soft (No. 2) black lead pencil.
- Make dark, heavy marks that fill the ovals.
- Mark ONLY the oval areas.
- Fill in only one oval per response on pages 3, 4, and 5.
- Erase completely any answer you wish to change.
- Make no stray marks.

EXAMPLES: Proper mark: ○ ○ ● ○
Improper marks: ⊘ ⊗ ⊙ ⊖

TO THE COUNSELOR:

1. Check that this booklet has been completed correctly.
   - Name (and/or identification number) boxes have been completed.
   - Gender has been indicated.
   - Marking instructions noted at left have been followed.
2. Complete the Request for CPP Scoring Services form.
3. Mail to the nearest CPP Scoring Center. (See the Request for CPP Scoring Services form for addresses.)

If you have any questions, please call 800-624-1765.

TO THE CLIENT: Complete the following steps.

1. Name: Print your name, one letter per box, in the boxes below. Print your last name first, skip one box, and print as much of your first name as possible. Fill in the appropriate oval below each box; fill in a blank oval for each box without a letter in it.

2. Identification number (optional)

3. Today's date — Jan. – Dec., Day, Year

4. Zip code (of your permanent home address)

5. IMPORTANT (mark one) Gender: ○ Female ○ Male

6. Age

7. Ethnicity (optional; mark all that apply)
- ○ African-American/Black
- ○ American Indian or Alaskan Native
- ○ Asian or Pacific Islander
- ○ Caucasian
- ○ Latino, Latina/Hispanic
- ○ Other (please specify): _____

8. Are you presently (mark all that apply)
- ○ Enrolled as a student
- ○ A homemaker
- ○ Unemployed, looking for work
- ○ Retired
- ○ None of the above

9. How many hours per week do you work in paid employment?
- ○ None
- ○ 1–20 hours
- ○ 21–29 hours
- ○ 30–40 hours
- ○ 41 or more hours

10. If you are currently employed, indicate how you feel about your work.
- ○ Very satisfied
- ○ Somewhat satisfied
- ○ Somewhat dissatisfied
- ○ Very dissatisfied

11. How many years have you been employed in your current or most recent occupation or line of work?

12. What is the highest level of education you have completed? (mark one)
- ○ Some high school
- ○ High school graduate
- ○ Trade/technical training
- ○ Some college (no degree)
- ○ Associate degree
- ○ Bachelor's degree
- ○ Master's degree
- ○ Professional degree (e.g., DDS, JD, MD)
- ○ Doctorate (e.g., Ph.D., Ed.D.)

NOTICE:
For this inventory to be scored properly, you must complete items 1 or 2 and item 5. The other questions on this page are optional. Responses on this form may be used in the aggregate for research and inventory revalidation and renorming.

DO NOT WRITE IN THIS AREA

***STRONG* PREPAID PROFILE**

DO NOT WRITE IN THIS AREA

INSTRUCTIONS

The *Strong Interest Inventory* is used to help you understand your work interests and to show you some kinds of work in which you might be comfortable. The following pages list many jobs, activities, school subjects, and so forth, and you will be asked to show whether you like, are indifferent to, or dislike each of them. Your answers will be compared with the answers given by people already working in a wide range of jobs, and your scores will show how similar your interests are to the interests of these people. The *Strong* is not a test of your *abilities;* it is an inventory of your *interests.* Your results will be presented to you later on a *Strong Interest Inventory* report. The report will provide information to help you understand your results.

Please answer every question. Do not spend too much time thinking about each one. Rely on your first impression.

PART I. OCCUPATIONS

Many occupations are listed below. For each occupation, show how you would feel about doing that kind of work.

- Mark on this sheet in the space labeled "**L**" if you think you would **like** that kind of work.
- Mark in the space labeled "**I**" if you are **indifferent** (that is, if you think you wouldn't care one way or another).
- Mark in the space labeled "**D**" if you think you would **dislike** that kind of work.

Don't worry about whether you would be good at the job or about not being trained for it. Forget about how much money you could make or whether you could get ahead. Think only about whether you would like to do the work done in that job.

1. Accountant
2. Actor/Actress
3. Advertising executive
4. Architect
5. Art museum director
6. Art teacher
7. Artist
8. Artist's model
9. Astronomer
10. Athletic director
11. Author of children's books
12. Author of novels
13. Author of technical books
14. Auto mechanic
15. Auto racer
16. Auto salesperson
17. Bank teller
18. Beauty and haircare consultant
19. Bilingual teacher
20. Biologist
21. Bookkeeper
22. Building contractor
23. Business teacher
24. Buyer of merchandise
25. Carpenter
26. Cartoonist
27. Cashier in bank
28. Chemist
29. City planner
30. Civil engineer
31. Civil service employee
32. Clothes designer
33. College professor
34. Computer operator
35. Computer programmer
36. Corporation lawyer
37. Courtroom stenographer
38. Criminal lawyer
39. Customer service representative
40. Dance teacher
41. Day care worker
42. Dental assistant
43. Dentist
44. Designer, electronic equipment
45. Dietitian
46. Editor
47. Electrical engineer
48. Electronics technician
49. Elementary school teacher
50. Employment manager
51. Factory manager
52. Farmer
53. Fashion model
54. Financial analyst
55. Flight attendant
56. Florist
57. Foreign correspondent
58. Foreign service officer
59. Forest ranger
60. Free-lance writer
61. Governor of a state
62. High school teacher
63. Hospital records clerk
64. Housekeeper
65. Hotel manager
66. Illustrator
67. Income tax accountant
68. Interior decorator
69. Jet pilot
70. Judge
71. Labor arbitrator
72. Laboratory technician
73. Landscape gardener
74. Librarian
75. Life insurance agent
76. Machine shop supervisor
77. Machinist
78. Manager, Chamber of Commerce
79. Manager, child care center
80. Manager, clothing store
81. Manufacturer
82. Mechanical engineer
83. Military officer
84. Musician
85. Newspaper reporter
86. Nurse
87. Nurse's aide/Orderly
88. Office clerk
89. Office manager
90. Opera singer
91. Orchestra conductor
92. Paralegal
93. Paramedic
94. Pharmacist
95. Photographer
96. Physician
97. Playground director
98. Poet
99. Police officer
100. Politician
101. Private secretary
102. Professional athlete
103. Professional dancer
104. Psychologist
105. Public relations director
106. Rancher
107. Realtor
108. Receptionist
109. Religious leader (e.g., minister, priest, rabbi)
110. Retailer
111. Sales manager
112. School principal
113. Scientific illustrator
114. Scientific research worker
115. Sculptor
116. Secret service agent
117. Security guard
118. Social worker
119. Special education teacher
120. Specialty salesperson
121. Sports reporter
122. Statistician
123. Stockbroker
124. Surgeon
125. Toolmaker
126. Travel agency manager
127. Traveling salesperson
128. TV announcer
129. Vocational counselor
130. Waiter/Waitress
131. Wholesaler
132. Word processor
133. X-Ray technician
134. Worker in religious vocation
135. Youth organization staff member (e.g., YMCA, YWCA, YMHA, YWHA)

SAMPLE

DO NOT WRITE BELOW THIS LINE

PAGE 3

PART II. SCHOOL SUBJECTS

As you did for the occupations on the previous page, show whether you are interested in these school subjects. You may have interest in some of the subjects even though you may not have studied them.

136 Ⓛ Ⓘ Ⓓ Acting
137 Ⓛ Ⓘ Ⓓ Agriculture
138 Ⓛ Ⓘ Ⓓ Algebra
139 Ⓛ Ⓘ Ⓓ Arithmetic
140 Ⓛ Ⓘ Ⓓ Ancient languages (Latin, Sanskrit, etc.)
141 Ⓛ Ⓘ Ⓓ Art
142 Ⓛ Ⓘ Ⓓ Bookkeeping
143 Ⓛ Ⓘ Ⓓ Botany
144 Ⓛ Ⓘ Ⓓ Business
145 Ⓛ Ⓘ Ⓓ Calculus
146 Ⓛ Ⓘ Ⓓ Chemistry
147 Ⓛ Ⓘ Ⓓ Civics (government)
148 Ⓛ Ⓘ Ⓓ Computer science
149 Ⓛ Ⓘ Ⓓ Economics
150 Ⓛ Ⓘ Ⓓ English composition/Writing
151 Ⓛ Ⓘ Ⓓ Geometry
152 Ⓛ Ⓘ Ⓓ Health education
153 Ⓛ Ⓘ Ⓓ Home economics
154 Ⓛ Ⓘ Ⓓ Industrial arts
155 Ⓛ Ⓘ Ⓓ Journalism
156 Ⓛ Ⓘ Ⓓ Literature
157 Ⓛ Ⓘ Ⓓ Mathematics
158 Ⓛ Ⓘ Ⓓ Mechanical drawing
159 Ⓛ Ⓘ Ⓓ Military drill
160 Ⓛ Ⓘ Ⓓ Modern languages (French, German, etc.)
161 Ⓛ Ⓘ Ⓓ Nature study
162 Ⓛ Ⓘ Ⓓ Penmanship
163 Ⓛ Ⓘ Ⓓ Philosophy
164 Ⓛ Ⓘ Ⓓ Physical education
165 Ⓛ Ⓘ Ⓓ Physics
166 Ⓛ Ⓘ Ⓓ Physiology
167 Ⓛ Ⓘ Ⓓ Political science
168 Ⓛ Ⓘ Ⓓ Psychology
169 Ⓛ Ⓘ Ⓓ Public speaking
170 Ⓛ Ⓘ Ⓓ Religious studies
171 Ⓛ Ⓘ Ⓓ Sociology
172 Ⓛ Ⓘ Ⓓ Statistics
173 Ⓛ Ⓘ Ⓓ Typewriting/Word processing
174 Ⓛ Ⓘ Ⓓ Zoology

PART III. ACTIVITIES

Show your interests by marking one response for each activity that follows. Give the first answer that comes to mind.

175 Ⓛ Ⓘ Ⓓ Making a speech
176 Ⓛ Ⓘ Ⓓ Doing research work
177 Ⓛ Ⓘ Ⓓ Repairing a clock
178 Ⓛ Ⓘ Ⓓ Cooking
179 Ⓛ Ⓘ Ⓓ Operating machinery
180 Ⓛ Ⓘ Ⓓ Writing reports
181 Ⓛ Ⓘ Ⓓ Discussing politics
182 Ⓛ Ⓘ Ⓓ Taping a sprained ankle
183 Ⓛ Ⓘ Ⓓ Adjusting a carburetor
184 Ⓛ Ⓘ Ⓓ Heading a civic improvement program
185 Ⓛ Ⓘ Ⓓ Raising flowers and vegetables
186 Ⓛ Ⓘ Ⓓ Interviewing job applicants
187 Ⓛ Ⓘ Ⓓ Teaching children
188 Ⓛ Ⓘ Ⓓ Teaching adults
189 Ⓛ Ⓘ Ⓓ Meeting and directing people
190 Ⓛ Ⓘ Ⓓ Learning more about the foods I eat
191 Ⓛ Ⓘ Ⓓ Making statistical charts
192 Ⓛ Ⓘ Ⓓ Operating office machines
193 Ⓛ Ⓘ Ⓓ Giving first aid assistance
194 Ⓛ Ⓘ Ⓓ Decorating a room with flowers
195 Ⓛ Ⓘ Ⓓ Interviewing prospects in selling
196 Ⓛ Ⓘ Ⓓ Drilling soldiers
197 Ⓛ Ⓘ Ⓓ Watching an open-heart operation
198 Ⓛ Ⓘ Ⓓ Repairing electronics equipment
199 Ⓛ Ⓘ Ⓓ Checking printed material for errors
200 Ⓛ Ⓘ Ⓓ Helping others overcome their difficulties
201 Ⓛ Ⓘ Ⓓ Cabinetmaking
202 Ⓛ Ⓘ Ⓓ Bargaining ("swapping")
203 Ⓛ Ⓘ Ⓓ Looking at things in a clothing store
204 Ⓛ Ⓘ Ⓓ Buying merchandise for a store
205 Ⓛ Ⓘ Ⓓ Displaying merchandise in a store
206 Ⓛ Ⓘ Ⓓ Taking care of children
207 Ⓛ Ⓘ Ⓓ Competing in activities
208 Ⓛ Ⓘ Ⓓ Working regular hours
209 Ⓛ Ⓘ Ⓓ Competitive sports
210 Ⓛ Ⓘ Ⓓ Continually changing activities
211 Ⓛ Ⓘ Ⓓ Interviewing clients
212 Ⓛ Ⓘ Ⓓ Participating in arguments
213 Ⓛ Ⓘ Ⓓ Developing business systems
214 Ⓛ Ⓘ Ⓓ Doing your own laundry work
215 Ⓛ Ⓘ Ⓓ Contributing to charities
216 Ⓛ Ⓘ Ⓓ Raising money for charity
217 Ⓛ Ⓘ Ⓓ Expressing judgments publicly, regardless of what others say
218 Ⓛ Ⓘ Ⓓ Climbing along the edge of a steep cliff
219 Ⓛ Ⓘ Ⓓ Living in a city
220 Ⓛ Ⓘ Ⓓ Discussing the purpose of life

PART IV. LEISURE ACTIVITIES

Show how you feel about these ways of spending your leisure time by marking one response for each of the following items. Do not think over various possibilities; instead, give the first answer that comes to mind.

221 Ⓛ Ⓘ Ⓓ Golf
222 Ⓛ Ⓘ Ⓓ Jazz or rock concerts
223 Ⓛ Ⓘ Ⓓ Boxing
224 Ⓛ Ⓘ Ⓓ Solving mechanical puzzles
225 Ⓛ Ⓘ Ⓓ Planning a large party
226 Ⓛ Ⓘ Ⓓ Religious music
227 Ⓛ Ⓘ Ⓓ Drilling in a military company
228 Ⓛ Ⓘ Ⓓ Shopping for the latest fashions
229 Ⓛ Ⓘ Ⓓ Conventions
230 Ⓛ Ⓘ Ⓓ Playing team sports with friends
231 Ⓛ Ⓘ Ⓓ Electioneering for office
232 Ⓛ Ⓘ Ⓓ Art galleries
233 Ⓛ Ⓘ Ⓓ Writing a one-act play
234 Ⓛ Ⓘ Ⓓ Symphony concerts
235 Ⓛ Ⓘ Ⓓ Young people's religious group
236 Ⓛ Ⓘ Ⓓ Sports pages in the newspaper
237 Ⓛ Ⓘ Ⓓ Poetry
238 Ⓛ Ⓘ Ⓓ Skiing
239 Ⓛ Ⓘ Ⓓ Business magazines
240 Ⓛ Ⓘ Ⓓ Popular mechanics magazines
241 Ⓛ Ⓘ Ⓓ Magazines about art or music
242 Ⓛ Ⓘ Ⓓ Attending lectures
243 Ⓛ Ⓘ Ⓓ Performing scientific experiments
244 Ⓛ Ⓘ Ⓓ Camping
245 Ⓛ Ⓘ Ⓓ Preparing dinner for guests
246 Ⓛ Ⓘ Ⓓ Entertaining others
247 Ⓛ Ⓘ Ⓓ Trying new cooking recipes
248 Ⓛ Ⓘ Ⓓ Being the first to wear the latest fashions
249 Ⓛ Ⓘ Ⓓ Organizing a play

PART V. TYPES OF PEOPLE

Most of us choose jobs that allow us to work with people we enjoy. Show how you would feel about having day-to-day contact with the following types of people. Don't think of specific people you know. Give the first answer that comes to mind.

250 Ⓛ Ⓘ Ⓓ Highway construction workers
251 Ⓛ Ⓘ Ⓓ High school students
252 Ⓛ Ⓘ Ⓓ Military officers
253 Ⓛ Ⓘ Ⓓ Artistic people
254 Ⓛ Ⓘ Ⓓ Ballet dancers
255 Ⓛ Ⓘ Ⓓ Nonconformists
256 Ⓛ Ⓘ Ⓓ People who assume leadership
257 Ⓛ Ⓘ Ⓓ Religious people
258 Ⓛ Ⓘ Ⓓ Aggressive people
259 Ⓛ Ⓘ Ⓓ Physically sick people
260 Ⓛ Ⓘ Ⓓ Babies
261 Ⓛ Ⓘ Ⓓ Very old people
262 Ⓛ Ⓘ Ⓓ People who have made fortunes in business
263 Ⓛ Ⓘ Ⓓ Musical geniuses
264 Ⓛ Ⓘ Ⓓ Physically disabled people
265 Ⓛ Ⓘ Ⓓ Outspoken people with new ideas
266 Ⓛ Ⓘ Ⓓ Prominent business leaders
267 Ⓛ Ⓘ Ⓓ Athletic people
268 Ⓛ Ⓘ Ⓓ Outstanding scientists
269 Ⓛ Ⓘ Ⓓ People who live dangerously

DO NOT WRITE IN THIS AREA
STRONG PREPAID PROFILE

PART VI. PREFERENCE BETWEEN TWO ACTIVITIES

Here are several pairs of activities or occupations. Show which one of each pair you like better.

- If you prefer the one on the **left**, mark in the space labeled "**L**." ● ⊜ Ⓡ
- If you prefer the one on the **right**, mark in the space labeled "**R**." Ⓛ ⊜ ●
- If you like or dislike **both the same**, or if you **can't decide**, mark in the space labeled "**=**." Ⓛ ● Ⓡ

Make one mark for each pair.

270	Airline pilot Ⓛ ⊜ Ⓡ Airline ticket agent
271	Taxicab driver Ⓛ ⊜ Ⓡ Police officer
272	Headwaiter/Hostess Ⓛ ⊜ Ⓡ Lighthouse keeper
273	Developing plans Ⓛ ⊜ Ⓡ Carrying out plans
274	Doing a job yourself Ⓛ ⊜ Ⓡ Telling somebody else to do the job
275	Dealing with things Ⓛ ⊜ Ⓡ Dealing with people
276	Working full time Ⓛ ⊜ Ⓡ Working part time
277	Taking a chance Ⓛ ⊜ Ⓡ Playing it safe
278	Drawing a definite salary Ⓛ ⊜ Ⓡ Receiving a commission on what is done
279	Outside work Ⓛ ⊜ Ⓡ Inside work
280	Working for yourself Ⓛ ⊜ Ⓡ Carrying out the program of a supervisor whom you respect
281	Superintendent of a hospital Ⓛ ⊜ Ⓡ Warden of a prison
282	Vocational counselor Ⓛ ⊜ Ⓡ Public health officer
283	Being friends with a research scientist Ⓛ ⊜ Ⓡ Being friends with a sales executive
284	Physical activity Ⓛ ⊜ Ⓡ Mental activity
285	Thrilling, dangerous activities Ⓛ ⊜ Ⓡ Quiet, safe activities
286	Physical education director Ⓛ ⊜ Ⓡ Free-lance writer
287	Statistician Ⓛ ⊜ Ⓡ Social worker
288	Technical responsibility (in charge of 25 people doing scientific work) Ⓛ ⊜ Ⓡ Supervisory responsibility (in charge of 300 people doing business-office work)
289	Going to a play Ⓛ ⊜ Ⓡ Going to a dance
290	Teacher Ⓛ ⊜ Ⓡ Salesperson
291	Experimenting with new grooming preparations Ⓛ ⊜ Ⓡ Experimenting with new office equipment
292	Being responsible for earning money to support the family Ⓛ ⊜ Ⓡ Being responsible for caring for children
293	Working in a large corporation with little chance of being president before age 55 Ⓛ ⊜ Ⓡ Working for yourself in a small business
294	Working in an import-export business Ⓛ ⊜ Ⓡ Working in a research laboratory
295	Music and arts events Ⓛ ⊜ Ⓡ Athletic events
296	Reading a book Ⓛ ⊜ Ⓡ Watching TV or going to a movie
297	Appraising real estate Ⓛ ⊜ Ⓡ Repairing and restoring antiques
298	Working for nonprofit organizations Ⓛ ⊜ Ⓡ Working for profit-oriented organizations
299	Work in which you move from place to place Ⓛ ⊜ Ⓡ Work in which you live in one place

PART VII. YOUR CHARACTERISTICS

Show here what kind of person you are.

- If the statement describes you, mark in the space labeled "**Y**" (for "**Yes**"). ● ⊙ Ⓝ
- If the statement does *not* describe you, mark in the space labeled "**N**" (for "**No**"). Ⓨ ⊙ ●
- If you cannot decide, mark in the space labeled "**?**." Ⓨ ● Ⓝ

(Be frank—both strong and weak points are important to consider in choosing a career.)

300	Ⓨ ⊙ Ⓝ Usually start activities of my group
301	Ⓨ ⊙ Ⓝ Prefer working alone rather than on committees
302	Ⓨ ⊙ Ⓝ Have mechanical ingenuity (inventiveness)
303	Ⓨ ⊙ Ⓝ Am concerned about philosophical problems such as religion, meaning of life, etc.
304	Ⓨ ⊙ Ⓝ Can prepare successful advertisements
305	Ⓨ ⊙ Ⓝ Stimulate the ambitions of my associates
306	Ⓨ ⊙ Ⓝ Can write a concise, well-organized report
307	Ⓨ ⊙ Ⓝ Can communicate easily with people of different cultures
308	Ⓨ ⊙ Ⓝ Enjoy tinkering with small hand tools
309	Ⓨ ⊙ Ⓝ Can smooth out tangles and disagreements between people
310	Ⓨ ⊙ Ⓝ Put drive into an organization
311	Ⓨ ⊙ Ⓝ Have patience when teaching others

PART VIII. PREFERENCE IN THE WORLD OF WORK

For each of the six pairs below, show which one of each pair you like better.

- If you prefer the one on the **left**, mark in the space labeled "**L**." ● ⊜ Ⓡ
- If you prefer the one on the **right**, mark in the space labeled "**R**." Ⓛ ⊜ ●
- If you like or dislike **both the same**, or if you **can't decide**, mark in the space labeled "**=**." Ⓛ ● Ⓡ

Make one mark for each pair.

Ideas are insights, knowledge, theories, abstractions, and new ways of expressing something. **Data** are facts, numbers, records, files, and systematic procedures. **Things** are machines, tools, materials, mechanisms, and physical and biological processes.

312	Ideas Ⓛ ⊜ Ⓡ Data
313	Data Ⓛ ⊜ Ⓡ People
314	People Ⓛ ⊜ Ⓡ Ideas
315	Things Ⓛ ⊜ Ⓡ People
316	Ideas Ⓛ ⊜ Ⓡ Things
317	Things Ⓛ ⊜ Ⓡ Data

DO NOT FOLD, STAPLE, OR SEPARATE THE PAGES OF THIS BOOKLET.

Strong Interest Inventory of the *Strong Vocational Interest Blanks*®, Form T317. Copyright © 1933, 1938, 1945, 1946, 1966, 1968, 1974, 1981, 1985, 1994 by the Board of Trustees of the Leland Stanford Junior University. All rights reserved. No part of this publication may be reproduced in any form or manner without prior written permission from Consulting Psychologists Press, Inc. Printed and scored under license from Stanford University Press, Stanford, California 94305. *Strong Interest Inventory* is a trademark and *Strong Vocational Interest Blanks* is a registered trademark of Stanford University Press.

is a trademark of Consulting Psychologists Press, Inc.

Printed in the United States of America
99 98 97 96 95   12 11 10 9 8 7 6 5 4

R9015-PFI

STRONG INTEREST INVENTORY

Profile report for: **ROBIN BYRD**
ID:
Age: **24**
Gender: **Female**

Date tested: **04/11/94**
Date scored: **04/15/94**

SNAPSHOT: A SUMMARY OF RESULTS FOR ROBIN BYRD

GENERAL OCCUPATIONAL THEMES

The General Occupational Themes describe interests in six very broad areas, including interest in work and leisure activities, kinds of people, and work settings. Your interests in each area are shown at the right in rank order. Note that each Theme has a code, represented by the first letter of the Theme name.

You can use your Theme code, printed below your results, to identify school subjects, part-time jobs, college majors, leisure activities, or careers that you might find interesting. See the back of this Profile for suggestions on how to use your Theme code.

THEME CODE	THEME	VERY LITTLE INTEREST	LITTLE INTEREST	AVERAGE INTEREST	HIGH INTEREST	VERY HIGH INTEREST	TYPICAL INTERESTS
A	ARTISTIC	☐	☐	☐	☑	☐	Creating or enjoying art
C	CONVENTIONAL	☐	☐	☑	☐	☐	Accounting, processing data
S	SOCIAL	☐	☐	☑	☐	☐	Helping, instructing
R	REALISTIC	☐	☐	☑	☐	☐	Building, repairing
I	INVESTIGATIVE	☐	☑	☐	☐	☐	Researching, analyzing
E	ENTERPRISING	☐	☑	☐	☐	☐	Selling, managing

Your Theme code is ACS—(see explanation at left).
You might explore occupations with codes that contain any combination of these letters.

BASIC INTEREST SCALES

The Basic Interest Scales measure your interests in 25 specific areas or activities. Only those 5 areas in which you show the *most* interest are listed at the right in rank order. Your results on all 25 Basic Interest Scales are found on page 2.

To the left of each scale is a letter that shows which of the six General Occupational Themes this activity is most closely related to. These codes can help you to identify other activities that you may enjoy.

THEME CODE	BASIC INTEREST	VERY LITTLE INTEREST	LITTLE INTEREST	AVERAGE INTEREST	HIGH INTEREST	VERY HIGH INTEREST	TYPICAL ACTIVITIES
A	WRITING	☐	☐	☐	☐	☑	Reading or writing
S	RELIGIOUS ACTIVITIES	☐	☐	☐	☑	☐	Participating in spiritual activities
A	ART	☐	☐	☐	☑	☐	Appreciating or creating art
A	CULINARY ARTS	☐	☐	☐	☑	☐	Cooking or entertaining
R	AGRICULTURE	☐	☐	☐	☑	☐	Working outdoors

OCCUPATIONAL SCALES

The Occupational Scales measure how similar your interests are to the interests of people who are satisfied working in those occupations. Only the 10 scales on which your interests are *most* similar to those of these people are listed at the right in rank order. Your results on all 211 of the Occupational Scales are found on pages 3, 4, and 5.

The letters to the left of each scale identify the Theme or Themes that most closely describe the interests of people working in that occupation. You can use these letters to find additional, related occupations that you might find interesting. After reviewing your results on all six pages of this Profile, see the back of page 5 for tips on finding other occupations in the Theme or Themes that interest you the most.

THEME CODE	OCCUPATION	VERY DISSIMILAR	DISSIMILAR	MID-RANGE	SIMILAR	VERY SIMILAR
A	LIBRARIAN	☐	☐	☐	☐	☑
AIR	TECHNICAL WRITER	☐	☐	☐	☐	☑
A	LAWYER	☐	☐	☐	☑	☐
A	TRANSLATOR	☐	☐	☐	☑	☐
CE	PARALEGAL	☐	☐	☐	☑	☐
SA	SOCIAL WORKER	☐	☐	☐	☑	☐
AES	CORPORATE TRAINER	☐	☐	☐	☑	☐
AE	ADVERTISING EXECUTIVE	☐	☐	☑	☐	☐
ASE	ENGLISH TEACHER	☐	☐	☑	☐	☐
SEA	SOCIAL SCIENCE TEACHER	☐	☐	☑	☐	☐

PERSONAL STYLE SCALES measure your levels of comfort regarding Work Style, Learning Environment, Leadership Style, and Risk Taking/Adventure. This information may help you make decisions about particular work environments, educational settings, and types of activities you would find satisfying. Your results on these four scales are on page 6.

CPP CONSULTING PSYCHOLOGISTS PRESS, INC. • 3803 E. Bayshore Road, Palo Alto, CA 94303

Understanding Your Results on the STRONG

Your answers to the *Strong Interest Inventory*—what you said you liked and disliked—determine your scores. These scores can help you identify general areas of interests as well as specific activities and occupations that you might want to explore further.

As you go over your Profile report, remember that the *Strong* measures your interests, *not* your abilities. It tells you about your pattern of interests and how your interests compare with those of people from a wide variety of occupations. For example, while your results may suggest that you will like how engineers spend their day, the *Strong* does *not* tell you whether you have the mathematics aptitude needed to become an engineer.

Keep in mind that choosing an occupation is not a single decision, but a series of decisions. Your results on the *Strong Interest Inventory* can help you identify options that may lead you to a satisfying career.

What You Can Learn from Your Results

There is a wealth of information available in your *Strong* results. Understanding your Profile will help you find your career focus and begin your career exploration. Your *Strong* results can be used to help you identify the following:

- How you might find a job or career consistent with your likes and dislikes in the world of work
- How similar (or dissimilar) your interests are to the interests of people who are working in 109 occupations
- Your leisure interests
- Additional alternatives or options related to work or leisure-time activities for you to explore
- General patterns in your interests
- Work or learning environments that fit your interests
- How your liking or disliking of risk taking and your preferences regarding leadership style might affect your options

Organization of the Profile

The *Strong* Profile is organized as follows:

1. The Snapshot (page 1 of the Profile) summarizes your results. You can use the Snapshot to quickly identify the areas in which you showed the most interest and to help you see your overall interest pattern. Still, you should examine carefully the more detailed results on the other five pages of the Profile.

2. The General Occupational Themes (page 2 of the Profile) show your interest in 6 general areas, types of occupations, or occupational environments.

3. The Basic Interest Scales (also on page 2 of the Profile) show your interest in 25 specific activities or areas.

4. The Occupational Scales (pages 3, 4, and 5 of the Profile) show how similar your interests are to those of men and women in 109 occupations.

5. The Personal Style Scales (page 6 of the Profile) show your comfort level regarding 4 personal characteristics that may affect your educational or career choices.

6. The Summary of Item Responses, including the Administrative Indexes, (also on page 6 of the Profile) provide information about how many items you answered and how many you said you liked and disliked.

The information on the reverse sides of each of these pages explains how to understand and use your *Strong* results.

Thousands of jobs exist in the world of work. Use your *Strong* results, as well as what you know about your values and skills, to help you find information about those occupational areas in which your interests and aptitudes are focused. Ask your counselor or a librarian for information on jobs in those particular areas and talk to people working in those fields.

You can find your results on the General Occupational Themes and Basic Interest Scales on page 2 of your Profile. The back of page 2 contains an explanation of these *Strong* scales.

Designed by *DBA Design & Illustration, San Carlos, CA*

STRONG INTEREST INVENTORY

Profile report for **ROBIN BYRD**
ID:

GENERAL OCCUPATIONAL THEMES
BASIC INTEREST SCALES

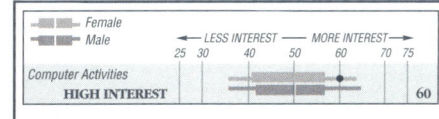
KEY (Sample Scores)

Female / Male ← LESS INTEREST — MORE INTEREST →
Computer Activities — HIGH INTEREST — 60

The phrase printed below the scale name compares your interests to those of people of your own gender. The upper bar shows the range of scores for a group of women from many occupations; the lower bar, the range of scores for a group of men. The number in the right-hand column, represented by the dot, is your score compared to both men and women.

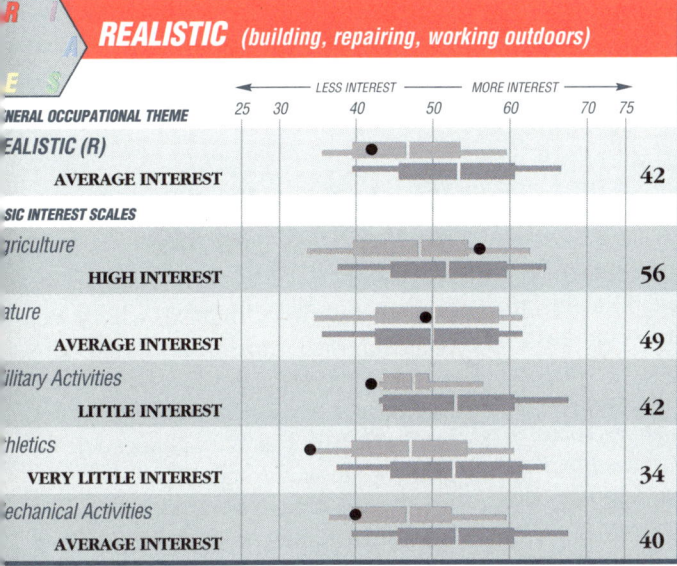

REALISTIC (building, repairing, working outdoors)

Scale	Level	Score
REALISTIC (R)	AVERAGE INTEREST	42
Agriculture	HIGH INTEREST	56
Nature	AVERAGE INTEREST	49
Military Activities	LITTLE INTEREST	42
Athletics	VERY LITTLE INTEREST	34
Mechanical Activities	AVERAGE INTEREST	40

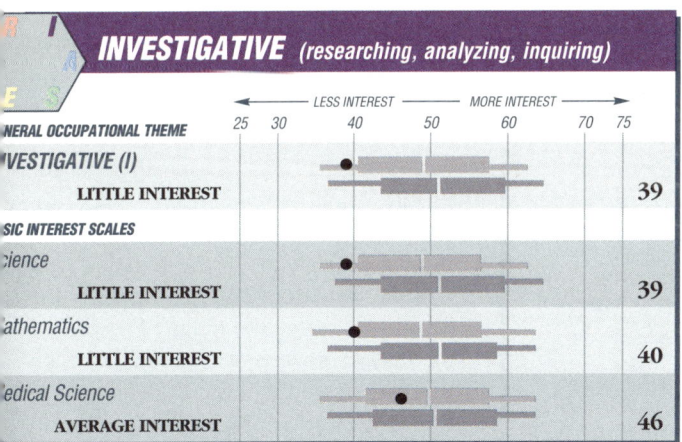

INVESTIGATIVE (researching, analyzing, inquiring)

Scale	Level	Score
INVESTIGATIVE (I)	LITTLE INTEREST	39
Science	LITTLE INTEREST	39
Mathematics	LITTLE INTEREST	40
Medical Science	AVERAGE INTEREST	46

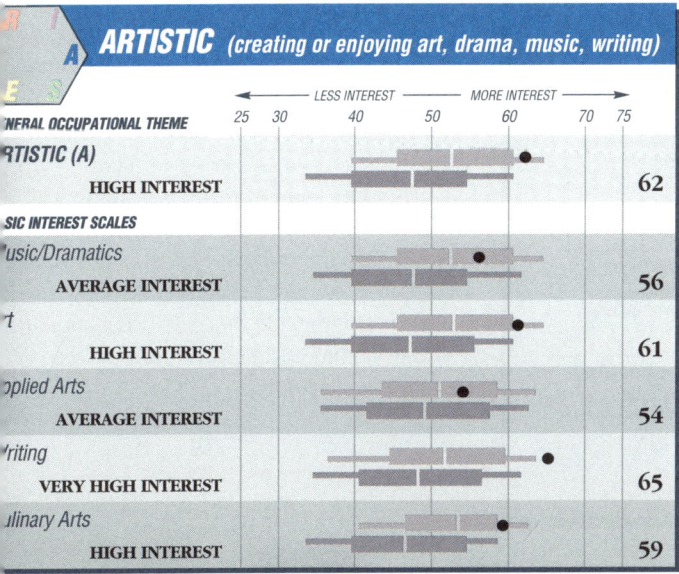

ARTISTIC (creating or enjoying art, drama, music, writing)

Scale	Level	Score
ARTISTIC (A)	HIGH INTEREST	62
Music/Dramatics	AVERAGE INTEREST	56
Art	HIGH INTEREST	61
Applied Arts	AVERAGE INTEREST	54
Writing	VERY HIGH INTEREST	65
Culinary Arts	HIGH INTEREST	59

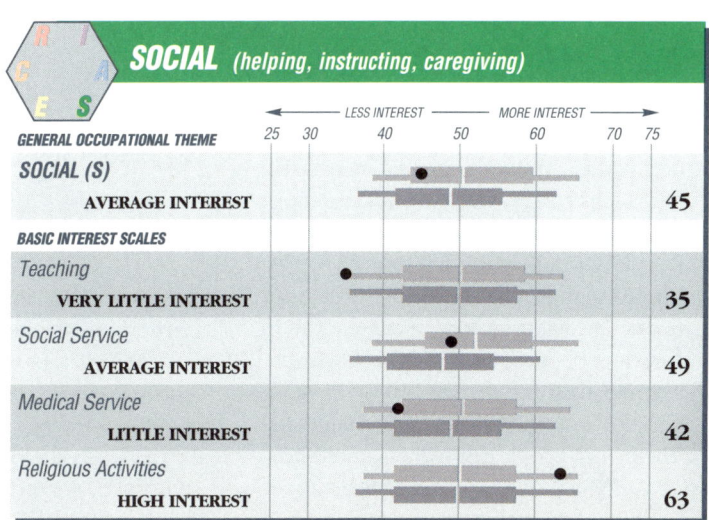

SOCIAL (helping, instructing, caregiving)

Scale	Level	Score
SOCIAL (S)	AVERAGE INTEREST	45
Teaching	VERY LITTLE INTEREST	35
Social Service	AVERAGE INTEREST	49
Medical Service	LITTLE INTEREST	42
Religious Activities	HIGH INTEREST	63

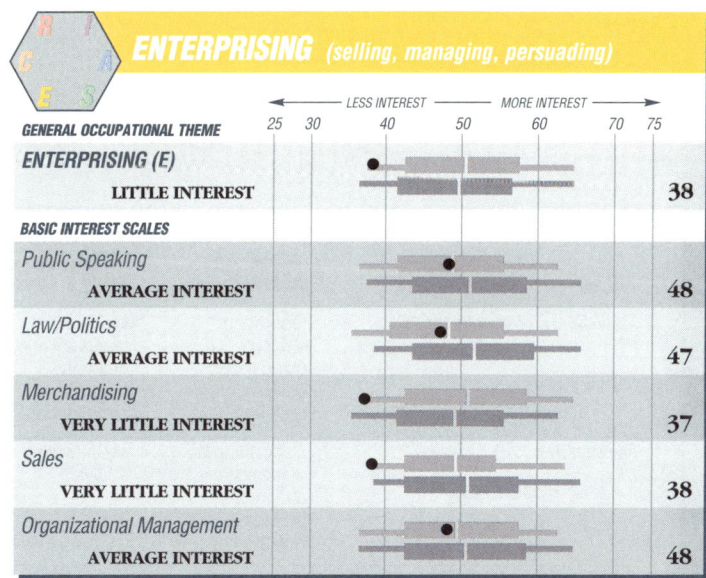

ENTERPRISING (selling, managing, persuading)

Scale	Level	Score
ENTERPRISING (E)	LITTLE INTEREST	38
Public Speaking	AVERAGE INTEREST	48
Law/Politics	AVERAGE INTEREST	47
Merchandising	VERY LITTLE INTEREST	37
Sales	VERY LITTLE INTEREST	38
Organizational Management	AVERAGE INTEREST	48

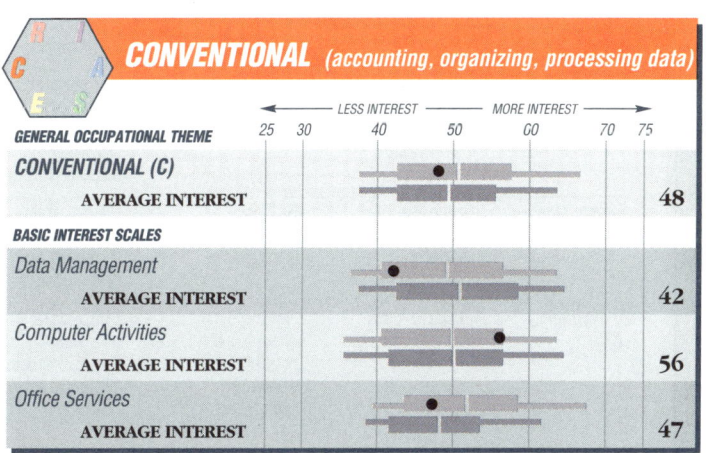

CONVENTIONAL (accounting, organizing, processing data)

Scale	Level	Score
CONVENTIONAL (C)	AVERAGE INTEREST	48
Data Management	AVERAGE INTEREST	42
Computer Activities	AVERAGE INTEREST	56
Office Services	AVERAGE INTEREST	47

CPP • CONSULTING PSYCHOLOGISTS PRESS, INC. • 3803 E. Bayshore Road, Palo Alto, CA 94303

The General Occupational Themes and the Basic Interest Scales

On the other side of this page, you saw your detailed results on the 6 General Occupational Themes (GOTs) and the 25 Basic Interest Scales (BISs).

General Occupational Themes

The six General Occupational Themes describe vocational or career interests, as well as occupations and working environments. The following chart provides you with examples of interests, activities, skills, and values of people who fall into each of the six Themes. These examples, however, are generalizations; none will fit any one person exactly. In fact, most people's interests combine several Themes to some degree. Although some people do not indicate interests in any of the Themes, or in only one of them, most show an average or a high degree of interest in two or three of them. In career planning, try to identify occupations whose typical activities combine the interests suggested by your General Occupational Theme scores.

These six themes can be arranged around a hexagon with the types most similar to each other falling next to each other, and those

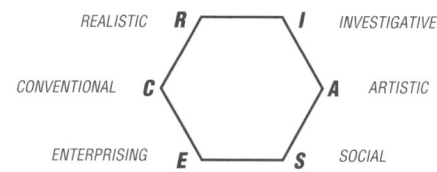

most dissimilar falling directly across the hexagon from one another. For example, as shown in the hexagon above, the Realistic and Investigative Themes are next to each other. People of these two types show some similarity—they generally like to solve technical problems and to work alone. On the other hand, the Realistic and Social Themes are opposite one another on the hexagon. Therefore, people of these two types usually have dissimilar interests. For example, unlike the Realistic types who like working through problems on their own, the Social types like to solve problems by discussing them with others in groups.

Basic Interest Scales

Each of these scales shows your interest in a specific activity or interest area. On the Profile, each Basic Interest Scale is categorized under the General Occupational Theme to which it is most closely related.

How to Read Your Scores on the GOTs and BISs

On each of these scales, your results are reported in three ways. The first result you see, printed under the name of the scale, is one of the following five phrases: Very Little Interest, Little Interest, Average Interest, High Interest, or Very High Interest. These phrases describe how your answers compare to a large number of people of your own gender. Your score is compared to the scores of members of your own gender because research has shown that men and women score somewhat differently on some of the General Occupational Themes and Basic Interest Scales.

Second, your scores on the General Occupational Themes and Basic Interest Scales are shown graphically on the Profile using boxes and lines. The upper box shows the range of scores for the middle 50 percent of the females with whom you are being compared; the lower box shows the range of scores for the middle 50 percent of the males. Each thin line extending from the ends of the boxes shows the range of scores for an additional 15 percent of the gender; therefore, each set of lines and boxes displays the middle 80 percent of the scores. The vertical line near the middle of the box is the average score for that gender. The dot, placed on or near the box for your gender, shows your score.

The third kind of result is a numerical score, which is printed to the right of the boxes. This score shows how your answers compared to a large sample of men *and* women from a wide variety of occupations. These combined samples score about 50 on each scale, on average.

THEME	INTERESTS	WORK ACTIVITIES	POTENTIAL SKILLS	VALUES
Realistic (R)	Machines, tools, outdoors	Operating equipment, using tools, building, repairing	Mechanical ingenuity and dexterity, physical coordination	Tradition, practicality, common sense
Investigative (I)	Science, theories, ideas, data	Performing lab work, solving abstract problems, researching	Math, writing, analysis	Independence, curiosity, learning
Artistic (A)	Self-expression, art appreciation	Composing music, writing, creating visual art	Creativity, musical talent, artistic expression	Beauty, originality, independence, imagination
Social (S)	People, team work, human welfare, community service	Teaching, explaining, helping	People skills, verbal ability, listening, showing understanding	Cooperation, generosity, service to others
Enterprising (E)	Business, politics, leadership, influence	Selling, managing, persuading	Verbal ability, ability to motivate and direct others	Risk taking, status, competition
Conventional (C)	Organization, data, finance	Setting up procedures, organizing, operating computers	Math, data analysis, record keeping, attention to detail	Accuracy, stability, efficiency

STRONG INTEREST INVENTORY

Profile report for **ROBIN BYRD**
ID:

OCCUPATIONAL SCALES

KEY (Sample Scores)

THEME CODES		YOUR SCORES		← DISSIMILAR INTERESTS — MID-RANGE — SIMILAR INTERESTS →
FEMALE	MALE	FEMALE	MALE	15 20 30 40 50 55
IES	(SEC)	Dietitian	25	(SEC)
*	R	Plumber	*	35

( ) You can find your score compared to this gender under the Theme represented by the first letter of this code. For example, your score compared to male dietitians is shown under the S or Social Theme.

• The position of the dot shows how similar your interests are to those of individuals of your gender who say they are satisfied in their occupation.

* Not enough people of this gender who work in this occupation could be found to make a good comparison.

REALISTIC (building, repairing, working outdoors)

THEME CODES FEMALE	THEME CODES MALE	Occupation	YOUR SCORES FEMALE	YOUR SCORES MALE
S	(SIR)	Athletic Trainer	–1	(SIR)
R	R	Auto Mechanic	16	–4
A	REA	Carpenter	9	1
A	RIC	Electrician	11	–13
CI	RI	Emergency Medical Technician	12	11
I	RI	Engineer	17	7
GE)	RC	Farmer	(CSE)	14
I	RI	Forester	34	24
C	RE	Gardener/Groundskeeper	32	30
EI	REI	Horticultural Worker	18	8
RE)	RCE	Military Enlisted Personnel	(CRE)	11
EI	REC	Military Officer	31	15
*	R	Plumber	*	19
E	R	Police Officer	27	10
S	RI	Radiologic Technologist	26	26
E)	RE	Small Business Owner	(CE)	20
SI	RSE	Vocational Agriculture Teacher	5	6

INVESTIGATIVE (researching, analyzing, inquiring)

THEME CODES FEMALE	THEME CODES MALE	Occupation	YOUR SCORES FEMALE	YOUR SCORES MALE
S	IA	Audiologist	32	35
RA	IA	Biologist	20	25
R	IR	Chemist	18	13
R	IRA	Chiropractor	20	22
R	IAS	College Professor	34	31
R	IAR	Computer Programmer/Systems Analyst	26	24
RA	IR	Dentist	14	15
S	(SEC)	Dietitian	23	(SEC)
RA	IA	Geographer	28	23
RA	IRA	Geologist	12	7
RC	ICA	Mathematician	0	–3
RC	IRE	Medical Technician	16	6
RC	IRC	Medical Technologist	12	15
R	IR	Optometrist	17	5
CR	ICE	Pharmacist	18	22
AR	IAR	Physician	18	5
RA	IRA	Physicist	7	9
A	IA	Psychologist	27	39
R	IRC	Research & Development Manager	4	–1
RA	IRS	Respiratory Therapist	12	12
RS	IRS	Science Teacher	4	6
R	(AI)	Sociologist	29	(AI)
RA	IR	Veterinarian	23	14

CONSULTING PSYCHOLOGISTS PRESS, INC. • 3803 E. Bayshore Road, Palo Alto, CA 94303

The Occupational Scales

The next three pages of your Profile show your results on the Occupational Scales. The 211 Occupational Scales representing 109 different occupations are also grouped within the General Occupational Themes. Page 3 of the Profile contains the Realistic and Investigative Occupational Scales; page 4, the Artistic and Social Occupational Scales; and page 5 the Enterprising and Conventional Occupational Scales. Your scores on these scales show how similar your interests are to the interests of people in each of these occupations. The occupations found on your *Strong* Profile include some of the fastest growing occupations, according to the latest figures from the U.S. Department of Labor. To create these scales, more than 60,000 people took the *Strong*. Because of such extensive research, you can feel confident that these scales are contemporary and reliable.

Although most people can identify some of their own interests, they're not sure how their interests compare with those of people actively working in various occupations. For example, you may not know what it would be like to work as a writer, marketing executive, plumber, or scientist. Your score on an Occupational Scale shows how similar your interests are to people who have been working in, and are satisfied with, that occupation. If you reported the same likes *and dislikes* as they did, your score will fall in the "similar" range and you would probably enjoy working in that occupation or in a closely related one. If your likes and dislikes are different from those of the people in the occupation, your score could be in the "dissimilar" range and you might not be happy in that kind of work.

SCORES OF:	MEAN THAT YOU:
40 or above	• Share both the likes and dislikes of people in that occupation, *and* • Would probably enjoy the day-to-day work in that occupation
30–39	• Share some of the likes of people in that occupation, *or* • Share some of the dislikes, *or* • Share some likes and some dislikes, *and* • May enjoy some of the work done in that occupation, but not enjoy all the work
29 or below	• Have few likes and dislikes in common with people in that occupation, *and* • Would probably not enjoy the work done in that occupation

How to Read Your Scores on the Occupational Scales

For each occupation listed on the Profile, two numerical scores are reported. The score in the "Female" column compares your interests to those of women working in that occupation, and the one in the column labeled "Male" compares your interests to those of men working in that occupation. The score that compares you to people of your own gender is then graphed with a black dot in one of the columns to the right of the scores.

These columns describe the similarity of your interests compared to those of people of your gender who work in that occupation. The higher your score, the more common interests you have with those people. Members of an occupation score about 50 on their own scale—that is, female dentists score about 50 on the female Dentist scale, male artists score about 50 on the male Fine Artist scale, and so forth.

The Purpose of Gender Scores

You may wonder why your interests are being compared to groups of men (male chefs, for example) and groups of women (female chefs) instead of compared to combined groups of men and women working in the same occupations (all the chefs who are in the *Strong* sample). Research has shown that men and women, even those in the same occupation, tend to answer some items on the *Strong* differently. Because both scores are reported—those comparing your interests to the males' interests and those comparing your interests to the females' interests—you can choose to compare your interests to those of either men or women. For a particular occupation, you may find that your interests are more similar to those of members of the opposite gender. In such cases, you should consider the occupation among those which you might explore. Generally, however, the scores for your gender—those that are graphed with the black dot—are more likely to be better predictors of occupations that you like than are the scores for the opposite gender.

Comparing Your Scores on Occupational Scales and Basic Interest Scales

You may find that your scores on some of the Occupational Scales on pages 3, 4, and 5 appear to be inconsistent with your scores on related Basic Interest Scales found on page 2 of the Profile. You might, for example, show high interest on the Mathematics Basic Interest Scale yet score in the dissimilar range on the Mathematician Occupational Scale. These results are not errors; they actually give you useful information. What they usually mean is that although you have a general interest in the subject matter of an occupation (as shown by your high interest on the Mathematics BIS), you don't share many of the specific likes or dislikes of people actually working in that occupation (shown by having dissimilar interests compared to the mathematicians who make up the Mathematician Occupational Scale). These results suggest that you probably would not enjoy the day-to-day activities involved with being a mathematician.

Your results can help you identify many more occupations in which you might be interested. To do this, you first need to understand the Theme codes for the occupations. The Theme codes are explained on the back of the next page of your Profile.

Profile report for **ROBIN BYRD**
ID:

OCCUPATIONAL SCALES (continued)

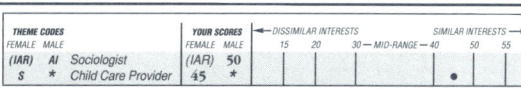

KEY (Sample Scores)

THEME CODES		YOUR SCORES	DISSIMILAR INTERESTS — SIMILAR INTERESTS
FEMALE MALE		FEMALE MALE	15 20 30 — MID-RANGE — 40 50 55
(IAR) AI	Sociologist	(IAR) 50	•
S *	Child Care Provider	45 *	

( ) You can find your score compared to this gender under the Theme represented by the first letter of this code. For example, your score compared to female sociologists is shown under the I or Investigative Theme.

• The position of the dot shows how similar your interests are to those of individuals of your gender who say they are satisfied in their occupation.

* Not enough people of this gender who work in this occupation could be found to make a good comparison.

ARTISTIC (creating or enjoying art, drama, music, writing)

CODES (F/M)	Occupation	YOUR SCORES FEMALE	MALE
AE	Advertising Executive	39	55
ARI	Architect	28	37
A	Artist, Commercial	15	35
A	Artist, Fine	28	38
AS	Art Teacher	14	29
AE	Broadcaster	38	46
AES	Corporate Trainer	41	43
ASE	English Teacher	39	46
AE	Interior Decorator	(EA)	37
A	Lawyer	47	51
A	Librarian	58	62
AIR	Medical Illustrator	11	15
A	Musician	34	47
ARE	Photographer	34	32
ASE	Public Administrator	35	37
AE	Public Relations Director	37	46
A	Reporter	38	50
AI	Sociologist	(IAR)	39
AI	Technical Writer	50	51
AI	Translator	47	51

SOCIAL (helping, instructing, caregiving)

CODES (F/M)	Occupation	YOUR SCORES FEMALE	MALE
SIR	Athletic Trainer	(RIS)	−5
*	Child Care Provider	26	*
SE	Community Service Organization Director	35	27
SEC	Dietitian	(IES)	30
S	Elementary School Teacher	22	21
SA	Foreign Language Teacher	25	37
SE	High School Counselor	32	35
*	Home Economics Teacher	6	*
SA	Minister	32	40
SCE	Nurse, LPN	10	20
SAI	Nurse, RN	24	33
SA	Occupational Therapist	26	35
SE	Parks and Recreation Coordinator	22	27
SR	Physical Education Teacher	−8	−10
SIR	Physical Therapist	18	20
SEC	School Administrator	29	25
SEA	Social Science Teacher	39	37
SA	Social Worker	43	51
SEA	Special Education Teacher	26	36
SA	Speech Pathologist	38	49

Page **4** of 6

NOTES

CPP CONSULTING PSYCHOLOGISTS PRESS, INC. • 3803 E. Bayshore Road, Palo Alto, CA 94303

The Occupational Scales (continued)

Understanding the Theme Codes

The Theme codes on the Profile show how alike or different occupations are from one another. To the left of each Occupational Scale name are two columns labeled "Theme Codes." In these columns, one labeled "Female" and one labeled "Male," you will see one to three letters. These letters are the first letters of the names of the six General Occupational Themes:

CODE	THEME
R	Realistic
I	Investigative
A	Artistic
S	Social
E	Enterprising
C	Conventional

Each occupation is assigned a code that shows the typical interests of the workers in that occupation. For example, the code for the English Teacher scale is ASE. This code means that the majority, but not all, of the English teachers who make up this group of teachers have a combination of Artistic, Social, and Enterprising interests, with Artistic interests primary. Similarly, the EA code for the Marketing Executive scale tells you that most marketing executives tend to have a combination of Enterprising and Artistic interests.

In some cases, the first letters of the codes for men and women from the same occupation are different. Different codes mean that the interests of the majority of men in this occupation are different from the interests of the majority of women in the occupation. Look at the two Theme codes for Small Business Owner. The code for males is RE, while the code for females is CE. These codes show that male and female owners of small businesses share Enterprising interests, which is not surprising, since the Enterprising Theme reflects an interest in business activities. As the first letters of the codes indicate, however, Realistic interests are primarily characteristic of men in this occupation, while Conventional interests better describe the majority of women who are small business owners. One explanation of why men and women of the same occupation would have different interests is that they probably enter the occupation for different reasons or that they work in different areas within the occupation.

The occupation of Dietitian provides another example. The code for male dietitians, SEC, suggests that they enter this field primarily to work with people or to provide a service, since Social is the primary Theme. In contrast, the code for females, IES, suggests that they are drawn to the occupation primarily because of interests in the scientific aspects of the occupation, since Investigative is the primary Theme.

Of course, the occupations listed on the *Strong* Profile are not all of the occupations available to you; there are thousands of others as well. No interest inventory can capture them all. Still, your results, along with the other information on the Profile, can help you to identify many more occupations in which you may be interested. On the back of page 5 you will find an explanation of how you can use the Theme codes in your career exploration. Before turning to that discussion, be sure that you have read the explanation of the Occupational Scales scores, which appears on the back of page 3.

STRONG INTEREST INVENTORY

Profile report for **ROBIN BYRD**
ID:

OCCUPATIONAL SCALES (continued)

KEY (Sample Scores)

THEME CODES		YOUR SCORES		← DISSIMILAR INTERESTS				SIMILAR INTERESTS →		
FEMALE	MALE		FEMALE	MALE	15	20	30 — MID-RANGE — 40	50	55	
EA	(AE)	Interior Decorator	46	(AE)				●		
CSE	*	Dental Assistant	15	*	●					

- The position of the dot shows how similar your interests are to those of individuals of your gender who say they are satisfied in their occupation.
- * Not enough people of this gender who work in this occupation could be found to make a good comparison.

( ) You can find your score compared to this gender under the Theme represented by the first letter of this code. For example, your score compared to male interior decorators is shown under the A or Artistic Theme.

ENTERPRISING (selling, managing, persuading)

THEME CODES FEMALE	MALE	Occupation	YOUR SCORES FEMALE	MALE
ECR		Agribusiness Manager	*	0
EC		Buyer	3	11
ER		Chef	15	25
*		Dental Hygienist	8	*
ESA		Elected Public Official	33	25
EAS		Flight Attendant	24	41
EAC		Florist	11	20
EA		Hair Stylist	14	21
ECS		Housekeeping & Maintenance Supervisor	28	25
ES		Human Resources Director	37	33
(AE)		Interior Decorator	16	(AE)
ECI		Investments Manager	23	15
E		Life Insurance Agent	25	22
EA		Marketing Executive	34	38
ER		Optician	11	12
ECR		Purchasing Agent	17	19
E		Realtor	7	18
ECR		Restaurant Manager	17	21
ECS		Store Manager	23	19
ECA		Travel Agent	20	32

CONVENTIONAL (accounting, organizing, processing data)

THEME CODES FEMALE	MALE	Occupation	YOUR SCORES FEMALE	MALE
CE		Accountant	25	15
CI		Actuary	13	16
CE		Banker	34	21
C		Bookkeeper	30	24
CES		Business Education Teacher	23	30
CE		Credit Manager	35	23
*		Dental Assistant	14	*
(RC)		Farmer	23	(RC)
CES		Food Service Manager	27	34
CIS		Mathematics Teacher	4	−3
C		Medical Records Technician	29	41
(RCE)		Military Enlisted Personnel	23	(RCE)
CES		Nursing Home Administrator	32	47
CA		Paralegal	45	44
*		Secretary	23	*
(RE)		Small Business Owner	28	(RE)

NOTES

Using Your STRONG Results in Career Exploration

Your *Strong* results may have already helped you to identify some specific occupations that you might find interesting. You can also use your results, however, to discover general patterns in your interests that can help you to further expand your job or career options.

Here are some specific steps that you can take to explore additional options. People who follow these steps sometimes find that they are considering occupations that they had never thought of before, simply because they had never been exposed to them. A more detailed set of steps for career exploration can be found in the booklet *Where Do I Go Next? Using Your Strong Results to Manage Your Career* or on the worksheet "Career Exploration: A Journey of Discovery," both of which are available from Consulting Psychologists Press, Inc.

1. **Examine the Occupational Scales on pages 3, 4, and 5 of the Profile.**

   Circle, or write in the "Notes" column, the names of those occupations in which your interests are similar to those of people working in that occupation. These occupations are the ones for which the black dot falls in one of the three right-hand columns labeled "Similar Interests" (scores of 40 and above). The farther to the right your dot appears, the more similar your interests are to those of people working in the occupation. Your career exploration should probably begin with these occupations. If you do not have any scores in the similar range, use those for which the dots appear in the mid-range column.

2. **Look for a pattern in the Theme codes.**

   Look at the Theme codes of the occupations that you just identified. These codes are found in the two columns to the left of the name of the occupation. Try to identify a code (one, two, or three letters) that summarizes or represents all or most of the occupations that you have identified. Don't be concerned about the exact order of the letters in the code for each occupation. Just look for common letters in the codes for the occupations for which your interests are similar.

   For example, if your results show that you have interests similar to people in a number of occupations that all have the letters *A* and *I* somewhere in their codes, (showing that people in these occupations have Artistic and Investigative interests), then you should explore other occupations that are also coded with these same letters, regardless of the order of the letters. So, for example, you would look for occupations coded *A, I, AI,* or *IA*. If, however, all or most of these occupations have codes that start with *A*, then focus on occupations whose Theme codes begin with *A*.

3. **Identify other occupations that have a similar code.**

   You can now use the code that shows your overall pattern of interests to look for other occupations that you may be interested in that are not on your *Strong* Profile. Whoever is interpreting your *Strong* can help you find resources that contain lists of occupations along with their Theme codes. Remember that when searching for similar occupations, you should not be too concerned with the order of the letters in the code. When you have finished this step, you will have a list of occupations from your *Strong* Profile and from materials providing related occupations. Focus your career exploration on these occupations.

4. **Find out as much as you can about those occupations whose codes are similar to your code.**

   Information about occupations can be found in a public library, in the career library of a college or university near you, or in a career center. You can also learn a lot about an occupation by talking to people who are working in that particular occupation. These people can describe their day-to-day work and tell you what they like and dislike about it.

5. **Use your results on the Personal Style Scales (page 6 of the Profile) to help you identify more specific alternatives.**

   Your results on the four Personal Style Scales can help you narrow your choices. (You can find a description of these scales on the back of page 6.) For example, no matter which occupations you have identified in the steps above, your results on the Work Style scale can help you tell whether you might be happier in a job in which there are a lot of opportunities for contact with other people than in a job that requires you to work alone or independently. Most of the time if you have identified an occupation that requires you to get more education, the Learning Environment scale can help you understand the type of educational settings in which you would be most comfortable. The other two Personal Style Scales help you to think about your preferences regarding risk taking and leadership style, factors that can be important in career decision making.

STRONG INTEREST INVENTORY

Profile report for **ROBIN BYRD**
ID:

PERSONAL STYLE SCALES

KEY (Sample Scores)

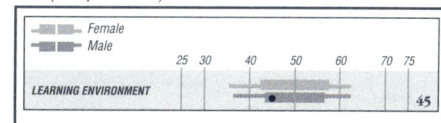

The upper bar shows the range of scores on this scale for a group of women from many occupations; the lower bar, the range of scores for a group of men. The number in the right-hand column, represented by the dot, shows your preference on this scale compared to both men and women.

PERSONAL STYLE SCALES

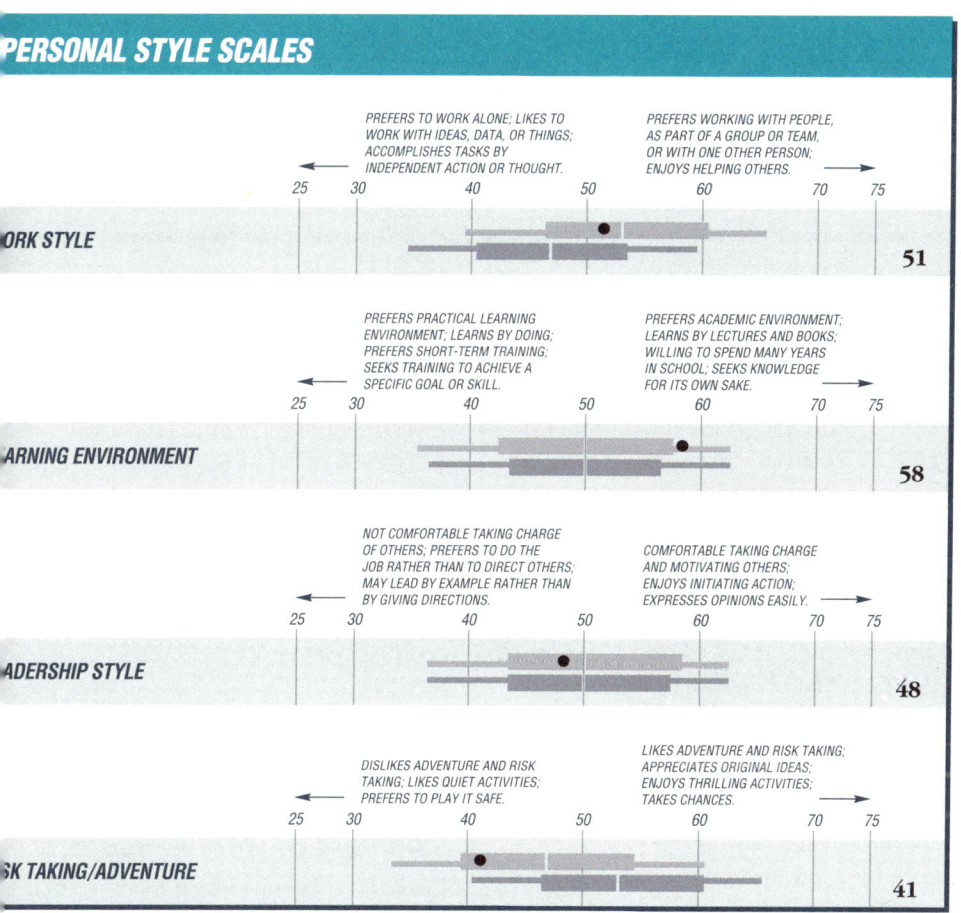

Scale	Score
WORK STYLE — Prefers to work alone; likes to work with ideas, data, or things; accomplishes tasks by independent action or thought. ← → Prefers working with people, as part of a group or team, or with one other person; enjoys helping others.	51
LEARNING ENVIRONMENT — Prefers practical learning environment; learns by doing; prefers short-term training; seeks training to achieve a specific goal or skill. ← → Prefers academic environment; learns by lectures and books; willing to spend many years in school; seeks knowledge for its own sake.	58
LEADERSHIP STYLE — Not comfortable taking charge of others; prefers to do the job rather than to direct others; may lead by example rather than by giving directions. ← → Comfortable taking charge and motivating others; enjoys initiating action; expresses opinions easily.	48
RISK TAKING/ADVENTURE — Dislikes adventure and risk taking; likes quiet activities; prefers to play it safe. ← → Likes adventure and risk taking; appreciates original ideas; enjoys thrilling activities; takes chances.	41

SUMMARY OF ITEM RESPONSES

Total responses out of 317: **317**
Infrequent responses: **5**

ADMINISTRATIVE INDEXES (response percentages)

OCCUPATIONS	25 % L		14 % I		61 % D
SCHOOL SUBJECTS	23 L		38 I		38 D
ACTIVITIES	35 L		28 I		37 D
LEISURE ACTIVITIES	45 L		28 I		28 D
TYPES OF PEOPLE	10 L		25 I		65 D
CHARACTERISTICS	25 Y		33 ?		42 N
SUBTOTAL	27 %		28 %		45 %
PREFERENCES: ACTIVITIES	50 L		20 =		30 R
PREFERENCES: WORK	50 L		50 =		0 R

The Personal Style Scales

The other side of this page shows your results on four Personal Style Scales. These scales can give you more insight into your interests and career or educational expectations.

Work Style Scale

This scale indicates a preference for working with people as opposed to working with data, things, or ideas. Your results on this scale can help you refine your job or career choice. For example, two people may have identical scores on one of the Occupational Scales—Accountant, for instance—indicating interests similar to those of people in that occupation. However, if these two people score toward opposite ends of the Work Style scale, then they should probably consider different organizations, different work settings, or different tasks within the accounting profession that will match their preferred work styles.

It is also important to understand that you might be very successful working in an environment that does not match your work style. However, you may need to find leisure or avocational activities that can help you "recharge" by offering you the opportunity to use your own style.

Learning Environment Scale

Your results on this scale show the kind of setting in which you may enjoy learning. It is important to understand that this scale does *not* measure academic ability or your chance of success in an academic environment.

You can use your results on this scale to help you make decisions about careers or educational options that you are considering. When exploring careers that interest you, find out what kind of education is typically required for people who work in that occupation. Then compare the educational requirements to the kind of learning environment that you prefer. However, you should not necessarily rule out an occupation just because of an apparent mismatch. For example, people who scored toward the practical pole have successfully completed doctorate programs by keeping in mind the practical goal motivating them to get their education.

How to Use the Personal Style Scales

Work Style	Determine how much contact with people you want in your job
Learning Environment	Decide what kind of education you want to achieve your work goals
Leadership Style	Determine what kind of leader you prefer to be
Risk Taking/Adventure	Use your preference regarding risk taking to choose career and leisure pursuits

Leadership Style Scale

Your results on this scale can help you to identify what kind of leadership style you prefer. This scale does *not* measure whether you are interested in leading or in following someone else's lead. Instead, it measures your interest in a certain type of leadership.

For example, people in the occupations Elected Public Official, Realtor, Public Administrator, and School Administrator tend to score toward the right pole of this scale. They like a directive, persuasive, and outgoing leadership style, and they enjoy being responsible for directing and motivating others.

Occupations that tend to score toward the left pole of the scale, on the other hand, include Physicist, Mathematician, Farmer, Veterinarian, and Auto Mechanic. For the most part, these occupations do not require as much people-contact, and those who score toward this pole are not comfortable assuming a high profile, outspoken leadership style. This does not necessarily mean that they are not interested in being leaders, or that they are not good leaders. Such people can be effective leaders, but their style may be one that is more team-oriented or one in which they lead by example.

It is important to note, however, that many of the people in the *Strong* occupational groups fall somewhere in the middle of this scale, rather than near the poles. Also, within a given occupation scores vary greatly among the people working in that occupation. This variety explains why different people choose different roles and tasks within an occupation. Use this scale to help you decide how you would function best in a particular job.

Risk Taking/Adventure Scale

This scale shows whether you like adventure and how much you enjoy taking risks. Your results on this scale can help you to identify career or leisure options that fit your style.

If you like to take risks, you may choose an occupation that directly places you in physical danger, such as law enforcement or the military. If your job does not challenge you sufficiently, you may seek out risk-taking opportunities in your leisure time.

If you prefer to play it safe, you may enjoy more quiet activities or the thrill of intellectual activities. Preferring to play it safe may not mean that you avoid taking risks, but rather you may weigh risks carefully before acting.

Summary of Item Responses

This section of results, which appears on the bottom of page 6, can help your counselor tell whether the inventory was administered properly and whether the answer sheet was marked correctly. The Administrative Indexes show in percentages how you answered the questions in each of the eight parts of the *Strong*. For example, you can see how many questions you answered with the response "Like," "Indifferent," or "Dislike."

The Total Responses index shows how many of the 317 *Strong* items you answered. It helps to identify whether you missed items when completing the answer sheet.

The Infrequent Responses index shows whether your interests are fairly typical, or whether they suggest a pattern of responses that is not often seen on the *Strong*. Your counselor can help you to understand the meaning of your score on this scale.

Strong Interest Inventory™
Quick Fact Sheet

Applications and Administration

- Administration: The Strong Interest Inventory has been used with high school students, college students, and adults for over 70 years.

- Length: The current form contains 317 items and takes 35-40 minutes to complete. The recommended reading level is between 8th and 9th grade.

- Multicultural and International Use: The Strong is validated with a variety of ethnic, cultural, and racial groups (See Chapter 15, Cross-cultural Use of the Strong, in the "Strong Interest Inventory: Applications and Technical Guide," pages 255 – 280). For specific foreign language information, see the International Distribution section of the current CPP Catalog.

Reliability

- **General Occupational Themes**
  Internal Consistency: Ranges from a low of .90 on Artistic to a high of .94 on Social.
  Test-Retest (adult sample 3-6 months): Ranges from a low of .84 on Enterprising to a high of .92 on Realistic.

- **Basic Interest Scales**
  Internal Consistency: Ranges from a low of .74 on Agriculture to a high of .94 on Mechanical Activities.
  Test-Retest (adult sample 3-6 months): Ranges from a low of .82 on Agriculture and Computer Activities to a high of .94 on Athletics.

- **Occupational Scales**
  Internal Consistency: N/A for empirically-derived scales
  Test-Retest (adult sample 3-6 months): Ranges from a low of .80 for female Dental Hygienists and female Opticians to a high of .95 on male Advertising Executives, female Auto Mechanics, and female Chemists.

- **Personal Style Scales**
  Internal Consistency: Ranges from a low of .78 on Risk Taking/Adventure to a high of .91 on Work Style.
  Test-Retest (adult sample 3-6 months): Ranges from a low of .85 on Risk Taking/Adventure to a high of .92 on Work Style.

Normative Data and Validity

- General Occupational Themes and the Basic Interest Scales Normative Data: The Normative or General Reference Sample consists of 9,467 women and 9,484 men. The average ages were 40.5 for men and 44.6 for women. The General Reference Sample is comprised of samples of approximately 200 members of each occupational group (Harmon, Hansen, Borgen, Hammer, 1994, p.110). General Occupational Themes and the Basic Interest Scales were normed on the General Reference Sample.

- Occupational Scales Normative Data: The 211 Occupational samples range in size from 60 to 1187; the median size is 250. The participants who make up the occupational samples ranged in age from 25 to 60 years old and had at least three years experience on the job. Those included in occupational samples performed their job duties in a manner typical of their occupational group and all reported being satisfied with their work. (p. 105-113, 120-130, 309-376, Harmon, 1994).

- Criterion Related Validity: Concurrent validity generally measures the ability of the psychological instrument to separate different groups. The concurrent validity of the Occupational Scales is measured by Tilton's overlap statistics. The occupational groups are differentiated from the General Reference Sample by an average of slightly less than two standard deviations. The best scale was male Medical Illustrator scale that had an overlap of only 15 percent between occupational sample and the male General Reference Sample. The poorest scale in terms of concurrent validity was male audiologist at an overlap of 61 percent (p. 130-148, Harmon, 1994). The validity of each of the Basic Interest Scales can be evaluated by ranking the means of the 109 occupational groups in the 1994 Strong on each scale. The results suggest substantial validity for the Basic Interest Scales, with mean occupational scores frequently spread out over 2 to 2.5 standard deviations (p. 91, 92-104, Harmon, 1994).

- Construct Validity – The Strong Interest Inventory has been said to be the best measure of Holland's interest themes (Rounds, 1995). Extensive construct validity information is provided in the *Strong Interest Applications and Technical Guide*.

Recommended Readings

Harmon, L. W., Hansen, J. C., Borgen, F. H., & Hammer, A. L. (1994). Strong Interest Inventory Applications and Technical Guide. Stanford, CA: Stanford University Press.

Schaeffer, E. L. & Usher, M. C. (1993). Terror Free Measurement: A Statistics and Psychometrics Supplement for Users of the Strong Interest Inventory. Palo Alto, CA: Consulting Psychologist Press. [In order to purchase this document, contact G/S Consultants in South Lake Tahoe, California at gstahoe@sierra.net, www.gsconsultants.net, or (530) 541-8587].

Savickas, M.L., & Spokane, A.R. (Eds.). (1999). Vocational Interests: Meaning, Measurement, and Counseling Use. Palo Alto, CA: Davies-Black Publishing.

Donnay, D. A. C., & Borgen, F.H. Finding passion in careers: Integrating your Skills Confidence results with your Strong Interest Inventory profile. Palo Alto, CA: Consulting Psychologists Press.

Donnay, D.A.C. (1997). E.K. Strong's Legacy and Beyond: 70 Years of the Strong Interest Inventory. Career Development Quarterly, Volume 46, 2-22.

Borgen, F.H. & Grutter, J. (1995). Where Do I Go Next?. Palo Alto, CA: Consulting Psychologists Pr

Betz, N.B., Borgen, F.H., & Harmon, L.W. (1996). Skills Confidence Inventory Applications and Technical Guide. Palo Alto, CA: Consulting Psychologists Press.

Hammer, A.L., & Kummerow, J.M. (1992). Strong and MBTI Career Development Guide. Palo Consulting Psychologists Press.

Grutter, J. (1998). Making it in Today's Organizations Using the Strong and MBTI. Palo A Consulting Psychologists Press.

Krebs Hirsh, S. (1995). Strong Interest Inventory Resource. Palo Alto, CA: Consulting Press.

Prince, J.P. (1995). Strong Interest Inventory Resource. Palo Alto, CA: Consulting Psychologists Press.

Rumpel, S.K. & Lecertua, K. (1995). Strong Interest Inventory Resource. Palo Alto, CA: Consulting Psychologists Press.

CPP Resources and Contacts

CPP Website: www.cpp-db.com
CPP Career site: www.careerhub.org
Customer Service: 1-800-624-1765

Regional Consultants:

West: Ann Alkire
phone: (619)-225-1135
fax: (619)-523-5639
e-mail: aea@cpp-db.com

Midwest: Sarita Bhakuni
phone: (773)-235-8151
fax: (773)-235-8161
e-mail: snb@cpp-db.com

Mid-Atlantic: Amy Ferris
phone: (301)-353-8806
fax: (301)-353-8807
e-mail: arf@cpp-db.com

South Central: Bonnie Hagemann
phone: (405)-844-6151
fax: (405)-844-6202
e-mail: bkh@cpp-db.com

Southeast: Catherine Holmes
phone: (803)-324-1737
fax: (803)-324-2306
e-mail: crh@cpp-db.com

North Central: Ralph Hundley
phone: (317)-244-9336
fax: (317)-244-9337
e-mail: rph@cpp-db.com

East: John Maketa
phone: (215)-489-6857
fax: (215)-489-6858
e-mail: jem@cpp-db.com

Southwest: Kelly O'Connor
phone: (719)-338-6633
fax: (719)-548-9007
e-mail: kko@cpp-db.com